RESEARCH METHODS

Visit the *Research Methods: A Practical Guide for the Social Sciences* Companion Website at **www.pearsoned.co.uk/matthews** to find valuable student learning material including:

- Video of two focus groups, showing this exciting data collection method in practise.
- Videos of interviews, with full transcriptions, to let you practise coding and analysing interview data.
- Animated maths walkthroughs talk you through the basics of collecting and interpreting data.
- Checklists and exercises from this book – print them out, fill them in, and watch your project come together!
- Interactive decision-making exercises to help you choose the best methods for your project.
- Real life questionnaire and a sample Excel dataset of results, to let you practise your question-building and analysis skills.
- Annotated weblinks to relevant organisations to help you take your own project further.
- An online glossary to explain key terms.
- Flashcards to test your understanding of key terms.

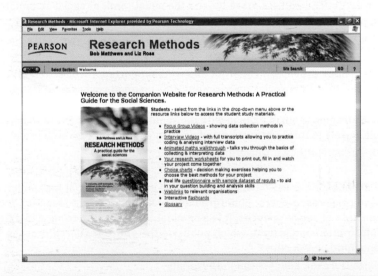

"A lively and accessible, practical guide on how to do social research. It takes the reader on a journey, from initial thoughts and questions through to the complexities of data collection, analysis and dissemination – a welcome and invaluable addition to the literature on research methods."
Professor Saul Becker, Head of the School of Sociology and Social Policy, The University of Nottingham

"Bob Matthews and Liz Ross have produced a research methods text that is highly accessible, but also takes people through the processes of planning, carrying out fieldwork and analysing research data without compromising the need for understanding complex ideas. They are not afraid to offer their own views about both theory and method, and link these to very practical suggestions about 'how to do' both data collection and analysis. Overall this is a refreshing approach to teaching research methods that will be welcomed by lecturers across the social sciences."
Professor Marian Barnes, University of Brighton

"This user-friendly guide to research methods is a great starting point for students and would-be social researchers. The book is thoughtfully organised and written in an accessible manner. I warmly recommend it for all those who want a lively and practical introduction to social research."
Professor Nick Ellison, University of Leeds

"Matthews and Ross have produced a welcome addition to a small but growing research literature that is accessible to new researchers without losing the essence of highly complex issues. The text also provides an excellent and detailed key to research terminology that offers a way in to denser and less user friendly writings on methodology. In short, a valuable tool for those seeking to mobilise research projects for the first time or those seeking to refresh and update knowledge of current research issues."
Dave Orr, University of Central Lancashire

"This book is an outstanding contribution to research methods literature. It embraces the whole research field by combining analytical rigour with descriptive richness. Its methodological presentation and analysis are clear, concise and effective. It is a very instructive book for beginners, helping students to develop research skills. Bob Matthews and Liz Ross have written a book that is a required reading for anyone doing social research. The authors move beyond the usual remit of social scientists and offer a fresh approach with their persuasive and forward-thinking ideas."
Professor György Jenei, Corvinus University, Budapest, Hungary

"This book provides a coherent and well supported introduction to research methods for the first time social researcher. Offering good coverage of important topics and guidance, it also talks clearly, concisely and in a friendly manner to the novice researcher encouraging them to engage with the required elements of the research process and ultimately to think, formulate and develop successful research projects of their own."
Dr Julian Matthews, University of Leicester

"The book is a must-have text for anyone involved in social research methods, including lecturers; researchers; undergraduate and postgraduate students and practitioners in the field of social sciences. It is a seminal textbook, glittering with extensive examples, information and insight, which publicise the entire research process from a new and engaging perspective."
Faiza Qureshi, Loughborough University

Bob Matthews and Liz Ross
University of Birmingham

RESEARCH METHODS

A practical guide for the social sciences

Longman
is an imprint of

PEARSON

Harlow, England • London • New York • Boston • San Francisco • Toronto
Sydney • Tokyo • Singapore • Hong Kong • Seoul • Taipei • New Delhi
Cape Town • Madrid • Mexico City • Amsterdam • Munich • Paris • Milan

Pearson Education Limited
Edinburgh Gate
Harlow
Essex CM20 2JE
England

and Associated Companies throughout the world

Visit us on the World Wide Web at:
www.pearsoned.co.uk

First published 2010

© Pearson Education Limited 2010

The rights of Bob Matthews and Liz Ross to be identified as authors of this Work have been asserted by them in accordance with the Copyright, Designs and Patents Act 1988.

All rights reserved. No part of this publication may be reproduced, stored in a retrieval system, or transmitted in any form or by any means, electronic, mechanical, photocopying, recording or otherwise, without either the prior written permission of the publisher or a licence permitting restricted copying in the United Kingdom issued by the Copyright Licensing Agency Ltd, Saffron House, 6-10 Kirby Street, London EC1N 8TS.

All trademarks used therein are the property of their respective owners. The use of any trademark in this text does not vest in the author or publisher any trademark ownership rights in such trademarks, nor does the use of such trademarks imply any affiliation with or endorsement of this book by such owners.

Pearson Education is not responsible for the content of third party internet sites.

ISBN 978-1-4058-5850-2

British Library Cataloguing-in-Publication Data
A catalogue record for this book is available from the British Library

Library of Congress Cataloging-in-Publication Data
Matthews, Bob, 1953-
  Research methods : a practical guide for the social sciences /
Bob Matthews, Liz Ross. — 1st ed.
       p. cm.
  ISBN 978-1-4058-5850-2 (pbk.)
 1. Social sciences—Research—Methodology—Handbooks, manuals, etc.
I. Ross, Liz. II. Title.
  H62.M3228 2010
  001.4'2—dc22

                                                    2010007217

10 9 8 7 6 5 4 3 2 1
14 13 12 11 10

Typeset in *9.5/12 Giovanni Book* by *73*
Printed and bound by Rotolito Lombarda, Italy

BRIEF CONTENTS

CONTENTS

LIST OF FIGURES, SCREENSHOTS AND TABLES

Figures and screenshots

Tables

GUIDED TOUR OF THE BOOK

CHAPTER A2
Knowledge, theories, paradigms and perspectives

Contents

In context

Have you ever wondered why people think and act in different ways? This chapter asks you to think about this from a research point of view. It discusses information and knowledge, how we know and understand things and how we use our knowledge and understanding to construct a particular way of looking at the social world. Though this might sound confusing and hard to comprehend, it is very important: if we don't understand how researchers look at the world, then we will probably have difficulty in understanding their research.

PART A: Thinking about research

- A1: What is research?
- A2: Knowledge, theories, paradigms and perspectives
- A3: The nature of data
- A4: Research questions, hypotheses and operational definitions
- A5: Research as an ethical and cultural issue

◀ Each chapter opens with a **Contents** box displaying the topics to be covered and is placed **In Context** with a brief introduction, which relates it to the other chapters in the part.

Examples, drawn from the headlines as ▶ well as from more familiar everyday situations, demonstrate how research theory translates into practice in our social world.

▯ **What is . . .**

Epistemology [1]

Epistemology is the theory of knowledge and how we know things.
[We offer slightly different definitions below in the sections on ontology and epistemology.]

- What are we trying to do when we do social research (see also A1)?
- How can theories help us in our social research?
- What does this mean for me as a student social researcher?

Example A2.1

'Number of marriages falls to record low' – *Guardian* 22 February 2007

'Worlds apart – poll finds parents out of touch' – *Guardian* 24 February 2007

'Teenage gang shooting blamed on family breakdown' – *Guardian* 23 February 2007

'Fathers told: do more for your children' – *Guardian* 27 February 2007

'Mothers bear brunt of discrimination at work – women with children are seen as less reliable' – *Guardian* 1 March 2007

This chapter includes some quite abstract material so an example is included to help your understanding of the key points. Throughout this chapter there are example boxes which will take you through some of the points being made in relation to a particular area of the social world – *the family*.

As we write this, a topic that is rarely far from the news in the UK has hit the headlines again. Throughout the latter part of the twentieth century and into the twenty-first, the family, with its changing composition and the role it is thought by some to play in many aspects of daily and social life, has been a topic of interest, concern and research and it is one of the social units that most people experience themselves in some way.

The family, as a social unit, encompasses a number of different elements:

- It can include people who are related to each other by blood, by law and by choice.
- It can include the relationship between parent(s) and child.
- It can include legal and choice relationships between adults.
- Members of a family may or may not live in the same household.
- And probably many others!

The family, as a social unit, is of concern to: policy-makers, economists, house builders, social and health care providers, the police, the retail industry, education providers, travel agents, car makers, lawyers and many others!

Some changes that have had an impact on the family as a social unit in the last 50 years include:

- laws relating to divorce, cohabitation and civil partnerships
- effective means of contraception and abortion
- education and employment opportunities for women
- lengthening lifespan.

CHAPTER A2 Knowledge, theories, paradigms and perspectives   25

actors (humans) who are involved. The social researcher's relationship to the social world and the social phenomenon he is studying is therefore one of objective observation.

The objectivist position derives from the approach often taken by natural scientists who study the way the natural physical world of animals, plants, cells, atoms, nuclei and chemical elements behaves. This approach values the objectivity and independence of the researcher and identifies the characteristics of the social world in terms of entities which are ordered and predictable and can be identified and recorded without affecting the entities themselves.

> **Think about it . . .**
> **The family from an objectivist position**
>
> The family can be seen as a social unit which includes people who are related to each other by blood or law. This may be extended to groups of people who, though not related by blood or law, live as if they were related and consider themselves to be a family. The relationships may be defined by law or custom to include responsibilities, for example, for financial arrangements and social behaviour, particularly of children. There are certain life events that mark changes within the family – a marriage, the birth of a child, a divorce and so on – which can be identified.
>
> Although each individual family will vary, the idea of a family as a social unit has a reality that is independent of the particular individuals who are members of it. The family represents a particular set of relationships and behaviours to which individual members conform to differing degrees.

constructivism
An ontological position which asserts that the social phenomena making up our social world are only real in the sense that they are constructed ideas which are continually being viewed and reworked by those involved in them through social interaction and reflection.

Constructivism

Constructivism asserts that the social phenomena making up our *social* world are only real in the sense that they are constructed ideas which are continually being reviewed and reworked by those involved in them (the *social actors*) through social interaction and reflection. There is no *social* reality apart from the meaning of the social phenomenon for the participants. However, the meanings attributed to and the understandings of a *social* phenomenon (like an organisation, the family, a community, social care, the law), which are constructed by the social actors, *are* available for study. Most importantly, the social researcher, as part of the social world herself, brings her own meanings and understandings to her study.

> **Think about it . . .**
> **The family from a constructivist position**
>
> The family is seen as situated within a particular time, space and culture. It is the product of the relationships of its performers. In other words, what is interesting – and can be studied – is what people themselves understand as 'family' and how they use this understanding to make sense of their lives together as a family.
>
> Relationships – like parent, child, brother, partner – are worked with on a day-to-day basis and what it means to be a parent, for example, is continually being reviewed and reworked through social interaction with each child and other members of the family *and* the experiences and understandings prevalent in their time and culture.
>
> This means that ideas about parenthood within the culture itself are also continually being constructed and reconstructed by its members and these ideas are demonstrated in the ways in which parenthood is discussed or written about.

Think About It... boxes contain questions and ideas to help you focus on core issues and practical considerations for your own research project.

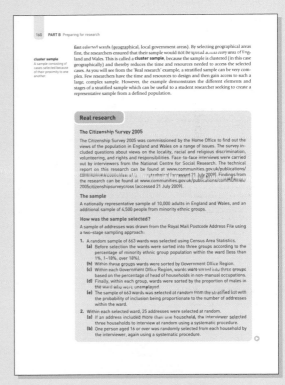

160   **PART B** Preparing for research

cluster sample
A sample consisting of cases selected because of their proximity to one another.

first selected wards (geographical, local government areas). By selecting geographical areas first, the researchers ensured that their sample would not be spread across every area of England and Wales. This is called a **cluster sample**, because the sample is clustered (in this case geographically) and thereby reduces the time and resources needed to access the selected cases. As you will see from the 'Real research' example, a stratified sample can be very complex. Few researchers have the time and resources to design and then gain access to such a large, complex sample. However, the example demonstrates the different elements and stages of a stratified sample which can be useful to a student researcher seeking to create a representative sample from a defined population.

> **Real research**
>
> **The Citizenship Survey 2005**
>
> The Citizenship Survey 2005 was commissioned by the Home Office to find out the views of the population in England and Wales on a range of issues. The survey included questions about views on the locality, racial and religious discrimination, volunteering, and rights and responsibilities. Face-to-face interviews were carried out by interviewers from the National Centre for Social Research. The technical report on this research can be found at www.communities.gov.uk/publications/communities/2005technical (accessed 21 July 2009). Findings from the research can be found at www.communities.gov.uk/publications/communities/2005citizenshipsurveycross (accessed 21 July 2009).
>
> **The sample**
>
> A nationally representative sample of 10,000 adults in England and Wales, and an additional sample of 4,500 people from minority ethnic groups.
>
> **How was the sample selected?**
>
> A sample of addresses was drawn from the Royal Mail Postcode Address File using a two-stage sampling approach:
>
> 1. A random sample of 663 wards was selected using Census Area Statistics.
>   (a) Before selection the wards were sorted into three groups according to the percentage of minority ethnic group population within the ward (less than 1%, 1–18%, over 18%).
>   (b) Within these groups wards were sorted by Government Office Region.
>   (c) Within each Government Office Region, wards were sorted into three groups based on the percentage of head of households in non-manual occupations.
>   (d) Finally, within each group, wards were sorted by the proportion of males in the ward who were unemployed.
>   (e) The sample of 663 wards was selected at random from the stratified list with the probability of inclusion being proportionate to the number of addresses within the ward.
> 2. Within each selected ward, 25 addresses were selected at random.
>   (a) If an address included more than one household, the interviewer selected three households to interview at random using a systematic procedure.
>   (b) One person aged 16 or over was randomly selected from each household by the interviewer, again using a systematic procedure.

Real Research from a wide variety of disciplines, including social work, social policy, and criminology lets you see your project in context and provides examples of best practice for first-time researchers.

---

154   **PART B** Preparing for research

An important note: although throughout this chapter we will often refer to and use examples that are based on selecting individual *people* to take part in research, much of what is included here is appropriate for the *selection of cases, documents* and *time* and *context periods* for observation. Selection is always part of research design, and you must be aware of the criteria and approach you are using when you decide to collect data from any sources. The relevant sections in **C3** and **D3** will provide material to consider in addition to this chapter.

Approaches to sampling

In Figure B5.1 we have arranged the different approaches to sampling in a spectrum. At one end of the spectrum are the sampling approaches that are based on statistical theory, and which aim to produce a sample that can be shown to be highly representative of the whole population – or all the potential cases – in terms of relevant criteria: **probability samples**. At the other end of the spectrum are approaches to sampling that are concerned with selecting (usually fewer) cases that will best enable the researcher to explore the research questions in depth, and to work with the data collected to identify and explore theoretical ideas: **purposive** and **theoretical samples**.

probability sample
A sample that can be shown to be highly representative of the whole population – or all the potential cases – in terms of relevant criteria.

purposive sample
A sample of selected cases that will best enable the researcher to explore the research questions in depth.

theoretical sample
A sample of selected cases that will best enable the researcher to explore theoretical ideas.

population
In statistical terms, population refers to the total number of cases that can be included as research subjects.

Probability samples				Non-probability samples	
Random sample	Stratified random sample	Quota sample	Convenience, snowball sample	Purposive sample	Theoretical sample

Figure B5.1 A spectrum of different approaches to sampling

Statistical sampling – or selecting a probability sample

One approach to sampling is to use probability or statistical theory to help you to select a sample that is representative of the **population** from which it is taken. This approach is most commonly used when designing experimental and survey research (B3) and where the data being gathered is quantitative in nature. Selecting a sample in this way enables the researcher to undertake a statistical analysis of the data (D3).

> **What is . . .**
>
> **Population**
> In statistical terms, population refers to the total number of cases that can be included as research subjects. For example, a population may be:
> - all the people who live in a country;
> - all the students studying at a particular university;
> - all the undergraduate students studying sociology at any UK university at a particular time;
> - all the newspaper articles published in the UK referring to student volunteering during a particular month.
>
> The key characteristics of a probability sample are as follows:
>
> - Each member of the population has a known (and usually equal) chance of being selected for the sample. This assumes that the members of the population are known – that is, that they can be individually identified. If this is not the case, then other sampling strategies may need to be adopted.

Throughout the book, the **What is...?** feature provides detailed explorations of important concepts and topics and is partnered with **key terms** and **definitions** in the margin for quick reference.

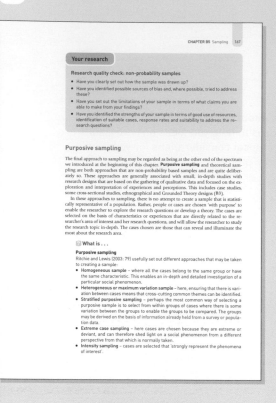

Your Research summaries present questions, activities and checklists to help you develop your ideas. Many of these are also available online at **www.pearsoned.co.uk/matthews**. Print them out and fill them in as your own research project takes shape.

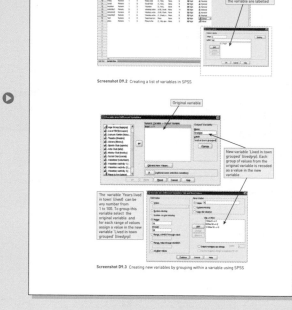

Annotated walkthroughs of SPSS, NVivo and Microsoft Excel and Word give you a truly visual guide to the most popular data analysis packages and processes.

In each chapter, full **References** and **Further Reading** guide you towards the best resources for taking your learning further.

GUIDED TOUR OF THE COMPANION WEBSITE

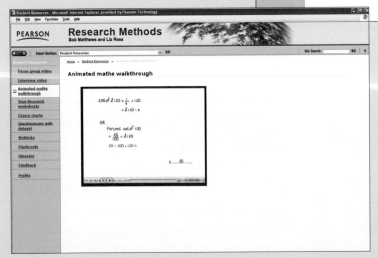

A **video of two focus groups** demonstrates this fascinating data collection method in practice. Neither is being presented as 'expert', but this is an invaluable chance to experience what a real focus group is like.

Videos of interviews with student participants give you an insight into this popular data collection method. Full **transcriptions** of the interviews are also available, giving you the opportunity to practise coding and analysing interview data.

If your maths is a little rusty, get some online help with the quantitative side of research from **animated maths walkthroughs**. These short animations talk you through the basics of working out averages and probabilities, collecting and interpreting data, and constructing survey questions.

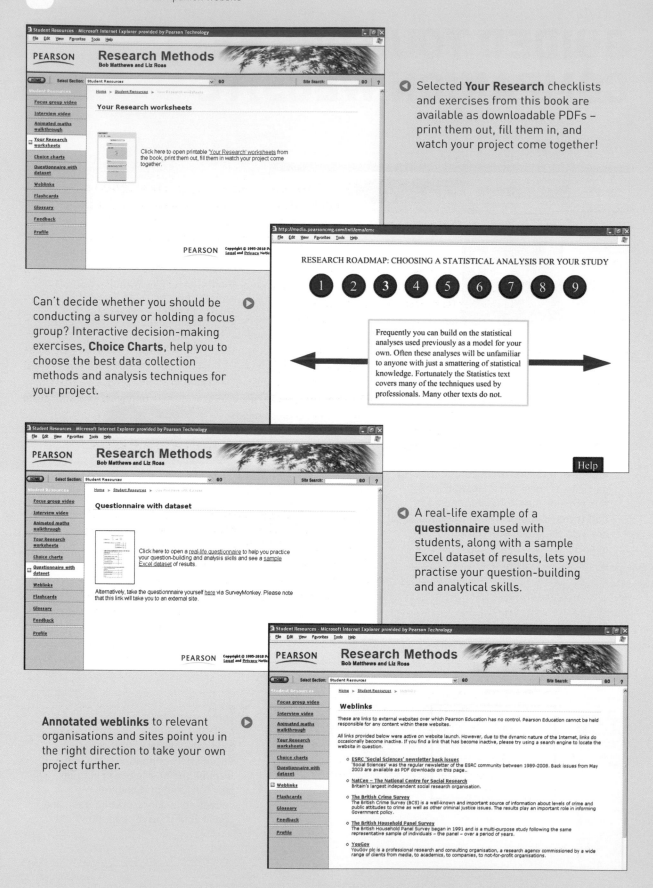

Selected **Your Research** checklists and exercises from this book are available as downloadable PDFs – print them out, fill them in, and watch your project come together!

Can't decide whether you should be conducting a survey or holding a focus group? Interactive decision-making exercises, **Choice Charts**, help you to choose the best data collection methods and analysis techniques for your project.

A real-life example of a **questionnaire** used with students, along with a sample Excel dataset of results, lets you practise your question-building and analytical skills.

Annotated weblinks to relevant organisations and sites point you in the right direction to take your own project further.

ABOUT THE AUTHORS

Bob Matthews

Bob was a latecomer to academia. He left school with a handful of GCE 'O' levels and worked for 25 years in the electricity supply industry as a surveyor until he decided that there were more interesting and worthwhile things to do. This decision made, he set out for higher education via an Access course (and with the support of his partner, Alison, to whom he is forever grateful).

In 1994, Bob began reading for an honours degree in Social Policy at the University of Birmingham (ironically perhaps, Liz Ross was the person who interviewed him and accepted him for a place there). Bob achieved a first-class degree in 1997, while working part-time for the Probation Service, winning the Social Study and the François Lafitte prizes along the way. With the support of an ESRC studentship, he was awarded a PhD in 2001 and became a lecturer at the Institute of Applied Social Studies (now part of the School of Social Policy in the College of Social Sciences) at Birmingham University, where he was Director of Undergraduate Social Policy programmes until 2008. Bob's academic duties have taken him to some interesting places, including Estonia, Siberia, Korea and China, where he is a visiting professor at Nankai University, Tianjin.

Bob currently teaches and researches in Comparative Social Policy, Social Inclusion, Health Policy and Research Methods and plays acoustic guitar whenever he can.

Liz Ross

Liz studied Sociology at London University and then worked as a researcher with the (then) Government Social Survey (now the Office of National Statistics). Here she learnt the basics of social research at a time when computers were just beginning to be used to process large quantities of survey data. After a time caring for her two young children she trained as a social worker and worked in community development for many years before returning to social research and taking a Masters in Advanced Educational and Social Research with the Open University. A research fellowship brought her to the University of Birmingham where she continues to research and teach at the Institute of Applied Social Studies.

For ten years she was the Director of Postgraduate Taught Programmes and continues to coordinate a postgraduate programme developed with the government of the Republic of Korea. Liz's research and teaching interests reflect her experience as a community development worker, her work in the voluntary sector and her connections with South Korea.

Over the years Liz has taught social research methods on both undergraduate and postgraduate programmes, introducing many postgraduates in the social sciences to qualitative social research methods, and has also trained local authority officers and community groups to use social research techniques in their work and their neighbourhoods as a means of involving local people in decisions about their lives and communities and making their voices heard.

ACKNOWLEDGEMENTS

Thanks and appreciation to the following reviewers for their insightful and constructive comments that have helped shape the contents of this book:

Ann-Katrin Backlund, Lund University
Fred Cartmel, University of Glasgow
Pauline Dooley, University of Gloucestershire
Jonas Edlund, Umeå University
Robert Evans, Cardiff University
Alice Feldman, University College Dublin
John Gelissen, University of Tilburg
Sheila Gilford, Staffordshire University
Jeni Harden, Edinburgh Napier University
Emma Head, Keele University
Adam Hedgecoe, University of Sussex
Monica Magadi, City University
Julian Matthews, University of Leicester
David Orr, University of Central Lancashire
Faiza Qureshi, Anglia Ruskin University
Emma Uprichard, University of York
Jon Warren, Durham University

PUBLISHER'S ACKNOWLEDGEMENTS

We are grateful to the following for permission to reproduce copyright material:

Figures
Figure C10.1: From The Higher Education Academy (www.heacademy.ac.uk/forum) reproduced with permission; Figure D3.6: From *Social Trends*, 38, ONS (Office for National Statistics, 2008) Figure 7.9, p. 98. Crown Copyright material is reproduced with the permission of the Controller, Office of Public Sector Information (OPSI) under terms of the Click-use Licence; Figure D7.1: Adapted from Content analysis in leadership: examples, procedures, and suggestions for future use, Leadership Quarterly, 8(1), 1–25 (Insch, G. S., Moore, J. E. and Murphy, L. D., 1997) with permission from Elsevier; Figure F3.8: From Center for Instructional Technology and Educational Support (CITES) (Fogel, C), (http://nursing.unc.edu/cites/presentation/ example_graphic.jpg) University of North Carolina – Chapel Hill, School of Nursing; Figure E3.9: From Dr. J. Goeppinger who was a Professor in the University of North Carolina School of Nursing when this poster was created with the school's Center for Instructional Technology and Educational Support (CITES), (http://nursing.unc.edu/cites/presentation/example_ncmap. jpg) University of North Carolina – Chapel Hill, School of Nursing; Figure E3.10: From Research Impact, (http://researchimpact.files.wordpress.com/2009/05/april-30-poster-v3mj. jpg). Reproduced with permission; Figure E3.11: From Department of Epidemiology and Community Health, University of Minnesota (www.epi.umn.edu/research/macc/2008_macc_ppt/EricksonSPR08_Poster.jpg). Copyright © 2009 Regents of the University of Minnesota. Reproduced with permission.

Screenshots
Screenshots D4.1, D4.2, D4.3, D4.4, D4.5, D4.6, D4.7: Presented from SPSS UK Ltd with permission (www.spss.com/uk); Screenshots D4.8, D4.9, D4.14: From Microsoft Corporation (www.microsoft.com). Microsoft product screenshots reprinted with permission from Microsoft Corporation; Screenshots D4.10, D4.11, D4.12, D4.13: From QSR International Pty Ltd. NVivo is designed and developed by QSR International Pty Ltd. NVivo is a trademark or registered trademark of QSR International, patent pending (www.qsrinternational.com).

Tables
Table A2.1: Adapted from *Investigating the Social World: The Process and Practice of Research*, p. 13 (Schutt, R. K., 1996). Copyright © 1996 by Sage Publications, Inc. Reproduced with permission of Sage Publications, Inc. (Books) in the format Textbook via Copyright Clearance Center; Table D4.23: Adapted from *Qualitative Research Practice: A Guide for Social Science Students and Researchers*, p. 240 (Ritchie, J. and Lewis, J. 2003). Copyright © Sage Publications 2003. Reproduced by permission.

Text
Page 75: Real Research: Informed Consent adapted from *Informed Consent in Health and Social Care Research*, p. 2 (RCN, 2005). Reproduced with kind permission of the Royal College of Nursing.

Photo
Page 45: © Andraz Gregoric / iStockphoto.

In some instances we have been unable to trace the owners of copyright material, and we would appreciate any information that would enable us to do so.

INTRODUCTION

This book is about doing social research, something that is fascinating, exciting, informative and enlightening. It can be time-consuming, challenging and, sometimes, frustrating too. It's the way we find out how the social world works.

There are a lot of books that claim to tell you how to do research for the social sciences. This one lives up to that claim – it is a genuinely *practical guide* for researchers, and though it is particularly aimed at those who are undertaking social research for the first time, the more experienced will find it an essential guide for more advanced work too.

The authors both teach research methods in the College of Social Sciences at the University of Birmingham and have used their combined experience as teachers, researchers and students to create an accessible text that takes you right through the research process from initial thoughts to the completion of the project, whether it is a successful dissertation or publication. Along the way you will find examples from many different social science disciplines of how research is used in the 'real world' and opportunities to see how you can apply these techniques to your research project.

This book is not designed to be read from cover to cover in one sitting. Instead, you can think of it as a series of guides targeted at five particular stages of research:

- Thinking about research
- Preparing for research
- Data collection
- Data analysis
- Data presentation and reports.

Each part is divided into a number of linked sections. All through the text you will find references to other sections (e.g. A2, B3, C4 and so on), which will help you to make the connections that can transform the quality of your work and support you in making the best possible use of your learning.

Throughout the book, research is seen as a *process* – something that is continuous (though it is made up of several linked stages) and ongoing. This helps the reader to appreciate that, for example, it is impossible to 'just' collect data. The researcher needs to understand that information and research do not exist in a vacuum but are part of a bigger whole that includes how we think about ourselves and our social world, our ideas and theories as well as more immediately practical issues like designing a questionnaire or analysing statistics. All through the text these links are emphasised in a way that helps the reader to comprehend both their individual significance and the way that they relate to each other.

Overall, it is the practical nature of this book that is its greatest strength; being able to see how others have used different theories and techniques (and how these work together) to increase our understanding of the working of the social world we live in and, of course, to change that world alongside thinking about how you can do your own research.

Undergraduate students writing a final-year dissertation will find this book useful, not only for guidance on how to research, but also for the specific section on presenting your findings in a variety of interesting ways, as well as support for the whole process of writing and presenting a dissertation.

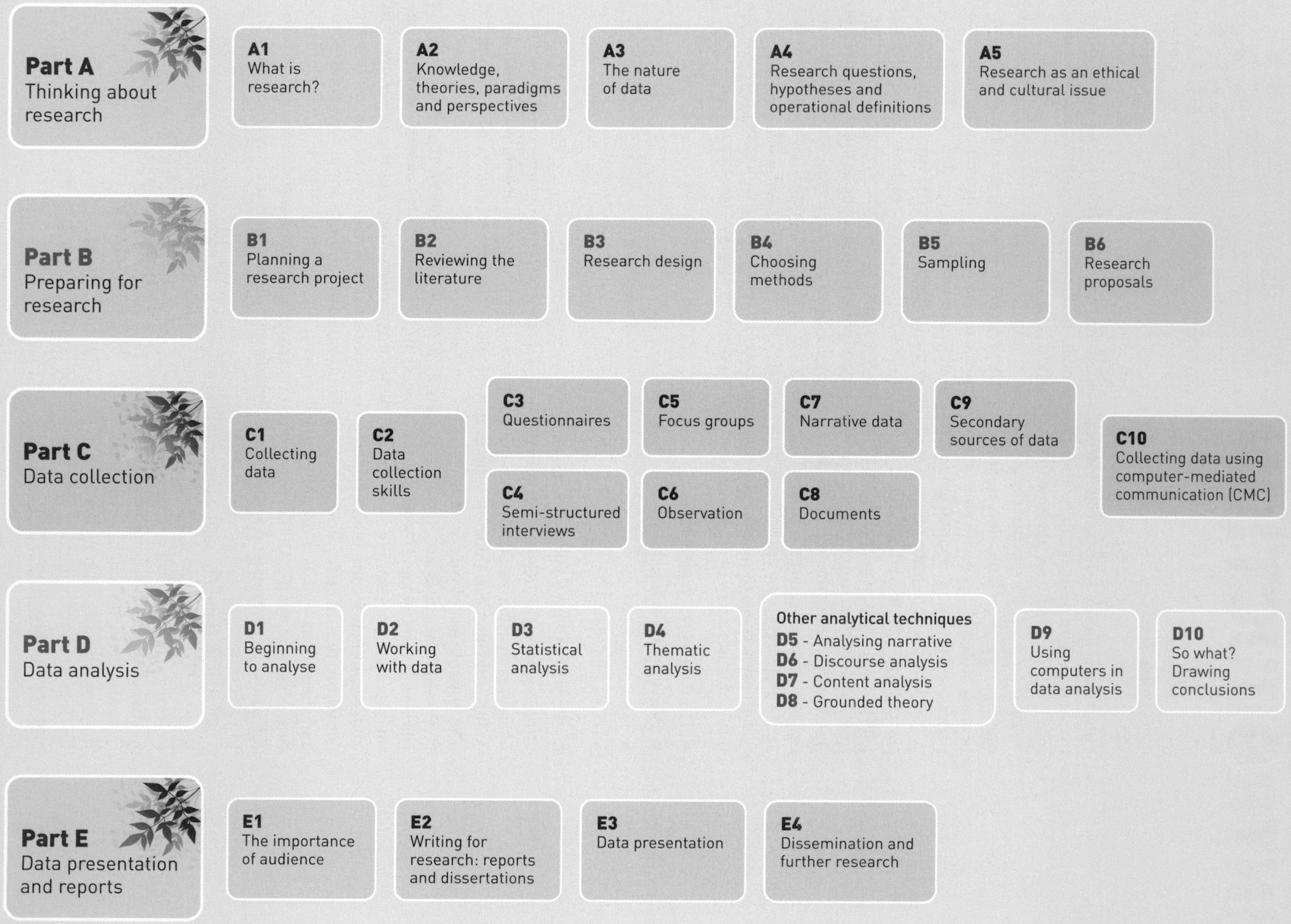

Part A
Thinking about research

A1
What is research?

A2
Knowledge, theories, paradigms and perspectives

A3
The nature of data

A4
Research questions, hypotheses and operational definitions

A5
Research as an ethical and cultural issue

Part B
Preparing for research

B1
Planning a research project

B2
Reviewing the literature

B3
Research design

B4
Choosing methods

B5
Sampling

B6
Research proposals

Part C
Data collection

C1
Collecting data

C2
Data collection skills

C3
Questionnaires

C4
Semi-structured interviews

C5
Focus groups

C6
Observation

C7
Narrative data

C8
Documents

C9
Secondary sources of data

C10
Collecting data using computer-mediated communication (CMC)

Part D
Data analysis

D1
Beginning to analyse

D2
Working with data

D3
Statistical analysis

D4
Thematic analysis

Other analytical techniques
D5 - Analysing narrative
D6 - Discourse analysis
D7 - Content analysis
D8 - Grounded theory

D9
Using computers in data analysis

D10
So what? Drawing conclusions

Part E
Data presentation and reports

E1
The importance of audience

E2
Writing for research: reports and dissertations

E3
Data presentation

E4
Dissemination and further research

Figure I.1 The book structure

The book

The structure of this book is a little unconventional because it is not written, as is commonly done, as either a large number of tangentially linked chapters or as a list of different data collection techniques. Instead, the book takes the reader on a self-guided journey through the five parts of the research process. Every reader can take his or her own path. Although we do recommend that you start at the beginning, it is likely that you will finish at a different point to others, depending on the requirements of your project.

Part A: Thinking about research

This first part is concerned with a series of linked issues, predominantly about the nature of the research process. First, the nature of research is discussed together with the importance of ensuring that research is of high quality, and this is followed by a section that looks at theories, paradigms and perspectives and links these intangibles with the real world of research practice. Then the complex nature of data is considered along with the ways in which it can be used to inform our understandings of social life. The subsequent section, A4, looks at the ways in which we can ask meaningful questions and the clear operational definitions that must be made if our work is to be valid and understandable to others. The final section examines ethical and cultural issues in research and the ways in which these need to be addressed to ensure that proper procedures are followed so that participants are treated with dignity and respect, that vulnerable people are not put at risk and that no harm comes to ourselves or others.

Part B: Preparing for research

This second part takes the reader through the first 'hands-on' stages of research, starting with how to plan your project and moving on to the process of reviewing the literature, one of the most important parts of undertaking any research. This section discusses the process of creating a *critical* literature review and covers all the issues of where to find the information, how to evaluate it and how to structure a useful literature review section. Subsequent sections in Part B examine different research designs, looking at how these might work for you, and reflects on how to choose research methods that fit with your project – of course, it also looks at the ongoing 'qualitative v. quantitative' debate and discusses mixed methods. This part concludes with sections on sampling, which is particularly important to understand if you want to make generalisations from your research, and how to write a research proposal.

Part C: Data collection

The third part talks about the processes of data collection and discusses the skills needed for this ultra-practical part of the research process. It then moves on to look at the most important data collection techniques, which include questionnaires, focus groups, interviews, observation, documents, vignettes, secondary data and narrative data collection. Each section includes details of the processes involved, real research examples and the advantages and disadvantages of the technique, and is presented so that readers will be able to choose the most appropriate techniques for their own research. There are interactive and reflective exercises together with multiple real-world examples to help you understand these complex issues and make choices that are right for your work. This part ends with a section on online data collection – a rapidly growing field.

Part D: Data analysis

This fourth part of the book is, arguably, the most complex. Its purpose is to describe not only the procedures necessary to analyse data, but also to ensure that the analysis has a purpose. Thus, it ends with a section (D10) on drawing conclusions and ensuring that people will not ask 'so what?' when they learn the findings of a research project.

The start of this part, however, talks about the reasons for analysis (many researchers seem to think that it is enough to collect data and present it – it isn't!) and the principles that underlie the process. It moves on through a section on working with data – which particularly examines the differences between structured and unstructured data and what to do with your data – to a series of linked sections about different analysis techniques and procedures. The main areas examined are statistical analysis (D3) and thematic analysis (D4) since these are the most common techniques used by students. There are also sections on other analytical techniques which include narrative analysis, discourse analysis, content analysis and grounded theory. A separate section looks at the use of computers in quantitative and qualitative analysis.

Part E: Data presentation and reports

This final part of the book talks about what happens when the research itself is completed; that is, what to do with the results, starting with a discussion of the importance of audience – a first, and crucial, step in how to present your data in different settings and to different people.

Section E2 is about writing and research. It pays particular attention to practical techniques and tips for writing reports and dissertations. It deals with the reasons that we do these different activities and also how to structure this sort of work. The examples and lessons from this section can be usefully applied to most of the writing tasks and assessments that students undertake.

The next section (E3) looks at the techniques for presenting data with some specific emphasis on practices that are becoming more popular including oral presentations and poster presentations. The final section is about disseminating your research to a wider audience and notes that no research project is ever really complete: there is always scope for further research in the future.

Throughout the book you will find:

- Real-life *examples* to help you to understand the points that are being made.
- *Real research* examples – examples of real research which has been carried out by social researchers in a wide variety of social science disciplines.
- *Think about it* boxes – questions and ideas to get you thinking more deeply about the subject.
- *Your research* – questions, activities and checklists for you to use to help you think through your own research project.
- *What is . . .* definitions of social research terms.

We are sure that you will find this book accessible, detailed and useful. We hope that you will come to understand, value and enjoy social research.

PART A
Thinking about research

CHAPTER A1
What is research?

Contents

In context

What do we mean by social research and why do we do it? In this introductory chapter we begin to look at these questions by thinking about what we mean by research and looking at some definitions. We introduce some of the characteristics and purposes of social research and suggest that it is helpful to think of social research as a process which needs to be planned and structured. How do we know if our social research is any good? We introduce the criteria used to check the quality of social research.

PART A: Thinking about research

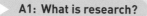 **A1: What is research?**

    A2: Knowledge, theories, paradigms and perspectives

    A3: The nature of data

    A4: Research questions, hypotheses and operational definitions

    A5: Research as an ethical and cultural issue

There is a sense in which we are all researchers. Every day we pose questions and we look for – or research – the answers.

> How do I get to the sports centre?
>
> What shall I have for lunch?
>
> Where shall we go for our holidays?
>
> Why have I got a headache?

In some cases we know where to find the answer; in other cases we may have to search or investigate the topic in more depth in order to locate our answer. How we find out more will depend on the resources – books, maps, internet and so on – we have, the people we can ask and our previous experience of the topic.

research quality
The reliability, validity, credibility and ethical practice of a piece of research.

While we are all familiar with this day-to-day personal researching it can only prepare us a little for the demands and challenges of social research which will enable us to ask questions and gain knowledge and understanding of the social world of which we are a part. In this chapter we introduce some of the key characteristics of such research and consider what we mean by **research quality**.

The 'what' of research

Think about it . . .
Why is research important?

Research in the social sciences is something very special: a **process** (we will return to this important term below) we use to understand our world in a way that goes far beyond simple description, common sense or anecdote.   (Pole and Lampard, 2002: 2)

process
An on-going, often continuous series of actions intended to achieve a specific result. This often requires the researcher to follow an established set of (usually) routine procedures.

It is easier to talk about *how* to do research than *what* it is. In part, that is because we all think we know what research is, so we often do not feel any necessity to define it clearly – this is not always helpful. The 'how' of research is the primary purpose of this book, so we do not intend to discuss it here.

Research does not always give us the results we expect or want – something J. R. R. Tolkien (author of *The Lord of the Rings*) noted when he (reputedly) said:

> *There is nothing like looking, if you want to find something. You certainly usually find something, if you look, but it is not always quite the something you were after.*

At the most basic level, research is the **process** we undertake when:

- we have a question to answer;
- we need to acquire knowledge;
- we want to extend our understanding of the social world.

Definitions of research

Just as **research** is carried out in a variety of contexts and by people with quite different understandings of and reasons for conducting research, so there are a variety of ways in which research itself is defined. We offer just a selection in the 'What is . . .' box on p. 8.

❓ What is . . .

Research

(1) . . . the systematic, controlled, empirical and critical investigation of hypothetical propositions about presumed relations among natural phenomena (Kerlinger, 1970: 8).

(2) 'Research' for the purpose of the RAE* is to be understood as *original investigation undertaken in order to gain knowledge and understanding*. It includes work of direct relevance to the needs of commerce, industry, and to the public and voluntary sectors; scholarship; the invention and generation of ideas, images, performances, artefacts including design, where these lead to new or substantially improved insights; and the use of existing knowledge in experimental development to produce new or substantially improved materials, devices, products and processes, including design and construction. It excludes routine testing and routine analysis of materials, components and processes such as for the maintenance of national standards, as distinct from the development of new analytical techniques. It also excludes the development of teaching materials that do not embody original research (www.rae.ac.uk, 2008; emphasis added).

(3) Research is a step-by-step process that involves collecting and examining information. We do research to improve our knowledge and understanding about the world we live in. It almost always involves finding out something new. (http://info.cancerresearchuk.org/cancerandresearch/aboutcancerresearch/whatisresearch)

(4) A search or investigation directed to the discovery of some fact by careful consideration or study of a subject; a course of critical or scientific inquiry. To search into (a matter or subject); to investigate or study closely (*OED*, 1989).

*The RAE is the *Research Assessment Exercise* which is used to judge the value of research undertaken by UK universities.

Think about it . . .

What do the definitions have in common? Now write your own definition, drawing on the key characteristics in our selection.

In each definition above, research is identified as a **process** or practice by which we can extend our knowledge or find the answers to our questions. Crucially, this process is transferable; that is, it is not usually specific to either the research topic or to the researcher. This is a blessing: at least we do not have to re-invent the wheel each time we start a new piece of research!

The 'why' of research

Research is undertaken for many reasons: perhaps we have an idea and want to know if it is true. For example, we might believe that house burglaries are more frequent when there is an increase in unemployment, but until we collect and analyse data to prove or disprove this notion, we cannot know for sure.

Real research

Burglary and unemployment

The Home Office publishes the British Crime Survey annually. In 2001, Tracey Budd looked at the results of the Survey and established that house burglaries *are* most frequent in areas that experience high rates of unemployment. For more details see: www.homeoffice.gov.uk/rds/prgpdfs/brf501.pdf.

But we might want to use research for other things too. We might, for example, want to establish the reasons that some particular event took place or we might want to understand more about how people react to social stimuli. There is really no limit to what we can research, though there are outside factors (such as time and money) that constrain our ability to do so.

Characteristics of research

In many ways, the process of research is quite simple. In its simplest form it can be thought of as having only three components:

1 The question
2. The research process
3. The answer.

Of course, it is item 2 that is the most complex and is the main purpose of this book (though research questions are critically important too and are discussed in several chapters of this book, particularly A4).

What is . . .

The nature of research IS:
- structured and purposeful (both in gathering and interpreting data);
- rigorous;
- robust and defensible;
- systematic.

The nature of research IS NOT:
- simply gathering information or facts (though this may be an important component of the process);
- divorced from practical life: some research deals with abstract ideas or theoretical development; other types change the 'real' world and our experience of it, often for the better.

Structured and purposeful

Research is not something that 'just happens'. It should always have a purpose. (This does not necessarily mean that the results of research *have* to have a practical application, though many do. The search for abstract knowledge is also a valid reason to research.) This does not mean that description, anecdote or common sense are useless; they make a significant contribution to our understanding of the world. But research should provide knowledge that is robust, defensible and useful (Pole and Lampard, 2002: 2).

Rigorous

Research should be strictly and scrupulously planned and conducted, not just in the obvious areas of data collection and analysis, but also in such things as design (B3) and ethical considerations (A5).

Robust and defensible

Research (particularly academic research) is often subject to the criticism of our peers or, in the case of students submitting work for assessment, our markers. Our research needs to be strong in all elements of its conception, design and practice so that our critics can understand how we arrived at conclusions and so that the researcher can defend those conclusions.

Systematic

This crucial term simply means that everything that is examined in the research (this could be people, or cases, or data sets, for example) is treated in the same way.

More than gathering facts

Research is not just gathering facts and/or data together and describing them; it is much more than this and is usually focused on explanation as well as description (D1).

Quality in research

In order that we can say that our research is rigorous and robust, we need to consider the issue of quality. What is a quality piece of research?

Research can vary considerably depending on the topic, the theoretical approach taken, the choice of data collection methods and so on, but there are some key concepts that help researchers to ensure that their research meets the quality standards expected by other researchers (and, in the case of students, those marking their research projects).

Real research

Quality criteria in research

Becker *et al.* (2006) undertook a complex research project to identify 'quality' in social policy research. They used mixed methods including an online survey and focus groups. The population was made up of social policy academics. They published a table (2006: 5) which ranked 35 quality criteria. The top five were:

1. Research written in ways that are accessible to appropriate audiences.
2. Research design that clearly addresses the research question(s).
3. Transparency in data collection and analysis.
4. A clear statement of how the research process was conducted.
5. That the research makes a contribution to knowledge.

Quality concepts

In social research there are four key aspects to research quality and these will be introduced here and discussed further in **A3**. They form the basis of the 'Research quality checks' which you will find at key stages throughout the book.

Reliability – or dependability (also sometimes called replicability)

In essence the question to ask of your research is:

Can my results be replicated by other researchers using the same methods?

In the natural sciences, for example, physics or chemistry, researchers would usually expect to get *exactly* the same results for the same experiment (however, see the 'Real research' box below – Whatever happened to cold fusion?).

In the social sciences, we mostly deal with people, not chemicals or falling weights. Every person is an individual and different. For this reason, no sane social science researcher would expect *exactly* the same result, but it should be similar for similar groups of people. Importantly, this means that *reliable* research is *not researcher specific*: it should be possible for any researcher to use the same methods on a similar group of people to achieve similar results. What we are concerned with in social research is that another researcher would expect to obtain the same findings if they carried out the research in the same way, or the researcher would expect to obtain the same findings if she tried again in the same way.

Real research

Whatever happened to cold fusion?

In 1989 two physicists in Salt Lake City, Utah, USA, announced that they had created controlled nuclear fusion in a glass jar in their laboratory (normally, this is something that happens either in the Sun, nuclear bombs or a very large, very specialised and very dangerous nuclear power station). The heat generated in the experiment promised a new power source for the planet and an end to global warming as well as huge financial rewards.

Unfortunately, other physicists have been unable to recreate the effect. Though there is no suggestion that the original experimenters were in any way attempting to mislead the scientific community, their experiment failed to demonstrate reliability and their personal credibility was seriously damaged (Taubes, 1993).

---

dependability
A measure of research quality, meaning, for example, that all data is included, and that no data is lost through unreliable audio recorders or inaccurate transcribers.

transparent
In a research context, this means that the research process and the decisions made by the researcher are recorded and available to others for scrutiny.

The concept of **dependability** is related and is often referred to in relation to qualitative research methods (**B4**) but is applicable to most research approaches. This usually applies to consistency in research practice, for example, ensuring that all data is included, and that no data is lost through unreliable audio recorders or inaccurate transcribers.

The reliability and dependability of a piece of research is demonstrated through the research process and the decisions made by the researcher being **transparent** and available to others for scrutiny.

Validity and credibility

This apparently simple quality concept is really asking the question:

> *Am I researching the thing that I think I am?*

and

> *Are the data that I am gathering relevant to my research question (will they help me to answer my research question or test my hypothesis)?*

Here the concern is with the researcher's decisions about what data to gather and interpretation of the data gathered. It usually refers to whether or not the researcher is measuring and finding out what she think she is and how that relates to her research questions.

Think about it . . .

What are you really asking about?

The Black Report of 1980 (Townsend and Davidson, 1982) was the first detailed investigation of the health status of people from different social classes in Britain. Its main finding was that people from the lowest social class were 2.5 times more likely to die before retirement than those in the highest social class.

If you were to try to bring their work up to date today, would it be enough to examine individuals' age at death and social class?

What else might be relevant? List your ideas below.

_____

_____

_____

_____

_____

_____

_____

_____

_____

(Suggested answers at the end of this section.)

---

credibility
The credibility (or believability) of the researcher's interpretations of the data she has gathered is tested by the analysis and interpretation of data being transparent, for example, by testing out the interpretation of the data with the research participants or by setting the interpretations alongside existing theory.

A related concept is **credibility**. The credibility (or believability) of the researcher's interpretations of the data she has gathered is tested by the transparency of the analysis and interpretation of the data, for example, by testing out the interpretation of the data with the research participants or by setting the interpretations alongside existing theory.

Generalisability and transferability

**generalisability/
transferability**
Measures of research quality in which the researcher asks 'How far am I able to claim that the results or findings from my research are true for or relevant to the wider population or a different context?'

Generalisability and **transferability** refer to the question:

> *How far am I able to claim that the results or findings from my research are true for or relevant to the wider population or a different context?*

For some research the claims will depend on a statistical demonstration that findings from a sample can be regarded as more or less true for the population as a whole. In other cases the claim that findings from one context or time can be transferred or say something about another context or time can be demonstrated by reference to relevant theory or other research. It is important to recognise that small-scale research can still have value, though it can rarely claim to be generalisable. It is equally important *not* to claim more for your research findings than can be clearly demonstrated to the satisfaction of other researchers.

Ethical practice

Here we are asking the question:

> *Have I given full consideration to the way I behave as a researcher with respect to the other human beings who are involved in my research?*

Social research practice involves the participation of human beings and working with information about people (A5). A quality piece of research can demonstrate that due consideration has been given to the ethics concerning research behaviour, the possible impact of the research on the research participants and the honesty and care of the researcher. For some researchers this would include considering the value of the research in terms of its potential benefit to the research participants or, more widely, to particular groups of people and making the findings as widely available as possible.

Who are social researchers?

Everybody who ever asks a question about the way we live, how something happens or why, is a researcher of sorts. However, as we say above, research is about much more than asking (or even answering) questions: it is about the way we do it.

Social researchers are everywhere. They work for local and central government, for charities, schools, clubs, football teams, etc. However, to be a 'good' researcher takes time and effort and an understanding of the quality issues involved.

The way forward

Doing social research isn't always easy. There are many difficult issues that we have to deal with along the way (the rest of this book tells you about them and how to overcome them successfully). With perseverance, however, comes success.

Your research

Some useful things to remember

- Research is a *process*.
- Research has to be planned. It does *not* happen by accident.
- Facts and data are not necessarily the same as knowledge.
- Description is *not* the same as explanation.
- Research must be robust and rigorous. It must be capable of withstanding criticism and challenge from individuals and organisations who may not agree with the methods used or the findings produced.

Think about it . . .

Some suggested answers

What are you really asking about?

The Black Report of 1980 (Townsend and Davidson, 1982) was the first detailed investigation of the health status of people from different social classes in Britain. Its main finding was that people from the lowest social class were 2.5 times more likely to die before retirement than those in the highest social class.

If you were to try to bring their work up to date today, would it be enough to examine individuals' ages at death and social class?

What else might be relevant?

The questions about age of death and social class are, obviously, central to this enquiry. However, they would only provide very basic information and probably would not be very helpful in explaining the difference in death rates. You may want to consider other ways of measuring health status. Anyway, to ask such simple questions suggests that you may not have thought the question through thoroughly. We think that there are issues such as income, employment, geography, environment, education, pollution, health, politics, genetics, social justice (and others) that are *hidden* in the two simple questions and these would need to be considered before a conclusion was reached.

References and further reading

Becker, S., Bryman, A. and Sempik, J. (2006) *Defining 'Quality' in Social Policy Research: Views, Perceptions and a Framework for Discussion*, SPA, Lavenham in conjunction with JUC.

Budd, T. (2001) Burglary: Practice Messages from the British Crime Survey, Home Office Briefing Note 5/01, July. Available from www.homeoffice.gov.uk/rds/prgpdfs/brf501.pdf (accessed 6 August 2009).

Cancer Research UK (2004) What is research? *Cancer and Research, About Cancer Research* (online), Cancer Research UK. Available from http://info.cancerresearchuk.org/cancerandresearch/aboutcancerresearch/whatisresearch/ (accessed 6 August 2009).

Corbetta, P. (2003) *Social Research: Theory, Methods and Techniques*, London: Sage.

Kerlinger, F. N. (1970) *Foundations of Educational Research*, New York: Holt, Reinhart & Winston.

Pole, C. and Lampard, R. (2002) *Practical Social Investigation: Qualitative and Quantitative Methods in Social Research*, Harlow: Pearson Education.

Research Assessment Exercise (2008) *Guidance on Submissions (Annex B)*, available from www.rae.ac.uk/Pubs/2005/03/rae0305.doc (accessed 6 August 2009).

Taubes, G. (1993) *Bad Science: The Short Life and Weird Times of Cold Fusion*, New York: Random House.

Townsend, P. and Davidson, N. (1982) *Inequalities in Health: The Black Report*, Harmondsworth: Penguin.

CHAPTER A2
Knowledge, theories, paradigms and perspectives

Contents

In context

Have you ever wondered why people think and act in different ways? This chapter asks you to think about this from a research point of view. It discusses information and knowledge, how we know and understand things and how we use our knowledge and understanding to construct a particular way of looking at the social world. Though this might sound confusing and hard to comprehend, it is very important: if we don't understand how researchers look at the world, then we will probably have difficulty in understanding their research.

PART A: Thinking about research

A1: What is research?

▶ **A2: Knowledge, theories, paradigms and perspectives**

A3: The nature of data

A4: Research questions, hypotheses and operational definitions

A5: Research as an ethical and cultural issue

Where do we start?

As we saw in **A1**, we are all researchers! Most people will be familiar with the idea of 'researching' a topic for an assignment or researching about something you want to buy or a holiday you want to go on. We are all everyday researchers – wanting to find out the facts or what someone else thinks of something or somebody, from a new girlfriend to the government's policy on nuclear power.

If you are researching a topic for an assignment you will probably be looking for a mixture of different types of **information** – perhaps in the form of statistics, the opinions and ideas of key academics and researchers in that area, the theories or sets of ideas that seem to underpin the way the topic is seen and understood and, depending on your discipline, you may be interested to find out more about, for example, the government's policy on this topic, the economics related to that topic, the specific cultural aspects and so on.

When you gather information for an assignment you are selecting that which will help you to address a question and to demonstrate your **understanding** of both the question and the information you use to discuss the issues raised by the question. In answering your assignment questions you are doing more than simply presenting the facts or a set of ideas – you will be expected to work with the information to enable you to discuss, explain, analyse critically and draw some conclusions.

So what is different about doing *social* research – and why do we need to think a bit more about it as students within our own disciplinary areas? As students in sociology, social policy, political science, economics, social anthropology, criminal justice, social work and so on, we need, first of all, to apply our everyday student research skills and experience to the topic of *social research* itself. This may be a bit surprising and may not be something that you expected to be doing – but we will try to make it worthwhile and to show you how important this is as you begin to think about your own social research. As with all good assignments, we begin with a title and an introduction – and will then include an example (introduced in Example A2.1) which will run through this section and serve to illustrate the points that are being made. We will also suggest some activities to help you to think about your own research topic. There will also be places where you are directed to other sections of the book which will help you to think through the points made in relation to your own social research.

So our assignment title might be something like:

What is social research and what are the ideas, theories and perspectives that influence the way in which social research is carried out?

To address this question we will be discussing the following in this chapter:

- The nature of the subject matter of social research – what is the **social world**?
- As part of that social world, what **do** we or what **can** we 'know' about it? As a human being – and part of the social world – what is the relationship of a social researcher to the social world he is studying?
- What is there to study, to find out about – **ontology**? And why do people see things differently?
- Thinking about what there is to study – how can we do that? What ways are there of 'looking' at the social world – **epistemology** – that can help us to think about what we want to study and how we can do it?

❓ What is . . .

Ontology
Ontology is the science of what is, of the kinds and structures of objects, properties, events, processes and relations in every area of reality (Smith, 2003: 155).

---

information
Knowledge gained through study, experience or instruction: what we are told.

understanding
Grasping the meaning of information.

social world
The setting or cultural surroundings in which social research takes place.

? What is . . .

Epistemology (1)

Epistemology is the theory of knowledge and how we know things.

(We offer slightly different definitions below in the sections on ontology and epistemology.)

- What are we trying to do when we do social research (see also A1)?
- How can theories help us in our social research?
- What does this mean for me as a student social researcher?

Example A2.1

'Number of marriages falls to record low' – *Guardian*, 22 February 2007

'Worlds apart – poll finds parents out of touch' – *Guardian*, 24 February 2007

'Teenage gang shooting blamed on family breakdown' – *Guardian*, 23 February 2007

'Fathers told: do more for your children' – *Guardian*, 27 February 2007

'Mothers bear brunt of discrimination at work – women with children are seen as less reliable' – *Guardian*, 1 March 2007

This chapter includes some quite abstract material so an example is included to help your understanding of the key points. Throughout this chapter there are example boxes which will take you through some of the points being made in relation to a particular area of the social world – *the family*.

As we write this, a topic that is rarely far from the news in the UK has hit the headlines again. Throughout the latter part of the twentieth century and into the twenty-first, the family, with its changing composition and the role it is thought by some to play in many aspects of daily and social life, has been a topic of interest, concern and research and it is one of the social units that most people experience themselves in some way.

The family, as a social unit, encompasses a number of different elements:

- It can include people who are related to each other by blood, by law and by choice.
- It can include the relationship between parent(s) and child.
- It can include legal and choice relationships between adults.
- Members of a family may or may not live in the same household.
- And probably many others!

The family, as a social unit, is of concern to: policy-makers, economists, house builders, social and health care providers, the police, the retail industry, education providers, travel agents, car makers, lawyers and many others!

Some changes that have had an impact on the family as a social unit in the last 50 years include:

- laws relating to divorce, cohabitation and civil partnerships;
- effective means of contraception and abortion;
- education and employment opportunities for women;
- lengthening lifespan.

What is the nature of the subject matter of social research – what is the 'social world'?

As social scientists we begin by thinking about what interests us in the world in which we live. We can say that we are interested in the 'social' aspects. We talk about human beings being 'social animals' – having the physical characteristics of many other animals but it is our social characteristics that make us human beings.

When social scientists talk about something being 'social' they are usually talking about a situation or context where there is relationship and interaction between two or more people. Interaction and social relationships depend on language – the main means of communication between people – as the way in which we are able to be *social* beings. It is the language of relating and interacting that enables us to act together, to organise ourselves into social groups and units and to make and put into effect group decisions. As human beings we have many social experiences in common with others who live in different geographical locations (or even in different times), for example, learning, work and family life. Although the particular form or set of ideas about such social experiences may be different, there are likely to be similarities and this enables us to identify some common and key aspects of a 'social world'.

However, we are not just social beings, we are also individuals. Each person, as a unique individual, has a sense of 'self' (the specific and personal way that he or she interacts with 'others'). This enables us, as individuals, to reflect on our relationships and interactions with others and to 'tell our own story', based on our own perspective of social reality as it appears to us. We are able to describe, try to explain, and sometimes challenge, other people's behaviour (and their behaviour may in turn affect the way we feel about them and about ourselves, just as our behaviour may affect them).

It is this that social scientists are interested in – the social relationship between individuals and the social world and how and why the social world is and becomes as it is. C. Wright Mills (a famous American sociologist) describes this as 'the sociological imagination':

> We have come to know that every individual lives, from one generation to the next, in some society: that he lives out a biography, and that he lives it out within some historical sequence. By the fact of his living he contributes, however minutely, to the shaping of this society and to the course of history, even as he is made by society and its historical push and shove.
>
> The sociological imagination enables us to grasp history and biography and the relations between the two within society. That is its task and its promise.   (Wright Mills, 1959)

Think about it . . .

The *family* is often studied and talked about as a social unit, one in which different members of the family have their own roles in relation to each other but together they make up a whole. But each individual has their own experience of the family unit itself.

If you have brothers and sisters you may already be well aware that they have had different experiences within your family to you and may recount common family stories with quite a different slant!

Whose story is the 'real' story?

It is clear then that one of the particularly interesting things about being a social scientist and a social researcher is that we are studying something of which we are a part. We are

natural sciences
The study of the physical world and associated phenomena, including such disciplines as chemistry, physics, etc.

social phenomenon
Anything that influences or is influenced by human beings who interact with and are responsive to each other.

members of the social world which provides the subject matter of our study. This distinguishes social sciences from the **natural sciences**.

While, of course, social human beings are engaged in the study of the physical world, the subject matter of their study is not social but physical and is independent of them and the way they understand it. In other words a tree has an entity and physical structure of its own, regardless of the scientist who is studying the way it grows. Can we say the same about a **social phenomenon** like an organisation, the family or a community?

As we shall see later, this is a key philosophical question which has always troubled social scientists and there are different sets of ideas about this which have underpinned the ways that social research has developed over the past hundred years and the ways we think about social research today.

A brief history of social research can be found on pages 38–40. We suggest that you read it alongside or after this chapter to enable you to place the discussion in the chapter within the framework of the history and development of social research.

As part of the social world ourselves, what *do* we and what *can* we 'know' about it?

As social human beings we already know a lot about the world in which we live and in particular we know about our own context, the historical time, the geographical place and the social settings in which we are situated – our home, our university department, our local shopping centre and so on. We also know that there is more to find out and that we have some of the means to get hold of that **knowledge**.

? What is . . .

Knowledge
(1) information about or awareness of something, an issue, a fact;
(2) an understanding of a matter, a fact, an issue.

We have access to books written many years ago or more recently, we can log on to current information gathered on the other side of the world via the internet, we hear of research being done that predicts what will happen in the future using, for example, climate change models.

Think about it . . . ✳

So how do we know what we know? Jot down five things you know about your family and think about how you come to have that knowledge.

My family	How do I know this?
1. _____	_____
2. _____	_____
3. _____	_____
4. _____	_____
5. _____	_____

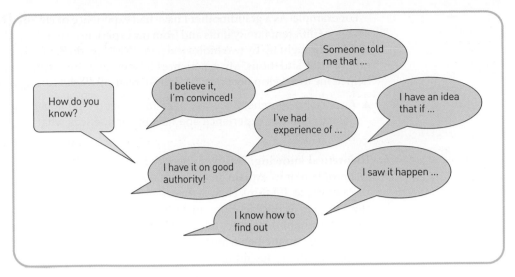

Figure A2.1   Ways of knowing

Depending on the type of statements you have made about your family, you may have already found that you are demonstrating that there are different ways of knowing about it (see Figure A2.1).

Becker and Bryman (2004) draw on the work of Burns (2000) and Brechin and Siddell (2000) to identify and classify five different ways of knowing. We have linked these to our own examples of knowledge related to the family below. But how useful is this knowledge to us as social researchers? See below and note that, as a social researcher, you may need to reflect on, question or challenge some of the knowledge you bring to your research.

Five ways of knowing

1. **Belief:** Sometimes we hold on to what we know because we believe it to be true. Strong beliefs may not be changed even when there is contrary evidence.

   For example: I may believe that it is always better for children to be brought up with two biological parents – my deeply felt belief may come from a combination of my own and observed experience, and perhaps my moral values or religious faith, and my belief may be strong enough for me to ignore other examples that differ from my own; when, for example, children brought up with only one parent present or in a stepfamily do well, or when a child is abused by one of its biological parents.

   ▲ As social researchers we may need to challenge our own beliefs and assumptions.

2. **Authoritative knowledge:** We may feel convinced that something is true because an authority (the Bible, Koran, a leader or teacher) tells us it is true. We perceive such knowledge to have a higher authority than knowledge gained from our own experience.

   For example: I may feel that I know it is true that marriage between a man and a woman is the best form of relationship because I have been told by a religious authority or a leader, or I may know because 'my mother told me'.

   ▲ As social researchers we may have to question the authority of such sources of knowledge.

3. **Experiential knowing:** Knowledge can be built up from experience over many years. This can be knowledge we do not realise we have – and it may be difficult to express to others.

For example: As a grandmother I have had experience of children being brought up in a range of different family units and from my experience I would find it hard to argue that children brought up by two biological parents always do better than those brought up in other family situations. My experiences of spending time with young children has also helped me to develop my practical skills in relating to and caring for young children.

▲ As social researchers we may need to reflect on the knowledge and skills we have gained from our experience and how this influences what we are interested in and what we do.

4. **Theoretical knowing:** Having a theory or set of ideas helps us to work out a response to a problem or to explain an aspect of our social world.

For example: If I think (have a theory) that there are a number of different factors that affect the way a child develops, including the people the child lives with on a day-to-day basis, the school they go to, the neighbourhood they live in and so on, then I am likely to try to explain the behaviour of young people in these terms and not simply in terms of their family composition.

▲ As social researchers we can begin to identify the theories we use in everyday life and the theories that are used by others studying the same aspects of the social world.

5. **Empirical knowledge:** This is knowledge based on available research evidence – data that have been gathered to answer research questions or test hypotheses which can be checked through further research.

For example: One of the headlines in Example A2.1: 'Teenage gang shooting blamed on family breakdown' heads a report on a piece of research that asked people what *they* thought was to blame for an increase in gun-related crime among young men. Eighty per cent of the 1,000 people (aged over 18) interviewed agreed with the statement that 'one factor is family breakdown and the lack of discipline in the home' (ICM Research, *Guardian February 2007 Poll* (online), available at www.icmresearch.co.uk/pdfs/2007_february_guardian_february_poll.pdf (accessed 6 August 2009)). This research tells us what people *think* – it does not tell us whether gun crime *is* caused by family breakdown and lack of discipline in the home. Another piece of research may help us to explore this further.

▲ As social researchers we need to develop the skills to enable us to gather data to answer research questions or test hypotheses, to develop knowledge-based theories.

Source: Adapted from Becker and Bryman (2004) p. 41. Reproduced with permission from Polity Press.

Your research

Look back at your five things you know about your family – which of the five ways of knowing are each of your statements? At this stage you might also like to try the same exercise again, putting your own research topic in place of 'your family'.

My research topic   How do I know this?

1. _____   _____

2. _____   _____

3. _____   _____

4. _____   _____

5. _____   _____

Knowledge and truth

It will be clear from the examples above that knowledge is not just a collection of facts. Rather it is about the *act of knowing* and what we feel we can say we know. It can also be the basis of being able to act. Without the knowledge we get from a timetable, we are unable to make sure we can catch the train. Without the knowledge gathered in research on the family which identifies the impacts of changes, we cannot decide whether a new policy or practice should be introduced to try to address these.

However, knowing something does not mean that we can say that it is true although the knower may believe it to be so. In everyday life, our knowledge is often sufficient for us to take action as if it were true. In some circumstances evidence may be provided to support a knowledge statement and attempt to convince us of its truth, as in a court of law, or we may be prepared to accept that the information we have been given is true because we trust the source of the information or we know from experience the chances of it being true.

In social research there is a concern for the truth in terms of how far we can say that our knowledge of a social phenomenon corresponds to, or is the same as, the reality of the social phenomenon itself. This then raises the question of the nature or reality of a social phenomenon and what there is about it that can be known and how we can know what there is to know.

Imagine that you have been invited to a family party (a social phenomenon) by your girlfriend's or boyfriend's family. At the end of the evening what would you be able to say you *know* about the reality of the party?

- You know what you have observed using your senses of sight and hearing (and, perhaps, taste and smell).
- You could use your own experience to interpret or make sense of your observations.
- You know what other people have told you, for example, their names, relationships, work, opinions about the government, etc.
- Your experience of similar occasions may help you to know what sorts of things may have been going on.
- Your experience of similar occasions may help you to identify what worked, what made it a good party, or what might have led to an argument.
- You may be able to put yourself into the shoes of some of the people there and try to understand how it was for them.

But how closely does your knowledge of the party then correspond to the true reality of the party? Does the party have a reality apart from the combined experiences and perceptions of the partygoers themselves?

ontology
The 'science or study of being'; in social research, ontology refers to the way the social world is seen to be and what can be assumed about the nature and reality of the social phenomena that make up the social world.

epistemology
The theory of knowledge and how we know things.

These are the central issues of **ontology** and **epistemology**. Few social researchers would claim in their research findings that they have discovered 'the truth' and most would agree that knowledge can only be partial because of the nature of the social world, and their own position as part of that social world. However, as we shall see, there are different views on the nature of the social world and what there is to know about it. This means that there are different positions or stances on the claims that can be made about the knowledge gained from studying it. Blaikie suggests that there are at least three approaches to truth, reflecting the different ways social researchers see the social world:

One typical and common approach adopts the view that there are truths to be known about the way the natural and social worlds work: regularities that make up the independently existing reality can be discovered, described and explained by theories, the truth of which can be reliably established. Another approach argues that all knowledge of these worlds is tentative; we can only approach the truth but never know when we have discovered it . . . Our knowledge is limited by the fact that reality cannot be observed directly, but only through concepts and theories we choose to use; change the concepts and theories and what appears to be reality will also change. A more radical position claims that all knowledge of the world, but particularly of the social world, is relative in time and space; there are no absolute truths.   (Blaikie, 1993: 6)

Situated knowledge

Knowledge is also *situated* with particular people or within specific contexts. It is held by the people who 'know' and we need to consider whose subjective knowledge we will gather as social researchers. We noted above, for example, that different members of the same family may have different stories (or knowledge) about family experiences they have shared. Similarly, if we consider the partygoers' accounts of the party, different people's views on the party are likely to vary significantly, but a dominant account of it having been a 'good party' may emerge from those whose opinions are seen to count for more, while the opinions and experiences of other members and 'outsiders' may count for little.

Some social researchers (see, for example, Example A2.7 on page 34) argue that knowledge held by more powerful groups dominates the way in which the social world is known and understood and the knowledge held by the less powerful is ignored or hidden; and, as we will see later, this influences the approaches they take to studying the social world and the methods used to collect data. The ethical and power relationships of social researchers with their data sources is discussed in **A5**.

Our ideas and perspectives on knowledge, what we know and how we know, will then impact on the way in which we think about and design social research, and we move on now to consider different ways of thinking about the social world, what there is to know and how we can know about it.

What is there in the social world to study, to find out about? And why do people see things differently?

Thinking about different ways of knowing helps us to begin to think further about what there is to know within the social world. We have already identified that people's own knowledge of their social world comes from a range of different sources: from their beliefs, perhaps associated with their values; from those whom they regard as authorities on different aspects of their social world; from their own experience; from their common sense of how things are; from the theories that they and others develop about how and why things happen as they do; and finally from organised collections of data or information to test out an idea or theory – or to see what is out there.

Ontology

To begin to think about what this means for us as social researchers, we now need to have a look at one of the terms already mentioned – ontology. Ontology refers to the way the social world and the social phenomena or entities that make it up are viewed. These social phenomena can include social groups of people like the family or a gender or ethnic group, institutions and organisations, as well as social situations, events and social behaviour (including social research itself). What can we know about these social phenomena? What is the nature of the knowledge available to us as social researchers?

There are different ontological positions that we are going to consider, namely, objectivism, constructivism and realism.

Objectivism

objectivism
An ontological position which asserts that the social phenomena that make up our social world have an existence of their own, apart from and independent of the social actors (humans) who are involved.

Objectivism asserts that the social phenomena that make up our social world have an existence of their own (rather like our tree!), apart from and independent of the social actors (humans) who are involved. The social researcher's relationship to the social world and the social phenomenon he is studying is therefore one of objective observation.

The objectivist position derives from the approach often taken by natural scientists who study the way the natural physical world of animals, plants, cells, atoms, nuclei and chemical elements behaves. This approach values the objectivity and independence of the researcher and identifies the characteristics of the social world in terms of entities which are ordered and predictable and can be identified and recorded without affecting the entities themselves.

> ## Think about it . . .
> ### The family from an objectivist position
>
> The family can be seen as a social unit which includes people who are related to each other by blood or law. This may be extended to groups of people who, though not related by blood or law, live as if they were related and consider themselves to be a family. The relationships may be defined by law or custom to include responsibilities, for example, for financial arrangements and social behaviour, particularly of children. There are certain life events that mark changes within the family – a marriage, the birth of a child, a divorce and so on – which can be identified.
>
> Although each individual family will vary, the idea of a family as a social unit has a reality that is independent of the particular individuals who are members of it. The family represents a particular set of relationships and behaviours to which individual members conform to differing degrees.

Constructivism

constructivism
An ontological position which asserts that the social phenomena making up our social world are only real in the sense that they are constructed ideas which are continually being reviewed and reworked by those involved in them through social interaction and reflection.

Constructivism asserts that the social phenomena making up our *social* world are only real in the sense that they are constructed ideas which are continually being reviewed and reworked by those involved in them (the *social actors*) through social interaction and reflection. There is no *social* reality apart from the meaning of the social phenomenon for the participants. However, the meanings attributed to and the understandings of a social phenomenon (like an organisation, the family, a community, social care, the law), which are constructed by the social actors, *are* available for study. Most importantly, the social researcher, as part of the social world herself, brings her own meanings and understandings to her study.

> ## Think about it . . .
> ### The family from a constructivist position
>
> The family is seen as situated within a particular time, space and culture. It is the product of the meaning given to it by the participants. In other words, what is interesting – and can be studied – is what people themselves understand as 'family' and how they use this understanding to make sense of their lives together as a family.
>
> Relationships – like parent, child, brother, partner – are worked with on a day-to-day basis and what it means to be a parent, for example, is continually being reviewed and reworked through social interaction with each child and other members of the family *and* the experiences and understandings prevalent in their time and culture.
>
> This means that ideas about parenthood within the culture itself are also continually being constructed and reconstructed by its members and these ideas are demonstrated in the ways in which parenthood is discussed or written about.

Realism

The objectivist and constructivist positions are often presented as incompatible opposites where each position rules out the other. This suggests that the two positions cover all there is to know about the social world.

However, some social scientists would suggest that there is more to the reality of the social world than can be observed by the senses. **Realism** accepts that the social world has a reality that is separate from the social actors involved in it and that this can be known through the senses. In addition to this, though, there is a dimension that is hidden from the senses, which cannot be directly observed. This hidden dimension relates to what we know about the social world as social beings who are part of the world and affects the way we behave and understand our social lives. This dimension is described as including structures and mechanisms that trigger or affect the social reality that can be observed. While the mechanisms and structures themselves are not observable, their impact can be observed in the way people behave.

realism (1)
An ontological position which asserts that the social world has a reality that is separate from the social actors involved in it, that can be known through the senses as well as the effects of 'hidden' structures and mechanisms.

Think about it . . .
The family from a realist position

On the face of it, the family is a group of people with an observable set of relationships among them. A realist position would suggest that there are hidden mechanisms and structures which need to be present in order for the family to take a particular form. These could include, for example: children's psychological need for security, physical care and continuity; biological reproduction requiring male and female involvement; formation of gender identity including sexuality, fathering and bearing children; human needs for emotional and social support.

We use theories about our social world and ourselves as social beings to help us to identify potential hidden mechanisms and understand how they work.

What ways are there of 'looking' at the social world that can help us to think about what we want to study and how we can do it?

Three positions on the nature of the social world and what there is to study have been identified and discussed – the ontological positions of objectivism, constructivism and realism. We will now use these to think about how taking different positions on the nature of the social world impacts on the ways we can gather knowledge about the social phenomena found in the social world. We need to introduce another term – **epistemology**. This refers to what can be regarded as knowledge about a social phenomenon and considers what sort of knowledge it is acceptable to use to help us to study that phenomenon as social researchers.

❓ What is . . .

Epistemology (2)

An epistemology is a theory of knowledge; it presents a view and a justification for what can be regarded as knowledge – what can be known and what criteria such knowledge must satisfy in order to be called knowledge rather than beliefs (Blaikie, 1993: 6–7).

Three different epistemological positions – positivism, interpretivism and realism – will be introduced and, as they unfold, you will begin to see how they may impact on your choice of research topic and in particular on the research questions you adopt.

Positivism

positivism
An epistemological position which asserts that knowledge of a social phenomenon is based on what can be observed and recorded rather than subjective understandings.

We mentioned earlier that some social scientists have argued that the approaches of the natural sciences can be applied to studying social phenomena and the first epistemological approach to be introduced is that traditionally taken by natural scientists – the **positivist approach**. This develops from the objectivist ontological position that there is a social reality to study that is independent of the researcher and the research subjects.

A positivist approach has a number of distinct features:

hypothesis
A proposal or statement that is intended to explain observations or facts; it can be thought of as an 'informed guess' about the social world that, if true, would explain the phenomenon being researched.

- Knowledge is defined as that which can be observed by the senses.
- Knowledge of the social phenomenon is based on what can be observed and recorded rather than subjective understandings.
- Usually data are gathered to test a **hypothesis** which has been generated from existing theory.
- The researcher is independent of and has no impact on the data – the researcher is objective.

What is . . .

Positivist approach
A positivist approach to social research typically means:
- *quantitative* data are collected;
- aspects of the social world, social phenomena, are measured;
- *causal relationships* between different aspects of the social world are sought;
- large *data sets* and *statistical analysis* are often used.

(See Chapters **A3** and **B4** for much more about this.)

Example A2.2

A positivist approach to studying the relationship between family breakdown and the increase in gun crime

Earlier we highlighted an opinion poll which found that 80% of adults questioned thought that family breakdown and the lack of discipline in the home are factors in the increase in gun-related crime among young men. How might we research the relationship between family breakdown and young men participating in gun-related crime?

Taking a positivist approach we might:

1. Set up a hypothesis that young men who have experienced family breakdown are more likely to be involved in serious crime than those who have not experienced family breakdown.

2. Define 'family breakdown' in terms of observable indicators, e.g. day-to-day presence or absence of two biological parents, divorce of parents, involvement of other members of the family in crime.

3. Consider other theories about young men and crime, e.g. young men who are not in employment or education are more likely to commit crime.

4. Collect data about a large sample of young men including evidence of 'family breakdown' and any criminal activity, and data relating to the other theories considered.

5. Use statistical analysis to identify relationships (which have the potential to be causal relationships) within the data.

Interpretivism

There is a longstanding debate within the social sciences with regard to the usefulness of natural science research positions to the study of the social world, and a significant part of that debate revolves around the use of the positivist approach to studying social phenomena. Many social scientists believe that social research must include understandings and explanations of social phenomena which are not necessarily observable by the senses but can be interpreted by a fellow human being, the social researcher. The epistemological position that has emerged and developed from this is called **interpretivism**.

interpretivism
An epistemological position that prioritises people's subjective interpretations and understandings of social phenomena and their own actions.

Thus this is a position that prioritises people's subjective interpretations and understandings of social phenomena and their own actions, and can be linked to the ontological position of constructivism – where the nature of a social phenomenon is in the understanding and meanings ascribed to the social phenomenon by the social actors:

> *knowledge is seen to be derived from everyday concepts and meanings – the social researcher enters the social world in order to grasp the socially constructed meanings and then reconstructs them in social scientific language. At one level these latter accounts are regarded as redescriptions of everyday accounts; at another level they are developed into theories.* (Blaikie, 1993: 96)

An **interpretivist approach** has the following features:

- Knowledge gathered includes people's interpretations and understandings.
- The main focus is on how people interpret the social world and social phenomena, enabling different perspectives to be explored.
- The researcher is interpreting other people's interpretations in terms of the theories and concepts of the social researcher's discipline – studying the social phenomenon as if through the eyes of the people being researched.
- The researcher works with the data gathered to generate theory.

⁇ What is . . .

Interpretivist approach
An interpretivist approach to social research typically means:
- *qualitative* (rich in detail and description) data is collected;
- uncovering and working with *subjective* meanings;
- *interpretation of meaning* within a specific *context*;
- *empathetic* understanding, 'standing in the other's shoes'.

(See Chapters A3 and B4 for much more about this.)

Example A2.3

An interpretivist approach to studying the relationship between family breakdown and the increase in gun crime

Earlier we highlighted an opinion poll which found that 80% of adults questioned thought that family breakdown and the lack of discipline in the home are factors in the increase of gun-related crime among young men. How might we research the relationship between family breakdown and young men participating in gun-related crime?

Taking an interpretivist approach we might:

1. Explore with young men who have been or are involved in activities that include having guns, how they see their own situation in relation to others involved with them and the people who are potential or real victims.

2. Enable young men to tell their own story of how they became involved in activities that include having guns.

3. Examine the ways in which young men talk and write about guns and crime on the internet.

4. Enable parents of young men who may have guns and be involved in gun-related crime to give their understanding of their role as parents.

5. From the rich and detailed data gathered, identify possible explanations for the participation of some young people in gun-related crimes.

Realism

Positivism and interpretivism have been seen to be in opposition to each other and social scientists coming to their research from one or other position have developed their own methodologies and methods (A4 and B4). However, social science continues to evolve and develop new ways of addressing the issue of studying a social world of which the researcher is a part and, as we have seen, realism offers another position on the nature of the social world and what can be known about it.

realism (2)
An epistemological approach that asserts that knowledge of a social phenomenon is based on both what can be observed and recorded and 'hidden' structures and mechanisms whose effects can be observed.

Realism starts from a position similar to positivism in acknowledging that there is a social reality that is external to the researcher and a belief that it can be researched using approaches similar to those used in the natural sciences. Realism, however, goes further and suggests that the apparent social reality is underpinned by invisible but powerful structures or mechanisms. These mechanisms are not directly observable but their effects are apparent so these can be gathered and used to provide evidence of the underlying structures or mechanisms. There is also a **critical realist approach** which prioritises identifying structures or mechanisms that result in inequality or injustice and thus offers the opportunity for social change by changing or negating the structural mechanisms that are identified as having these impacts. This position does not fit neatly into an objectivist or a constructivist ontological position as it focuses on the identification of knowledge that is real but unobservable other than in the effects it has. Thus the main aim of a critical realist is to identify both the hidden mechanisms and the observable effects.

❓ What is . . .

Critical realist approach
A critical realist approach to social research typically means:
- revealing hidden *structures and mechanisms;*
- uncovering *power* relations and *dominant ideologies;*

- research that leads to *action*;
- collecting *qualitative and/or quantitative* data.

(See Chapters A3 and B4 for much more about this.)

Example A2.4

A critical realist approach to studying the relationship between family breakdown and the increase in gun crime

Earlier we highlighted an opinion poll which found that 80% of adults questioned thought that family breakdown and the lack of discipline in the home are factors in the increase of gun-related crime among young men. How might we research the relationship between family breakdown and young men participating in gun-related crime? Taking a critical realist approach we might:

1. Start with the observed reality that young men's participation in gun-related activities has increased and seems to be associated with coming from a situation of family breakdown.

2. Think about and find out about other research in this area in terms of identifying possible mechanisms that may lead to *some* young people who experience family breakdown becoming involved with gun-related crime.

3. Identify possible social mechanisms associated with family breakdown that may trigger participation of young men in activities connected to gun crimes, e.g. social exclusion, stereotyping or labelling, role models and masculine identity.

4. Explore, by gathering qualitative and quantitative data, whether the hidden mechanism is present and *how it works* to trigger participation of some young men in gun-related activity.

What are we trying to do when we do social research?

We have begun to think about ways of studying social phenomena and the different forms of knowledge that may be appropriate for different epistemological positions. Now we need to look at what it is we are trying to do when we undertake a piece of social research.

> Social research is about 'exploring, describing, understanding, explaining, predicting, changing or evaluating some aspect of the social world . . . 'what', 'why' and 'how' questions.
> (Blaikie, 1993: 4)

Basically, as social researchers we are trying:

(a) *to describe* and *explore* a social phenomenon (or social phenomena);

(b) and, usually, to *understand* and *explain* how and why the phenomenon is – or is understood – as it is.

Put simply, we are trying to describe and explore the phenomenon using questions like *What? Who? Where? When?* and understand and explain the phenomenon using questions like *How?* and *Why?* (see A4).

In practice, we may be answering more than one of these questions in a piece of research as they can be interlinked or one question may depend on another. Schutt (see Table A2.1) suggests that typically there are four types of research and these can be illustrated using the example of researching young men and gun crime.

Table A2.1   Four types of research

Descriptive research	Who are the young men who are involved in gun crime?
Exploratory research	What is it like to be a member of a gang?
Explanatory research	Why do young men join gangs that participate in gun-related crime?
Evaluation research	What changes in policy and practice would best help young men not to join such gangs?

Source: Adapted from Schutt (1996: 13). Reproduced with permission.

Your research

Think about your own area of research and identify four questions or aspects you might address.

Descriptive research

Exploratory research

Explanatory research

Evaluation research

We look at this in more depth in A4 when we discuss research questions.

In most social research we can expect there to be at least an attempt at *explaining* what is happening and the nature of the social phenomenon, in terms of why and how it is as it is. This is what we are doing when we work with our data during the analysis stage of our research (Part D).

The explanations may take a number of different forms:

variable
An attribute or characteristic of cases (for example, individuals, organisations, objects or situations) which can vary from case to case.

- could be in terms of *this* phenomenon, incident, condition (often called a **variable**) causing *that* phenomenon – a **causal relationship** (A4);

- could be in terms of getting a better understanding of how people attribute meaning and understanding to what happens to them;

- could be in terms of looking for the conditions or structures that appear to determine what people do or think.

causal relationship
The assertion that a change in 'A' causes a change in 'B'.

You will see that these three forms of explanation correspond to the three epistemological positions identified above – positivism, interpretivism and realism – and that the explanations use different types of knowledge. While this is generally the case, as we shall see when we begin to consider developing research questions and choosing methods, these approaches to explanation are not necessarily mutually exclusive (A4 and B4).

How do theories help us in our social research?

Social research is primarily about gathering data and working with it in ways that will help us to understand and explain social phenomena. We have seen that there are different ways of knowing and that social scientists have different ways of looking at the social world and accept different types of knowledge as useful in attempting to understand and explain.

We have already encountered **theories** – in this case theories relating to knowledge, what knowledge there is about the social world and how knowledge about the world can be used to help us to understand and explain social phenomena. Ontological and epistemological positions are themselves theories of knowledge. And as we have seen, there are different theories, or sets of ideas, about the nature of knowledge and how it can be 'known'. The epistemological positions we identified are based on theories of knowledge and, as such, provide us with theories of social research, which attempt to explain the nature of social research itself.

❓ What is . . .

Theory

A set of ideas or related concepts which can be used to explain and understand an event, situation, social phenomena.

Concept

An abstract idea which encapsulates a way of describing or thinking about a social phenomenon, for example, family, poverty, power, health. (See **A4** for more about working with concepts.)

Whatever approach we take to our research theory will be part of it. Just as we are all researchers, so we are all everyday theorisers. Theories are sets of ideas which attempt to explain something – the relationship between two characteristics, why particular events occur, how some people come to hold particular views or behave in particular ways. In an everyday way we draw on our own theories to explain what is happening to us.

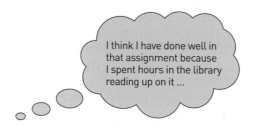

I think I have done well in that assignment because I spent hours in the library reading up on it …

Theory – the more time you spend reading, the better the assignment (a theory that could quite easily be disproved!).

She's not got such good marks this year because she's had a hard time, her parents have divorced and her grandmother has been ill.

Theory – academic work can be affected by personal worries and stresses.

In conversation, we often try to explain ourselves to others by drawing on ideas about the way things are, or ought to be, and how things work; these depend on our shared common experience of being social human beings. We use our own experience, ability to empathise and understandings to apply our theories to others.

In addition to using theories of social research, social scientists (and natural scientists) develop and use theories to attempt to explain the nature of the phenomena they study. Just as there are different ways of explaining the nature of social research, so there are different ways of explaining how a social phenomenon like 'the family' comes to be seen or understood as it is. As social researchers we need to both identify our own theories about our research topic and to find out about the theories other researchers have used or developed from their own research findings.

O'Brian (cited in Gilbert, 1993: 11) uses the example of a kaleidoscope to demonstrate the way theories help us to study the social world:

> *When you turn the tube and look down the lens of the kaleidoscope the shapes and colours, visible at the bottom, change. As the tube is turned, different lenses come into play and combinations of colour and shape shift from one pattern to another.*

Theories are like lenses which bring different aspects of the social world into view and can help us to see the social world in new ways.

Think about it . . .

Earlier we highlighted an opinion poll which found that 80% of adults questioned thought that family breakdown and the lack of discipline in the home are factors in the increase of gun-related crime among young men.

What theory or theories do you think the people who held this opinion may have been using?

Example A2.5

Examples of theories relating to the example of teenage gangs and family

- Masculinity is socially constructed (understood and given meaning) in different ways in different times and cultures *(social constructionist theory)*.
- A child's development is influenced by culture, neighbourhood and family *(known as the ecological–transactional model)*.
- One function of the family is to socialise the children *(functional theory)*.
- Some groups of boys are expected to fail at school *(stereotyping/labelling theory)*.
- Some young men join gangs because it gives them a sense of belonging and identity which may be lacking in other aspects of their lives *(identity theory)*.
- A child who witnesses violence may become aggressive and see violence as normal *(social learning theory)*.

macro theories
Theories that attempt to cover all aspects of the social world in general terms (also known as grand theories).

meso theories
Middle-level theories relating to social phenomena usually found, such as organisations, institutions, community and family.

micro theories
Local theory relating to a specific area, group of people or aspect of the social world.

Social theories are often described as being at different levels relating to the areas of the social world they can be said to cover: **macro**, **meso** and **micro**.

- *Macro* (or sometimes *grand*): theories that attempt to cover all aspects of the social world in general terms.
- *Meso*: middle-level theories relating to social phenomena usually found, such as organisations, institutions, community and family.
- *Micro*: local theory relating to a specific area, group of people or aspect of the social world.

Macro-level theories influence the way social scientists think about the social world as a whole and can provide the basis for the development of theories at a lower level and related to more specific aspects of the social world.

Example A2.6

Theory levels relating to the example of teenage gangs and family

Macro theory – Masculinity is socially constructed (understood and given meaning) in different ways in different times and cultures.

Meso theory – If within a particular culture masculinity is socially constructed as powerful and dominant, this will be evident in the way families and organisations are structured.

Micro theory – Young men who join gangs often lack power over other aspects of their lives and seek power through membership of a gang and committing crime.

Paradigms

Theories at a macro level that attempt to encompass the social world also cover the social phenomena of social research itself and include within the theory ideas about the nature of the social world and the acceptable ways of studying it. This means that a particular theoretical approach can include its own ontological and epistemological position. Bringing together theory about the social world with particular ontological and epistemological positions in this way is sometimes referred to as a **paradigm**.

❓ What is . . .

Paradigm

(1) The entire constellation of beliefs, values, techniques and so on shared by members of a given (scientific) community (Kuhn, 1970: 175).

(2) A cluster of beliefs and dictates which for scientists in a particular discipline influence what should be studied, how research should be done, how results should be interpreted and so on (Bryman, 1988: 4).

As the definitions suggest, paradigms tend to reflect the interests and focus of research communities, or of social scientists from a particular discipline or sharing a set of theory-informed beliefs about the social world. Within the social sciences we can identify, for example, feminism, postmodernism and post-structuralism as paradigms (see Example A2.7 below for a discussion of feminism and the ontological and epistemological positions implicit within feminist theory). Researchers sometimes talk about the way a paradigm supports their research as a **theoretical framework**. This suggests that the theoretical ideas and approaches to viewing and gathering knowledge provide the basic ways of addressing the topic. Marlow describes a paradigm as a map, helpfully 'directing us to the problems that are important to address, the theories that are acceptable, and the procedures needed to solve the problems' (Marlow, 2001: 7).

theoretical framework
The ideas and approaches to viewing and gathering knowledge, and which provide the basic ways of addressing a topic.

Example A2.7

Feminism – theory, ontology and epistemology

In the latter part of the twentieth century, feminists – people who held a set of ideas and approaches to studying and explaining the social world that prioritised the experiences and perspectives of women – challenged social researchers to approach their research from a feminist perspective. For feminist researchers the relationship between the genders and gender differences is fundamental to understanding and explaining the social world and, from a feminist perspective, much social research

▶

has been focused on the study of men and their social world with the voices and experiences of women being hidden or ignored. A new approach to social research was put forward which incorporated the feminist ideas within the ontology and epistemology.

The nature of the social world (ontology) is described by feminist researchers as socially constructed and both the natural and social worlds have been predominantly constructed by men – the meanings and understandings of the nature of social phenomena given by men have been prioritised in attempts to understand and explain the social world. A feminist ontology includes multiple constructions and, in particular, emphasises the differences in meanings and understandings between men and women.

A feminist epistemology prioritises women's experience as the basis of knowledge of a social phenomenon and focuses on experiences, feelings and emotions that are held in common. There is an emphasis on data-gathering methods that place the researcher alongside the research participant working collaboratively to generate knowledge (see participatory research methods in **C1**, and power in social research in **A5**). There is often an explicit commitment for change in the gender relations between women and men.

Studying our example within a feminist paradigm or theoretical framework

1. The research may focus on gathering the experiences and feelings of women linked to the young men involved in gun crime, particularly mothers and siblings.

2. The research may take a critical approach to studying power and influence within the family relationships of those involved.

3. The research may look at the ways in which ideas about masculinity are constructed in opposition to ideas about femininity.

4. The research may look critically at ideas that families, and particularly the mother, are to blame for the behaviour of young men.

Alongside the feminist paradigm other critical approaches to studying the social world have developed which Cresswell terms 'advocacy' or *participatory* research (Cresswell, 2003: 9). As in the case of feminist social research, these include approaches that study the social world from the perspective of groups of people whose understandings and experiences of the social world have been ignored or hidden, for example people with disabilities, black people, gay and lesbian groups (A5). Research within such theoretical frameworks may focus on the discourse or language that is used by other people, who are perceived to be more powerful, to describe the group. There may also be an emphasis on the empowerment of the research subjects and on research that will challenge current discourses and practice and initiate change.

Your research

Each discipline within the social sciences has different sets of theoretical positions which are both taught and inform research in that disciplinary area.

Thinking about your own discipline, can you identify any macro-, meso- and micro-level theories that are used?

Macro

Meso

Micro

Using theory in social research

So how do you use theory in thinking about and developing your social research? There are five key ways.

Using existing theories of your own and of others

As you are beginning to think about your research topic you will be reading about the research topic area, familiarising yourself with other work that has been done on the topic and reflecting on how your own experience and knowledge feeds into your study. Your reading will probably introduce you to theories that have been developed by other researchers in this area, perhaps in your own discipline, perhaps in other disciplines. Here you will be finding sets of ideas about a particular topic that attempt to explain what is happening. Of course, you may find a number of different or competing theories on your topic (see the Example boxes for different theories on youth and crime) and you will need to think about your own position and whether you find one or another more plausible or acceptable to you. You will also be drawing on your own preliminary theories, ideas that you have which might explain what is going on. These may come from experience or study or may just be a combination that gives you a 'hunch'. Check out at this stage whether your ideas are actually similar to those already written about. You may also want to check out work that has been done in adjacent areas, for example, if you are looking at issues of age discrimination you may want to look at work done within the gender and disability discrimination fields. Sometimes theories are transportable to different topics that have some similarity (**B2**).

Using theories of social research and knowledge

In the early stages of your research you will also be drawing on theories about social research itself. What we have been discussing so far in this section are theories, or sets of ideas about how we see and study the social world. You may find it hard to decide on an ontological or epistemological position but, drawing on your discipline knowledge, you can begin by thinking about what aspects of your study really interest you and this may help you to reflect on the position you are taking on the nature of the social world and how it can be studied. One way of doing this is illustrated in the examples in this section. By thinking through what each epistemological approach would mean for the study of your research topic you may find you are opening up different aspects of the topic and a wider range of potential research questions from which to choose (**A4**).

Working with theory

Theories, as sets of ideas that attempt to explain aspects of the social world, are central to your research methodology and the nature of the data (**A3**) you collect. Depending on your epistemological position you may work with theory in different ways (**A4**). If, for example, you take a positivist, or possibly a critical realist, approach you may set out to test a hypothesis that is based on an existing theory. This is called a *deductive* approach to using theory. If, however, you are taking an interpretivist approach, you are likely to start with research questions (which may be informed by existing theory) and you will then gather data and derive your explanations – tentative theories – from the data itself; this is an *inductive* approach.

In most research, theory is used both inductively and deductively. If we think of research as both informed by theory and as generating theory, the research process can be described as a cycle as shown in Figure A2.2.

Developing research questions or hypotheses

Whichever epistemological position you take, theories will be explicit or implicit in your hypothesis or research questions (**A4**). Here you are setting out clearly what you are going to be gathering data on and you will be developing research questions or hypotheses to

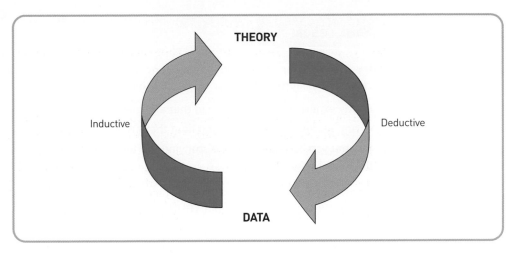

Figure A2.2   Inductive and deductive approaches

help you to explain aspects of your research topic. If you are developing a hypothesis, you may be drawing on an existing theory, or developing one of your own, to set up and test by gathering data. If you are developing research questions you will be posing questions that draw on existing theory and knowledge and set out questions to be addressed by the data collected (A4).

Explaining your data

And finally, when you have gathered your data and worked with it, analysed it and discussed the findings (Part D) you will be able to demonstrate how far your hypothesis was proved or disproved, how far your data helped you to explain and address the questions you have posed, and you may be able to develop your own theory, set of ideas or add to an existing theory.

What does this mean for me as a student social researcher?

We have been looking at some of the theories or philosophical ideas behind the development of particular positions on studying the social world and at the way in which different ways of thinking about our study are necessary because we are studying something of which we are a part. Our discussion of the ontological positions highlights the ways in which social scientists view the social world and why many of them take issue with the objectivist approaches of natural science. While these are basic positions and are likely to be closely linked to the epistemological approaches we might take, it is important to recognise that there are other things that the social researcher brings to his study which he needs to explore and perhaps be explicit about at least to himself.

All social researchers, students, leading academics, government officers and independent consultants come to their research with a certain amount of theoretical, cultural and disciplinary baggage as well as other suitcases full of very creditable values, beliefs and desires to change the world. Social researchers are, after all, social beings and it is worth thinking a bit about quite how and why someone gets into studying and researching in this area. For some researchers social research that is not linked to social change or action is meaningless and frustrating; for others the desire for a more sophisticated understanding of the way the social world works is underpinned by a hope that their development of theory will impact on those who are more practically orientated.

Your research

Try writing to (or have an imaginary conversation with) a friend to explain how you came to be interested in your research topic, including:

- any experiences you have had that are relevant;
- any values or convictions you hold that are related to the topic;
- what you have learnt while studying the topic;
- any theories or sets of ideas you have about the topic.

What have you learnt about your own interests, values and motivations that might inform the way you think about YOUR RESEARCH?

In this section we have been looking at the ideas that social researchers use to help them to think about their research topic, identify research questions or hypotheses and design research that will enable them to address those questions. We have attempted to provide these starting points for you in the initial stages of your research:

- As members of the social world you are studying, you each bring your own knowledge to your research and it is helpful to begin thinking about your research topic by reviewing and reflecting upon what you know.
- There are different ways of looking at the social world and different approaches to gathering knowledge about social phenomena. Before you decide on the approach you will take, try thinking about how your topic may be approached from various ontological and epistemological positions.
- If you think about the social world and social phenomena in different ways you will begin to identify the variety of types of data that may be available to you in your research. (See A3 for more about the nature of data.)
- Thinking about different ontological and epistemological positions can open up the possibilities of using other research methodologies and data collection and analytical methods. While qualitative and quantitative methods are typically associated with particular epistemological positions, research using a mixture of methods is becoming more common, and qualitative and quantitative data can be worked with in a variety of ways. (See B4 for a discussion of this.)
- Reviewing other research and literature in terms of the theoretical ideas and approaches used by other researchers in your topic area will help you to identify theories that may provide a starting point, or even a theoretical framework for your own study. (See B2.)

Real research

A brief history of social research

The roots of social research are in philosophy and a concern to establish authentic and valid approaches to the study of human beings. Concerns with truth and objectivity, and how the researcher studies the world of which he is a part, can be found in the writings of Descartes in the seventeenth century. In his *Discourse on Methodology* (1637) (Descartes, 1999) he set out his thinking on searching for truth and emphasised objectivity and the importance of supporting evidence, while David Hume (1711–76), writing in the eighteenth century, maintained that knowledge of the world comes from human experience and is objectively gathered through the senses (Williams and May, 1996: 16).

Augustus Comte (1798–1857) proposed that the social world can be studied using the same approaches as the natural world, in particular that there are general discernible 'laws' about the way the social world works which do not vary. This is clearly recognisable as the basis for the positivist position which was the predominant position of social scientists during the late nineteenth and much of the twentieth centuries, and early sociologists including Durkheim (Durkheim, 1982), who considered social phenomena as objects to be observed and studied, developed this position in their attempts to discover and demonstrate overarching theories that explained the social world.

There were, however, other thinkers who focused more on human understanding and interpretation, including, for example, Kant who argued in his *Critique of Pure Reason* (1781) that the social world can be known through thinking about and interpreting what is observed and experienced, and Dilthey writing in the latter half of the nineteenth century who focused on the importance of people's 'lived experiences' (Williams and May, 1996: 62). This was taken up by Max Weber (1864–1920) who focused on the social meaning of people's actions within different contexts and their understandings (*verstehen*). While he acknowledged that understanding can come from direct observation, he maintained that understanding also comes from interpreting subjective experiences and meanings and defines sociology as

> *a science which attempts the interpretative understanding of social action in order thereby to arrive at a causal explanation of its course and effects.*   (Weber, 1949: 88)

In the early twentieth century Schutz (1899–1959) introduced the ideas of phenomenology – a philosophical approach which is concerned with how individuals make sense of the world around them – into the social sciences. These ideas were built on in the twentieth century as social research became more common and developed new approaches and methods. Social researchers drew on the work of anthropologists, for example, Margaret Mead and Malinowski, and saw the development of participant observation (**C6**) and the ethnographic work of, for example, the Chicago School (see Whyte's study of a Boston slum in *Street Corner Society* (Whyte, 1955) and Becker's study of deviance, *Outsiders* (Becker, 1963) and **B3**), ethnomethodology (Garfinkel, 1967) and symbolic interactionism (Blumer, 1969).

The late nineteenth and early twentieth centuries saw social research methods being applied in the more practically oriented work of social reformers like Henry Mayhew, Charles Booth and Joseph Rowntree. These men were aware of the problems of poor people and sought to gather data to demonstrate the extent and nature of the poverty in industrial cities in the latter part of the nineteenth and early twentieth centuries. Their work contributed significantly to the development of methods of collecting data and to the recognition of the value of research data as evidence to support changes in policy and practice and highlight the situation of particular groups of people.

Large-scale survey methods developed and their use by academic, government and market researchers grew rapidly in the second half of the twentieth century. Positivism, with its use of large-scale surveys and increasingly sophisticated statistical techniques was the dominant social research position in the middle of the twentieth century, and more interpretive and qualitative approaches were regarded as 'soft', unscientific and lacking rigour.

Alongside this there were discussions among social scientists about the nature of social theory and its early attempts to develop 'grand' or overarching theories were challenged in terms of their limited usefulness in themselves as frameworks for social research. The reality was that social researchers were working with what Merton (1957) called 'theories of the middle range'. Alongside Merton, Berger and Luckmann's *The Social Construction of Reality* (Berger and Luckmann, 1967) developed theory based on a constructivist approach to the social world and an emphasis on there being multiple meanings or perspectives on social phenomena. The interpretivist position on studying the social world was clearly associated with this theoretical approach, and related research methodologies and data collection methods (usually referred to as qualitative methods) began to develop and to be more widely used. (See, for example, Lincoln and Guba, 1985; Bogdan and Taylor, 1975; Glaser and Strauss, 1967.)

During the 1970s positivism was also challenged by social scientists who questioned the appropriateness of using experimental approaches to study human beings and, in particular, whether social research that ignored the meanings and understandings of the social actors involved could itself be meaningful, particularly when there was evident diversity in people's understandings of common situations, events and behaviour. Challenges came particularly from feminist researchers who maintained that the scientific-positivist approach itself represented a masculine understanding and interpretation of the social world and that the dominance of male perspectives and understandings of the world led to inequality. Feminist approaches to social research developed which focused on the relationship between the researcher and the researched and engaged with the complexities of women's experiences (see, for example, Stanley's *Feminist Praxis*, 1990, and Roberts' *Doing Feminist Research*, 1981). Other researchers taking a similarly critical perspective maintained that material conditions and inequality of power have a major impact on people's lives and understandings and that findings should be analysed in terms of, for example, race, gender and class and the understandings of groups of people with different experiences and perspectives prioritised.

Other social scientists questioned the ontological dichotomy of objectivism and constructivism and claimed that reality is both external to social human beings and 'at the same time a dimension which includes our socially determined knowledge about reality' (Danermark *et al.*, 2002). This has become known as the critical realist position and Bhaskar (1978) and Pawson and Tilley (1997), among others, have developed research approaches that look below the surface of actions, organisations and language to expose mechanisms and structures that are not directly observable, and look critically at how these mechanisms work to affect the social world.

As the twentieth century drew to a close the debates within social research still focused on the nature of knowledge and data and its context with a significant emphasis on the power relations associated with language and meaning and the ownership of knowledge. Some researchers emphasised the power relationships within social research itself and called for greater equality between the researcher and the research subjects, and advocated participative and collaborative approaches to carrying out research (see, for example, Reason, 1994, on participative research and Greenwood, 1998, on action research). This brought an increased focus on the perspective of the researcher and a more reflexive and less neutral approach was advocated by some, alongside narrative and biographical methods developed to enable research participants to tell their story (see, for example, Plummer, 2001, and Miller, 2000).

The twenty-first century has already seen a growing emphasis on more pragmatic approaches to social research based on the purpose of the research, the values and perspective of the social researcher, the nature of the research question and the data required to address it. The use of mixed methods (quantitative and qualitative), to gather and work with data is increasingly advocated as an approach to knowing the social world (see, for example, Cresswell, 2003).

References and further reading

Becker, H. (1963) *Outsiders: Studies in the Sociology of Deviance*, New York: Free Press.

Becker, S. and Bryman, A. (eds) (2004) *Understanding Research for Social Policy and Practice: Themes, Methods and Approaches*, Bristol: The Policy Press and the Social Policy Association.

Berger, P. and Luckmann, T. (1967) *The Social Construction of Reality*, London: Allen Lane.

Bhaskar, R. (1978) *A Realist Theory of Science*, Leeds: Leeds Books.

Blaikie, N. (1993) *Approaches to Social Enquiry*, Cambridge: Polity Press.

Blumer, H. (1969) *Symbolic Interactionism*, Englewood Cliffs, NJ: Prentice Hall.

Bogdan, R. and Taylor, S. J. (1975) *Introduction to Qualitative Research Methods: A Phenomenological Approach to the Social Sciences*, New York: John Wiley.

Brechin, A. and Siddell, M. (2000) Ways of knowing, in R. Gomm and C. Davies (eds) *Using Evidence in Health and Social Care*, London: Sage.

Bryman, A. (1988) *Quantity and Quality in Social Research*, London: Routledge.

Burns, R. B. (2000) *Introduction to Research Methods*, London: Sage.

Cresswell, J. W. (2003) *Research Design: Qualitative, Quantitative, and Mixed Methods Approaches*, London: Sage.

Danermark, B., Ekstrom, M., Jakobsen, L. and Karlsson, J. C. (2002) *Explaining Society: Critical Realism in the Social Sciences*, London: Routledge.

Descartes, R. (1999) *Discourse on Method and Related Writings*, London: Penguin.

Durkheim, E. (1982) The rules of sociological method: and selected texts on sociology and its method, in S. Lukes (ed.) *Contemporary Social Theory*, London: Macmillan.

Garfinkel, H. (1967) *Studies in Ethnomethodology*, Englewood Cliffs, NJ: Prentice Hall.

Gilbert, N. (ed.) (1993) *Researching Social Life*, London: Sage.

Glaser, B. G. and Strauss, A. L. (1967) *The Discovery of Grounded Theory: Strategies for Qualitative Research*, Chicago, IL: Aldine de Gruyter.

Greenwood, D. (1998) *Introduction to Action Research: Social Research for Social Change*, London: Sage.

Kuhn, T. S. (1970) *The Structure of Scientific Revolutions*, University of Chicago Press.

Lincoln, Y. S. and Guba, G. E. (1985) *Naturalistic Inquiry*, Beverly Hills, CA: Sage.

Marlow, C. (2001) *Research Methods for Generalist Social Work*, Belmont, CA: Brooks/Cole.

Merton, R. (1957) *Social Theory and Social Structure*, New York: US Free Press.

Miller, R. L. (2000) *Researching Life Stories and Family Histories*, London: Sage.

Pawson, R. and Tilley, N. (1997) *Realistic Evaluation*, London: Sage.

Plummer, K. (2001) *Documents of Life 2: An Invitation to Critical Humanism*, London: Sage.

Reason P. (ed.) (1994) *Participation in Human Enquiry*, London: Sage.

Roberts, H. (ed.) (1981) *Doing Feminist Research*, London: Routledge & Kegan Paul.

Schutt, R. K. (1996) *Investigating the Social World*, Thousand Oaks, CA: Sage.

Smith, B. (2003) Ontology, in L. Floridi (ed.) *The Blackwell Guide to the Philosophy of Computing and Information*, Oxford: Blackwell.

Stanley, L. (ed.) (1990) *Feminist Praxis: Research, Theory and Epistemology in Feminist Sociology*, London: Routledge.

Weber, M. (1949) *The Methodology of the Social Sciences*, New York: Free Press.

Whyte, W. F. (1955) *Street Corner Society: The Social Structure of an Italian Slum*, University of Chicago Press.

Williams, M. and May, T. (1996) *Introduction to the Philosophy of Social Research*, London: UCL Press.

Wright Mills, C. (1959) *The Sociological Imagination*, New York: Oxford University Press.

CHAPTER A3
The nature of data

Contents

In context

In Chapter A2 we considered the theories that underpin social research and the way researchers look at and study the social world, and we identified different positions on what can be known about a social phenomenon. In this section we move on to think about the material that social researchers have to work with – data. We will consider the characteristics of data and the different types of data that may be available to social researchers and then introduce some of the criteria or standards social researchers apply to the data they gather and work with.

PART A: Thinking about research

    A1: What is research?

    A2: Knowledge, theories, paradigms and perspectives

    ▶ **A3: The nature of data**

    A4: Research questions, hypotheses and operational definitions

    A5: Research as an ethical and cultural issue

social phenomenon
Anything that influences or is influenced by human beings who interact with and are responsive to each other.

Data stands in place of the social reality we wish to study. We cannot simply know a **social phenomenon**, but we can attempt to capture it as data which represent the reality we have experienced, observed, asked questions about or are trying to explain. As social beings we all gather and work with data every day as we take part in the social world through conversations, reading, observing and writing. This section is about the data that is produced by social beings in the social world and how we can begin to think about collecting and working with that data as social researchers.

❓ What is . . .

Data

A collection of facts (or other information, such as opinions or values) which can be analysed and from which conclusions can be drawn.

(Although 'data' is the plural of 'datum' it is recognised by the *Oxford English Dictionary* that the plural form – data – is typically used in a singular form, as it is in this text.)

Human beings create many different ways of communicating social experiences and ideas, and these form the data at our disposal as social researchers. The ways in which we are able to gather and work with the data will depend on our approach to studying the social world and what can be known about it (**A2**), our research questions (**A4**) and the nature of the data itself, and it is this that we consider in this chapter. Throughout the chapter there will be signposts to relevant data collection methods in **Part C** and examples of data drawn from the 'family party' example introduced in **A2**.

Characteristics of data

Language as data

The data we work with as social researchers (and as social beings) is usually in the form of language because this is the means we have of capturing, reflecting on and describing social reality. For example, as individuals we can physically feel pain – but we need words to actually call it 'pain' and to tell other people (and ourselves) that pain is the reality we are experiencing. In fact it is through giving something a name that it is created as an entity or concept. We may then need to find other words to describe the nature of the pain and to communicate this to other people in a way that they recognise as a description of something they understand and may have experienced themselves.

Sometimes we use other media than words to express what we feel – colour, pictures, music, movement, facial expressions, behaviour – in an attempt to communicate without words. However, in social research such attempts will usually, at some point, be turned into words because words are the means by which researchers work with the data and then communicate their findings and explanations to others.

Spoken and written text

Verbal data, or text, can be either spoken or written and there are differences in the nature of spoken and written data. Written communication can be undertaken alone, take time, be amended and crafted, while spoken words are less likely to be so carefully prepared. We usually write with a purpose in mind, for example, to convey a message, to report an event or activity, to summarise what has been said, to express feelings or an opinion. Spoken communication, though it can be prepared and rehearsed in a similar way, for example for a speech or a lecture, is more likely to be interactive and responsive to at least one other person. Compare the different accounts of the family party in Example A3.1.

Example A3.1

Party data A

You were invited to a family party for your girlfriend's great-grandmother and after the party you write a letter of thanks to her

Dear Mrs Jones,

I am writing to thank you for the most enjoyable party last night. It was lovely to meet you and other members of your family and to share in this important event. The food was delicious!

I would like to wish you a very happy birthday and hope that you will continue in good health.

With best wishes

How was the party?

It was OK really, better than I expected. Great grandmother was lovely and enjoyed a joke! And the food – ummm – really good and lots to drink too ... I had a bit too much!

gr8 party
gg kwl
cu l8r lol

Spoken communication is usually associated with being in the physical presence of the recipient of the spoken words and being able to gauge the impact of and response to the words spoken. When words are spoken to another who is present, there is the possibility of using non-verbal communication, including tone of voice, and the listener hears the words as part of a communication package which will influence the impact and response to those words. Telephone discussions take away the visual aspect of this response and the speaker is dependent on aural communication which can include silences as well as changes in the tone of the voice. In the case of written words, the writer may be anticipating the response of the reader or wider audience, or may be unaware of some of the people who may read it. Similarly the reader may or may not be aware of the writer's identity, characteristics or status.

Recently, written and spoken communication have merged in the production of, for example, electronic messaging, emails and mobile phone texting, where a written format is used drawing on conventions that are more usually used in direct speech and including pictures to express emotions (emoticons) (see Example A3.1). Other technical developments in communication mean that, for example, communication takes place using the internet and other systems which enable people to both hear and see each other even though they are in different geographical locations.

Think about it . . .
The characteristics of data (1)

- Written text is usually more structured and considered than spoken text.
- Spoken text is usually more responsive to the audience.
- Spoken text is often supplemented by non-verbal communication visible to the listener.

Non-verbal communication

Communication also takes place non-verbally and this can be available to us as observed data (**C6**) although the process of non-verbal expressions of social reality becoming data usually includes it becoming verbal or expressed in words. Non-verbal simply means that words are not used and other (usually visual, but also aural) means are used. Non-verbal communication can include facial expressions, sounds that are not words, pictures that are drawn or painted, photographs, behaviour, movement, non-human sounds – music or other noises. As with verbal data, as social researchers we need to consider:

- What does the person want to communicate?
- Why have they chosen this means of communication?
- How does the receiver of the communication understand it?

Example A3.2

Party data B

Source: © Andraz Gregcric/iStockphoto

Think about it . . .

Write a short verbal description of the photograph. What do you think the photographer wanted to communicate?

A photograph of the family party may be useful as visual data in terms of both the content of the photograph as a record of a moment in time – for example, the number of people included and what they are doing – as well as considering the meaning of the photograph for the person who took it.

Think about it . . .
The characteristics of data (2)

- Non-verbal communication is usually interpreted using words.
- Non-verbal communication often accompanies spoken text.
- Non-verbal communication depends on common understandings in the same way as verbal communication.

Factual and value statements as data

Data can be factual – evident by observation or stated by the owner of the knowledge:

I am female, I am aged 30, I have lived in the UK since 2000.

Or it can have value attached to it:

I am young, I enjoy being a woman, I am glad I came to live in the UK.

Factual data

Data that can directly represent what can be observed is referred to as factual data. For example, we can observe (usually) whether a person is male or female and count how many men and how many women are attending the family party. Here the data we gather depends on an observation that draws on the observable physical differences between male and female and our ability to quantify or count the number of instances of each.

We could gather more information along similar lines: how many glasses of wine each person drank or how many women wore red dresses. However, we may find that if we asked two participants to do some research and each gather this data they may take different approaches and there may be some discrepancies in their findings. For example, one may position himself next to the bottles of wine and make a note each time a person comes to fill up their glass. The other may go round to each person at the end of the party and ask them how many glasses of wine they have drunk. In the first case we cannot be sure that each person has actually drunk the wine they took, and in the second we are depending on people's memories and honesty! If we want accurate factual information, we will need to find a different way of measuring the amount drunk.

When counting how many women wearing red dresses are present, they may agree on some but disagree when they come to consider a dress that is a mixture of colours or which is, in the eyes of one of the researchers, pink. If we want factual information, the observers will need to agree on the criteria they are using to decide whether a dress is red.

Value statements

value statements
Statements, usually from an individual, that are indications of each person's opinion where they are using their own judgement and criteria.

The two researchers may also want to find out whether people enjoyed the wine and whether other people there thought the red dresses were flattering and fashionable. There are likely to be different opinions on these two matters and the data gathered will be in the form of **value statements** like those in Example A3.3.

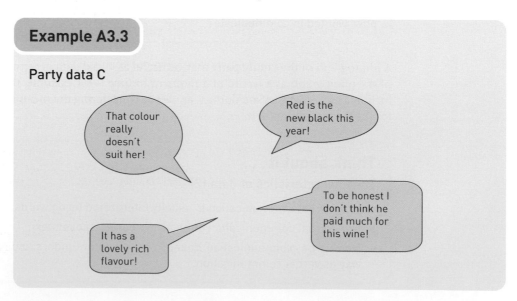

Example A3.3

Party data C

That colour really doesn't suit her!

Red is the new black this year!

To be honest I don't think he paid much for this wine!

It has a lovely rich flavour!

These statements are indications of each person's opinion and they are using their own judgement and criteria to explain to the researchers how they value the wine and the dresses. A social researcher may want to find out how many people share similar opinions but is also likely to want to explore these opinions in more depth rather than accept them at face value, to find out what criteria people are using when making a judgement, how strongly they hold an opinion, how people come to their views and why they hold these opinions.

Think about it . . .

The characteristics of data (3)

- Factual data depends on agreed definitions, criteria and measurements.
- Value statements often need to be explored further to discover how and why the statement was made.

Constructing and structuring data

Data can be organised and structured to meet particular needs. When we describe an event to somebody else we usually select and structure the data we share with them about the event in a way that will help them to understand the nature of the event even though they were not present. Some people may organise their data chronologically and give an account of what happened hour by hour, or day by day. Others may focus on one aspect of the event and explain that in detail before moving on to describe the surroundings and context, or they may start with the context and setting so that the listener can 'picture' the event. Others may tell the story of their own involvement in the event, what they were doing, how they were feeling and so on. Alternatively they may extract some key facts about the event, the number of people present, the length of time it lasted, the activities included and so on and present these to their listener. Take a look at Example A3.4 which includes four different accounts of the family party.

Example A3.4

Party data D

1. *There were about forty people there, equal numbers of men and women and most were under 30. During the first part of the evening the older people sat talking while the younger people danced. Then at nine o'clock we had a buffet meal and a toast to great-grandmother whose ninetieth birthday it was. Then the music started again and there was dancing until about midnight.*

2. *It was a lovely house with large rooms interconnecting so we could have music in one room while the others could find a quiet corner for a chat, and then another room where all the food was set out – it looked fantastic, quite a spread and lots to drink . . .*

3. *I had a great time. I met lots of new people, relatives of my girlfriend who I hadn't met before. She has lots of cousins of about the same age and some are at university too – I met Simon who's doing Sociology like me so we were comparing notes . . .*

4. *It was a party to celebrate my girlfriend's great-grandmother's ninetieth birthday so it was really a family occasion with lots of relatives and friends of all ages. She's a lovely old lady and obviously really enjoyed having all her family there to celebrate . . .*

Our accounts of a social phenomenon or experience can be structured or organised in a variety of ways and to different degrees. A written report to a manager is likely to be more structured, for example, than a spontaneous conversation with a friend, when we may move from one topic to another in a relatively unstructured way.

> ## Think about it . . .
>
> Think of an event you have been to recently and try structuring your account of the event in different ways.

As we will see in Parts **C** and **D**, the social researcher can both determine the way data gathered is structured by using different data collection tools (**C1**), for example, questionnaires (**C3**) and interviews (**C4**), and use different analytical techniques to work with structured, semi-structured or unstructured data (**D2**). This is discussed in more depth in **B4** in relation to quantitative and qualitative research.

> ## Think about it . . .
> ### The characteristics of data (4)
>
> - Most data is structured by the person or group who produces it.
> - Data representing a social phenomenon can be structured in many different ways.
> - Data gathered by social researchers is structured to different degrees by the researcher as part of the data collecting process.

Data – content and meaning

Data is itself constructed by an individual or group. An account of an event or experience is produced by the account giver who decides not only what information is included but also how the data will be presented, which aspects will be emphasised, which omitted, whether a particular image of the event will be presented (for example, was it exciting? disappointing?). It will probably include both factual and value statements and take account of the listener or audience. The language used by the speaker or writer is chosen (consciously or subconsciously) to present a specific account of the event.

Much of the data that is exchanged between social beings is either spoken or written using a language that is, at least to a degree, shared. We talk sometimes about people 'not speaking the same language' when we mean that they are not understanding each other even if they are both speaking English. Language is not simply made up of words that have dictionary definitions which are used precisely by everyone. Words are used to share meanings and understandings, some of which are common and easily understood and others that are not, and words are used in different ways by different groups of people, in different times and places. There can be misunderstandings through individuals understanding the language used in different ways. Language can be used to exclude those who do not understand the words used. What is doubly challenging is that, as social researchers, we are also using language to work with, interpret and explain the data we have gathered. So the nature of language is problematic as well as central to our work.

As social researchers we are often interested not only in the content of what people say or write – the factual and value statements – but also how they use language to explain their understanding and meaning. Consider the different ways the word 'family' is used in the data in Example A3.5. In each case we need to consider how the word is being used, what meanings and understandings are packaged into the word 'family' and how the speaker came to use the word in that particular way.

> ### Example A3.5
>
> #### Party data E
>
> **1.** It was a *family* occasion really, everyone else was related to each other.
>
> **2.** There was a lot of *family* stuff going on I didn't really understand!
>
> **3.** It had a lovely *family* feel to it, I really felt part of it.

> ## Think about it . . .
> What do you think 'family' means to the speaker in each of the statements in Example A3.5?

Language is used and understood differently across cultures and times. For example, the word 'family' may encapsulate different perceptions and experiences for two men living in the UK in the twenty-first century if one is a Sikh and the other an Afro-Caribbean (see A5 for a discussion on social research as a cultural issue). To find out how the word is being used, we need to find out more about the speakers, their experiences and their understandings.

> ## Think about it . . .
> #### The characteristics of data (5)
>
> - Data can include the meanings and understandings expressed through the words (and non-verbal communication) used.
> - Data can include the way language is used by data producers to present their meaning and understanding.

Individual- or group-created data

Data can be created by individuals or by groups of people. An individual can describe an event or experience (spoken or in writing, verbal and non-verbal) to other people who provide an audience. His account of social reality may be influenced by the people to whom he is speaking or writing and the context in which the data is produced. In other situations a group may work together to produce data, for example, in a conversation, an argument, a meeting, or working together on a document, a speech or a dramatic presentation. Data is produced as people interact, share or challenge facts and opinions, agree or disagree. While an individual has more control over the data he produces himself, interaction with others, hearing other people's opinions and experiences is likely to influence his contribution to the group production of data. Some of his own experience and knowledge may be hidden, some may be ignored by other members of the group, some may be built on and developed by others. The data specific to an individual may no longer be attributable but be subsumed within the group data. Much of the data we work with on a day-to-day basis as social beings is group rather than individual.

Example A3.6

Party data F

Laura, her boyfriend Sam and her cousin Rachel are discussing the family party for Laura and Rachel's great-grandmother's ninetieth birthday.

Laura: I suppose it wasn't bad considering . . .

Sam: I enjoyed it!

Rachel: It was lovely to see Great-Gran enjoying herself so much. She really likes having all the family and it's worth it just to see her happy.

Laura: Yes, but you would have thought they could have had some better music and all those oldies sitting in the corner going on about the old days and all this family stuff . . .

Rachel: That's families for you! We don't do it very often and it is good to catch up and to meet Sam and see Joanne's new baby and . . .

Laura: But it's only family, frankly I wouldn't care if I never saw some of them ever again – I mean, Joanne and I have nothing in common.

Sam: I thought the baby was cute!

Rachel: I think it's good for families to get together, these sort of occasions are really important – it's traditional.

Laura: Oh come on! All that stuff about where we've come from, how well we've all done and the odd ones we don't talk about – I just don't want to know!

Sam: I wish I had a family like yours . . .

Rachel: There, you see? Someone agrees with me . . .

Think about it . . .

For each of the participants in the group discussion above, what have you learnt about what 'family' means to them?

As social researchers we may be interested in the way pairs or groups of people produce an account of a social phenomenon together (**C5**) including:

- how different information, experiences and perspectives are contributed to the discussion;
- how the individuals interact, who takes a lead, who contributes most and who contributes least;
- what words are used and what shared understandings are apparent in the words that are used.

Think about it . . .

The characteristics of data (6)

- Data produced by a group includes data that relates to the way the group members interact.
- Data produced by a group is group data rather than a set of individual data.

Reflexive data

This is the data produced by individuals themselves as they think about what they are doing, experiencing and feeling and try to understand their social reality. As social human beings who are part of the social world they are studying, social researchers bring their own biography, experience and empathy to the data they observe, hear and work with and can reflect on how they make sense of what they themselves are doing and experiencing as social researchers. This **reflexive data** can include the researcher's own feelings about and experience of the research topic, her thinking about the issues involved, her own reactions to her research subjects and research data and how she made decisions about data collection and analytical methods. These reflections may be recorded in research notes or a research diary and discussed in supervision and can be critically analysed alongside other social research data.

reflexive data
The data produced by individuals themselves as they think about what they are doing, experiencing and feeling and try to understand their social reality.

Think about it . . .
The characteristics of data (7)

- Reflexive data is produced by the social researcher.
- Reflexive data can include the thinking, understandings and actions of the researcher in relation to his research.

Primary and secondary data

Social researchers can work with both data that they have gathered specifically for their own research – **primary data** – and data that has already been produced by others – **secondary data**.

Primary data is gathered by a social researcher using a data collection method appropriate to the type of data that is being collected. A range of data collection methods are discussed in detail in C3 to C9. Primary data is collected specifically for the social research project using a data collection method that has been chosen by the researcher and using a data collection tool, e.g. a questionnaire or interview guide, which has usually been designed by the researcher (occasionally a researcher may use a questionnaire or other tool that has been designed by another researcher but is suitable for her research).

There are a number of types of secondary data:

primary data
The data that a researcher gathers specifically for their own research.

secondary data
The data that a researcher uses which has already been produced by others.

1. Data that has been gathered by another social researcher using a research method of data collection, for example, a questionnaire or interview. The data is then made available for further analysis.

2. Data that has been gathered by government or another organisation for their own research or recording purposes, for example, census data, hospital patient data.

3. Data that is produced in the course of an organisational activity, for example, policy documents, legal documents, doctors' or social workers' case notes. Here the data has been produced for a particular purpose and may or may not be available in the public domain.

4. Data produced by individuals or groups as their own means of communication, for example, letters, diaries, poems, art work, videos. Again this data has been produced for a particular purpose and may or may not be in the public domain.

Although secondary data has not been produced primarily for the social researcher, he must still consider how the data has been selected, gathered and analysed and how he will select and work with the data himself. In **Parts C** and **D** we will look in more detail at how we can both collect and work with secondary data (**C9**, **D2**) and the particular issues raised for the social researcher of using data that has not been collected as part of his own research and to address his own research questions.

Think about it . . .
The characteristics of data (8)

- Primary data is collected by the researcher specifically to address the research questions.
- Secondary data may have been collected by others for research or other purposes.
- Secondary data has been produced for purposes other than to address the researcher's questions.

Using data as a representation of social reality

The purpose of this chapter has been to introduce you to a range of types of material that we all work with as social human beings on a day-to-day basis and which are available to a social researcher as data that can be collected and worked with to help us to study social phenomena. The chapter forms a link between thinking about the theory underpinning social research in **A2** and moving on to develop research questions (**A4**) and designing research (**B3** and **B4**). In **A2** we considered different ways of knowing the social world and it will be becoming clear that each epistemological position introduced in **A2** will require and work with different types of data. In particular, research that takes a positivist approach is likely to work primarily with data in terms of it being facts or values which can be observed, measured and counted. This approach to social research is often called a **quantitative** approach and is discussed in **B4**. A researcher who takes an interpretivist approach will gather data that enables the researcher to capture and interpret the meanings and understandings attributed to a social phenomenon through a consideration of the way the data is constructed and the language used within a social context. This approach to social research is often called a **qualitative** approach and is discussed in **B4**. Increasingly social researchers are drawing on a variety of types of data to enable them to address their research questions and this is sometimes referred to as a **mixed methods** approach (**B4**).

mixed methods
Methods that combine qualitative and quantitative methods in a way that is best for a specific research project.

Is the data good enough?

As data is the material through which we can demonstrate what we understand of social reality, we need to assess whether the data is doing a good job as a stand-in for the social reality it represents. Social researchers have to apply certain standards and criteria to the data itself: the way it is collected, analysed and presented. These form the basis of social research methodology and the methods of data collection and analysis which are included in this book.

We introduced these in **A1** but they will arise again in **Parts C** and **D**, depending on the nature of the data and the methods of data collection and analysis used, the appropriate criteria or quality checks that need to be applied.

validity
A measure of research quality, meaning that the data we are planning to gather and work with to address our research questions is a close representation of the aspect of social reality we are studying.

credibility
The credibility (or believability) of the researcher's interpretations of the data she has gathered is tested by the analysis and interpretation of data being transparent, for example, by testing out the interpretation of the data with the research participants or by setting the interpretations alongside existing theory.

reliability
A measure of research quality, meaning that another researcher would expect to obtain the same findings if they carried out the research in the same way, or the original researcher would expect to obtain the same findings if they tried again in the same way.

Our first concern as social researchers is how far we can say that the data we are planning to gather and work with to address our research questions is a close representation of the aspect of social reality we are studying. This is usually called its **validity.** We have already encountered this issue in relation to our small research project concerning the amount of wine drunk and numbers of women wearing red party dresses. The two researchers took different approaches to assessing the amount of wine drunk by each person and they each came up with a different answer to the question – and we noted that neither answer was probably a correct representation of reality. As social researchers we need to find ways of collecting data that ensure that the data closely reflects the reality it represents.

In this chapter we have considered data that depends on the interpretation of content and an understanding of the way language itself is used, as we saw, for example, in the different uses of the word 'family' and the different ways the party was described. As social researchers we have to be able to show how we have interpreted the data and demonstrate that our interpretations and understandings are **credible** – they make sense and are believable to others.

Unlike our two researchers at the party, as social researchers we have to ensure that our data collection and analysis processes are consistent, in that the same procedures and definitions (for example, of a 'red dress') are used – **reliability** – and that our research processes are transparent and can be understood and (possibly) reproduced by others – **replicability**.

We want to be able to check that our findings have not been affected by the way in which the data was collected, or the type of data collected. If different types of data are collected to address the same research question, each set of data can be used to check the findings from the others. This process is called **triangulation** (B4).

What sort of data will you gather and work with?

triangulation
A measure of research quality, meaning that if different types of data are collected to address the same research question, each set of data can be used to check the findings from the others.

You are likely to want, and need, to gather a range of data with different characteristics in order to be able to study your research topic. The data you gather may have a range of different characteristics and there will be different issues to consider in terms of the way the data is gathered, the quality of the data and how you are able to work with it. As a social researcher you must decide the nature of the data you will gather and work with and you will need to demonstrate that it does a good job of standing in for the social reality it represents.

Your research

Thinking about your research topic – what sort of data could you gather and work with?

Spoken or written?

- Written text is usually more structured and considered than spoken text.
- Spoken text is usually more responsive to the audience.
- Spoken text is often supplemented by non-verbal communication visible to the listener.

Fact or value?

- Factual data depends on agreed definitions, criteria and measurements.
- Value statements often need to be explored further to discover how and why the statement was made.

How is the data structured?

- Most data is structured by the person or group who produces it.
- Data representing a social phenomenon can be structured in many different ways.
- Data gathered by social researchers is structured to different degrees by the researcher as part of the data collecting process.

Primary or secondary?

- Primary data is collected by the researcher specifically to address the research questions.
- Secondary data may have been collected by others for research or other purposes.
- Secondary data has been produced for purposes other than to address the researcher's questions.

Verbal or non-verbal communication?

- Non-verbal communication is usually interpreted using words.
- Non-verbal communication often accompanies spoken text.
- Non-verbal communication depends on common understandings in the same way as verbal communication.

Meanings and understandings?

- Data can include the meanings and understandings expressed through the words (and non-verbal communication) used.
- Data can include the way language is used by data producers to present their meaning and understanding.

Individual or group created?

- Data produced by a group includes data that relates to the way the group members interact.
- Data produced by a group is group data rather than a set of individual data.

Reflexive?

- Reflexive data is produced by the social researcher.
- Reflexive data can include the thinking, understandings and actions of the researcher in relation to his research.

WILL THE DATA DO A GOOD JOB AS A 'STAND-IN' FOR THE SOCIAL REALITY IT REPRESENTS?

References and further reading

Bachman, R. and Schutt, R. K. (2001) *The Practice of Research in Criminology and Criminal Justice*, Thousand Oaks, CA: Pine Forge Press.

Coolican, H. (1996) *Research Methods and Statistics in Psychology*, London: Hodder & Stoughton.

Graziano, A. M. and Raulin, M. L. (2004) *Research Methods: A Process of Inquiry*, 5th edn, London: Pearson Education.

Leedy, P. D. and Ormond, J. E. (2005) *Practical Research: Planning and Design*, Upper Saddle River, NJ: Pearson Education.

Patton, M. Q. (2002) *Qualitative Research and Evaluation Methods*, London: Sage.

CHAPTER A4
Research questions, hypotheses and operational definitions

In context

This chapter is about how you begin to put your research ideas into words and, in doing so, think about the questions you want to ask about your research topic. Social researchers often begin with an area or aspect of social life that interests them, perhaps from their own experience or study or because a social issue has hit the headlines.

   As you begin to think about the topic it will become obvious that there are many different questions that you could ask about any subject and you will need to decide exactly what it is about the topic that you wish to research. In doing this you are beginning to formulate research questions. Initially these questions may be quite broad and general but, as you begin to focus more clearly and to unpack the questions, the research questions are likely to become narrower and more carefully defined. These research questions form the basis of your decisions about the research design (B3) and methods of data collection you will use (B4).

PART A: Thinking about research

   A1: What is research?

   A2: Knowledge, theories, paradigms and perspectives

   A3: The nature of data

   ▶ **A4: Research questions, hypotheses and operational definitions**

   A5: Research as an ethical and cultural issue

What are research questions?

The idea of a question will not be new to you; we become familiar with questions and answers at an early age. When we want to find out about something, get some information or read a chapter to help us write an essay, we construct questions to help us to find and then focus on the information we need. Often this is a process that we do without explicitly thinking about it, but in the case of research questions we need to think carefully and clearly about our questions to ensure that we design research that will enable us to answer the questions. Basically, if there is no question, you cannot find an answer. Research questions are central to your project and provide the focus of your research. A research question, therefore, both states the purpose of your research project and guides you through the process of research. Obviously, then, it is more than a simple statement because it has to include some detail of the complete nature of the research. This means that research questions are specific to a particular research undertaking.

Asking and designing research questions

As we showed in A2, as social researchers we are trying:

(a) to *describe* and *explore* a social phenomenon (or social phenomena);

(b) and usually to *understand* and *explain* how and why the phenomenon is – or is understood – as it is.

Our research questions, therefore, will usually begin with *What? Who? Where? When? How?* and *Why?*

Types of research questions

As we saw in A2, there are, basically, four different types of research question: exploratory, descriptive, explanatory and evaluative.

1. *Exploratory.* That is, an initial attempt to understand or explore some social process or phenomenon when you (maybe as an individual, but possibly the social research community to which you belong) have limited prior understanding of the area or issues.

2. *Descriptive.* This sort of question usually follows on from exploratory questions. Descriptive questions are often concerned with quantifying an area, issue or phenomenon, for example: How big is it? How many are there? Where are they? What proportion of the population is affected?

3. *Explanatory.* This could be described as the 'why' question. It asks about causes and effects: Why has this happened? How did this happen? What processes are at work here?

4. *Evaluative.* Evaluative questions are concerned with the value of a particular social practice or phenomenon and asks questions like: What works best? How good (or not so good) is it? How effective is this? This type of research often includes making recommendations about how something may be improved or changed and this aspect may be included in the research questions.

Your research may fall into more than one of these categories and that does not have to be a problem as most research projects have more than one research question.

Think about it . . .

One example used in **A2** focused on possible research questions relating to gun crime and gangs and suggested four possible research questions, as follows:

Descriptive research	*Who are the young men who are involved in gun crime?*
Exploratory research	*What is it like to be a member of a gang?*
Explanatory research	*Why do young men who join gangs participate in gun-related crime?*
Evaluative research	*What changes in policy and practice would best help young men not to join such gangs?*

A social researcher is interested in researching possible relationships between unemployment and mental health. Can you suggest some research questions for her?

Descriptive research	
Exploratory research	
Explanatory research	
Evaluative research	

In **A2** we suggested that you identify four questions relating to your own research – you might want to look back at those now.

Hypotheses

Hypotheses are a specific type of research question which actually are not questions but rather statements or assertions about relationships between two or more concepts. The question is implied rather than stated and could be in the form 'Can I prove (or disprove) that there is a relationship between these two concepts?' The purpose of the research then is to test the asserted relationship with a view to proving or disproving it.

❓ What is . . .

Hypothesis

A *testable assertion* about a relationship or relationships between two or more concepts (this is not necessarily a statement about reality; it is something to be proved or disproved).

Example A4.1

Hypotheses – crime and ethnicity

A hypothesis

People from ethnic group A are more likely to commit crimes than people from ethnic group B.

This hypothesis asserts that there is a relationship between ethnicity and committing crimes.

We could say that the research question is:

Is there a relationship between ethnicity and committing crimes?

And an additional or sub-question might be:

Are people from ethnic group A more likely to commit crimes than people from ethnic group B?

Hypotheses are most commonly used to look at relationships between concepts that are statistically testable, in other words:

- each concept can be identified and measured (see below *operational definitions*);
- data can be gathered relating to each concept;
- the data can be tested using statistical theory to ascertain whether the hypothesis can be statistically proved or disproved – that is, whether there is (or is not) a statistically demonstrable relationship.

causal relationship
The assertion that a change in 'A' causes a change in 'B'.

association or **associative relationship**
The belief that there is a relationship between two concepts, but not necessarily that the relationship is causal.

There are two main types of **relationship** that are investigated in social science research in this way. These are **causal** and **associative**.

As you will see in Example A4.2 below, establishing the nature of relationships in social research is rarely straightforward and hypotheses are likely to provide only a starting point for social research. A statistical relationship between, for example, two concepts, characteristics or events will initiate further questions to try to establish the nature of the relationship and explanations for it.

Thinking about the possible relationships – in this example, the reasons that students may (or may not) get high examination marks – at this stage will help to ensure that you gather data on all those relationships that may be of interest and relevance to your research. If, for example, you only asked students their examination marks and how many hours they spent on 'focused' reading you may establish that there is (or is not) an association between the two but you would not be able to then look at possible reasons for the association unless you had gathered data on other aspects of students' study which may have affected the examination mark. You may therefore have a series of hypotheses or combine a number of simple hypotheses into a more complex assertion.

Hypotheses, as assertions that can be tested, are not only used in research where data is collected that can be statistically tested. They can form the basis of research where the data that is collected and worked with is less structured and quantifiable. Possible causal and associative relationships can be identified between different experiences, characteristics and events in, for example, semi-structured interview data and narratives (D1, D2, D4, D5). Possible causal and associative relationships can be identified and traced through the data from a number of cases by the researcher and then further cases can be analysed to test whether the same relationships are present.

Example A4.2

Relationships

Causal relationships

Causal relationships are often shown diagrammatically as:

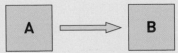

For example, we could assert that an increase in focused reading results in higher exam marks for university students. We would show this as:

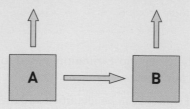

Here an increase in A – focused reading – causes an increase in B – exam marks.

Associative relationships

However, although there may be a statistical relationship between increased fo-cused reading and higher exam marks, we may not be able to prove that A causes B. This could be for a number of reasons:

1. There are many reasons that a student gets high exam marks and it would be difficult to prove that it was focused reading alone that caused the high marks.

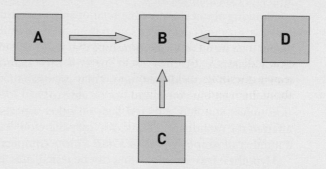

2. It may be the case that students who perform well in examinations are also the students who find focused reading suits their way of learning.

3. A third factor may be at work, influencing both the amount of focused reading and the high exam marks. For example, some of the students may have had a lecturer who has expected her students to undertake regular reading prior to seminars and has set the exam questions. She suggested that they use these readings as revision.

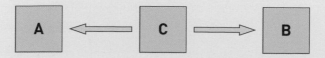

Developing research questions and operational definitions

Unpacking the research questions

You may begin with tentative research questions, as in the 'Think about it . . .' box on p. 58, but before you can produce research questions or hypotheses that will help you to design your research and choose your data collection methods you need to unpack your initial questions to ensure that you know exactly what you are researching and that you will be able to gather data that will help you answer them. This involves creating some **operational definitions** which we discuss below. Alongside this you are advised to begin to review the literature on your research topic (**B2**) as this will help you with the process of operationalising your definitions, refining your research questions and, probably, developing some **subsidiary research questions**.

Operational definitions

Before we can ask useful questions about an issue or topic, we need to *define* the exact nature of that topic.

We attempt to do this by making an operational definition, a definition we can work with. We need operational definitions to help us to focus the question and to decide what data we are going to gather to address those questions. This process is sometimes called operationalisation. Jupp *et al.* (2000: 62) describe this process as referring to

the laying down of rules which stipulate when instances of a concept have occurred.

In slightly clearer language, the purpose of the operational definition is to give you a clear indicator so that you can tell when the thing you are researching happens. Most research questions include and are about **concepts**, the way we want to find out more about them and the way they relate to each other. Concepts are ideas that can be defined or understood differently by different individuals or groups or at different times so it is essential that you have a clear definition of the concepts you use and that the definition is workable for your research – it is operational.

An operational definition:

- must be valid for and specific to the research – it must be able to be used to gather data to help you to address your research question;

- is always context-specific, designed for each research project and may be of no use in other research projects.

operational definitions
Definitions that the researcher can work with and adapt to help to focus the research questions and to decide what data to gather to address those questions.

subsidiary research questions
These are questions that help you to specify more precisely the areas of the research topic that you will focus on.

concept
An idea, abstraction or construct that encapsulates a way of describing, thinking about or labelling a social phenomenon.

Example A4.3

Unemployment and mental health – operational definitions

Earlier we asked you to think about research questions relating to the possible links between unemployment and mental health.

The research is looking at the relationship between two concepts – *unemployment* and *mental health.* Before we are able to develop our research questions and design our research we need to create operational definitions of these two concepts.

In this research what do we mean by being *unemployed*?
Here are some suggestions:

1. An adult who is not in paid work.
2. An adult who has been in paid work but is not now.

3. An adult aged between 16 and 65 years who has been in paid work but has not been in paid work for more than one year.

4. An adult who is receiving unemployment welfare benefits – 'on the dole'.

5. An adult who is not in paid work and is looking for paid work – 'signing on'.

6. An adult who does not work.

We need to know the focus of the research and the research question before we can choose the definition that is going to be used.

For example: If the research question is:

A. What are the impacts of long-term unemployment on people's mental health?

operational definition 3 would be appropriate and could be used to identify a suitable sample of research participants.

OR COULD IT?

We have fallen into the trap of operationalising one concept – *unemployment* – using another – *paid work.* We now need a definition of paid work. This could be 'employment of at least 35 hours per week for which payment is received'. This would exclude people who are working for less than 35 hours but for our research, which is looking at long-term unemployment, this would probably be an acceptable definition.

B. Are people who are not in paid work happier or unhappier than those who are?

On the face of it, operational definition 1 would be most appropriate here but this group – adults not in paid work – includes a very wide variety of people: those who do not want or need to take paid work, those who are retired, those who are unable to take paid work as well as those who want to work and those who volunteer. It would be advisable to refine the definition by deciding which groups of people this research is going to focus on.

Think about it . . .

What is meant by *mental health*?
  Here are some suggestions:

1. Presence or absence of clinically diagnosed mental disorders.

2. State of mind which can be measured using psychological tests.

3. How we feel about ourselves and our lives.

Which operational definition would you use to research each of the questions? And can you suggest other ways of operationalising *mental health*?

A. What are the impacts of long-term unemployment on people's mental health?

B. Are people who are not in paid work happier or unhappier than those who are?

Operational definitions are not only used to help researchers refine their research questions. They are also necessary when we begin to think about how we will gather data in order to address our research questions. We need to be able to gather the data in terms of our operational definitions. In the example we need to:

- be able to find people or find out about people who meet the criteria of the definition – in this case, *adults aged between 16 and 65 years who have been in paid work (for at least 35 hours per week) but have not been doing any paid work for more than one year;*
  - In this case the operational definition chosen has implications for the selection of the sample, identifying people who meet the criteria or gaining access to secondary data that can be used.

- be able to collect data from them or from others that will enable us – in this example – to 'measure' their mental health
  - In this case the issue is one of measurement and how the data will be collected. For example, taking the three suggested operational definitions of *mental health*:
    - *Operational definition 1* would require access to medical information (or a self-report of the diagnosis).
    - *Operational definition 2* may require the researcher to develop a psychological test – or use a test designed by psychologists – and administer the test to the research participants.
    - *Operational definition 3* would require the development of questions designed to elicit people's feelings about their own mental state. This is a subjective issue and people are likely to have different ideas about, for example, what they mean when they say they are happy. Of course *happiness* is also a concept and requires operationalising so that we can gather data that will help us to see whether it is present or not.

Think about it . . .

What questions would you ask a research participant to find out:

(a) whether they consider themselves to be *happy*?
(b) what they mean by being *happy*?

We have seen that when we try to operationalise a concept we can easily fall into the trap of using another concept as part of the definition, and that as we develop our data collection methods we sometimes introduce more concepts which need to be operationalised to ensure that we are collecting data that answers the questions we think they are answering. A few more examples will help to illustrate the care with which you need to word your research questions and the questions you address to your research participants.

Question wording

If, for example, we are interested in people's experiences of visiting their doctor and one of our questions is:

Have you had to wait too long to see your doctor?

then there will be a number of problems. The most significant is that individuals will define *too long* in different ways. For some, five minutes may seem a very long time (especially if they have parked on double yellow lines outside the health centre) and answer *yes*; for others, a wait of 40 minutes in an air-conditioned waiting room may be a welcome relief from the heat of a summer's day and answer *no*. When we look at the two replies we will learn little about the waiting time and why it is seen to be *too long* (or not). Whatever the reasons, individuals will give different and disparate answers that will be of little use to us when we begin our analysis. To get the data we are interested in, we may need to ask more questions:

> How long did you have to wait in the waiting room before seeing the doctor?
>
> Were you satisfied or dissatisfied at having to wait this length of time?
>
> Why were you satisfied/dissatisfied at having to wait this length of time?

Context and culturally specific concepts and wording

Operational definitions are usually context- and culture-specific. This aspect of operational definitions needs to be considered to ensure that questions are able to be understood and answered by all those who may be research participants and to ensure that their use results in valid data – that is, that all the research participants have the same understanding of the questions and are, effectively, answering the same question. For example, if people who belong to white, middle-class, British culture are asked to list the *immediate members of their family*, it would probably be unusual for the number to exceed 15. If this question is asked of, for example, a Sikh, it would not be unusual for the list to exceed 100 (www.jamardaresources.com) because different cultural groups have different family concepts. This indicates the need to ensure that operational definitions are informed by the context and culture of the research participants and that the research design must be able to accommodate very different answers to the same question.

Getting the same type of answer

One of the purposes of creating operational definitions and using them in questions is to make sure that the question always gets the same *type* of answer. For example, a question that asks 'Where do you live?' can be answered in a variety of ways. Your respondent could say:

- in Birmingham;
- in a house;
- with my parents;
- near the park;
- etc.

A researcher faced with this variety of answers would be unable to use the data from the question as people had understood and answered the question in different ways. Questions must be worded precisely to ensure that there is a common understanding. For example:

- Which local authority area do you live in?
- Do you live in a house, bungalow, flat or other type of accommodation?
- Who lives with you in the same household?
- Which street do you live in / what is your postcode?

Using other people's definitions

When you are working with secondary data (**C9**) or using someone else's research to develop your ideas (**B2**) you will find other researchers' or data collectors' operational definitions which you may consider using. The difficulty with this is that you may not know enough about the way in which the other researchers operationalised their definition/question; in many circumstances, you will not even know the exact question that was asked, so it is possible that you will misinterpret their results. Even when you know the exact research question, the operational definition(s) that underpin it may not be known so you are advised to proceed with care and use these definitions to inform the development of your own definitions rather than simply adopting them.

Pilot-testing operational definitions

It *is* difficult for an individual to create valid, reliable operational definitions. Most of us do not have the ability to take account of many perspectives and possibilities at the same time. Accordingly, the recommended course of action is to **pilot-test** your definitions. This could mean, at its most simple, asking a few colleagues or friends to consider whether the definition makes sense and check whether it always results in the same type of answer.

If you have the opportunity to pilot your questions on a small group of research participants you can check the validity of your questions and amend the wording, clarify your definitions and ensure that you are gathering useable data before you embark on your main research stage. It is common practice for researchers to ask research participants at the pilot stage to reflect on the experience, to identify questions that are not clear and to discuss any potential misunderstandings.

pilot-test
A trial run or an opportunity to try out a data collection method on a small sample of cases before the main research data gathering takes place; question wording, research participant understanding and data collection procedures can all be tried out and amended if necessary before the main research stage.

Your research

The giraffe and tortoise approach to writing operational definitions

One way of creating operational definitions is to take the giraffe and tortoise approach. By this we mean breaking down the process of creating the definition into two phases.

1 The giraffe

As a giraffe your head is a long way above the ground, giving you a great overview of everything around you. This is comparable to the first stage of making an operational definition: getting the big picture, the concept, the idea of what you need to measure. Maybe it's *crime* or a hypothesised relationship between *poverty and crime*. It could be anything that you're interested in.

So while you're a giraffe, you're browsing through the treetops, you're taking an overview, but you're not too interested in details.

This first (or giraffe) stage of producing a research question or hypothesis about poverty and crime might result in something like:

There is a link between poverty and crime.

That's fine, but it lacks a lot of detail. A sarcastic lecturer might say something like: *Well, what is crime? How do you measure it? Do you just mean crimes against property or people? Do you include traffic offences? If so, what about parking tickets?* Similar things can be said about poverty. *Do you mean absolute or relative poverty? How will you measure it?*

Giraffes can't answer questions like that – they're ideas people. So we move on to the second phase:

2 The tortoise

Suddenly, we're right down at ground level. We move slowly. We can't see very far, but what we can see, we see in a *lot* of detail, because it's right under our noses and we spend a long time looking at it.

Now we can get on with constructing the detail of our operational definition. We can decide if we're looking at quantities or feelings: official definitions or self-definitions. There are lots of possibilities, a lot of detail, but in practice, you're after something that you can use and decisions have to be made. The end result that we want is to have made the intangible measurable.

(NB The giraffe/tortoise analogy may seem a bit childish. You may prefer to look at the front cover of this textbook. If you look at a forest from a distance, then all you see is a mass of barely distinguishable trees. If you look more closely at a tree, what do you see – branches, maybe? And if you look at a branch? Operational definitions are complex, often multi-layered and essential to the conduct of research. Don't just be a giraffe!)

Developing your research questions

For most researchers, developing and refining research questions is a process that goes on alongside reviewing the literature (**B2**), thinking about research design (**B3**) and choosing methods (**B4**). As we indicated above, the process is likely to start with a general (giraffe-level) question which needs unpacking to enable you to begin defining concepts in ways that are going to be operational. As the operational definitions are developed it is likely that your research question(s) will become more focused and precise and that you begin to generate **subsidiary research questions**. These are questions that help you to specify more precisely the areas of the research topic that you will focus on. As you will see from Example A4.4, the subsidiary research questions spell out more clearly the data you will want to gather and how you will identify and measure, in this example, people's *mental health*.

Earlier we specified four different types of research question and suggested that many research projects include more than one research question. If you approach your research topic in two or more different ways – for example, both describing the nature and extent of a problem or situation and looking for explanations of certain aspects of the topic – you may have two, or more, main research questions, each with their own subsidiary questions.

Example A4.4

Developing research questions using operational definitions

Initial research question

What are the impacts of long-term unemployment on people's mental health?

Operational definitions

Unemployed:
An adult aged between 16 and 65 years who has been in paid work within the last two years but has not been in any paid work for more than one year

Mental health:
How you feel about yourself and your life

Ways of asking questions about this definition of *mental health* could include:

- How would you describe yourself?
- Have you sought help because of the way you feel about yourself and your life from a doctor, counsellor or adviser?
- What would improve your life?

Refinement of the research question

What are the impacts on how people who have had paid work feel about themselves and their lives when they have been without any paid work for more than a year?

Subsidiary questions

Using the operational definition and suggested ways of asking questions, some subsidiary questions can be developed:

- How do people in this situation describe themselves?
- Have they sought help because of the way they feel about themselves during the period of unemployment?
- What type(s) of help have they sought and for what reasons?
- What changes would people in this situation like to see in relation to themselves and their lives?

This chapter has taken you through a process that goes alongside the other preparations for your research. At each stage of this process the focus of your research will become clearer – you will be getting nearer to the data gathering itself. The process is one of focusing, defining and refining and is primarily concerned with the validity of your research – that is, that you are able to demonstrate that you are researching what you think you are researching and gathering data that will help you to address your research questions.

Your research

Research quality check – validity

- Have you operationalised the concepts in your research questions or hypotheses?
- Do your operational definitions enable you to get data that will answer your questions?
- Do your operational definitions help you to describe the concept in terms you can identify and measure?

- Will you be collecting data from or about the cases, people, situations you say you are?
- Are your operational definitions specific to the context and culture setting of your research?
- Are your operational definitions meaningful to your research participants?
- Are you sure you are getting the data you think you are getting?

Your research

My initial research question is . . .

Operationalising the concepts

Concept _____

Operational definitions:

Concept _____

Operational definitions:

Refinement of the research question:

Subsidiary research questions:

-
-
-
-

References and further reading

Campbell, J. P., Daft, R. L. and Hulin, C. L. (1982) *What to Study: Generating and Developing Research Questions*, London: Sage.

Jamarda Resources (2007) Sikhs. Available at http://jamardaresources.com/Training%20Sikhs.php (accessed 1 August 2009).

Jupp, V., Davies, P. and Francis, P. (eds) (2000) *Doing Criminological Research*, London: Sage.

Kimchi, J., Polivka, B. and Stevenson, J. (1991) Triangulation: operational definitions, *Nursing Research*, 40(6): 364–6.

King, G., Keohane, O. and Verba, S. (1994) *Designing Social Inquiry: Scientific Inference in Qualitative Research*, Princeton University Press.

Miles, M. and Huberman, A. (1984) *Qualitative Data Analysis*, London: Sage.

Punch, K. F. (1998) *Introduction to Social Research: Quantitative and Qualitative Approaches*, London: Sage.

Silverman, D. (1997) *Qualitative Research: Theory, Method and Practice*, London: Sage.

CHAPTER A5
Research as an ethical and cultural issue

Contents

In context

This chapter discusses the issues of ethics in research. We offer some definitions of ethics and some examples of ethical issues that social researchers may encounter. We discuss the notions of informed consent, power relationships, protection from harm, vulnerable groups and cultural issues in detail and we offer some suggestions for ways in which student researchers can comply with ethical requirements.

PART A: Thinking about research

    A1: What is research?

    A2: Knowledge, theories, paradigms and perspectives

    A3: The nature of data

    A4: Research questions, hypotheses and operational definitions

▶ A5: Research as an ethical and cultural issue

All social research has ethical implications and dilemmas. So, what we are doing when we think about **ethics** is looking at the social and moral values involved in undertaking social research and, in particular, asking ourselves how we should treat our participants.

❓ What is . . .

Ethics

Ethics can be thought of as a set of rules by which individuals and societies maintain moral standards in their lives.

McAuley (2003: 95) says:

The ethics of social research is about creating a mutually respectful, win-win relationship in which participants are pleased to respond candidly, valid results are obtained, and the community considers the conclusions constructive.

The Economic and Social Research Council (2009) say:

'Research ethics' refers to the moral principles guiding research, from its inception through to completion and publication of results and beyond – for example, the curation* of data and physical samples after the research has been published.

*The supervision by a curator of a collection of preserved or exhibited items.

Frankly, most social science research ethics are common sense: as a first stage, ask yourself how you would want to be treated when you are invited to take part in someone else's project. However, social research *is* becoming more and more subject to restrictions and controls, and it is therefore always wise to find out if there are explicit requirements in your discipline or research area (see Example A5.1).

Example A5.1

Ethical guidelines

Many organisations have formal ethical guidelines for their members. These can also be useful for you! Check whether your own discipline or profession has its own ethical guidelines. Here are some examples:

British Sociological Association
www.britsoc.co.uk/equality/Statement+Ethical+Practice.htm (accessed 10 August 2009)

Social Research Association
www.the-sra.org.uk/documents/pdfs/ethics03.pdf (accessed 10 August 2009)

British Association of Social Workers
www.basw.co.uk/Portals/0/CODE%20OF%20ETHICS.pdf (accessed 10 August 2009)

Barnardos
www.barnardos.org.uk/resources/research_and_tips/research_and_publications_research.htm (accessed 10 August 2009)

Economic and Social Research Council
www.esrc.ac.uk/ESRCInfoCentre/Images/ESRC_Re_Ethics_Frame_tcm6-11291.pdf (accessed 10 August 2009)

Government Social Research Unit (Civil Service)
www.civilservice.gov.uk/networks/professional/gsr/professional-guidance/GSR_Code_Legal_and_Ethical.aspx (accessed 10 August 2009)

While different sets of guidelines and advice on ethics can vary, there are a number of issues that should be considered every time we undertake research. However, it is important to remember that ethics are, in part at least, context-specific. It is not so much that they change, but rather that we need to take special care when we research in some areas or if we are interested in particular groups of people; after all, even though everyone is worthy of our care and respect, some people are more vulnerable than others. Because of this, you will find specific references to ethical considerations elsewhere in this book and this chapter should be thought of as a baseline for ethical considerations/approval, rather than the complete story.

The sections that follow comprise what we think are the basic areas that need consideration *before* you start your research; you need to be looking at these at the design stage. At this stage you may need to gain ethical approval for your research plans and if you are preparing a research proposal (**B6**) you will need to demonstrate in the proposal that you have considered and addressed any ethical issues.

Example A5.2

Ethical guidelines

The Economic and Social Research Council, which funds much of the academic research in the social sciences, sets out the following as the key principles of research ethics:

- Research should be designed, reviewed and undertaken to ensure integrity and quality.
- Research staff and subjects must be fully informed about the purpose, methods and intended possible uses of the research, what participation entails and what risks, if any, are involved.
- The confidentiality of information supplied by subjects, and their anonymity, must be respected.
- Any participant must do so on a voluntary basis free from coercion.
- Harm to participants must be avoided.
- The independence of the research must be clear and any conflicts of interest or partiality explicit.

Source: Economic and Social Research Council (2009).

Ethical approval

Most social research projects, including those undertaken by students gaining qualifications, are now subject to an ethical approval process that must be completed before the research starts. These processes differ widely between organisations and levels and types of research. So if, for example, you were planning to do 'health' research on human beings that involved the administration of drugs or some surgery, you would (rightly) expect there to be strong safeguards in place to protect your participants. Although that is an extreme situation, there is still a need for safeguards even where research is simply about seeking people's opinions or answers to questions. The process of ethical approval, then, is basically to make sure that your participants are not put at any risk by your research, or more usually to make sure that, among other things, the risks are 'reasonable' and that the participants understand them.

The ethics approval process is more useful than it might sound. Certainly, its final purpose is to ensure that the research complies with appropriate ethical guidelines, but it also creates an opportunity for the researcher to think the process through in detail, something that can be beneficial in terms of improving and refining the data collection methods. At the very least, the ethics process will raise the researcher's awareness of all the details of the research process.

When you first try to find out about ethics in research, you can be swamped with information about 'medical' research, which is governed by very strict rules. Approval for medical research in the UK is usually controlled by the NHS research ethics committees and gaining approval can be a long and complex process – for more detail, see www.nres. npsa.nhs.uk/ (accessed 7 August 2009). University-based research is, as a rule, controlled by a system of ethics committees too, but often they require different levels of approval depending on the nature of the research. It is not unusual for a proposal for undergraduate social research (such as you might undertake for a module or dissertation) to be approved by your supervisor in a (relatively) informal way. Of course, different institutions will have different requirements. If you are undertaking research at a university or college then you should check what approval process you must follow at your institution.

Below we highlight the most important considerations when thinking about the ethics of your research and you will find a 'checklist' at the end of the chapter.

Informed consent

informed consent
Making sure that the people who are going to take part in the research understand what they are consenting to participate in.

The basis of **informed consent** is making sure that the people who are going to take part in the research understand what they are consenting to participate in. This may sound obvious, but there are a number of things that the researcher must do to make sure that an ethical process is followed (see the 'Real research' box on page 75 which sets this out in detail).

- *Consent should be freely given.* It is not acceptable to coerce people into participating. This can be an issue of power; maybe people will want to please you by helping or maybe they find you so scary that they are frightened to refuse! When you are thinking about recruiting your sample, you need to consider how you will encourage people to participate without coercing them.

- *You must provide clear, adequate information.* Make sure people understand what they are consenting to. People who are going to be part of your study deserve your respect and consideration. Most likely they will be giving up their time without compensation. The reasons for this can be complex, but could be that they feel that your project is interesting and worthwhile or that they think that you are worth some of their time. We think that the best way to do this is to use a formal information sheet and consent form along the lines of our examples. So, at the least, they need to know the following:
  - *What's in it for them.* Often, this will be the satisfaction that they have helped someone's research, but sometimes it will be more complex (they might have a strong personal involvement in the topic, for example). Sometimes, research participants are paid or rewarded for their participation; if your project wants to do that, then you will need to find funding and decide whether the reward should be in cash or, perhaps, in something like gift vouchers (paying participants is a bit of a minefield and can have important implications such as income tax liability or an effect on someone's benefit payments).
  - *Why you are doing this research.* A clear explanation and justification here will often encourage people to participate, particularly if they feel that your work will be valuable to them or their social group.
  - *What the practical implications are for them.* Will they, for example, be asked to give up a lot of time? Or maybe to do complicated mental exercises? Or perhaps to meet other people in a focus group?
  - *Participation is voluntary and they have the right to withdraw at any time.* It can be really frustrating if people choose to exercise this right, especially if your sample is small, but it is important to understand that there can be no penalty for this – your participant is simply deciding to withdraw their consent. You need to consider in the design stage of your research what you will do with any data collected up to the time that someone withdraws.

- *Are there any risks?* Your research participants need to know if there are any risks from their participation in your work (see the section on protection from harm, on page 77).
- *What you will do with the data.* People need to know what you plan to do with the information that you collect about them (see the section on protection from harm, on page 77).
- *What authority you have.* Often, people will want to know what 'authority' you have to undertake this research. Most ethical approval processes will require you to have a 'sponsor' who vouches for your reliability (for students, this will usually be your department, tutor or supervisor). Participants should also know how to contact you and your sponsor.

- *Respondents must be able to give informed consent.* There are times when you may need to know that your respondents are able to give informed consent. Mostly, students should not expect this to be a big issue, but you should be aware that some individuals are not considered competent to give consent, usually because it is thought that they are unable to understand the implications of doing so. In such cases other adults may be asked to give consent by proxy – on behalf of – them. This would include parents giving consent for their children's participation and could include consent being given by proxy for people with, for example, dementia. (For further reading on this, see Norman *et al.*, 2006: 228–33.)

Example A5.3

Research participant consent form

University of Anywhere
Department of Social Sciences

Date

<u>CONSENT FORM</u>

Title of Research Project:

Name of Researcher:

Address Email and Telephone Number of Researcher:

1. I confirm that I have read and understood the information sheet for the above study and have had the opportunity to ask questions.   YES/NO*

2. I understand that my participation is voluntary and that I am free to withdraw at any time, without having to give any reason, and without my care or legal rights being affected.   YES/NO*

3. I agree to take part in the above study.   YES/NO*

_____   _____   _____
Name of Research Participant   Date   Signature

_____   _____   _____
Name of Researcher   Date   Signature

* Please delete as appropriate

Figure A5.1   Example of a research participant consent form

Your research

Here is a list of headings that you will probably need to include on your information sheet. Write a sentence or paragraph about each to complete the form.

University of Anywhere
Department of Social Sciences

INFORMATION FOR PARTICIPANTS

Title of the project:

The project is being carried out by:

The project is about:

What will I have to do?

What are the benefits of participating in the study?

Are there any risks for me if I agree to participate?

Will the study cost me anything?

What if I do not want to take part?

What happens to the information collected?

What if I change my mind and decide to withdraw from the study?

What if I have any questions or do not understand something?

What happens at the end of the study?

If you have any concerns about the study and wish to contact someone to discuss them please telephone:

Figure A5.2   Example of an 'Information for Participants' form

Real research

Informed consent

The Royal College of Nursing says:

> *Informed consent is an ongoing agreement by a person to receive treatment, undergo procedures or participate in research, after risks, benefits and alternatives have been adequately explained to them . . .*

Freely given informed consent is central to research involving human participants or the use of human tissues or genetic material. This is because it is essential to ensure that those who participate in research understand exactly what the research involves for them. This applies equally whether they are patients or healthy volunteers.

Informed consent helps to ensure that people are not deceived or coerced into participating in research.

In order to give truly informed consent, potential participants need to understand the following:

- the purpose of the research;
- the practicalities and procedures involved in participating;
- the benefits and risks of participation and, if appropriate, the alternative therapies;
- how data about them will be managed and used;
- the consent form;
- their role if they agree to participate in the research;
- how information will be provided to them throughout the study;
- that their participation is voluntary;
- that they can withdraw from the study at any time, without giving any reason and without compromising their future treatment;
- the insurance indemnity arrangements for the conduct of the research where appropriate;
- that the research has been approved by a research ethics committee.

They should also be given the following information:

- contact details, should they have further questions or wish to withdraw;
- details of the research sponsor and research funding body.

Continued consent

Informed consent is an ongoing requirement, so researchers must ensure that participants:

- continue to understand the information above and any changes in that information;
- continue to consent to participate throughout the study.

Source: Adapted from Royal College of Nursing (2005) *Informed Consent in Health and Social Care Research*, p. 2. Reproduced with permission. Available at www.rcn.org.uk/__data/assets/ pdf_file/0003/56703/informedconsentdec05.pdf (accessed 7 August 2009).

You should remember that it is not always possible or meaningful to try to obtain informed consent, for example, if the research is concerned with observing the behaviour of football crowds (**C6**). However, this should not be used as a way of avoiding the issue; wherever possible, it is the researcher's duty to obtain informed consent.

Power relationships

We mentioned this in the discussion about informed consent, but there are further ramifications that you should consider and which can have an effect on your data collection.

Does the participant see you as 'powerful'? (Of course, this can happen without the participant realising it as well!) This could be in a number of different ways, for example, you may be seen as 'the expert' on the research topic and thus your respondent will not want to disagree with you. You might also be perceived as someone who has access to something (for example, expertise, contacts) that would be useful to the participant; this, again, can change a person's responses to your enquiries.

There are more general things too. For example, if your research is with young people, you may be seen as their superior because you are older (this can sometimes have special implications when working with people from different cultures too and we discuss it in more detail on page 182). As a social researcher you must try to be aware that different groups of people will see you in different ways. Some may be intimidated by your research skills or feel superior to you because they are older. It is important that you try to 'think through' the implications of this before you start your data collection so that you can take proper account of any impact it may have on your work.

Protection from harm (participant)

It should be quite obvious that anyone who participates in your research should be safe while doing so. There are a few things that it is worth thinking about so that this is an explicit practice, rather than just something that happens by chance:

Physical harm

Your participants should not be at risk of any physical harm (we assume here that you are *not* conducting any medical or other physical experiments on them, otherwise you will be subject to specific rules). At the least, this means that the places where your data collection sessions take place should be safe (not just in terms of the building's roof staying on, but also in terms of their travel to and fro). The researcher should not simply assume that a participant will feel that a suggested venue is safe, but common sense is useful here: many people will be happy about being invited to a place where there are lots of other people, for example, a neighbourhood or town centre. Be flexible about where research can be done.

Psychological harm

Your participants also have the right to be protected from any risk of psychological harm. This is more difficult. If we are researching sensitive subjects, then there is always the risk that a respondent may be affected by consideration of such issues. Most of us are not trained counsellors or psychologists and are therefore not properly equipped to deal with this sort of reaction. However, there is a solution and that is to make sure that participants have an opportunity to discuss any uncomfortable issues outside the data collection setting. Perhaps this will be with you as the researcher, but it might be with some other support that you have access to.

Think about it . . .

Suppose you were undertaking research about the services used by people with a particular chronic health condition, e.g. diabetes or a heart condition. Your questions about the services used, e.g. clinics, hospitals and specialists, may leave the respondent feeling that he is not receiving all the services he needs or that his condition is more serious than he had thought. This could cause him to feel anxious.

You are probably not a medical expert but you can ensure that your respondent receives advice and support by, for example, providing information leaflets produced by medical experts, including a suggestion that the respondent contacts his own doctor with any queries.

Other consequences

There are other potential forms of harm that may need some thought. What would you do, for example, if, as a result of taking part in your research, a participant lost his job? Such a thing is not impossible (though highly unlikely). The participant needs to be certain that any personal information divulged will remain confidential (see 'Real research' below); they are also likely to be more willing to participate if they understand both the purpose of the research and who may read the report/dissertation. The situation also arises where a respondent discloses some illegal behaviour: what will your response be? (See 'Your research' on p. 80.)

Real research

It can be difficult to protect people from harm when researching organisations. Rogers (2001) carried out a research project into management structures in a mental health services delivery organisation. Because the staff team was quite small, there were specific problems to overcome and, to some extent, it became impossible to preserve complete anonymity and confidentiality because 'everybody knows everybody'. It would not be surprising if employees felt that they were 'exposed' to managers and that their jobs might therefore be at risk. This was overcome by having clear understandings with participants about how they would be described and how their identities would be masked.

Risk

There is an ongoing debate about whether participants should be allowed to take risks in research projects, even if they are fully explained. (For a detailed discussion, see Larossa *et al.*, 1981: 303–13.) For the purposes of most (maybe all) undergraduate research, this should not be an issue as it would be very unusual to allow participants to take any risks.

Confidentiality/anonymity

Participants should, usually, be assured that they will not be identified in the research and that their input to the project will be confidential. They should also be informed about the way that the findings of the research will be disseminated, so that they can make a proper decision about participation.

Although it is quite easy to offer anonymity, researchers need to understand that it may not always be possible. If, for example, your data collection involved talking to the teaching staff at a school, there is a potential problem with reporting your findings anonymously because there is only one head teacher and so any data attributed to the head teacher would not be anonymous. Researchers need to consider these issues when they plan how to report findings (in this instance, it might be possible to say 'a senior member of the teaching staff said . . . ') and to ensure that the participants themselves understand how the researcher intends to ensure their anonymity.

There is also an implicit constraint on the use of the data you gather for any other purpose than that which you told your participants. Generally, this would be considered unethical.

Honesty

overt methods
Open methods of investigation in which participants are aware that they are part of your research.

covert methods
Methods of investigation in which participants are not aware that they are part of a research project, or are perhaps being observed in secret.

Generally, you should be honest with your participants and not mislead or deceive them about your methods or purpose. This argues that you should use **overt** or open methods of investigation. However, there can be situations when overt methods would not be successful and **covert** methods are required. For example, you might wish to observe the honesty behaviour of people working in shops. Clearly, if people know they are being observed, then they are likely to ensure that their behaviour is above reproach. What must be decided is whether it is ethical to use subterfuge and whether this can be justified: it is probable that this would require significant justification in a research proposal before ethical approval would be given. Conducting your data gathering covertly may also involve you in observing or gathering data about (in this example) dishonest, perhaps illegal behaviour. We discuss the ethical issues this may raise below.

Data Protection

You may have obligations under the Data Protection Act (1998) which covers *personal data* in any form (so paper records and computer records are subject to the Act). In summary, it requires that all personal data shall:

- be obtained and processed fairly and lawfully and shall not be processed unless certain conditions are met;
- be obtained for a specified and lawful purpose and shall not be processed in any manner incompatible with that purpose;
- be adequate, relevant and not excessive for those purposes;
- be accurate and kept up to date;
- not be kept for longer than is necessary for that purpose;
- be processed in accordance with the data subject's rights;
- be kept safe from unauthorised access, accidental loss or destruction;
- not be transferred to a country outside the European Economic Area, unless that country has equivalent levels of protection for personal data.

Source: University of Birmingham Legal Services 'Summary – Data Protection Act', available at www.legalservices. bham.ac.uk/data_protection_policy/ (accessed 7 August 2009)

Vulnerable groups

As we noted above, some groups are seen as 'vulnerable' and therefore worthy of additional care. In part, this is to ensure that members of such groups are not exposed to any risks or dangers, but also to make certain that they are not exploited.

Making lists of such groups is not necessarily a very productive way forward, but we suggest that, at the very least, you give extra thought to all the issues above when you are considering undertaking research with people who:

1. are young: by this we mean (as a general guideline) people aged 16 years or less;
2. are older, especially older people who live alone: it is more difficult to give an age range here, but we would suggest that you give additional thought to your plans when involving people above the statutory retirement age;
3. have physical or learning disabilities;
4. have mental health issues: there is specific legislation, the Mental Capacity Act (2005), in place to protect people with mental health issues; this legislation is complex – if your research is taking you in this direction, then you will need specialist advice from an expert.

This is not a complete list. You need to think about this issue when you design your research and endeavour to treat any vulnerable group appropriately.

Ownership of data

Though it may not, at first, seem to be an ethical issue, the ownership of data is important. If you own data, then (usually) it is yours to do with as you will (within the constraints that we discuss above). However, you need to be certain of the ownership. Though it probably will not be an issue for most students, contracts for research that is externally funded, by the ESRC or a charity, for instance, will often contain explicit conditions about the ownership and dissemination of data and findings. The ESRC, for example, requires that reports be lodged in central, publicly accessible databases (www.esrcsocietytoday.ac.uk/ESRCInfoCentre/index.aspx, accessed 7 August 2009). Other organisations do not want the data – which, after all, they have paid for – to be accessible to anyone else. It would, of course, be unethical, and probably illegal, to break these requirements.

Illegal behaviour

One of the things that always surprises researchers when they start out is that participants will tell you the most astonishing things! It is quite usual for people to tell you intimate details of their lives and relationships and, to some extent, the better you are as a researcher, then the more of this sort of information will come your way. There is a big potential problem, though: what if a participant tells you that they have committed some illegal act? What will you do?

Your research

If you become aware of illegal acts that come within the scope of the Children Act (2004) or the Terrorism Act (2006), then you are *required* to report them to the police.

As with many ethical issues, you need to have made the decision about your actions at the design stage, rather than when the event takes place. It is difficult to advise on the proper course of action, because all of these cases are different. However, we suggest that you take the following points into consideration when making the decision on what your action will be:

1. We think that the first consideration is to remember that you are a human being and a member of society and that this will take precedence over your role as a researcher.
2. If you decide to report your participant's actions to the police, then it is probable that you will not be able to use this person's contribution to your project. It is also possible that the entire project will be put in jeopardy.
3. If you decide not to take any action, have you thought the process through and justified it in the design stage of your research? How do you decide what to report? (See the 'Think about it . . .' box below.)
4. Remember, too, that you need to be comfortable with your decisions.

One way of dealing with issues of illegal behaviour is to be explicit with your participants at the outset. You might, perhaps, choose to make a statement in your information sheet (or include it verbally in your initial meeting) along these lines:

> *You need to be aware that if you disclose details of illegal behaviour, then I will report them to the police.*

You may not want to be this strict, of course. For some, there would be a difference between the declaration of breaking a speed limit where no one was harmed and the armed robbery of a Post Office (a real example from the work of one of the authors in the Probation Service). However, it is difficult to draw that line: an ethical dilemma in itself

The statement is clear and easy for everyone to understand. However, there are a couple of major drawbacks:

1. It is possible that your participant will decide to withdraw from your research.
2. A statement of this sort makes it impossible for you to research illegal behaviour – and this can include a lot of research associated with sociology, cultural studies and criminology, for example – and might make it difficult even to research attitudes towards such behaviour.

Think about it . . .

Ethical dilemmas and the law

Below are some questions for you to ask yourself while you are designing your research. They are all drawn from 'real-life' situations:

1. Would you report someone to the police who told you that he had been speeding in his car on the morning of your interview?
2. Would your decision be different if he told you that he had been involved in an accident where someone was injured as a result of the speeding?
3. What will you do if your participant tells you that she smokes marijuana?
4. What will you do if she tells you that she deals crack cocaine?
5. What will you do if your participant tells you that he used to steal chocolates from the newsagents?
6. What will your decision be if your participant tells you that he robbed a Post Office?

Cultural considerations and diversity in research

This section is not about how to undertake research concerning different cultures or minority groups, but rather some of the ethical implications of cultural difference and diversity within your research.

Most research texts do not include any discussion of diversity or cultural difference, even though there is a growing body of evidence (for example: Smaje, 1995: Alexander, 1999; Sheldon, 1992) that suggests that researchers do not pay enough attention to cultural difference and diversity when they undertake their projects. In terms of ethics, it is apparent that people from different cultures will respond in different ways to requests to participate, provide informed consent and so on (Ryen, 2007); some cultures will not have the same understanding of privacy as you do and others will be unfamiliar with the notion of, for example, written consent (Ryen, 2007: 220).

It is important to keep the nature of your population in mind (see **B5**). In the UK, we live in a very varied and diverse society which includes people of many different social, ethnic and religious groups. People vary in many other ways too, for example, by gender, age, social class, sexuality, location and physical characteristics. If our research purposes and questions require us to reflect this, then it is clearly vital that we take account of this diversity in our research design (**B3**) and choice of methods (**B4**). However, this is not always the case and perhaps we only want to research the characteristics of white men aged 18 who live in Shrewsbury; if so, our task is probably more straightforward (though this includes the unspoken assumption that the researcher is a white man too!). It is a good idea to remember that people may not have had the same experiences as you and, because of this, their view of the world may not be the same as yours. This is probably particularly true in the UK for anyone who belongs to a 'minority' or 'oppressed' group.

One of the purposes of the ethics process is to ensure that we do not *accidentally* exclude part of our population through the way we select our participants and engage them in our research. Below, we set out a few ethical issues of culture and diversity that we think should be considered when designing research.

Language

It may seem obvious, but the researcher and the participant need to share a common language. The assumption that everybody in the UK speaks English fluently is both dangerous and wrong. Relying on the use of a single language in some research settings can result in the exclusion of significant groups of participants.

Ethnicity and 'race'

Which ethnic and 'racial' groups are included in your research is, largely, an issue of design. However, one of the purposes of ethics is to ensure that you – as the researcher – have considered the issue and the impact that it has (or does not have) on your project. If you are concerned with the parameters of a broad population (the inner-city population of Birmingham, for example) and your sample consists entirely of white males, then you have a problem and you should reconsider your research design, choice of methods and sampling approach.

Similar issues can exist for the other social divisions such as, *gender, age, sexuality, location, social class* and *disability*, depending on the subject matter and purpose of your research.

Visibility

We have included this slightly strange term, not to suggest that your research subjects are physically transparent, but to point out that sometimes people can be difficult to locate or contact. This can be for a variety of reasons: some groups are very small or geographically dispersed; others may not want to be 'seen' (think, for example, about people who may be in the country illegally). This is probably best seen as a 'diversity' issue in ethical terms; making sure that people are not unintentionally excluded from your research is important.

'Culture'

culture
Culture is the set of social ideas and behaviours, customs and norms that constitute the way of life of people in a particular society.

There are different meanings of the word **'culture'**, and 'cultural differences' cover the wide and diverse field of social behaviours and understandings. We can only raise some of the issues to consider when planning a research project.

When considering your research ethics and cultural difference, it will be up to you to make sure you understand what the implications are for your particular project. We offer some examples below to stimulate your thinking.

Think about it . . .

- Many cultures (but particularly those of East Asia such as China, Korea and Japan) venerate older people and defer to them. This can have implications for you as the researcher:
  - Are you older than your participants? If so, they may not want to disagree with you (being older, you will be perceived as wiser).
  - Are you younger than your participants? Perhaps they will think that you are unimportant and will not want to help you.
- Some cultures (one might think of some Islamic nations or people from the parts of India where Hinduism is the dominant religion) have different ideas about 'modesty' and gender roles:
  - Are you a woman trying to interview a man? Or a man trying to interview a woman? Communication may be difficult if you have stepped outside the gender role that your participant thinks of as 'normal'.
- In some societies (some parts of the UK, for example) social class is an important division:
  - Are you a member of a 'higher' social class trying to interview a member of a 'lower' social class (or vice versa)? You may be perceived as having no credibility or understanding of individuals' situations.
- Some people (for example, many from Arab countries, Canadian First People) have cultures in which hospitality and 'politeness' are highly valued and it may be very difficult for someone to refuse to help you.
  - Have you really given your participant(s) the opportunity *not* to be a part of your research?

A solution to some of these difficulties (at least in bigger, well-financed research projects) is to consider recruiting and training researchers from the communities involved since this has the potential to overcome some of the barriers or to seek advice from fellow students, staff or friends who belong to the cultural community you hope to include in your research.

Protection from harm (researcher)

Though perhaps not quite in the same class ethically, the researcher, too, has the right to be safe while conducting the research. If you have designed your research carefully, then you will have taken account of this. Ensure that you do not put yourself at risk:

- In physical terms this means (at least):
  - Do not undertake your data collection anywhere that is obviously unsafe.
  - Do not travel alone at night or in areas that are known to be unsafe.
  - Make sure that someone knows where you are, what you are doing and when you should return.
  - When giving contact details, it is wise to refrain from divulging your home address or telephone number.
- In psychological terms, you should be aware that some data collection can be upsetting or even emotionally disturbing. You should make sure that someone is available to offer you support. In education, this will usually be your personal tutor or supervisor.

Ethics and your research

Social research is about human beings and because most social research involves human beings, their experiences, their attitudes and their ideas directly, and because participation in social research is itself a social activity which will have an impact on both the researcher and the research participants, ethical issues are important considerations when planning any social research. The ethical issues we have raised cannot be avoided but rather can be used to help ensure that your research is of good quality.

Think about it . . .

The statements below are common objections to the ethical approval process. Now that you've read this section, what do you think?

1. I don't have time to go through all this – my project needs to be finished in eight weeks.

2. My research does not raise any ethical issues or problems.

3. I don't think the Ethics Committee understands my subject area.

4. No one can agree what ethics are, so why should I bother?

Ethical guidelines and ethics approval processes have been developed to help social researchers to think through the issues for their particular research topic and context and in most cases this can be a helpful part of the process. In some cases the ethical issues can be more challenging and require more thought and preparation – perhaps changes in research design – but may result in a better quality piece of research. Think about the ethics issues that may be involved in your research using our checklist.

Your research

Ethics checklist

Here are some questions that we hope will help you think through and address the ethical issues in your research and to gain ethical approval:

- Does the title of your research give a proper description of the work that you plan to do?
- Do you know how long your project will take? (Do you have a timetable?)
- Have you prepared yourself properly in terms of research knowledge and skills?
- Do you know why you are doing this research (e.g. you think little research has been done on this topic, you want to evaluate a policy initiative, you want to understand how theory and practice go together, etc.)?
- Do you have a clear, operationalised research question(s)? (A4)
- Have you planned and designed your research? (**Part B**)
  - Do you know what sample you need? (**B5**)
  - Do you know what data collection methods you will use? (**Part C**)
  - Have you designed your research instruments (e.g. questionnaire, interview schedule, etc.)?
  - What about anonymity and confidentiality?
  - Will your data be secure (Data Protection Act 1998)?
- Have you thought about the risks to your participants?
  - Will they be physically safe?
  - Are there potential psychological risks?
  - Could participation in your project put their jobs, relationships, financial situation, etc. at risk?
  - Can you ensure their confidentiality/anonymity?
- Have you considered how to get informed consent?
- Have you thought about power relationships between researcher and participant?
- How are you dealing with diversity issues in your research (e.g. gender, 'race', sexuality, disability, age, mental health issues)?
- Are there risks to you as the researcher?
- What will you do if the participant discloses something like:
  - criminal activity?
  - child abuse?

References and further reading

Alexander, Z. (1999) *Study of Black, Asian and Ethnic Minority Issues*, London: Department of Health.

Economic and Social Research Council (2009) *Research Ethics Framework*, Swindon: ESRC. Available at www.esrc.ac.uk/ESRCInfoCentre/Images/ESRC_Re_Ethics_Frame_tcm6-11291.pdf (accessed 7 August 2009).

Gallagher, B., Creighton, S. and Gibbons, J. (1995) Ethical dilemmas in social research: no easy solutions, *British Journal of Social Work*, 25: 295–311.

Homan, R. (1991) *The Ethics of Social Research*, London: Longman.

Hood, S., Mayall, B. and Oliver, S. (eds) (1999) *Critical Issues in Social Research: Power and Prejudice*, Buckingham: Open University Press.

James, T. and Platzer, H. (1999) Lesbians' and gay men's experiences of health care: a personal perspective, *Nursing Ethics*, 6: 73.

Larossa, R., Bennett, L. A. and Gellese, R. J. (1981) Ethical dilemmas in qualitative family research, *Journal of Marriage and the Family*, 43(2): 303–13.

Leathard, A. and McLaren, S. (eds) (2007) *Ethics: Contemporary Challenges in Health and Social Care*, Bristol: Policy Press.

McAuley, C. (2003) Ethics, in R. L. Miller and D. Brewer (eds) *The A–Z of Social Research*, London: Sage.

Minkler, M. (2004) Ethical challenges for the 'outside' researcher in community-based participatory research, *Health Education & Behavior*, 31: 684–97.

Minkler, M., Fadem, P., Perry, M., Blum, K., Moore, L. and Rogers, J. (2002) Ethical dilemmas in participatory action research: a case study from the disability community, *Health Education & Behavior*, 29: 14.

Norman, R., Sellman, D. and Warner, C. (2006) Mental capacity, good practice and the cyclical consent process in research involving vulnerable people, *Clinical Ethics*, 1: 228–33.

Oliver, P. (2003) *The Student's Guide to Research Ethics*, Maidenhead: Open University Press.

Rogers, H. J. (2001) *Partnership Working: A Case Study of Adult Mental Health Services*, University of Birmingham.

Ryen, A. (2007) Ethical issues, in C. Seale, G. Gobro, J. F. Gubrium and D. Silverman (eds) *Qualitative Research Practice*, London: Sage.

Sheldon, T. A. (1992) The use of 'ethnicity' and 'race' in health research: a cautionary note, in W. I. U. Ahmad (ed.) *The Politics of 'Race' and Health*, University of Bradford & Ilkley Community College.

Smaje, C. (1995) *Health, 'Race' and Ethnicity: Making Sense of the Evidence*, London: King's Fund Institute.

University of Birmingham Legal Services (1998) Summary – Data Protection Act 1998, Birmingham. Available at www.legalservices.bham.ac.uk/data_protection_policy/ (accessed 7 August 2009).

Walker, B. and Haslett, T. (2002) Action research in management: ethical dilemmas, *Systemic Practice and Action Research*, 15(6): 523–33.

PART B
Preparing for research

CHAPTER B1
Planning a research project

Contents

In context

This second part of the book is concerned with the preparations you need to make to carry out a successful research project. It is divided into a series of practical sections which will enable you to take your project forward. This first chapter is about planning – an important topic that can sometimes be overlooked – and provides an outline of the process that you need to complete before you can create your research proposal (B6).

PART B: Preparing for research

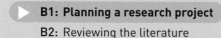 **B1: Planning a research project**

B2: Reviewing the literature

B3: Research design

B4: Choosing methods

B5: Sampling

B6: Research proposals

planning
To arrange in advance (an action or proposed proceeding); to devise, contrive, or formulate (a project or manner of proceeding).

A detailed plan is an essential part of your research strategy and proceeding without one can be unwise. We want to persuade you that thinking about and **planning** the whole project at the beginning (the *holistic* approach) is important, and though the design may still be modified after this stage it is worth spending some time getting it as complete as you can so that you will not suddenly find gaps in your processes as you get further through the project. Time spent on planning is never wasted!

If you have read **Part A**, 'Thinking about research', then you have probably already made some choices which you will be able to include in your planning process.

Every individual takes a different approach to planning: some will use 'mind-mapping', others will use bubble diagrams, lists, sticky notes, etc. We recommend that you use a process that works for you without worrying about what other people do. Your target, though, is to produce a workable plan that will:

- guide your writing of the final research proposal;
- enable you to manage your project in the real world.

Each research project will be different in detail of course, but the same planning processes apply. To keep this all straightforward, we have divided the processes into two categories: defining, and practical planning/managing.

Defining

The first thing to consider is the purpose of, or the reason for, your research. As a student, it may simply be that it is a requirement of your programme (and that *is* a sufficient reason!). If you are progressing further along an academic or commercial route, then it might be about market or attitude research, or maybe you are trying to obtain research funding. We recommend trying to be a clear as possible about the driving force for your project and making sure that you are certain of the requirements you must fulfil to complete, for example, your dissertation successfully.

> ## Your research
>
> Try to summarise the purpose of your research in a single sentence.

Although, at this stage, you probably will not know exactly what you will need to do your research, as you continue your preparations you will need to think about:

- what resources you need to do this research (and what you will have access to): things like time, recording devices, photocopying facilities, interview rooms, etc.;
- what research has already been done in the area you plan to study and how your project will relate to it (**B2**);
- how you are beginning to think about:
  - collecting your data (**Part C**);
  - analysing your data (**Part D**);
  - presenting your findings (**Part E**);

- what you think the outcome of your work might be: for example, a completed dissertation is probably the first priority of undergraduate students, but you might also think about how your work could be used by policy-makers or how it might influence people's attitudes.

Practicalities

Second, you should consider the practical planning of your project:

- *Are you working (a) alone or (b) as part of a team?* If it is (b) then you should try to be clear about who is responsible for each part of the research (clarity here will be very useful in the case of disagreements or in the unlikely event that one team member does not 'pull their weight').
- *What is your timetable?* As a student, the end-point, when you submit your work for assessment, is probably beyond your control. However, it will be useful for you to try to identify the different events that should occur during the project and work out when they are likely to happen. All researchers have some time constraints and need to work out how they will complete the project within the time allowed. Overall, your timetable must be realistic (so you will need to try to assess and estimate how long the different stages might take).
- *How will you make sure that your project is progressing properly?* Perhaps you will need to arrange meetings with your tutor or supervisor to discuss progress. In any event, you need to think about what constitutes success for your work and, maybe, set yourself some targets along the way. For example, you could decide that your literature review section should be complete one month after you start work.

Depending on the project you are undertaking, you may also need to consider:

- organising resources (voice recorders, cameras, computer time, etc.);
- how to manage the rest of your time to meet the deadline (you may have other studying and assessed work to complete at the same time).

Be holistic

In general, we think that student researchers are very good at defining the nature of their project and deciding on a data collection method. However, our experience suggests that – often – not enough thought is given to planning data analysis (Part D). We want to emphasise how important it is to try to think about your project as a *whole*. This book is organised to help you to think in this way and we encourage you to use the links to other chapters to help you to think about different aspects of your project at the same time.

In order to complete your planning successfully, you need to make a series of decisions about the processes you will follow. To help you through this, we have designed a checklist that you could use as part of your planning process. So, as we have suggested above, don't leave reading about the subsequent stages of your research until the moment when you need to do them: plan your work sequentially using this book – for example, don't leave deciding your analysis strategy (D) until after you have collected your data (C).

Your research

Project planning checklist

	Section/part	✓
Have you thought about your research and do you understand about theories, paradigms and perspectives?	A2	
Are you clear about the nature of the data you will need to collect and the data collection methods you will use?	A3	
Have you defined the nature of your research?	B1	
Have you considered the practicalities of your research? (In particular, have you considered resources and funding?)	B1	
Have you thought about accessing and assessing existing literature?	B2	
Have you decided on a research design (for example, case study, experimental, ethnographic, etc.)?	B3	
Have you chosen your data collection methods?	B4, C	
Have you thought about your population and sample?	B5	
Do you have a research question or hypothesis?	A4	
Have you considered ethical implications?	A5	
Have you obtained any formal approval that you need for your research?	A5	
Have you thought about how you will analyse your data?	D	
Have you thought about how you will present and disseminate your findings?	E	

This checklist is, necessarily, very simple and cannot take account of all the variables that may be present in your research project. However, when you can tick all the boxes then you are probably in a good position to write your research proposal and start your project.

References and further reading

Beins, C. B. (2004) *Research Methods: A Tool for Life*, Harlow: Pearson.

Leedy, P. D. and Ormond, J. E. (2005) *Practical Research: Planning and Design*, Boston MA: Pearson Education.

Sharp, J. and Howard, K. (2002) *The Management of a Student Research Project*, 3rd edn, Aldershot: Gower.

Walliman, N. (2001) *Your Research Project: A Step-by-Step Guide for the First-time Researcher*, London: Sage.

CHAPTER B2
Reviewing the literature

Contents

In context

A review of literature is one of the foundations on which any social research project is constructed. From a review of the literature associated with your research topic, you will be able to set your own ideas about the research topic in context, learn how other people have researched in your research area and begin to think critically about the implications for your own research project. This can seem like a huge task as, on almost any topic, there is a wealth of books, papers, research and other documents that we could read. However, we need to take a focused and critical approach to reviewing the literature and in this chapter we will introduce you to a range of literature sources and discuss how you can achieve a critical and focused literature review in practice.

PART B: Preparing for research

> B1: Planning a research project

> **B2: Reviewing the literature**

> B3: Research design

> B4: Choosing methods

> B5: Sampling

> B6: Research proposals

Part of the process of preparation for research is to consider how your topic has been researched, thought about and written about by others and how this knowledge will help you to develop and refine your own research ideas. Alongside your thinking about research questions, methodologies and data collection methods will go a review of the varied forms of literature that are relevant to your research topic. Reviewing the literature begins early in the process of thinking about and preparing for research and may continue alongside the development of your research questions and decisions about your research design and data collection and analysis methods.

Reviewing the literature is itself a process and there are usually four stages:

1. *Background* reading 'around' the topic; looking for ideas and seeing what has already been done and using this information to focus your own project.
2. Doing a *detailed search* of sources of information and compiling a comprehensive record of this information.
3. *Reading and evaluating* what you have found.
4. *Structuring and producing* the finished review.

Why is a review of the literature part of the preparation for research?

There are a number of reasons for undertaking a critical literature review. The list below highlights some of the most common reasons with the most important first.

A review of the literature will enable you to:

- Critically analyse the current situation in your research area:
  - You will be able to find out what is already known about your research area. Usually, you do not want to repeat work that has already been done (unless you want to look at the same issue or data in a different way). One aim of the literature review is to see what the current state of knowledge is, what has already been done and what might still be accomplished in the future. Sometimes, we say that we are looking for the 'gaps' in research, the parts that have been missed or ignored in the past. You can also think of this as familiarising yourself with the current state of knowledge.
  - You can learn about the different theoretical and methodological approaches that have been used in the past (and how successful they were, so that you do not repeat others' mistakes).
  - You can see what sort of analytical frameworks and strategies other people have used and decide whether they are right for your work.
- Compare and contrast different sources and the opinions of experts.
- Put your research into a context. In the social sciences our work is usually linked to other issues and events in society, for example, the introduction of a new policy, an economic recession, changes in ideas on ethical issues or climate change.
- Learn the 'language' or vocabulary of your topic.
- Find the important issues or variables in your topic. Maybe the literature review will lead to you including things that you might otherwise have left out.
- Think about and define research questions and maybe identify further questions or issues that could be investigated.
- Inform the way that you deal with your research findings and, probably, enable you to relate them to work that has gone before.

- Help you identify links between practice and theory (depending on your research area).
- Provide a synthesis of all the relevant information in a way that the reader of your dissertation or report will be able to understand and which will properly support your work.

What is literature?

A few years ago we would probably have said that **literature** was the *published written word* and this would have meant that it was something that was printed on paper. We would have talked about books, journals, periodicals and newspapers. This is still a good place to start but we must now also include electronic sources and visual and audio media.

> ### ❓ What is . . .
>
> **Literature**
> Literature is a complex and inclusive term and to make a comprehensive list would (a) take too long, and (b) be soon out of date. However, the main components are listed below:
>> Books
>> Refereed journals
>> Non-refereed journals
>> Theses and conference papers
>> Newspapers
>> Television/radio
>> 'Grey' literature
>> Official documents
>> Research reports
>> The internet.

Books

Times have changed dramatically over the last 15 years or so. In the 1990s, the main source of information for undergraduate students was textbooks. Easier access to journal papers, official documents and other online sources now means that students *can* use a wider range of sources but academic books are still one of the most useful sources. Most universities have large libraries of textbooks and new ones are still being added year by year. Most academic books are written by expert academics and researchers in a particular field and often bring together research and scholarship to provide a useful overview of a particular topic. Textbook authors usually draw on and refer to other experts, nationally and sometimes internationally.

They are often an excellent starting point for your review of the literature because reference will be made to other sources, research and ideas which you can follow up as you develop your own ideas. By their nature, most are produced by reputable authors, have useful indexes and are easy to use. The downside of books is that they can very quickly become out of date and are often expensive to buy (though, of course, they are in libraries – even if not in your local library). However, they will continue to be useful sources for the foreseeable future and even the older editions are frequently of use because they can show the state of a topic, and the thinking around it, at a particular time.

Journals and periodicals

peer review
In academic settings, the process by which articles and papers are reviewed and selected for publication.

This paper-based literature (though much is now available in electronic form on the internet) comes in what we call a *hierarchy of value* which is based on the notion of **peer review**. In an academic setting, peer-reviewed articles or papers are considered to be the 'best' because of the way that they are chosen for publication. Most peer-reviewed articles are written by academic staff, and when an article is submitted to a peer-reviewed journal it is sent to a number of people who are experts in that particular field who comment to the journal editor on the article's quality and suitability for publication. Based on these reports, the editor will decide whether the piece of writing is included in an edition of the journal. Even among peer-reviewed journals there is a hierarchy with *international* journals usually regarded as the most prestigious because these journals have a global readership and are open to appraisal by academics worldwide. Most journals include papers that are based on research that the writer has carried out as well as papers that demonstrate the author's scholarship, that is their expertise in the area and their ability to develop original and often theoretical ideas. Sometimes academics present papers at conferences prior to publication and these may be available, though not, at this stage, peer reviewed.

Examples of peer-reviewed journals include: *Journal of Social Policy, Sociology, Policy Studies, Culture, Criminology, Health and Social Care in the Community, International Economics, Social Policy and Society*. Of course, there are many more and a cursory internet enquiry (see 'Searching for literature', on p. 100) will return a list of literally hundreds.

Editors of journals and periodicals that are not peer reviewed print what they want to, usually based on their editorial policy (for example, *New Statesman, The Economist*). The editor may request or commission articles from a range of writers and then decide which to publish. The published articles will not usually have been scrutinised by experts but may still be useful as they can provide different perspectives on a particular topic or area and may be written by people with experience, for example, of practice or work in that area. Professional journals (e.g. *Health Service Journal, Management Today, Nursing Times, Community Care*) come into this category.

Media

Newspapers and other media are at the next level in the hierarchy of value and here we think there is a need to proceed with some care. If you use information from newspapers (or magazines like *Marketing* or *Country Living*) then you need to think about how much you can rely on the accuracy of the information they contain, bearing in mind that their prime purpose is to make money from selling newspapers, magazines and advertising. The main advantage of newspapers is that they are current and can help you to keep up with social, political and economic issues, policy and practice on a day-by-day basis. Newspapers tend to focus on aspects of issues that are seen as particularly interesting or problematic and may help you to identify issues, people, research reports and so on that you could follow up.

It is important to understand that other sources can be regarded as literature too. If we extend our definition a little so that it includes *material that is in the public domain*, then more becomes available to us, such as television programmes, radio, video, audio recordings, podcasts and other media. They all have potential as sources of information, but because they are not in a format that can be used directly in most student work, the user needs to think about different ways of processing them (for example, you might choose to transcribe part of a recorded radio interview or television documentary).

'Grey' literature

grey literature
Documents that are produced by (and for) organisations or companies.

One, often overlooked, type of literature is known as **grey literature**. Usually, this refers to documents that are produced by (and for) organisations or companies. They are usually printed (and now sometimes available on the organisation or company's website), but are generally not in the public domain. (In the UK the Freedom of Information Act 2000 now means that access to many of these documents is comparatively easy, though there may be costs involved.) There is a problem about access too: you need to know that the document exists, or – at least – be able to ask a carefully worded question to get the information you want. This is often a rich source of information for those investigating, among other areas, the public sector or the implementation of policy.

Official documents

Depending on your research topic and discipline, you may want to include in your review of literature some of the many and varied documents produced by the government and other official sources. These include policy documents like Acts of Parliament, Royal Commission reports, practice guidelines, White and Green Papers, Audit Commission reports, government research and so on.

Research reports

One of the reasons for conducting a review of the literature is to identify and learn from research that has been carried out in your topic area by others. These may include academics researching in universities, people working for research organisations (the Joseph Rowntree Foundation, for example) and researchers within public, private or voluntary sector organisations. Some of these reports may be effectively 'grey' literature and only accessed by contacting the organisation or searching their websites. Others, like those produced by the Joseph Rowntree Foundation (www.jrf.org.uk), are easily available from their website.

Another type of research report is the thesis or dissertation. These are produced by students for the award of a degree and may range from an undergraduate dissertation to a thesis submitted for a doctorate, the highest level of accredited study. Theses are publicly available, as are some dissertations. While these may be of value if they focus on your research area, you must be aware of the level of award given to the work and that in relation to dissertations you will not know how the dissertation was assessed.

The internet

First of all, it is important to distinguish between different types of 'literature' you may find on the internet.

First, many of the literature sources discussed above are now available on websites. In some cases these are in the same format as they would be if produced on paper. For example, many academic journals, newspapers and research reports are available in this way and consequently are much easier to access than was previously the case. Some can be downloaded onto your own computer and saved for future reference.

Second, some of the literature you may wish to use may only be available on a website. For example, some official documents are now produced only for the government websites and may be difficult to access in any other way.

Third, websites themselves are a form of literature you may want to review. For example, the websites of organisations like Age Concern, the Alzheimer's Society and the National Institute of Clinical Excellence all include interesting and potentially relevant material for someone looking at the impacts of dementia on older people which is not available in any other format.

Fourth, the internet gives you the facility to search your research topic across a very wide range of sources including pieces written by a wide range of people from across the world. This means that a search can identify thousands of potential sites and that a great deal of care is needed in identifying potential sites of interest. There is a vast amount of information out there. Search engines can find hundreds of thousands of references for any enquiry, even if you use a search engine that is targeted on academia such as Google Scholar. No one has the time to look at or evaluate all the responses and it is easy to miss something important or to be diverted towards sites that are inaccurate and misleading.

Note that:

- Most search engines list material in the order of websites that are most popular (and, increasingly, those who have paid to be high on the list). Unfortunately, this does not always mean that they are the most accurate.

- A general search of the internet will return information from many different sources and countries. This is quite often a problem for students: how do you tell if the information is relevant to the issue that you are investigating? Even if you restrict your search to English-language documents, it is unlikely that a quote on employment regulations in Australia will be directly relevant to your work in the UK.

- Anyone can publish anything on the internet. Wikipedia, for example, makes a virtue of the fact that its content is provided and edited by the people that use it – and some of the content is not as accurate as it could be. Such sites can be useful pointers to research or researchers working in your research area, providing that you then trace the original papers or research rather than relying on the information given on the site.

This does not mean that the internet is useless to the researcher. On the contrary, if carefully used, it is an extremely valuable resource, always provided that we are careful, critical – and perhaps a little suspicious – about the provenance of the information. This is in fact the case with all the literature we may use, and we now turn to the issue of the critical evaluation of literature.

Think about it . . .
Evaluating internet sites

Because there are so many different websites and sources of information on the internet, and anyone can publish material on the internet, there are some additional questions you should ask when using websites:

- Who has provided the information? Individual or organisation?
- Why are they providing this information?
- Are details provided about the authors and the publishers?
- When was the information provided?
- When was the material first published on the internet?
- How frequently is the site updated?
- Will it still be there tomorrow?
- Where is the information held?
- Where is the information from?

You can use the URL (Uniform Resource Locator) or address of a website to get some clues as to its source.

URL

The URL will give you an idea of:

- which organisation the site belongs to;
- what type of organisation it is;
- the country where the organisation is located (though this can sometimes be the country where the website is hosted).

Organisations

The name of the organisation is often the first term in the website address and the type of organisation is shown in the latter part of the address, e.g.

- academic sites: .ac.uk or .edu
- commercial sites: .co.uk or .com
- voluntary and other non-profit organisations' sites: .org.uk or .org
- government sites: .gov.uk or .gov

> **Countries:**
> The last part of the address usually tells you the country where the site originated
> (apart from the USA which has no country suffix), e.g.
>
> - .uk = United Kingdom
> - .au = Australia
> - .ca = Canada

Critically evaluating the literature

There are two stages to evaluating the literature and deciding whether it is of value to you in developing your research ideas. First, you need to assess the value of the literature in terms of its source and purpose – its provenance. Essentially this is about who produced the piece of literature and why it was produced in that way. Second, you need to look at the content of the literature in terms of the information and ideas it contains.

 What is . . .

Critical approach

The way in which we use judgement (and other things such as experience or observation) to evaluate data, information, knowledge, etc.

When we say 'critical' we do not mean it in a negative sense: we mean 'evaluate'. Usually, we will be looking at one of the forms of literature we talked about earlier and we have a number of suggestions for the things that you should be looking for.

What is the purpose of the literature?

To help us to establish why a particular paper, report, website or TV documentary was produced, we need to ask some questions of the author or producer and then ask some questions of ourselves. Of course we cannot ask the author or producer directly so we have to look carefully at the source of the literature and think about how and why it has been written or produced in that way, what information or experience the writer or producer probably brought to its production and whether issues have been clearly set out and addressed. Then address the questions to yourself in terms of your own research questions and use your own knowledge and experience to assess the value of such a source to you as a researcher.

QUESTIONS TO ASK

The author/producer	Yourself
Why did you write this?	Why am I reading this?
Who did you write it for?	Was it written for 'me'?
What was your purpose?	What am I looking for?
What questions were you asking?	What questions am I asking?
What answers did you find?	Do I find the answers credible?
What is your evidence?	Do I accept the evidence?
What is your conclusion?	Do I agree with the conclusions?

Asking these questions will help you to decide what type of source you have found and why it was written. Asking yourself questions will help you to decide whether and how you might use the source in your literature review.

Your research

Select a book, a journal paper and a newspaper report on your research topic and ask the questions above of the authors and yourself.

What is the literature about and how useful will it be in thinking about your research?

What questions you ask about the content of the literature depend on the type of source you are evaluating. One of the types of source you are most likely to want to include in your review of literature is other research carried out in your area of interest. Here you will be particularly interested in why and how the research was carried out and may ask a series of questions to help you to get a fuller understanding of the research. These will be different for each article, depending on the type of research that is reported. It is worth remembering that the editing process and word limits on published work can sometimes mean that some parts of a project may not be reported in the detail you might expect. When research is reported in journal papers, for example, the paper may focus on just one aspect of the research or may focus more on a discussion of the findings rather than a detailed methodology.

So, the following are questions that you could ask yourself:

- Are the aims and objectives of the research clear?
- Do the authors explain their hypotheses, research questions and underlying theories? (A2, A4)
- Is it clear who paid for the research (i.e. is there a possibility of a conflict of interests)?
- Are research questions and operational definitions plainly stated? (A4)
- Are the methodology and methods clear and appropriate? This will probably also include:
  - a discussion of ethical issues (A5);
  - an explanation of why the research was designed this way (B3);
  - explanation and discussion of data collection methods and analytical processes (for example, whether a pilot study was carried out, the appropriateness of any statistical analyses);
  - definitions of variables (if appropriate);
  - sample design and sampling processes (B5);
  - discussion of research instruments (for example, questionnaires, interview schedules, etc.) and their development.
- Are the limitations of the methods used discussed?
- Are the results understandable and well discussed?
- Is the conclusion clear?
  - Is there a discussion of whether the conclusion(s) can be generalised (i.e. applied to the whole population rather than just the sample)?
  - Are there links between the conclusion(s) and the theoretical perspective?
  - Is there a discussion of the implications of the conclusion(s)? (For example, is there a need to change policy because of what was found?)

Your research

In **A1** we introduced some research quality checks and these are developed and feature in **B3**. When reading reports of research for your literature review, use these to assess the quality of the research you are reading.

Not all of your sources will be focusing on research and you will need to use a slightly different set of questions to enable you to assess the value of a particular source. Here are some suggestions:

- Are the aims of the book, paper, article or programme clear?
- Do the authors explain why they are writing or producing it? Do they have a particular skill, interest or expertise?
- Is it written from a particular perspective or does it include different perspectives?
- Are other authors, papers or research referred to?
- Are the key issues and arguments understandable and well discussed?
- Is evidence provided to support statements that are made? Is the evidence itself credible and accessible to you?
- Are there any conclusions?
- Is there a discussion of the implications of the conclusion(s)? (For example, are changes in policy or practice suggested? Are particular events or situations predicted?)

In summary, taking a critical approach to evaluating your literature sources is about asking questions of them. You may not be able to answer all of your questions from the information that you have and some of your answers may not be satisfactory. This does not mean that a particular source should not be used. Rather, it means that you should take care when using information from the source and ensure that you refer to the limitations as well as the value of the source within your review.

Searching for literature

Starting points

The starting point is usually background reading, informed by what you already know about the topic. So, for example, if you were going to research the causes of poverty in childhood, your starting place would probably be a textbook such as *The Student's Companion to Social Policy* (Alcock *et al.*, 2008) which would tell you some of the important issues and ideas around poverty and childhood, give you some ideas that are interesting and list further reading that you could pursue. If you follow this course of action, very likely you will come across the names of prominent writers in the field. You can then search for work by these experts by means of a variety of techniques. In most cases you will be using electronic catalogues or databases to help you to search and you will need to use keywords to help you to find books, articles, media, etc., on your research topic.

❓ What is . . .

Keyword
Keywords are the terms that tell a database (such as a library catalogue, or a citations search engine) what to look for. Clearly it is important to choose keywords with care and to combine them with others to narrow your search.

Different databases and search engines allow different *operators* to be used (some like '&' or '+' or 'AND' to combine words, and 'OR' or '/' to allow the choice of both) – you must check which ones work for the system you are using.

1. *Library catalogues*: always a good place to start. Most catalogues are now computer-based so are easy and quick to use. You might choose to search for **keywords** or authors' names or even by date. If you are using a flexible, up-to-date system, you will be able to combine them.

2. *Textbooks, journals, other printed material*: library catalogues will lead you to both printed and electronic resources. Looking at journal articles and textbooks to see what sources were used by the author is a very useful way of extending your search.

3. *Online databases*: are usually discipline-specific. For example, ASSIA (Applied Social Sciences Index and Abstracts) is an index that contains references and abstracts (a short summary) of journal articles. There are many of these services. At the time of writing, these are some of the current services:

ISI Web of Knowledge: http://wos.mimas.ac.uk/
BIDS (Bath Information and Data Services): www.bids.ac.uk/
SSCI (Social Sciences Citation Index): http://library.wellcome.ac.uk/
ASSIA (Applied Social Sciences Index and Abstracts): contact through your university library

(If you are at university or college, you should first try to access these services through the university or college library. Some of them need an authenticated log-in which you will get from your library and in many cases there will be links from the database to a downloadable copy of the full article, paper or even ebook.)

4. *Talking to experts*: if you are studying at a school, college or university, then it is likely that there are 'experts' among the teaching team who may be able to throw new light on your thinking. Library staff, who are often experts in their own particular fields, are also frequently willing to share that expertise.

Example B2.1

Causes of childhood poverty: choosing keywords

Selecting keywords on which to search usually requires some imagination! This is simply because we do not all use the same terms to describe the topics we are interested in and sometimes researchers and writers use different definitions in their work.

Start with the key terms in your research question – in this case, 'childhood' and 'poverty'.

Searching for them separately is likely to produce a lot of sources that are not relevant to you – for example, 'childhood' may bring up research on childhood diseases, psychological development, play activities and so on.

Searching for 'poverty' is likely to bring up research on poverty in different countries, different types of poverty and poverty relating to adults as well as children.

So it makes sense to start by combining the terms with 'AND' to show that you want to search for sources that include the term 'childhood AND poverty'.

You may then want to focus on 'childhood poverty' in the UK and include 'UK' as one of your keywords.

However, there may still be articles and research that would be of interest to you but which do not contain the term 'childhood poverty' in the title or even in the article itself. This may be because the writer has used other terms – e.g. 'poor children' – or it could be that the article is about something close to your area of interest but not expressed in the same way – for example, it could be about 'children of poor households', 'children living in deprived areas' or 'children of lower social classes'. So you may want to conduct some further searches.

And are you interested in young people as well as children? If so, there may be literature relating particularly to 'young people', 'teenagers' and 'youth' that would be relevant for your research.

> ### Think about it . . .
>
> If you were undertaking research about the leisure activities of older people, what keywords would you use to search for other research on this topic?

A search strategy

Having made a start on gathering and reading literature it is advisable to give some thought to and plan:

(a) what you are looking for – in terms of keywords and topics;

(b) what types of sources you will include;

(c) how you will search.

Initially student researchers are often either overwhelmed by the number of sources they find that appear to have some relevance to their research or can find very few potentially relevant sources. In both situations it is now time to ensure that you are focusing on the literature that is going to be most relevant for *your research*.

One approach to this is to start by drawing a spider diagram of all the aspects of your research topic that you might want to explore. In many cases there will be two or more main areas referred to in your research questions. For example, if you are interested in researching the connection between *child poverty* and *educational achievement* (perhaps inspired by the headline news in the 'Real research' box below) you may need to explore some of the literature relating to both child poverty and educational achievement separately initially. However, you will not need to look at literature relating to every aspect of each. In Example B2.2 we show at least some of the aspects of your topic that you would need to include in your literature review. The topics at the edge of the circle are likely to provide background contextual material for your review, while those nearer the centre of the circle are likely to be the aspects of your topic that you will need to focus on as you begin to look at the relationships between the two topics.

Real research

Reported in the media: social mobility in Britain

> ## WEALTH AND PRIVATE SCHOOL REMAIN KEY TO PROFESSIONS
>
> *The report by an all-party panel chaired by the former cabinet minister Alan Milburn paints a damning portrayal of a country in which family wealth, private education and privileged access to university remain the key to well-paid professions. . . .*
>
> *. . . It is estimated that only 29% of students – and just 16% at the Russell group of universities – come from lower socio-economic backgrounds, even though they make up 50% of young people.*
>
> The *Guardian* is referring to a 2009 Cabinet Office report, *Unleashing Aspiration: The Final Report on Fair Access to the Professions,* available from www.cabinetoffice. gov.uk/strategy/work_areas/accessprofessions.aspx (accessed 10 August 2009).

Source: Wintour (2009).

Example B2.2

Childhood poverty and educational achievement: searching the literature

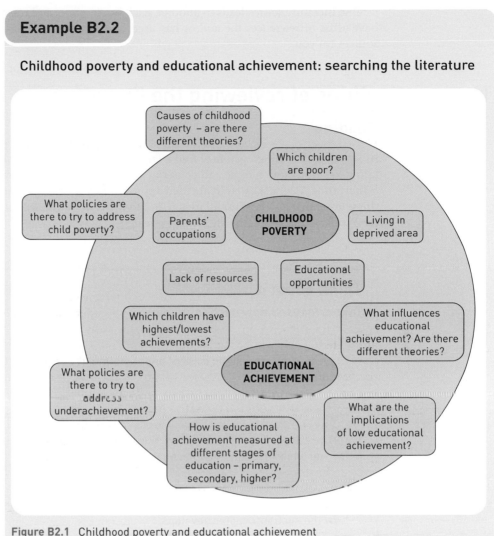

Figure B2.1 Childhood poverty and educational achievement

Most literature searches become more focused as they progress and as the research questions are more clearly defined. For many student researchers the initial research topic is quite wide and general – as in the example of childhood poverty and educational achievement. As the literature is found and studied, the focus of the research is likely to become narrower and more clearly expressed. In the example, the researcher may decide to focus on one stage of education – primary, secondary or higher – and may decide to focus on the experiences of children of a particular minority ethnic group. Another student may decide to focus on the impact of educational opportunities in areas of deprivation or on the influence of parents from different socio-economic backgrounds on their children's educational achievement. The diagram in Example B2.2 provides just a starting point.

Your choice of research topic will determine the range of different types of resource you may want to include in your literature review. A literature review focusing on policy is likely to include some official documents while, if the focus is on a current social issue, you may want to search the recent media for material. It can be useful to explore the possible sources of literature, in addition to the library catalogue and online databases, initially to establish the range and type of literature that may be available to you.

One literature source leads to another. Each book, paper and research report is likely to have a list of references the author has used in writing it and these can provide further sources for you.

The practicalities of reviewing the literature

Reading

As we suggested earlier, you may find a large number of potentially interesting sources relating to your research topic and consequently have quite a pile of reading to complete in a short time. Taking a carefully focused approach to your reading can help you to identify the sources that are most useful to you and to focus in on the sections of the article, chapter or report that relate directly to your research.

Think about it . . .

Take a focused approach to reading

Before you start reading:

- Look quickly through the book or paper, noting how it is structured, and headings are used.
- Read any introductions, abstracts or contents pages.
- Use an index – if there is one – to point you to sections that are likely to be of interest.
- Ask yourself, why am I reading this?
- Decide which sections/chapters you will read.

THEN:

- Do a 'quick read' looking at the beginning of each paragraph to get a sense of how the section/chapter develops.
- Check again – is this going to be useful to me?
- With your research topic in mind, read the section/chapter carefully, only making notes that relate to your research.
- Note down the page numbers of any key points or quotations you may wish to use and sections you may want to return to for further study.
- Note down the full reference of the source.

Keeping records

It may seem obvious, but there is no point in doing all this reading and evaluation if you do not keep good records. Nor is it enough just to keep a list of titles and authors. At the very minimum, you need to record all the bibliographic information that you will need later on to construct your bibliography or reference list, as well as the body of your literature review. To ensure that you record all the information, you need to check which referencing system you are required to use and the various pieces of information required to complete a full reference.

However, this is a minimum and you are likely to want to record additional information about the sources, your own notes, possible quotes and key arguments so that you can come back to these later when you are writing the literature review. The method you choose for your records should suit the way you, as an individual, work. For many people, some sort of paper record system will be fine. How complex this needs to be is governed by the size and complexity of the project. For an essay, many people will use a notebook; for a dissertation it may be that index cards are more useful.

There are other ways of keeping these records and there is computer software to help. Packages include Endnote, Citation, Bookends, Biblioscape, Papyrus and Procite. They all provide a pre-formatted database for you to enter the information about the source that you will need while writing. The strength of such packages is the ability to output this information in different referencing styles such as Harvard or APA. There is a drawback, though: all of these packages are expensive, and can be time consuming to learn. Check whether your university or college has a licence that will allow you to use the software for free (or at a low cost) while you are a student.

We do not make particular recommendations as to what system you should consider, as on-site support may be more important than individual software features. And pen and paper or file cards can be equally as effective; use a system that suits you. Students who are particularly IT-literate may like to design their own bibliographic database using something like Microsoft's Access database program.

Presenting the review of literature

Once you have reviewed the literature, there are different ways in which the review may be presented, depending on the nature of your research project. If you are undertaking research for a student dissertation or thesis which will be examined then you are likely to be required to include a literature review as part of that. If you are writing a research project report, then the requirement may be different and you may be expected to use your literature as background, contextual material or to include an annotated bibliography. We will look briefly at each of these formats.

Literature review

A literature review forms a significant section or chapter of a student dissertation or thesis and usually comes near the beginning of the written work, following the introduction and before the methodology section. In this case the literature review is the point where the initial introductory ideas are developed and explored in more depth using the literature and particularly focusing on existing research. As such the section or chapter provides a link between your introduction and your research questions and methodology. There are various ways in which the literature review can be structured but the most common approach is to provide an overview of the subject matter of your research, including perhaps a historical and then a current context before moving on to explore your research areas in more depth, increasingly becoming more focused on your own research area.

In a literature review short discussions, or mini-essays, are developed around the key areas of the research topics and the literature is drawn upon to provide supporting evidence for the points made. The material from the literature should be presented critically, with care and recognising the value of the source and the strengths and limitations of it in relation to your discussion.

Example B2.3

Childhood poverty and educational achievement

Structuring a literature review

1. Overview of context historically and identification of current issues.

2. What is childhood poverty?
   (a) Different ways of defining poverty
   (b) What type of children live in poverty?
   (c) What are the theories about the causes of childhood poverty?
   (d) What are the implications of childhood poverty?

3. What is meant by educational achievement?
   (a) How is educational achievement measured? At different stages?
   (b) Who are the low/high achievers?
   (c) What are the influences on a child's educational achievement?
   (d) What are the implications of this for children living in poverty?

4. Review of research work linking childhood poverty and educational achievement.
   (a) What are the key findings? Issues raised?
   (b) What policy and practice issues are there related to these links?
   (c) What are the possible implications of this research, policy and practice for children from a particular ethnic group who experience childhood poverty?

5. Conclusions, drawing together the literature review and introducing the research questions.

Background and contextual review

A research report will typically have a much shorter review of the literature and will usually focus on the background to the research being carried out, why the research was thought to be necessary and the context in which the research is set. Reference would be made to a number of sources and the main points made within them, or research findings would be presented briefly with a list of references to enable the reader to follow up the sources if they wish.

An annotated bibliography

An annotated bibliography may sometimes be required as part of an academic or other report. This is simply a list of a range of sources that usually inform the study of a particular subject, with a short paragraph on each which includes a brief summary, key findings or arguments and an assessment of its value to a student studying the topic. Each source is evaluated independently and there is no opportunity to compare findings or consider the differences between sources.

The process of reviewing the literature

Reviewing the literature is an ongoing activity to which you may return at numerous points during your research. Initial reading helps to inform and develop your ideas about your research topic and the hypotheses and questions you pose (A4). More detailed searching and reviewing helps to clarify the research area and to narrow the focus of the research questions, enabling you to begin to identify your research design (**B3**), sampling approaches (**B5**) and data collection methods (**Part C**). The review of the literature will also inform your analysis and help you to plan your analytical approach and identify themes or issues you will look for in your findings (**D1**). A discussion of the research findings can usefully refer back to the literature to demonstrate ways in which your findings are similar or different to others, or to help you to explain your findings in relation to theories or research findings presented by others.

Your research

Searching the literature

Research topic ....

Initial reading

'Spider' diagram

Your topic

Keywords

Catalogues, databases, search facilities

Structure of literature review

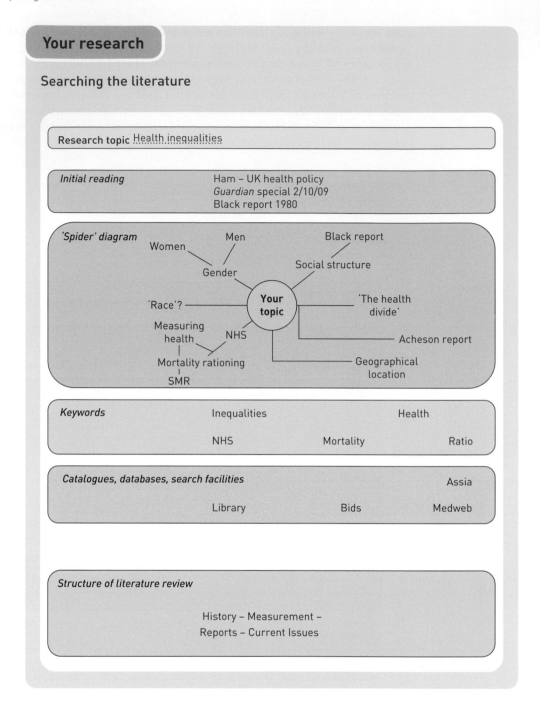

Your research

Searching the literature

Research topic <u>Health inequalities</u>

Initial reading
Ham – UK health policy
Guardian special 2/10/09
Black report 1980

'Spider' diagram

Women   Men   Black report
Gender   Social structure
'Race'?   **Your topic**   'The health divide'
Measuring health   NHS   Acheson report
Mortality rationing   Geographical location
SMR

Keywords
Inequalities   Health
NHS   Mortality   Ratio

Catalogues, databases, search facilities
Assia
Library   Bids   Medweb

Structure of literature review

History – Measurement –
Reports – Current Issues

References and further reading

Alcock, P., Erskine, A. and May, M. (eds) (2008) *The Student's Companion to Social Policy*, 3rd edn, Oxford: Blackwell.

Berg, B. L. (2007) *Qualitative Research Methods for the Social Sciences*, Boston: Pearson Education.

Hart, C. (1998) *Doing a Literature Review: Releasing the Social Science Research Imagination*, Buckingham: Oxford University Press.

Hart, C. (2001) *Doing a Literature Search: A Comprehensive Guide for the Social Sciences*, London: Sage.

Pole, C. and Lampard, R. (2002) *Practical Social Investigation: Qualitative and Quantitative Methods in Social Research*, Harlow: Pearson Education.

Ticehurst, G. W. and Veal, A. J. (2000) *Business Research Methods: A Managerial Approach*, Frenchs Forest: Longman.

Wintour, P. (2009) Britain's closed shop: damning report on social mobility failings, *Guardian*, 21 July.

CHAPTER B3
Research design

Contents

In context

We now begin to move from thinking about choosing your research topic to thinking about how you are going to research your topic. Research design draws on all the preparation you have done and helps you to set out an overall framework for your research. Based on your research design, you can then go on to choose your data collection methods (B4) and how you will select your research participants or cases (B5) before bringing it all together in a research proposal (B6).

PART B: Preparing for research

    B1: Planning a research project

    B2: Reviewing the literature

  ▶ **B3:** Research design

    B4: Choosing methods

    B5: Sampling

    B6: Research proposals

Designing research means going back to your research questions (A4) and thinking about what you are hoping to be able to do with the data you collect in order to be able to address those research questions. Throughout this chapter we will take the research topic of *alcohol and students in higher education* as our research example.

Real research

Alcohol and students in higher education

From *BBC News*, 31 March 2008:

The [University of Liverpool] Guild of Students has said it will no longer promote offers for heavily discounted drinks amid concerns for the health of young binge drinkers.

From the *Guardian*, 27 March 2009:

The government yesterday faced fresh calls to increase the price of alcohol, after research showed young people in the UK reported some of the highest levels of teenage binge drinking, drunkenness and alcohol-related problems in Europe.

Sources: BBC News (2008); Smithers (2009).

Depending on the research question or hypothesis you have chosen, you may be seeking to gather data that will help you to:

(a) *describe* the current (or past) situation – that is, in this example, set out the nature and extent of alcohol consumption between different groups of students and in different situations;

(b) *explain* the differences and similarities between different groups of students and situations by looking for possible causal relationships;

(c) *explore* your data, looking for possible reasons for differences between students and situations, for ideas about why some students drink alcohol and what opinions they have on whether and why this is regarded as a 'problem'.

Broadly speaking, what you can do with social research data falls into two categories – looking for similarities and differences and looking for relationships – these form the basis for your research design.

Similarities and differences

You may choose to look at differences between two or more groups of people or situations, or you may want to look at changes over time. In these cases, you need to collect comparable data about the different groups, situations or periods of time, so that you can look for differences or changes.

Example B3.1

Students and alcohol

Similarities and differences

You may want to look at the differences in the amounts of alcohol drunk by students at different universities, by students taking different subjects, or at different times. For example, you could select a sample of students taking Sociology and a sample of students taking Physics and look for similarities and differences between the two groups of students – and then look for possible explanations of these.

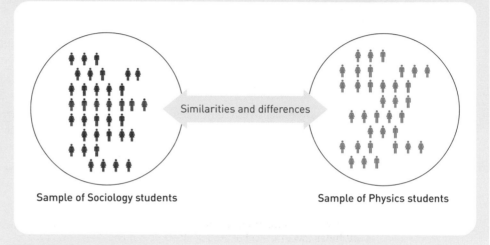

Sample of Sociology students   Similarities and differences   Sample of Physics students

Figure B3.1 Two samples

Relationships

Second, you may wish to look for relationships between different characteristics or variables, for example, age group, gender, ethnicity, religion, financial situation and so on.

When looking for relationships, you may be exploring data collected from a number of cases for any indications that certain characteristics or variables tend to be found together (or not). You may underpin this type of research design with a hypothesis which puts forward a proposition about the relationship between two variables. Alternatively, you may have a research question which seeks to explore the possible relationships between variables and aims to build a **typology**, or typical model, of the way variables tend to be found in relation to each other.

typology
A typical model of the way variables tend to be found in relation to each other.

Example B3.2

Students and alcohol

Relationships between variables

You may want to find out whether particular characteristics of individual students are associated with attitudes towards alcohol consumption. To do this, you may decide to look at the potential relationships between, for example, the variables of religion, family background and gender, and different attitudes towards alcohol consumption.

This is quite a complex research design because you are:

(a) looking at the possible relationships between holding a particular attitude towards alcohol and the student's religion, gender and family background;

(b) comparing (looking for similarities and differences between) students holding this attitude with students holding other attitudes.

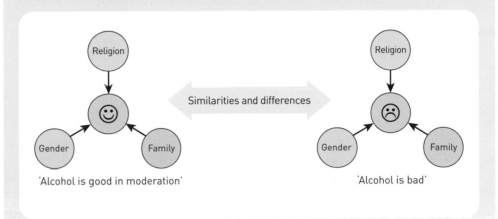

Figure B3.2 Comparing relationships between religion, gender and family background and attitudes towards alcohol among students holding different attitudes

As shown in Example B3.2, research will often incorporate aspects of both of these approaches in order to address the complexity of the research questions.

Your research

Thinking about your own research topic and your research questions, try using the diagrammatic format used in Example B3.2 to show the relationships and similarities and differences you are interested in.

Qualitative or quantitative?

Research design does not depend on whether you intend to use quantitative, qualitative or mixed methods (B4) of data collection and analysis. The decision to take a qualitative or quantitative approach should be based on your research question, and the nature of the data you need to collect and analyse in order to address the question (A3 and B4). All of the research designs discussed here can form the overall framework of either quantitative or qualitative data collection and analysis, or indeed a mixed-methods approach. However, as you will see, some research designs are much more likely to include *either* qualitative *or* quantitative methods.

Level and unit of study

unit
The individual respondent or subject about whom a researcher collects data, for example countries, universities, families or individuals.

Your research topic can probably be studied at a number of different levels. You may be interested in how countries, universities, religions or cities compare regarding how your research topic is perceived or how policy is made to address an issue. On the other hand, you may be interested in the behaviour, experiences or opinions of individuals, families or households. Part of your research design is to consider the level and unit of data collection and analysis required to be able to address your research question. Will you collect data about countries, universities, families, individuals – what is the **unit** about which you will have data? Usually, social research is conducted at either:

micro level – focusing on the individual as a 'social actor'

or

macro level – focusing on the organisation, social entity, system or structure

Research questions often cannot be adequately addressed without collecting data from individuals, as well as data about the organisation or context in which they are set. Some research designs (for example, see the case study design below) usually do include the collection of data at more than one level, for example at the macro level of the organisation and at the micro level of the individuals who work for that organisation. Consequently, data is gathered from more than one unit of analysis. However, the methods of collecting and analysing data from each of the different levels and units of analysis are likely to be different, so you will need to consider how you will analyse the different sets of data and present your findings.

Example B3.3

Students and alcohol

Level and unit of analysis

Possible levels and units of analysis

Macro level:
    countries
    universities
    departments
    student groups and societies

Micro level:
    year groups
    undergraduate students
    postgraduate students
    students living at home
    students living in halls of residence on campus / off campus

Your research

Thinking about the topic you are hoping to research, list the possible levels and units of analysis.

Macro level:

Micro level:

Research quality checks

Throughout the processes of research design, choosing methods and sampling, you must consider aspects of research quality. Basically this means checking the value of your research against certain social research criteria to ensure that your research will be of a good standard. You must ultimately be able to demonstrate that the research you have done, and the findings and discussion you present, are based on research that has been designed and carried out according to these criteria. Researchers use data as a measure for understanding social reality (**A3**) – we need to assess whether the data is doing a good job as a stand-in, or proxy, for the social reality it represents. To be able to assess the quality of the data, we must consider the way the research is designed so that the collection, analysis and presentation of the data is really addressing the research questions or hypotheses in the ways we claim it is. The research design has therefore to be assessed alongside your research questions and hypotheses on the criteria of validity or credibility, reliability or dependability and generalisability or transferability. In this chapter we will use these concepts to check the research quality issues for each of the research designs discussed. You will also find them referred to in relation to data collection (**Part C**) and analysis (Part D) as well.

Your research

An important note

When considering the quality of your research design, remember: quality criteria are there to help you to look critically at your research plans and to recognise the strengths and limitations of your research design and your data collection and analysis methods. You will not be able to 'tick all the boxes'. The claims that you will be able to make about your research findings will be limited, and this should be acknowledged and explained. For this, you will be given more credit than for an uncritical presentation of results that claim much more than can actually be justified.

Research designs

In this chapter, we consider four major types of research design: **experimental**, **cross-sectional**, and **longitudinal** and **case studies**. We then go on to look at four research strategies which are considered as particular variations on these research designs, and which are appropriate for specific types of research question: **comparative**, **evaluation**, **ethnography** and **Grounded Theory**.

Experimental research design

We begin with the experimental research design that, paradoxically, is the research design you are least likely to find or use when conducting social research! However, there are good reasons for beginning here, as some of the features of an experimental design form the basis for variations that meet the criteria of quality research and are useful to social researchers.

The experimental research design underpins much scientific research, and begins with the assumption that the material or cases that are being studied can be manipulated by the researcher in some way so that some change or difference can be measured. For example: a chemical is added to a test tube of water and an identifiable gas is given off and the amount measured; a series of identical plants are exposed to different amounts of light and their growth rates measured and related to the amount of light exposure. In experimental research examples like these, the researcher deliberately *does* something *to* something, in order to provoke and then *measure* a reaction.

However, often we cannot manipulate the data sources used most frequently in social research in this way. We cannot, for example, deliberately deprive a child of schooling to see how far they would develop without that sort of education. This is because such a course would, on the one hand, be regarded as highly unethical, but it would also be impractical since there are so many other aspects of a normal child's life which we would be unable to control. Children will have inherited different skills and attributes; some children may be educated by their parents at home; others may be neglected by their parents. The results of our experiment would be inconclusive because we would not be able to control all the possible influences on each child.

However, there are ways in which the principal characteristics of an experiment can be helpful in designing social research that approximates to an experiment.

An experiment usually has two key elements:

experimental group
In a research design, the group of people or materials that are manipulated or changed in some way.

control group
In a research design, this is a group of people or materials that are the same as the experimental group in every way *except* the aspect of manipulation or change.

1. **Experimental group** – this is the group of people or materials that are manipulated or changed in some way.
2. **Control group** – this is a group of people or materials that are the same as the experimental group in every way *except* the aspect of manipulation or change.

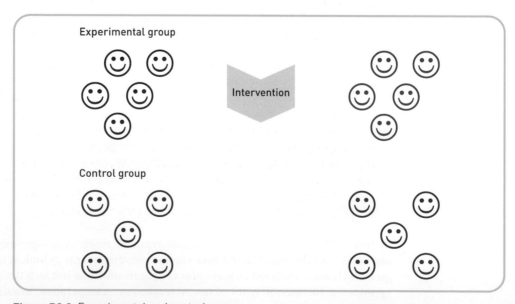

Figure B3.3 Experimental and control groups

An experiment typically is set up to test a hypothesis that is related to the change that is introduced:

> If *A* is added to *B*, then *C* (change) will occur.

If an experiment is carefully conducted and the variation between the two groups is confined to the intervention or change, then the experiment can claim that it is likely that the effect of the intervention or change on the experimental group has been caused by the intervention or change.

In order to control such experiments and eliminate any other variation between groups, most experiments are carried out under controlled conditions, for example, in a laboratory, and indeed some of the most significant social research experiments in the field of social psychology have been carried out in such controlled conditions (see the 'Real research' box below).

Real research

Experimental social research

S. Milgram (1963) Behavioral study of obedience, *Journal of Abnormal Social Psychology* 67: 371–8

Following the Second World War, people brought to court for war crimes in, for example, concentration camps, often claimed that they were 'acting under orders' when they tortured or killed their victims. Will people do anything to obey orders? The psychologist Stanley Milgram set up an experiment to answer the following question: 'For how long will someone continue to give shocks to another person if they are told to do so, even if they thought they could be seriously hurt?'

What the researcher did

Forty men were recruited to participate in an experiment about 'memory and learning' for which they would be paid. Each of the participants met with the researcher and another research participant. In fact this was not a participant but, unknown to the research participant, was an actor playing the part of a research participant. The real participant was allocated the role of 'teacher' and the actor was the 'learner'.

The 'teacher' saw the 'learner' being strapped to a chair and having electrodes attached to their body. The 'teacher' was then seated in another room in front of a shock generator, unable to see the 'learner'. The 'learner' was given a series of questions and the 'teacher' was instructed to punish the 'learner' each time he made a mistake by giving him an electric shock. The voltage was raised each time a mistake was made. The 'learner'/actor was heard to scream in pain and plead with the 'teacher' to stop. Of course, in reality no electric shock was being given but the 'teacher' did not know that. The experiment ended after three shocks given at '400 volts' and there was silence from the 'learner'. The researcher was in the room with the 'teacher' and encouraged him to obey the orders.

Findings

Most of the 'teachers' were uncomfortable about inflicting pain but all 40 obeyed up to 300 volts. Twenty-five of the 40 'teachers' continued to give shocks until the maximum level was reached.

> ### The research design
>
> The research question could only be carried out in laboratory conditions and in a situation where conditions were created to simulate a real social situation. The experiment could be carefully prepared to ensure that all the participants had the same experience. Although the 'learners' were not harmed, there are ethical concerns about the effect the experience may have had on the research participants/ 'teachers', some of whom showed considerable stress when being asked to inflict pain on others.

Random controlled trials

One of the difficulties with studying people is that they vary so much. This means that it is impossible to find people who can be matched on a wide range of criteria so that you can then have a control person and a person on whom the experiment is conducted. It is possible to match on a few criteria – age, gender, occupation or ethnicity, for example – but if we need to consider whether someone is extrovert or introvert, compliant or rebellious, calm or excitable, depressed or happy, then it quickly becomes too complex. The characteristics we have as human beings can be attributed to an almost limitless variety of factors and though we may know, for example, that someone is depressed, we cannot know all the variety of reasons that may be causing the depression.

One way to address this, and to take some account of the many and random ways in which we differ, is to set up large-scale experiments which allocate people to either the control or the experimental group on a **random** basis.

❓ What is . . .

Random

Unpredictable, without regard to particular characteristics. In the case of **statistical sampling** (B5), a **random sample** is selected from a **population** (see B5) where every case has an equal chance of being included in the sample and the composition of the sample cannot be predicted.

random controlled study
A research design that divides the research participants into broad groups relating to age, gender or ethnicity or other characteristics that are relevant to the research topic, and then randomly allocates people to control and experimental groups.

A **random controlled study** may first divide the research participants into broad groups relating to age, gender or ethnicity or other characteristics that are relevant to the research topic. This ensures that the experimental and control groups will be similar on broad characteristics and avoids, for example, having an experimental group made up entirely of people aged over 65 years. Then people are allocated to the control and experimental groups randomly. If sufficiently large groups of people are included in the experiment (random controlled studies usually include over 1,000 cases), then the variation between people in each of the experimental and control groups can be assumed to be similar.

Random controlled trials are commonly held when testing medical drugs or treatments, and often include 'blind testing' wherein the participant (and sometimes the doctor) does not know whether they are receiving the medication or a placebo (a replacement for the medication which appears the same but has no medicinal effect). This is to ensure that the effect of the medication on the participants is unrelated to how they feel about the medication.

Occasionally opportunities for random controlled studies present themselves to social researchers. For example, let us suppose a new method of teaching children how to read is being introduced across a number of schools. Within each school, children could be randomly assigned to classes where the new method was being used (thereby becoming the experimental group), or to those where teaching continued as before (the control group). Children's reading skills could be tested before and after the teaching period, and the overall differences between the two groups assessed. Of course, there may be other associated issues that may need to be considered. It is human nature to show more interest in something that is new and different, and the teachers using the new methods may be more (or possibly less!) enthusiastic in their teaching and the students may be more excited and engaged. The first experience of a new activity is often different from subsequent experiences and the new method may lose some of its initial charm for both children and teachers once they are used to it.

Example B3.4

Students and alcohol: experimental research design

While it is difficult to imagine a controlled experiment in relation to students and alcohol consumption, it may be possible to design research that considers the impact of alcohol within student life. For example: leaflets inviting freshers to a student society event are given out randomly, but some leaflets specifically say that there will be free alcoholic drinks while the other makes no mention of alcohol. Those who come to the meeting are then asked which leaflet they received and what attracted them to the society.

Quasi-experiments

As social researchers, we are generally looking for opportunities to collect data in 'natural' situations – in other words, to collect data about situations, issues or opinions that exist in everyday life rather than constructing laboratory simulations. A **quasi-experimental research design** can be used in some situations where two or more 'naturally' different groups of participants or data can be identified, and one used as the control and the other as the experimental group.

In our earlier example of the new teaching method for reading, it may not have been possible to allocate children at random to the class groups – this could be deemed very disruptive to the children and might risk affecting their learning in other ways. Yet it would still be possible to consider one class as a control group (using the traditional method) and the other as the experimental group (using the new method), and to compare the outcomes in terms of the measurement of levels of reading skills before and after the teaching has taken place. This would be regarded as a quasi-experiment because the make-up of the control and experimental groups would be pre-arranged. However, it would be more 'natural' because the children would not be aware of any changes.

quasi-experiment
Literally, 'almost the same as an experiment' but lacking some of the attributes of an experiment.

quasi-experimental research design
A research design used in situations where two or more 'naturally' different groups of participants or data can be identified, and one used as the control and the other as the experimental group.

Real research

A naturalistic quasi-experiment

R. Fischer, J. Maes and M. Schmitt (2007) Tearing down the 'Wall in the head'? Culture contact between Germans, *International Journal of Intercultural Relations*, 31: 163–79

The reunification of Germany in 1990 gave researchers the opportunity to test out their theories about the effect of personal contact between people from different cultures. Germany had been divided for 45 years, and East and West Germany experienced different political, economic and socio-cultural systems, with little opportunity for individuals to have contact with people from the other part.

Fischer *et al.* focus on the effect of contact between people from different cultures on the individuals themselves. Do people who have contact with people from the other part of Germany experience well-being and satisfaction with their own lives?

What the researchers did

As a random sample, over 3,000 people were selected from across both parts of Germany. This was also a longitudinal study, and questionnaires were sent to them in 1996, 1998 and 2000 to see how people's experiences might change as more opportunities for contact with people from the other part of Germany arose. The questionnaires asked about the amount and type of contact each individual had with people from the other part of Germany, and about their own well-being and satisfaction with their life.

The findings

While the effects of contact with people from a different culture were generally positive, there were differences between those from West Germany and those from East Germany. In particular, while contact was generally seen to be more beneficial for those from East Germany, it also made them more aware of their own disadvantages.

The research design

The researchers were primarily interested in the theory that contact between people from different cultures is beneficial for those involved. The reunification of Germany provided a unique opportunity to explore this because:

(a) the two parts of Germany had developed different socio-cultural systems;

(b) there had been virtually no opportunities for personal contact for 45 years;

(c) after 1990 contact was encouraged as the two parts became one country.

A longitudinal design was introduced to enable researchers to gather data on the ways that people's experiences and perceptions of well-being and satisfaction changed over time as more opportunities for contact arose.

Example B3.5

Students and alcohol

A quasi-experimental research design

The impact of receiving information about the possible effects on health of excessive consumption of alcohol could be studied using a quasi-experiment involving medical students (who would be the experimental group) and sociology students (who would fulfil the role of the control group).

The researcher would gather data from both groups of students about their alcohol consumption and attitudes at the beginning of term, then collect data again at the end of the term after the medical students had been taught about the effects of drinking alcohol on their bodies as part of their lecture programme.

Your research

Research quality check: experimental research designs

- Are the control and experimental groups the same apart from the intervention or change?
- Will you be able to justify any claims made about causal relationships – for example, that the intervention caused the outcome?
- Could your research design be replicated by another researcher?
- Does the research design enable you to claim that your research findings can be generalised to a wider population or different setting? This will depend on the way you have selected your experimental group.
- Does the research design enable you to collect data that 'stands in' for social reality – data that reflects the social reality of natural social settings?
- Does the research design enable you to collect data in a consistent and reliable way?
- What are the ethical implications of your research design for your research participants?

Cross-sectional studies

In reality most social research is conducted after the event we are interested in or at a particular point in time. We are likely to be looking at people's expressed history or reporting on their experience and opinions, and comparing the differing characteristics of their experience and the outcome or current state. We can work with data about past and current experiences to try to identify possible cause-and-effect associations. It is to this research design – cross-sectional studies – that we now turn.

Cross-sectional studies are often associated with large-scale surveys using questionnaires (C3). This is a common, but by no means the only, way of carrying out a cross-sectional study. A cross-sectional research design:

- includes more than one case;
- collects data at one particular time;
- includes within its research participants groups of people or cases that can be compared, e.g. men and women, people of different ages or ethnicities, or people from different cities.

Example B3.6

Students and alcohol

A cross-sectional study design could be used to find out more about the differences and similarities between students with regard to the consumption of alcohol and their attitudes and opinions. Such a design would enable the researcher to build up a picture of the reported levels of consumption and how students feel about alcohol.

The data could be collected for a large number of students using a questionnaire, or a more in-depth study could be designed using semi-structured interviews to collect data from a selected range of students. The researcher could then look for relationships between consumption of alcohol and a range of different variables, such as age, gender and social class.

Alternatively, a cross-sectional study using a different-level unit of analysis could be designed which included a sample of universities. In this case, data about university policies and practice regarding students and consumption of alcohol could be collected from published documents and websites. The researcher could then look for relationships between the policy and practice of universities, and variables like size of institution, proportion of international students or mature students, 'old' or 'new' university, and the level of serious alcohol problems among students.

Cross-sectional studies often take the form of questionnaire surveys, with participants selected using random sampling processes (**B5**). However, the data may be collected in many other ways, through observation, or from documents or interviews, and, as noted above, may be both quantitative and qualitative (using purposive sampling – **B5**). The scale of the studies can also vary from a small number of cases to a survey including thousands of people.

Usually, the focus of the research is on the possible relationships between the variables (or different pieces of information about a person or case) about which data is gathered. The data is often in a quantifiable form so that the differences between cases – the variation – can be measured using statistical tests (**D3**). Depending on the research question, though, this research design can include the gathering of qualitative data where participants are selected purposefully to include a specified range of people. Here the differences may be explored through the identification of themes and the relationship between these and emerging groups within the data (**D4**) (see the 'Real research' box below).

Real research

A cross-sectional study gathering qualitative data

K. Rowlingson (2006) 'Living poor to die rich'? Or 'Spending the kids' inheritance'? Attitudes to assets and inheritance in later life, *Journal of Social Policy*, 35(2): 175–92

What do people do as they get older? Do they spend as much of their money as possible while they are still alive, or do they save their money to pass on to their kids? Older people generally have lower incomes, as they are no longer in paid employment, but may have significant capital assets in the form of property. How do they decide what to do with these?

What the researcher did

The researcher worked with two sets of qualitative data. The first was interview data which had been collected by the researcher for two earlier studies which focused on wealth and future planning. The sample was selected to include people of different ages, income and wealth.

Focus groups were then brought together to discuss inheritance and assets. Each group included people of the same age group, and groups were held in two areas of the same city. In one area house prices were relatively high: house prices were relatively low in the other.

The findings

The findings from the interviews and focus groups suggest that most people want to take a 'balanced and pragmatic' approach to the use of their money as they get older, spending some and having some to leave to their children. The researcher also discussed some of the policy implications in terms of introducing ways of helping people to do this.

The research design

The research design ensured that people of different ages, income and wealth were included so that the experiences and opinions of different groups could be compared.

Real research

Cross-sectional survey

C. Vogler, M. Brockmann and R.D. Wiggins (2008) Managing money in new heterosexual forms of intimate relationships, *Journal of Socio-Economics*, 37: 552–76

Managing money within a relationship can be problematic. Do couples share all their money, or keep their own separate? In this research, the researchers were interested in possible difference between couples who were married and those who were not married but were living together.

What the researchers did

The researchers worked with secondary data that had already been gathered as part of the International Social Survey Programme. This is an annual programme of surveys across many countries, and includes an occasional survey on family and changing gender roles. The data was collected by interview and questionnaire from a large representative sample within the UK. The data collected had already been analysed and published, but it was still available for other researchers to use to explore their own research questions.

The survey included many different types of household, so the researchers first had to identify the sub-groups in which they were interested – households where there were married or cohabiting heterosexual couples. Using data collected by other researchers for other purposes may raise some problems. In this case, the 2002 survey had not asked about previous marriages, so it was not clear whether people who were now cohabiting had been in a married relationship previously.

The researchers selected data on four groups for analysis: 'childless cohabiting respondents, cohabiting parents, childless married respondents and married parents'. The survey had included questions about the couples' socio-economic status and their views on marriage and relationships, working women and managing money.

The findings

The researchers found that cohabiting couples who had children managed their money in very similar ways to those who were married, typically pooling their money in a household pot. Young childless cohabiting couples were more likely to manage their money partly or completely separately.

The research design

A large-scale representative survey was used to enable the researchers to identify the smaller sub-groups in which they were interested. A range of data had been collected about each couple, and this enabled the researchers to look for relationships between different variables.

The original research had collected data at the level that the researchers were interested in – the household. So, in this case, the unit of analysis was the household.

Your research

Research quality check: cross-sectional research designs

- Will you be able to use your data to look for possible causal associations between variables?
- Are you able to select a sample that reflects a cross-section of the population you are interested in? Are any groups likely to be excluded by your research design?
- Could your research design be replicated by another researcher?
- Does the research design enable you to claim that your research findings can be generalised to a wider population or different setting? This will depend on the way you have selected your research participants.
- Does the research design enable you to collect data that 'stands in' for social reality – data that reflects the social reality of natural social settings?
- Does the research design enable you to collect data in a consistent and reliable way?
- What are the ethical implications of your research design for your research participants?

Longitudinal study

A cross-sectional study gathers data from one point in time, but if your research questions relate to changes over time you may wish to consider designing a **longitudinal study**. This will enable you to look at the same people or situations at key points in time and to consider how the changes over time have affected different groups of people. Data is gathered on at least two occasions separated in time.

Many longitudinal studies are large scale and are set up as longitudinal studies from the beginning (**prospective longitudinal studies**). There are a number of well-known examples of longitudinal studies which look at babies born at a particular time (**cohort studies**) and then gather data about them at set points throughout their early years – or indeed their lifetime. A popular example of this is the television documentary '7 Up' which follows the lives of 14 children, selected from different socio-economic backgrounds, who were 7 years old in 1964 when the programme was first shown. Every seven years a documentary is made about them in the *World in Action* series, the last one being screened in 2005 showing them as 49 year olds. Longitudinal studies are major research undertakings and involve numerous, and often changing, social researchers.

prospective longitudinal studies
Research studies that are initially designed to be longitudinal.

cohort studies
A type of longitudinal study which looks at a group of people of the same age and then gathers data about them at set points throughout their lives.

Real research

The Millennium Cohort Study

Following two major cohort studies during the twentieth century – the 1958 National Child Development Study and 1970 British Cohort Study (both of these studies are still gathering data from their cohorts) – the Centre for Longitudinal Studies (www.cls.ioe.ac.uk/) set up the Millennium Cohort Study involving children born in the year 2000, for which 18,818 children were selected using a stratified sample. By 2008, data had been gathered from the families of the children on four occasions.

The research design for the Millennium Cohort Study (MCS) was based on the following five principles:

1. The MCS should provide data about children living and growing up in each of the four countries of the UK.

2. The MCS should provide useable data for sub-groups of children, in particular those living in advantaged and disadvantaged circumstances, and for children of ethnic minorities and those living in Scotland, Wales and Northern Ireland.

3. As well as data about children, the MCS should provide data about their family circumstances and the broader socio-economic context in which the children grow up.

4. The MCS should include children born throughout a single 12-month period.

5. All children born as members of the MCS population should have a known and non-zero probability of being included in the selected sample.

Source: Center for Longitudinal Studies. www.cls.ioe.ac.uk/studies.asp?section=0001000200010010 (accessed 12 August 2008).

However, it is also possible to design smaller-scale studies over quite short time periods. Interviewing people before, during and after a particular event could be regarded as a longitudinal design, if the focus of the research is to track how each individual research participant anticipated, experienced and reflected on the event.

Example B3.7

Students and alcohol: longitudinal study

A longitudinal study could be designed to look at the way students' drinking patterns changed over the course of their university programme. This could include collecting the same data from a sample of students at the key points during their three-year degree programme.

A retrospective longitudinal study may be designed which asks final-year students to recall their drinking patterns at key times during their time at university (for example, during freshers' week, at exam time and during the vacation), and to identify changes over the three-year period. But, as with all retrospective studies, people's memories are not always accurate and may be coloured by their current situation and perceptions. We may gain more accurate data if we choose to include students from each of the three years of a degree programme at one particular point in time, and compare the different year groups.

Real research

Longitudinal and cross-sectional research

B. Milton, S. E. Woods, L. Dugdill, L. Porcellato and R. J. Springett (2008) Starting young? Children's experiences of trying smoking during pre-adolescence, *Health Education Research*, 23(2): 298–309

Why do children try smoking when the risks to health are now well known? The researchers wanted to hear from children their own accounts of their first experiences of smoking.

What the researchers did

The study is part of a prospective longitudinal study of smoking in a large city in the UK. The study is following a cohort of children from six primary schools in areas selected to include variation in terms of health and socio-economic status. This study gathered data from children when they were aged 9, 10 and 11. The data was collected using questionnaires, interviews and focus groups.

Children were asked about any experiences of smoking they had had, family smoking habits and their opinions of smoking.

Findings

By the age of 11, 27 per cent of the cohort had tried smoking: curiosity and peer influence were important factors in prompting experimentation. The researchers emphasised that approaches to preventing children from smoking must take account of social factors (including friends and family) which play a significant role in whether a child tries smoking. Account must also be taken of the different ages at which pre-adolescent children tried smoking, as different approaches to prevention needed to be taken.

The research design

The study was designed to include a cross-section of children born in the same specific year, ensuring that children from areas of different social and economic backgrounds were included.

As data was gathered each year between the ages of 9 and 11, children were asked about their first experiences of smoking near in time to the event. The same children were involved on each occasion, enabling researchers to look at the changes and processes within children's lives during pre-adolescence.

retrospective longitudinal study
A type of longitudinal study where data is available from the past, for example, where participants can be asked to provide data about their past experiences, or where records may be available.

life history approach
A data collection method where participants are asked to tell their life story focusing on common events.

For practical reasons some longitudinal studies cannot involve the same participants on each of the data-gathering occasions. This may be because the participants have died or moved and cannot be contacted or because they no longer want to take part. A study may therefore include different samples of people but using similar criteria for selection. Similarly, while a longitudinal study is usually planned as such, there are some situations where data is available from the past (a **retrospective longitudinal study**) which can be used: for example, where participants can be asked to provide data about their past experiences; or where records may be available – for example, medical records or social work case notes. A **life history approach** to gathering data, where participants are asked to tell their life story focusing on common events, could be considered a longitudinal research design if participants are asked to report and reflect on the same key points in their life.

While many large-scale longitudinal studies depend on the gathering of quantitative data from large numbers of participants, a longitudinal study may also be based on gathering in-depth data from a small number of selected participants on a number of occasions.

Real research

Longitudinal and qualitative research

A. Corden and K. Nice (2007) Qualitative longitudinal analysis for policy: Incapacity Benefits recipients taking part in Pathways to Work, *Social Policy and Society*, 6(4): 557–69

When a new policy is introduced, there is naturally some interest in how it is put into practice and how people experience the changes. The Pathways to Work Pilot was a new approach to helping people who were receiving Incapacity Benefit to take up paid employment. Policy-makers wanted to hear about service users' experiences of using the new project.

What the researchers did

The study focused on the service users' experiences of using the service over a period of time, while also gathering data about changes in people's lives, their employment, financial situation and so on. Data was collected initially through an in-depth interview and then by telephone after three and then six months. There were three cohorts of research participants, starting at six-month intervals. This ensured that people were included who joined the project when it had been running for some time as well as those involved at the very beginning. A total of 105 people were involved.

Findings

Though people's experience of the service varied, this longitudinal study was able to show how different groups of people experienced the service over time and also gave some people the opportunity to reflect on the experience after a year. The researchers were able to give feedback to the policy officers throughout the process, and to demonstrate at the end of the study that changes through time are complex, with changing family, financial and employment situations.

Research design

The use of a longitudinal design enabled the researchers to look at the changes and processes involved in the introduction of the project and the experience of the service users. The use of qualitative interviews to gather data enabled service users to discuss and reflect on their experience at different stages in the process.

The use of three cohorts of research participants starting at different stages in the initial year of the project enabled the researchers to study any changes that were introduced as the project settled down, and to compare the experiences of each cohort.

Your research

Research quality check: longitudinal research designs

- Will you be able to collect data on the same variables on each occasion?
- Will you be able to gather data from the same people/cases on each occasion? What will you do about people who drop out, cannot be found?
- Could your research design be replicated by another researcher?

- Does the research design enable you to collect data that 'stands in' for social reality – data that reflects the social reality of natural social settings?
- Does the research design enable you to collect data in a consistent and reliable way on each occasion?
- What are the ethical implications of your research design for your research participants?

Case study

Unlike the research designs discussed above, a case study includes either a single case or a small number of cases but each case is explored in detail and great depth. A variety of different types of data about the case may be gathered, and both cross-sectional and longitudinal data may be included.

The subject of the case may be a person, an organisation, a situation or a country, but the study must relate to a particular aspect of the case as demonstrated in your research question. There are usually boundaries to the case, making it clear what is within the case to be studied and what is not. In this sense, it takes a holistic approach to the study, as the relationship between the component parts of the case and the case as a whole – the social context – are all of interest to the researcher. However, a case study is not simply an in-depth study of a community, organisation or group. The case itself must be pertinent to the research topic. The selection of the case is therefore significant, in terms of its potential to produce data that will enable you to address your research question. The focus of research interest must be included in the case itself, not simply in the range of data that has been collected about it. Yin (2003) sets out a number of criteria for the selection of case studies which may help you to understand the nature of a case study better.

1. *Critical case.* Here the case is chosen as one that will enable the researcher to test a theory or hypothesis. The case includes the potential to show whether the theory holds up or not. This could be a case where an event or change has occurred which provides the researcher with the opportunity to study what happens as a result.

2. *Extreme or unique case.* Here the focus is on a situation or group that is perceived to be different to any other and the focus is on its uniqueness. It may be the only case where a particular combination of people and events are found.

3. *Representative or typical case.* This is effectively the opposite of the unique case. It is a case that is chosen because it is seen to represent many other similar cases – in a sense it is the everyday, ordinary case, which has similarities to others and is chosen on these grounds.

4. *Revelatory case.* This is a case that has the potential to shed light on the research topic. It may be that the researcher has access to a situation that has been hidden.

5. *Longitudinal case.* Many case studies offer the opportunity for research at different time points and case studies may be chosen on the basis of being able to carry out successive studies over a period of time (as discussed above).

Real research

Case study research

C. Chapain and A. Murie (2008) The impact of factory closure on local communities and economies: the case of the MG Rover Longbridge closure in Birmingham, *Policy Studies*, 29(3): 305–17

There have been a number of studies over the last 50 years of the impact of the closure of factories or mines on the local area. However, most are focused on industries where people live and work in the same area. The researchers sought to examine the impact of a different type of closure, where workers were more geographically spread, and the reduction in workforce took place over a period of at least eight years. The eventual collapse of the car manufacturing company MG Rover, and the closure of its main plant at Longbridge in Birmingham, UK, in 2005, with the loss of 5,900 jobs, provided a case example.

What the researchers did

The researchers gathered secondary data from different sources, including payroll data from 1998 and 2005 (this included information about where workers lived), monthly data about claimants of unemployment benefits, census data and data relating to business activities within the wards.

Findings

The researchers found that the impact of the closure had been felt across a wide geographical area as workers commuted from other parts of Birmingham and towns to the south of Birmingham, although there was a significant local impact.

The research design

The focus of this research was on the wider spatial impact of the closure of a large industrial plant and the case of the Longbridge factory provided a critical case study opportunity.

Example B3.8

Students and alcohol

Case study design

The focus of the case study may be on the way alcohol is consumed within a social group and the way alcohol consumption is perceived to be part of the societal group activity. A university society could be chosen as a typical social group. An alternative may be to choose two contrasting examples of university societies based on whether the predominant membership is male or female.

Clearly, the selection of a case study can include elements of more than one of these criteria, and the case study can include within it elements of other research designs. This means that, for instance, a cross-sectional study of people living within the case study area may form part of the overall design, or that there may be an opportunity for a quasi-experimental study within the case study.

A case study design may include just one case, or multiple cases may be selected. This may then form the basis for a comparative study (see below).

Your research

Research quality check: case study designs

- Are you able to identify a case that will enable you to address your research question or test your hypothesis?
- What claims are you able to make about your case study – is it a critical case, a typical case, etc.?

- Are you able to identify clear boundaries to your case study?
- What will you be able to claim for your findings in terms of how they might be generalised or their theoretical value, and their explanatory value?
- Does the research design enable you to collect data that 'stands in' for social reality – data that reflects the social reality of natural social settings?
- Does the research design enable you to collect data in a consistent and reliable way?
- What are the ethical implications of your research design for your research participants?

The four research designs – experimental, cross-sectional, longitudinal and case study – provide the data collection and analysis frameworks with which we can begin to put together our own research plans. We now need to revisit our research questions and, bearing in mind these four designs, look at the overall research strategy needed to address these.

Your research

In this section we have taken the example research topic of 'students and alcohol' and suggested example research designs which could be used to study the topic. Taking your own research topic, can you suggest how you might study it using each of the designs?

Quasi-experimental

Cross-sectional

Longitudinal

Case study

Research strategies

A research strategy is essentially a research plan. It may be that the four basic research designs we have considered are sufficient for you to be able to plan your research. However, it may also be useful to consider some variations or specific developments of these designs, which have emerged during the history of social research from researchers who have sought to refine and experiment with different ways of studying social phenomena.

We will consider comparative research, evaluation, ethnography and Grounded Theory. Within each of these approaches to research, one or more of the four research designs already introduced will usually be found.

Comparative research

Comparative research designs are often used to study two or more countries or two or more cultures, and are perhaps most commonly used within policy studies. Typically, the research design will include a detailed examination of a particular aspect, policy, issue or characteristic within each of the countries or cultures, and compare these on the basis of a set of common criteria. The researcher is interested not just in the similarities and differences between the two cases, but also in the differences in the two contexts. These may include the history, customs, institutions, ideologies, values and lifestyles of the country, culture, organisation or community. The researcher is likely to be interested in how these impact on the research area.

Comparative research often uses a multiple case study design, allowing in-depth study of each case (country or culture), and aims to explain the similarities and differences between the cases.

Why use a comparative research strategy?

In cases of cross-national and cross-cultural comparative research, the study of another country or culture to one's own is seen to produce greater awareness and understanding of one's own country or culture, as it provides the opportunity to look 'through different eyes' at a familiar situation. Comparative research may also be used as the basis for developing typologies or models of the ways different countries or cultures organise or think about themselves. For example, Esping-Andersen has developed a typology of states with regard to their approach to social welfare (Esping-Andersen, 1990). Other comparative social policy researchers can then test out the usefulness of the model in not only understanding different countries but also how they change through time.

The overall comparative framework typically draws on both cross-sectional and case study designs. The criteria for comparison must reflect the research questions and point to the nature of the data that needs to be gathered. This may be a mixture of individual data, documents and statistics – often largely secondary data.

harmonised data
Data gathered from a range of different sources but which take account of the differences in the way the data has been collected, enabling researchers to access comparative data.

Gathering data for a comparative cross-national study has become more accessible to students with the development of a number of sources of **harmonised data**. One of the difficulties of undertaking cross-national research has been securing access to a range of comparable data from each country. Organisations like the OECD (www.oecd.org, accessed 20 July 2009) and European Union (EuroStat, http://epp.eurostat.ec.europa.eu/, accessed 20 July 2009) now gather similar data from a range of countries and set out the differences in the way the data has been collected, enabling researchers to access comparative data from countries around the world. The Survey of Health, Ageing and Retirement in Europe referred to in the following 'Real research' box is an example of research that is taking place across the countries of Europe, and which can provide comparable data on particular issues for a student interested in this topic.

Real research

Comparative study

M. Albertini, M. Kohli and C. Vogel (2007) Intergenerational transfers of time and money in European families: common patterns different regimes, *International Journal of European Social Policy*, 17: 319

Given the ageing population of most European countries and the cost of supporting older people, this research looked at how money and resources flow between generations in ten European countries.

What the researchers wanted to find out

They wanted to know more about the transfer of money and other resources, including social support and care of grandchildren, between parents and their adult children. Do patterns differ in different welfare regimes?

What they did

They used data from 22,777 people from ten European countries (excluding the UK) gathered as part of the Survey of Health, Ageing and Retirement in Europe (SHARE, www.share-project.org/), a longitudinal, multidisciplinary and cross-national survey representing the population of individuals aged 50 and over in Europe. They then looked for differences between countries using a welfare regimes typology.

Findings

They found that across all countries there was a net outflow from parents to adult children, particularly among the younger parents. However, money and resources were transferred from parents to adult children less frequently but 'more intensely' in Southern European countries and differences were found to reflect differences in welfare regimes.

The research design

The researchers were able to use data already collected in a large-scale cross-sectional survey which asked the same questions of people aged over 50 years from ten different European countries. The research could be regarded as opportunist in that the data was available through this large-scale survey and appropriate for their research questions. They were also able to draw on existing theoretical models of welfare regimes to help them to explain the differences they found.

Your research

Research quality check: comparative social research

- How will you justify your choice of cases? What is the basis of your comparison?
- Have you identified the criteria on which you will compare the two cases?
- Will you be able to identify comparable data about your two research foci?
- How will you address issues of difference in language, culture and interpretation?
- Will you be dependent on secondary data – data collected by others and for different purposes? How will you justify and explain this?
- Will you be able to collect data in a consistent and reliable way from both cases?
- Are there any ethical implications of your study?

Evaluation

To 'evaluate' essentially means to assess the value of something in terms of the impact that it has on a situation, individual(s) or organisation. Evaluatory social research usually relates to an intervention or change that has been made, and whether the intervention has achieved the change or outcomes that were intended. The key issue is to decide how those outcomes are to be identified and measured. Value may be defined in terms of observable or measurable benefit to particular groups of people, efficiency, satisfaction, value for money or improvement in practice.

A quasi-experimental design may be appropriate for evaluatory research where an intervention has been introduced in one situation but not in another (control). Alternatively, a longitudinal design may be appropriate where data is collected before and after an intervention. On the other hand, there are likely to be elements of both cross-sectional design and possibly case study design within a piece of evaluatory research as well.

Why do evaluatory research?

1. To find out whether an intervention or change has had the desired outcomes.
2. To assess how well a process (policy implementation, practice) is working.
3. To consider how a process or intervention might be improved.
4. To assess whether the costs of the process (service, policy implementation, etc.) is value for money or 'best value'.
5. To find out what works (or doesn't work) and why.

Often a range of data is collected to provide evidence of 'value'. This may include both quantitative and qualitative data, from a range of individuals. For example, an evaluation of the introduction of a new service may include:

- quantitative data showing how many and what type of people use the service;
- satisfaction data from people who use the service;
- in-depth data from people who use the service, relating their experience and perceptions;
- opinions of service deliverers – practitioners and managers on how well the service has been delivered and their perceptions of the impact;
- documentary evidence of the way the service has been designed and delivered, e.g. plans, minutes of meetings.

Real research

Evaluation

J. Hirst, E. Formby, S. Parr, J. Nixon and C. Hunter (2007) *An Evaluation of Two Initiatives to Reward Young People*, York: Joseph Rowntree Foundation, available at www.jrf.org.uk/knowledge/findings/housing/ 2149.asp (accessed 11 September 2008)

Concern about the behaviour of young people in some neighbourhoods led the Joseph Rowntree Housing Trust to devise a scheme whereby young people would be rewarded for 'good' behaviour by collecting points for activities that were socially helpful. The points could be used to claim rewards, for example, cinema tickets. The scheme was set up in areas of two British towns.

What the researchers did

The researchers were asked to evaluate the scheme in terms of how the scheme had worked in the two towns, the young people's perceptions of the scheme and whether there was any growth in tolerance towards young people and their activities.

Data was collected using a variety of methods – interviews, focus groups and participatory research – and involving the different stakeholders (including young people who had participated and some who had not), staff and residents.

Findings

The scheme had operated with different levels of success in the two towns. Neither had been successful in engaging young people over 15 to the scheme. There was some evidence in one town that young people had become more involved in community activities. However, the evaluation was unable to show whether there was any growth in tolerance towards young people, or that the scheme would have longer-term success.

The research design

The initial design of the project that set up the scheme in two towns provided the basis for the evaluation. This ensured that the specific contexts in each town (including the level of resources) and how this might have impacted on the scheme could be considered. A range of stakeholders were included in the evaluation, including young people who had not participated (a sort of control group).

Evaluation research is usually – but not always – designed to be of value to its commissioners, or to others working in similar areas. It may be carried out with a view to identifying areas for improvement or to identify lessons for others in similar situations.

Within social policy and social work arenas, evaluatory research is often linked to the assessment of the impact of new policies, practices or projects and is designed to assess both whether it has worked in the way that was intended and why. UK academics Pawson and Tilley (1997) have introduced the idea of realistic evaluation which follows the underpinning ideas of critical realism (A2). They suggest that the research needs to be designed so that the question 'why did/didn't it work?' can be answered.

Your research

Research quality check: evaluatory research

- Will the data that you collect help you to address the evaluation questions?
- Do you have comparable 'baseline data' – data gathered before the intervention or change was introduced?
- Are you able to gather data from a range of 'stakeholders', people with different interests in the focus of the evaluation?
- What is your position with regard to the evaluation and the participants? Are you external to the situation or an 'insider'?
- Does the research design enable you to claim that your research findings can be generalised to a wider population or different setting? This will depend on the way you have selected your evaluation participants.
- Does the research design enable you to collect data that 'stands in' for social reality – data that reflects the social reality of natural social settings?
- Can you ensure that data has been collected in a consistent and reliable way?
- What are the ethical implications of the evaluation for the various stakeholder participants?

Ethnography

What makes an ethnographical study different from other types of study is the relationship of the researcher with the data that is collected. In ethnographical research the researcher spends time (sometimes a number of years) immersed within the research context, seeing and hearing the data at first hand. This is often called 'the field' or 'a natural setting'. Typically the researcher takes a role within the setting that will allow him to participate in the research context as a researcher and as a participant. Popular media/documentary examples would be Louis Theroux (see for example, http://news.bbc.co.uk/1/hi/magazine/7753282.stm, accessed 20 July 2009) and Bruce Parry (www.bbc.co.uk/tribe/bruce/index.shtml, accessed 20 July 2009).

The researcher keeps a reflective diary and his reflections become part of the data that is worked with. Data is analysed as it is collected, and this may then influence the way further data is collected. Data is typically collected using participant observation, conversations and sometimes more formal interviews. Relevant documents may also be included. Data may also be gathered using visual recording through photographs or videos. (If you are interested in this, see the further reading suggestions at the end of this chapter.)

Effectively, ethnography follows a case study design. However, there is the added dimension of the researcher participating in the social phenomenon under study and seeking, through that participation and regular data collection and reflection, to gain a deeper understanding of the culture of the group, organisation or community. This is gained by observing how people construct social meaning and actions in everyday life.

Although a lengthy ethnographical study is unlikely to be feasible for most students, it is possible to design a shorter study, perhaps focused in an organisation or group of which you are already a member or in a part-time job, over a period of weeks rather than years.

An ethnographical study is not about just gathering as much data as possible. There must be a focus – a research question to address – which may be related to the way people interact, what hierarchies can be observed in the way people work together and how participants organise themselves.

Real research

Ethnographical study

Judy Yuen-man Sui (2008) The SARS-associated stigma of SARS victims in the post-SARS era of Hong Kong, *Qualitative Health Research*, 18: 729

In 2003 there were outbreaks of SARS (severe acute respiratory syndrome) in Hong Kong. This new life-threatening disease is highly contagious, and there was worldwide concern about it spreading, and the ability of medical personnel to contain it. Around 1,700 people were infected, of whom 299 people died. Those who were infected but survived found themselves stigmatised and discriminated against, and many continued to suffer from physical and psychological difficulties. For example, some still wore face masks in public places because others feared they were infectious.

What the researcher did

The researcher was interested in how the stigma and discrimination associated with SARS victims had been constructed in the society. She wanted to understand the experiences and perceptions of SARS victims, and chose to spend some 16 months in close contact with a SARS self-help group. She collected data through participant observation, interviews, attending meetings and conversations. All the participants were informed about the research. A research diary was kept and the reflections and interpretations of the researcher were checked with participants.

Findings

The researcher found that the stigma attached to being a SARS victim was experienced and understood related to the way that medical doctors, the government and the public still treat SARS victims as different.

The research design

The ethnographical approach enabled the researcher to build trusting relationships with people over time and to observe how they related and shared their experiences with each other.

Your research

Research quality check: ethnographical research

- Will you be able to gain access to a situational context that will help you to address your research questions?
- Will you conduct the research overtly or covertly and what are the implications for your study?
- How will you record and demonstrate your own reflections and interpretations?
- How will you check out your interpretations with others?
- What are the boundaries of your study within the situational context?
- What will you be able to claim for your findings in terms of their generalisability, their theoretical value and their explanatory value?
- Does the research design enable you to collect data in a consistent and reliable way?
- What are the ethical implications of your study for your research participants?

Grounded Theory

The last of our four research strategies is Grounded Theory. Grounded Theory is a bit unusual. In many ways, Grounded Theory is 'just' another data collection method. However, it is of such unusual popularity – particularly in the USA – that we decided to include it as an approach you might take to your research. However, we hope that readers will view this section with a measure of care since, while we have some serious concerns about this particular method as a whole, we are convinced that the specific processes involved in gathering and analysing data are useful in a range of research – even if they are not theory generating.

The normal course of action is for researchers to start out with a theory (or, maybe, a hypothesis) or a research question and then gather data to test or answer it (A2 and A4). Grounded Theory does the opposite. It is a systematic research approach in which theory is developed – or generated – from data. This is, to say the least, rather unusual and quite problematic. It has become widely accepted in the social sciences that research can never be **atheoretical**, that is, there is always some sort of underpinning (or over-arching, depending on your point of view) theory or set of ideas about the way things are. Grounded Theory rejects this, causing a philosophical problem. Other criticisms of Grounded Theory usually concentrate on its status as 'theory' arguing that what it produces is not 'theory'. For an up-to-date discussion of this and other criticisms, see Thomas and James (2006).

atheoretical
Refers to the absence of an underpinning theory or set of ideas.

What is a Grounded Theory approach?

Grounded Theory is best described as a systematic research method which generates theory from data. It was 'discovered' by Anselm Strauss and Barney Glaser who were American sociologists (Glaser and Strauss, 1967). They described the approach as an attempt to bridge the gap between theory and research. Strauss and Glaser subsequently had a fairly major disagreement about the application of Grounded Theory which, ultimately, led to Glaser forming the breakaway Grounded Theory Institute (www.groundedtheory.org) which is worth a virtual visit. Strauss died in 1996 at the age of 79, which made a resolution of their differences impossible, though to some extent his work has been carried on by Julia Corbin.

There is no doubt that Grounded Theory as a research method has a number of advantages, partly because it is a very detailed and meticulous process. As a result, the researcher needs to have considerable experience and a significant amount of insight. On the whole, we feel that novice researchers should only use Grounded Theory with great care and under careful supervision. However, the detailed processes used in this method are very useful and can, with some modification, be used in other data collection and analysis scenarios.

The Grounded Theory approach has two key and useful aspects. First of all, the last item in our explanation of Grounded Theory above was the inference that many researchers use the method without 'buying in' to the theory generation aspect. In part, at least, this is because many researchers feel that the 'groundedness' (we use this term in relation to qualitative analysis to mean *remaining in touch with the raw data*) of this method is a significant advantage. This means that it is a data collection and analysis approach which works with the data in the form it is observed, heard and recorded. In this sense it takes an **inductive approach** to working with the data, at least in the initial stages of analysis.

And secondly, in practice in Grounded Theory data collection, theory generation and analysis all happen simultaneously. (Many social researchers would argue that data collection and analysis (Part D) are always concurrent, but they are not always explicitly so.)

Data can be collected for Grounded Theory analysis in many different ways. Generally, the technique is used only for qualitative research, though there is no real reason that it should not be utilised for mixed-methods research.

The Grounded Theory process

Grounded Theory research starts when you are in a research setting. As the researcher, your role is to understand the processes that are happening and the ways in which the various actors conduct themselves. The most common methods used are interviews and observation, though there is no reason that other qualitative methods should not be utilised. At the end of each data collection session (whatever methods are used), the 'results' are recorded (these could be data, key issues, etc.) and immediately used as part of the **constant comparison** which, along with **coding** and **memoing**, is central to the analytical process. Initially, you compare data from different sources (which, of course, may include literature as well as empirical findings). At the same time, the researcher searches for **negative cases** (instances that seem to contradict or disprove the emerging theory). As (and if) these are found, this is seen as an indicator that more research is required (which will, in turn, modify the emerging theory) and that **data saturation** (see below) has not been achieved.

As the process continues it is contended that theory will emerge and that it is then possible to compare data and theory. Whether this can be achieved is contested, but there is no doubt that the processes employed are useful and, for example, constant comparison is often a very good way to identify themes and categories. The analytical process is developed in more detail in D8.

Why use a Grounded Theory approach?

Grounded Theory has some unique components and processes which may be of value in other research, including the following:

- The ideas of relevance, modifiability and workability might be useful as alternatives to validity.
- The idea that data collection and analysis occur simultaneously.

---

inductive approach
A data collection and analysis approach that works with the data in the form it is observed, heard and recorded.

constant comparison
Comparing data from different sources and from different places and times to support the analysis, along with the search for negative cases.

coding
The process of 'marking' or identifying data for later analysis.

negative cases
Instances that seem to contradict or disprove the emerging theory.

data saturation
The idea that that there are ways in which the researcher can be sure that 'enough' research has been done.

- The approach enables the researcher to work with different sources and types of data simultaneously.
- The meticulous way in which the research is structured, undertaken and recorded – an inspiration to us all.
- The processes of:
  - constant comparison – the comparing of data from different sources and from different places and times to support the analysis, along with the search for negative cases
  - coding – the process of 'marking' or identifying data for later analysis, but split into three useful dimensions (open, axial and selective) in this instance
  - memos – ways of recording, thinking about and analysing data
  - data saturation – an important concept, arguing that there are ways in which the researcher can be sure that 'enough' research has been done.

Your research

Research quality check: Grounded Theory approach

In practice, the research quality checks you should be aware of in relation to a Grounded Theory strategy are the same as those for an Ethnographic strategy. However, the creators of Grounded Theory argue that the value of this sort of research is best evaluated by a series of terms that they call 'relevance', 'modifiability' and 'workability' (Glaser and Strauss, 1967). Though we might wonder about the method's originators' innovative and inventive use of language, their definitions are certainly worth thinking about and can have application in other sorts of research.

Relevance – if a study is to be relevant in Grounded Theory, then it must be both of academic interest and also be important to the participants.

Modifiability – because it is impossible to apply the concepts of 'right' and 'wrong' to grounded theories, the theory can always be altered when 'new' data is compared to existing data.

Workability – is a measure of how the Grounded Theory explains the issue being researched.

Grounded Theory also claims to provide a system of judging whether the resultant 'theory' is 'good' or not (readers will, of course, realise that these terms are contested). It does this in ways that are different from those with which we may be more familiar. Strauss and Corbin (1990) set out four main requirements for the process:

1. The theory must fit the phenomenon under examination.
2. The theory should be understandable and provide understanding.
3. The theory should fit a wide variety of contexts.
4. The theory must include a statement of the conditions under which it applies.

Which research design is for you?

As this section illustrates, research design is a complex matter – perhaps the most crucial aspect is to make sure that the design you develop is right for *your project*. Just because someone else has done something similar in the past, or because a particular design is popular at the moment, does not mean it is right for you. Take time to consider different designs and strategies.

Your research

Thinking about your research topic and research questions: which research design will you choose?

An experimental or quasi-experimental design may:

- enable you to look at the impact of a change or an intervention;
- enable you to explore causal relationships between different characteristics, changes and interventions;
- help you to test a hypothesis.

A cross-sectional design:

- may enable you to compare the experiences, views and characteristics of different groups of people or cases;
- may enable you to explore the possible relationships between the experiences, views and characteristics of different groups of people or cases;
- usually includes data from a sample selected to represent different groups within the population and the findings may be generalisable to the population.

A longitudinal design may:

- enable you to look at changes over time;
- enable you to identify key differences over time and look for possible explanations;
- enable you to look at the impact of key events or changes using data collected before and after.

A case study design may:

- enable you to look at a small number of cases in depth;
- enable you to look at your research topic within a particular or different contexts;
- enable you to take a holistic approach to your research and explore your topic in context.

References and further reading

Banks, M. (2001) *Visual Methods in Social Research*, London: Sage.

BBC News (2008) Ban on student alcohol promotions *BBC News*, 31 March (http://news.bbc.co.uk/l/hi/england/merseyside/7323578.stm) (accessed 20 July 2009).

Brewer, J. D. (2000) *Ethnography*, Buckingham: Open University Press.

Esping-Andersen, G. (1990) *The Three Worlds of Welfare Capitalism*, Cambridge: Polity Press.

Glaser, B. G. and Strauss, A. L. (1967) *The Discovery of Grounded Theory: Strategies for Qualitative Research*, New York: Aldine de Gruyter.

Kennett, P. (2001) *Comparative Social Policy*, Buckingham: Open University Press.

Moser, C. (1958) *Survey Methods in Social Investigation*, London: Heinemann.

Pawson, R. and Tilley, N. (1997) *Realistic Evaluation*, London: Sage.

Pink, S. (2001) *Doing Visual Ethnography: Images, Media and Representation in Research*, London: Sage.

Smithers, R. (2009) UK teenagers among heaviest drinkers in EU, *Guardian*, 27 March (www.guardian.co.uk/society/2009/mar/27/teenage-drinking-alcohol-binge) (accessed 20 July 2009).

Strauss, B. and Corbin, J. M. (1990) *Basics of Qualitative Research: Grounded Theory Procedures and Techniques*, London: Sage.

Thomas, G. and James, D. (2006) Re-inventing grounded theory: some questions about theory, ground and discovery, *British Educational Research Journal*, 32(6): 767–95.

Yin, R. K. (2003) *Case Study Research: Design and Methods*, 4th edn, London: Sage.

CHAPTER B4
Choosing methods

Contents

In context

In this chapter we begin to look in more practical terms at the methods or approaches that can be taken to collecting and working with data. In developing a methodology you are drawing on your research questions and operational definitions (A4) and the nature of the data (A3) you will need to collect in order to be able to test your hypothesis or answer your research questions. Research methodologies are often grouped into quantitative and qualitative approaches. However, researchers often use more than one data collection method and it is becoming increasingly common to used a mixture of methods. We begin by looking at the quantitative, qualitative and mixed-methods approaches before going on to consider some ways of choosing methods.

PART B: Preparing for research

> **B1:** Planning a research project
>
> **B2:** Reviewing the literature
>
> **B3:** Research design
>
> ▶ **B4: Choosing methods**
>
> **B5:** Sampling
>
> **B6:** Research proposals

Choosing methods

The approach taken in this book is that the choice of research data collection methods should be determined by the hypotheses or research questions and the aspects of the research topic that are the prime focus and interest of the researcher. The choice of methods therefore depends on the type of data you need to collect to be able to test your hypotheses or answer your research questions. We do need to recognise, however, that there are debates between social researchers in terms of the overall approaches to gathering data which derive from different ontological and epistemological perspectives on the social world and how we can study it. This has been described as the qualitative/quantitative debate.

Qualitative v. quantitative: the debate

A look at the history of social research and the development of social research methods (see our brief history in A2) would suggest that there is a qualitative/quantitative divide between social researchers and that there has been heated debate over the past 50 years with regard to the value of quantitative or qualitative approaches to collecting and analysing data. As we have seen in A2, the different approaches are typically linked with different views on how the social world is seen and understood and how we can know about the social phenomena within our social world. Social research methods have developed along with these views. For example, quantitative methods in the social sciences were developed from those used in the physical sciences. These are predicated on the notions that: (a) the world has a physical reality, (b) it is possible to measure all the phenomena that occur, and (c) the results of such experimental measurement will be the same whenever it is repeated. Within some social sciences (particularly psychology and, to some extent, sociology) these processes have been successfully adapted as social research approaches.

Alongside this in other disciplines, most notably anthropology, methods of studying societies developed which involved the researcher closely with the members of the society themselves, in some cases living alongside for a time. These researchers were observing and listening to people within their own context and the data they were gathering came directly from the naturally occurring events and situations of the social world. An early example, written originally in 1955, is *Street Corner Society: Social Structure of an Italian Slum* (Whyte, 1993). This approach to studying the social world evolved into what has become known as a qualitative approach to collecting and working with data and methods of data collection have been developed that enable social researchers to gather and work with data produced by the research participants themselves.

The latter part of the twentieth century saw developments in both the quantitative (use of computers and the development of statistical analysis) and qualitative approaches (development of feminist research, new data collection and analysis methods and computer software to aid analysis). However, some boundaries between the two approaches remain and within one discipline or area of research a particular approach can still be dominant and thus can influence the choice of methods that are acceptable for use by student researchers. Recent years have seen some of these disciplinary boundaries broken through with, for example, increasing numbers of research projects within the medical sciences, which have traditionally designed research based on gathering statistical data, taking a qualitative approach to research.

What is . . .

The difference between quantitative, qualitative and mixed methods
- *Quantitative research methods* are primarily concerned with gathering and working with data that is structured (A3) and can be represented numerically. As we

saw in **A2**, quantitative data is typically gathered when a positivist epistemological approach is taken and data is collected that can be statistically analysed.

- *Qualitative research methods* are primarily concerned with stories and accounts including subjective understandings, feelings, opinions and beliefs. As we saw in **A2**, qualitative data is typically gathered when an interpretivist epistemological approach is taken and when the data collected is the words or expressions of the research participants themselves (**A2**, **A3**).
- *Mixed methods* can best be thought of as combining qualitative and quantitative methods in a way that is best for a specific research project.

As shown in **A2** and **A3**, the data about the social world that is available to us does depend on the ontological (the way the social world is seen to be and what can be assumed about the nature and reality of the social phenomena that make up the social world) and epistemological (what can be known about the social world) approaches the researcher takes. In practice, different approaches do result in the collection of different types of data which in turn require different data collection methods. In **A3** we looked at different types of data, and the distinctions between structured (quantitative) and semi-structured/unstructured (qualitative) data are the most relevant here. We can use these ideas to set out the key features of quantitative and qualitative approaches to data collection and analysis before going on to consider ways of choosing the methods that will help you to answer your research questions or test your hypotheses.

Table B4.1 Features of quantitative and qualitative approaches

Quantitative	Qualitative
Ontological and epistemological approaches are **positivist** (assumes that the social world is real)	Ontological and epistemological approaches are **interpretivist** (assumes that reality is a social construct)
Research questions may be set out as testable hypotheses	Research questions may be developed using subsidiary questions
The research question can be answered (or hypothesis tested) by counting events and using statistical analysis	The research question can be answered by describing and explaining events and gathering participants' understandings, beliefs and experiences
Researcher normally knows what he is looking for	Researcher may only have a general idea of what he is looking for
Research design/strategy is usually fixed before data collection	Research design/strategy may be fluid and evolutionary
Objective (researcher is not part of the research)	Subjective (researcher is involved as a social being)
Often uses tools (such as surveys or questionnaires) to collect data	Usually no use of tools: the researcher can be seen as the main instrument for collecting data
Data is often represented by numerical or named codes	Data may be in any form
It may be possible to generalise from the data	Not usually possible to generalise from the data

Example B4.1

A darts match

It is Wednesday evening at 9.45 p.m. Steve and Tony, who are second-year students at the University of Anywhere, are playing darts in the Students' Union bar. Steve is reading Sociology and Tony is studying Social Policy. It is the end of the summer exams and they are both feeling relieved that another year is over. To celebrate, they have had several drinks. The bar is busy and quite noisy. There is a crowd of rugby players at the bar who are very loud.

Tony has found it a difficult year. He has had a number of personal issues that have meant that he needed to go home more often than he would have liked and he has found some of the academic work quite challenging. He is feeling short of money because he has not had time to have a job this term. Steve has had a busy year too (he works part-time in the library) but is in a really good mood because he has a new girlfriend whom he will be seeing later in the evening.

They are playing 301 (starting and ending on a double). Both are good players, but Tony has won many more games during the last year. The throws they make are as follows:

Throw	Steve	Tony
1	Double 20, 18, 12 (231 left)	20, 20, 5 (301 left)
2	19, double 19, treble 7 (153 left)	Double 19, bull, 19 (194 left)
3	20, treble 1, treble 20 (72 left)	19, 19, 19 (137 left)
4	Treble 20, 6, double 3.	

Steve wins the game and Tony buys him a drink. Soon afterwards they go their separate ways.

Some things to think about:

1. If you wanted to research the events set out above, what are you trying to find out?
2. Would you choose qualitative or quantitative research methods?
3. Would your results be different depending on your choice of methods?

Some reasons for using quantitative methods:

- The actual game of darts is easy to research in this way.
- The variables (number of darts thrown, score for each dart) are numeric and it would be possible to use statistical analysis.
- It would be possible (over time) to calculate a player's chance of winning and to produce details (for example) of average scores.
- Darts leagues use quantitative analysis if they need to calculate a player's handicap.

Some reasons for using qualitative methods:

- It would be possible to learn more about the context of the game (timing, location, players' mood, and so on).

- It may be possible to learn how external influences (for example, the noise made by other people in the bar) impacted on the individual players.
- It may be possible to understand why one player did better than the other in this setting.

Some reasons for using mixed methods:

If the two methods above were combined, then we would have two sorts of information which we could use together, which would make our research better.

Mixed methods

While some researchers will primarily (or in some cases, totally) research using one approach, increasingly social researchers are drawing on either qualitative or quantitative approaches to gathering data or using both in mixed-methods approaches. Example B4.1 illustrates that studying any social phenomena (in this case a darts match) can be undertaken from different perspectives and to get a holistic picture of what is happening we may need to gather a range of different types of data using different methods. Which methods we choose depends on our research questions and how we define the concepts within them (A4).

In our example, we could choose to analyse the success of the darts match in numeric terms (quantitative), but we could also choose to analyse it in terms of the players' moods, stresses, preoccupations and so on. To do either would give us interesting results. However, if our main focus is to consider why, in this case, Tony lost the match, then we need both types of data as well as perhaps some historical data about previous matches. The most useful way to study the situation would be to include a combination of qualitative and quantitative procedures – or mixed methods.

A mixed-methods approach to choosing data collection methods should come from the research questions and show that the research questions can best be answered using both types of data. Sometimes one research question (or subsidiary) question demands quantitative data while another requires qualitative data; in other cases both qualitative and quantitative data may be required to answer one research question.

Think about it . . .

In **A4** we developed a research question concerning unemployment and mental health.

What are the impacts of long-term unemployment on people's mental health?

1. After operationalising the concepts of *unemployment* and *mental health* we refined the question to:

What are the impacts on how people who have had paid work feel about themselves and their lives when they have been without any paid work for more than a year?

What type of data do you think you would need to gather (and from whom) to answer this question?

2. Another way of operationalising *mental health* suggested in **A4** was:

Presence or absence of clinically diagnosed mental disorders

What type of data do you think you would need to gather (and from whom) to answer the question if this was your operational definition of mental health?

Now see our suggested answers on p. 146.

Qualitative and quantitative methods can be used in combination in a number of different ways.

Qualitative methods can be used:

- *before* quantitative

  Qualitative approaches enable the researcher to explore concepts in more depth with the research participants and to hear them talk about concepts in their own words (like mental health – see the 'Think about it . . .' box above). This can be a useful way of beginning to research a topic with which the researcher is unfamiliar or about which little research has already been done. Operational definitions can be developed or tested and this can be helpful in ensuring that the wording of structured questions in, for example, questionnaires, is commonly understood and meaningful to the research participants. From such qualitative data more structured data collection questions can be developed. Taking a qualitative approach can also help the researcher to identify and check out which aspects of a topic are most important and meaningful to the research participants and this may then provide the ideas for developing hypotheses or subsidiary research questions (**A4**).

- *alongside* quantitative

  Both approaches can be used alongside each other with each type of data contributing to answering either the same or different research questions.

- *after* quantitative

  Qualitative approaches may be used after quantitative ones to enable the researcher to explore some of the issues raised in the quantitative data in more depth. Quantitative data may be gathered that helps the researcher to identify small groups of people who are different or have interesting experiences and a more in-depth approach to collecting data from them will enable the researcher to explore issues in depth. In the example in the 'Think about it . . .' box above, an initial questionnaire to unemployed people might be used to identify those who perceive themselves as having mental-health problems and qualitative approaches may then be used to explore these perceptions in more depth with a small group of individuals (**C4**) or in a focus group (**C5**).

While a mixed-methods approach often means gathering both quantitative and qualitative data, this is not necessarily the case. It may be that you choose two different ways of gathering quantitative data – for example – using a questionnaire survey and working with secondary data. Or you may decide to gather qualitative data using both semi-structured interviews and participant observation (**C6**). Using two or more ways of gathering data to help you to answer your research question(s) can help you to check the validity of your data. This process is called **triangulation** as it reflects the process of triangulation used in mapping – pinpointing one point by measuring the distance and angle from two other points. In social research, collecting and working with data from different sources but on the same topic can help us to cross-check our findings.

triangulation
A measure of research quality, meaning that if different types of data are collected to address the same research question, each set of data can be used to check the findings from the others.

If we find that there are discrepancies or anomalies in the data from different sources or using different approaches then we need to consider why this may be so. In some cases this may be explained by the intentional use of different operational definitions as in the 'Think about it . . .' example, or it may be that there are different perspectives or understandings on the issues that using different methods of collecting data has highlighted. For example, people may discuss some issues quite differently in a focus group from the way people will talk about the issue when interviewed individually. This, in itself, may be an interesting finding or it may make us question whether our data collection tools – in this case our interview and focus group guides – have produced different responses because of wording differences, a different emphasis on questions by the interviewer or the use of different interviewers.

Think about it . . .
Suggested answers

Question 1

In the refined research question the emphasis is on how people who are unemployed feel about themselves and their lives. This suggests that the data should come from the unemployed people themselves and that the data would be best gathered in a semi-structured format – that is, allowing people to use their own words to describe their experience.

Appropriate methods

- Semi-structured interviews (**C4**)
- Focus groups (**C5**).

An alternative may be a questionnaire to unemployed people which included a set of questions (e.g. Likert scaled statements) relating to self-perceptions of mental health (**C3**).

Question 2

Data may be available from unemployed people themselves or (perhaps more accurately) from medical records. In order to be able to establish whether there were significant numbers of unemployed people with clinically diagnosed mental disorders, large numbers of cases would be needed (**B5**).

Appropriate methods

- Secondary data may be available (**C9**)
- Questionnaire to unemployed people (**C3**)
- Questionnaire to doctors/psychiatrist concerning their patients (**C3**).

So what is the way forward?

If your research topic is about possible links between unemployment and mental health, you may well want to include data that relates to mental health as a clinical diagnosis *and* to self-perceptions of mental health. This would enable you to both describe the extent of diagnosed mental (ill) health among people who are unemployed *and* to explore in more depth how unemployed people feel and experience unemployment and how they do or do not link this to how they feel about themselves and their lives.

So if your research questions required data relating to both approaches to operationalising *mental health*, then you may want to choose the method that enables you to include both aspects in one data collection method – *a questionnaire.*

However, this approach would require you to develop a series of questions to measure each person's perceptions of their mental health and would not enable you to hear some unemployed people describe and explain their feelings about themselves and their lives *in their own words*.

What approaches would you take?

Choosing methods

In terms of data collection and analysis the key difference between quantitative and qualitative approaches is the way the data that is collected is structured and by whom.

Quantitative approaches gather and work with data that is:

- structured – categorised or coded so that it can be counted;
- structured by the researcher – the researcher decides on both the questions that are asked and the type of answer that can be given (often a choice between a set of categories or answers).

Qualitative approaches gather and work with data that is:

- constructed by the research participant in their own way;
- interpreted and structured by the researcher as part of the analytical process.

Data collection methods are designed to best produce the type of data that can be worked with taking each approach and some are listed in Table B4.2.

Table B4.2 Matching quantitative and qualitative approaches to data collection methods

Approach	Data collection methods
Quantitative	Surveys and questionnaires which ask the same questions of usually large numbers of people or cases
	Secondary quantitative data which is available for further analysis
	Content analysis - counting the number of cases of different words or ideas in written or spoken material
	Observation - counting the number of occurrences of different events
	Case records/formats with ready structured information
Qualitative	Semi-structured/unstructured interviews which enable research participants to talk about a set of questions or topics in their own way
	Focus groups - a semi-structured facilitated discussion with a small group of people
	Gathering documents relating to the research questions and asking questions of the documents
	Narrative - gathering people's stories to analyse how the story is told
	Participant or non-participant observation of a situation or social context

Choosing a qualitative, quantitative or mixed-methods approach is only one of the decisions you need to make about what data collection methods to use. In A3 we identified different ways of thinking about data and these provide some useful ideas about the way we can use different data collection methods. At the end of A3 we suggested that you think about your own research topic in terms of the sort of data you could gather and work with. At this stage we can begin to link thinking about the sorts of data you might collect with the practicalities of choosing data collection methods that will enable you to do this. The data collection methods are each discussed in detail in **C3–C9** and we suggest that you read about each of the methods you are considering before making your final decision.

Choosing methods is also a practical, and to some extent pragmatic, decision. All researchers work within limited resources, with a variety of skills and with access to some, but not all, potential sources of data. If you are a student researcher you will need to choose your methods on the basis of the resources, particularly of time and money, your skills and the access you may have to data sources.

Use the checklist below to help you think about the methods you might use.

Your research

Thinking about your *research questions*: what sort of data could you gather and work with?

PRIMARY OR SECONDARY DATA?	Yes ✓
Has data that would help you to address your research questions been collected by others?	
What sort of data is it?	
Do you have access to the data?	
Do you know how it was collected?	
If you want to know more about using secondary data read C9	
Are you able to collect data yourself?	
Do you have access to people, situations or cases from which you can gather data?	
Which data collection methods do you have the skills and resources to use?	
Do you want to include reflexive data (your own understandings and experiences of the research)?	
Read C2 and the methods you are interested in C3–C9 with your own skills and resources in mind	

SPOKEN, WRITTEN OR NON-VERBAL/VISUAL?	Yes ✓
Is there written material that may be used as data, for example, policy documents, diaries, case notes?	
Do you have access to the data?	
Do you know how and why the material was produced?	
Read C8 and C9 on collecting documentary and secondary data	
Will you be able to collect written answers to your questions?	
Have you considered using questionnaires to gather data? Read C3	
Is there visual data that may be used?	
Is there data that is communicated non-verbally?	
Can events be observed?	
Are there photographic or video records?	
Have you considered using observational methods? Read C6	
Do you have access to people who can talk about the research topic in ways that will help you to answer your research questions?	
Read C4 and C5 and consider using semi-structured interviews or focus groups	

INDIVIDUAL OR GROUP?	Yes ✓
Do you want to collect information about and/or from individuals?	
Do you need factual, attitude, opinion data from different groups of people?	
Do you have information that will enable you to identify the people you need to gather data from?	
Do you have the resources to gather data from a large number of people (say, more than 50)?	
Read C3 and consider using a self-completion questionnaire	
Do you want to gather people's stories, experiences and understandings?	
Do you have access to people who have experiences, ideas and opinions that are relevant to your research topic?	

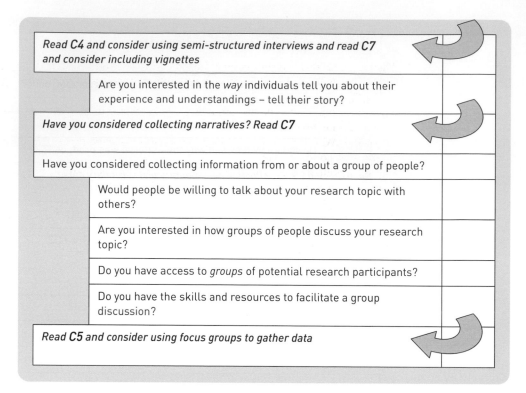

	Read **C4** and consider using semi-structured interviews and read **C7** and consider including vignettes	
	Are you interested in the *way* individuals tell you about their experience and understandings – tell their story?	
	*Have you considered collecting narratives? Read **C7***	
	Have you considered collecting information from or about a group of people?	
	Would people be willing to talk about your research topic with others?	
	Are you interested in how groups of people discuss your research topic?	
	Do you have access to *groups* of potential research participants?	
	Do you have the skills and resources to facilitate a group discussion?	
	*Read **C5** and consider using focus groups to gather data*	

Having considered a number of different data collection methods, you should return to your research questions and think about how those research questions can best be addressed – how you are going to gather data that, when analysed, will enable you to at least begin to answer those questions. Having chosen your methods you should also be able to justify your choice of methods in relation to your research questions – to show that you have made an informed choice and that you are aware of the strengths and limitations of the methods you have chosen. The relevant chapter in **C3–C9** will help you to do this.

Your research

List your research questions/hypotheses and any subsidiary questions, the types of data you might gather to answer/test each, and the data collection method you are thinking of using.

Research questions	Types of data	Data collection methods
1.		
2.		
3.		
4.		

References and further reading

Bryman, A. (2006) Integrating quantitative and qualitative research: how is it done? *Qualitative Research*, 6: 97–113 (online version available at: http://qrj.sagepub.com/cgi/content/abstract/6/1/97).

Burke Johnson, R. and Onwuegbuzie, A. J. (2004) Mixed methods research: a research paradigm whose time has come, *Educational Researcher*, 33(7): 14–26.

Creswell, J. W. (2003) *Research Design: Qualitative, Quantitative and Mixed Methods Approaches*, 2nd edn, London: Sage.

Foss, C. and Ellefsen, B. (2002) The value of combining qualitative and quantitative approaches in nursing research by means of method triangulation, *Methodological Issues in Nursing Research*, 40(2): 242–8.

Plano, V. L. and Cresswell, J. W. (eds) (2008) *The Mixed Methods Reader*, London: Sage.

Silverman, D. (2004) *Qualitative Research: Theory, Method and Practice*, 2nd edn, London: Sage.

Whyte, W. F. (1993) *Street Corner Society: Social Structure of an Italian Slum*, 4th edn, Chicago University Press.

CHAPTER B5
Sampling

Contents

In context

In this section we look at the ways of deciding which data to gather to include in your research. We are rarely in a position to collect data from all the cases, contexts and situations that are relevant to our research questions. If we are going to select only some of the potential data sources – people, documents, cases – then we have to make some decisions about how we are going to do that. Only in the ten-yearly census is data collected about every member of the UK population, and even then there are some groups – for example, homeless people – who are often excluded. If you are using secondary data or documentary data you will still need to think about how you decide what to include, and to be aware that somebody else – a researcher or an official perhaps – has already made some decisions about who or what is included in the data or document. Broadly speaking, there are two ways of approaching the task: a probability sample or a purposive sample, and which way you choose depends on the nature of your research question, the data you want to gather and whether you are gathering quantitative or qualitative data (or both). However, while the two approaches are quite different, they can be regarded as being at two ends of a spectrum, and you may find that you are using a combination of approaches – particularly if you are using a mixture of data collection methods.

PART B: Preparing for research

- B1: Planning a research project
- B2: Reviewing the literature
- B3: Research design
- B4: Choosing methods
- ▶ **B5: Sampling**
- B6: Research proposals

The selection of some cases from a larger group of potential cases is called sampling. Our approach to sampling is closely related to our choice of research design and methods, and reference will be made to research designs and choice of methods considered in B3 and B4. Throughout this section we will use researching volunteering as the basis of our examples.

Example B5.1

Is volunteering good for you?

[Volunteering is] an activity that involves spending time, unpaid, doing something that aims to benefit the environment or individuals or groups other than (or in addition to) close relatives. (Commission on the Future of Volunteering, 2008)

A report prepared for the Office of the Third Sector in the Cabinet Office by the National Centre for Social Research and the Institute for Volunteering Research found that in 2007 just under three-fifths of their population sample had been involved in formal volunteering with an organisation, with two-fifths doing so at least once a month. Volunteers said that the benefits of volunteering were enjoyment, personal achievement and satisfaction in seeing the results of their volunteering; 51 per cent said that it made them feel less stressed and 44 per cent said it improved their physical health (Low *et al.*, 2007).

We will also bear in mind throughout this chapter that time and other resources are important factors in the choice of data collection methods and approaches to sampling. Research can be undertaken at many different levels, with researchers bringing a wide range of skill resources, time and financial support. Here we aim to provide guidance on the choice of sampling approach for a university student undertaking research as part of a programme of study, but we will also refer to larger-scale and more heavily resourced research examples. This will enable you to have a better understanding of other research which you may read and use as part of your study.

Your research

Research quality check – generalisability and transferability

One of the first questions we need to address when thinking about how we are going to choose our data sources is how we will want to use the data when we have gathered it.

1. Do we want to be able to use the data from our sample to tell us about the population from which it was drawn? If, for example, we are collecting data about school pupils, do we want to be able to show how the data from our sample can be *generalised* – that is, said to be likely to be similar to that of *all* school pupils in the UK, in our local town or to school pupils in state-run schools?

2. Do we want to be able to collect data that will enable us to explore in depth the experiences, opinions or behaviour of particular people, cases or situations? Are we, for example, asking questions about the way particular educational settings impact on the behaviour of particular groups of school pupils? We may then want to consider how far our findings could be *transferred* to other similar situations or settings.

We will consider these questions in relation to each different approach to sampling.

An important note: although throughout this chapter we will often refer to and use examples that are based on selecting individual *people* to take part in research, much of what is included here is appropriate for the selection of *cases*, *documents* and time and context *periods* for observation. Selection is always part of research design, and you must be aware of the criteria and approach you are using when you decide to collect data from any sources. The relevant sections in **C3** and **D3** will provide material to consider in addition to this chapter.

Approaches to sampling

In Figure B5.1 we have arranged the different approaches to sampling in a spectrum. At one end of the spectrum are the sampling approaches that are based on statistical theory, and which aim to produce a sample that can be shown to be highly representative of the whole population – or all the potential cases – in terms of relevant criteria: **probability samples**. At the other end of the spectrum are approaches to sampling that are concerned with selecting (usually fewer) cases that will best enable the researcher to explore the research questions in depth, and to work with the data collected to identify and explore theoretical ideas: **purposive** and **theoretical samples**.

probability sample
A sample that can be shown to be highly representative of the whole population – or all the potential cases – in terms of relevant criteria.

purposive sample
A sample of selected cases that will best enable the researcher to explore the research questions in depth.

theoretical sample
A sample of selected cases that will best enable the researcher to explore theoretical ideas.

population
In statistical terms, population refers to the total number of cases that can be included as research subjects.

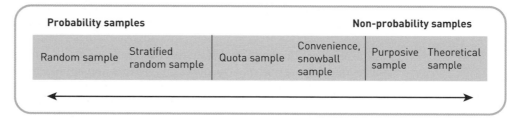

Figure B5.1 A spectrum of different approaches to sampling

Statistical sampling – or selecting a probability sample

One approach to sampling is to use probability or statistical theory to help you to select a sample that is representative of the **population** from which it is taken. This approach is most commonly used when designing experimental and survey research (**B3**) and where the data being gathered is quantitative in nature. Selecting a sample in this way enables the researcher to undertake a statistical analysis of the data (**D3**).

❓ What is . . .

Population
In statistical terms, population refers to the total number of cases that can be included as research subjects. For example, a population may be:
- all the people who live in a country;
- all the students studying at a particular university;
- all the undergraduate students studying sociology at any UK university at a particular time;
- all the newspaper articles published in the UK referring to student volunteering during a particular month.

The key characteristics of a probability sample are as follows:

- Each member of the population has a known (and usually equal) chance of being selected for the sample. This assumes that the members of the population are known – that is, that they can be individually identified. If this is not the case, then other sampling strategies may need to be adopted.

- Each sample member is chosen at random and it cannot be predicted which members will be chosen.
- The sample is usually selected to be representative of the population on the basis of certain known characteristics, for example, age, gender, socio-economic group and so on, which are relevant to the research study.

Random samples and stratified samples

In a random sample every case has an equal chance of being selected.

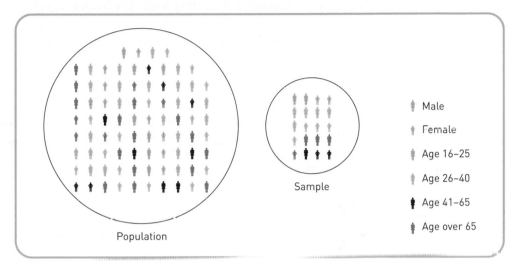

Figure B5.2 Selecting a random sample from a population of men and women aged over 16 years (A)

A random sample may or may not include cases with particular characteristics in the same proportions as they are found in the population. So in Figure B5.2 the sample does include the age groups represented by colours and male and female symbols in similar (but not exact) proportions.

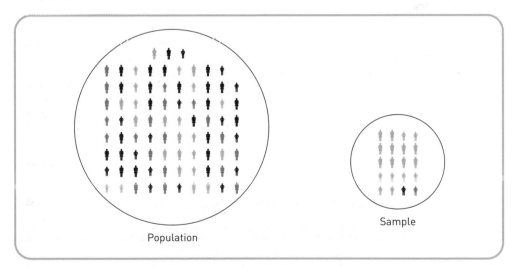

Figure B5.3 Selecting a random sample from a population of men and women aged over 16 years (B)

In Figure B5.3, you will see that the random sample includes all the green symbols and only two others. Taking a random sample can *potentially* produce this type of result, and would clearly have implications for research that was designed to look at the different experiences of, for example, people aged 16 to 25 years and those aged 41–65 years, as only one of the second group has been included.

The probability of selecting a sample that is so unrepresentative of the population is low, but it is one that must be considered (see below). To improve the representativeness of the sample we can introduce some **stratification**, while still ensuring that all the population cases have an equal chance of being included in the sample.

stratification
A method of organising a population in order to improve the representativeness of a sample.

Think about it . . .
Statistical probability of selecting a sample from a population

There are many possible samples of 20 people that could be selected from 100 people. The possibilities increase if the population is much larger – for example, there are even more ways of selecting 1,000 people from 50,000,000. Statistical probability theory can be used to show that most of these samples will closely resemble the characteristics of the population. If, for example, we found from our sample that, on average, people who visited their doctor infrequently undertook volunteering activities five times a year, how likely is it that people in the whole population (in this case, the doctor's patient list) who visit their doctor infrequently also have an average of volunteering five times a year?

Using statistical theory, we can say that if we took lots of different samples from the same population, we would find that the distribution of the average (mean) number of volunteering activities would be a normal distribution. This is a bell-shaped curve graph, as shown in Figure B5.4 below. If we assume that the population mean is at the high point of the bell curve (that is, coinciding with the highest numbers of sample means), then we can say that our particular sample mean will lie within two **standard deviations** of the central point in 95 per cent of cases. The standard deviation is a statistical measure of how the cases – in this case the averages (means) of each of our samples – are distributed around the mean (in this case the assumed population mean).

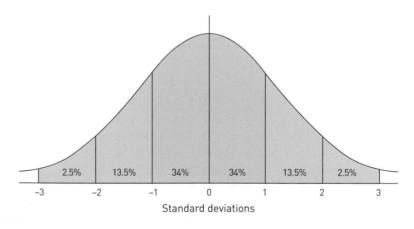

Figure B5.4 A normal distribution

🔍 What is . . .

Standard deviation
The standard deviation is a statistical measure of how the cases – in this example the averages (means) of each of our samples – are distributed around the mean (in this case the assumed population mean).

Your research

Further reading for students who want to understand more about statistical sampling: D. B. Wright and K. London (2009) *First (and Second) Steps in Statistics*, 2nd edn, London: Sage.

Example B5.2

Sampling: volunteering and health

A doctor wants to explore the links between volunteering and physical and mental health among her adult patients who are aged 65 or under. She has heard of some research that shows that people who volunteer tend to be healthier. She would like to find out which of her patients do volunteer, but does not have the resources to survey all of them.

She has two ideas about how she might sample her 5,000 patients.

(a) She might ask her administrator for an alphabetical list of all her patients aged between 16 and 65 years and then select 500 (1 in 10) patients at random using random number tables to decide which patients to include (random number tables are lists of numbers generated at random, usually by a computer).

(b) She might devise a questionnaire and ask her receptionist to give this out to the first 500 patients aged between 16 and 65 years to come to the surgery during a particular month.

Which of these, (a) or (b), would be a random sample?

In Example B5.2, approach (a) is a good method for selecting a random sample – although it still may not be the best way of getting a useful sample, as we shall see. First, though, let us consider what the problem is with approach (b). Although we cannot predict who would be the first 500 people to visit the surgery, people who have chronic diseases or who need to see their doctor on a regular basis would have a much higher chance of being included in the sample than those who rarely have cause to visit their doctor's surgery. As the research is trying to distinguish between people on the basis of their physical/mental health and ill health, this sample would not be an appropriate way to select people for this research.

Let's now consider sample approach (a) in a little more depth by thinking about the research question. The researcher is interested in people who do and do not volunteer, and in their health. From what she knows about the subject, she suspects that there will be differences that relate to people's ages, genders and perhaps ethnic group. She also knows that most younger people are in good health, and that as people get older they are less likely to be so. If she wants to be able to explore these questions, she needs to ensure that her sample is going to include all of these different combinations of people. To do this, she will need to know more about her population, so that she can select a sample that is representative of the population in relation to these characteristics.

proxy definition
A 'rule of thumb' definition which stands in for a more detailed and sophisticated way of defining something.

To do this, the doctor will first need to find out the proportions of her patients who are in each of the categories. She might start by drawing this diagrammatically, as in Example B5.3. Note that she has decided to use a **proxy definition** of health by separating her patients into two groups – those who visit the doctor's surgery infrequently, and those who are frequent attenders. This proxy definition is standing in for a more detailed and sophisticated way of defining health, as a means of ensuring that the sample includes the range of people she needs in order to be able to address her research questions.

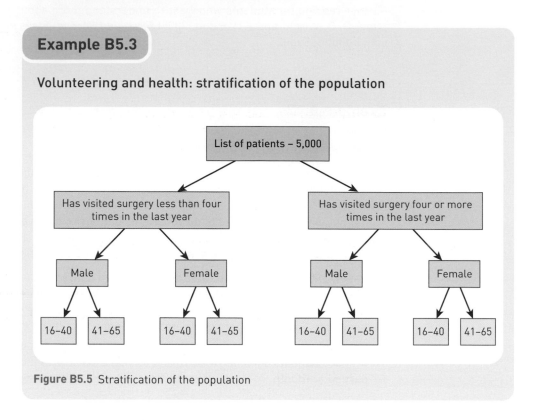

Example B5.3

Volunteering and health: stratification of the population

Figure B5.5 Stratification of the population

Her sample, then, should include the sample proportions of people in each group. For example, if there are 500 women aged between 41 and 65 years who have visited the surgery less than four times during the last year, then:

$$500/5,000 \times 500 = 50$$

So 50 women in this category should be included in the sample. These women can be selected at random from the list of 500 women in this category.

Think about it . . .

If there are 300 men aged 16–40 who are frequent attendees, how many should be included in a sample of 500?

What if there were just 30 men in this age group who were frequent attendees? Do you think this would be a sufficient sample of this group?

In this example, the population has been stratified, or organised into categories at three levels, to enable the doctor to select a sample that will help her to address her research questions. The levels of stratification are:

1. Frequency of visiting the surgery
2. Gender
3. Age.

Example B5.4

Volunteering and health

The doctor is also interested in the experiences of people from two minority ethnic groups among her patients. One group have lived in the area for many years, while the others are recent migrants who have lived in the area for only a year or so. Their ethnicity is recorded on their case notes. Each group is only a small percentage of her total patient list (both groups together make up about 5%, or 250), so her initial sample is likely to include just a few of each group. The doctor therefore decides to take an additional sample, made up of people from these two minority ethnic groups. In this case she selects a higher proportion of the total population, 1 in 2, to ensure that her sample is large enough to enable her to analyse her findings on the same variables of age and gender as her larger sample.

However, when she comes to analyse her data, she cannot simply add the two samples together, because the samples have been drawn using different **sampling fractions**, and patients of the two ethnic groups had the chance of being selected in both samples. The doctor can analyse the two samples and present the findings for each sample separately, and the findings from the two samples can be compared using percentages rather than raw numbers.

An alternative, or additional, approach would be to select two samples:

A: from the total population excluding the two ethnic groups – using a sampling fraction of 1 in 10;

B: from the two ethnic groups using a sampling fraction of 1 in 2.

Each sample would then be analysed separately and compared using percentages. Then, to analyse both samples together as representative of the total patient list, the doctor would need to reduce the weight of sample B. To do this she would need to divide any results from sample B by $10/2 = 5$ as the patients from the two ethnic groups were five times more likely to be selected than the other patients.

Table B5.1 Volunteering and health sample data

Gender	(1) Data from sample A	(2) Data from sample B	(3) Weighted data from sample B Column 2/5	(4) Total of sample A and weighted sample B Column 1 + Column 3
Male	225	75	15	240
Female	250	50	10	260
Total sample	475	125	25	500

Note that the data gathered from *all* those included in sample B is used and the weighting is applied to it. Do not be tempted to simply select, for example, 25 out of the 125 patients from the small ethnic groups to include and exclude the remainder.

Stratified samples are also used to enable researchers to minimise the time and resources required, particularly in large-scale interview surveys which draw samples from across a large geographical area. Most large-scale surveys undertaken by government departments take this approach, as the 'Real research' box on p. 160 shows. In this example, the researcher first selected wards (geographical, local government areas). By selecting geographical areas first, the researchers ensured that their sample would not be spread across *every* area of England and Wales. This is called a **cluster sample**, because the sample is clustered (in this case geographically) and thereby reduces the time and resources needed to access the selected cases. As you will see from the 'Real research' example, a stratified sample can be very complex. Few researchers have the time and resources to design and then gain access to such a large, complex sample. However, the example demonstrates the different elements and stages of a stratified sample which can be useful to a student researcher seeking to create a representative sample from a defined population.

cluster sample
A sample consisting of cases selected because of their proximity to one another.

Real research

The Citizenship Survey 2005

The Citizenship Survey 2005 was commissioned by the Home Office to find out the views of the population in England and Wales on a range of issues. The survey included questions about views on the locality, racial and religious discrimination, volunteering, and rights and responsibilities. Face-to-face interviews were carried out by interviewers from the National Centre for Social Research. The technical report on this research can be found at www.communities.gov.uk/publications/communities/2005citizenshipsurveytechnical (accessed 21 July 2009). Findings from the research can be found at www.communities.gov.uk/publications/communities/2005citizenshipsurveycross (accessed 21 July 2009).

The sample

A nationally representative sample of 10,000 adults in England and Wales, and an additional sample of 4,500 people from minority ethnic groups.

How was the sample selected?

A sample of addresses was drawn from the Royal Mail Postcode Address File using a two-stage sampling approach:

1. A random sample of 663 wards was selected using Census Area Statistics.
    (a) Before selection the wards were sorted into three groups according to the percentage of minority ethnic group population within the ward (less than 1%, 1–18%, over 18%).
    (b) Within these groups wards were sorted by Government Office Region.
    (c) Within each Government Office Region, wards were sorted into three groups based on the percentage of head of households in non-manual occupations.
    (d) Finally, within each group, wards were sorted by the proportion of males in the ward who were unemployed.
    (e) The sample of 663 wards was selected at random from the stratified list with the probability of inclusion being proportionate to the number of addresses within the ward.

2. Within each selected ward, 25 addresses were selected at random.
    (a) If an address included more than one household, the interviewer selected three households to interview at random using a systematic procedure.
    (b) One person aged 16 or over was randomly selected from each household by the interviewer, again using a systematic procedure.

The additional minority ethnic groups sample was drawn as follows:

1. The wards that had a relatively high proportion (over 18%) and medium proportion (1–18%) of people from minority ethnic groups were used for this sample.

   (a) In each of the medium density wards, the two addresses before and after the addresses already chosen were selected for screening. Respondents at the chosen addresses were asked if there were people from minority ethnic groups living at these addresses. If so, then the interviewer called at these addresses.

   (b) In the high density wards, an additional 110 addresses were chosen and screened by the interviewer for respondents from people from minority ethnic groups.

2. An additional sample of wards was drawn from a further 150 wards (not included in the core sample) with a high density population of people from minority ethnic groups. The same stratification process was used, and 110 addresses were selected for each ward. These were then screened for people from minority ethnic groups.

What was the response rate achieved?

Core sample

Of the 16,575 addresses selected:

  1,543 addresses: were not suitable – e.g. empty, non-residential, demolished

  338 addresses: no contact – unable to establish eligibility

  3,923 addresses: refused to take part

  595 addresses: unable to take part through e.g. illness, language

A total of 9,691 interviews were carried out.

Minority ethnic groups sample
7,171 households selected including eligible adults (i.e. from a minority ethnic group)
4,390 interviews were carried out

Probability sampling – the practicalities

If you are thinking of using probability sampling, there are a number of questions to think about at this stage.

What are the relevant characteristics of the population that should be represented in the sample?

At this stage, you should already be thinking about how you will analyse the data you gather, and be able to identify the characteristics or variables that you will be using to distinguish between different cases. For example, if it is clear from your research question or hypothesis that you will be looking for similarities and differences between people of different age groups, or between articles from different types of newspaper, then you will need to ensure that cases are selected to include these. By stratifying your population using these characteristics, you can ensure that you include similar proportions of each group in your sample to those in the population (as the doctor did in the example). If you keep in mind both your research questions and your plans for analysis, your sample will be designed to ensure that you are collecting data from cases that will provide data that can be used to address those questions.

Is there an accessible list – or sampling frame – of all the members of the population from which a sample can be drawn, and which gives the information required to be able to draw a stratified, representative sample?

sampling frame
A list of all the members of a population from which a sample may be drawn.

In many cases it will not be (easily) possible to draw up or have access to a list of all the members of the population from which the sample can be drawn (a **sampling frame**). This could be because, quite simply, no such list exists. When drawing a sample for the Citizenship Survey, the researchers were unable to use a list of all the addresses in the UK where people from minority ethnic groups lived, because no such list existed. Instead, the researchers used census data to identify the wards where people from minority ethnic groups were most likely to be found.

Even if a list of your population exists, you may not have access to the details about the people or cases on the list that you need in order to draw the sample. This may be because the information is confidential, or because the person who holds the list, sometimes called the 'gatekeeper', is unwilling to give you access to it. While the doctor in the earlier example did have access to her own patient list, she may be unwilling to give a student researcher access to the information required for the student to undertake the research on volunteering. There are a number of reasons that a gatekeeper may not give you access to the information you need to draw a sample. The data may be confidential and covered by the data protection legislation or the gatekeeper may have a professional or other responsibility for the people you wish to involve in your research and may be concerned for their well-being (A5). These are ethical issues and you may need to consider whether you will be able to access the people or settings in the way that you wished. Other reasons for denying access may relate to the gatekeeper's lack of time to help you or lack of interest in the research you are proposing, particularly if the research is not seen to be of value to the gatekeeper or her organisation.

If you do not have access to a population list, you may need to consider other approaches to gathering a sample, including **quota sampling** and **snowball sampling**, which are discussed later in this chapter – see pp. 164 and 166.

quota sampling
A sampling technique that selects a certain number, or quota, of cases, on the basis of their matching a number of criteria.

snowball sampling
A sampling technique where members of an initial sample are asked to identify others with the same characteristics as them, who the researcher then contacts.

sampling error
The likely variation of the sample mean from the population mean.

How large a sample should be drawn?

This is not an easy question, as a number of different aspects need to be taken into account. First of all, thinking statistically, it is generally the case that if you are selecting a representative random sample from a known population, increasing the sample size means that the generalisability of the sample data to the population increases, and the **sampling error**, or likely variation of the sample mean from the population mean, decreases. However, it is not the case that the bigger the population, the bigger the sample required. Market research and opinion poll organisations often depend on a sample size of 1,000 from the adult population of the UK as the basis of their research. It can be shown that the additional benefits derived from increasing the sample size become smaller as the sample size increases and the time and resource implications of increasing the sample size begin to take precedence over the marginal reduction of the sampling error.

However, for a student undertaking research with limited time and resources, the sample size is more likely to be influenced by the resources available and the ease of access to the sampled cases. Seek advice from your tutor or supervisor on this, as she will be able to advise you of any guidelines and look with you at the particular issues relating to your research. It is important, though, to be aware of the limitations of a smaller sample and to discuss these in your research report or dissertation.

A further matter to consider with regard to sample size: remember that, like the doctor in Example B5.2, you are likely to want to analyse data for groups within the sample – for example, look for differences between men and women of different age groups. If your overall sample is small, you will find that the data relating to (for example) men aged 16–24 years is based on very few cases. This will limit the usefulness of the data and may mean that you are not able to undertake the analyses you have planned.

A final point to remember is that there will be some non-responders – people who do not agree to take part in your research – and some whom you may not be able to contact.

It is advisable to select your sample with this in mind and to select at least 10% more than you hope to gain responses from.

Is there any bias within the sampling frame or the method of sampling which may affect the sample?

When considering your sampling frame – that is, the list of people or cases that may be included in your sample – you need to check that the list has not been compiled in such a way as to exclude particular cases or groups. It was noted earlier that even the official UK census cannot claim to include every member of the population. You need to be aware of cases and groups of people who may be missing from the list. In the volunteering example, we saw that collecting a sample by giving questionnaires to the first 500 patients to come to the surgery could **bias** the sample towards people who made more frequent visits to the doctor. In this example we might also consider the gender of the doctor and question whether male and female patients were equally likely to choose a female doctor. By selecting the sample from only her own patient list, the doctor may be selecting a sample that is biased towards people who made a particular choice.

Is the sample accessible? And likely to participate or respond?

Before drawing the sample, you also need to think about how accessible the sample you have chosen will be. Will the selected people or cases be available to you at the time you are required to carry out your data collection? Will you need to travel? If you are planning an email survey, will all of your sample have access to and be regular users of email? Are there likely to be any language or comprehension difficulties?

Here we are highlighting another source of potential bias, because you may not have the same access to all of your sample, and they may not all have the same opportunity to participate in your research. You should expect that there will be some people who will not participate in your research, and record evidence of the **non-response**. Non-response can occur for a variety of reasons:

- non-contact – the researcher is unable to contact the selected person;
- refusal – the selected person does not wish to take part in the research;
- the selected person is unable to take part through, for example, ill health, language or holidays;
- the selected person is not appropriate   usually because the information about the person was inaccurate.

As a researcher, you need to do what you can to minimise non-response. This is best done through good preparation and forethought.

bias
Prejudice in favour, or against, a group individual, perspective, etc.

non-response
This occurs wherever an invited participant declines to be involved in a research project, perhaps because they refuse, are ill or are inappropriate.

Your research

Research quality check: probability samples and generalisability

- Are there significant omissions from the population list which may lead to bias?
- Is the sample selected randomly?
- Are your analysis groupings sufficiently large (at least five cases in each group)?
- Have you considered bias that may be introduced through lack of access and non-response?
- Is the probability sample of sufficient size to support statistical analysis and claims of generalisability to the population?
- Have you included a discussion of the limitations of your sample in your research report or dissertation?

Non-probability sampling

We have already noted that when you are embarking on a small piece of research with limited time and resources, you are unlikely to be able to create a sample that is (a) large or (b) meets all the requirements of a random probability sample. In this section we introduce some approaches to sampling that are perhaps more suited to the scale of research work most students undertake. These approaches may be suitable for small-scale experimental and cross-sectional survey research designs.

Convenience sampling

With limited time and resources, student researchers may have little choice but to select a sample on the basis of its convenience or ease of access. In fact, if we look at a selection of research studies, we will often find that the context in which the research is set has been selected from a much wider range of possibilities because the researcher has easy access to it. Typically a student researcher may select an appropriate setting from which to obtain as many responses as possible, for example, her own university department, a community centre or meeting place, a shopping centre or a sports club.

Example B5.5

Volunteering and health

The doctor in our example begins by defining the population for her study as all her own patients; in other words, the patients to whom she has easy access. She is not attempting to draw a sample from the total adult population of the UK. However, she does go on to select a probability sample from her 'convenient' population.

Example B5.6

Student volunteering

A student interested in researching the prevalence and nature of volunteering among the student population decides to select participants from his own programme group and his hall of residence and email a questionnaire survey out to all those listed. He hopes for a good response, particularly from those he knows well!

In his dissertation, he shows that he understands the limitations of this approach by pointing out that, by using this sampling approach, those who live at home or in private lettings are likely to be under-represented and those who are on his programme, Social Policy, are over-represented. He discusses the possibility that Social Policy students are more likely to volunteer than others and that those students living at home may have different opportunities to volunteer from those who live in a hall of residence.

Quota sampling

This approach to sampling includes some of the features of a **stratified sample** (a sample that is selected to ensure that certain categories and groups of people and cases are included proportionate to their presence in the population) without the use of a complete list of all the people or cases in the population and can be a more convenient way of developing a sample. In fact, it is an approach taken by many market research organisations. If you have ever been approached in the street by an interviewer with a clipboard, asking you to be involved in some research about a new brand of crisps or detergent, it is likely that the interviewer has been given a quota of interviews to complete. You may have been approached because, for example, you are male, look as if you are aged between 18 and 25 years, and have a middle-class background. The interviewer will have been given a set of criteria which she has to meet, which may include:

Five male

Five female

Three aged 18–25

Four aged 26–45

Three aged 46–65

Six middle-class

Four working-class.

Interviewers will then look for individuals who fulfil at least one, but probably more than one of these criteria. In this example, the interviewer could achieve her quota by conducting just ten interviews, provided that all of her criteria are met according to the quota she has been given. The criteria are usually derived from population data, for example, local census data, and the quotas are worked out so that the sample of individuals selected will be in proportion to the prevalence of a particular characteristic (gender, age, ethnicity, etc.) in the population. The interviewer continues approaching potential interviewees until all the quota have been filled. The interviewer will, of course, sometimes get it wrong and approach people who look as if they fulfil the quota but, on questioning them, find that they fall into the wrong age or social class grouping for her quota. The interview will then usually be ended.

Example B5.7

Volunteering and health

The doctor could use a quota sample to gather a sample of patients by giving the receptionist a quota of patients, using age and gender as the criteria, to approach and ask to take part in the survey of volunteering. This would ensure that a range of patients were included on the basis of age and gender. However, it would not include information about the frequency of visiting the doctor, and the sample would be biased towards those who attend more frequently.

Can you think of a way that this frequency of visiting could also be included in the quota criteria?

The example has given us some clues to the limitations of quota sampling.

(a) *Choice of criteria.* It may be difficult to choose criteria that are both useable in practice and relate to the research questions. For example, how would you decide whether a person in the street was middle-class or working-class?

(b) *Bias towards particular groups of people.* The choice of place and time to select the sample of participants is likely to exclude certain groups and give other groups a much higher chance of being included. Market research is often carried out in town centre shopping areas during working hours, i.e. between 9 a.m. and 5 p.m. People who are busy or are in a hurry to catch a train or go to a meeting are more likely to refuse to take part in an interview, while those who are not busy, or are perhaps unemployed, may have more time and be more willing to participate. In addition, interviewers (and researchers!) may be more likely to approach people who look to them as if they are likely to take part, or who look friendly and less likely to refuse.

(c) *Non-random selection.* Data from a quota sample of people cannot be regarded as statistically generalisable to the population, because the way the sample is collected does not give every member of the population a calculable chance of being included.

Snowball sampling

As we noted above, some populations are quite hard to find because there are no lists of such people or cases, nor are there obvious places where the cases may be found. These 'hidden' populations are sometimes associated with behaviour that is seen as less socially acceptable or criminal. However, all sorts of other behaviour and characteristics can be hidden from the researcher, for example, their 'informal volunteering' as in Example B5.8. A snowball sample starts with a few people who are known to be the type of people the researcher wants to involve in the research. The researcher may make contact with them through a shared meeting place, an internet site or through personal contacts of her own. Then each member of the initial group is asked to suggest others with the same characteristics, and the researcher will then contact them, and so on. Given that people who have certain characteristics or behaviour are often part of a network of similar people, this approach to sampling can be quite fruitful, particularly if it is combined with a quota sampling approach which seeks out people with specific characteristics, for example different ages and ethnicities.

Example B5.8

Informal volunteering

A researcher wants to include 'informal' volunteers in her research. She has defined an 'informal' volunteer as someone who carries out tasks and activities for others who are not family members, without payment. She is particularly interested in people who help out their neighbours on a fairly regular basis by, for example, doing their shopping or gardening.

She selects a neighbourhood and begins by identifying a few 'informal' volunteers through visiting the local church, mosque and community centre. She then asks them if they know other people in their street or nearby who are also 'informal' volunteers, and so on, until she has built up a sample that covers most of the streets in the neighbourhood.

Comparing a non-probability sample with the population

The characteristics of a non-probability sample can in some cases be compared with those of the total population. If comparable data about the whole population is available – for example, the proportions of male and female and the proportions in each age or socio-economic group for the area in which the research is carried out – this can be used to see how closely the sample resembles the population. Although a non-probability sample cannot be used to generalise to the population *statistically* as a probability sample can, in research where the non-probability sample does resemble that of the population closely, this should be discussed in the research report.

Your research

Research quality check: non-probability samples

- Have you clearly set out how the sample was drawn up?
- Have you identified possible sources of bias and, where possible, tried to address these?
- Have you set out the limitations of your sample in terms of what claims you are able to make from your findings?
- Have you identified the strengths of your sample in terms of good use of resources, identification of suitable cases, response rates and suitability to address the research questions?

Purposive sampling

The final approach to sampling may be regarded as being at the other end of the spectrum we introduced at the beginning of this chapter. **Purposive sampling** and theoretical sampling are both approaches that are non-probability based samples and are quite deliberately so. These approaches are generally associated with small, in-depth studies with research designs that are based on the gathering of qualitative data and focused on the exploration and interpretation of experiences and perceptions. This includes case studies, some cross-sectional studies, ethnographical and Grounded Theory designs (B3).

In these approaches to sampling, there is no attempt to create a sample that is statistically representative of a population. Rather, people or cases are chosen 'with purpose' to enable the researcher to explore the research questions or develop a theory. The cases are selected on the basis of characteristics or experiences that are directly related to the researcher's area of interest and her research questions, and will allow the researcher to study the research topic in-depth. The cases chosen are those that can reveal and illuminate the most about the research area.

 **What is . . .**

Purposive sampling
Ritchie and Lewis (2003: 79) usefully set out different approaches that may be taken to creating a sample:
- **Homogeneous sample** – where all the cases belong to the same group or have the same characteristic. This enables an in-depth and detailed investigation of a particular social phenomenon.
- **Heterogeneous or maximum variation sample** – here, ensuring that there is variation between cases means that cross-cutting common themes can be identified.
- **Stratified purposive sampling** – perhaps the most common way of selecting a purposive sample is to select from within groups of cases where there is some variation between the groups to enable the groups to be compared. The groups may be derived on the basis of information already held from a survey or population data.
- **Extreme case sampling** – here cases are chosen because they are extreme or deviant, and can therefore shed light on a social phenomenon from a different perspective from that which is normally taken.
- **Intensity sampling** – cases are selected that 'strongly represent the phenomena of interest'.

- **Typical case sampling** – here cases are selected that can be regarded as typical or 'normal'.
- **Critical case sampling** – cases are selected on the basis of the way they are 'critical' to a process or phenomena.

Theoretical sampling

theoretical sampling
A sampling technique in which the initial cases are usually selected on a relatively unstructured basis: as 'theory' begins to emerge from the initial data, further cases are selected to explore and test the emerging theory; this continues until there is no new theory emerging and theoretical 'saturation' is reached.

Theoretical sampling is a variation of purposive sampling which is based on the ideas and processes of Grounded Theory (**B3**). It assumes that data collection, analysis and the sampling of cases are going on concurrently, and that sampling of new cases for data collection continues until there is no further data emerging from each additional case. The process is described by Glaser and Strauss (1967: 45) as

> data collection for generating theory whereby the analyst jointly collects, codes, and analyses his data and decides what data to collect next and where to find them, in order to develop his theory as it emerges.

Thus the initial cases are usually selected on a relatively unstructured basis. As 'theory' begins to emerge from the initial data, further cases are selected to explore and test the emerging theory. The researcher is also interested in identifying 'negative cases' – cases that do not conform to the emerging theory, as it is from these cases that the theory can be amended and developed. This continues until there is no new theory emerging and theoretical 'saturation' is reached.

Purposive sampling – the practicalities

The approach to designing and gathering a purposive sample draws on other non-probability techniques which we discussed earlier in this chapter. Convenience, quota and snowballing samples are all commonly used approaches to gathering participants or cases for a purposive sample. As we have seen in the sample and volunteering example, it may be possible to use data gathered using a probability sample, as data is then available to help the researcher to purposefully select participants for the more in-depth study.

What is the population from which the sample will be selected?

When designing a purposive sample, we are using population in a similar way to when drawing a probability sample, in that it needs to be defined in terms of its characteristics, and particularly in terms that are relevant to the research study. However, we are not seeking to identify all possible members of the population in order to be able to draw a sample from them. Rather, we are looking at the relevant characteristics and thinking about the context in which a population with those characteristics may be found.

Example B5.9

Volunteering in hospitals

A researcher is developing a study of people who volunteer in hospitals. He starts by considering the context – the hospital – and finds out about how hospitals are organised through reading and searching the internet. By visiting a local hospital, he is able to find out more about the opportunities for volunteering in the hospital. This helps him to identify people and organisational structures that may help him to identify potential participants for his study.

Thinking a bit more about his research questions and the hospital, he then wonders whether volunteering in a large city-centre hospital is different from volunteering in a small local hospital, so he finds a smaller hospital and finds out more about the context before deciding to include volunteers from both hospitals in his study.

What are the characteristics or criteria for selection?

The criteria for selection within a purposive sample usually derive from the research questions themselves and the type of purposive sample. For a small-scale piece of research undertaken by a student, a sample that is stratified – or a quota sample – based on the key areas and issues you are identifying in your research questions is the most common approach to take.

As with probability sampling, it is important at this stage to also be planning the initial stages of your analysis. In particular, you should be aware of groups of cases, based on such variables as age, gender and ethnicity, that you may wish to compare for similarities or differences. You should also think about the differences and similarities you might expect to find based on your reading of other research and theory in the topic area, and ensure that you are including cases within your example that will enable you to explore these initial ideas. From this, a sample matrix (see Ritchie and Lewis, 2003: 101) can be developed, as shown in Example B5.10, which will enable you to identify potential participants.

How many cases should be included?

Purposive sampling is usually used as part of research designs that include in-depth study, gathering and working with qualitative, in-depth and detailed data. The number of cases is typically small by comparison with a probability sample, for the following reasons:

(a) Research that uses qualitative data is not usually concerned with being able to generalise to a population, or the prevalence of a particular characteristic in the population.

(b) There are diminishing returns to be gained from the data gathered from each additional case. Because we are not attempting to demonstrate the prevalence of a particular characteristic in the population, there is no requirement to go on looking for further examples.

(c) Gathering qualitative data is very time- and resource-consuming, and the data gathered is itself rich in detail. Few researchers have the resources, or the need, to include large numbers of cases.

That said, the question of how many cases to include remains. For most student projects, it is likely that a maximum of around 20 individual interviews will be feasible (though in some circumstances it may be less – check your regulations), and for many it will be unnecessary to include even as many as this. Much will depend on time and resources. Perhaps even more, it will depend on the access to participants and their willingness to participate in the research. Setting out the criteria for selection as shown in the matrix in Example B5.10 can be very helpful in terms of identifying the minimum and maximum number of cases you want to include.

Of course, if you are using purposive sampling to sample for a focus group, then you may be seeking to include rather more individuals (C5). And if you are using a case study design, you will want to first consider your selection of cases (B3) before perhaps gathering a sample of individuals or groups from within each case.

Example B5.10

Volunteering and health – a mixed-methods approach

The doctor who is interested in her patients' volunteering experience primarily wants to study the way volunteering and mental well-being are linked. She is interested in the effect the volunteering experience has on the way her patients feel. To undertake research on this, she wants to explore patients' experiences and perceptions in depth and so decides to select a small sample of patients from those who completed her questionnaire who do volunteer.

NOTE: At this stage she does not want to spend time and resources interviewing people with no volunteering experience and who are unable to shed any light on the research questions.

She is interested to see whether men and women of different ages have different experiences and perceptions of volunteering, and she still feels it would be interesting to include some people who visit the surgery frequently and some who visit infrequently. However, she also wants to ensure that she includes people who are in paid employment as well as those who are not. She is able to use her initial questionnaire to identify potential participants on the basis of a matrix. She has the resources to interview about 16 people.

Table B5.2 Volunteering and health – a purposive sampling matrix

Age	Frequent visits to surgery		Infrequent visits to surgery	
	Male	Female	Male	Female
16–40	2 or 3	2 or 3	1 or 2	1 or 2
41–65	2 or 3	2 or 3	1 or 2	1 or 2
Total	10		6	
Not in paid employment	4–6		3	
Paid employment	4–6		3	

Is the sample accessible?

The initial research regarding the sample context will usually include the opportunity to find out how accessible the potential participants in the research are likely to be. When using purposive sampling we are not so concerned with non-response as we are seeking to fulfil the selection criteria rather than ensuring that our sample is based on probability of inclusion. However, you do still need to minimise the possibilities of non-response by ensuring that you consider how best to encourage informed participants. The research report or dissertation will usually include a discussion of the ways that access to participants was achieved, any difficulties in terms of refusals to participate and how any difficulties were overcome.

Your research

Research quality check: purposive sampling

- Have you a good understanding of the research context and the potential participants?
- What type of purposive sample are you using?
- How do the criteria for selection relate to your research questions?
- Have you justified your sample size and composition in terms of the analytical approach you plan to take?
- Have you identified the strengths of your sample in terms of your research questions and the claims you hope to be able to make for your analysis, the development of theory or the transferability of your findings to other contexts?

Choosing a sampling approach

At the beginning of the chapter we said that the approach you take to sampling will depend on your research questions, the nature of the data you want to collect, whether the data is quantitative or qualitative and the methods of data collection you decide to use. We also suggested that the different approaches to sampling can be thought of as a spectrum. In Figure B5.6 we have mapped each of the research designs and data collection methods across the sampling spectrum. This shows that for each research design you have a range of approaches you can take to sampling and selecting your research cases, people, documents or observations. In practice any researcher faces limitations to the possibilities available to them and these will significantly determine the eventual sample used in the research. The research quality checks for each approach can be used to help you to assess the strengths and limitations of the approaches available to you.

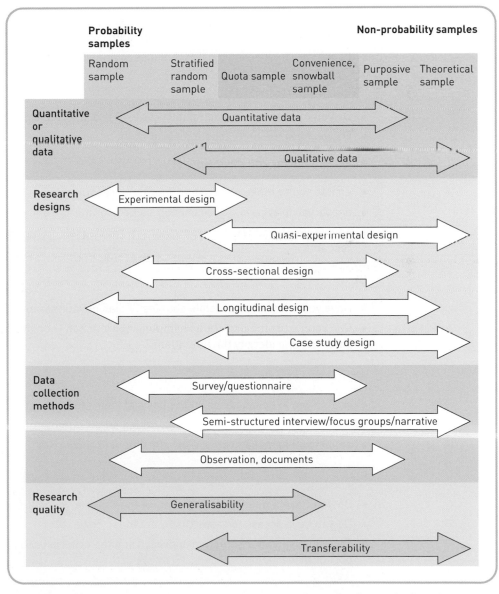

Figure B5.6 The sampling spectrum and research design, data collection methods and quality

The sampling approach chosen determines the claims you can make for your findings in relation to the wider social context from which they were drawn. In general terms we can say that the findings from probability samples may be generalisable to the population from which the sample is taken whereas the findings from a purposive sample can be considered in terms of their transferability to other settings or cases. However, in most small-scale research, including student research projects, great care must be taken in terms of the claims you can make for your findings on the basis of the sample you have selected.

Your research

Thinking about your research topic and research questions: which sampling approach (or approaches) will you choose?

A probability sample may:

- enable you to generalise to your population;
- enable you to use statistical techniques to analyse your data.

BUT

- Do you have access to population lists – all the selected cases?
- Do you have the time, resources and skills to carry out the research in this way?

A non-probability sample may:

- enable you to make good use of your time, resources and skills;
- enable you to achieve a 'good enough' sample for the size and scale of your research;
- enable you to target the cases that are most likely to be of relevance to your research.

BUT

- Have you considered possible sources of bias in your sample?
- Can you justify the use of this sampling approach in your research report or dissertation and identify the limitations?

A purposive sample may:

- enable you to select cases on the basis of your research questions;
- enable you to gather in-depth data from a small number of cases;
- enable you to make good use of your time and resources.

BUT

- Do you have a good understanding of the criteria you will use to select cases?
- Do you have access to cases that meet those criteria?
- Can you justify your sampling approach and the criteria used in your research report or dissertation?

References and further reading

Commission on the Future of Volunteering (2008) *Report on the Future of Volunteering and Manifesto for Change,* London: Volunteering England.

Glaser, B. G. and Strauss, A. L. (1967) *The Discovery of Grounded Theory: Strategies for Qualitative Research,* New York: Aldine de Gruyter.

Low, N., Butt, S., Ellis Paine, A. and Davis Smith, J. (2007) *Helping Out: A National Survey of Volunteering and Charitable Giving,* London: Office of the Third Sector.

Moser, C. (1958) *Survey Methods in Social Investigation,* London: Heinemann.

Ritchie, J. and Lewis, J. (eds) (2003) *Qualitative Research Practice: A Guide for Social Science Students and Researchers,* London: Sage.

Wright, D. B. and London, K. (2009) *First (and Second) Steps in Statistics,* 2nd edn, London: Sage.

CHAPTER B6
Research proposals

Contents

In context

This section is about writing a research proposal. A research proposal brings together all the preparatory work that has gone into developing the research and is often written as a precursor to being able to actually start collecting and working with data. The section discusses the purpose of the research proposal and its typical structure, while noting that proposals must be focused on a particular audience (**E1**) and that the proposal needs to set out the research project clearly.

PART B: Preparing for research

  B1: Planning a research project

  B2: Reviewing the literature

  B3: Research design

  B4: Choosing methods

  B5: Sampling

▶ **B6: Research proposals**

What is a research proposal and what does it do?

A research proposal can serve several purposes, but essentially it is how the researcher tells someone else about a piece of proposed research.

To do this, the proposal must say:

- what the research is about: that is, a description of the research issue;
- how it will be undertaken: a discussion of methods and other issues;
- why it is worthwhile: a discussion of why the issue is important or relevant;
- how long it will take;
- why it should be funded (this is, probably, not a major issue for students, but is crucially important for some researchers, particularly academics).

It is important to remember that a research proposal will be targeted on a specific audience. For students this is probably a lecturer or tutor who will either:

- be marking a 'research proposal' assignment; or
- be agreeing that a piece of student research can take place; often this will be research for a dissertation.

A third possibility is that you are applying for a place on a research degree programme. If this is the case, it is likely that you will be asked to write a research proposal that will be evaluated and the result used to judge your suitability for the course.

This means that writing a successful proposal is important to you, at the very least so that you will not have to do additional work to achieve your objective.

Structure of a research proposal

Although there is no 'fixed' structure for a research proposal, your institution may have specific rules and requirements: please check before embarking on such a project. You may notice that this suggested structure is quite similar to the dissertation structure discussed in **Part E**.

Research proposals are often constrained by short word limits: be careful to adhere to them.

❓ What is . . .

Basic research proposal structure
1. Introduction*
2. Literature review*
3. Methodology/methods
4. Dissemination
5. Timetable.

*Don't forget to state the research question!

Introduction

The introduction for a research proposal is similar to introductions to essays and reports, with which you may already be familiar. Its purpose is to set the scene for your research by describing the issue that you plan to investigate and the objectives of your project, i.e. answering your research questions. You can take this opportunity to give definitions if you need to and you can also say why you, personally, are interested in the issue.

You may also need to say why this area is important or topical and, therefore, worth researching. You might also suggest who or what will benefit from the research findings and say how your research fits within the discipline or area that you are studying in.

At some point in the proposal you will need to state the research question(s) (A4) and associated operational definitions. (Note: we have used the word 'question' for convenience. It could be that you will state a hypothesis that you will test in your research.). Opinion is divided on where this should be placed in a proposal, and there is no concrete answer. Your choices are threefold:

1. in the introduction;
2. in the literature review;
3. as a separate section between literature review and methodology/methods.

Our personal preference is to put the question(s) after the literature review as the introduction and literature review set the scene for the research questions before moving on (in the methodology) to show how you will answer the research question(s).

Literature review

(For details of literature reviews in general, please see **B2**.)

In a research proposal, the literature review is often the largest component. However, it is important to understand that it is only *indicative* of the available literature for a topic. At this stage in the research process you will probably not have completed you review of the literature.

In a research proposal, the literature review performs a number of important tasks:

1. It positions the research in terms of the real world and puts the research into context.
2. It may provide a conceptual and theoretical framework for the study.
3. It discusses the research issues. In doing this, it:

    (a) demonstrates that the researcher has an understanding of the issue in terms of existing literature and research;

    (b) identifies and discusses the limitations of earlier research;

    (c) identifies and discusses the 'gaps' in existing knowledge that the research will fill.

4. It leads to the definitive research question(s).

A short summary at the end of the literature review helps to clarify for the reader both what you have included and how the literature relates to your research.

Methodology/methods

Although we have put these two headings together in one section, it is important to know the difference. Essentially, *methodology* is about the epistemology and ontology of your research (A2) but perhaps more focus in a research proposal will be on the sort of research design and methods you are planning to use (**B3, B4**).

Once you have stated your methodological position, the next step is to talk about the practical issues that will be important in your research. These are the *methods* and are likely to include the following:

- *Data collection.* A statement of the data collection processes that you propose to use (**Part C**) and, if space permits, a discussion of why you have chosen particular method(s) of data collection and the appropriateness for your research should be included. You may want to (or be required to) include a draft data collection instrument (for example, a questionnaire or interview schedule).

- *Population and sampling.* You will need to state the nature of the population you are studying, the size of the sample and the sampling procedure you will use (**B5**).
- *Data analysis strategy.* It is important to make clear at this stage that you know what you will do with your data once you have collected it (**Part D**) and that your analysis strategy is compatible with your collection process. This is part of the process of making your research reliable and valid. For example, it would be inappropriate to carry out structured interviews and then attempt a narrative analysis of the data.
- *Ethical issues.* An ethical statement needs to be included at this point (if your institution requires you to submit to an ethical approval process, you could include that approval here) to ensure that your reader knows that you understand the ethical issues and possible implications that could ensue from researching with individuals (**A5**).

Dissemination

You need to say what you will do with the results of your research (sometimes, you will have been instructed on what is permissible). So, for example, you might say that you plan to publish the results on your college's website, or simply that your research is only for the purposes of your dissertation.

Timetable

A timetable of your proposed work will show the different stages that your project will go through, with clearly indicated time periods for different stages of the research and significant dates. Check that you know the key dates (e.g. hand-in dates for drafts and final copies) and that you are using the timetable formats required by your institution or organisation. The format of the timetable can be simple, as shown in the example below.

Example B6.1

A research timetable

Table B6.1 Research timetable

From*	To*	Task*
5 January	19 January	Write literature review; design interview schedule; submit proposal for ethical review.
19 January	26 January	Contact participants; arrange interviews; book interview rooms.
26 January	9 February	Conduct interviews; start transcription and analysis.
9 February	16 March	Transcription and analysis.
16 March	6 April	Complete analysis; begin writing up results and recommendations.
4 May		Submit final report.

*Please note: these dates are entirely fictitious – they are not suggestions about how long these tasks should take.

Summary

Overall, your proposal is trying to influence someone and persuade them that you are capable of completing a research project. We suggest that you re-read your completed proposal with this outcome in mind and that you refer to the research proposal checklist in the box below.

Your research

Check your research proposal

RESEARCH PROPOSAL CHECKLIST

	✓
Look at your document. Does it look professional and interesting?	
Have you addressed all the important issues?	
Have you written at the appropriate level for your audience?	
Have you checked the spelling and grammar?	
Are your arguments clear?	
Are the research questions/hypotheses supported by the literature review?	
Are your methodology, data collection and analysis strategies compatible?	
Is your timetable complete and accurate?	

References and further reading

Baxter, L., Hughes, C. and Tight, M. (2001) *How to Research*, Buckingham: Open University Press.

Bell, J. (1999) *Doing Your Research Project: A Guide for First-time Researchers in Education and Social Science*, Oxford University Press.

Cryer, P. (2000) *The Research Student's Guide to Success*, Buckingham: Open University Press.

Silverman, D. (2005) *Doing Qualitative Research*, 2nd edn, London: Sage.

PART C
Data collection

CHAPTER C1
Collecting data

Contents

In context

In **Part C** we introduce a range of different approaches to collecting the data you need in order to be able to address the research questions (**A4**) you are investigating in your research study. This part introduces the idea of a 'research tool' and considers some of the features of different research tools. To do this we need to remind you of the characteristics of data introduced in **A3** and then go on to consider how we develop the 'right tools for the job'.

Collecting data is a practical activity and in **C2** we look at some of the practical skills you will need to develop to collect data effectively, before going on in **C3–C9** to discuss some of the most common ways of collecting data in turn.

It is now common to use computers in a number of ways to facilitate the collection of social research data, and **C10** looks at some of the current approaches to data collection which use, for example, email and discussion groups as means of collecting social research data.

PART C: Data collection

▶ **C1:** **Collecting data**

   C1: Data collection skills

   C3: Questionnaires

   C4: Semi-structured interviews

   C5: Focus groups

   C6: Observation

   C7: Narrative data

   C8: Documents

   C9: Secondary sources of data

   C10: Collecting data using computer-mediated communication (CMC)

Collecting data – a practical activity

In **A3** we explored the idea that data is a 'stand-in' for the social reality we wish to study. It is as close as we can get to a true representation of the facts, values, opinions and experiences of the people and social phenomena we are interested in for our research. We identified a number of characteristics of social research data:

- It can be spoken or written words.
- It can be non-verbal – pictures, gestures or sounds – which can then be expressed as words.
- It can be structured in different ways.
- It can be constructed or produced by individuals and by groups.
- It can include factual statements and value statements.
- It can include what people say (the content) and the language they use to express the content.
- It can include the researcher's own thoughts and reflections.

Having formulated one or more research questions or set up a hypothesis (**A4**), the social researcher is faced with the task of designing research that will enable her to gather data to address the research question or hypothesis, bearing in mind the characteristics of social data and the relationship of the social researcher, as a social human being and part of the social world, with that data.

Data collection is a practical activity, one that has to be carried out within time, spatial and resource constraints. It is therefore important to consider how valid social research data can be collected effectively and efficiently within those constraints. The history of social research has included the development of a range of research 'tools' to help social researchers to organise and manage the task of data collection. A **research tool** is simply the means by which the data is collected, for example, a questionnaire, a format or, in the case of semi- or unstructured interviews, the researcher herself, as they are the means through which the data is gathered.

research tool
Something used to collect data, e.g. a questionnaire, the researcher her/himself or an interview schedule.

In this section we will consider three characteristics of social research data collection tools and the implications of these for both the data that is collected and the way in which data collection is carried out. Each aspect is presented as a continuum along which different research data collection methods can be found. These are:

A: structured/semi-structured/unstructured data;

B: present/absent researcher;

C: active/passive researcher.

A: Structured/semi-structured/unstructured data

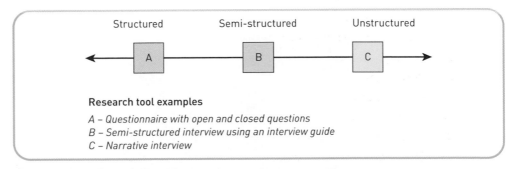

Figure C1.1 Continuum of structured/semi-structured/unstructured data

The first continuum relates to the format in which data is collected. In **A3** and in our discussions about quantitative and qualitative research (**B4**), we considered the nature of data. Quite simply, is the collected data ready packaged into age groups, degree of satisfaction, opinions or experiences which can be counted (structured), or is the data in its 'raw' state – as the respondent spoke or wrote it or the researcher observed it (unstructured)? Of course, it may be somewhere along a continuum between these two, i.e. semi-structured. Note that it is the researcher who decides where on the continuum the structural format of the data is to be and then designs a research tool that will facilitate the collection of the data in that format. Example C1.1 shows how the respondent can construct and deliver the data in different formats depending on the structural format the researcher has devised.

Example C1.1

Structured, semi-structured and unstructured data

A social researcher is studying patient satisfaction with the service they receive when they visit their family doctor. Here are three ways in which the data could be collected.

Structured data

	Satisfied	Not sure	Dissatisfied
Receptionist			√
Waiting time	√		
Time with doctor	√		
Treatment		√	

Semi-structured data

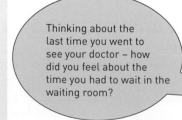

Unstructured data

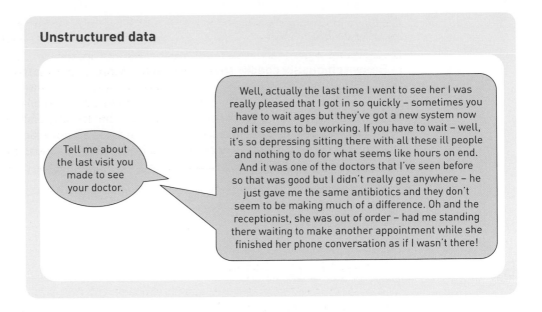

Tell me about the last visit you made to see your doctor.

Well, actually the last time I went to see her I was really pleased that I got in so quickly – sometimes you have to wait ages but they've got a new system now and it seems to be working. If you have to wait – well, it's so depressing sitting there with all these ill people and nothing to do for what seems like hours on end. And it was one of the doctors that I've seen before so that was good but I didn't really get anywhere – he just gave me the same antibiotics and they don't seem to be making much of a difference. Oh and the receptionist, she was out of order – had me standing there waiting to make another appointment while she finished her phone conversation as if I wasn't there!

Although the examples given in Example C1.1 relate to collecting primary data from a person, similar structural formats can be used to interrogate and record documentary data, visual data or secondary data. You will find examples of these in Chapters C3 to C9.

Things to think about: structured/semi-structured/unstructured data

In terms of the practicalities of collecting data there are different things to think about in relation to the degree of structure of the data being collected. These will be highlighted and discussed in relation to specific data collection methods in chapters C3 to C9 but there are three general points to think about at this stage:

- The validity of the data collection tool – by this we mean ensuring that the research tool is designed in a way that is going to best collect data that can 'stand in' for the social experience it represents. This is particularly important when considering structured formats like questionnaires (C3) as the data is collected in categories or groupings and the researcher does not have access to the raw data (the respondent's spoken words or thoughts). This means that attention and time have to be given to the preparation of the structured format – the research tool – into which the data is to be collected.

- In the case of less structured data, consideration has to be given to the management of potentially large amounts of 'raw' data, from, for example, interview transcripts (C4), audio and video recordings, documents and narratives. The collection of semi-structured or unstructured data must be planned with the approach to working with (analysing) the data in mind, as analysis of this type of data usually works with the data in the form in which it is gathered, for example, the words spoken by a respondent or the account as it is written in a document (D2).

- Different data collection skills are needed depending on the way the data production is structured. For example, if you are gathering structured data you need to be able to create research tools like forms/formats or questionnaires into which the data can be entered (C2). If the data is semi-structured or unstructured, you may use audio or video recording (C2) and will need to transcribe or turn the oral or written data into written text (C2).

Your research

Research quality check: structured/semi-structured/unstructured data

- Have you decided how the data should be structured for your project?
- Are you clear on the reasons for this and the potential impact on validity?
- Have you designed a data collection tool that takes account of this? (Do you need access to raw data later, for example, or is structured data enough?)
- Are your operational definitions appropriate for this sort of data collection?
- Can you manage the data properly (transcription, storage, etc.)?

B: Present/absent researcher

This continuum refers to the physical (and virtual) presence or absence of the researcher at the point when the data is being collected and, as such, relates in part to the degree of human relationship between the researcher and the respondent. If the researcher is not present when the data is being produced – as, for example, in the case of a self-completion questionnaire – then the researcher must ensure that the respondent has all the information they need in order to be able to produce the requested data. This could include detailed instructions about the completion of a form, how to record an event or how to access a website, as well as a comprehensive and comprehensible description of the research, its aims and purpose, and such issues as confidentiality and what will happen to the data and the findings.

If the researcher is physically present when the data is being produced, then there are different issues to consider. What impact will the researcher as a person have on the respondents in terms, for example, of gender, ethnicity, age and perceived social status? This may affect the willingness of the respondent to participate or perhaps to answer questions that are personal or sensitive. Building up a rapport may be important before gathering data. On the other hand, depending on the context, a more formal approach may be required, if, for example, an interview is taking place within a work context or with a respondent who is perceived to have a high status or is very busy.

You may not think of this as a continuum – after all, the researcher is either present or not. However, as communication increasingly takes place via telephone, email and other computer-based means, it is still possible for the researcher and respondent to have a sense

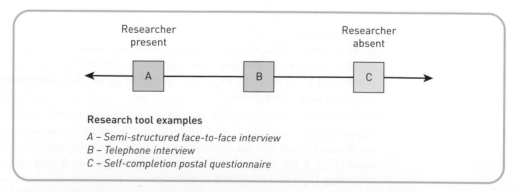

Research tool examples

A – Semi-structured face-to-face interview
B – Telephone interview
C – Self-completion postal questionnaire

Figure C1.2 Continuum of present/absent researcher

of the other person through oral and written communication. The researcher, for example, could be participating in a virtual focus group (**C10**) where participants only know each other through virtual discussion, or monitoring a chat room without the participants being aware that he is 'in the room'. There are therefore different degrees of 'presence' and the impact of this on the way data is produced needs to be considered.

Think about it . . .

In which of these scenarios do you think you would get the most accurate (closest to the truth) data on how often and why teenagers go out 'binge drinking'?

1. A self-completion questionnaire which is anonymous and delivered to 16–18 year olds through their school/college and returned to the university-based researcher in a sealed envelope.

2. A focus group (group discussion) of teenagers at a youth centre with a researcher aged around 20.

3. A virtual discussion group on a website used by teenagers which the researcher has joined and is monitoring, having assumed the identity of an 18 year old.

Can you suggest other data collection approaches that could be used?

Things to think about: present or absent researcher

In terms of the practicalities of collecting data, there are different things to think about in relation to whether the researcher is present or absent when the data is collected. These will be highlighted and discussed in relation to specific data collection methods in Chapters **C3** to **C9** but there are some general points to think about at this stage:

- If the researcher is not present (physically or virtually), then particular attention needs to be given to the instructions given to the respondent or other data collectors; to the language used in the data collection tool, for example, a questionnaire or format, to ensure that it is easy to understand; and to the explanation of the research.

- It may be more difficult to ensure a good response rate if the researcher does not have any personal contact with the respondents and consideration needs to be given to ensuring that delivering the data is not onerous, time consuming or difficult for the respondents. It is easier for some respondents, for example, to send back their response by email rather than by post. However, some people may not have email and so will need a stamped, addressed envelope to encourage them to reply, or a dropping-off point could be provided at a place where the respondents are likely to go regularly, for example, a shop or community venue.

- If the researcher has face-to-face contact with the respondent, then consideration has to be given to the impact the researcher as a social human being may have on the respondent, including thinking about the impact of gender, age and ethnicity on both the interaction between the researcher and the respondent and the way the research topic is discussed.

- If the researcher does not have face-to-face contact with the respondent but does have a virtual, oral or written 'presence', then the researcher will need to consider the form of communication and the way in which he presents himself to the respondents through this medium of communication as each medium has its own characteristics, use of language and etiquette (see **C10** for a discussion of computer-based communication).

Your research

Research quality check: present/absent researcher

- Are you clear on the reason for being present or absent in your research?
- If absent, have you given particular thought to participant instructions so as to maintain validity?
- Have you taken steps to maximise response and reduce bias (particularly in returning questionnaires and ensuring access to computers, for example)?
- Have you considered your impact as the researcher?
- Are you aware of communication conventions and etiquette if you have decided to be a virtual researcher? Have you considered the impact of these issues on your research?

C: Active/passive researcher

The third continuum relates to the role of the researcher as a 'research tool' – a means by which the data is collected. You may not think of yourself as a research tool but some data collection (and analysis) methods depend on the researcher being an active and effective data collector himself. In the semi-structured example in Example C1.1, the researcher was playing quite an active role, asking a question and then following this up with a probing question to find out more about the changes to the waiting system. Here the researcher was developing a conversational interaction to facilitate the production and delivery of data by the respondent. However, the researcher's participation in the interview is limited to using a range of prompts and probes which are designed to encourage the respondent to develop their ideas and explanations in their own way. The researcher's role was less active in the unstructured example, with the respondent being encouraged to tell the story as they wished ('Tell me about . . .'). Here the respondent is more in control of the production and selection of data and the way it is delivered. On the other hand, some researchers (see, for example, Oakley, 1981) advocate developing a relationship with the respondent such that both the respondent *and* the researcher introduce their own experiences and ideas into the **data production** process – this is usually called a collaborative interview (C4).

In Example C1.1 the tool for gathering structured data is a self-completion questionnaire (C3). Here the researcher has devised the research tool – the questionnaire – but plays a passive role in the actual data collection and may not even be present while the respondent is completing the questionnaire. Even if the researcher was present and asking

data production
The way in which social experiences, thoughts, feelings, behaviour and other social phenomena are expressed in words – thus making them available as social data. Individuals and groups can produce data by talking, writing and thinking – using language. This data can then be shared with others using a common language.

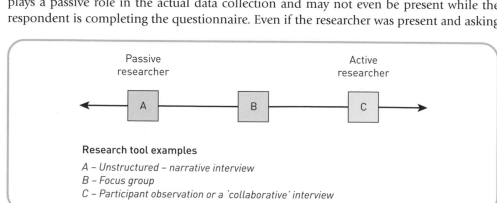

Figure C1.3 Continuum of active/passive researcher

the questions of the respondent, using this type of structured format leaves a limited role for the researcher beyond reading out the questions and recording the answers.

Let's think about a different example – that of collecting data using observation (C6). Collecting data through observation can take a number of forms, from observing a situation from a distance, or on a video, through to observing while being an active participant in the situation. One of the key variables in observational data collection is the degree to which the researcher is a participant in the situations she is observing. Observation can be carried out covertly by, for example, observing via a concealed video camera, or by a researcher participating as a member of the group, workplace or context that she is observing. In the first case the researcher could be described as taking a passive role, having no impact on the research site or the participants under observation (there are ethical issues you may wish to consider if you are videoing people without their awareness or consent – see A5). In the second the researcher is a participant herself and, whether or not the participants know that she is also a researcher, she will be actively involved in the production of the social data that is being collected and recorded. Typically in research where the researcher is actively involved in the data production process through an interactive interview or participant observation, some reflexive data (A3) would also be included to enable the researcher to:

(a) reflect on the impact her presence and participation has had on the data generated;

(b) reflect on what it felt like to be part of the social world that is being researched;

(c) note down any ideas and interpretations that may contribute to the analysis of the data.

Things to think about: active or passive researcher

In terms of the practicalities of collecting data there are different things to think about in relation to how actively the researcher participates in the data collection process. These will be highlighted and discussed in relation to specific data collection methods in Chapters C3 to C9 but there are some general points to think about at this stage:

- If the researcher is actively participating in the production of research data then consideration needs to be given to how the data will be recorded as he is unlikely to be able to take notes or complete forms while also engaging in the activities associated with the data production. Audio and video recording (C2) may be used or the researcher may keep a detailed diary which can be written up whenever it is convenient (C2).

- The degree and flexibility of participation should be decided as part of the research design. For example, in preparing a semi-structured interview possible ways of probing and prompting need to be included in an interview guide (C4).

- If the researcher is actively participating in the production of data he will also be engaged in the interpretation of the data as it is being produced. In fact the analysis process is already beginning as the researcher is working with the data as it is being collected. A reflexive account, using, for example, a diary or research journal, with notes of interpretations and ideas that may be useful in the analysis process should be kept.

Your research

Research quality check: active/passive researcher

- Are you clear on the reason for being active or passive in your research?
- Have you designed a data collection tool that takes account of this?
- Are you sure that your research design is treating each participant the same?
- Have you considered your impact as the researcher?

Using the three continua to help in the design of research tools

In this section we have introduced three continua along which different research data collection tools may be found. Thinking about where on each of the continua a particular data collection tool is found can help you to be aware of the issues that are raised for you as a researcher in terms of both the practical skills needed and the implications for the quality of the research.

Each data collection method, and the research tools associated with it, can be found on each of the continua and it is helpful to plot their position on each so that you are aware of the various implications of using a particular data collection method. There are always a number of different sorts of practical issues to consider in designing and planning data collection, including the constraints of time, skills and (usually) financial and other resources. Thinking about the implications of using particular data collection methods and research tools before you embark on your data collection will help you to work as effectively as possible within these constraints.

From what you know of the different data collection tools, try to place them on the continua in the 'Think about it . . .' box below, and then think about your own research and the data collection tools you are planning to use and plot these in the 'Your research' box that follows. You may find it helpful to refer back to the three continua while reading about your data collection methods in Chapters C3 to C9, consider where on the three continua a particular data collection method can be found and check the 'Things to think about'.

Think about it . . .

Put X where you think the data collection tool is on each of the three continua.

Virtual focus group

Structured	Unstructured
Present	Absent
Active	Passive

Self-completion questionnaire

Structured	Unstructured
Present	Absent
Active	Passive

Semi-structured telephone interview

Structured	Unstructured
Present	Absent
Active	Passive

Your research

For each of your data collection tools, plot their position on the three continua.

Data collection tool 1:

Structured _____ Unstructured

Present _____ Absent

Active _____ Passive

Data collection tool 2:

Structured _____ Unstructured

Present _____ Absent

Active _____ Passive

Data collection tool 3:

Structured _____ Unstructured

Present _____ Absent

Active _____ Passive

References and further reading

Denscombe, M. (2007) *The Good Research Guide: For Small-Scale Social Research Projects,* Buckingham: Open University Press.

Gilbert, N. (ed.) (1993) *Researching Social Life,* London: Sage.

May, T. and Williams, M. (eds) (1998) *Knowing the Social World,* Buckingham: Open University Press.

Oakley, A. (1981) Interviewing women: a contradiction in terms, in H. Roberts (ed.) *Doing Feminist Research,* London: Routledge & Kegan Paul.

CHAPTER C2
Data collection skills

Contents

In context

Data collection for social research is a series of practical activities requiring skills that are transferable from and to other situations. What skills do you bring to the process and what skills may you need to learn and develop?

In this chapter we look at some of the skills a researcher needs and give some practical advice to help you to best use the data collection methods you are most likely to choose.

PART C: Data collection

C1: Collecting data

▶ **C2: Data collection skills**

C3: Questionnaires

C4: Semi-structured interviews

C5: Focus groups

C6: Observation

C7: Narrative data

C8: Documents

C9: Secondary sources of data

C10: Collecting data using computer-mediated communication (CMC)

You have chosen your data collection methods – now you need to think about how you will actually do it, what skills you bring to the task and what you may have to learn. Each data collection method requires its own particular skills and processes but there are common skills which are likely to be required regardless of the methods you choose.

Think about it . . .

You are planning to use a questionnaire to gather data from other students face to face. What skills do you think you will need to actually do this?

Look at the checklist in the box below – which of the skills listed do you think you would need to use a questionnaire to collect data?

It is helpful at this stage to take stock and think about your own experience and skills, and be aware of the resources you have to draw on. Below are listed some of the main skills we think you are likely to need to be able to collect social research data. Use the checklist to identify the skills you think you have at this stage.

Your research

Which skills will you need to carry out your data collection?

Skills		I have this skill ✓	Where/how did I learn this skill?	I need this skill for my data collection methods ✓
Keeping records	Using a database			
	Using cards			
	Using a diary			
Creating forms/ formats using computer software	Creating tables			
	Using boxes/shapes			
	Using colour/fonts/ shading, etc.			
Creating posters/information leaflets/ letters using computer software				
Taking notes	From documents/books			
	From spoken words			
	From observation			
Communicating with a variety of types of people	By letter			
	By email			
	Face to face			
	By telephone			
Interviewing	Individuals			
	Groups of people			
Recording audio	Tape recorder			
	Digital recorder			
Recording video				
Transcribing/taking notes from recordings				
Reflecting on actions/learning	Using a diary			
	Using a learning journal			
LIST ANY OTHER SKILLS YOU THINK YOU WILL NEED				

Keeping records

Any data collection method will produce a quantity of data. Organising and keeping a record of the data you have will help you to manage the process and will probably save you time and work when it comes to the analysis stage. Tables C2.1 to C2.3 give some examples of records you may want to keep.

If you are familiar with and skilled in using databases you could devise your own record system. However, the records could be kept on cards or in a table or spreadsheet format (e.g. Microsoft Excel). Alternatively, a diary system could be used to keep a record of all that has been done on a particular day. This will enable you to check back for information when needed but does not have the advantage of being able to see the information relating to each source of data in one place.

You may also want to keep your own research notes, literature and interview notes or your learning journal (see below) in a set of standardised documents. Using a standard

Table C2.1 Keeping records of questionnaires

Questionnaire no.	Date sent by email	Date of follow-up email	Received	Complete Y/N	Checked
101	02/04/10		03/04/10	Y	✓
102	02/04/10	16/04/10			
103 etc.	02/04/10	16/04/10	16/04/10	N	✓

Table C2.2 Keeping records of interviews

Interviewee	Transcript number	First contact	Date of interview	Place of interview	Length of interview	Notes
Anne	01	15/03/10	22/03/10	University	30 min	International student
Steve	02	16/03/10	23/03/10	Hall	40 min	First year
Kate etc	03	16/03/10	29/03/10	Coffee bar	10 min	Kate had to leave before the end of interview – will try to arrange another time

Table C2.3 Keeping records of secondary sources

Document	Newspaper	Date of publication	Title/headline	Accessed
1	*Guardian*	13/02/10	Young people have little hope of work	Online
2	*Daily Mail*	13/02/10	It's not working!	Paper copy
3 etc	*Independent*	13/02/10	Rise in unemployment for third month	Online

template or layout and then saving each as a separate file which is dated or labelled will enable you to refer back easily to particular records or events. The design of the layout can be tailored to your own needs and the information you want to record, and the record can include a variety of different types of information.

Creating formats

Recording data and information about the data collection are most effectively done using forms or formats into which information can be entered. In some cases, like the examples above, the formats are designed for the use of the researcher, and while they should be clear and easy to use, the detail of the design is less important. However, if the format being created is for use by your research respondents then more care is needed to make sure that it is clear, easy to use and attractive to them. This is particularly important for self-completion questionnaires and other forms that you may want your respondents to complete.

Take the opportunity to develop your computing skills and in particular to use the features available to you in your computer software. Most word-processing packages, like Microsoft Word, include design features that enable you to produce tables (the examples above use tables), boxes and other shapes, check boxes and drop-down lists, and to apply colour, shading and borders. (In Microsoft Word 2007 you will find these features in the *Insert* and *Developer* tabs.) Some packages, such as Microsoft Publisher, include a wide range of features designed to produce posters, leaflets and forms. Time spent exploring the possibilities of the software available to you will probably be time well spent in terms of both producing an effective and attractive data collection format and developing your own skills for the future. Most software packages include tutorials and help features and, if you are a student, your university or college may have training sessions or online tutorials.

Note-taking

There are numerous situations in research, and in studying more generally, when you need to take notes. It may be taking notes in a lecture, from a book, in an interview with a research respondent or as you observe an event.

> ### Think about it . . .
> **Taking notes**
>
> Think about a situation in which you have had experience of taking notes.
>
> - How did you take notes?
> - What worked for you?
> - What did not work?

The key to effective note-taking is to think about the following:

- What you are taking notes about?
- Why you are taking notes?
- Which information is 'worthy of note' or needed for future use?
- How will you take notes? In what form will your notes be?

If you prepare well, then note-taking will be focused on the subject matter and in a form that means your notes are easily useable at a future point.

Your research

Note-taking tips

- At the top of your note-taking sheet, write the topic of your note-taking clearly. This may be an essay question, your research question or the particular focus of an interview or observation.
- Only write notes that relate to your topic.
- Devise a format that will help you to take notes under headings or in different boxes or sections. This could be, for example, based on your interview topic guide with space for notes on each of the issues discussed.
- Label your notes with the details you will need in order to put those notes into context, e.g.
  - a full reference of a document or text, including where you accessed it – library, website, etc.
  - respondent name/number, date and place of interview
  - observation point, date and time of observation, focus of observation.

Active note-taking

Many people will have had the experience of sitting in a lecture or reading a book and making notes without actively thinking about the information that is being recorded. It is easy to feel that if you have a set of notes you do not need to think actively about the topic at the time. Unfortunately this passive note-taking can be counterproductive because little of the information is retained by the listener or reader and the notes in themselves are unlikely to be sufficient to remind him of the full content of the information. An active listener, reader or watcher and note-taker will be doing three things:

1. reading, listening or watching;
2. thinking about what is read, heard or observed and deciding what to note;
3. making notes.

As we are unable to do more than one thing at a time, these three activities are happening in rapid succession when we actively take notes. Active note-taking usually results not only in a useful set of notes but also good recall of the event itself. If you spend some time soon after the event checking and adding to your notes from your memory, you should find that you have a fully useable record.

Memos

A different sort of note is often called a memo. A memo is effectively a short note to yourself – the sort of note you might write on a Post-it note. In social research these are used in a number of ways. First of all, it is useful to have a small notebook, diary or set of Post-it notes with you at all times as you may want to jot something down about your research at any time – it may be an idea, a reminder to yourself, or a note about something that has happened. These sorts of notes will probably need transferring to different places according to the type of note. Dates will go into your diary, reminders need to go into a diary at the time when you want to be reminded. Ideas about your research, a suggested research participant, a question you want to come back to when you are analysing your data, or a book you want to follow up, will all need to be transferred to places in your research diary or plan where you will come back to them at the right time. If you work with an electronic diary you could use the 'To do' or task feature to make sure you are reminded of these on the appropriate day.

Memos can also be attached to your research diary, your research proposal or report using either Post-it notes or the 'comment' feature found in Microsoft Word software (this can be found in the 'Review' menu in Word 2007). This enables you to add an aside or comment to your writing as a reminder of something you want to add or change. Or it could refer to an idea that you have about your research that you want to come back to.

Some data analysis software, for example NVivo (**D9**), include the facility to add these notes or memos at any point in the analysis of your data (and in fact you can even include your memos as part of the analysis).

Communication

Most social researchers will need to communicate with others in some way and at some point in their research. The preparation of a research proposal (**B6**) and the presentation of your findings in a report or dissertation (**E2**) are both ways in which you will be telling others about your research. Most researchers also have some communication with the people who take part in their research face to face or by letter, email or telephone. Typically the communication will relate to:

- telling people about the research;
- asking them to take part or to give you access to their data;
- assuring them of confidentiality and other ethical issues;
- making arrangements for them to participate;
- collecting the data;
- thanking them for taking part;
- telling them what will happen next.

You may find yourself needing to communicate with people you do not know, with different types of people and with people who know very little about social research.

Your research

Good communication tips

- Think about the purpose of your communication.
- Plan and rehearse what you are going to say or write.
- Avoid specialist or technical language.
- Speak clearly and audibly.
- Take care with grammar and spelling in written communication – including emails.
- Think about the person you are communicating with:
  - What are they likely to know about the topic of your research?
  - What are they likely to think about you as a researcher?
  - Are they from a different age group, culture or social class from you?
  - Is the time when they receive the communication convenient for them?
- Listen to the other person and read emails and letters carefully before responding.

Interviews

Interviews with individuals or groups are special forms of interactive communication and social research interviews and focus groups are special forms of interviews. As such they are designed to facilitate the collection of research data and have particular characteristics and techniques to enable the researcher to do this effectively. These include questionnaire formats (C3) and interview (C4) and focus group topic guides (C5) and techniques for encouraging respondents to tell their stories (C7).

The respondents will often look to you, as the researcher and interviewer, for guidance on the way the interview is expected to develop and for reassurance that they are providing the type of data you need for your research. Remember: you have planned the interview and know how it will develop, while your respondent knows only what you have told them. Make sure that you explain what will happen clearly and check their understanding of the research and the interview. If appropriate, spend some time developing a rapport by talking about general topics, for example, the weather or travel to the venue, before starting the interview, and spend a short time together at the end after you have turned off the recorder or finished taking notes.

Think about the setting for your interview or focus group and how this will help the interaction between you and your research respondents. People are more willing to participate and communicate if they are comfortable and able to give their whole attention to the interview. Primarily you are looking for a venue that will suit the respondent and will allow you to spend as much time as is necessary on the interview, preferably without interruptions. If possible, arrange the chairs so that – if it is a one-to-one interview – you are sitting at right angles to each other. This enables both you and the respondent to make eye contact and look away as you talk. This can provide for a variety of intensity within the interview conversation and can enable the respondent to speak more easily than they might if faced directly by the interviewer across a table or desk. It can be rather intimidating to face an interviewer directly, although if you are interviewing someone in, for example, a work situation this may be necessary.

A focus group or group interview will require a larger venue. Make sure that there will be enough chairs for everyone and arrange these in a circle or around a table. Try to ensure that each person can see and hear all the others. Check whether there are other facilities that your participants may use – refreshments, toilets, waiting areas and so on. If you require flipcharts, pens or other equipment, check whether these can be provided or whether you need to bring your own. When using equipment you are not familiar with, make sure that you arrive with enough time to check that it is working before your first participant arrives. Be ready to welcome your participants – and be prepared to chat to the one or two who turn up first while you are waiting for the others. Few people have experienced taking part in this type of activity and most will need some reassurance about what will happen.

Remember that your research participants are giving their time voluntarily and that they deserve your full attention and consideration. Show your interest with encouraging comments and nods, concentrate on them and listen to what they say.

Active note-taking and listening is particularly important if you collect your data using interviews or focus groups and are unable to record these in any other way. In an interview you should be interacting with the interviewee and this includes looking at and listening to them as well as making notes. It can be disconcerting for the interviewee if they are faced with an interviewer who spends most of the interview looking down and writing every word that is being said. A good interviewer will focus on the interviewee and listen as well as taking notes of key points during the interview, and then after the interview will write up a full account of the interview drawing on the notes and her recall of the interview content.

You are advised to read about the data collection method you are using and to plan with your own skills and experience in mind. It is valuable to rehearse with friends or colleagues and to pilot the data collection method if possible. Try to learn from each experience using a reflective diary or learning journal. After each interview, reflect on what went well and what could have been done better.

Recording audio and video

Some data can be recorded using audio or video recording equipment, and if you have access to, and are experienced in using, these devices then you may wish, for example, to record your focus groups or individual interviews, or video a situation or event for analysis. If you have limited experience of using recording equipment, you should be aware of the time it may take to learn how to use the equipment confidently and effectively to gather your data and you may want to weigh up the advantages and disadvantages compared with the alternative of note-taking.

If you are using recording equipment you should:

- be familiar with the equipment;
- plan how you will use the equipment in the data collection situation, thinking about the place and space where it will take place;
- ensure that the equipment and any other resources, e.g. batteries, tapes, microphones or tripods, will be available when you require them;
- rehearse with friends or colleagues to check that the equipment is working and is suitable for the data collection situation.

Using recording equipment to gather social data

The main advantage of using recording equipment is that you, as the researcher, are able to take away a recording of the event to work with. You have a copy of the data as it was being produced, as the event happened. You are then able to work with the raw data as you begin the analysis process. However, there are other issues that you must consider, including the impact of the recording process itself on the collection of data and the people who will be providing the data, your interviewees, or the people you are observing.

Audio recording is acceptable to many people, but their permission to record must be given and there may be those who do not wish to be recorded (A5). In case of this event you will need to prepare an alternative way of recording the data, usually note-taking. Interviewees must have the option to change their mind about the recording at any point during the interview and should also have information about who will listen to the recording and when and how the recording will be destroyed or deleted. Some researchers return the recording of an interview to the interviewee at the end of the research or sometimes at an earlier stage to ask them to check whether they have anything to add to what they said during the interview.

It is good practice to show the interviewee how to pause the recorder if they do not wish the recording to continue. An interviewee may find some subjects difficult to talk about and may prefer to talk about them without being recorded, although (and you should check this) they may still be prepared for the data to be used in the research. Sometimes an interviewee may simply want a break and after a few minutes is prepared to start the recording again and continue with the interview.

Group interviews can be more difficult to record and a high quality microphone is needed to ensure that all members of the group will be recorded clearly. If there is overlap between different speakers it can be difficult to distinguish voices. Although focus groups (C5) are regarded as group data and individuals are usually not identified, it can be helpful when working with the data to be able to distinguish different voices. If you hope to be able to do this, then participants may need to be encouraged to speak one at a time.

Recording an interview means that the interviewer is not distracted by the necessity to take notes. However, the interviewer should still be an active listener, remaining alert to the words being said, thinking about what the interviewee is saying and preparing follow-up probes or questions as appropriate to the style of interview.

Videoing an occasion in which a number of people are involved can be a useful source of observed data. However, you must be aware of the impact of the recording on the behaviour of those being recorded and in some situations it will be necessary to obtain the permission of all those involved (**A5**). This will depend on whether your observation is overt or covert (**C6**) and the nature of the situation being recorded.

Using recording equipment

A variety of types of audio and video recording devices are available. The key difference between models is whether they are recording to tape or recording digitally. Digital recording has a number of advantages as the recordings are saved as files and can be transferred to a computer. Each recording has a numerical index or time attached to it which means that you are able to move within the recording quickly and easily and can also use the index as a means of attaching flags or pointers to particular points in the recording. This can be used in the analysis process (**D2**). While tape recorders also have a numerical system they are less accurate and usually more difficult to work with.

Transcribing recorded data

If you want to be able to work with the full verbatim (word-for-word) data you record in an interview or focus groups, it will be necessary to transcribe each interview – that is, put the audio data into written form. This is a time-consuming activity which is sometimes undertaken by the researcher themselves or may be done by a trained transcriber at a cost. If you hope to transcribe your recorded data yourself, you should be aware that each hour of audio recording could take three to four hours to transcribe.

Although it is possible to transcribe directly from your recording device by listening to short sections and then typing the words as you hear them, it is advisable to obtain the use of a transcribing machine if possible. This is a recording device which plays the recording back in short sections, allowing time for the words to be typed. A foot pedal and other controls help to facilitate the process.

If transcription of all the interviews is too time consuming, it is advisable to adopt a process of listening to the recording of each and making detailed notes under headings or themes (**D4**), including verbatim quotes where particularly pertinent points are made or the interviewee uses words or expresses conceptual data in an interesting or relevant way.

Reflective skills

Data collection is a learning process. Regardless of the experience of the researcher, each piece of research is new and different. Some researchers keep a research diary throughout the research process; others use a recording format that includes their own notes, ideas and reflections.

A learning journal or research diary can serve any or all of these purposes:

- To provide a record of the researcher's thoughts and ideas through the research process. This may include initial ideas about theories, ideas to come back to later in the process, and changes in thinking or plans and the reasons for these.

- To provide a dated record of each stage in the research: decisions made, activities completed, literature searches, coding systems, analyses undertaken.
- To provide a record of the researcher's own observations on the research as it is in progress: what has worked well and why; what has had to be changed.
- To provide a record of the researcher's own learning: identification of skills or limitations; feelings about the research and progress; learning from mistakes and from good and not-so-good experiences; identifying how to improve skills and performance.

A journal or diary is most useful when it is added to on a regular basis and when it is personal to the researcher. Writing a journal provides an opportunity for honest reflection on all aspects of the research and to identify ways forward. It should focus primarily on what has worked well and why, so that those lessons can be applied to the aspects of the process that are not working so well. Acknowledging that doing social research is a learning process, especially if the research is being undertaken as part of a study programme, helps you to learn through the experience and identify your strengths as well as the areas in need of development.

Your research

Start your research diary

Look back at the skills checklist and use the format below to begin your research diary.

Research topic	Date

Possible data collection methods

Skills I will need	What are my strengths and my limitations in relation to this skill?	How can I improve and develop this skill?
1.		
2.		
3.		
4.		
5.		

CHAPTER C3
Questionnaires

Contents

In context

We all know what questionnaires are – or, at least, we think we do because they are so common in daily life. We have all completed questionnaires about different topics and issues.

Questionnaires are very popular among students as a means of data collection, possibly because they are perceived as 'easy' (they're not!). In this chapter we discuss the construction of questionnaires and talk about the advantages and limitations of using them.

PART C: Data collection

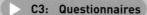

    C1:   Collecting data

    C2:   Data collection skills

   ▶ **C3:**   **Questionnaires**

    C4:   Semi-structured interviews

    C5:   Focus groups

    C6:   Observation

    C7:   Narrative data

    C8:   Documents

    C9:   Secondary sources of data

    C10: Collecting data using computer-mediated communication (CMC)

Questionnaires are, perhaps, the most common way of gathering data from research participants. The use of questionnaires as a means of gathering social data grew rapidly during the twentieth century alongside the development of statistical techniques which enabled researchers to work with large numbers of cases and complex sets of data. One of the first questionnaires used in the UK was the census (first held in 1831). Census enumerators went from door to door with formats on which they listed the name, age, place of birth and occupation of each of the inhabitants. No doubt they asked a series of questions of each householder to help them to fill in the form. During the nineteenth century and into the twentieth, factual data about people was gathered not only by government but also by medical, industrial and charitable organisations to try to find out more about social conditions, particularly of people in the industrialised cities (for example, Henry Mayhew, Charles Booth and Seebohm Rowntree). Prior to and during the Second World War, mass sample surveys were instigated, including the New Survey of Life and Labour in London and studies of unemployment, housing and health (Bulmer, 1982).

❓ What is . . .

Questionnaire
(1) a list of questions each with a range of answers;
(2) a format that enables standardised, relatively structured, data to be gathered about each of a (usually) large number of cases.

Most of the data collected in these early surveys was factual data about people and their experiences. However, social researchers also wanted to find out about people's opinions and values and began to develop ways of measuring these using a series of questions. The most well known is Rensis Likert, an American psychologist (1903–81) who was interested in human organisations and devised the Likert scale (see 'Types of question' on page 201) to enable his respondents to evaluate idea or attitude statements along a (usually) five-point scale, from 'strongly agree' through to 'strongly disagree'. Other ways of rating statements have since been developed, particularly to be used in psychological testing, marketing and evaluative research.

Alongside this, market research was developing and increasingly using questionnaires as the means of finding out about people's opinions and wishes. Following the Second World War, the Government Social Survey was set up to undertake large-scale surveys on behalf of government departments, typically using long and detailed questionnaires. As the statistical techniques developed and computers were introduced, more sophisticated analyses of data were feasible. Some ongoing large-scale surveys were set up during the latter part of the twentieth century, for example the Family Expenditure Survey (now the Expenditure and Food Survey, available at www.esds.ac.uk/government/efs/, accessed on 15 August 2009) and the General Household Survey (available at www.statistics.gov.uk/statbase/prep/5756.asp, accessed on 15 August 2009), and teams of interviewers still interview a sample of households with detailed questionnaires throughout the year.

Questionnaires are now commonly used at all levels of social research, from small-scale student and community projects through to large-scale international surveys. What they all have in common is the formulation of a set of questions (and answers) which are going to help the researcher to answer his research questions or test his hypothesis.

structured
Describes data, or a data collection method (such as an interview or questionnaire), in which the questions are the same for each participant, and typically there is a common set of answers for each question.

What is a questionnaire?

A questionnaire is a set of questions which can be answered by the research participants in a set of ways. Most questionnaires are designed to gather already **structured** data (A3 and B4) and so include a set of answers which the respondent can choose from, although some

open questions
Questions that allow the
respondent to answer
the question in their
own way.

may include more **open questions** which allow the respondent to answer the question in their own way. All the participants are asked the same questions, in the same order and using the same wording and have the same set of answers to choose from.

Real research

The decennial Census of Population

In the UK, a census of the population is carried out every ten years. The first Census was carried out in 1831, and it has been repeated every ten years (with the exception of 1941, during the Second World War) up to the present. The most recent Census was on 29 April 2001 and the next is scheduled for 27 March 2011.

The Census of Population is a survey of all the households and people in the country and is used to provide statistics that are utilised by government (and are also often available to other organisations, including industry and commerce). For a history of the Census, see: www.ons.gov.uk/census/census-history/index.html.

The Census is a large questionnaire which is delivered to every house in Britain (there is a complex system of support for people who find the completion of the Census difficult). The Census is used by government in particular for three main purposes:

1. monitoring the size, composition, age, ethnicity, etc., of the population;
2. planning the provision of services in the future;
3. monitoring the delivery of existing services and policies.

However, it is unusual for two reasons:

- Completing the Census is *compulsory*! This means that the issue of poor response rates should not arise.* (Currently, those who fail to complete the Census can be fined £1000.)

- The sample and the population are the same (B5). This is very unusual, because of the scale (approx. 60,000,000 participants) and resources required.

*The 'missing million': about 1,000,000 people failed to complete the Census in 1991 (see, for example, www.independent.co.uk/news/uk/missing-million-indicates-poll-tax-factor-in-census-1557887.html). This is said to be because the government was planning a 'poll tax' and they believed that if they were not recorded in the Census, then they would not have to pay!

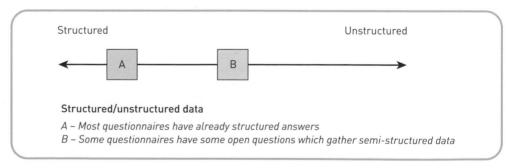

Structured/unstructured data

A – Most questionnaires have already structured answers
B – Some questionnaires have some open questions which gather semi-structured data

Figure C3.1 Questionnaires on the continuum of structured/unstructured data

As the data is in a standard form, it can be counted and worked with as coded or numerical data. However, this means that the design of the questionnaire is the most important stage as the design determines both the questions and the answers that the researcher has to work with. Ask the wrong questions – or give the respondent the wrong set of answers to choose from – and you will not gather the data you want and need to answer your research questions. The validity – ensuring that you are gathering the data you think you are gathering – of your questionnaire (or research tool – **C1**) is one of the key research quality issues to consider (see 'Research quality check' on p. 216).

A questionnaire, as the name implies, is usually a series of questions, for example:

Do you live in Ladywood?

How many children aged under 16 years live with you?

How satisfied are you with the service provided by your health centre?

But data-gathering formats that do not include questions but ask for information can also be regarded as questionnaires as they have similar features. These could include forms that gather a set of information about a person or situation, for example, forms drawn up to record student achievement, the number and type of people in a workforce, the characteristics of people joining a particular club or information taken from documents. Formats are also used to record observations, for example, the number of people eating alone in a café, the number of times each person smiles, or the number of times a student speaks in a seminar (**C6**). These recording formats include implicit questions and, as such, have similar characteristics to a questionnaire.

Questionnaires can be used in a number of ways. Sometimes a questionnaire is used as the basis for an interview so there is some interaction between the respondent and the researcher (or at least an interviewer). This may be face to face, over the phone or via email. In other situations the questionnaire is designed as a self-completion questionnaire for the respondent to complete themselves without the researcher present. The respondent may be given the questionnaire by the researcher, or sent the questionnaire via the post or email, or may access the questionnaire on the internet (**C10**). However, in whatever situation the respondent answers the questions, the questions and the choice of answers will be the same. If the questionnaire is used as an interview, then the interviewer must read the questions and responses in the same way for all the respondents and not offer additional help, prompts or comments to the respondent because this may affect the way the respondent hears and replies to the questions. Effectively the interaction between the interviewer and the respondent is limited to the questions and answers.

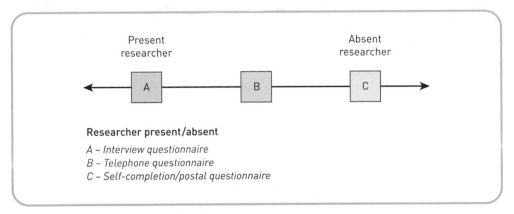

Figure C3.2 Questionnaires on the continuum of present/absent researcher

Using questionnaires in social research

Questionnaires are used in a wide range of social research situations and to find out about all sorts of social issues and phenomena. Although questionnaires are particularly useful for gathering factual data, for example, people's ages, genders, incomes or use of services, they can also be used to gather people's opinions, ideas, attitudes, knowledge and experiences. Different ways of asking questions have to be devised to enable this value data (A3) to be gathered and we will consider below some of the approaches you might take.

Questionnaires are most often chosen to gather data within a cross-sectional or longitudinal research design (B3) and where the data is being collected from a sample (B5) of a larger population. The purpose of the research may be to compare the characteristics and experiences of different groups of people or to look for relationships between different characteristics (B3, B4).

Real research

The British Crime Survey

The British Crime Survey has been carried out at intervals since 1982 (and annually since 2001). It is one of the largest cross-sectional surveys in England and Wales. It is currently carried out by the British Market Research Bureau for the Home Office. The survey is designed to find out the extent and nature of crime in England and Wales (occasional similar surveys are carried out in Scotland and Northern Ireland) and asks people about their experiences of crime (including crimes against property and against the person) during the previous year. This includes crimes that have not been reported to the police, and it has come to be regarded as a good estimate of the real extent and nature of crime. Questions are also included that elicit the views of the respondents on current government and legal policies on crime.

The sample

About 40,000 people aged over 16 years are included each year.

The questionnaire

The survey questionnaire is administered by interviewers who ask most of the questions. The answers are entered into a laptop computer during the interview. A self-completion section is given to the respondents for them to answer themselves on the computer. This section includes questions about the respondents' own behaviour, including whether they have taken illegal drugs and how much alcohol they drink. (The questionnaire for British Crime Survey 2007–8 is available at www.data-archive.ac.uk/doc/6066/mrdoc/pdf/6066questionnaire.pdf, accessed 15 August 2009.)

Like many other large-scale surveys, information, reports and copies of the questionnaires used are available at the Economic and Social Data Service (www.esds.ac.uk/about/about.asp, accessed 15 August 2009). The data from the British Crime Survey is also available for secondary analysis from the Economic and Social Data Service.

The advantages of using questionnaires to gather this data

- Data to be gathered is in a standardised format.
- A large-scale survey is needed to ensure that a wide range of people and experiences are included and that results can be generalised to the whole population.
- Most of the information gathered is factual.
- Using the same questions year on year enables comparisons to be made longitudinally as well as cross-sectionally.
- Data can be entered into a computer and be ready for statistical analysis.

Selecting participants for questionnaire surveys

Questionnaires are usually used when a random sample has been drawn from a population, or using a quota sample. The sample chosen will depend on the research question and what the nature of the data is that is being gathered. However, it is also quite common to use a questionnaire to, for example, gather information about all the people attending a particular event or who have a certain medical condition. In terms of size, the two main points to remember are: (a) if it is a random sample from a population, consideration must be given to size and ensuring that small groups are represented sufficiently; and (b) if it is not a random sample, that the groups you want to compare are included in sufficient numbers (B5).

Real research

Community researchers

A group of local community activists in a deprived area were concerned about the lack of leisure activities within the neighbourhood for both adults and children. They were also aware that information about local activities and services did not always reach those who needed it.

They devised a short questionnaire which included questions about:

- current use of leisure facilities, local clubs and activities by the adult and their children (if they had children aged 16 or under);
- a measure of their satisfaction with leisure facilities in the area;
- leisure activities that they (and their children) would like to be able to do in the neighbourhood;
- the ways people found out about activities and events in the area;
- their use of different forms of communication – posters, leaflets, newspapers, internet and local radio.

Two open questions were included to allow respondents to put forward their own ideas and opinions. If the respondent wished, the community researchers helped them to complete the questionnaire by using it as an interview.

Using a quota sampling approach based on the age, sex and ethnicity groupings within the neighbourhood, they gave out the self-completion questionnaire in doctors' surgeries, outside schools, in the shopping centre and community centre and at a local 'Fun Day' event. The group aimed to have 100 questionnaires completed.

Advantages of using a questionnaire

- The questionnaire enabled the group to gather data from a range of people in a standard format, making it easy to analyse.
- The questionnaire could be designed to be completed easily in a variety of situations.
- Given the limited resources of the group, the questionnaire was the most effective way of gathering data from a range of people who lived in the area.

Questionnaires and ethical issues

Questionnaires can be anonymous and it is not usually necessary to have a name or identifying feature. If you do, you should have a good reason for doing so – perhaps that you may wish to contact some of your respondents for a further stage of the research. However, you do need to take care that individuals or small groups of people are not identifiable when you present your findings. If you intend to analyse your findings by comparing, for example, the opinions of people of different ages and occupations, you should ensure that you have sufficient people in each small group (in this case of a particular age and occupation) both to make any claim for that group and to avoid particular people being identified.

Questionnaires can be exclusive. A self-completion questionnaire will exclude people who are unable to read or write and people who do not speak the language of the questionnaire. Those without email or telephone will be excluded from email or telephone questionnaires and you may need to consider alternative means of getting questionnaires to such people. Instructions and information on questionnaires must be clear to ensure that people can fill them in correctly. If the researcher is present when the questionnaire is completed, then the introduction must be clear and the respondent's understanding should be checked. Take care with the wording of questions so that they will not be perceived as being judgemental or insensitive and people can answer them without embarrassment or shame. In the 'Real research' example of the British Crime Survey (on p. 204), which uses an interviewer to ask most of the questions, respondents are handed the laptop computer to enter their answers to sensitive questions on drug use and alcohol consumption themselves. If the researcher is present while the questionnaire is being completed, care must be taken with regard to the power relationships between the researcher and the respondent (A5) and to ensure that the respondent is not pressurised to take part or to give particular answers.

Practicalities

Designing a questionnaire

Designing the questionnaire is the most important stage in this type of research because once the questionnaire is designed you have determined the questions and the answers and you will not be able to go back and get further information. You need to be sure that the questions you ask are going to enable you to gather the data that you need – here you need to refer back to your operational definitions. How do you ask a set of questions that will show you whether a person is happy or not? Or has had a 'good' holiday? Or even whether they have really eaten what they said they have eaten?

Designing a questionnaire is both about working out how you are going to measure the presence of something and about the practicalities of finding a set of questions and answers that will enable you to do that and be meaningful to and answerable by all your respondents.

Your research

Thinking about your research topic and designing a questionnaire to gather data:

- What do you want to know?
- Who will be able to answer the questions?
- Will they understand the questions?
- How will they answer the questions?
- Will they be able to give the answers they want to give?

Different types of data

A questionnaire is usually designed to collect a number of different types of data including:

- facts – about people or events;
- descriptions – people's descriptions about something that, for example, has happened to them;
- knowledge – what people know about something;
- opinions – what their opinion is about something they have experienced or know about;
- attitudes/values – their attitudes towards other people, institutions, ideas and so on;
- background information about the respondent which may be linked to the research topic.

Different types of answer

Questionnaires include ways of answering questions as well as ways of asking them. The two are clearly linked – the way the question is asked will determine the range of answers the respondent has to choose from. While this may seem obvious, it may not be immediately apparent that when designing the questionnaire you need to have the data you will gather in mind as well as the questions you have to ask to get that data. The nature of the data you gather will determine how you are able to work with it when you come to analyse it. These are the main types of answer – or data – you will get from a questionnaire:

- quantity – number of times, number of brothers, etc.;
- category – age category, e.g. 16–25 years; job category, e.g. manual worker;
- answers chosen from a list of possible answers, e.g. yes/no/don't know;
- position on a scale – for example, from 'very satisfied' to 'very unsatisfied';
- rank position – for example, your first choice, your second choice, etc.;
- open data – answers in respondents' own words.

Types of question

There are different ways of asking almost any question. The following are just some of the most commonly used questions in questionnaires.

Yes/no

The most simple question asks for a 'yes' or 'no' response and is used as a way of distinguishing between different groups of respondents. Basically there is no point in asking a yes/no question if all your respondents are likely to answer one or the other unless you are using it as a check question to ensure that you have the respondents you want. All of your respondents should be able to answer 'yes' or 'no' but it is sometimes advisable to add a 'don't know' or 'not applicable' category for any respondents who are unable to answer the question. In the example below it could be that the respondent has not been at home for the last six months because she has been in hospital.

Have you been away from home on a holiday for a week or more during the last six months?

Yes	☐
No	☐
Not applicable	☐

Which category? How many? How much?

You will probably want to ask questions about the respondents themselves or about a situation. This (usually) factual data needs to be collected in a way that makes it easy for the respondent to give the data accurately.

(a) *What is your age? Please tick the age group you are in.*

16-25 years ☐

26-40 years ☐

41-60 years ☐

Over 60 years ☐

(b) *We are interested to know more about who people go on holiday with. Please tell us about the people who went with you on your last holiday*

Person	Age last birthday	Sex (please circle)	Relationship to you, e.g. child, sister, friend, partner
1		M/F	
2		M/F	
3		M/F	

When asking for this information you should think carefully about why you need the information and how you will use it. This is particularly pertinent if you are asking for information that may be sensitive, for example, a person's ethnic group, religion or income. Organisations that gather this type of data as part of, for example, employment or health data, use standard sets of categories and you may be able to make use of them. (You can find out more about the questions on the topics used in the National Census 2001 at www.statistics.gov.uk/about/ethnic_group_statistics/introduction.asp, accessed 15 August 2009).

However, the first question for you as a researcher to ask is whether, with your research questions in mind, you need this information about your respondents. If you do need the information you must explain on the questionnaire why you are asking for it and give your respondents the opportunity to opt out of the question. Bear in mind that if a significant number of your respondents do not answer the question, you may not be able to use the data from the question in your analysis, and just asking the question may lead to people refusing to take part in your research.

You should also think carefully about the groupings or categories you will use. For example, when designing a question asking respondents their age, think about how you will want to use that information in your analysis. If you are unsure of the age groupings you will want to work with, then it may be better to ask respondents for their age at last birthday rather than ask them to put themselves in an age group. However, you will then probably need to group the data at the analysis stage (D2) and so it is worth thinking at this stage about the age groupings you are interested in.

Think about it . . .

Age groupings

Note that your age groups may or may not be equal in length. This depends on how you will use the age groupings and how they relate to your research questions.

If you are interested in asking teenagers about their experiences of school, you will probably want to ask them which school year they are in rather than their age.

If you are interested in how, for example, unemployment affects people at different stages in their lives, you can choose your age groups to correspond to those stages, e.g. 16–25 years, 26–40 years, 41–50 years, 51–65 years, over 65.

Why do you think we have chosen these age ranges?

Choose from a list

If there are a set of answers we want respondents to choose from, it is common to list them and ask them either to select one or more or to 'tick all that apply'. Think carefully about what information you want from the question. An 'other' category is often included so that respondents can add any other answers which they feel do not fit in the categories you have given them to choose from as in the first example below. In the second example this would not be appropriate.

a) During the last six months have you been on any of the following types of holiday?

Tick all that apply to you

✓

City-based holiday   ☐

Seaside holiday   ☐

Holiday in a rural location   ☐

Other   ☐

What type of holiday was it?

b) When you are choosing a holiday, which of these factors is the <u>most important</u> to you?

Tick one box

The location   ☐

The accommodation   ☐

Length of journey   ☐

Who I will go with   ☐

The people I will meet   ☐

The activities I will be able to   ☐
take part in

A variation on this question would be to ask respondents to choose their two or three most important factors – or to ask them to *rank* them in order of importance: 1 (most important) to 6 (least important).

Agree/disagree with a statement

If you want to gather data about people's ideas, values, opinions or attitudes, you can ask respondents whether they agree or disagree with a statement which you have devised. The statements themselves need some careful thought on a number of counts:

- How does this statement relate to your research question – what are you hoping to find out by including this statement?

- Will all the respondents understand the statement in the same way – will it mean different things to people from different cultures or with different experiences?

- Do you need a number of statements on a particular topic in order to find out what people think or how people feel?

- Is the statement unambiguous and clear in its meaning?

The use of the Likert scale gives the respondents the opportunity to show how strongly they feel about the factors you have raised in the statement and can helpfully distinguish between people. However, unless you have the opportunity to test your statements and establish whether there are real differences in degree of agreement between people, you do need to be cautious about what you are able to claim about such distinctions. You should also consider how people may use the middle (neutral) category (sometimes this can be 'neither agree nor disagree' or, as in the example, 'not important'). In these examples the choice of the middle category is significant because it is indicating that the factor raised in the statement is not important to that respondent.

Please circle the answer that most reflects your opinion on each of these statements

The food is the most important part of a holiday for me

| Strongly agree | Agree | Not important | Disagree | Strongly disagree |

I like to meet local people when I go on holiday

| Strongly agree | Agree | Not important | Disagree | Strongly disagree |

Hot sunny weather is essential for a good holiday

| Strongly agree | Agree | Not important | Disagree | Strongly disagree |

I enjoy making new friends on holiday

| Strongly agree | Agree | Not important | Disagree | Strongly disagree |

I like to have my holiday organised for me

| Strongly agree | Agree | Not important | Disagree | Strongly disagree |

Rating scale

Another way of asking about respondents' opinions or attitudes is to use a rating scale. In this case they are asked to place their answer on a scale which can be from 1 to 5, to 7, or to 9. It is usual to have an odd-numbered scale as this gives respondents the option of choosing the midpoints.

How important are the following to you when choosing a holiday? Please circle the number that reflects the importance of each factor to you.

	Very important						Not at all important
Cost	1	2	3	4	5	6	7
Accommodation	1	2	3	4	5	6	7
Being able to do what I want	1	2	3	4	5	6	7
Being with my family/friends	1	2	3	4	5	6	7

Open question

Sometimes a questionnaire includes questions that allow respondents to answer as they wish. If the questionnaire is self-completion, a box is included for the respondent's answer and the size of the box is usually an indication to the respondent of the length and detail of their expected answer. An interviewer may use probes and prompts in a similar way to those used in a semi-structured interview (**C4**) to make sure that the question is answered fully but is not usually looking for the depth and detail of a semi-structured interview. Data gathered in this way will be categorised and coded (**D2**) so that it can be included in a quantitative or statistical analysis (**D3**).

Open questions can be used in a number of ways:

(a) *To explain an answer to a previous question.* An open question can give the respondent the opportunity to give more detail or explain an answer they have given to a previous question. We have already seen this above in relation to 'other' categories.

Have you ever made a formal complaint about a holiday to a travel agency or other organisation?

No ☐

Yes ☐ ⟶

What was the complaint about?

(b) *What do you think about . . .?* These are often exploratory questions which can allow the respondents to give their own ideas.

What do you think are the most important factors for a family with young children when choosing a holiday?

(c) *Anything else you want to say . . . ?* It is good practice to include a question at the end of the questionnaire that allows respondents to add anything else they want to say about the topic. This sometimes produces interesting and useful data on aspects of the topic that have not been covered or the researcher has not considered. It also provides an opportunity for the respondent to say what is important to them if the researcher has not included this in the questionnaire. While the data may not be of relevance to the research, this opportunity may ensure that the respondent can complete the questionnaire feeling satisfied that his opinion or experience has been recorded.

Filter questions

filter questions
Questions that are used to help people to find their own way through a questionnaire, and to select respondents according to whether a question is relevant to them.

Sometimes within a questionnaire you want to ask certain types of people some questions and others a different set of questions. There is no point in asking people to answer questions that do not apply to them or about subjects they know nothing about, so **filter questions** are used to help people to find their own way through the questionnaire and usually include *signposts* to tell the respondents which question to answer next.

2. **Do you have children aged 16 years or under living with you?**

Yes ☐ ⟹ go to Q3

No ☐ ⟹ go to Q8

3. **How many children aged 16 or under live with you?** ☐

Wording questions

Your questions must be clear and understandable by the people who you expect to answer them and, as such, should enable you to gather the data you need. The 'awful' questionnaire (see the 'Think about it . . .' box on p. 213) highlights some of the most common mistakes made in designing questionnaires. We include some tips below to make this process easier.

> ### Your research
>
> #### Tips for writing questionnaire questions
>
> ✓ Use language that is familiar to your respondents – avoid jargon.
> ✓ Ask questions in a neutral form – avoid 'leading' questions.
> ✓ Two or three simple questions are usually better than one long or complex question.
> ✓ Ensure that all possible answers are included – add an 'other' category if appropriate.
> ✓ Ensure that answers are mutually exclusive if only one answer is required.
> ✓ Include a few open questions to give people the opportunity to say what they want to say.
> ✓ Ask people about things they know about rather than things they may or may not be able to imagine.
>
> ✗ Avoid questions that are ambiguous or imprecise.
> ✗ Avoid questions that assume specialist knowledge the respondent may not have.
> ✗ Avoid words or phrases that may cause offence.
> ✗ Avoid asking two questions in one.
> ✗ Avoid questions couched in negative terms, e.g. 'Would you rather not go to Italy for your holiday?' (People may be unsure whether to answer yes or no.)
> ✗ Avoid questions that depend on memory of events in the distant past.

Ordering questions

The order of the questions in a questionnaire should make sense to the respondents. This usually means that each question will lead on to the next or there will be an introduction to a new set of questions on a different topic or aspect. A typical design includes a general question followed by a number of more detailed sub-questions. It can be helpful for respondents to answer more descriptive and factual questions about the topic before being asked for their opinion, as this helps them to bring their own experience, events and people to mind before being asked their opinions about them.

If the questionnaire covers sensitive topics it is usually advisable to place these in the middle or towards the end of the questionnaire, as respondents are likely to have a better understanding of the questionnaire and the reasons for asking these questions by this stage. Background characteristics like ethnicity, age and occupation are usually placed at the end of a questionnaire with an explanation for their inclusion.

A general question at the end of the questionnaire that gives the respondent the opportunity to add anything else they want to say about the topic can ensure that respondents feel that their opinions are valued.

Layout and presentation

The layout and presentation of the questionnaire depends on whether it is to be completed by the respondents themselves or whether the researcher is completing it in an interview. However, even if you are recording the answers yourself, it is helpful to have an attractive layout, a typeface that is easy to read, instructions and signposting to help you find your way through the questions, and clear boxes in which to record the answers.

A good questionnaire should:

- include an introduction to the research, an explanation of what will happen to the answers, a note about the confidentiality of the information and a contact number for people who may have questions following the survey;
- include instructions on the completion of the questionnaire and instructions within the questionnaire to help people move through it;
- be laid out clearly and attractively using a legible typeface (**C2**);
- take account of the needs of all the groups who will be completing the questionnaire, including the visually impaired, those with reading difficulties, those who speak other languages and those who have special needs;
- be as short as possible.

Think about it . . .

Spot the deliberate mistakes in this awful questionnaire and then check your answers over the page.

User involvement

THIS QUESTIONNAIRE IS TO BE COMPLETED BY ALL CLIENTS WHO ATTEND THE DAY CENTRE

1. Male ☐   Female ☐

2. Age   *0–16*
            17–20
            20–30
            30–45
            45–50
            over 50

3. Do you come to the day centre often?   Yes ☐   No ☐

4. What is your opinion of the day centre?

5. Which of the following statements do you agree with?
   a) I like the food and the activities at the centre   AGREE/DISAGREE
   b) I feel involved in the policy- and decision-making processes   AGREE/DISAGREE
   c) I feel I belong   AGREE/DISAGREE
   d) I don't like the way we are never told about what's happening   AGREE/DISAGREE
   e) This is a really nice place   AGREE/DISAGREE
   f) The staff are kind and cheerful   AGREE/DISAGREE
   g) Women make better care staff but it is better to have a man
      at the top   AGREE/DISAGREE

7. What is your ethnic group?

6. Is this day centre better than Mayfields Centre?

7. What do you think about the *Area User Involvement Policy Document?*

8. Do you agree that it would be better if users were involved more?   Yes ☐   No ☐

9. What is your total weekly household income from all sources, including any wages, benefits and pensions?

Attendance at Day Centre   Monday   Tuesday   Wednesday   Thursday   Friday

PLEASE GIVE THE QUESTIONNAIRE TO A MEMBER OF STAFF

Answers

Title: use of a font that may be difficult to read and title may not be understood. No introduction to the questionnaire, no explanation or assurance of confidentiality. Respondent is ordered rather than asked to complete.

1. No instructions – fussy boxes.

2. No boxes. Age ranges overlap. Age ranges are varied and do not appear to make sense. Unlikely to be respondents aged under 16.

3. No definition of 'often' – respondents will understand this differently.
4. Very open question with no indication of which aspects of the day centre are of interest.
5. Question asks which statements are agreed with but the statements have AGREE/DISAGREE as answers.
5a) The statement includes two different things – food and activities – but respondent may like one and dislike the other.
5b) Also includes different things – policy- and decision making. Will respondents understand what policy- and decision-making processes are?
5c) Belong to what?
5d) A very complex statement with two negatives – difficult to know what you are agreeing with!
5e) What does 'really nice' mean?
5f) Another statement with two ideas but also unclear what is meant by 'the top'.
7. Wrong numbering. No guidance on how to determine ethnic group. No explanation of why this information is needed or how it will be used.
6. Open question with no indication of the criteria the respondent should use to assess whether the day centre is better. Respondent may not know the Mayfields Centre.
7. Another open question referring to a document the respondent may not have read. Title of document is in technical jargon and fussy font may be unreadable.
8. This question is likely to lead respondents to answer 'yes' and it is not clear what users would be more involved in.
9. An impossible question for most people to answer without spending a lot of time and no reason is given for asking for this information. Not clear how respondents are to record their attendance or how respondents who vary their attendance week by week should answer this.

The questionnaire asks for personal information and for opinions about the day centre and yet respondents are required to hand the completed questionnaire to a member of staff. The layout lacks consistency and clarity with different fonts, spacing and boxes used.

Think about it . . .

Did you spot the mistakes?

User involvement

THIS QUESTIONNAIRE IS TO BE COMPLETED BY ALL CLIENTS WHO ATTEND THE DAY CENTRE

1. Male ☐   Female ☐

2. Age   0–16
            17–20
            20–30
            30–45
            45–50
            over 50

3. Do you come to the day centre often?   Yes ☐   No ☐

4. What is your opinion of the day centre?

5. Which of the following statements do you agree with?

   a) I like the food and the activities at the centre   AGREE/DISAGREE

   b) I feel involved in the policy- and decision-making processes   AGREE/DISAGREE

   c) I feel I belong   AGREE/DISAGREE

   d) I don't like the way we are never told about what's happening   AGREE/DISAGREE

   e) This is a really nice place   AGREE/DISAGREE

   f) Women make better care staff but it is better to have a man
      at the top   AGREE/DISAGREE

7. What is your ethnic group?

6. Is this day centre better than Mayfields Centre?

7. What do you think about the *Area User Involvement Policy Document?*

8. Do you agree that it would be better if users were involved more?   Yes ☐   No ☐

9. What is your total weekly household income from all sources, including any wages, benefits and pensions?

Attendance at Day Centre   Monday   Tuesday   Wednesday   Thursday   Friday

PLEASE GIVE THE QUESTIONNAIRE TO A MEMBER OF STAFF

Getting a good response rate

Part of the process of designing a questionnaire is to consider who you will target as respondents – particularly, in some cases, how you will choose a sample from a population (B5) and how you will then contact them and invite them to be your questionnaire respondents. Not everyone you approach will want or be able to take part in your research and you need to take account of this when determining how many respondents to aim for. Depending on the type of questionnaire, your response rate (percentage of questionnaires given to respondents that are completed) could range from as little as 10% up to 100%. There are a number of practical issues to consider:

1. Making contact with potential respondents

   (a) *Face-to-face questionnaire interviews.* If you are aiming to interview all of your respondents then you need to plan how, when and where you will do this and make arrangements to meet people at times and places that are convenient and accessible to them. You may know who you want to interview in advance and be able to make arrangements directly with them, or you could, for example, be in a place at a time when there are likely to be people who would be willing to answer your questionnaire. This could be in a shopping centre, a doctor's surgery (while people wait for their appointment), a youth centre or a pub. Make sure you have a clipboard for your questionnaire and, if possible, somewhere to sit with your respondent.

   Keep your questionnaire as short as possible and give potential respondents a clear introduction to yourself and your research before asking them if they are willing to take part.

   (b) *Telephone questionnaire interviews.* These are similar to face-to-face interviews in terms of gaining access to potential respondents.

   (c) *Self-completion questionnaires.* Self-completion questionnaires can be given personally to potential respondents for them to complete, can be left in prominent places for people to pick up and complete, or can be sent through the post or via email (see **C10** for much more on email questionnaires). The introduction to the research and engaging the interest of potential respondents are particularly important when the researcher is not present. The first contact with potential respondents should be carefully thought through in terms of the target group of people and what will be interesting and attractive to them. Clear instructions and explanations will help the potential respondents to decide whether to respond or to ignore the questionnaire.

2. Follow-ups and reminders

   If respondents are completing the questionnaire themselves then they must be able to return the questionnaire to the researcher with the minimum of effort. A postal questionnaire must include a stamped, addressed envelope, an email questionnaire must include clear instructions on how to return the answers, and if self-completion questionnaires are given out then there must be a point to which they are to be easily returned. You should also consider whether you will send out reminders by post, email or telephone to those who do not respond by a set time. Postal questionnaires can get lost and sending a second copy may elicit more responses.

In practical terms you should aim to get the best response you can and plan this stage of the research process carefully. Realistically, depending on the scale and level of your research, your response rate may be quite low – 25% is typical for a postal questionnaire. The data you have from the completed questionnaires will still be useable but:

- Consider whether there are any possible explanations of why the response is low. Was it the summer holiday period? Or was it a time when people may have been busy with other matters?

- Have you had a better response from some groups than others? Are most of the completed questionnaires from younger people? Is there a possible reason that more older people have not responded?

- If particular groups have not responded, what implications does this have for your analysis and your findings?

- You must state your response rate and discuss these issues in your report or dissertation.

Your research

If you are thinking of using a self-completion questionnaire to collect data for your research project:

> Who will you target?
>
> How will you contact them?
>
> How will you attract their interest in your questionnaire?
>
> How will you make sure you get as good a response as possible?

The nature of questionnaire data and analysis

As we have seen, the data collected using questionnaires is already structured and, apart from data from open questions, is already in a form that can be worked with. Data is categorised and coded and statistical techniques can be used in the analysis. Because the data gathered in this way is already structured, it is particularly important to think about the analysis of your data at this stage and to make sure that the data you are gathering can be worked with in ways that will help you to answer your research questions. We therefore advise you to read **D2** and **D3** at this point.

Research quality

The questionnaire is a research tool or instrument (**B4**) and the means of gathering data about a particular research topic or concept. The validity of the questionnaire rests on whether your research tool measures what it purports to measure. The design of questionnaires includes working with operational definitions to try to find questions and answers that will distinguish between the presence or absence of a particular characteristic, opinion or experience. A pilot – or pre-test – of your questionnaire involving a few respondents, friends or colleagues can help to identify issues of validity as well as other possible problems with the questionnaire which can be changed prior to the main research study. There are a number of ways that the validity of questions can be assessed (see research quality check below), and while it is not always feasible within the constraints of a small piece of research to carry out tests of validity it is useful to bear these in mind when you are designing your questionnaire.

Your research

Research quality check: using questionnaires

- Do the questions and answers produce the data you need to address the research questions or test the hypothesis?
- Do the questions and answers provide data about the research concepts as they have been operationally defined (**A4**)?
- Have you considered the following in assessing the validity of the questionnaire?
  - *Face validity.* A question has face validity when it seems obvious that the question will elicit a correct answer, e.g. 'How old are you?' (But what if there may be a reason for not giving the correct age?)
  - *Convergent validity.* This depends on asking the same question in two ways, e.g. for their age and their date of birth, or finding another source of the data, e.g. checking school records.

- *Concurrent validity.* A test or questionnaire is said to have concurrent validity if it produces similar findings to other studies that use different measures of the same concept.
- *Construct validity.* Refers to the extent to which a set of questions appears to result in findings that conform to what would be predicted from theory.
- *Triangulation* Refers to the collection of a variety of data on the same phenomena, or the collection of data by different investigators or by different methods to ensure that the method of collecting data is valid. Questionnaires are often used in conjunction with other data collection methods.

- Would the data collected be the same if collected again under the same circumstances or if collected by another researcher?
- Have you piloted your questionnaire?
- Have you considered whether any groups of people will be excluded by the use of a questionnaire?
- Have you considered the implications of low response rates on your findings?

Your research

Advantages of questionnaires

- Can be used to effectively gather data from large numbers of people or cases.
- Data is gathered in the same way for all the respondents or cases.
- The questions and range of answers are determined by the researcher.
- Data is ready coded for analysis.
- If the data is gathered from a statistical sample (B5), the findings may be generalisable to the population.

Limitations of questionnaires

- Give the researcher only limited access to in-depth experience and feelings.
- Limited opportunities for respondents to answer questions in their own way.
- Most effective with a large sample.
- Low response rates may result in a biased sample.
- May exclude some groups of people.

References and further reading

Bulmer, M. (1982) *The Uses of Social Research*, London: George Allen & Unwin.
Moser, C. and Kalton, G. (1993) *Survey Methods in Social Investigation*, 2nd edn, Aldershot: Dartmouth.
Munn, P. and Drever, E. (2004) *Using Questionnaires in Small-scale Research: A Beginner's Guide*, Glasgow: SCRE Centre.

CHAPTER C4
Semi-structured interviews

Contents

In context

Interviews are one of the commonest forms of collecting data from participants and have probably been used by social researchers throughout the history of research. While the interview can take a number of forms, the use of interviews as a face-to-face method of asking questions and gathering answers is common in both quantitative and qualitative research. This section looks at different types of interview and discusses their use in social research and then focuses on the practicalities of conducting semi-structured interviews.

PART C: Data collection

    C1: Collecting data

    C2: Data collection skills

    C3: Questionnaires

▶ **C4: Semi-structured interviews**

    C5: Focus groups

    C6: Observation

    C7: Narrative data

    C8: Documents

    C9: Secondary sources of data

    C10: Collecting data using computer-mediated communication (CMC)

*By the 1920s the interview, in a recognisably modern form, both structured and unstruc-
tured, had become established as a data collection method in sociology.*   (Lee, 2004: 870)

One of the earliest explicit uses of interviews to gather data was by the nineteenth-century
social reformer Charles Booth who attempted to survey the nature and extent of poverty in
London. One of his assistants, Beatrice Potter (later Beatrice Webb), described his approach:

*Charles Booth, or one or other of his secretaries, would extract from the school atten-
dance officer, bit by bit, the extensive and intimate information with regard to each family,
the memory of those willing witnesses amplifying and illustrating the precisely recorded
facts in their notebooks . . .*   (Webb, 1938: 278, quoted in Bulmer, 1982: 12)

The key feature of an interview is that there is direct contact between the interviewer, who
may be the researcher and the participant, and that there is an interaction. As a means of
collecting social data it has been recognised as a means of gathering people's opinions, experiences and characteristics by governments, market researchers and academics for much
of the last century. Although most of the government research and market research during
the latter half of the twentieth century used questionnaire-based structured interviews, less
structured interviews designed to gather qualitative data were also used during that time by
some social scientists and were increasingly accepted as a useful means of gathering data.

What is an interview?

As we have seen in A3, human beings use language to communicate their knowledge and understanding to each other and this is commonly through spoken words. When two or more
people talk to each other a conversation can develop with each speaking in turn, or sometimes
both speaking at once. While one is speaking, the other is (perhaps not always!) listening
before taking their turn while the other listens. In some conversations, one person may dom-
inate, do more of the talking and determine the way the conversation develops. The other may
be unable to 'find a space in which to speak' or may simply 'stop participating'.

What is . . .

Interview
A data collection method which usually:
- facilitates direct communication between two people, either face to face or at a
  distance via telephone or the internet;
- enables the interviewer to elicit information, feelings and opinions from the interviewee using questions and interactive dialogue.

An **interview** is a particular type of conversation between two or more people. Usually the
interview is controlled by one person who asks questions of the other. Interviews are used
to find out more by asking questions in a wide range of contexts, for example, when considering someone for a job, by doctors trying to diagnose a patient's illness, by counsellors
trying to help people with problems and by social researchers who want to find out more
about what people think, feel or experience.

Interviews are one of the main data collection methods used by social researchers, providing the opportunity for direct interaction between the researcher and the research participants. As leading social researchers Hammersley and Atkinson highlight:

*The expressive power of language provides the most important resource for accounts.
A crucial feature of language is its capacity to present descriptions, explanations, and
evaluations of almost infinite variety about any aspect of the world, including itself.*
(Hammersley and Atkinson, 1995: 126)

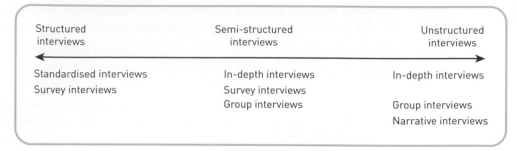

Figure C4.1 Interviews on a structured/semi-structured/unstructured continuum

However, interviews used as a data collection method are different in two ways. First of all, they differ in the degree of structure and standardisation within and between interviews. Usually three types of interview are identified (although it is possible that a research interview will include two or more of these types).

Using a similar continuum to the first we introduced in **C1**, we can show how the degree of structure and standardisation of interviews varies along a continuum rather than as three discrete types.

There is a second dimension to interviews which interacts with this continuum. This relates to the roles that the researcher and the participant play in the interview. These can vary, again along a continuum, from the researcher being in control of the interview, through asking a set of questions to which the research participant replies (known as **participant interviews**), through to the participant being substantially in control of the interview and being enabled by the researcher to tell their own story, in their own way (sometimes known as **informant interviews**). The role of the researcher is quite different in unstructured interviews. For example, in narrative data collection (**C7**) the researcher says little and the data is created and structured by the research participant. This is shown in the third of our continua from **C1** (see Figure C4.2).

The focus of narrative data analysis is on the way in which research participants construct their story without researcher intervention, and so the researcher says little and records the narrative as the research participant tells it. On the other hand, some, particularly feminist, researchers suggest that as the interview becomes less structured and the informant is more in control of the interview, the researcher can become more actively involved in the interview, working with the research informant to create the data. In some cases feminist researchers would go so far as to suggest that the researcher brings into the

participant interviews
A type of interview in which the researcher is in control of the interview, asking a set of questions to which the research participant replies.

informant interviews
A type of interview in which the participant is in control of the interview, and is able to tell their own story, in their own way.

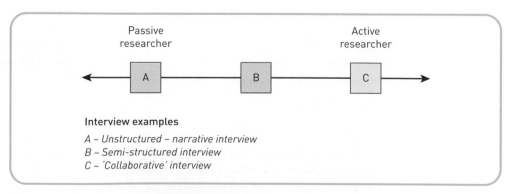

Figure C4.2 Continuum of active/passive researcher

interview their own experiences and ideas. Ann Oakley, a notable exponent of this point of view, undertook research with women throughout their pregnancies and worked in this way (Oakley, 1981). These are called 'collaborative interviews', reflecting the fact that while the interview itself is not pre-structured by the researcher (as in a structured interview), the researcher does have an active involvement in the creation of data.

Think about it . . .

A standard, structured interview effectively uses a questionnaire as an interview format. Here the interviewer uses a questionnaire structured format to interview the participant using carefully prepared questions and answers. For more about designing a questionnaire that can be used as a structured interview, see **C3**.

For a discussion and guidance on the use of unstructured interviews as a data collection method, see **C7**. In this case the 'interview' is structured by the research participant rather than the researcher.

Characteristics of interviews

A: Standardised structured interviews

- Follow a common set of questions for each interview.
- Ask the questions in exactly the same way, using the same words, probes etc for each interview.
- Present the participant with a set of answers to choose from.

B: Semi-structured interviews

- Follow a common set of topics or questions for each interview.
- May introduce the topics or questions in different ways or orders as appropriate for each interview.
- Allow the participant to answer the questions or discuss the topic in their own way using their own words.

C: Unstructured interviews

- Focus on a broad area for discussion.
- Enable the participant to talk about the research topic in their own way.

Semi-structured and unstructured interviews are regarded as 'non-standardised'.

In this section the focus is on the use of semi-structured interviews to gather data in a face-to-face or telephone interview (see **C10** for a discussion of interviews carried out online or via email).

Using semi-structured interviews to collect social research data

Semi-structured interviews are used to collect data in a wide variety of research designs (**B3**). They are most typically associated with the collection of qualitative social data when the researcher is interested in people's experiences, behaviour and understandings and how and why they experience and understand the social world in this way. The researcher is interested in both the information the participant can give about the research topic and how the participant talks about their experiences and attitudes. In other words, the researcher is interested in both the content of the interview conversation and the way the participant expresses themselves – the words they use.

Semi-structured interviews can be used in the following ways:

exploratory research
Research that aims to discover what participants think is important about the research topic.

pilot-test
A trial run or an opportunity to try out a data collection method on a small sample of cases before the main research data gathering takes place; question wording, research participant understanding and data collection procedures can all be tried out and amended if necessary before the main research stage.

1. **Exploratory research** (and **pilot-testing**): for example, to discover what participants think is important about the research topic and to find out how people use language to talk about the research topic. Exploratory research of this kind is common in areas where there has been little research or where the researcher is exploring a new angle or perspective on the research topic. Semi-structured interviews may be used in this way at the pilot stage of research to help the researcher to formulate more structured ways of gathering data.

Real research

An example of research using semi-structured interviews: exploratory research

K. Badlan (2006) Young people living with cystic fibrosis: an insight into their subjective experience, *Health and Social Care in the Community*, 14(3): 264–70

Cystic fibrosis is an inherited chronic medical condition which affects sufferers in a number of ways that require daily therapy. The condition usually results in early death but successful management techniques are now enabling people to live longer, to manage their own care and to live more independently for longer. However, the management of the disease is complex and interferes with 'normal life'. The research aimed 'to explore the experiences of young people living with cystic fibrosis and the impact of these experiences on their compliance to treatment regimen'.

What the researchers did

The researchers interviewed 13 individuals aged between 17 and 39 years and held seven group interviews. They wanted to find out how the young people coped with everyday living and the practical and social issues that their disease posed.

The findings

Most of the young people interviewed did feel that they were in control of their own care. Living a 'normal' life was difficult but most had attempted to have similar lives to their peers. There were different levels of compliance to the medical care regimen and it appeared that some non-compliance was part of trying to live a normal life. The findings from the research would be useful to medical professionals who treat young people with cystic fibrosis and would enable them to have a better understanding of their experiences.

The advantages of using semi-structured interviews

- Young people had the opportunity to talk about their personal experiences of managing their own care.

- Individual, rather than group, interviews may have provided a more confidential situation in which to 'admit' to non-compliance.

- In this research, individual interviews were necessary in some cases to ensure that there was no cross-infection between participants.

- Face-to-face interviews enabled the interviewer to be sensitive to the needs of the participant in talking about potentially distressing subjects.

explanatory research
Research that aims to explain why people experience or understand a social phenomenon in a particular way.

2. **Explanatory research**: semi-structured interviews are used to gather data which will help the researcher to explain why people experience or understand a social phenomenon in a particular way. A common use of semi-structured interviews is where the researcher seeks to explore participants' experiences, opinions and feelings and collects data to help him to gain a better understanding or explanation of behaviour or attitudes. The focus of the research is on how research participants explain their behaviour and understandings in their own words.

Real research

An example of research using semi-structured interviews: explanatory research

S. Cater and L. Coleman (2006) *'Planned' Teenage Pregnancy: Views and Experiences of Young People from Poor and Disadvantaged Backgrounds*, York: Joseph Rowntree Foundation

One of the aims of the Labour Government elected in 1997 was to halve the rate of conception to under 18 year olds by 2010. The UK has one of the highest rates of teenage pregnancy in Europe and the researchers point out that research has found that teenage pregnancy is often linked to poverty and disadvantage. It has also been observed that pregnant teenagers from more affluent backgrounds and who have education and career plans are more likely to have an abortion than those from more deprived areas, with lower expectations. However, it is not clear how many teenagers plan to become pregnant and, if they do plan the pregnancy, how that decision can be explained.

What the researchers did

The researchers wanted to interview young people who had recently been pregnant and who described their pregnancy as 'planned'. First of all they had to define what they meant by a 'planned pregnancy' and devised a set of questions that they could ask of young parents to identify those whose pregnancies had been 'planned'. The four criteria were: intending to become pregnant, stopping contraception, the agreement of their partner and it being the right time for them in terms of their lifestage/lifestyle. A screening questionnaire was devised and administered to young parents in different areas. From this questionnaire 41 young women and 10 young men were identified who had had a planned child and they were then interviewed using a semi-structured interview. The interviews lasted on average 45 minutes. The interview included talking about the pregnancy and the participant's childhood, family background, educational achievement, future ambitions and influences of family and friends. The interview closed by asking participants to reflect on their life prior to pregnancy (and how different their life may be now), and also to imagine their life in the future.

Findings

The researchers identified a number of possible explanations for the planned pregnancy, including:

- Young parents' backgrounds and experiences at school led to wanting to 'change direction'.
- Limited employment and training opportunities locally and a local acceptance of young parents.
- Parenthood is an opportunity to create a family, sometimes compensating for their own bad experiences.
- Many said that their lives would have been worse if they had not become a parent.
- Young fathers wanted to 'be there' for their children and some lacked a 'father-figure'.

> **Advantages of using a semi-structured interview**
>
> - Little previous research had been done and the semi-structured interview allowed for unanticipated explanations to emerge and be explored.
> - An informal and flexible interview guide enabled young parents to talk about their experience in their own way.
> - The semi-structured interview format allowed the researchers to talk to the participants in-depth and to explore, for example, young parents' definitions of a 'planned pregnancy'.
> - Face-to-face interviews enabled the interviewer to be sensitive to the needs of the participant in talking about potentially distressing subjects.

evaluation
A research strategy that usually relates to an intervention or change that has been made, and whether the intervention has achieved the change or outcomes that were intended.

3. **Evaluation**: semi-structured interviews allow the researcher to find out what people think about a social phenomenon they have knowledge of, for example, a service, a new policy or a proposed plan. The format of the semi-structured interview allows the researcher to explore with the participant different aspects of the social phenomenon and to identify and elaborate on, for example, perceived advantages and disadvantages. A semi-structured interview allows the participant to talk about their experiences, perceptions and values in their own way. (See the example in the 'Real research' box below.)

Social research is often a combination of any of the above types, for example exploratory and evaluatory research (see the example in the 'Real research' box below).

Real research

An example of research using semi-structured interviews: exploratory and evaluatory research

L. Ross and A. Witz (1993) 'From surviving to thriving', Department of Social Policy and Social Work, University of Birmingham

Earlier research had showed that women who have been sexually abused as children (termed 'survivors' in this research) can be affected by this in their adult lives in a variety of ways, including, for example, their mental health and their ability to relate to others. This research was undertaken for a large local authority to *explore* survivors' experiences of seeking help as adults and to *evaluate* the helping services these women used now used as adults and in particular to assess the value of the services in terms of helping them as survivors of childhood abuse.

What the researchers did

Estimates of the numbers of adult survivors using various helping services were gathered from the services using a standard questionnaire. Twenty-five women who had been sexually abused as children were identified using snowball sampling. An interview guide was designed to enable women to talk about their adult experience. Particular attention was given to ensuring that the participants were comfortable and well supported through the interview which was a distressing experience for some (see Example C4.1 on p. 228.)

The findings

Most of the women interviewed had used a range of social, health and counselling services to try to find help with the effects of the abuse on them as adults. Different 'routes' through services were identified: for example, some used services sequentially while others used a number of services at the same time. Self-help groups of women who had been abused and 24-hour services were seen to be most helpful. The survivors stressed the importance of 'listening, empathising and establishing what the survivor herself wanted to do'.

The advantages of using semi-structured interviews

- Women who were survivors of childhood sexual abuse had the opportunity to talk about their experiences of using services.
- A flexible interview guide enabled survivors to talk about their experience in their own way.
- Having an interview guide helped to ensure that the same areas were covered in each interview.
- In-depth data about a sensitive topic was collected within a clear framework set out in the interview guide.
- Face-to-face interviews enabled the interviewer to be sensitive to the needs of the participant in talking about potentially distressing subjects.

Settings and contexts where interviews can be used

Semi-structured interviews can be used in a wide variety of settings, from interviewing an elderly person in their own home through to interviewing a government minister or the chief executive of a company. Each setting brings its own particular challenges and you need to think about the setting and context when you are preparing your interview guide and preparing for the interview. For example, you must ensure that you and your interviewee can hear and understand each other (**C2**) and you may need to consider whether an interpreter, signer or advocate may help to improve the communication between you and your participant. Remember that a semi-structured interview is a conversation, and for it to be successful in terms of producing the data you require for your research, there needs to be interaction between you and your interviewee. If you are interviewing your participant at work in their work role, time may be limited and the participant may ask for prior notice of the questions to be asked so that they can prepare for the interview.

Sampling

As we have already noted, semi-structured interviews are usually regarded as a means of collecting qualitative data. In terms of the selection of participants, this will usually mean that purposive sampling (**B5**) is employed and that participants are chosen because of their experience or opinions on the research topic. People are chosen 'with purpose' to enable the researcher to explore the research questions or develop a theory. The participants are selected on the basis of characteristics or experiences that are directly related to the researcher's area of interest and her research questions, and will allow the researcher to study the research topic in depth. Usually semi-structured interview participants are chosen who have something to talk about. It would be difficult to interview someone in this way if they knew nothing about the research topic area.

Ethical issues relating to semi-structured interviews (A5)

Semi-structured interviews are often used to elicit people's experiences and feelings. Care should be taken therefore to ensure that all information data given is confidential and not able to be accessed by others. For more discussion of ethical issues see A5. Here we highlight three specific issues:

1. Semi-structured interviews are often recorded and then transcribed (**C2**). This can mean that the data collected in the interview remains accessible for some time and may be seen or heard by other researchers or transcribers. Recorded and transcribed data must be kept in a secure place and if others are involved they must agree to securing the confidentiality of the data.

2. Semi-structured interviews are often used as part of a research design that includes interviewing small numbers of people, selected specifically because of their experience or opinions, and collecting detailed information about them. Care must be taken to ensure that research reports and dissertations do not include data that could lead to the identification of research participants. As verbatim quotes from interview data are sometimes used to illustrate findings, care must be taken when selecting quotes that may include identifying information. For example, if you are interviewing people who are using a particular health service and the service providers may read the report, care must be taken to ensure that the people interviewed cannot be identified by those providing the service.

3. As we will see, semi-structured interviews can be used to gather data about sensitive and sometimes distressing topics. One of the strengths of the semi-structured interview format is that it is flexible and adaptable to the needs of the participant and can enable people to talk about such issues. However, care must be taken to consider the well-being of the participant and to ensure that participants do not suffer ongoing distress as a result of the interview. There are a number of ways that the researcher can address this:

    (a) make sure that the participant is aware of the research topic and the issues you are likely to raise in the interview;

    (b) provide a comfortable, secure environment in which to hold the interview;

    (c) give the participant control of the recorder – they can then turn off the recorder if they are upset or do not wish to have personal experiences or opinions recorded;

    (d) design the interview to 'lift' the participant out of the more sensitive discussion in the middle of the interview – that is, try to end on a positive note (see Example C4.1 on p. 228);

    (e) provide the participant with a contact phone number, or perhaps access to a website, where further support and information may be accessed if necessary after the interview.

The researcher as the 'primary instrument'

In the semi-structured interview the researcher is usually concerned with gathering detailed and in-depth data, i.e. data that gets beneath the surface of people's experiences and opinions to explore the reasons for behaviour and attitudes. The researcher can be thought of as the 'primary instrument'; that is, the researcher herself both asks the questions and enables the research participant to give their answers. This is what we mean when we speak of the researcher as the 'research tool'. Because the researcher can develop and work with the questions within the interview itself and be responsive to the way in which the research participant tells 'their story', semi-structured interviews are a particularly effective means of gathering data when the subject matter of the interview is complex, sensitive or not well understood.

Think about it . . .

Designing semi-structured interviews

When designing a semi-structured interview we are looking for an approach that will:

- enable research participants to reply in their own way and their own words;
- allow the researcher to explore issues with the participant;
- encourage the participant to express their opinions and feelings;
- be flexible and adaptable to different participants; *but*
- ensure that the same aspects of the research topic are discussed with each participant.

Designing and using an interview guide

interview guide
An agenda for an interview with additional notes and features to aid the researcher.

An **interview guide** is designed to help the researcher to conduct a semi-structured interview. Unlike a questionnaire, an interview guide is not simply a list of questions to be worked through. Rather, the guide acts as an agenda for the interview with additional notes and features to aid the researcher. For face-to-face interviews it is best to limit the guide to one side of a sheet of paper so that it can be easily referred to.

Think about it . . .

The interview guide:

- helps the interviewer to remember the points to cover;
- suggests ways of approaching topics;
- reminds the interviewer about probes and ways of asking questions;
- includes an introduction and a way of ending the interview;
- ensures that the interviewer covers all the topics;
- gives a possible order of topics;
- helps the interviewer to enable people to talk in their own way and as fully as possible;
- is *not* a list of questions!

Here is an interview guide designed for a piece of research carried out by Liz Ross and Anne Witz (Ross and Witz, 1993) (see the 'Real research' box on p. 224). The research focused on women who had been sexually abused as children and who were now, as adults, seeking help and support. We were interested to find out more about how women sought help and how they felt about the support services they used. Although we did not want to discuss their childhood experiences in the interview, participation in the research was likely to trigger memories and deep feelings. The interview guide was carefully designed to try to ensure that participants felt comfortable and able to contribute to the improvement of services for themselves and for others.

Example C4.1

Interview guide

Interviewing women who were survivors of childhood sexual abuse about their use of helping services

1. *Introduction*
   Chat about getting to interview etc.　How are things going with you today?
   Explain confidentiality – nobody else knows you are being interviewed – tapes will be destroyed.
   Interview will be a conversation - explain tape recorder and that she can switch it off at any time if not comfortable.

2. **Can you tell me a bit about yourself: how old you are, where you live, who lives there with you? Children, etc.?**

3. *Use of services*
   Begin by asking about the service known to be used at present.
   Points to cover:
   - What sort of service?
   - How often?
   - What happens there?
   - When did you first go?
   - How did you hear about it?
   - Do the people there know you are a survivor?
   - How do you feel about going there?

4. *First disclosure*
   I want to ask you now about the first time as an adult you told someone that you had been abused as a child.
   Points to cover:
   - Who did you tell?
   - Can you describe what happened?
   - Can you remember why/how you came to tell that person?
   - What were you hoping would happen?
   - What sort of help did you get?
   - What happened next?

5. *Subsequent use of services*
   Points as for current service.

6. *Good/not-so-good points of services used*

7. *Check other service use*

8. *Other support*
   Help from family, partner, friends, other survivors?

9. *Future*
   Help needed in future? Type? How long?

10. *Ending*

Any ways in which you would like services improved both for yourself and for other survivors?   Anything else that you would like to say about the help survivors need?

11. Switch off tape – make sure participant is comfortable, reassure about confidentiality and interest, chat, tea, etc.

Notes on the interview guide

1. Ensure that your research participant is comfortable and fully informed about the nature, length and format of the interview. Time spent building rapport helps the participant to feel more relaxed and willing to engage in the interview. If your subject matter is personal or sensitive then the confidentiality of the interview should be stressed – particularly thinking about what will happen to any information the participant shares in the interview.

2. Initially it is important to encourage your research participant to talk, to help them to feel that they have experiences or opinions to contribute to the interview and to show them that you expect them to do the talking! So the first question or topic you introduce should be something you know they can answer – and to which they have to say more than just 'yes' or 'no'.

3. Early in the interview it can be helpful to talk about events or situations that are likely to be in the participant's mind: current use of service, for example, is a good place to start.

   PROMPTS – here we put in a list of questions to prompt the interviewer to cover all of these points about the current service. This is not a list of questions to be put to the participant – rather, it is a list to remind the interviewer to ask about these aspects if the participant does not include the information in their answer.

4. We are now moving to the middle of the interview and more sensitive and personal aspects of the topic can be introduced. Here we want to encourage the participant to share more and deeper feelings about a key event.

   PROBES – to encourage the participant to share their feelings without asking a lot of detailed questions we used probes – general searching questions which give the participant the opportunity to say more about the event.

5. Now we want to move from the first disclosure through to the present and to discuss each service used in between. Asking the participant to work through a series of events chronologically can be helpful as it helps them to remember and in this research it helped us to understand how the experience of using one service can lead to similar or different experiences when using another. Note that the same prompts are used as in item 3.

6. At this point in the interview, having shared a lot of detailed experience and, in some cases, deep feelings, participants are asked to begin to draw out some general points about the range of services they have used. It is useful to do this late in the interview because participants have by this stage recalled and thought about all the services they have used. Having brought their experiences and feelings to mind, they are in a good position to assess those services and identify 'good' and 'not so good' experiences.

7. A check question to gather anything that has been overlooked.

8. Now the discussion is widened to include other forms of support.

9. As the end of the interview is drawing nearer, the participant is encouraged to look to the future rather than the past.

10. Another question which helps to move the focus away from what may have been a distressing or uncomfortable discussion about the past to looking at ways in which services can be improved for the participant and for others – and for the researcher to find out what ideas people have about improving services. And an opportunity for the participant to say anything else about the topic that has not been included so far.

11. The end of the interview is signalled by turning off the recorder. The participant is reminded of the confidentiality of what has been said and the purpose of the research. The researcher thanks the participant and ensures that she is OK.

Think about it . . .

The semi-structured interview is a bit like doing a jigsaw!

Imagine you are doing a jigsaw. You have been given the pieces but no picture on the box to follow. However, you are told that the picture is about your research topic. Together you and the participant are making the jigsaw.

What do you do first?

Find the edge and corner pieces and put them together.

As researcher, you set the boundaries of the interview – say what you are going to talk about and show, by your initial questions, how you want the participant to take part.

Next?

Sort out the pieces into colours or shapes that seem to match.

You have already decided on ways of dividing up the research topic in designing your interview guide. However, when you start to do this you may find that your participant is sorting in a different way or perhaps has different perceptions of colour – is that blue or purple?

Next?

Begin to put some pieces together and put them within the frame.

Sometimes the participant may start working on a different part of the interview (jigsaw) to you and it will probably be best for you to leave your questions (pieces) on one side and help them to complete the part they want to work on before coming back to your bit.

And?

Sometimes we assume pieces fit together or all the blue pieces belong to the sky and then discover they don't fit so we have to think again, move pieces around, perhaps ask for help or clarification.

You get the picture? An interview is a collaborative activity although the two participants do have different roles.

Conducting a semi-structured interview

Some tips for successful interviewing

- The semi-structured interview is like a conversation where one person (the researcher) focuses on the other (the participant) and does all they can to enable them to talk about the events, feelings and opinions that relate to the research topic. A comfortable setting, with no other distractions, where the researcher and participant can sit so that they can see each other's faces (ideally a seating position that does not feel confrontational, so usually not face to face), facilitates this.

- As the researcher you should approach each interview with a naïve curiosity. Leave any assumptions you might have about the participant or the situation behind and use prompts and probes to always encourage your participant to tell you rather than assume you know what he thinks.

- Use neutral probes (see Example C4.2 below) to ensure that you do not lead your participant to make 'acceptable' comments.

- Encourage your participant with responses (even non-verbal grunts and 'ummms'!) to let them know you are listening,

- Be prepared for surprises: in what people say, for disturbances, for the recorder turning off, and so on. Stay calm!

- Be prepared for participants to tell their story in a variety of different ways (and some will not follow your nicely planned interview guide). You have to be flexible and adaptable to each participant rather than expecting them to conform to your agenda.

- Use your interview guide to ensure that all the research questions have been covered, to remind you of prompts and probes, and as a reminder when your mind goes blank!

Example C4.2

Useful probes for semi-structured interviews

- Can you tell me more about that?
- Can you tell me how you feel about that?
- In what way was that a good/bad experience?
- How did you feel when that happened?
- What happened next?
- Can you tell me more about …?
- You said earlier that . . . . Can we talk a bit more about that?
- How do you mean?
- In what way?

Recording the interview

Semi-structured interviews are often recorded (C2) and then transcribed (C2). Where recording is not possible, notes can be taken during the interview and then fully written up as soon as possible after the interview. A note-taking format can be devised based on the interview guide (see **C2** for more on this).

Reflective interviewing

As you are the 'primary instrument' gathering the data directly from your participants, you can also gather data from yourself and your own experience. After each interview, take some time to reflect on the interview in two ways:

1. Note down your observations of the interview:
   - How did the participant seem to be feeling about the interview?
   - Did the participant show their feelings through non-verbal actions, hand movements or facial expressions?

2. Note down your observations of yourself as interviewer:
   - What surprised you?
   - What worked in terms of interview structure and your interviewing style?
   - What didn't work?
   - What would you do differently?
   - What are your tentative interpretations/ideas for analysis?
   - What didn't you find out? What do you need to clarify – check out with the participant?
   - Do you want to amend your interview guide?

Nature of data collected and implications for analysis

The data gathered from a semi-structured interview is in the words of the participant and as such is 'raw' data. It is usual to record and keep the data in this form in the initial stages of analysis so that the analysis can use the participants' own words (D2). The data gathered is then analysed with regard to the research questions. For student researchers a thematic analysis (D2 and D4) using a set of charts is a useful way to begin to work with such data. Other approaches used may include Grounded Theory, discourse analysis and content analysis (D6–D8).

Your research

Advantages of semi-structured interviews

- Particularly useful for exploring topics with research participants.
- Can explore experiences and feelings in some depth.
- Researcher is in direct contact with the participant.
- Flexibility to allow participants to talk about research topics in their own way.
- Some structure ensures that the same research topic areas are covered with all participants.
- Can be combined with other data collection methods.
- Data is 'raw' (in participant's own words).
- With careful preparation, sensitive or potentially distressing topics can be explored in a comfortable, secure environment.

Disadvantages of semi-structured interviews

- Data gathering is time consuming.
- Researcher needs to develop interviewing skills.
- Potential implications of mismatch between participant and researcher in terms of gender, ethnicity or age.
- Large amounts of 'raw' data may be generated.
- Participants may focus on issues that are not of interest to the researcher.

References and further reading

Badlan, K. (2006) Young people living with cystic fibrosis: an insight into their subjective experience, *Health and Social Care in the Community*, 14(3): 264–70.

Cater, S. and Coleman, L. (2006) *'Planned' teenage pregnancy: views and experiences of young people from poor and disadvantaged backgrounds*, York: Joseph Rowntree Foundation. Available from www.jrf.org.uk/publications/planned-teenage-pregnancy-views-and-experiences-young-people-poor-and-disadvantaged-bac (accessed 12 August 2009).

Hammersley, M. and Atkinson, P. (1995) *Ethnography: Principles in Practice*, London: Routledge.

Lee, R. (2004) Recording technologies and the interview in sociology, 1920–2000, *Sociology*, 38: 869–89.

Minichiello, V., Aroni, R., Timewell, E. and Alexander, L. (1992) *In-depth Interviewing: Researching People*, London: Routledge.

Oakley, A. (1981) Interviewing women: a contradiction in terms, in H. Roberts (ed.) *Doing Feminist Research*, London: Routledge & Kegan Paul.

Ross, L. and Witz, A. (1993) From surviving to thriving, Departmental Paper, Department of Social Policy and Social Work, University of Birmingham.

Webb, B. (1938) *My Apprenticeship*, Harmondsworth: Penguin. Quoted in Bulmer, M. (1982) *The Uses of Social Research*, London: George Allen & Unwin.

CHAPTER C5
Focus groups

Contents

In context

Focus groups can be thought of as an adaptation of interviews (**C4**), that is, they are a type of group interview, when a number of people (usually between 5 and 13) are brought together to discuss a topic. Data generated from the discussion is collected by the researcher.

Focus groups allow researchers to do more than simply collect the factual data generated by the discussion – they also allow the collection of data associated with the focus group itself (that is, the researcher may have an interest in how a group, rather than an individual, reacts to a situation).

PART C: Data collection

    C1: Collecting data

    C2: Data collection skills

    C3: Questionnaires

    C4: Semi-structured interviews

    ▶ **C5: Focus groups**

    C6: Observation

    C7: Narrative data

    C8: Documents

    C9: Secondary sources of data

    C10: Collecting data using computer-mediated communication (CMC)

The **focus group** has been used by researchers for much of the second half of the twentieth century. For example, in the 1940s focus groups were used to assess the impact of propaganda programmes put out on the radio in the USA. The sociologist Robert Merton coined the term 'focused interview' (Merton and Kendall, 1946; Merton, 1987) to describe an interview involving around 12 people. Although the techniques developed by Merton were initially mainly used as a basis for individual interviews, focus groups emerged as a popular tool for market researchers by the 1960s (Bloor *et al.*, 2001) and certainly from the 1980s they were beginning to be widely used within the public sector to ascertain political opinions and to assess the impact of services. More recently, focus groups have become popular (some would say fashionable) in the social sciences (see, for example, a journal paper, written in 1984, by Morgan and Spanish entitled 'Focus groups: a new tool for qualitative research'), and focus groups achieved some favour with the Labour Party (and some notoriety in the press) as a tool to test public opinion and develop their policies in the years prior to their 1997 election victory.

What is a focus group?

Essentially, a focus group is a qualitative data collection method which is an adaptation of the interview technique. The change is that the focus group (as the name implies) departs from the one-to-one interview and becomes a group interview. However, this does not mean that it is simply a way of interviewing a number of people together. (Some researchers may interview a number of people together simply to save time and resources but still collect individual data from each respondent – this is sometimes called a group interview and isn't really a focus group.) Rather, focus groups are used to gather data that is generated in a discussion between the focus group members with the help of the focus group facilitator.

> **? What is . . .**
>
> **Focus group**
> A data collection method that usually:
> - brings together a group of between 5 and 13 people;
> - who have something in common, which is connected to the research topic;
> - to take part in a discussion on that topic, which is facilitated by the researcher.

Although it is difficult to generalise, focus groups usually consist of between 5 and 13 participants plus a facilitator and often a recorder or note taker. Importantly, members are usually *selected* to participate (see below and B5) and the group is made up of people who have something in common which links them to the topic of the focus group. Typically, members of a focus group take part in one organised discussion lasting between one and two hours, often based on a single specified topic. Indeed, it is an intrinsic feature that such groups must have (at least) a focus or objective and, in addition, are often expected to undertake specific tasks, for example, ranking a number of alternatives.

Using focus groups in social research

A focus group is a way of collecting data that draws on group dynamics to acquire deep, rich, often experiential qualitative data (A3 and B4) and can be used within a variety of social research designs. They can be either the sole data collection method used or part of a more complex data collection strategy.

semi-structured
Describes data, or a
data collection method
(such as an interview or
questionnaire), in which
questions and answers
may vary in wording and
length; answers to
questions are often in
the respondent's own
words.

As with other methods of collecting qualitative data (and focus groups have a lot in common with **semi-structured** interviews), the data generated within a focus group is relatively unstructured and uses the words and concepts of the participants. In most cases focus groups are used to find out how people experience and understand the issues raised by the research topic. In particular, though, there is an emphasis on how people interact within the group and how they construct their understanding of the topic together. In this sense the focus group attempts to mimic everyday conversations between groups of people (for example, at the pub, around the dinner table, in a self-help group or in an internet chat room) and reflects the way in which people come to an understanding of an issue or experience through both telling their own 'story' and listening to others. Unlike a one-to one interview, a focus group can provide the opportunity for people to explore and challenge the experiences and opinions of others and to reflect on their own within a facilitated environment, and much of what happens within the group is in the hands of the participants. The researcher acts as a facilitator to, rather than an interviewer of, the group and the emphasis is on enabling the group of people to discuss with each other rather than simply answer a set of questions posed by the researcher.

Focus groups are an appropriate method of data collection to use when the researcher is interested in gathering qualitative data about people's experiences, ideas and understandings and has an interest in why they experience their social world in this way. This is achieved through listening to, observing and recording their discussion and the way the group works with the topic issues. So the researcher is often interested both in the content of the discussion (*what* is said) and also in *how* the subject is discussed.

As focus groups have grown in popularity and been acknowledged as a bona fide data collection method in social science, researchers have found them useful in a range of different research methodologies, settings and contexts. In fact, focus groups are being used in more settings and for more purposes than their originators ever envisaged. Here are just some of the ways focus groups are used:

1. *Exploratory*: or pre-pilot stage of social research, e.g. to discover what participants think is important about an issue or topic and what sort of language and concepts are used in the discussion. Focus groups may be used in this way to assist in the design of further research data collection tools, for example, a questionnaire or a structured interview. However, exploratory research using focus groups alone or alongside other data collection methods is also quite common, particularly among student researchers or when studying an area on which little research has been carried out. In the 'Real research' box below ('Exploratory research using focus groups'), research on young people's physical activity explores the differences between boys from different socio-economic backgrounds (Humbert *et al.*, 2006). (You might also want to look at Grogan and Richards' (2002) exploratory research on male body image and Wong *et al.*'s (2006) study of gender differences in doctors' attitudes and practice towards women who had been abused by their partners.)

Real research

Exploratory research using focus groups

M. L. Humbert *et al.* (2006) Factors that affect physical activity participation among high and low socio-economic status youth, *Qualitative Health Research*, 16: 4

The researchers wanted to *explore* the relationship between physical activity and high or low socio-economic status (SES) among young people aged 12–18. In particular they wanted to find out what the young people thought would help to increase physical activity and were looking for differences between young people from high and low SES backgrounds.

What the researchers did

The researchers selected 160 young people from four schools (two in an area of lower and two in an area of higher SES) in Canada on the basis of their level of physical activity and their willingness to respect the views of others and talk in a group.

Twenty-nine focus groups, of about one hour each, with between 5 and 7 participants, were held. The groups focused on the question: 'If you could be the one in charge of increasing physical activity levels of kids your age, what would you do?'

Each group was recorded and transcribed. The data was analysed using a **content analysis** (D7) approach to develop categories and themes.

content analysis
A technique for examining the categories that the data comprise and condensing them into fewer numbers so that they are easier to understand.

The findings

Having fun with friends, developing competence and having adults involved were important to both groups but there were differences between the two groups with regard to time barriers, choice of activity, costs and facilities. For example, higher SES young people discussed the importance of different choices while lower SES young people highlighted cost, proximity and facilities as important.

The advantages of using focus groups in this research

- Young people had the opportunity to talk about their experiences and opinions.
- Young people with different levels of physical activity could share their experiences and ideas with each other and listen to other young people's perspectives.
- The researchers could explore the differences between higher and lower SES boys by identifying the variations between the focus group discussions.
- More young people could be involved in the research than would be feasible if one-to-one interviews had been undertaken.

2. *Generating a hypothesis or developing theory*: focus groups can be used to gather data that will enable the researcher to look for tentative explanations as to why or how people come to experience or understand a social phenomenon in a particular way. In the 'Real research' box below ('Research using focus groups and developing theory'), research is described that looked at how people's own theories about ageing are connected to their experiences of health as people grow older (Fairhurst, 2005). (You might also take a look at a paper by Davidson *et al.* (2006) which studies lay perceptions of health inequalities and at Munday's (2006) paper on the Women's Institute and the construction of collective identity.)

Real research

Research using focus groups and developing theory

E. Fairhurst (2005) Theorizing growing and being older: connecting physical health, well-being and public health, *Critical Public Health*, 15: 1

As people grow older they have their own ideas – theories – about what being older means. This research looks at how 'ordinary' people (rather than 'experts') connect ideas about their physical health, well-being and public health with their theories about growing older. The research was carried out for Age Concern, a large charity concerned with the needs of older people.

What the researcher did

Officers of Age Concern were trained as facilitators and carried out focus groups with people aged between 40 and 80 years, in ten-year cohort groups, in seven areas of a UK city. Participants were selected through local Age Concern offices and on the basis of age. Many members of the groups knew each other through other activities.

The findings

Health was a key element in the way people discussed and theorised about growing older and how healthy older people were seen as more important than chronological age because good health brought well-being. Some public health aspects like transport and housing contributed to this.

The advantages of using focus groups in this research

- Limited resources and time available.
- Research focused on shared (rather than individual) views and understandings of growing older.
- The focus group replicates everyday conversations – which is where 'ordinary' people 'theorise' about their social world.

3. *Observing and recording how a group interacts*: here the emphasis is on the way the group discusses the issue – who participates, who takes a lead, how dialogue is developed, how language is agreed and the concepts defined when discussing a particular subject. Focus groups are often used in this way in research about sensitive or challenging current issues. Kitzinger's (1994) study of adolescent boys and their knowledge of HIV/Aids was one of the first studies to use focus groups explicitly to study interaction and the construction of meaning within a group. The example in the 'Real research' box below ('Using focus groups to study group interaction') describes research about young people and sexuality (Hyde *et al.*, 2005), but in particular considers how far the focus group itself mimics the everyday interactions of a group of teenagers and the questions this may pose for the researcher.

Real research

Using focus groups to study group interaction

A. Hyde *et al.* (2005) The focus group method: insights from focus group interviews on sexual health with adolescents, *Social Science and Medicine*, 61: 2588–99

The researchers were interested in the perspectives of teenage boys and girls on sexuality and sexual health with a view to developing health education programmes that would help teenagers to develop responsible and healthy sexual behaviour. As part of this they wanted to explore how far interaction in a focus group reflected peer group conversations, as these conversations with their 'jokes, insults, innuendoes, responses, sensitivities and dynamics in the group might offer new insights into the . . . topic under investigation'.

What the researchers did

Girls and boys, aged 14–16 years and 17–19 years, from ten schools in Ireland were invited to participate in one of 29 (single-sex) focus groups. A total of 226 teenagers took part. Members of each group knew each other and were often from the same school class. An interview guide was used to trigger discussion and the focus groups were recorded. The data was analysed using Grounded Theory (D8) techniques to identify key themes. A post-interview questionnaire was given to each individual participant which included questions about the focus group and whether the discussion had been a 'true' reflection of participants' real experiences and opinions. Further analysis of the interactions within the group was carried out.

The findings

Most of the teenagers, when asked individually, said that the information given in the focus group was mostly true, although more girls than boys thought this to be the case. The researchers argue that, from their analysis and experience, the focus groups may be a 'valid representation' of a peer group conversation, that researchers need to be aware of ways in which the composition of the group may affect the variation in the discussion and that during a focus group members may be 'acting out' and 'managing impressions' as well as sharing information. They found that members were able to share anxieties and uncertainties about sexual matters and that some members challenged the views of others.

The advantages of using focus groups in this research

- The researchers could observe how teenagers interact when discussing the topic.
- The focus groups may have mimicked everyday peer group conversations as participants knew each other.
- Participants were able to challenge information shared.
- Participants may have been more at ease than in a one-to-one interview and more willing to share their experiences and views.

BUT this research sets out to question how far the *content* of these focus groups – what people said – can be regarded as 'true'.

4. *Consultation and evaluation*: focus groups may be used to find out what people think about a proposed or existing social phenomenon, for example, a proposed new policy, an existing public service or an event. When focus groups are used in this way, discussion is generated about the phenomenon and participants are encouraged to consider the advantages and disadvantages, good and not-so-good aspects of, perhaps, a residential care service or the policy to ban smoking in public places, through sharing opinions, experiences and ideas. This type of focus group often includes a group task (see below). An evaluation of services for children who are carers, where focus groups were used as part of a multi-method approach, is described in the 'Real research' box below ('Evaluation research using focus groups' – Butler and Astbury, 2005). Focus groups are sometimes used as a means of involving people who may otherwise be excluded from a consultation or evaluation – see, for example, Cambridge and McCarthy's (2001) study which included people with learning disabilities in an evaluation of 'best value' within social care services.

Real research

Evaluation research using focus groups

A. H. Butler and G. Astbury (2005) The caring child: an evaluative case-study of the Cornwall Young Carers' Project, *Children and Society*, 19: 292–303

A variety of different data collection methods were used to evaluate this project including a focus group with service users – that is, 'children and young people who provide . . . a substantial amount of care on a regular basis' (The Carers Act, 1995, p.1). The evaluation findings were to inform future services for young carers.

What the researchers did

They gathered national and local statistics and project monitoring data and a focus group was held with seven young carers aged between 11 and 18 and two facilitators.

The findings

The main themes emerging from the focus group were that the young carers experienced:

- isolation and stigma
- problems at school
- lack of time for leisure
- lack of recognition/praise.

The focus group also discussed the benefits and limitations of the project and other services. While the project had been quite effective in supporting young carers, the evaluation highlighted some aspects for improvement including helping young carers to feel less isolated.

The advantages of using focus groups in this research

- Qualitative data was gathered alongside quantitative data.
- Young carers who are often isolated were able to share their stories and listen to others'.
- Young carers were able to suggest and discuss service improvements.
- Information gathered informally within the project could be 'checked out' with the focus group participants.

5. *'Checking back'*: focus groups are sometimes used as reference groups for the researcher following some analysis of data collected perhaps through interviews or questionnaires, or indeed earlier focus groups. The researcher then reports to the focus group on her analysis and interpretation of the data and checks with the participants that her interpretations make sense to them. Bloor reported that he used focus groups to discuss the findings from his ethnographic study of therapeutic communities with the staff of those organisations (Bloor *et al.*, 2001: 14). Focus groups can also be used in situations where data gathered using another method, for example, a survey questionnaire, has produced surprising findings or findings that cannot be explained with the available data. A focus group allows the researcher to explore the findings with the group and may help the researcher to better interpret the findings.

6. *Empowering/involving participants*: focus groups are also used as a means of involving people in decisions that are to be made (perhaps about a service they use or new

facilities in their neighbourhood) and to give the participants a sense of 'ownership' in the research. This may be as part of a consultation or evaluation process but includes an emphasis on participation. Such focus groups may meet more than once over a period of time (for example, as a 'citizen jury' or a consumer or service user panel).

Focus group settings

Focus groups can take place in many settings or contexts: some 'natural' (or pre-existing), where the participants already know each other because they, for example, go to the same club, live in the same street or go to the same school; and some 'artificial' or created for the purpose of collecting data. With the growth of modern communication, but particularly the internet, it is possible to have an online focus group (**C10**) where the participants never meet face to face. Indeed, the participants could easily be in different parts of the world. This adds a new dimension to the range of information that can be accessed in this way as an online focus group can bring together groups of people who would otherwise be unable to interact, e.g. people from different cultures and nationalities.

The focus group setting is about more than just a physical location. Thinking about the setting means thinking about the composition of the group too. Therefore, we have to think about the topic of the research and settings and contexts within which people can be brought together to discuss that topic. So typical settings/contexts for focus groups might include:

- the workplace: with participants who do particular types of work;
- a community centre, school or similar public building: with people who live in the local area and who use a particular local service, group, etc.;
- groups of people with common interests who may or may not live in the same locality;
- geographical communities: people who live in the same locality, neighbourhood or town and share a common interest in the area;
- non-spatial communities: people with shared interests or experiences who do not usually come into physical contact;
- online: an online focus group can bring together people who are geographically near or far and can bring together people with a particular experience or interest which is relevant for your research (an artificially created group), or can include people who are already involved in online discussion (a natural, pre-existing group) (**C10**).

Size and selecting participants for focus groups

So, how big should a focus group be? And how many focus groups should you run?

> **Your research**
>
> If you are thinking of using focus groups to collect data for your research:
>
> - How big is the population you want to research?
> - How many participants do you have access to (and how many will consent to participate)?

- If you wanted to use focus groups to collect data, do you need to run separate groups because of gender/age/cultural/power etc., differences?
- What resources do you have to do this work (e.g. funding, premises, equipment, etc.)?
- Are you using other data collection methods as well as focus groups?
- How much time have you got?

Student research, especially at undergraduate level, is often affected by constraints (some of which are mentioned above) and sometimes pragmatic decisions have to be made. It seems to us that it is impossible to have a group of less than three participants and, equally, we think it would be difficult to facilitate a group with more than 13.

Probably the first thing that you should remember is that members of a focus group *must* have some knowledge of the topic that is being researched. There is no point otherwise. In most cases, focus groups bring together groups of peers, that is, people who are 'equals' in terms of abilities, experiences, achievements, etc., which are related to the research topic. This notion of a group of peers can get rather stretched to perhaps include people from the same geographical location, who are employed by the same organisation, or who have shared some similar experience (Asbury, 1995). Of course, you might want to construct a focus group that is not composed of peers, but if you do you will need to take special care that each participant has an opportunity to contribute, particularly if some members of the group are seen by other members to be more important, higher in an employment hierarchy or to hold more power.

Focus group data, particularly that resulting from a small number of groups with few participants, is often criticised for its lack of reliability and generalisability when the researcher is not actually trying to achieve reliability and generalisability in the sense these terms are used when working with quantitative data (**A3** and **B4**). Remember that data collected from focus groups is qualitative data and you will usually be selecting participants on the basis of the experience or interest they bring to discussing your research topic. Most focus groups are conducted with purposive samples (**B5**): samples that are chosen purposefully to include people who have an experience, situation or opinion that is related to your research topic and, sometimes, to deliberately include people with potentially different experiences or perspectives. The researcher needs to be aware of potential bias within the sample and to try to ensure that relevant different experiences and perspectives are included. However, as Morgan points out, this is not always possible:

> *If a particular recruitment source does limit the nature of the data that are available, then this forces the choice between living with those limitations or finding other sources of participants that will reduce these biases.* (Morgan, 1997)

An additional matter to consider when selecting participants for a focus group is how the group will get along together – the group dynamics. It is rarely possible to predict just how a group will work together, particularly when the participants are unknown to the researcher. However, from your own experience and knowledge of your research topic you can make some assessment of what is likely to work.

For example, if the topic is related to some aspect of teenage behaviour, for example, smoking, sexual knowledge or binge drinking, running a focus group that includes both teenagers and parents of teenagers could mean that the teenagers are inhibited about what they contribute, and the parents may be less likely to express their anxieties. Separate focus groups, one for teenagers and one for parents, may be more effective in generating useful data.

Similarly, there may be cultural practices and assumptions that govern what can and cannot be said within a group and which may impede participation. These must be considered when bringing together, for example, men and women, people from different ethnic groups or people with disabilities (A5).

It is fine to use a group that already exists, though you need to be aware that the group dynamics within a group where people know each other will be different from one where they don't, and there may be existing power relationships, dominant personalities and differences of opinion that you are unaware of (see Example C5.3 on p. 248).

Focus groups and ethical issues

Generally, ethical issues for face-to-face focus groups are the same as those for other social research methods (Homan, 2004) and centre around the notions of safety, confidentiality/ anonymity and informed consent (A5). There is a special issue with regard to using focus groups and this concerns the way in which sensitive or confidential material is handled within the group and by group members (Gibbs, 1997) since there will always be multiple participants. Participants in the group may be reluctant to disclose information about themselves to the other members of the group. This may be particularly worrying for participants who know each other or who will meet up again after the focus group. Confidentiality within the group cannot be guaranteed by the researcher who can have no control over how information disclosed within the group may be used outside the group. However, the researcher can ask group participants to respect the confidential nature of all information shared within the group on the assumption that each individual would wish their information to be kept confidential within the group and should therefore respect the similar wishes of other members. This situation is best dealt with by ensuring that participants clearly understand what, if any, information can be shared outside the group. Researchers have their usual duty to maintain anonymity and confidentiality.

There are additional ethical issues to be aware of in relation to virtual focus groups carried out on the internet or through email discussion groups (C10).

Practicalities

Recruiting focus group participants

Having decided on the size, number and composition of the focus groups you are aiming for, you will probably need to be quite creative in devising ways of recruiting people to your groups. Here are some ideas:

1. Check out whether there are any existing groups or meeting places where the people you want to recruit will be, for example, a youth club, day centre for older people, health centre, school (for parents, teachers or students), hall of residence or workplace. You may be able to put up a poster (you may need to get permission) asking for volunteers, or go along and talk about your research with a group and then ask for volunteers. It will be helpful in recruiting if you can also hold the focus groups at this venue: check out that possibility too!

2. Snowball! Ask your first recruits to recommend you to a friend or contact who also has an interest in the research topic (B5).

3. Check out whether there are existing groups meeting regularly at community centres, religious buildings, in the workplace, etc., where the members may be willing to take

part in a focus group as part of their regular programme of meetings. One advantage of this is that you automatically have a venue for the group.

4. Advertise your groups, for example, in the local newspaper, through email groups or on websites likely to be used by potential participants, and ask people to contact you for more information so that you can then check their eligibility and, perhaps, which of your groups would be most appropriate for them.

It is usually a good idea to invite more people than you need as it is likely that some people will not turn up. To encourage people to attend, prepare an attractive handout which gives all the information they need.

Example C5.1

Invitation to a focus group

Dear Focus Group Participant

Thank you for agreeing to take part in the focus group.

What you need to know about my research:
I am doing some research on ....
as part of my studies at ....
When I have finished the research the results will ....
You are invited to a focus group discussion with other people from ....
on ....at ... pm
at ....
It will last about .... and light refreshments will be provided.

I hope that the members of the group will have a good opportunity to share their varied experience and opinions on this important topic. You will not be personally identified in anything that is written or reported about the research and what you say will be confidential within the group.

If you have any questions now or later you can contact me by phone – .... or email – ....

Thank you for your help – your participation is valued.

I look forward to seeing you.

Jack

Some researchers send reminder letters or emails, or text or phone participants close to the time of the group.

In practice, it is often difficult to persuade people to participate in focus group sessions unless some incentive is offered. This may be a small payment or voucher or the opportunity to take part in a prize draw. Alternatives, particularly for researchers with limited funds, can include providing refreshments or an information pack; linking the focus group with some other activity such as a school parents' evening, a community event or a presentation or exhibition; or linking the focus group to an existing group meeting or gathering, perhaps at a day centre, a residents' meeting or a youth club.

Where and when?

Where and when a focus group takes place depends on who is in the group and whether the group is meeting face to face or 'virtually' using an online facility (**C10**). Either way, the group should meet at a time and in a place that suits the group participants. Potential participants can be excluded from participating in the group through the choice of venue and time.

Face-to-face focus groups

In planning a group it is important to think about the participants in terms of places where they will be comfortable and that are accessible and convenient for them. For example, many people may feel uncomfortable if the group is held in a church or mosque; some groups may prefer familiar surroundings close to their home; others will value the anonymity of a town centre venue. For some groups, for example, older people or people with a disability, transport may need to be provided. If it is clear to the potential participants that the researcher has not thought about their needs then they are unlikely to agree to take part in the group.

The timing of the group is also important. Groups held during the day are likely to exclude those who are in employment – a form of bias (B5) – while evening groups may deter people who do not like to be out after dark through fear of crime or lack of suitable transport, and people with young children may find early evenings difficult because of meals and bedtimes.

A light and airy room with comfortable chairs arranged in a circle helps people to feel relaxed and refreshments will add to the creation of a friendly and informal atmosphere. Ensure that the room is prepared well before the first participant arrives and that you (and perhaps a co-facilitator) are available to welcome people as they arrive and give them a name badge. Make sure that the room is signposted from all the entrances to the building and latecomers are introduced and included in the discussion as soon as possible. If you are using recording machines, flipcharts or other materials, these should be prepared before the participants arrive and you need to familiarise yourself with their use (C2) so that there is no delay in starting the group or interruption to the group discussion. Always remember that people who take part in focus groups are giving their time and sharing their experiences with others for the benefit of your research.

Online focus groups

This is a growing area for social researchers (see Kenny, 2005) and there are a number of different approaches that can be used. (This is discussed in C10.)

Facilitating focus groups

The first characteristic of a focus group is that it is just that – a group – and you as the researcher are (usually) also the facilitator of the group. This means that you are responsible for the group and particularly for enabling the group to talk about your research topic and interact with each other and you. To do this you will need to have an insight into what is going on in the group as well as ensuring that you are able to gather data that will help you to address your research questions.

The facilitator's (or moderator's) role has been described as 'interactional choreography' (Puchta and Potter, 2004), suggesting that the facilitator's role is to find ways of directing the members of the group to best perform as a group. And focus groups are about performing! Whatever is said, however a point of view is presented or a story told, there is an audience and the audience is full of other performers. Social psychologists have suggested that, rather than people presenting their individual pre-formed attitudes, they perform evaluations, opinions and experiences in relation to the situational context (in this case, the focus group) and the people with whom they are interacting (Puchta and Potter, 2004). The focus group is designed to enable them to do just that.

The second characteristic of focus groups is that they are interactive and not simply a way of asking each person the same question. Rather, group interaction is facilitated (made easy, or enabled) by the researcher.

So, as the facilitator, you need to ensure that:

- members of the group interact;
- the discussion stays focused on your research topic;
- you do not 'lead' or influence the discussion;
- you are aware of the group dynamics and how the participants are experiencing the group.

Most focus group facilitators use a **topic guide** to help them to do this.

? What is . . .

Topic guide

A set of questions, key points or prompts to be included in a focus group or interview which:

- helps the facilitator to remember the issues/questions to introduce;
- suggests ways of approaching topics and phrasing questions;
- reminds the facilitator to probe and follow up comments;
- includes an introduction and a way of ending;
- ensures that the same topics are covered in each group, if you are holding more than one focus group or two or more facilitators are involved.

The topic guide in Example C5.2 is an example that includes the following features:

- a format for *introducing and ending* the focus group, to make sure that you cover all the important information about confidentiality, the purpose of the research, what will happen to the findings and the recordings, and to ensure that participants are thanked for taking part;
- an *introductory question* to get people talking: the first question is directed to each participant in turn so that everyone has an early opportunity to say something in the group;
- four or five *broad questions* to introduce the different aspects of the topic you want the group to discuss;
- follow-up *probes* (for example, 'In what way?', 'Can you tell us more about . . .?', 'How do you mean . . .?') and *prompts* (for example, 'What about other people who live with you? at home? in the neighbourhood?') to encourage people to go into more detail and share more experiences and ideas (see **C4** which includes some useful probes for interviews that could be used for focus groups);
- a way of drawing the focus group to a close using a task (see below for more task ideas).

Example C5.2

A focus group topic guide: what makes a place a 'healthy place' to live?

> Thank you for coming along, this will take about one hour, and anything you say here will be confidential in that none of you will be identified in any report about the meeting and we ask you to respect other people's confidentiality when you leave the group. We are working with other people in Westwood to find out what people think makes a place a healthy place to live. We are talking to a number of groups of people like

	this and the findings from the groups will be used to help policy-makers and local people to make Westwood a healthier place to live. **I'd like to start by asking each of you to introduce yourself by just saying your name and saying about how long you have lived/worked in Westwood and something that you like about living here.**
B E G I N N I N G	1. **I'd like to start by talking about what being healthy means to you.** Physical well-being Mental well-being Free of illness Lifestyle • **What about the other people who live with you?**
M I D D L E	2. **What sorts of things do you think are good for your health?** At home? In your neighbourhood? • **What about the other people who live with you?** 3. **What sorts of things are not so good for your health?** At home? In your neighbourhood? • **What about the other people who live with you?** 4. **What stops you <u>as parents</u> living a healthy life?** • **What could be done to change this?** 5. **What stops your <u>children</u> living a healthy life?** • **What could be done to change this?**
E N D T A S K	6. **Can you suggest one thing that would significantly improve your health and well-being?** (gather on flipchart) 7. **Can you suggest one thing that would significantly improve the health and well-being of <u>your child or children</u>?** (gather on flipchart) 8. **What would make <u>Westwood</u> a healthier place to live?** (gather on flip chart) • **Prioritising task – each person chooses their top three priorities and marks with a star sticker** 9. **Anything else you would like to add?** *Thank you for taking part in this discussion. We are holding a number of discussions like this one and then will be feeding back our findings to people who live and work in the area by the end of the year. Please help yourselves to the healthy eating pack and vouchers.*

Tasks help participants to interact and work together and allow individuals to have their say. Here are some ideas:

● *Buzz groups.* During the group, ask people to discuss an issue in pairs, then fours, before discussing it in the whole group. This can help people to think through the issue before presenting it to the whole group.

- *Prioritising*. List all the different things people have said on a flipchart, then ask people to show which are most important to them by asking them to put a sticker next to their top one, two or three. This gives people the opportunity to say what is important to them as an individual.
- *Group prioritising*. Give the group an amount of 'money' tokens to 'spend' on health services for different groups of people, for example. How will they decide to allocate the 'money'? This can help the group to interact with each other rather than the facilitator.
- *Discussion stimulators*. During the group, introduce a piece of information, a controversial idea, a picture or a short video and then ask for immediate responses. This can be a means of introducing opposing views, information that may not be known by all the group or aspects of the issue that may not otherwise be raised.

Your research

Thinking about your research topic – how would you get people talking about it?

Focus groups, by their nature, are very varied and the way that each group discusses your research topic will be different depending on the make-up of the group, whether people know each other, what types of experience people bring to the group and how they as individuals, or perhaps as an ethnic or gender group, are affected by the research topic. As the facilitator, you have to work with the group to enable all the participants to take part as they want to and to ensure that individuals feel comfortable and valued within the group setting. This is not always easy and you need to be prepared to help the group to work.

So what if . . .

- . . . some people don't take part?
- . . . two people start arguing?
- . . . someone is upset by the subject matter?
- . . . etc., etc.

Example C5.3

So what if you are facilitating a focus group and the discussion is developing quite well but . . .

. . . after a while you notice that one person is always the first to answer when you put a question to the group and occasionally interrupts other people while they are speaking – what do you do?
Tips:

- *Look away from the person and look towards another participant, inviting them to contribute.*
- *Raise your hand slightly in a 'stop' gesture while looking towards another participant.*
- *Say 'Perhaps we could hear from someone else now'.*

. . . after the first few minutes three of the women who are sitting together sit silently. Then they begin to talk very quietly to each other, occasionally laughing – what do you do?

Tips:

- *Look towards them, inviting them to contribute.*
- *Address a question directly to them by name.*
- *Invite them to share their ideas with the group.*

. . . as the discussion develops, two people take the lead and they take opposite points of view. As the argument develops, other people withdraw, leaving the two to 'fight it out' – what do you do?

Tips:

- *Interrupt, saying 'OK, it seems to me that (person A) takes one view and (person B) takes another – what do others think?'*
- *Invite each in turn to say what their main point is and then open the discussion to others.*

. . . one of the men makes a remark about women which upsets some of the women, who object and call him 'a sexist ......' – and other members then defend him. What do you do?

Tips:

- *Interrupt, saying 'OK – sometimes people say things that may be upsetting to others and have different ideas about what is acceptable to say in a group. Can I suggest that we continue our discussion about (the research topic) and agree that we will all be sensitive to the other members of the group – can I check that is OK with everyone?'*
- *If some participants do not wish to continue with the group discussion, give them an opportunity to leave and have a short break before continuing.*

. . . one woman has been very quiet for the early part of the discussion and then, when there is a break in the conversation, starts to tell her personal story which is related to the topic of the focus group. It is a distressing story and she becomes tearful. Some members of the group are very sympathetic and make expressions of concern; others are silent. What do you do?

Tips:

- *Thank her for telling her story.*
- *Suggest a short break before resuming the discussion and check that she wants to continue in the group.*
- *Be prepared with information about sources of help and advice that can be given to participants as they leave the group.*

Recording the group

Ideally, a focus group is recorded using a suitable digital or tape recorder with a surround sound microphone. This will enable the various voices in the group to be recorded clearly. However, this is often not possible and the researcher may be dependent on his notes, flipchart lists and notes made immediately after the group. In either case, as full an account as possible of the focus group needs to be prepared as soon as possible after the group, either through transcribing the recording or assembling and elaborating on the notes taken. It will not always be possible to note who says what in a focus group, although it is helpful to do this when you can (**C2**).

The nature of focus group data

The data collected from a focus group is qualitative data which may include audio or video recordings, transcripts of the recordings, notes taken by the facilitator and co-facilitator, or notes gathered on a flipchart or from a group activity within the focus groups. While it may be possible to identify different speakers in the recordings and notes, this will not always be the case as sometimes people speak over one another or the recording equipment does not pick up the range of voices. As it is not always possible to discern who said what, it is not possible to analyse the data in terms of each individual contribution or to quantify the data in terms of, for example, how many people hold a particular opinion. In any case, focus groups are not usually used to gather individual opinions or experiences but rather to generate data that represents the interaction of the group.

As with other data collection methods, the data gathered is analysed with regard to the nature of the data and the research questions. Focus group data may therefore be analysed using, for example, analytical induction approaches, Grounded Theory, conversational analysis or content analysis (D7). Many student researchers will begin with a thematic analysis using a chart to begin to organise the data (D2 and D4).

Your research

Advantages of focus groups

- Particularly useful for exploratory research and idea/theme generation.
- Group membership can be empowering/liberating for the members.
- Can combine interview and observation.
- Can provide a relaxing, 'safe' setting that is, potentially, disinhibiting and *may* allow groups to be researched in their 'natural setting'.
- Gives access to group dynamics and may indicate how people arrive at their decisions/choices.
- Can be relatively low cost and 'economical': lots of opinions/information at one time.
- Whether there is consensus or disagreement can (often) be ascertained quickly.
- Can usefully be combined with other methods and may enhance them, for example, 'checking back'.
- Works particularly well with groups that have oral traditions.
- Flexible: allows the use of different formats and techniques.
- High *apparent validity*, that is, this is an approach that is intuitively obvious in intent/content and therefore easy for everyone to understand. Thus, the results will be credible (Marshall and Rossman, 2006; Merton, 1987).

Limitations of focus groups

- Success of the group often depends on the skill of the facilitator.
- The researcher has limited control over the data generated.
- Failure to consider the relative power, social positions, cultural issues etc., of group members can affect results.
- An artificial setting may be uncomfortable and 'unnatural' for participants.

- The actions of dominant or subservient personalities can affect validity.
- It is intrinsically difficult to record focus group data.
- Group opinion and individual opinions may be different and can be hard to separate.
- Can be costly, particularly if participants do not attend.
- Usually only possible to ask a few questions or deal with a limited number of topics.
- There are potential problems with confidentiality.
- It is often difficult to do more than identify major themes (Krueger, 1994).
- Focus group outputs may not be generalisable.

Your research

Research quality check: using focus groups

- Does your research need group or individual opinions, attitudes and evaluations?
- Do you want the group to generate themes and ideas?
- Will the data you gather help you to answer your research questions?
- Do you want (or need) to gather a lot of information in a limited time?
- Are group interactions important to your project?
- Have you considered:
  - how the group will be composed?
  - where you will meet?
  - how you will record sessions?
  - how you will 'manage' the group?
  - if you can do this on your own?

References and further reading

Asbury, J. E. (1995) Overview of focus group research, *Qualitative Health Research*, 5: 414–20.

Barbour, R. S. and Kitzinger, J. E. (1999) *Developing Focus Group Research*, London: Sage.

Bloor, M., Frankland, J., Thomas, M. and Robson, K. (2001) *Focus Groups in Social Research*, London: Sage.

Butler, A. H. and Astbury, G. (2005) The caring child: an evaluative case study of the Cornwall young carers project, *Children and Society*, 19: 293–303.

Cambridge, P. and McCarthy, M. (2001) User focus groups and best value in services for people with learning disabilities, *Health & Social Care in the Community*, 9: 476.

Davidson, R., Kitzinger, J. and Hunt, K. (2006) The wealthy get healthy, the poor get poorly? Lay perceptions of health inequalities, *Social Science & Medicine*, 62: 2171.

Fairhurst, E. (2005) Theorising growing and being older: connecting physical health, well-being and public health, *Critical Public Health*, 15: 27–38.

Finch, H. and Lewis, J. (2003) Focus groups, in J. Ritchie and J. Lewis (eds) *Qualitative Research Practice: A Guide for Social Science Students and Researchers*, London: Sage.

Gibbs, A. (1997) Focus groups, *Social Research Update*, 19.

Grogan, S. and Richards, H. (2002) Body image: focus groups with boys and men, *Men and Masculinities*, 4: 219–32.

Homan, R. (2004) Ethical considerations, in S. Becker and A. Bryman (eds) *Understanding Research for Social Policy and Practice*, Bristol: Policy Press/Social Policy Association.

Humbert, M. L., Chad, K. E., Spink, K. S., Mahajarine, N., Anderson, K. D., Bruner, M. W., Girolami, T. M., Odnokon, P. and Gryba, C. R. (2006) Factors that affect physical activity participation among high and low socio-economic status youth, *Qualitative Health Research*, 16: 467–83.

Hyde, A., Howlett, E., Brady, D. and Drennan, J. (2005) The focus group method: insights from focus group interviews on sexual health with adolescents, *Social Science & Medicine*, 61: 2588–99.

Kenny, A. J. (2005) Interaction in cyberspace: an online focus group, *Journal of Advanced Nursing*, 49: 414–22.

Kitziuger, J. (1994) The methodology of focus groups: the importance of interaction between research participants, *Sociology of Health and Illness*, 16: 103–21.

Kreuger, R. A. (1994) *Focus Groups: A Practical Guide for Applied Research*, 2nd edn, London: Sage.

Marshall, C. and Rossman, G. B. (2006) *Designing Qualitative Research*, London: Sage.

Merton, R. K. (1987) The focussed interview and focus group: continuities and discontinuities, *Public Opinion Quarterly*, 51: 550–6.

Merton, R. K. and Kendall, P. (1946) The focused interview, *American Journal of Sociology*, 51: 541–57.

Morgan, D. L. (1997) *Focus Groups as Qualitative Research*, London: Sage.

Morgan, D. L. and Spanish, M. T. (1984) Focus groups: a new tool for qualitative research, *Qualitative Sociology*, 7: 253–70.

Munday, J. (2006) Identity in focus: the use of focus groups to study the construction of collective identity, *Sociology*, 40: 89–105.

Puchta, C. and Potter, J. (2004) *Focus Group Practice*, London: Sage.

Wong, S. H., De Jonge, A., Wester, F., Mol, S. S. L., Romkens, R. R. and Lagro-Janssen, T. (2006) Discussing partner abuse: does doctor's gender really matter? *Family Practice*, 23: 578–86.

CHAPTER C6
Observation

Contents

In context

For as long as there have been people, there has been observation. It is one of the primary, and most basic, ways in which everyone gathers information about the world in which they live and its many component features. Observation offers researchers the chance to collect data as it is generated in the real world and, if they want, to be part of that process as participant observers.

Observation can be quite complex and involves other senses than just sight, since observational data might be collected through any of the five senses (sight, hearing, touch, taste, smell), or, indeed, any combination of them. (For a discussion of the history of observation in research, see Adler and Adler, 1998.)

PART C: Data collection

    C1: Collecting data

    C2: Data collection skills

    C3: Questionnaires

    C4: Semi-structured interviews

    C5: Focus groups

 ▶ **C6: Observation**

    C7: Narrative data

    C8: Documents

    C9: Secondary sources of data

    C10: Collecting data using computer-mediated communication (CMC)

Observation is probably the most basic (not the *simplest*) way to collect data: the researcher records what he or she observes. In social research, observation is often presented as being associated with qualitative data. However, this is not really the case. At the simplest level, counting is clearly a form of observation and is most likely to be linked with quantitative research designs.

❓ What is . . .

Observation

1. The collection of data through the use of human senses.
2. The act of watching social phenomena in the real world and recording events as they happen. In research, observation is usually divided into *participant observation* and *simple observation*.

What do you observe?

So, observation is watching things happen, which sounds like a simple enough task. Reality is, unfortunately, much more complex and we need to ask 'What is it that we are watching?' The answer to this question may be obvious, but not necessarily easy. You are watching (or listening, or whatever) for instances of whatever it is that you are researching. You should be able to tell when these things occur, because you will have specified them in your research question(s) and operational definition(s) (A4).

In real life, observation is complex (and often very time consuming).

Think about it . . .

How complex is observation?

Imagine that you have been commissioned to evaluate crowding in the Student Union café at the University of Anywhere. The café operators are keen to know when (or if) the café is crowded and get some ideas of what to do about it. The café has 45 tables and a total of 180 seats.

How will you start?

Of course, you will plan your project carefully, decide on some research questions and make operational definitions for them (A4) – this isn't easy, of course, and it will probably take some time (and maybe some trial and error) to get these right.

   What would your operational definition of 'crowded' be?

How do you collect your data?

Well, if you've got the operational definitions right, then all you have to do is watch, OK? And you'll need some way to record your findings (C2) as well.

   What would you watch for and record?

Consider the practicalities

For example:

- It probably isn't feasible for one person to do this, so how many observers will you need?
- How will the presence of your observers impact on the process you're watching? (At the very least, you're likely to be occupying seats that customers could otherwise use.)

- Does the shape of the room matter? Will it affect observations?
- How will you make sure that the observers don't overlap, i.e. how will you tell that each observation is separate and that the same data is not recorded by more than one observer?
- How long can an observer work without getting bored?

  What other issues would be important?

Observation of any type (see below) can be carried out either *overtly* (the research participants know that they are being observed) or *covertly* (the research participants do not know that they are under observation). Obviously, this poses some ethical questions that must be addressed before proceeding with your project (A5).

Is it ethical to research when the participants do not know that it is happening? There is no clear answer to this, but one way to think about it is to ask yourself if the data *could* be obtained by overt observation. If the answer is 'yes', then it seems unlikely that a covert project would be ethically sound. If the answer is 'no', then you will still have to decide whether it is appropriate to proceed, and to make some assessment of the risks involved. For example (see the 'Think about it . . .' box below), what happens when you have started a covert participant observation project of a gang of football hooligans and you are 'uncovered'? Perhaps nothing obvious happens (although maybe the gang will ensure that you discover nothing of note, thereby probably rendering your findings useless), but you could have placed yourself in a very dangerous situation. We accept that this is an extreme example, but you should always consider your own safety, as well as that of your participants when undertaking this sort of research.

Think about it . . .
Covert participant observation

Scum Airways

John Sugden (2002) used covert participant observation to infiltrate gangs of football hooligans and discover fascinating background information and links to criminal activities and some of the driving forces behind football violence. It is unlikely that this information could have been unearthed by overt means, but the process carried significant personal risks for the researcher.

Manchester gangs

Peter Walsh (2005) does the same sort of thing in this book, again using sources 'inside' some violent and frightening gangs in Manchester. Again, the risks to the researcher were very high.

Spend a few minutes reflecting on the value of this sort of research, particularly when contrasted with the risks that the researcher experiences (both texts describe violent beatings and illegal killings).

Would you undertake this sort of research?

Types of observation

simple observation
A data collection method in which the researcher/observer is not part of the process that is being researched, but is an objective outsider.

participant observation
A data collection method in which the researcher/ observer achieves intimate knowledge of the group of people who are the subjects of the re-search, in the group's natural setting.

Researchers often divide observation into two distinct types: **simple observation** and **participant observation**, with simple observation seen as very much the 'poor relation'. Adler and Adler (1998) argue that this is because participant observation has a particularly strong theoretical basis in the discipline of symbolic interactionism, noting that

> *interactionist observers usually want to gather data from their subjects while interacting with them.*

In fact, simple observation is a very useful data collection tool and, to some extent at least, it can be quite difficult to differentiate between the two techniques (see Figure C6.1 on p. 259).

Simple observation

In simple observation, the observer is not part of the process that is being researched, but is an objective outsider. Simple observation (in common with all observation types) collects original primary data as it is created. It is important to make certain that the operational definitions (**A4**) that are used to identify the events to be observed are clear and to ensure that proper strategies are in place to record the data (**C2**).

Participant observation

The main purpose of participant observation (and the main way it differs from simple observation) is to achieve intimate knowledge of the group of people who are the subjects of the research (it may be very specific, so that it seeks to understand cultural practices, for example, or it might be quite general) and for that knowledge to be gathered in the group's natural setting. Often, participant observation extends over long periods of time (sometimes years). Participant observation originated with social anthropologists and was subsequently used by ethnographers: it has spread more widely in recent years (see the 'Think about it . . . ' box on p. 256).

There are three main reasons for using participant observation:

1. It is argued (see De Walt, 2002, for example) that using participant observation means that researchers are less likely to try to impose their own social reality and interpretations on the social world they are investigating.

2. Participant observation can sometimes gain access to areas that could not normally be studied (see the 'Think about it . . . ' box on p. 256). However, you should note that there are sometimes significant risks and dangers attached to this sort of study.

3. It tries to understand why specific practices occur (which might be cultural, for example, but could also include working practices – see, for example, Mayo, 1933), and how these practices originate and change over time.

Gold (1958) describes four styles of observation, which he calls: complete participant, participant as observer, observer as participant and complete observer.

- *The complete participant.* In this instance, the researcher will try to become a complete member of the group of people being researched. To achieve this, their role will always be covert (or sometimes the group may know that they are being researched but do not know the real purpose of the research). It is believed that this method will produce the most accurate data because the subjects will react 'normally', that is, as if no researcher were present. Additionally, using this method can sometimes allow the researcher to gain access to otherwise inaccessible groups. There are disadvantages too: the most obvious is that it is not always possible to infiltrate a group in this way (think about white people trying to research a 'black' group or women trying to research a men's group, for simple examples). Concerns are sometimes expressed that the researcher will lose objectivity by becoming a member of the group and (this argument assumes) adopting all its values and practices. To some extent, this is a real risk which would have to be addressed in each individual instance.

Real research

Participant observation: a model for organisational involvement

G. Vinten (1994) Participant observation: a model for organizational involvement, *Journal of Managerial Psychology*, 9(2): 30–9

In this paper, Gerald Vinten (1994) discusses a series of examples describing how covert participant observation can sometimes be the only way in which some behaviour can be discovered. He describes stealing from the workplace, posing as a homosexual to research homosexual behaviour, unusual/unconventional work practices and (rather frighteningly) posing as a patient in a psychiatric hospital so as to observe the medical treatment of people diagnosed with schizophrenia. (He also notes that the use of observation as a data collection method is often criticised, though he contends that it is rigorous and useful.)

- *The participant as observer.* This is different from being a complete participant in that the researcher takes an overt stance and reveals both her presence and her research role to the group. The advantages of this process are similar to the first, that is, the opportunity to study a group in its natural environment. For the researcher, there is no ethical issue arising from misleading the group about the researcher's role. There are some additional disadvantages which are not usually present with the complete researcher: chief among these is the issue that, if people know they are being researched, then it is likely that their behaviour will change (see the 'Real research' box on p. 259).

- *The observer as participant.* Now the researcher is starting to move away from the idea of participating in the research group and the process of data collection is likely to be more formal and structured than in the previous two strategies. Advantages are that it is likely to require a significantly smaller time commitment and, in principle, will increase the objectivity of the researcher as he distances himself from the people. Disadvantages include the possibility that interactions will not be understood so fully and that other issues may not be noticed because the researcher will be unaware of their significance.

- *The complete observer.* Here we have the antithesis of the complete participant. In this role the observer attempts complete objectivity and remains detached from and uninvolved with the activities under observation (ideally, the researcher would be invisible too). Claimed advantages are that the observer will be neutral and unbiased (because of their lack of involvement) and will have only a small influence on the objects of the research. Disadvantages are, essentially, those stated for the observer as participant, plus the fact that, if the researcher does remain completely divorced from the observed group, there is no possibility of discussion to eliminate misunderstandings.

We prefer to think of Gold's roles as points on a continuum rather than as separate positions, giving an infinite variety of possible variations. In addition, it is possible for the researcher to observe herself (auto-observation), adding yet another possible observation type.

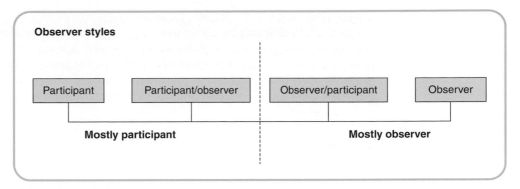

Figure C6.1 Observer styles
Source: Developed from Gold (1958)

It is worth spending a few minutes thinking about these different types of observation, so that you will be able to assess how useful they may be for your research project.

Your research

Thinking about your research questions and operational definitions:

- What observational data might you gather?
- How could you gather the data:
  - as a simple observer?
  - as a participant observer?

Observer effects (Hawthorne effect)

There can be no doubt that, if people know that their behaviour is being observed, then it will change. We all have experience of this. Consider the behaviour of drivers who have seen a police car at the side of the road! That the observer changes the thing that is being observed is a problem that cannot easily be overcome and can have far reaching effects. There is evidence that some behaviour shifts persist even after the observation is over (see the 'Real research' box below) which, again, raises an ethical issue: is it ethical to conduct research when there is a possibility that doing so will change the participants' behaviour permanently?

Real research

The Hawthorne effect

Interestingly, the Hawthorne effect is named after a place rather than the person who discovered it. Mayo (1933) used overt observation to research the effect that working conditions had on employees' performance in the Western Electric Hawthorne Works in Cicero, Illinois (a suburb of Chicago), between 1927 and 1932. He was interested in many aspects of the workplace: lighting, temperature, comfort and also psychological conditions.

His main finding can be summarised as: *employees work harder and are more productive when they know they are being observed*. No surprises here, perhaps. However, Mayo also found that these productivity changes persisted even when the research study had ended and suggested that being the subjects of a study in itself made the employees feel better and work more productively because of the interest of the observer.

Practicalities

There are a number of issues that require thought before embarking on observational research:

Sampling

It is rarely possible or necessary to observe everything for all of the time. Perhaps surprisingly you can apply the same sampling procedures to selecting the times and places you will observe as you might to choosing people to take part in a survey or semi-structured interviews, and your sampling approach will depend on the nature of the data you are gathering.

The first stage is to establish when and where the event to be observed is occurring. Then, bearing in mind your research questions and operational definitions, you will need to decide which times and places will be included in your sample. There are a number of approaches you might take:

- Your sampling may be based on time periods – you could, for example, make and record an observation every 15 minutes.
- Maybe you are interested in how the event you are observing changes during a particular time period and so choose a period for your observation and observe continuously, recording changes as they occur.
- If you are a participant observer you may not be able to record at specific time points but, with your research questions in mind, will identify and note the events, activities and interactions that are of interest to you and record these at the end of your session.

Think about it . . .
Sampling in the Student Union café

What approach to sampling would you take?

- You might observe the whole café every 15 minutes throughout the day.
- You might observe the whole café continuously for an hour at the times known to be busiest and record the flow of people through the café (this would probably require more than one observer to cover the whole café).
- You might observe every tenth person to come into the café and record their experience, waiting time, choice of seats, how many people they were with, etc.

Can you think of other approaches you might take?

Recording data

In the same way as you might design a questionnaire to gather data from a person, or an interview guide to ensure that you cover all of the aspects of your research topic in your interview, you need to design a format into which you can enter your observations. This may be a form, which records each event that is observed in terms of numbers, or it may be a description or a note that you make about what is happening – what you are observing (C2). The design of your format should allow you to record each event in the detail you require and be easy to complete as you are likely to be recording *in situ*.

Validity

In all research it is crucial that you understand what you are researching and are certain that your research processes really get you to the data you need. This is particularly difficult with observation. There is so much to see, hear, touch and smell! This means that you – as the researcher – must be more careful than ever that you know what it is you must observe. It is very easy to be distracted by peripheral events which will detract from the validity of your research (A1). We urge you not to try to collect too much different information when observing. Many researchers try to collect such disparate observations (for example, they may try to collect spoken words, people's positions, body language, facial expressions, etc.). It isn't impossible, but it is very difficult and very time-consuming. You will also need to devise special record-keeping strategies to manage this vast amount of data: and don't forget, you must analyse it all at some point. We urge caution.

Complexity

In part, this is the point made above, but all observational research is complex and time-consuming. As part of the complexity issue, reflect on how you may have to manage multiple observers for complicated or large projects. (This is not always a problem, you can use multiple observers to observe the same phenomenon/person and use this as a sort of triangulation to support your validity.)

You also need to understand that it is difficult for a single researcher to observe more than one thing (or one person) at a time. Even though this can sometimes be partially overcome by using video recording, the difficulties remain and need careful management.

The nature of observational data and implications for analysis

As we have seen, observational data can take a range of different forms from structured through to unstructured. The analytical techniques that you use will depend on the nature of the data you have gathered and may include both quantitative and qualitative approaches. You may be working with both data that you have counted – how many times an event happens, for example – and data that is more descriptive and needs to be interpreted as part of the analysis process. As the observer, the researcher is advised to keep their own notes on the observations including their own impressions of and, if appropriate, feelings about what they are observing.

Your research

Advantages of using observation

- Takes place in the real world.
- Can provide detailed, rounded pictures of social phenomena.
- Data is reliable and has high validity (providing operational definitions are clear).
- Data collected with participant observation is often very rich.
- The technique does not rely on the use of participants' words and therefore it does not matter if the participants are articulate.

Disadvantages of using observation

- Can be difficult to decide what to observe and record.
- Can be very time-consuming.
- Researchers can become bored and lose objectivity.
- The challenge of trying to 'observe everything' can be daunting and lead to loss of motivation.
- Ethical issues, especially around the use of covert participation.
- In simple observation, data may be shallow.
- Researcher effects (e.g. the Hawthorne effect).

Your research

Research quality check – observation

- Have you considered the ethical issues inherent in covert observation?
- How will you ensure that (as the observer) you remain objective?
- Are your operational definitions clear (you know *what* you are trying to observe)?
- Have you got enough time to carry this out?
- If working covertly, how will you gain access to the participant group?
- Do you understand the implications of observer effects?

References and further reading

Adler, P. A. and Adler, P. (1998) Observational techniques, in N. K. Denzin and Y. S. Lincoln (eds) *Collecting and Interpreting Qualitative Materials*, London: Sage.

De Walt, B. R. (2002) *Participant Observation: A Guide for Fieldworkers*, Walnut Creek, CA: Alta Mira Press.

Denzin, N. K. and Lincoln, Y. S. (eds) (1998) *Collecting and Interpreting Qualitative Materials*, London: Sage.

Ely, M. (1991) *Doing Qualitative Research: Circles within Circles*, London: Taylor & Francis.

Gold, R. L. (1958) Roles in sociological field observations, *Social Forces*, 36: 217–23.

Jorgensen, D. L. (1989) *Participant Observation: A Methodology for Human Studies*, Applied Social Research Methods Series, vol. 15, London: Sage.

Mayo, E. (1933) *The Human Problems of an Industrial Civilisation*, New York: Macmillan.

Sanger, J. (1996) *The Compleat Observer? A Field Research Guide to Observation*, London: Falmer Press.

Sugden, J. (2002) *Scum Airways: Inside Football's Underground Economy*, Edinburgh: Mainstream Publishing.

Vinten, G. (1994) Participant observation: a model for organizational involvement, *Journal of Managerial Psychology*, 9(2): 30–9.

Walsh, P. (2005) *Gang War: The Inside Story of the Manchester Gangs*, London: Milo Books.

CHAPTER C7
Narrative data

Contents

In context

Narrative is a technique of data collection and analysis usually associated with qualitative research and very strongly associated with the interpretivist paradigm. The idea of listening to people's stories sounds interesting and, when first seen, seems very easy to use. In fact, it can be very complex, both in the data collection and analysis phases.

PART C: Data collection

C1: Collecting data

C2: Data collection skills

C3: Questionnaires

C4: Semi-structured interviews

C5: Focus groups

C6: Observation

▶ **C7: Narrative data**

C8: Documents

C9: Secondary sources of data

C10: Collecting data using computer-mediated communication (CMC)

Narratives – that is, stories – have probably been around as long as humankind. Certainly, they pre-date writing as a means of record-keeping and many societies still use these 'oral histories' today. Narratives used this way (rather than as stories to entertain) are really the basis for narrative research, which we will look at in this chapter.

? What is . . .

Narrative

The depiction of a sequence of past events as they appear in present time to the narrator, after they have been processed, analysed and constructed into stories.

Narrative as *research*, rather than record-keeping, has been used, in some fields, for the last 100 years at least, notably for analysing literature. However, its modern social science usage probably dates from the 1920s (Elliot, 2005: 3). In the 1960s, French literary critic and semiologist Roland Barthes famously wrote on the importance of narrative, saying:

> The narratives of the world are numberless . . . narrative is present in every age, in every place, in every society . . . . All classes, all human groups, have their narratives . . . narrative is international, transhistorical, transcultural . . .   (Barthes, 1977)

Even with this strong support, it took time for the idea of narrative research to spread throughout the social sciences, but during the last 20 years or so this technique of collecting and analysing data has become more and more popular (Lieblich *et al.*, 1998).

What are narratives?

Narratives are socially constructed stories. A narrative is the *depiction* of a sequence of past events as they appear in present time to the narrator, after they have been processed, analysed and constructed into stories. This notion of *depiction* is of vital importance; narratives are *not* records of events, they are *representations of series of events*. So, on a very simple level, we can often easily establish the *facts* of a particular occasion (we could check the weather records to see if it was raining, for example), but whether the issue of weather was significant to the *story* must be left to the narrator.

How is narrative research different from other qualitative research?

There is something quite unusual and important about this type of data collection; something that makes it different from most of the other methods. This is because the data that we collect, and will later analyse, is not quite the sort of data with which we are most familiar. Instead of collecting 'facts' (and more of this below), what we are *actually* collecting is the way in which the participant(s) have organised the information into a story. It is, therefore, the *story* (and the process of organisation) that is our data.

So, what is a narrative? When we asked this question before, we gave a simple answer. However, this question really needs a relatively complex answer. Narratives – as far as social research is concerned – are generally more than just a simple story. Usually we find that the narrator has 'processed' the data – that is, that he has arranged and interpreted what happened to depict the happenings as a sequence of past events, usually in chronological order, more or less, as they appear to the narrator in the present. The complicated thing here is that (remembering that we are interested in the *story*) we may not really care very much about the 'facts', except, maybe, as a means of comparing participants' viewpoints with fixed things that we know took place. Some theorists, Foucault for example, even go as far as to say 'there are no facts, only interpretations' (Megill, 1985). Riessman argues that our aim, as researchers, is

> to see how respondents in interviews impose order on the flow of experience to make sense of events and actions in their lives. The methodological approach examines the informant's story and analyzes how it is put together, the linguistic and cultural resources it draws on, and how it persuades a listener of authenticity.   (Riessman, 1993)

We think that there can be a lot of confusion about this. Some experts (see, for example, Bryman, 2004: 322) seem to think that *life history* or *oral history* interviews generate narrative data. We are not so sure, since there is an issue about the nature of that data. If it is just about the information (the 'facts', if you like), then these are *not* narrative data. However, if it is about the ways the data is *organised* and the *purpose* of the story, then it *is* narrative research. We think that researchers should always ask themselves, 'Can data collected by non-narrative techniques be subject to narrative analysis?' We do not think it can, though this does not mean that it is impossible to use the *content* of the narrative for analysis.

So, why would someone want to tell us their story? Many theorists suggest that people need to impose some sort of order on their experiences in order to explain and understand them. So the argument is that, basically, we know that our experiences are complex and intertwined and the stories we construct help us to make sense of this chaos. Gee says: 'One of the primary ways – **perhaps the primary way**– human beings make sense of their experience is by casting it in narrative form' (Gee, 1985; emphasis in the original) and Abma says something similar: 'People give meaning to chaotic experiences and try to persuade others of their perspectives by telling stories' (Abma, 1998).

However, even if we accept that 'sense-making' is often the prime purpose of narrative, we can be sure that there are other reasons that people tell their stories too. As researchers, we need to be aware of some of the different possibilities because it will aid our understanding,

We need to be aware that people may have different motives for their storytelling. Not that this is a bad thing – in many ways it can be a strength – but like so many research findings, there is no harm in looking at people's motives for telling stories, which may include:

- persuading others;
- justifying past behaviour/decisions;
- rationalising;
- explanations/understandings of events;
- 'Set[ting] off on their own paths for their own purposes' (Riessman, 1993);
- raising pity or concern (Gergen, 1994).

Think about it . . .

Party narratives

Read the short narrative below. We have selected five places in the story for you to decide what is going on (you will find our interpretations on p. 274).

Researcher: 'Tell me about the party.'

Narrator: 'It was so boring. All the old people sat in one room and talked about the war or something.[1] I wanted to use my Playstation but Dad said that'd be rude. I ask you, is that fair?[2] Anyway, I went looking for Jason [name changed] but he was doing some college work and didn't want to be disturbed, so I thought I'd go and kick the ball in the garden. I mean, I didn't mean to break the glass in the greenhouse. I mean, what a stupid place to put it anyway,[3] you could see that someone would kick a ball through it. It wasn't my fault, it was granddad's for putting it there. So I patched it up with tape and didn't think it was worth telling anyone about it.[4] How was I supposed to know there'd be frost that night and all the flowers would die? I mean, what do people think I know about gardening?'[5]

1. _____
2. _____
3. _____
4. _____
5. _____

Styles of narrative

It is possible to group narratives in different ways which reflect their basic purposes, which we discussed above. This sounds a bit more 'scientific' than our earlier list, and so may be more useful in academia. We include a list below of *possible* narrative styles. It is unlikely that any one story will contain all of these, but it is common for stories to include several.

Example C7.1

Narrative styles

History

Overt agenda

Covert agenda

Seeking legitimation

Seeking researcher approval

Seeking information

Imparting information

Criticising

Think about it . . .

Narrative style

Return to the short narrative in the previous 'Think about it . . .' box. What style of narrative do you think this is? Why?

Why would you want to use narrative?

Many people like the idea of narrative; it sounds easy and pleasant to sit and listen to people's stories. Of course, those are not the greatest reasons for choosing a data collection method! However, if, for example, you want to hear how people make sense of their world (see the list above) and you're interested in that storytelling process *and* the story – if you want to investigate the differences between 'fact' and somebody's 'truth' – then this could be for you. It is often an exciting process: how the narrator created her story is fascinating, and it is absorbing to discover the purposes it is put to. Seeing people's perspectives and how they relate to the social world is always interesting, often illuminating and sometimes exciting! Probably the best feature of narrative research is that, properly applied, it finds out what the *narrator* thinks is important.

Practicalities

Different ways of collecting the data

Collecting narrative data is often called *narrative interviewing,* but that is not very accurate and can lead to confusion since we argue above that interviews per se do not necessarily collect narrative data even though the procedure (a person who is a data source and some-one listening to them) is superficially similar (**C4**).

There are two main ways of collecting narrative data. These are:

1. Non-interrupting
2. Interrupting (interview style).

In both of these techniques, participants will normally have been told what the research is about, have had discussed with them some details of the process, and the usual seating and recording strategies will be in place. However, in the first (non-interrupting) process, the re-searcher will use a single phrase or question to start the data collection session. This might be, for example, 'Tell me about . . . '. The researcher then sits back and listens to the partic-ipant tell their story *and does not interrupt.* Clearly, the design of the research needs to have been thorough and detailed – as is always the case. The researcher needs to have decided whether non-verbal prompts (sometimes called *non-lexical prompts,* because, after all, a grunt is audible but is not a word) are acceptable or what to do when the narrator asks him a direct question during the story. At some point, the story will stop (often when the narra-tor has brought it up to date) and the data collection session is over.

This non-interrupting technique is based upon the idea that stories are *self-terminating,* that is, they come to their own ending (usually) when they've been brought up to date *or* when they've completed the purpose they were started for (Connelly and Clandinin, 1990; Riessman, 1993; Matthews, 2001). It follows from this that, if a narrative is interrupted (and the most likely source of interruption in this setting is the researcher – so long as she has been careful to eliminate the possibility of telephones ringing, people bursting into the room, and so on), then it stops and – even though it may seem to continue – in fact a new story has begun. We think the reasons that this happens are too complex to go into great detail here – and not everyone will agree about how important it is.

With the 'interrupting' method, the researcher will ask for clarification, more detail or, perhaps, a return to the topic from a 'sidetrack'. Although this may mean that more of the collection session is spent focused on the topic and therefore that there is less extraneous material to be transcribed, it is the big difference from the 'non-interrupting' method where the narrator is left to do as he pleases. It can mean that the narrator may be constantly restructuring his story using the interviewer's questions and comments as prompts. This is not necessarily a bad thing, although it is clearly quite different from the non-interrupting method and could result in a very different story. For example, what if the narrator is seek-ing approval (see above) and uses the researcher's comments to tell the story with a differ-ent emphasis?

Settings

The setting (**C2**) in which your research takes place is important and, potentially, can be a significant factor in your success. There is no doubt that a participant's physical and mental comfort can impact on their production of narratives. Although there are other important issues, especially around personal safety (**A5**), we think that there are some fairly basic things that can make your narrative data collection more successful:

- make sure that your participant knows who you are and how to get in touch with you (or your organisation, or supervisor);
- make sure you have informed consent (**A5**) and that your participant understands the purpose of the research and what will happen to the data;
- send participants some basic information before the event (this could include contact details, information about the research, and so on);
- make sure that your participant is in a place where they are comfortable. This may mean meeting them on their 'home ground' or allowing them to choose the place. This should mean that the narrator is more at ease and therefore more willing to cooperate;
- make the room that you use for the session as comfortable as possible. Put chairs as close together as you can while avoiding a face-to-face confrontation;
- check that participants are happy with being recorded and show them how to turn off the recorder if they feel the need. Try to have unobtrusive recording equipment;
- no matter whether you're 'interviewing' or 'non-interrupting', make sure that your participant has time to say everything he needs to.

Skills

The skills needed for narrative research are really no different than those for other qualitative data. It is more a case of making sure that your research design is clear (i.e. interrupting/non-interrupting) and that you stick to the design.

The narrative data

These days, narrative data collection sessions (a clumsy term perhaps, but we think it is preferable to 'interviews') are usually recorded either on cassette or with a digital audio recorder. What happens then is, of course, dictated by the design of the research and its analysis strategy (**B1**, **B3** and **D2**) but, typically, the researcher will transcribe the recording for analysis (**C2**). This is a very time-consuming operation, although we believe that there is no better way of becoming immersed in the data. The downside, of course, is the length of time taken by this laborious process.

Be warned: narrative research tends to be pretty 'wordy'. People given the chance to talk will often do so at length and this can mean huge transcriptions! You need to be aware of this potential difficulty at your planning and design stage so that you do not fall into the trap of not having enough time in your schedule to finish the work properly.

The decision on the actual type of analysis will have been taken already at the planning stage, so will not be discussed here (**D5**).

Criteria for 'good' narrative research

In **A1** we write about the nature of 'good research' and talk about some of the criteria that can be used to judge it. With narrative research we hit a bit of a problem. Narrative is less interested in the 'facts' and much more interested in the subjective story that the narrator has constructed from the facts. The usual things like reliability, validity and generalisability which are such useful characteristics of some research designs (A1) are not always useful for judging the quality of narrative research (see, for example, Koch and Harrington, 1998). We think that there are still useful ways to evaluate the quality of this sort of research and that this can be done by examining the self-consistency of the story (we would make an argument that, with advanced work, this should be done in relation to the underpinning theoretical perspective's concept of 'truth') and on Koch and Harrington's (1998) notions of 'credibility' and dependability.

Advantages and disadvantages of narrative research

Advantages of narrative

One of the best things about well-executed narrative research is that it gives participants a chance to 'tell their story'. Experience of using this method suggests that this is often the first time that this happens, or at least the first time that the listener is willing and interested.

Telling the story also allows and encourages participants to make choices and, perhaps, to make definitions, both of themselves and of the events that they are describing. This can help them to feel that they are involved in and therefore 'own' part of the research. That this really happens is often seen in the depth and nature of the data collected.

Real research

'Early motherhood and Black women': sharing information

Ann Phoenix wrote about attitudes towards young black mothers (1994) narrating their stories of the overt racism to which they were subjected. A notable feature of these narratives is that they are presented in a manner that suggest that the narrators believe that – if they share their information – it will be used by others to alleviate the problem.

There are rewards for us, the researchers, too. Narrative tends to be cross-disciplinary and gives us access to multiple situations at the same time. While researching for a PhD, Matthews (2001) often found that participants would talk about the sensitive issues of 'race' and racism in a variety of social and professional settings which led to insights that might otherwise not have been made. (It also meant that there was a need to review a series of assumptions that the researcher had made, which underlines the usefulness of narrative for exploratory research.)

As well as this, it is almost impossible for the researcher to avoid 'putting himself into the shoes' of the narrator. This reflexivity helps to locate the researcher as part of the research process (Mason, 1996).

The different ways in which narrative can access 'sensitive' information are important too. Ward (2005) used narrative to access the life histories of lesbians, and Daiute and Turniski (2005) accessed young people's stories in post-war Croatia. These were complex, moving and painful stories that would be difficult to access and analyse with other techniques (see the 'Real research' box opposite).

Real research

Young people's stories of conflict and development in post-war Croatia

(This is an extract from a real narrative, demonstrating that they can be moving, even heartbreaking and disturbing – something that researchers need to be aware of.)

This conflict started between me and my friend because she lied. I felt awful. She was from a different nation, but I have never made any difference because we are all from flesh and blood, and we have the right to say our opinion. While we were going to the 'Suncokret' from school, she told me some terrible things about me and my family which have really moved me and I started to cry. I didn't say anything to her in order to cool the situation. But the quarrel continued. Then she threw a snow ball and hit me in the eye. My eye got red and I was in pain. I left for home and I told everything to my mother. My mother was very angry and she wanted to call her grandmother, but I told her to wait until her mother gets back to Gvozd.

The day after, I came to school and I was getting ready for the class when my class-teacher asked me to come talk to her. I was surprised because I didn't know why she would want to see me. But, my 'friend' had complained about me to the class-teacher. She asked me why did I swear at her Serbian mother and why am I saying bad things against Serbs. I started to cry and I tried to explain that that isn't true, that it doesn't matter to me whether someone is Balkan, Romanian, African, Serb, Croat, Bosnian, white, has long hair, has big nose . . . it only matters to me that he is a good person. It doesn't matter how he looks like, it is important to have a good heart

(Daiute and Turniski, 2005: 218)

Disadvantages/limitations of narrative

When participants tell their stories they take a risk, because they are 'exposing' themselves to the researcher and, ultimately, to whoever reads the research. Of course, they will not be identifiable in a report, but there can still be feelings of vulnerability that need to be taken into account.

Some people may be concerned that the researcher will find their story embarrassing or silly. Others may be worried that if they disclose some criminal act, then action might be taken against them. (This is a significant ethical issue which should be discussed with a supervisor at an early stage so that the researcher's approach to any such issue is both systematic and in accord with any appropriate legislation. At the moment, any disclosure of terrorism or of an offence under the Children Act *requires* the researcher to report it to the police.) We look at these issues in more detail in A5.

New researchers are often surprised at the things that participants tell them. It is not unusual to hear about driving offences, the use of illegal drugs and other such things. Being prepared for this is important and is discussed in more detail in A5, together with the associated power issues.

Quite often, the narrator feels a bit uncomfortable or unsettled that his story has been 'taken' by the researcher, and so no longer belongs to him. It is not clear whether people think this is always a bad thing or not. Some authorities argue that it can be a liberating experience (Atkinson *et al.*, 1993: 443; Zimbardo, 1988: 469), but we think that this suggestion should be viewed with caution. A particular problem is that, quite often, participants see researchers as 'experts' and will frequently seek their opinion on the content of the narrative (this happens in other qualitative inquiry too). There are many possible reasons for this, ranging from the need to legitimate past actions to gaining third-party advice on the future. While it is difficult not to respond to such questions and requests, the researcher should always take care not to respond inappropriately.

Unexpected findings

Quite often in narrative research something a bit unusual happens. A fairly common experience is that – no matter what the focus of your research is – you get unexpected findings.

One of the reasons for this is that the nature of narrative research is quite uncontrolled – at least, it is not usually as controlled by the researcher as some other methods are (**C1**). Certainly, it is very flexible and – even though there is a clear centre of attention – it is the narrator who is in control – much more so than the researcher. However, as with most qualitative data collection, the issue of choice (see Parts **A** and **D**) is of great significance.

So there is likely to be a lot of supporting, sometime extraneous, material in a story. But that material might be very useful in ways that you'd never imagined.

Real research

Unexpected findings in health research

When I was researching health experiences of people of mixed race (Matthews, 2001), I was using non-interrupting narrative collection which meant I just sat and listened; the method didn't allow me to interrupt. One participant used that session to disclose a history of her own experiences of physical and psychological abuse. This was alarming and distressing, as I'm sure you can imagine, and raised a number of issues for me – not least that I hadn't expected this to happen!

However, when that initial hurdle was overcome it became apparent that this was a data collection session that was really useful for my project, because it opened a number of doors that I hadn't even realised were there – things to do with power in domestic relationships that had an ethnic dimension.

It is important in all research with people that you prepare yourself as well as possible for the unexpected. For example, you have a duty to report certain activities to the police (these are things like child abuse under the provisions of the Children Act 2004, and the Terrorism Act 2006). How might that affect your research?

Your research

Advantages of narrative

- Story/narrator is central.
- Opportunity to tell the story.
- Narrator can exercise choice.

- Narrators 'own' the storytelling.
- Accesses interpretations and 'what matters'.
- Accesses information that may not be available elsewhere.
- Accesses sensitive information.
- Accesses 'unknown' information.
- Excellent for exploratory work.
- No need for prior understanding of issues.
- No prompting = no interruption.
- Collects *lots* of data.
- Wide 'range' of data.

Disadvantages of narrative

- Needs participants' willingness to tell their story.
- Can be difficult to access narrators.
- Narrators 'expose' themselves.
- Loss of ownership once told.
- May be cathartic for the narrator – this may be an advantage or a disadvantage.
- Ethical issues on disclosure.
- Difficult to analyse.
- Does 'truth v. fact' matter?
- Choice – selecting for analysis.
- No talking = no checking back.
- No time to develop relationship.
- Researcher may be seen as an expert.
- Difficulties of shared understanding.
- Very long transcriptions, large amounts of data.
- May be some irrelevant content.

Your research

Research quality check: narrative

- Are you interested in facts or interpretations?
- Do you want to collect information that the participant has processed?
- Do you want to know how the story relates to fact?
- Are you interested in the reasons behind the story's creation?
- Are you looking for 'unusual' or difficult-to-access information?
- Have you thought about how to deal with unexpected content?
- Have you considered how to manage very large quantities of data?

Think about it . . .

Party narratives

There are many possible interpretations of the narrative. These were ours:

Researcher: 'Tell me about the party.'

Narrator: 'It was so boring. All the old people sat in one room and talked about the war or something.[1] I wanted to use my Playstation but Dad said that'd be rude. I ask you, is that fair?[2] Anyway, I went looking for Jason [name changed] but he was doing some college work and didn't want to be disturbed, so I thought I'd go and kick the ball in the garden. I mean, I didn't mean to break the glass in the greenhouse. I mean, what a stupid place to put it anyway,[3] you could see that someone would kick a ball through it. It wasn't my fault, it was granddad's for putting it there. So I patched it up with tape and didn't think it was worth telling anyone about it.[4] How was I supposed to know there'd be frost that night and all the flowers would die? I mean, what do people think I know about gardening?'[5]

1. This probably has nothing to do with the 'facts' that people were talking about. But it is a way of someone describing their experience.

2. This is an attempt to generate pity at (supposedly) bad treatment.

3. This is justifying behaviour – it's someone else's fault.

4. Now the participant is rationalising – it was such a small event it wasn't worth bothering people!

5. This time a mixture of rationalising and raising pity!

References and further reading

Abma, T. A. (1998) Storytelling as inquiry in a mental hospital, *Qualitative Health Research*, 8: 821–38.

Atkinson, R. L., Atkinson, R. C., Smith, E. E. and Bem, D. J. (1993) *Introduction to Psychology*, 11th edn, Fort Worth, TX: Harcourt Brace Jovanovich.

Barthes, R. (1977) Introduction to the structural analysis of narratives, in *Image-Music-Text*, Glasgow: Collins.

Bryman, A. (2004) *Social Research Methods*, Oxford University Press.

Clandinin, D. J. and Connelly, F. M. (2000) *Narrative Inquiry*, San Francisco: Jossey-Bass.

Connelly, F. M. and Clandinin, D. J. (1990) Stories of experience and narrative inquiry, *Educational Researcher*, 19: 2–14.

Czarniawska, B. (2004) *Narratives in Social Science Research*, London: Sage.

Daiute, C. and Turniski, M. (2005) Young people's stories of conflict and development in post-war Croatia, *Narrative Inquiry*, 15(2): 217–40.

Elliot, J. (2005) *Using Narrative in Social Research: Qualitative and Quantitative Approaches*, London: Sage.

Gee, J. P. (1985) The narrativization of experience in the oral style, *Journal of Education*, 167: 9–35.

Gergen, K. J. (1994) *Realities and Relationships: Soundings in Social Construction*, Cambridge, MA: Harvard University Press.

Koch, T. and Harrington, A. (1998) Reconceptualising rigour: the case for reflexivity, *Journal of Advanced Nursing*, 28(4): 882–90.

Lieblich, A., Tuval-Mashiach, R. and Zilber, T. (1998) *Narrative Research: Reading, Analysis and Interpretation*, London: Sage.

Mason, J. (1996) *Qualitative Researching*, London: Sage.

Matthews, R. N. (2001) Mixed ethnicity, health and healthcare experiences, Department of Social Policy and Social Work, University of Birmingham.

Megill, A. (1985) *Prophets of Extremity: Nietzsche, Heidegger, Foucault, Derrida*, Berkeley, CA: University of California Press.

Miller, R. L. (2000) *Researching Life Stories and Family Histories*, Sage: London.

Phoenix, A. (1994) Early motherhood and Black women, in M. Wilson (ed.) *Healthy and Wise: The Essential Health Handbook for Black Women*, London: Virago.

Riessman, C. K. (1993) *Narrative Analysis*, London: Sage.

Ward, N. J. (2005) Social exclusion and mental wellbeing: lesbian experiences, University of Birmingham.

Zimbardo, P. G. (1988) *Psychology and Life*, 12th edn, New York: HarperCollins.

CHAPTER C8
Documents

Contents

In context

This section is about the use of documents in social research. We introduce the things that can be seen as documents and try to define them.

   We then discuss the use of documents as a rich source of data, while noting that they can sometimes be difficult to access and to interpret. Nevertheless documents are, potentially, very useful.

   If you are using documents in your research, we recommend that you look at **B2** and **C9** as well.

PART C: Data collection

   C1:   Collecting data

   C2:   Data collection skills

   C3:   Questionnaires

   C4:   Semi-structured interviews

   C5:   Focus groups

   C6:   Observation

   C7:   Narrative data

▶ **C8:**   **Documents**

   C9:   Secondary sources of data

   C10: Collecting data using computer-mediated communication (CMC)

The nature of the material that we discuss below means that this chapter is about both data *collection* and data *analysis*, although general analysis is dealt with in more detail in Part D.

Documentary analysis has probably been around since writing was invented by the Sumerians in Southern Mesopotamia about 4,000 years BC (www.ancientscripts.com/sumerian.html). Certainly, historians have used it for as long as their discipline has existed and it has always been popular in social research.

For the purposes of this chapter, we have assumed that most of the **documents** used will be relatively modern. That is, we have not gone into the issues of translating from, for example, Chaucerian English to contemporary language. This presents a different set of issues and difficulties which we do not have the scope to explore.

⍰ What is . . .

Document

Documents are difficult to define, but we believe that they are best described as *written records about people and things that are generated through the process of living*. This includes things like film, audiotape and video, but excludes such things as oral histories.

Probably the image that comes to mind for most of us when we think 'document' is that of a bundle of papers, maybe held together by a staple or in a folder. This is only part of the truth and we discuss this further below.

What are documents good for in social research?

[Documents] are 'social facts', in that they are produced, shared and used in socially organised ways. They are not, however, transparent representations of organisational routines, decision-making processes or professional diagnoses. They construct particular kinds of representations within their own conventions. We should not use documentary sources as surrogates for other kinds of data.   (Atkinson and Coffey, in Silverman, 1997: 47)

Every document has been written or produced by someone, in a specific context and for a particular purpose. The contents of a document do not become fact or truth simply by being written down. The focus in social research may be on the factual content within a document but is also likely to be on why and how it has been produced in a particular form and in a specific context.

Using documents in research is very like using other data collection methods. The most important difference is that the data in documents, in theory at least, is fixed at the time that it is written. In fact, this may not entirely be the case as it is not unknown for authors to try to 'rewrite' history – for a discussion, see Southgate, 2001. Possibly the most familiar examples of this are seen in war histories which are almost always written by the victors, and tend to gloss over their shortcomings while highlighting those of the losers. Some 'electronic' documents (see p. 278) are less robust than we might first think and are often subject to deletion and/or change by the author or others. Nevertheless, most documents can be accepted as providing a fixed record of something that happened at a particular time.

Documents can contain very different sorts of data, depending on their type, purpose and medium. This can range across the spectrum of social life and, although the list is long, could include, for example:

- news items (and commentary);
- numerical data (Census of Population, surveys);
- qualitative data (reports and findings of research projects);
- policy (government and other 'official' documents);
- personal information and interpretation (diaries, letters or shopping lists);

- history;
- visual material (films, photographs or video);
- audio material;
- 'other' material (see below).

Of course, documents are not restricted to one sort of data and it is possible for many different forms to be present in a single document.

Why use documents?

1. Documents are often readily available and can contain large amounts of information.
2. Documents are static and present a 'snapshot' of a particular time.
3. As least as important as the first two points, they are something more than just a source of data, since it is possible to research documents in their own right as a 'field' of research (Prior, 2003: 26).
4. Documents are socially constructed: this means that they can tell us more than just the data and information that they contain.
5. Documents can be very useful to triangulate data: that is, to get a picture of the data already collected for research from different sources.

Types of documents

To make life easier, we have divided documents into two main groups: 'written' and 'other'. This was not an easy decision, since some 'other' documents inevitably include words. However, we think that everyone is familiar with the idea of the 'written' document: the diary, committee minutes, official records, etc.

There is a complication, though. For most of recent history, 'written' records have consisted of some form of writing on paper (we include printing and typing in this notion). However, since the early 1990s more and more records are kept either in electronic form (in computer memories and disk drives) or in a form that can be accessed only by computer (CD-ROM, DVD-ROM, flash drives, memory sticks and cards, etc.). This is a complication, but we think that, mostly, this change of format is best ignored and the easiest way to approach these documents is to think of the medium in which they are created. Thus a word-processed document can be seen as its paper equivalent, or a digital picture seen as a photograph. This is not without some problematic issues around permanence, longevity and access, which we discuss these later. There are also separate issues concerning the security of electronic data, some of which are discussed in A5.

There are a number of other different ways, or typologies, that can be used to organise documents other than the simple 'written/other' dichotomy we have set out above (and which forms the first group below), which can be used in addition. We think that the best typologies are the following:

1. *Medium*: that is, the type of document and the material it is made of (which now includes non-material electronic forms such as the internet).
2. *Origin*: why the document was created and by whom.
3. *Purpose* (sometimes the same as 'origin', but not always – see below): which includes archiving and information transfer.

These include:
- *Medium* (1):
  - *paper*: with writing/printing;
  - *electronic*: computer memory, CD, DVD, flash, etc.

- *Medium* (2):
    - photograph (including digital photographs);
    - film;
    - video (tape, disk or solid-state memory);
    - audio (tape, disk or solid-state memory);
    - official inscriptions (commemorative plaques, foundation stones, inscriptions on buildings, etc.);
    - other writing (slogans on clothing, graffiti, gravestones, etc.);
    - mass media (newspapers, magazines, television, radio, etc.);
    - the internet.

(This list is not exhaustive and it would easily be possible to make it unnecessarily complex.)

- *Origin* (1):
    - *primary*: documents created by the person/people who observed/participated in the events described;
    - *secondary*: reports of things seen or recorded by others.

    It is also possible to have:

    - *tertiary*: compilations based on secondary documents and other data.
- *Origin* (2):
    - *personal*: documents created by 'private' individuals;
    - *official*: documents created by 'organisations' like governments, companies, transnational organisations (such as charities like Oxfam), supranational organisations (such as the EU, United Nations or NATO),
    - *historical*: documents specifically created to record 'history' (there is a debate about the existence of this category, some arguing that such documents fall into the 'personal' or 'official' categories; we include it for completeness).
- *Purpose*: some purposes are the same as origin (2) above; that is, official or historical. The other main purpose of the creation of documents is to make information available to others. Sometimes, this is a branch of 'official' and is then called an 'archive'. Archives are, usually, large quantities of data stored in some sort of organised manner to enable searching and access. Two examples are:
    - the Mass Observation Archive (www.sussex.ac.uk/librarymassobs);
    - Qualidata (www.essex.ac.uk/qualidata/).

    Modern archives are almost all computer based. Older archives are usually paper based. There are obvious implications for access and searching.

Think about it . . .

Something to think about

It is unlikely that the original purpose for creating the document is the same as that which drives your research (indeed, the original purpose may be unknown) – this sometimes makes it difficult (or impossible) to use the document in your research.

Most researchers will decide which typology, or combination of typologies, is appropriate for their project depending on what they are trying to find out and their research design (Part B). However, there are other issues that need consideration.

Permanence/longevity

Nothing lasts forever. This is particularly true of documents. Paper documents are fragile, flammable and subject to water and insect damage. Some inks fade over time or through exposure to light. Documents get lost, misplaced, hidden or destroyed (sometimes deliberately). Even apparently more permanent media, such as CDs, degrade over time.

The life of magnetic media (this includes audiotape and cassettes, videotape and cassettes, computer floppy disks, etc.) is limited and most have a useable lifespan of about 30 years (Bogart, 1995). Less is known about optical media (CD-ROM, DVD-ROM, etc.) though manufacturers claim lifespans between 50 and 200 years (Marken, 2004). Film degrades at different rates depending on what it is made from and how it is stored. Under good conditions 100–150 years may be possible.

But some documents are even more ephemeral. Personal letters may be destroyed after reading or disposed of in house clearances after the owner's death. Diaries are often destroyed at the end of the year. But there is one medium to which we have become accustomed that is the most short-lived of all: the internet. Documents on the internet may have a life of years, but only if they remain unchanged or undeleted. Even websites that we may believe are permanent (Wikipedia, for example) are actually changing all the time as they are updated and edited. Documents that exist one day are gone the next. Researchers therefore need to treat these sources with care and should also record the date that a document is accessed.

Access

Access to documents is often complex. Clearly, internet access is required for all web-based documents, but other requirements are less clear. Some government records are available to the public (for example, certificates of births, marriages and deaths, some census records and probated wills) but often a fee is charged. The Freedom of Information Act (2000) gave everyone access to documents published by a wide range of 'authorities' (for example, central and local government, the NHS, universities and schools) but there is a long list of exceptions: see www.justice.gov.uk/guidance/foi-exemptions-about.htm (accessed 22 August 2009) for details. It is worth noting that some official documents in the UK are kept secret under the '30-year rule', created by the Public Records Act (1958). Thus it is often impossible to research sensitive subjects while they are still relevant.

Often the problem with locating documents (and one for which we have no reliable solution) is knowing that they exist in the first place. Obviously, it is possible to pay specialist companies to locate documents for you, but it is a very expensive process and likely to be beyond the means of most, if not all, students. Searching the internet can be productive too, as can the technique of simply asking potential data holders if they keep the information that you want. A persistent, multi-pronged strategy is likely to be the most successful.

Context

Because documents are social constructions, their context is important. Researchers need to ask a series of questions when using documents so that as much of the context as possible can be understood (see the 'Your research' box on p. 282).

Authenticity

Whether or not a document is authentic is, obviously, important in research (even if your research is concerned with forged documents, it is still important to understand origins).

It is not always possible to assess the authenticity of documents and there have been some famous instances where mistakes have been made (see the 'Real research' box on p. 281).

We think that the best approach is to be fairly cynical, particularly if you think you have discovered something earth-shattering. In general, we think that it is possible to establish the authenticity of most official documents (though this, too, changes over time and with the advent of new administrations – it has become quite difficult to establish the veracity of some documents from the former East Germany, for example). However, the likelihood of the student researcher discovering forged or fraudulent documents is, we believe, very low.

Real research

The Hitler diaries

In 1983 a German news magazine published parts of what was claimed to be the diaries of Adolph Hitler. The magazine paid a vast sum of money for these documents and they were accepted as authentic by eminent historians. However, it was subsequently proved that they were forgeries and there was some suspicion of collusion in the deceit by one of the historians. (The diaries were written in modern ink on contemporary paper. The forger was later convicted and served nearly four years of a prison sentence.)

Why do you think that people were so easily convinced that the diaries were authentic?

Problems with official documents and statistics

Although we are not suggesting that governments and other official sources set out to mislead the readers of their documents, there are some problematical issues which are worth thinking about:

- It is not unusual for definitions to change over time. This can often be the case in official documents. For example, the names of 'racial' categories have changed significantly over time. The group of people who were once known as 'West Indian' may now be known as 'African-Caribbean' or 'Black' (these terms are different in other countries as well, for example, the ethnic group we refer to as African-Caribbean is usually known as 'African-American' in the USA). The very nature of the base term 'race' has changed and is often used (wrongly, in our opinion) as a synonym for 'ethnicity', and vice versa.

- In the UK it is not unusual for administrative boundaries to change. The county boundaries in England changed significantly in 1974 with the creation of 'new' counties. Further changes have taken place since then as well. This makes it very difficult to compare the information in some documents, simply because the things they refer to have changed – even though they (sometimes) still have the same name.

- Sometimes official documents are 'wrong' for unusual reasons. The first deaths from HIV/Aids in the UK were probably in the late 1970s. Certainly deaths were recorded from this cause in the early 1980s. However, there is a belief that many deaths from HIV/Aids were wrongly recorded as being from other causes (typically pneumonia). It is not clear whether this was:
  - because of ignorance on the behalf of the doctors who certified death;
  - a process to hide the real cause;
  - simply the truth because people suffering from HIV/Aids often die from associated infections.

The point we are trying to make here is that it is important to understand as much as you can about a subject before forming a judgement.

Think about it . . .

In each of the following research scenarios, ask the following questions about the data:

(a) Who is the author?

(b) What is the author trying to say?

(c) To whom is the author speaking?

(d) Why has this account been written?

(e) What does the author want to achieve?

1. Suppose your research on the way young people communicate with each other in the UK in the early twenty-first century included, as part of your data gathering, a sample of personal ads from an internet (or newspaper) dating site.

2. Suppose your research on the way political parties present themselves to the public included, as part of your data gathering, looking at the party manifestos of all the main parties taking part in an election.

Your research

Questions you should ask yourself when using documents in research

- What is the origin of this document?
- Is the document authentic? Can I trust it?
- How old is it?
- Who wrote the document?
- What was happening in the social/political/economic world when it was produced?
- Why has this document survived (or been preserved)?
- Does the context have an impact on the reliability/accuracy of the data?
- What was the purpose of the document?
- Who were the original audience?
- Does the original purpose render it unfit for use in my research?
- What is the value of the document to my research?
- Do I understand how definitions or boundaries might have changed since this document was created?

Ways of interpreting/analysis

You can ask questions of documents in the same ways as you might ask questions of your research respondents and the nature of the data you gather can be quantitative or qualitative. As with other data collection the starting points are the research questions and the operational definitions. From these a series of questions to put to each document can be drawn up and it can be useful to design a format into which the data can be recorded. The data could be quantitative – how many times particular words, phrases or concepts are used, for example – or more qualitative – what ideas are expressed in the document, and what is the underlying approach or 'agenda' of the document?

There are many ways of interpreting and analysing documents and their data. The simplest is reading the document to extract the information. However, most other forms of analysis can be applied to the contents of documents and these are dealt with in more detail in Part D.

Your research

Advantages of using documentary data

- Documents are readily available and often contain large amounts of information.
- Documents can be used to triangulate data gathered from other sources.
- Documents are long-lived, so can be researched across time.
- Documents are useful to provide context to the research.

Disadvantages of using documentary data

- Documents can be lost or altered.
- Definitions used in documents can change over time.
- The things documents refer and relate to (for example, English counties) change.
- Documents can be misleading if the full context is not known.

Your research

Research quality check: documents

- Do you understand the origin of your documents?
- Are you certain of their authenticity?
- Do you understand the original purpose of the documents and whether, because of this, they can be useful to your research?
- Have definitions and other terms changed since the document was written? Can you compensate for this?
- Can the document data be triangulated with other materials?

References and further reading

Bogart, J. W. C. (1995) *Magnetic Tape Storage and Handling: A Guide for Libraries and Archives*, Washington, DC: National Media Laboratory.

Marken, A. (2004) CD and DVD longevity: how long will they last? *Audioholic Magazine* available online at www.audioholics.com/education/audio-formats-technology/cd-and-dvd-longevity-how-long-will-they-last (last accessed 21 August 2009).

Prior, L. (2003) *Using Documents in Social Research*, London: Sage.

Silverman, D. (1997) *Qualitative Research: Theory, Method and Practice*, London: Sage.

Southgate, B. C. (2001) *History: What and Why? Ancient, Modern and Postmodern Perspectives*, 2nd edn, London: Routledge.

University of Liverpool and The Wellcome Trust (2008) *Understanding Epidemics* available online at www.liv.ac.uk/geography/research_projects/epidemics/HIV_intro.html (last accessed 21 August 2009).

CHAPTER C9
Secondary sources of data

Contents

In context

This chapter is about secondary sources of data. It is not specifically about the analysis of these sorts of data, because we deal with this elsewhere, particularly in Part D.

Data sources can be conveniently divided into two categories (for other definitions and typologies see A3):

1. *Primary data*: this is data that we (the researcher or a member of our team) collects directly.
2. *Secondary data*: this is data collected by someone else (who is not part of our project).

This chapter discusses secondary sources and focuses particularly on the use of 'organisational data' and 'official statistics'.

PART C: Data collection

    C1: Collecting data

    C2: Data collection skills

    C3: Questionnaires

    C4: Semi-structured interviews

    C5: Focus groups

    C6: Observation

    C7: Narrative data

    C8: Documents

    ▶ **C9: Secondary sources of data**

    C10: Collecting data using computer-mediated communication (CMC)

The great joy of working with **secondary data** sources might be that someone else has already done the work for us! Regrettably, this is not always the case.

Large amounts of data are recorded in a variety of places. For example, much of our lives are a matter of (semi)-public record (we say 'semi-public' because it is likely that the data that we will be able to access is anonymised in some way so that it is usually not possible to identify individuals).

Although it might initially be thought that most of the data available for secondary use is numeric (and, therefore, most likely to be the results of quantitative research or data gathering), this is not necessarily the case and extensive qualitative data on many subject areas is also available. For example, in the UK, government-funded research councils require data that is collected using their support to be deposited in the UK Data Archive (www.data-archive.ac.uk, accessed 21 August 2009) where it is readily available for use by other researchers.

What is . . .

Secondary data
The data that a researcher uses which has already been produced by others.

The nature of secondary data

Public records (which are often documents too) include: births, marriages and deaths; NHS and HM Revenue & Customs records; university admissions; censuses of population; police national computer files; and so on. Quite often these days, the information is stored in computer files which are available to authorised users. Clearly this represents a great deal of personal information. The internet has revolutionised access to secondary data. Information that – less than ten years ago – would have been available only in print or on computer disk is now accessible to anyone with an internet connection. In addition, much more detailed information is available on the internet at quite low cost. For example, it is now possible to access the full results of the 1911 Census of Population electronically, a process that would have been fiendishly time-consuming to do on paper.

Real research

Secondary data sources

The National Archives (available at www.nationalarchives.gov.uk/, accessed 21 August 2009) is the UK government's official archive. Records go back almost 1,000 years and much has now been digitised (including the Domesday Book) and is available on the internet. For a social researcher the archive includes both secondary data and documentary data.

Recent projects include census maps from 1871, public health films and posters from the twentieth century, a history of women in the army, a history of prisons, archives from workhouses and Poor Law Union papers.

Many other organisations (large companies, educational institutions, charities, youth organisations and so on) collect information as well. Broadly, we refer to this collection of data by official and unofficial institutions as 'organisational data'. We have kept this category separate from 'official/unofficial statistics' for reasons that will become clear a little later. Organisational data is, clearly, a vast resource.

Your research

The advantages of using organisational data

- The sample sizes can be very large both numerically and as a proportion (for example, the Census is supposed to be 100 per cent of the UK population).
- They are often well organised and searchable by other computers.
- It can be a very cheap method of gathering data! (Census information, for example, is available on the internet to any university, and many other researchers, usually free of charge.) There are many other sources of large-scale data similarly available: the UK Data Archive (www.data-archive.ac.uk/) website is well worth a visit, if only to see the types of data that are available.
- It can be possible to combine primary and secondary data to gain more depth and insight.
- Sometimes it is possible to use secondary data to conduct longitudinal research that would not otherwise be possible (but see the warning in the 'Your research' box on p. 288).
- It may be possible to combine a number of previous studies to produce new results. (This may be useful in cross-national work in particular.)

Your research

Problems with using organisational data

- Records may not be well kept or accurate: partly this is because record-keeping is seen as a low-status activity, if records are not well written originally by, for example, doctors or civil servants, the record-keeper (and those who rely on the records later) may not understand them; technical or professional jargon may be used which is not understood by the researcher.
- The researcher cannot assess or control the accuracy of the records, so it is important to have an understanding of how they are generated.
- Files (particularly manual/hard copies) can get lost – it might be by accident, but it could be deliberate too. The loss may be helping the record-keeper's hidden agenda.
- It is vitally important to know the reasons that the records are kept and the context in which the information is gathered.

- Organisational data may not provide the information you need.
- Definitions used may not be explicit enough or appropriate for your work.
- You have no control over the quality of data and, often, no way to assess it.

Real research

Secondary data and business ethics

In 1998 Christopher Cowton noted that, although there was a lot of research into business ethics going on, almost all of it made use only of primary data. Cowton investigated both the nature and availability of secondary data in this field and came to the conclusion that researchers were ignorant of the benefits of utilising secondary sources (Cowton notes that the primary benefit is in cost-effectiveness), but also that there were advantages in using existing data for comparison with the present day.

His final conclusion said:

as a general rule it seems to be the case that researchers are not as aware as they might be of the potential of secondary data for providing valuable insights into a whole range of questions in a cost-effective manner. Stewart (1984), for example, suggests that individuals and organizations do not take full advantage of the array of secondary information available to them, perhaps because of the great explosion that has occurred in recent times. A further reason for under-exploiting secondary data is that social scientists tend to think in terms of collecting new data when initiating a research project. (Cowton, 1998: 431)

Official statistics

The government collects vast quantities of statistics and produces analyses of them. Official statistics have many of the same characteristics as organisational data: they provide large samples at low cost; they are cheap and accessible; and they tend to be repeated over time, allowing the study of ongoing processes.

However, using official statistics can be problematic. It is important for the researcher to remember that the main purposes of official statistics are to inform government about its own performance and the development and performance of society. Thus, official statistics are produced to inform the need for policy change/implementation or to provide monitoring and management information. However, official statistics can also be seen as part of safeguarding the democratic process. That is, they can be used by the public to assess whether the government is doing its job well, for example, in reducing the length of hospital waiting lists. This means that the two roles described above are in direct conflict: the government may not wish to disclose information because it may generate 'bad press'. The cynical would suggest that data is manipulated to tell 'happy stories' and more contentious information is suppressed. However, the data may still be there for a conscientious researcher to discover.

Potentially even more problematic is that the researcher who wishes to use the information gathered in official statistics has no control over the context in which the data is collected and/or the design of the questions and definitions used.

Your research

Possible problems with official statistics

1. The way the government represents the information and the critical questions it asks may not fit precisely with the questions/information you want. This might mean that you have to redefine your operational definition to fit the data available. It may be necessary to estimate, calculate or infer from the information.

2. Problems may arise from the context in which official statistics are produced.

3. There can be major methodological problems with some work. For example, it is now well known that around 1,000,000 people are not represented in the 1991 Census. This was around the time of the introduction of the Community Charge (poll tax), when people believed that if they were not recorded in the Census then they would not have to pay!

Using secondary data

There are two issues that must be addressed when researchers want to use secondary data. First of all, you need to find out if the data exists. Most students will probably use an internet search engine as a first step, and it is likely that this strategy will be successful. However, the situation can be more difficult if the information sought is old or has not been 'officially' published. It may be that the best course of action in this case is to try to discuss your enquiry with an 'expert' (for example, a lecturer or tutor, a representative of a company that works in the appropriate field or a librarian).

Once you have decided that the information you want is *likely* to exist (and, of course, discovering that it does not exist is in itself an important research finding), the next task is to locate and access it. Some useful first steps are shown in Example C9.1.

Example C9.1

Internet gateways

- Directgov (the official government website for citizens): 'Easy access to the public services you use and the information you need, delivered by the UK government' (Directgov, 2008), http://direct.gov.uk/en/index.htm

- UK Data Archive: a collection of UK humanities/social sciences data, with some links to other archives, www.data-archive.ac.uk/

- Intute: 'a free online service providing you with access to the very best Web resources for education and research, evaluated and selected by a network of subject specialists' (Intute, 2008), www.intute.ac.uk/socialsciences/

- Europa: 'Gateway to the European Union' (Europa, 2008), http://europa.eu

There are also many subject-specific databases that may be useful to you. Your university/ college library should be able to help you.

> **Your research**
>
> Would your research benefit from the use of secondary sources of data?
>   Think about the possibilities of:
> - effectively increasing your sample size (**B5**);
> - being able to compare previous times with the present;
> - using cost- and resource-effective data;
> - combining primary and secondary data to give your work new insights.

Combining primary and secondary data

The idea of combining primary and secondary data is attractive to many researchers. In fact, most research projects will do this to some degree, typically setting the context of the project by stating what has already been done and including background data – perhaps national statistics relating to the research topic or data from the past which shows how the nature of the research area has changed.

However, researchers can also use secondary data as a supplement to the data they will collect themselves. The reasons for this vary, but include:

- having access to a larger body of data or sample size;
- longitudinal work: researchers will often try to use earlier work to extend the time span of their own project.

If this is to be done successfully, then the researcher should address two questions:

1. *Are the questions/contexts/definitions compatible?* This is the difficulty that we mentioned earlier. It is important to know that the questions asked and the definitions used in collecting the secondary data are compatible with the research being undertaken. If this is not the case, then it is probably impossible to use both sets of data together. However, the secondary data can still provide the background and contextual data discussed above so long as the differences in the nature of the data are clearly stated.
2. *Are the samples compatible?* Usually, the size of the sample is not important, unless there is to be an attempt to generalise from the results. However, the selection and composition of the sample may be of great importance: if the original sample was collected in a major city, then it is unlikely that the results will be useful for work that is based in a rural location (it may be useful for comparison, of course). Similarly, if the samples are of different age groups, genders or religions, or in fact different in any significant way, then the earlier data may not be useful for secondary analysis.

The researcher must always approach these issues critically, to avoid creating misleading findings, simply because a wealth of *apparently* relevant data was available.

The nature of secondary data and implications for analysis

As we have seen, secondary data can come in as many forms as primary data and, as such, should be worked with and analysed using the appropriate analytical techniques. Some secondary data has already been analysed and it is not always possible to get back to the original 'raw' data. If this is the case then the researcher must also be aware of the ways in which the data has been changed and worked with during the analysis process and must assess whether the data is still useful to her in addressing *her* research questions.

Real research

Using secondary data

C. E. Cronk and P. D. Sarvela (1997) Alcohol, tobacco, and other drug use among rural/small town and urban youth: a secondary analysis of the monitoring the future data set, *American Journal of Public Health*, 87(5): 760–4

Christine Cronk and Paul Sarvela (1997) looked at data collected about the use of drugs, alcohol and tobacco by high school seniors in the USA for the period 1976–92 (bear in mind that high school seniors are, usually, ages 16–18 and that, for most of the USA, the minimum age for purchasing and consuming alcohol is 21; most states also have a minimum smoking age of 18).

They examined many existing data sets and concluded that, although substance use varied between rural and urban high school seniors, by 1992 the patterns of consumption were essentially the same.

This research would not have been possible without the use of secondary sources.

Your research

A warning!

When using any data that you do not collect yourself, it is always necessary to ask where the data comes from, who wants you to have access to it and why, and why it is available now.

Nevertheless, secondary data is important, readily accessible and often easy to adapt for other purposes. It is an important research resource.

References and further reading

Cowton, C. J. (1998) The use of secondary data in business ethics research, *Journal of Business Ethics*, 17(4): 423–34.

Cronk, C. E. and Sarvela, P. D. (1997) Alcohol, tobacco, and other drug use among rural/small town and urban youth: a secondary analysis of the monitoring the future data set, *American Journal of Public Health*, 87(5): 760–4.

Hakim, C. (1982) *Secondary Analysis in Social Research*, London: Allen & Unwin.

Huston, P. and Naylor, D. (1996) Health services research: reporting on studies using secondary data sources, *Canadian Medical Association Journal*, 155(12): 1697–709.

Mort, D. (ed.) (2006) *Sources of Non-Official UK Statistics*, 6th edn, Aldershot: Gower.

Office for National Statistics (2000) *Guide to Official Statistics*, www.statistics.gov.uk/downloads/theme_compendia/GOS2000_v5.pdf (also available in hard copy from Palgrave Macmillan).

Reed, J. (2006) Secondary data in nursing research, *Journal of Advanced Nursing*, 17(7): 877–83.

CHAPTER C10
Collecting data using computer-mediated communication (CMC)

Contents

In context

This chapter looks at the use of computers and the internet for collecting research data. This is a rapidly developing area which is undergoing constant change. It seems bizarre that, as recently as 1998, only 9% of households had access to the internet – about 70% do so now in 2009 (Office of National Statistics, 2009a, 2009b). Using computers to gather data and to communicate has changed the world in which we live. We can now conduct research projects in remote locations that we cannot afford to visit and can even process the data in ways that were unimagined in the 1990s.

This (relatively) easy access to people and data has extended the scope of social research enormously, but has also required that we – as social researchers – develop new techniques to manage the data collection so that the quality of our results remains high.

The focus of this chapter is on computer-mediated communication (CMC) and the use of the internet for research.

PART C: Data collection

- C1: Collecting data
- C2: Data collection skills
- C3: Questionnaires
- C4: Semi-structured interviews
- C5: Focus groups
- C6: Observation
- C7: Narrative data
- C8: Documents
- C9: Secondary sources of data
- ▶ **C10: Collecting data using computer-mediated communication (CMC)**

The development of the internet, and the communication systems such as email, chat rooms and blogs that have come with it, has offered new potential to social researchers. These opportunities fall into four categories:

1. As social researchers you now have access to a much wider range of information than before. This includes books, journals, research reports, newspapers, statistics and so on, but also access to information about your research topic area from sites such as organisation websites, self-help discussion groups and sites that give advice to particular groups of people or for people experiencing something in common, for example, old age or parenthood or a particular illness. These sites can help you to develop your literature and research review and to think about your research questions and the issues associated with them. This use of the internet is considered in **B2** and **C9**.

2. We may want to study the internet environment itself: how do people 'talk' to each other in the virtual environment of a chat room or café? What sorts of issues are raised in email or web-based discussion groups and how do people discuss these? What sort of virtual environment do internet users create? And how do they present themselves in an environment where there is rarely any face to face contact?

Real research

Studying the way people use the internet

J. Hillier and J. Harrison (2007) Building realities less limited than their own: young people practising same-sex attraction on the Internet, *Sexualities*, 10: 82–100

The research of Hillier and Harrison looked at the way young people use the internet as a 'space' in which to practise different aspects of their social and sexual lives.

3. The internet and other new technologies have had a significant effect on how we live together, interact and organise our social world. And this is itself a subject for research. For example, the ESRC E-Society is a large programme of academic research (ESRC, 2007) which is studying the impact of digital technologies, particularly the internet, with a view to informing policy-making and practice within all sectors of society. The project ended in October 2007, but the website currently remains and links to their projects can be found at www.york.ac.uk/res/e-society/projects.htm (accessed 21 August 2009).

4. The internet also offers opportunities for data collection using, for example, online questionnaires, email interviews or virtual focus groups.

Think about it . . .

The internet and social research

There are four main ways in which you can use the internet for research:

1. Access to resources and 'literature' (B2).
2. Researching the internet itself and the environments it creates.
3. Researching the impact of the internet on society.
4. Collecting data: *computer-mediated communication*.

computer-mediated communication (CMC) The use of computers and the internet for communication between people.

This chapter will focus mainly on item 4: the use of **computer-mediated communication (CMC)** and internet communication tools to collect social research data – and this includes, of course, collecting data to help us to explore the questions raised in items 2 and 3.

❓ What is . . .

Online social research

Online social research is the computer-mediated collection of data and typically adapts traditional data collection methods, for example, questionnaires, interviews, focus groups, etc., for use in an online virtual environment.

Note, however, that using CMC to collect data is not necessarily the best way to find out how people use the internet – face-to-face interviews or focus groups may actually at least make a useful contribution to a study of internet behaviour. And if we are looking at methods of data collection that use the internet we will also need to consider studies that have been done about the way people use and behave on the internet. So here we will mainly be looking at the use of computer-based tools to gather data that will enable us to study human behaviour and perceptions in general.

Your research

A word of warning!

One of the problems in writing a chapter like this is that information technology, computers and other means of communication like mobile phones are continually changing and new services and ways of doing things are being introduced. This means that much of what is being written now may seem a little dated by the time you read it. What we will try to do is to highlight the key approaches to gathering data using the internet that are available now and the issues you need to consider when deciding whether to use a particular approach, and give you some starting points. What is clear to us at the time of writing is that the use of CMC is likely to continue growing and that social researchers will increasingly consider using the data collection tools it offers.

Before looking at the different data collection approaches you might use, we need to look at some of the features of the internet which can potentially be useful to social researchers.

Computer-mediated communication

Email

Communication between two or more people via email has become one of the favoured ways of keeping in touch. Essentially this is a text-based mode of communication which sends messages instantly (or almost) from one computer to another. Physical distance is not an issue and a message will be received on the other side of the world as quickly as one from the room next door. The message then has to be opened and read by the recipient before, perhaps, replying or sending the message on to others. An email can be sent to a number of recipients at the same time.

The email itself can have computer-generated files attached – these can be text documents, photographs, video clips, spreadsheets and so on. And the email message may include hyperlinks to websites or other email addresses.

To use email each person needs an email address, usually provided by their internet service provider (ISP) and needs to know the email address of the person they are emailing. At present there are no national or international databases that include all email addresses. However, most large organisations like universities will have their own email directory.

Email discussion groups – lists

An email discussion group provides the opportunity for people with a common interest to 'chat' using their ordinary email facilities.

Email discussion groups usually link together people with something in common – perhaps they are researching in the same area or are interested in the same hobby or support the same band. Each person subscribes to the email list (this is usually free) and receives all the emails posted by the members of the group. Sometimes the groups are used to generate discussion about a particular issue and sometimes mainly to exchange information. One person will be responsible for monitoring the emails and may or may not be able to stop emails that are deemed to be inappropriate or offensive, for example, being circulated, depending on how the group list has been set up.

An email list can be very simply set up among a group of people by adding all their addresses to a group email address in their email contacts list. However, where the list of people is more diverse and the group is looking for new members to join, a mail list server using software like LISTSERV may be used. New members may then be recruited by targeted emails or through a website. If you want more detailed information, try the LISTSERV website: www.lsoft.com/manuals/1.8d/userindex.html (accessed 21 August 2009).

asynchronous communication
Communication between people where all the communicants are not, necessarily, in contact at the same moment in time.

An important point to note here is that the 'discussion' between people using an email discussion group is **asynchronous communication** – that means that the members of the group who are participating in the discussion are not necessarily all sitting at their computers at the same time. A member may reply to an email or add to a discussion at any time.

Web-based discussion groups

These fall into two distinct categories. First there are web discussion groups (sometimes called forums) which are similar to email discussion groups except that they take place on an internet website. This can mean that they are open to participants to read without the need to register an email address. Having said that, many websites do ask potential participants to register before allowing them to 'post' messages. Note that these are asynchronous too. Sometimes the discussions are organised under different topics – often chosen by the website organisation. This can allow participants to contribute to discussions that particularly interest them – or sometimes to set up their own discussion thread.

chat rooms
Online discussion forums allowing synchronous or asynchronous communication.

synchronous communication
Communication between people where all communicants are taking part at the same time and can 'chat'; also known as real-time communication.

Then there are **chat rooms**. These are discussions in real time– or **synchronous communication**. Participants are able to 'chat' through text-based messages which are visible to all the other members of the group online at that time as soon as they have been (sometimes while they are being) typed in. Response can be immediate and can be from more than one member of the group. It is quite easy to set up your own chat room. A quick search on the internet will find a number of sites that let you do this and your chat room can be private to those you invite by email. Some internet service providers also offer the facility for instant messaging (e.g. MSN, Yahoo) and conferencing where a number of people can be 'chatting' online together.

This is now being taken further with the growing use of webcams and PC-to-PC voice connections and it is likely that social researchers of the future will be able to make increasing use of these facilities (while phone-based conferencing has, of course, been possible for

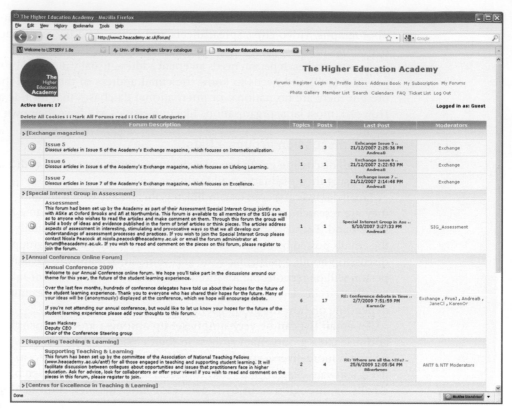

Figure C10.1 A web discussion group – The Higher Education Academy Forum

Source: The Higher Education Academy Forum (www2.heacademy.ac.uk/forum/). Reproduced with permission.

many years, online conferencing is now becoming accessible to more people). Conferencing software can be downloaded and currently there are free packages available which enable you to set up your own conferences. Again, a quick search of the internet will produce a number of sites that provide these services (some free) although these are primarily aimed at business organisations rather than the sole social researcher!

Diaries, blogs and websites

A wide range of material is published on the internet, from archived diary material produced by people who lived in the past to the blogs – current diaries or commentaries being posted on the web by politicians, celebrities and ordinary people on a day-to-day basis. Material published in this way is easily available to any internet user and some may have associated discussion groups or opportunities for communication between the writer and the reader. Many MPs, for example, have blogs (including the current prime minister, Gordon Brown: http://gordon-brown.blogspot.com/) and Conservative MPs contribute to the Conservative Party Blue Blog, www.conservatives.com/News/Blogs.aspx (both accessed 21 August 2009).

Real research

Internet use

In early 2007 it was estimated that 62% of the UK population used the internet (www.internetworldstats.com/stats9.htm#eu, accessed 14 August 2009) – and that it had grown by about 218% from 2000–08.

Using computers to gather data

There are examples of social researchers using computers to gather data from the early 1990s onwards (Fricker and Schonlau, 2002; Mann and Stewart, 2000), each using the techniques and technology available at the time and within the context of the research. As more researchers gained and shared their experience, research has been undertaken that looks at the value of these data collection approaches and how they can be used in different social research contexts and paradigms (see, for example, Fricker and Schonlau, 2002; Roster *et al.*, 2004; Stewart and Williams, 2005). As in other areas of social research, market research organisations have played a key role in developing methods of using the internet to gather data but there are now increasing numbers of academic studies that have been carried out using online data collection techniques.

In 2004, the Economic and Social Research Council sponsored a research training project entitled 'Exploring online research methods in a virtual training environment'. The project included designing a set of online tutorials to help social researchers to use online data collection methods (www.geog.le.ac.uk/ORM/site/home.htm, accessed 21 August 2009).

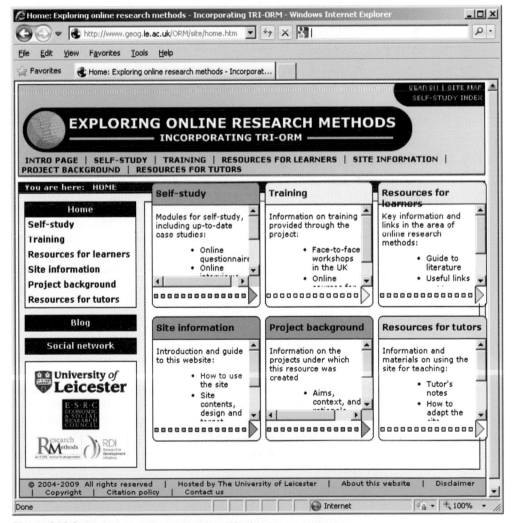

Figure C10.2 Exploring online research methods

Source: Department of Geography, University of Leicester (www.geog.le.ac.uk/ORM/site/home.htm).

A second ESRC project is the National Centre for e-Social Science (www.ncess.ac.uk/, accessed 21 August 2009) which has an interactive web page detailing research results and ongoing projects.

Clearly, the ability of a social researcher to make use of the web-based facilities described above will depend on a number of things:

1. The researcher's own knowledge and skill in using information technology.

2. The researcher's access to hardware and software which will enable her to carry out the research – and the resources if there are costs involved.

3. Whether the potential participants in the research also have access to and the skills to use the required technology.

The third point is the most important. While the researcher may be able to develop her own knowledge and skill and have access to the necessary technology, if the participants in the research do not have easy access to email and the internet and are unfamiliar with the use of this technology, they will be unable – and probably unwilling – to participate. This could, of course, lead to a significant group of people being excluded by the data collection method. Although internet usage is growing rapidly and now includes a broad and diverse range of the population, there remains some variation in internet usage with regard to such characteristics as education, age, gender and wealth and this could lead to a significant bias within the sample of respondents. As the use of computers and particularly the internet spread, this is likely to become less of a problem for social researchers.

Of course, just because it is possible to use the technology, it does not mean that this will be the most appropriate way of gathering data.

Why choose CMC to collect data?

So what might be some of the reasons for choosing CMC to collect data?

1. It's cheap! Most of the services listed above are free, or at least the researcher may have free access to them, having, for example, already paid for their broadband connection or having access as a student at a university or in the workplace. An emailed questionnaire does not have to be printed, posted or filed and the researcher does not have to travel to different parts of the town to conduct 20 face-to-face interviews. Participants in a virtual focus group can take part from their own homes with no transport, childcare and refreshment costs. Note, though, that there may be costs to a research participant who does not have easy access to a computer and perhaps has to travel to a library or pay to use an internet café.

2. Participants who are widely spread geographically can be invited to take part, for example, from different parts of the country or from anywhere around the world just so long as the participants have access to the technology. This can open up possibilities of undertaking comparative studies, including using larger samples and collecting data over a period of time or at a number of stages.

3. It may be particularly appropriate when researching certain groups of people. For example:

   (a) People who are unable to meet the researcher or other participants for some reason. Some people may simply be very busy. For such groups a time-limited opportunity to participate from their own home or workplace may be more likely to encourage them to participate.

Real research

Researching people unable to participate in person

N. Bowker and K. Tuffin (2004) Using the online medium for discursive research about people with disabilities, *Social Science Computer Review*, 22: 228–41

Bowker and Tuffin studied the online experiences of people with disabilities using internet-based interviews.

H. O'Connor and C. Madge (2001) Cyber-mothers: online synchronous interviewing using conferencing software, *Sociological Research Online*, 5

O'Connor and Madge gathered data from mothers with new-born babies using an online focus group.

(b) Some groups of people may be more likely to discuss sensitive or less socially acceptable topics using CMC rather than face to face because of the anonymity of internet-based interaction.

(c) Some groups may be less likely – or very unlikely – to respond to a researcher with particular visible characteristics – age group, gender or ethnicity. Online these characteristics are not so obvious and it may be possible to disguise yourself – although this does raise some ethical issues (A5). Online data collection does offer the possibility of reducing the effect of the researcher on the responses given.

hidden or invisible population
Groups who are not easy to identify.

4. It may be a useful approach to take when potential participants in the research come from a **hidden or invisible population**, that is, groups who are not easy to identify, e.g. drug dealers.

Real research

Finding hidden populations

R. Coomber (1997) Using the internet for survey research, *Sociological Research Online*, 2

Coomber's study targeted illicit drug dealers across international borders.

S. Scott (2004) Researching shyness: a contradiction in terms? *Qualitative Research*, 4: 91–105

Scott's study used face-to-face and CMC methods to talk to people who saw themselves as shy.

virtual communities
Groupings of people who share some experience but meet virtually online rather than face to face.

The internet is a source of, and a home for, **virtual communities**: groups of people who meet others with the same experiences or characteristics virtually online rather than face to face. If you are researching groups like this, then the internet may be a good place to find your research participants and *may* be the appropriate place to collect your data.

5. If your research is about the internet itself – how people use the internet, how particular groups discuss issues in chat rooms, etc. – then you will probably be collecting at least some of your data online.

6. The data can be in a text format. This means that an interview does not need to be transcribed or a questionnaire may be able to be downloaded directly into a statistical package, spreadsheet or database for analysis without having to copy the data from the questionnaire (a potential source of error).

Four methods of collecting data online will be considered, each drawing on the facilities currently available to most computer users. As with **face-to-face** methods the role of the researcher in the data collection varies, although the researcher will rarely have face to face contact with the research participants. And the data collected may be structured, semi-structured or unstructured.

face to face
Research methods which involve researcher and participant meeting in person.

Your research

An important note

We are assuming that most students will be familiar with standard computer procedures and packages but we do not expect that students will be skilled and experienced programmers or web designers. If you have these skills you will probably be able to use these data collection methods more easily and more effectively – if not, we still think that it is possible for a student with average familiarity with using a computer, email and the internet to make use of these data collection methods. For those with an interest in the more technical aspects of, for example, designing your own web-based survey, there are references to sources of advice on this in the 'References and further reading' section.

Survey questionnaires using CMC

Survey questionnaires can be distributed and completed electronically quite easily in at least three different ways.

1. If you have the email addresses of people you wish to include in your sample, you can quite simply send the questionnaire as an email with the questions printed within the body of the email. The respondent can then hit the reply button, add their answers to the questions and return it to you.

   There are some limitations to this approach. Email, currently, does not always have the same editing and formatting tools as, for example, word-processing packages and this means that the questionnaire may not be as clearly and attractively presented as one produced by other software. On the whole, people expect emails to be quite short – and with all the content visible within one screen – and they may be put off by the appearance and apparent length.

2. A variation on the above is to email your potential respondent with a questionnaire attached to the email. This is how it works:

   electronic questionnaire
   A questionnaire that is designed by the researcher, and completed by the participant, via computer-mediated communication (CMC).

   (a) You design your **electronic questionnaire** using a word-processing package that has text boxes, tables and a 'form' feature, e.g. Microsoft Word (Microsoft Word has facilities to create forms using the Forms toolbar (Word 2003) or the Developer toolbar (Word 2007) which respondents can then complete electronically) **(C2)**.

   (b) You save (lock) the form and email it as an attachment to your potential respondents.

   (c) They open the attachment and answer the questions.

(d) They save their completed questionnaire using a different filename which you have given them (or they could, if they wished, print off the questionnaire and return it to you by post).

(e) They reply to your email and attach the saved file.

(f) You can then open the attachment and record their answers or, with some software, import the data directly into a spreadsheet or database.

This has both advantages and disadvantages. You can produce a more attractive, easier-to-complete electronic questionnaire using the full facilities of your software. This can include features like text boxes into which your respondent can type, use **check boxes** and complete **drop-down lists** (C2). Depending on your skill you can design an attractive and easy-to-complete questionnaire in this way.

But can you assume that your respondents are familiar with the software and attaching documents to emails? And some respondents may also be unwilling or unable to accept emails with attachments because they fear computer viruses which are often spread in this way. A preliminary email advising respondents that an email with an attachment will be coming, and clear instructions on the completion and return of the questionnaire, may help to address this.

3. Taking this a stage further, if you have the skills and access to the resources you can create an electronic questionnaire on a website. This could be a personal website, an organisational website or possibly a website that is used by your target research population (*with the permission of the web administrator*). A web-based questionnaire can be designed using standard word-processing software and if you are familiar with techniques such as macros you will be able to design a format that includes checks on the data as it is input – for example, if the respondent enters a date of birth that does not match an age, this can be highlighted – or reminders if some questions are not answered. Questions can be presented to respondents one at a time – and any questions that are 'skipped' for particular groups of respondents can be filtered out and not shown. If you do not have these skills yourself, there are a number of websites that will help you to create a questionnaire and provide a web link to which you can direct your respondents, for example, go to Smart Survey (www.smart-survey.co.uk/, accessed 21 August 2009) and look at one of their sample surveys. Survey monkey (www.surveymonkey.com/, accessed 21 August 2009) does much the same thing. Both of these providers currently allow free (if limited) use of their sites and software and have instructions on their use. Figure C10.3 shows part of a survey about volunteering for undergraduates. This shows how the questionnaire would appear to the student answering the questions.

If you are able to consider this as a data collection method then you must first think about how your respondents will find the questionnaire (you could email them with a web link, have a link from a website used by your target population to your website, or restrict access to your questionnaire to users of a particular website where the questionnaire is sited).

As technology develops and more and more people use email and the internet as one of their main means of communication, the use of electronic questionnaires within social research is likely to grow and it will be possible to evaluate the effectiveness of using the medium in this way. A few studies have been conducted comparing computer-mediated surveys with face-to-face, phone and postal questionnaires – here are some of the findings:

- How people respond may vary with the media used to gather the data – for example, Fricker found that face-to-face interview questionnaires tend to get more socially acceptable answers than online self-completion questionnaires (Fricker and Schonlau, 2002).

check boxes
On an electronic questionnaire, boxes that can be ticked by respondents in response to a question.

drop-down lists
On an electronic questionnaire, a set of possible answers presented as a list from which respondents select one or more applicable responses.

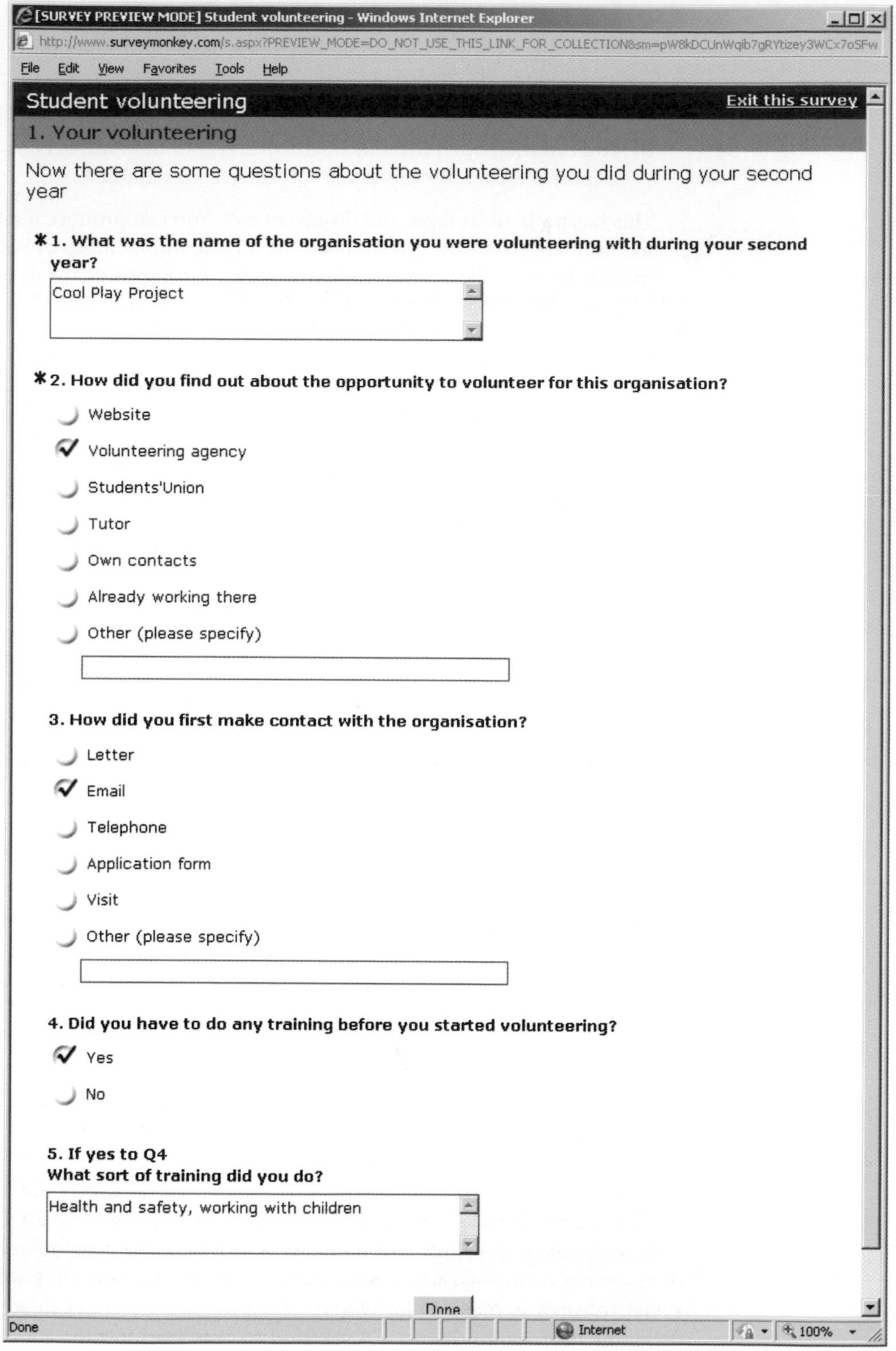

[SURVEY PREVIEW MODE] Student volunteering - Windows Internet Explorer

http://www.surveymonkey.com/s.aspx?PREVIEW_MODE=DO_NOT_USE_THIS_LINK_FOR_COLLECTION&sm=pW8kDCUnWqib7gRYtizey3WCx7oSFw

File Edit View Favorites Tools Help

Student volunteering   Exit this survey

1. Your volunteering

Now there are some questions about the volunteering you did during your second year

*1. What was the name of the organisation you were volunteering with during your second year?

Cool Play Project

*2. How did you find out about the opportunity to volunteer for this organisation?

- Website
- ✔ Volunteering agency
- Students'Union
- Tutor
- Own contacts
- Already working there
- Other (please specify)

3. How did you first make contact with the organisation?

- Letter
- ✔ Email
- Telephone
- Application form
- Visit
- Other (please specify)

4. Did you have to do any training before you started volunteering?

- ✔ Yes
- No

5. If yes to Q4
What sort of training did you do?

Health and safety, working with children

Done

Done   Internet   100%

Figure C10.3 An online survey

- Respondents may be more willing to leave questions out or not complete the question-naire when they are completing it electronically (Roster *et al.*, 2004).

representative sample
A sample that has been selected in order to be representative of a wider population.

- Response rates may not be as good (Roster *et al.*, 2004).
- And it may be difficult – if not impossible – to gather a **representative sample** (see below and **B5**).

Interviews using CMC

An interview is an interactive means of collecting data for social research. While it may take a simple question–answer format, we usually expect that an interview will provide the opportunity for the researcher to be more proactive within the interview and use the inter-action as the means of gathering data. The degree to which an interview is structured can be seen as a continuum (**C1**) – from a structured, face-to-face questionnaire through to an unstructured interview where the presentation of data is very much in the hands of the research participant. Although not physically present in online interviews, the researcher can still be the primary **research tool** as in face-to-face interviews and can seek to generate data by finding ways to encourage the interviewee to 'talk'.

research tool
Something used to collect data, e.g. a questionnaire, the researcher her/himself or an interview schedule.

So how far is it possible to reproduce the features of a face-to-face interview using email and facilities on the internet?

There are basically two different types of online interview:

1. *Synchronous*: where the interviewer and interviewee are 'talking' in real time. This type of interview usually takes place within a chat room or using a live messenger or conferenc-ing programme. A synchronous interview is more akin to the face-to-face interview and the researcher can prepare for the interview in a similar way to a face-to-face interview, preparing an interview guide and noting appropriate prompts and probes.
2. *Asynchronous*: where the interviewer and interviewee are not necessarily online at the same time and may not respond immediately to each other. This type of interview is typically carried out using email or a message programme.

Building up an interactive discussion online, either synchronously or asynchronously, is quite challenging. While the synchronous interview provides opportunities for probing and encouraging the interviewee to 'tell their story', the asynchronous interview can become a series of questions and answers. To counter this it can be useful to send one or two questions to the interviewee at a time and to respond directly to their answering message rather than simply sending the next question. This enables the interviewer to tailor the questions to the interviewee's responses and to generate some discussion, giving more of the 'feel' of a semi-structured interview (Bampton and Cowton, 2002).

An asynchronous interview does give respondents more time to think about their replies or to gather information and this is not necessarily a bad thing. Respondents may appreciate not being under pressure to respond immediately, as they are in a face-to-face or synchronous interview. One problem, though, is that interviewees may need prompting to respond and it may not always be clear why someone is not responding to a particular question. Gentle reminders may be appropriate but may also be seen as pressure to continue with the inter-view. The introductory material to interviewees should include an indication of the likely length of time over which the interview will be conducted and the broad areas to be covered in the discussion.

Researchers can, of course, run a number of asynchronous interviews by email at the same time and this can be helpful as data gathered from one interview may feed into questions in another – a process of cross-fertilisation (Bampton and Cowton, 2002).

Conducting an interview remotely (either synchronous or asynchronous) from your interviewee is a very different experience from a face-to-face interview because a human interaction includes more than spoken or written words. An email or online interview lacks the physical clues of body language, tone of voice and demonstration of emotion that the researcher can recognise, note and respond to in a face-to-face interview. It must also be noted, of course, that these clues are not available to the interviewee either and this may mean that there is less interviewer effect on the data generated within the interview, but some researchers have found that it is more difficult to build rapport and trust within the interview without such visual clues (see, for example, Orgad, 2005). Some researchers have found that it can help to engage in some more personal exchanges (see, for example, Kivits, 2005, and O'Connor and Madge, 2001), including information about yourself and what you are doing, as this helps the interviewee to engage in conversation rather than simply answer the questions. However, as with electronic questionnaires, people may be more prepared to give answers that are seen as less socially acceptable or to discuss sensitive issues more openly online.

Online, email and text messaging have their own languages and this includes ways of addressing the lack of face-to-face visual clues. Emoticons and other text expressions have been created by users to get over this and researchers may well find themselves using these.

One advantage of conducting interviews electronically is that the data is already in text form and there is no need to record and transcribe. Interview data can be cut and pasted into analytical software or a word-processing document in preparation for analysis.

Focus groups using CMC

Focus groups bring a group of people together to talk about a research topic and it is, of course, possible to do this virtually where people are not in the same physical space. As with online interviews, online focus groups can be either synchronous or asynchronous although we would usually expect a virtual focus group to be synchronous, with all the participants online at the same time, using an existing or specially created chat room or conferencing software.

Real research

Online focus groups

A. J. Kenny (2004) Interaction in cyberspace: an online focus group, *Journal of Advanced Nursing*, 49: 414–22

Kenny used WebCT (software that is used as a teaching medium in many universities and includes discussion group and chat-room facilities, also known as a *virtual learning environment*) to set up an asynchronous virtual focus group among student nurses.

H. O'Connor and C. Madge (2001) Cyber-mothers: online synchronous interviewing using conferencing software, *Sociological Research Online*, 5

O'Connor and Madge made use of a free downloaded conferencing software package to involve new parents in an online synchronous focus group.

K. Stewart and M. Williams (2005) Researching online populations: the use of online focus groups for social research, *Qualitative Research*, 5: 395–416

This is a useful review of the use of online focus groups in research, drawing on two examples – an asynchronous focus group and a synchronous focus group held in a 3D graphical environment.

As with face-to-face focus groups, a topic guide can be prepared with questions and prompts which can help to focus the discussion, with the researcher taking the role of facilitator. Some experienced researchers suggest that it may be useful to have ready-typed questions and prompts to cut and paste into the group discussion as needed, although of course the facilitator will also be responding to the data inputted by the participants.

An asynchronous focus group can be run involving members of a discussion group where all the participants can read what other members have written and respond at any time, and there may be periods when more than one, but not all, of the members are online and contributing at the same time. Typically the discussion group will be set up specifically for the focus group and the nature of the discussion topic will be clearly set out. Here the facilitator is likely to have more of an observer role as she is not able to be online to respond all the time, although it is likely to be necessary to stimulate the discussion at times with new questions, comments or responses to what the members have written.

Think about it . . .

Virtual focus groups

- It can be difficult getting everyone online at once and some negotiation is likely to be needed by email or online to ensure that times are convenient.

- An exchange of some socio-demographic data at the beginning of the group can be a useful ice breaker and provide helpful background information. It can also help the discussion if the researcher is prepared to exchange something about herself as well.

- As there are no visual clues, it may be helpful to spend some time either before or during the group getting to know each other and finding out how different participants express themselves, e.g. using emoticons or web or cultural group language.

- Some people will think and type more slowly than others and, as a facilitator, you need to look out for people who always seem to be one step behind and ensure that you acknowledge or respond to them in some way.

- As the facilitator you will not know whether the participants are who they say they are, nor will you know whether there are other people with them or other activities going on which may distract them.

- It is easy to opt out of a virtual focus group, either before or during the group, simply by logging off. Will you know when this has happened and will you know why? This is much easier than walking out of a face-to-face group.

- And what about silences? As a facilitator, what do you make of the pauses before the responses begin coming in?

Observation on the internet

The internet offers enormous potential for observation as a participant in chat rooms or discussion groups or as a 'lurker' – someone who observes a chat room or discussion group without participating. For the social researcher there is the potential to gather data to address research questions that concern ways in which people use the internet, ways in which people discuss issues on the internet and issues that are raised by participants. The data gathered is usually in the form of text conversations between participants. Participants may be selected, so that material is gathered about a particular group of people, or a site may be sampled over a time period. Observation of a chat room or 'lurking' is advised by some researchers as a preliminary stage prior to recruiting participants for questionnaires, interviews or focus groups.

The main issues for you to consider if you are thinking of gathering data in this way concern research ethics and your role as a researcher either participating or 'lurking' in a group. Essentially the issues are similar to those raised by face-to-face or 'real-world' participant observation or covert observation (A5 and C6) and many experienced social researchers would argue that it is OK to gather data as an observer without informing your research subjects in some situations. Indeed the argument is made that by informing people that you are observing their behaviour, you risk changing that behaviour or not being able to proceed with data collection at all because you do not have the informed consent of your research subjects (see below for a further discussion of ethical issues in research using CMC).

Sampling and recruitment for online questionnaires, interviews and focus groups

The internet and email lists can be used as sources of research participants for both online and offline data gathering.

Example C10.1

Deciding to gather data online or offline

A student researcher wants to look at how students studying social sciences decide on their future careers and decides to use her own social science department as the source of respondents.

The department's student email directory could be used as the population from which a (stratified by year and gender perhaps) random sample is drawn. Students could then be written to, phoned or emailed to invite them to participate in a piece of research.

Data gathering could take place offline in face-to-face interviews with times arranged by email (A), or online using an online questionnaire or focus group with the students being directed in the email to a website (B).

Table C10.1 Online and offline data collection methods

	Data gathering offline	Data gathering online
Recruiting offline	A	B
Recruiting online	C	D

Alternatively, a web link to information about the research or the researcher's email address could be included on the department's website and students asked to click on it if they are interested in taking part in the research. Data gathering may again take place offline through face-to-face interviews or focus groups (C) or the students may be directed to an online questionnaire or sent an electronic questionnaire by email (D).

Here we are concerned with the issues around sampling and recruiting research participants online (see B5 for a full discussion of sampling). Let's think about the recruitment process for C and D in Example C10.1 above. Who might be included and who excluded from the research?

1. In this example it is quite likely that most students will have access and the skills to be able to visit the departmental website.
2. But unless they are required to do so, for an assignment for example, some students may rarely log on.
3. Those who do, may be logging on for a very specific purpose and miss the web link to the research.
4. Others may think it looks interesting, click on the link and then discover they have to email the student researcher or complete details about themselves and decide not to bother just then as they have an assignment due in a couple of hours.
5. Those who do take the first step to participating in the research by emailing or filling in information may then find that they are being asked to take part in a focus group, and they don't have the time, or they start on the questionnaire and then are distracted by a text message or a friend calling in.
6. So the response may be quite small and, what is more, the student researcher will not know why others have not responded. Those who do take part will be self-selected, albeit from a clearly identified population.

The method of recruitment has introduced particular types of bias (B5) into the sample and this means that the sample cannot be regarded as representative but the data gathered from the sample could still be regarded as 'indicative' of the group of people from whom the sample has been drawn.

In this case the population from which the sample has been drawn is known. In many instances when respondents are recruited online it is not possible to even estimate what the size of the population might be. For example, if respondents are gathered from an existing website used by people who are interested in a particular band, there is unlikely to be any way of knowing how many people have visited the site or how many have considered taking part in the research. Again, the respondents are self-selected, and without some incentive to take part the sample is likely to be small. The researcher will not know whether those who responded are representative of those who follow the band or of those using that particular website.

Is it 'good enough'?

We have to consider whether there are any other ways of gathering recruits for the research given the time, resources and access to the research population and also the nature of the data the researcher wants to collect – this may be the best available means of finding research participants for the study and 'good enough'.

As we have seen, using the internet to find hidden populations may mean that a study can be carried out that would otherwise not be possible. And some groups of people may be more likely to respond if they can take part using CMC rather than face to face. This may be particularly the case when sensitive subjects are being studied.

The ethical issues of using CMC in social research

Undertaking any social research raises ethical issues because social research involves human beings and information about them, their circumstances, feelings and opinions, and there is a social relationship between the researcher and the research subject as fellow human beings.

These issues are explained and explored in A5 and here we will simply identify a number of issues that are raised in relation to CMC.

Informed consent (A5)

If the interaction between the researcher and the research subject takes place online, how can the researcher be sure that the subject has all the information needed to give consent to participation in the research? And how can the researcher know that the participant has consented without a signature or face-to-face assurance?

Full information about the research can be made available on websites and through email and should include a contact email or postal address for respondents who wish to follow up with questions or comments. Potential participants in the research can be given an opportunity to email an agreement or click an acceptance box showing their willingness to participate. It could be argued that where subjects have self-selected themselves, this is in itself a form of informed consent to take part. But it is the researcher's responsibility to ensure that all the information about the research is drawn to the participants' attention.

Note also that participants have easier options to withdraw when CMC is being used – they can simply not answer and log off.

Confidentiality, anonymity and privacy (A5)

When CMC is being used to gather data, the respondents may be known only by an email address and possibly a username chosen by the respondent themselves. Some participants may already be disguising themselves in some way within the chat room or discussion group and may have one or more 'virtual identities'. Cho and Larose (1999) note that false identities are commonly used on the internet and we think that the researcher needs to think about why this may be so. This in itself can provide a level of anonymity and confidentiality both while collecting the data and in any reports of the research. However, the internet is a public place and even data from private chat rooms or personal emails can be intercepted, 'overlooked' by others in the room, or inadvertently passed on to others, and the researcher must make sure that great care is taken to ensure confidentiality.

If a number of people are participating in asynchronous or synchronous focus groups, for example, it must be clearly understood by the members that all participants will read their postings and possibly be able to identify the email addresses of others. If it is a public chat room, then the data being gathered is already public, as is material from blogs and personal websites which should be referenced as published material. Some chat rooms and discussion groups have their own privacy requirements and you must ensure that you abide by the rules and conventions.

Deception (A5)

In CMC interactions between a researcher and his research subjects, the researcher as well as the research subjects may have a virtual identity. The researcher can never be certain of the age, gender or ethnicity of online research subjects (Hewson *et al.*, 2003) – and they may not be certain about the identity of the researcher! If you are participating or lurking in a chat room you may deliberately seek to deceive the members of the group in order to observe and gather data. This is regarded by some researchers as unethical and you should think through the issues involved carefully and discuss them with your supervisor or ethics board before embarking on such deception.

Even when the researcher is open about the research, the research subjects will lack the visual clues that would be there in a face-to-face interview or focus group, which may help them to decide whether to participate or what to say and what not to say and whether they trust the researcher. It can be helpful, particularly in a group that is closed to all but research participants, to include, for example, a photo of the researcher and to provide background information about the research *and* the researcher. However, care must also be taken to ensure your own personal security and you should consider carefully the possible effects of sharing personal information with unknown people on an open website.

Real research

Privacy in internet surveys

Cho and Larose (1999) looked at privacy in social science internet surveys. Their research

> examines the issue from the perspective of social science research on privacy in an effort to understand the unique privacy context of Internet-based survey research. Online surveyors commit multiple violations of physical, informational, and psychological privacy that can be more intense than those found in conventional survey methods. Internet surveys also invade the interactional privacy of online communities, a form of privacy invasion seldom encountered with traditional survey methods.

They base this finding on the analysis of some 15 internet surveys carried out by academics over a period of 12 years (one survey was conducted in 1986 and should really be thought of as ground-breaking since this is a very early date to be researching by email!).

They finish their article with some useful recommendations for improving online survey response rates, which include the following:

- Offer incentives such as gift certificates (great if you have funding available, but not many students do; there are ethical issues, too).

- Collect data through a web page. This is easier for the participant as, usually, there will be less effort involved than, say, having to respond by email.

- Use multiple-response options in surveys.

- Be credible. If you can use your university/college website as the basis for your survey, it is more likely to be seen as 'real' and 'useful'.

- Think about security. Don't expect participants to give you sensitive information if you cannot guarantee that it will be protected from third parties.

We suggest that you also take account of the ethical issues discussed in A5.

Validity of data gathered online

While the same issues regarding the validity of data apply to both data gathered online (A3 and A4) and data gathered in other ways, the anonymity of the internet and the potential to leave the research site easily without any face-to-face contact with the researcher or other participants could mean that it is easier for respondents to lie to or at least mislead the researcher. While checks can be built into online questionnaires, it may be more difficult to challenge discrepancies or explore respondents' accounts in depth in online interviews or focus groups when the respondent can simply withdraw from the research. As with most data collection methods it is always possible that the data collected is a deliberate distortion of the social reality it purports to represent and the researcher must be aware of this possibility, while noting also that the anonymity of the internet may result in some respondents being willing to share more of their experiences and opinions than they would face to face.

Netiquette

CMC is still relatively new and developing rapidly, and it crosses national and cultural boundaries so it is not always clear what is legal and acceptable when communicating online. However, codes of behaviour and rules are being developed in many online contexts, primarily to deter abusive or insulting language (flaming), and these include advice for good practice within different online environments. Check out some examples online. The user guide for LISTSERV (www.lsoft.com/manuals/1.8d/userindex.html, accessed 21 August 2009) is useful, or you might look at the Albion guide (www.albion.com/netiquette/, accessed 21 August 2009), and make sure you are aware of any netiquette specific to your data-gathering context.

Your research

Netiquette for social researchers

- Messages and postings in private emails or public chat rooms should not include abusive or insulting language and you should consider challenging research participants if they use such language.
- Be sensitive to the culture of your research subjects in terms of the language, humour and tone you use.
- Try to use the 'language' of your research subjects – emoticons, abbreviations, short sentences, etc. – but only if you are sure that you are not excluding people who may not understand.
- Take care to respect the privacy of private emails – particularly when forwarding or replying to emails within an email discussion group.
- Be sensitive to the skills and resources available to your research subjects in terms of computer and software access.
- Always check your own messages and postings for content, language and 'tone' – it is easy to 'sound' abrupt or cross!
- Avoid mass mailings which may be regarded as spam.

Your research

Advantages of using CMC to collect social research data

- Useful for research that includes people who are geographically distant from each other and/or the researcher.
- Useful for research with hidden populations.
- Useful for research involving groups of people who cannot meet face to face.
- Anonymity and confidentiality may be easier to ensure.
- Some people find it easier to discuss sensitive or personal issues online than face to face.
- There may be less 'researcher effect' in terms of visual characteristics, e.g. age, gender or ethnicity.
- Respondents may be less likely to give the more socially acceptable answers.
- It can be much cheaper than paper or face-to-face methods if the researcher and the research subjects already have access to cheap or free CMC.
- Interviews and focus groups do not need to be recorded and transcribed.
- If you have the skill and resources, you may be able to import your survey or interview data directly into analytical software (for example, Excel, SPSS, NVivo).
- A wide variety of personal and social data is available publicly on the internet, including chat-room discussions and blogs.
- Data is usually already in text form, so no need to transcribe.

Limitations of using CMC to collect social research data

- Both the researcher and the research subjects must have the skills and resources to use CMC.
- Some groups of people may be excluded from the research because they lack the skills or resources, leading to biased sample.
- It is unlikely that a representative sample will be achieved if research subjects self-select online.
- The researcher will have little or no information about people who do not participate or who 'leave' the research before completion.
- Online interviews and focus groups lack the visual clues, tone of voice and expressions of feeling that are often present in face-to-face data collection.
- It may be more difficult to ensure that participants have given their informed consent.
- Research subjects may not be who they say they are.
- Researchers wishing to observe or 'lurk' on the internet need to consider the ethical issues involved when collecting data without the informed consent of research subjects.

> **Your research**
>
> **Research quality check: CMC data collection**
>
> - Is the data you can gather 'good' enough?
> - Are you OK with not seeing participants face to face? (Does this have an impact on validity and replicability?)
> - Are you concerned that many internet users utilise false identities? (Does this have an impact on validity and replicability?)
> - If response rates are particularly low, is it important that you may have no way to find out why?

References and further reading

Bampton, R. and Cowton, C. J. (2002) The e-interview, *Forum Qualitative Social Research*, 3.

Bowker, N. and Tuffin, K. (2004) Using the online medium for discursive research about people with disabilities, *Social Science Computer Review*, 22: 228–41.

Cho, H. and Larose, R. (1999) Privacy issues in internet surveys, *Social Science Computer Review*, 17: 421–34.

Coomber, R. (1997) Using the internet for survey research, *Sociological Research Online*, 2.

ESRC (2007) E-society – Innovative Academic Research on the Digital Age, available online at www.york.ac.uk/res/e-society/projects.htm (accessed 21 August 2009).

ESRC Virtual Online Research Methods Modules, www.geog.le.ac.uk/ORM/site/home.htm (accessed 21 August 2009).

Fricker, R. D. and Schonlau, M. (2002) Advantages and disadvantages of internet research surveys: evidence from the literature, *Field Methods*, 14: 347–67. Available from www.websm.org/uploadi/editor/advantages%20and%20disadvantages%20of%20internet%20research%20surveys.pdf (accessed 21 August 2009).

Hewson, C., Yule, P., Laurent, D. and Vogel, C. (2003) *Internet Research Methods*, London: Sage.

Hillier, L. and Harrison, L. (2007) Building realities less limited than their own: young people practising same-sex attraction on the internet, *Sexualities*, 10: 82–100.

Higher Education Academy (2009) www2.heacademy.ac.uk/forum/ (accessed 15 August 2009).

Internet World Stats (2009) Internet Usage in European Union, available online at www.internetworldstats.com/stats9.htm#eu (accessed 12 December 2009).

Johns, M. D., Chen, S. S. and Hall, G. J. (eds) (2004) *Online Social Research: Methods, Issues, and Ethics*, New York: Peter Lang.

Kenny, A. J. (2004) Interaction in cyberspace: an online focus group, *Journal of Advanced Nursing*, 49: 414–22.

Kivits, J. (2005) Online interviewing and the research relationship, in C. Hine (ed.) *Virtual Methods: Issues in Social Research on the Internet*, Oxford: Berg.

Madge, C. (2006) Online Questionnaires, available from www.geog.le.ac.uk/ORM/questionnaires/quescontents.htm (accessed 22 February 2007).

Madge, C. (2006) Online Research Ethics, available from www.geog.le.ac.uk/ORM/ethics/ethcontents.htm (accessed 22 February 2007).

Mann, C. and Stewart, F. (2000) *Internet Communication and Qualitative Research*, London: Sage.

O'Connor, H. (2006) Online Interviews, available from www.geog.le.ac.uk/ORM/interviews/intcontents.htm (accessed 22 February 2007).

O'Connor, H. and Madge, C. (2001) Cyber-mothers: online synchronous interviewing using conferencing software, *Sociological Research Online*, 5.

Office for National Statistics (2009a) Statistical Bulletin: Internet Access 2009, available online at www.statistics.gov.uk/pdfdir/iahi0809.pdf (accessed 12 December 2009).

Office for National Statistics (2009b) Historical Households with Access to the Internet dataset, available online at www.statistics.gov.uk/StatBase/Product.asp?vlnk=5672_ (accessed 12 December 2009).

Orgad, S. (2005) From online to offline and back: moving from online to offline relationships with research informants, in C. Hine (ed.) *Virtual Methods: Issues in Social Research on the Internet*, Oxford: Berg.

Roster, C. A., Rogers, R. D., Albaum, G. and Klein, D. (2004) A comparison of response characteristics from web and telephone surveys, *The International Journal of Market Research*, 46. Available from www.websm.org/uploadi/editor/advantages%20and%20disadvantages%20of%20internet%20research%20surveys.pdf (accessed 21 August 2009).

Scott, S. (2004) Researching shyness: a contradiction in terms? *Qualitative Research*, 4: 91–105.

Stewart, K. and Williams, M. (2005) Researching online populations: the use of online focus groups for social research, *Qualitative Research*, 5: 395–416.

PART D
Data analysis

CHAPTER D1
Beginning to analyse

Contents

In context

It is not enough to have some questions and collect some data (even when you understand the theory behind what you're doing). The data you collect is the raw material for the answers to your research questions but, unfortunately, those questions will not answer themselves and you now need to conduct the analysis phase of your research. This chapter introduces the notion of analysis as a precursor to the detailed analytical techniques that are illustrated in the following chapters.

PART D: Data analysis

▶ **D1: Beginning to analyse**

   D2: Working with data

   D3: Statistical analysis

   D4: Thematic analysis

   D5: Analysing narrative

   D6: Discourse analysis

   D7: Content analysis

   D8: Grounded Theory

   D9: Using computers in data analysis

   D10: So what? Drawing conclusions

analysis
A process of working with the data to describe, discuss, interpret, evaluate and explain the data in terms of the research questions or hypothesis of the research project.

The good news is that you've *already* begun your analysis! **Analysis** starts as soon as the project is conceived. By the time that the project is designed and planned, the analysis strategy and process should be clear (see **Part B**). This is particularly important where certain data collection methods are used (see **Part C**) since the data collection method is linked to your choice of analytical approach; for example, structured interview data cannot normally be analysed using narrative methods (**C7**).

Collecting data is, obviously, important. However, there is no point in the collection itself. One cannot, sensibly, simply collect data and present it as research (though people quite often try this, usually with unfortunate results). Research data is not 'self-explanatory' and does not (ever!) speak for itself: analysis is required.

Since our research projects collect data (**A3**), we tend to talk about *data analysis*. However, data analysis is not a single 'thing' or process; rather, it is a collection of methods that we can apply to the data we have collected in order to describe, interpret, explain and evaluate it (we may not do all of these things – see **A4**). We can also use some of these processes to look for patterns in the data (different participants having similar experiences, for example), to answer our research questions and to test our hypotheses; and, sometimes, analysis is used to transform data so that it can be understood more clearly (or perhaps by more people). Every science, social or otherwise, uses data analysis, and it is also used in sales, administration, business and policy-making.

This part of the book is about different analysis techniques and how they might be applied. However, no matter which of the data analysis processes you use, there will be features that they have in common.

Analysis features

The purpose of data analysis is to *describe, discuss, evaluate* and *explain* the content and characteristics of the data that has been collected in your research project. This stage (or chapter in a dissertation) is generally called the *findings*. Note that there is no requirement to have a separate findings chapter, though many people do. Others will combine the findings section with the *discussion*. Finally, the analysis should lead to a *conclusion*.

The two most important features that are shared by all analysis methods are that they are:

1. *Systematic*: each piece of data (whatever that may be: case study, person, event, etc.) in the project is treated in the same way.

2. *Comprehensive*: all the data collected for the project is included in the analysis.

There is a third point which, although it is as important as the first two, needs to be viewed separately. This is:

3. Remember that you are answering your research question (or, perhaps, testing a hypothesis). We emphasise this need to answer your question because in almost every research project, many interesting things are discovered that do not relate to the research question (you don't have to ignore these discoveries, but it is critical to remember the focus of the project you are undertaking and not to allow yourself to be sidetracked: see **C7**, for example).

How to start your analysis

The following chapters (**D3–D9**) describe a series of different analytical techniques that you might use. However, we want to say a few words about the *general* idea of analysis and how you might begin the process.

1. *Think about what you are doing.* Remember that this is a specific research project and that you have been collecting data to answer the question(s) that you thought about at a much earlier stage.

2. *Go back to your research questions.* It is important that you remind yourself what your research questions were and how you operationalised them (A4). If you do not do this, then you run a risk of losing your focus and wasting time and effort.

3. *Revisit your plan.* Your research design should, of course, be familiar to you. Nevertheless, it cannot hurt to look at it again and make sure that you are following the outline you decided on (**Part B**).

4. *Remember.* The purpose of analysis is to describe, discuss, interpret, explain and evaluate the data and to *reach a conclusion*.

5. *Check.* Review your understanding of the process you will use for the actual data analysis:
   - Statistical analysis (D3)
   - Thematic analysis (D4)
   - Narrative analysis (D5)
   - Discourse analysis (D6)
   - Content analysis (D7)
   - Grounded Theory (D8)
   - Using computers in analysis (D9).

6. *Read* (D2). Ensure that you prepare your data for your analysis.

A brief note about findings

We would all like our research to change the world. There is a huge sense of achievement in discovering something new and significant; maybe something that makes the world a better place. Unfortunately, such discoveries are few and far between, so it is good to remember:

- even if you did not find anything new, you will have extended the range of knowledge by confirming work that others have done before;

- don't worry if you didn't discover anything. *Not* finding an event can be just as important as finding it. It is as important to know what *does not* happen in the social world as it is to know what *does*.

Analysis is often the most rewarding part of a research project. There is excitement as you finally understand the significance of your data (as well, usually, as a sense of relief that your work is meaningful) and a feeling of satisfaction as the project enters its concluding phases.

Your research

Starting-to-analyse checklist

Have you . . .

- thought carefully about what you need to do to begin analysis?
- returned to your research question(s)/hypothesis to ensure that you are clear on what needs to be done? (A4, B1)
- checked the details of the technique you are using? (D3 to D9)

- checked your operational definitions so that you know what you are looking for in the data? (A4)
- revisited your research plan to remind yourself of the analytical strategy you planned? (B1, B6)
- remembered that the purpose of analysis is to *reach a conclusion*? (D10)

References and further reading

Cramer, D. (2003) *Advanced Quantitative Data Analysis*, Buckingham: Open University Press.

Miles, M. B. and Huberman, A. M. (1994) *Qualitative Data Analysis: An Expanded Sourcebook*, London: Sage.

Ritchie, J. and Lewis, J. (2003) *Qualitative Research Practice: A Guide for Social Science Students and Researchers*, London: Sage.

Wright, D. B. and London, K. (2009) *First (and Second) Steps in Statistics*, 2nd edn, London: Sage.

CHAPTER D2
Working with data

Contents

In context

It's good to have collected data, but, on its own, data collection is only one stage in the process. Now you will need to begin to work with the data you have collected so that it can be used to find answers to your research questions or test your hypothesis.

This chapter looks at how you can begin to work with your data. We advise you to read this chapter before looking at the relevant chapter for specific analytical techniques:

D3 Statistical analysis

D4 Thematic analysis

D5 Narrative analysis

D6 Discourse analysis

D7 Content analysis

D8 Grounded Theory

D9 Using computers in analysis

PART D: Data analysis

D1:   Beginning to analyse

▶ **D2:   Working with data**

D3:   Statistical analysis

D4:   Thematic analysis

D5:   Analysing narrative

D6:   Discourse analysis

D7:   Content analysis

D8:   Grounded Theory

D9:   Using computers in data analysis

D10: So what? Drawing conclusions

However you have collected your data, you will need to work with this data in order to be able to use it to help you address your research questions or test your hypothesis. Working with data means a number of things:

1. It means ensuring that the data is *complete*.
2. It means getting to *know your data*, becoming really familiar with what you have got.
3. It means getting your data *organised* in a way that will help you to be able to find what you want when you want to use it.
4. It means getting the data organised in a way that will help you to begin to *use it* for your research.
5. It means setting up a plan for your *analysis* which you can follow through, and which can provide the basis for a record of all your analytical activity.

There are a number of ways of working with data, some of which depend on the type of data you are working with and some that are useful for a range of different types of data. Even if your data is either all quantitative or all qualitative, we think you will find it useful to read through all, or most, of this chapter.

Nature of the data and working with data

In A3 we looked at the nature of data and noted that the data we can collect and analyse as social researchers can have the following characteristics:

- be written or spoken or non-verbal data;
- relate to facts or values;
- be structured/semi-structured/unstructured data;
- have both content and meaning;
- be produced by an individual or group;
- be reflexive data produced by the social researcher herself;
- be primary data collected by the researcher or secondary data produced for some other purpose.

In **Part C** we introduced a number of different ways of collecting data and the techniques that can be used to ensure that the data is both an accurate representation of the social reality we are studying and useful in addressing our research questions or testing a hypothesis.

Now you need to consider the nature of the data you have gathered in terms of how you are able to work with it to address those research questions. The main issues we need to consider here are whether your data is complete and reliable and how you can begin to organise it so that you can use different analytical procedures to help you to explore and explain the social phenomenon you are studying.

It is helpful initially to think in terms of whether the data you have gathered is structured or semi-structured/unstructured as this influences the analytical approaches you will be able to take to your data.

Structured data

Structured data is usually collected using a questionnaire or other structured format which asks a set of questions of an individual or situation. The key characteristics of structured data are:

(a) the questions are the same for each participant or case; and
(b) typically there is a common set of answers for each question.

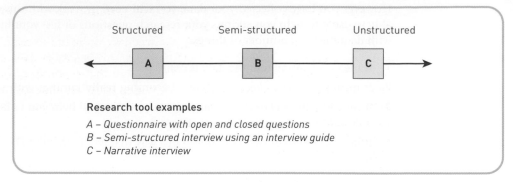

Figure D2.1 Continuum of structured/semi-structured/unstructured data

The nature of structured data is such that the analytical approaches most often used are based on *counting* the number of cases with particular characteristics or answers. The statistical techniques that are available to you to use depend on the consistency of your data collection tool – in other words, that the data has been collected in the same way for all your participants or cases.

Semi-structured/unstructured data

While data is rarely, if ever, unstructured by either the researcher or the participant, there are different degrees of data structure along a continuum (**C1**) from structured to unstructured.

The data collected using semi-structured or relatively unstructured methods usually has a number of characteristics:

(a) The questions may not always be worded in the same way and different follow-up probes and prompts may be used to suit each situation.

(b) The answers to questions are varied.

(c) The answers to questions are often in the words (or actions) of the participants.

(d) The overall structure of the data may vary from case to case; for example, questions may be addressed in a different order and some questions may not be answered in every case.

raw data
Data that has not been analysed in any way, but is presented in the form it was collected in.

The nature of semi-structured data is such that the analytical approaches available to you need to be able to work with data that is varied, often extensive and in a variety of formats. Furthermore the analytical approach needs to allow you to work with the data in the form it is collected, for example, the words as they were spoken by the participant in an interview. This is often called **raw data**.

Preparing to analyse data

This section introduces a number of techniques which will be helpful to you as you prepare to analyse your data, in each case looking at preparing both structured and semi-structured data.

Familiarising yourself with the data

It may sound rather strange to suggest that you will be *unfamiliar* with your own research data! However, the research process itself can be at least a few months long and quite complex, with different things going on at the same time. You will, of course, also have other things going on in your life. In addition to this, you may also find that your own thinking about your research study develops, or changes perhaps, during the time you are reading, collecting data and beginning to work with the data.

If you have collected your data using a structured format, you may have done so without any direct (for example, face-to-face) contact with the participant or case situation. In this case you will probably be eager to look at the responses of the first returns, but you may find, though, that as more arrive, you have less time and inclination to read each one, so your own natural enthusiasm (or lack of it!) can be a factor when you work with the data.

Alternatively, if you have collected your data yourself using, for example, interviews, focus groups or documents, you may feel that you already know your data well because you 'were there'. You may find, though, that as you conduct more interviews or read more documents, you are less able to distinguish between each one and significant points made in the first interview are forgotten as more and more data is added.

Re-familiarising yourself as you begin your analysis is important and there are two things that you will find helpful, whether your data is structured or semi-structured:

1. Read through *all* the questionnaires, transcripts and your research notes (or, if you have recorded video or audio material, watch and listen again) to get a good feel for what is there.
2. Write memos (**C2**, **D4**, **D8**) to yourself as you read, with notes about:
   (a) anything you want to come back to or to check, for example, missing information, inconsistencies, illegible writing or inaudible recording;
   (b) interesting comments, answers and points (when you say to yourself 'That's interesting!') – write them down to come back to later;
   (c) analysis you may want to do, questions you want to consider, tables you want to produce, relationships you want to explore.

Ensuring that your data is complete and accurately recorded

Before you start working with your data you need to ensure that it is as complete and accurate as it can be. Even the most well prepared and fully designed research will probably have some small problems with completeness and accuracy, and at this stage you need to be aware of potential problems and how to address them. While reading through your data to re-familiarise yourself, you may have found inconsistencies or that there is information missing. You now need to check through your data carefully and make some decisions about what to do. The following subsections deal with most of the situations you are likely to find in your research project.

Checking questionnaires
Identifiers

Each questionnaire or case needs a unique identifier. Sometimes this will be assigned prior to collecting the data by numbering the questionnaires or forms before use. If this has not been done, then an identifier should be given to each data source at this point. The identifier may itself include information. For example, all questionnaires received from people in London may start with '1' (101, 102, 103, etc.) and those from Birmingham with '2' (201, 202, 203, etc.). This will make it easier to sort out where questionnaires have come from and allow, for example, for analysis to be carried out on the two sets of questionnaires separately.

Any information that could lead to the identification of individual people, groups or organisations by name should also be removed at this point (**A5**). Often this information is retained by the researcher to enable him to refer back to his participants (if, for example, he wishes to involve them in further research, or to inform them that they have won a prize if he has used a prize draw to encourage people to participate in the research). To ensure confidentiality and anonymity, any identifying information must be kept separate from the data itself but can be numbered with the same identifier so that the researcher (and *only* the researcher) can match the identifying information with the data.

What to do with missed questions/information

There are three main reasons that a question may not have been answered.

Table D2.1 Reasons that a question may not have been answered

Problem	Action
1. The participant may have been 'filtered out' (**C3**) of that part of the questionnaire at a previous question	In this case the participant has correctly not answered the question and an answer of *Not Applicable* (NA) can be recorded
2. The participant may have (mistakenly or deliberately) not answered the question	In this case, the fact that the participant has not answered needs to be recorded – a code of 99 (see below) is often used. If significant numbers of participants have not answered the question you should consider item 3 below
3. The question or question instructions may be worded ambiguously, incorrectly or insensitively and significant numbers of participants may have omitted the question	In this case you will need to consider whether you will be able to use the answers to the question in your analysis, as the validity (**A3** and **C3**) of the data is in question

What to do with partial responses

If a questionnaire or data form is only partially completed there may be a number of reasons for this and you need to consider the points made above and also consider whether there may be reasons that information is missing for a significant portion of the questionnaire. It may be that the length of the questionnaire deterred your participants from completing it, or that they did not wish to answer a particular question or section on, for example, a sensitive topic and decided not to complete the questionnaire from that point (though you may never know why this has happened – one of the major frustrations of undertaking social research!). What you do with the data that you do have depends on:

- the number of cases;
- the possible reasons for incompletion;
- whether the data you have can be used, perhaps to address part of your research question – in this case you must make it clear when writing up and discussing your findings that this is the case.

At this point you will need to decide whether to reject some incomplete questionnaires or whether to include the partial information.

Inconsistent data

Sometimes you will find that the information given by a participant within, for example, a questionnaire or interview, is inconsistent. This can be the case with both factual and value data and it can be difficult for the researcher to decide what to do with this. For example, a participant may give their date of birth as 1990 but also record that they have children born in 2000. This type of inconsistency could have occurred for a number reasons. Either (or both) of the dates given may be incorrect or may have been misread or misheard. Or perhaps the participant has misunderstood the question and recorded his brothers and sisters who live with him as his children, or is referring to his stepchildren.

As with missing information, you will need to consider whether:

- the data can be checked in some way (perhaps by referring to other questions where information about children is given or by contacting the participant);
- similar inconsistencies occur in other responses;
- the data is useable in your analysis.

You may also find that participants give what appear to you to be inconsistent answers to questions asking them for an opinion or value statement. One participant may say, for example:

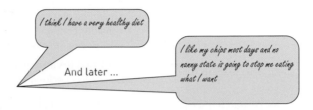

> *I think I have a very healthy diet*

And later ...

> *I like my chips most days and no nanny state is going to stop me eating what I want*

This is interesting! While the two statements may appear to be inconsistent, the researcher will need to consider both how the participant has understood the questions asked and, importantly, how his answers can be *interpreted*.

The researcher should also look for other similar, and different, perspectives from other participants.

Checking recorded interviews/focus groups/transcripts
Identifiers

Qualitative data can be varied and you may be collecting, for example, a number of different types of data about a particular person or situation (including your own notes). You will find it helpful to have a clear system of identification, with each data source given a unique identifier. You may also consider whether to include in that identifier some information that either says something about the data source (for example, a system that indicates the gender of the participant: F1, F2, F3 . . . and M1, M2, M3 . . .) or that shows how different data sources are linked. For example, you may have a number of individual interviews, a focus group, some documents and your own notes from each of three organisations and each set of documents could be identified by a letter or number prefix and data type: 3FG = 3 (organisation) FG (focus group); 3D4 = 3 (organisation) D (document) 4 (document 4).

When you have large quantities of qualitative data to work with, it is often important to be able to see the source of the data easily, and if you are using computer software to help you to work with the data this identifier can easily be attached to any of the data within that data source (D9).

For completeness, you should also ensure that information about when and where the data was collected and by whom is attached to each source of data.

Checking records

If you have carried out data collection methods like interviews, focus groups and observation yourself, you will probably be aware of potential problems with recording the data immediately. It is advisable to allow time after each data collection session to check the recording (whether it is an audio or video recording or your own notes). If someone else is collecting or providing the data (for example, if someone else is conducting focus groups, or if participants are completing daily diaries), then you should ensure that you allow yourself time to check the data for completeness and accuracy as soon as possible after receiving it.

Table D2.2 Checking records

Problem	Action
Incomplete or inaudible recording	Check the extent of the problem: • if a significant amount of the recording is unuseable or not available, consider whether the data could be collected again • if researcher's notes (and memory) are available, consider whether the gaps can be filled with data from the notes (this should be distinguished as such in any transcript) • consider contacting the source of the data (for example, interviewee) to check the missing data **Ensure that the problem does not occur in future data collection sessions by checking equipment and settings (C2).**
No researcher's notes or notes illegible or incomprehensible	Check the extent of the problem: • consider rewriting the notes, working with any other recording and memory • consider contacting the source of the data (for example, interviewee) to check the missing data **Ensure that this does not happen in future cases by improving your note-taking skills (C2) and allowing time after each data collection session to complete your notes.**

Organising your data

Beginning to organise quantitative data

Structured data is just that: already structured according to the way in which it was collected. There may, therefore, be little more to do to get it ready for the analysis process. It may simply be a matter of counting how many people gave each answer to each of the questions included in a questionnaire, or counting how many times a particular event occurred or a word was used.

> **Your research**
>
> At this point you should consider whether you will use a software package to assist you in your analysis, as each package will have slightly different ways of entering and preparing the data for analysis (D9).

However, even the simplest of analytical processes needs a clear description of what is being counted. If the analysis demands more complex statistical processes, it is important to be able to clearly identify the data with which you started. To be able to do this, you need to look at each set of answers to a question, or each activity you have recorded, and assign an identifying name to it. This is usually called a variable because each question has a range of different, or variable, answers. The variable is the name given to that *set* of answers.

The usual practice is to start by giving variable names to each of the questions you have answers to or the activities you have counted.

Example D2.1

Variables and codes

		Code	Variable name
Are you	male ☐	1	GEN
	female ☐	2	
What is your age?	16–25 ☐	1	AGE
	26–45 ☐	2	
	46–65 ☐	3	
	over 65 ☐	4	

Thinking about what you eat on a typical day would you say that your diet is (tick the box):

DIET

Very healthy	Fairly healthy	Neither healthy or unhealthy	Fairly unhealthy	Very unhealthy
1	2	3	4	5

Of course, you could simply call the variables VAR1, VAR2, etc., but some people find it helpful to use variable names like AGE, GEN (gender), etc., to remind them what the variable means or relates to.

For each variable there will be a range of answers or characteristics: this is the data you will want to work with so each answer or characteristic also needs some identification. When working with structured data this is usually called coding, as a **code** (identifier) is attached to each answer.

Usually a numbering system is used to code answers, as shown in the questionnaire example above. For each variable name there will be a list of codes and the answers or characteristics they represent. For each variable, the number, for example, of people giving each answer can be counted. This is called the **frequency** – that is, the number of times – that each answer has been given.

Multiple codes

Some questions can ask for more than one answer (see Example D2.2). In this case there is more than one variable attached to the question. You can regard each of the listed foods as a variable and code each variable as 1 if it is ticked, 2 if it is not ticked. You could then count how many people eat, for example, cereal more than twice a week.

---

code
A way of identifying a specific answer or characteristic. It may be numeric or alphabetic.

frequency
The number of times that each answer has been given, or that a particular outcome occurs.

Example D2.2

A multi-coded question

Which of these foods do you eat more than twice a week?
(Tick all that apply)

	Code 1 or 2	Variable name
Cereal		*CER*
Bread		*BRE*
Fresh fruit		*FFR*
Fresh/frozen vegetables		*FVG*
Egg		*EGG*
Meat		*MEA*
Fish		*FSH*

There is another way of dealing with questions that have a number of answers and this can be useful when coding open questions (see below). In this case a number of variables – for example, OPIN1 (opinion 1), OPIN2, OPIN3, etc. – are assigned to a particular question. The same range of codes is used for each of the variables as shown in Example D2.4.

Creating new variables

As you plan and develop your analysis you may find that you want to create new variables by combining the answers to two or more questions or by grouping up the answers to one question. This can enable you to explore the relationships between different questions and to develop more complex analyses. New variables typically have a set of codes that specify the way the data from, in some cases, two or more questions is to be combined (see Example D2.3).

The simplest form of new variable is where the answers to one question are grouped or combined to simplify the analysis. For example, you may have asked participants to give their age in years but you do not want to analyse all your data by individual age years so you need to create a new variable which groups the ages into age ranges chosen to reflect your interest in the differences or similarities in people of each age group.

Think about it . . .

You could group up the answers given in Example D2.1 above. The DIET variable could be simplified by combining the codes 1 & 2 and 4 & 5 to give a simpler variable which showed whether people thought they had a 'healthy' or an 'unhealthy' diet.

Example D2.3

Creating a new variable

Suppose you wanted to know whether men eat a more healthy diet than women but you also suspected that there may be differences in the way people eat at different stages in their lives. It would probably be helpful to create a new variable which combined the gender and age variables as follows:

New variable name = GENAGE
Codes
Male/aged 16–25 years	=	*1*
Male/aged 26–45 years	=	*2*
Male/aged 46–65 years	=	*3*
Male/aged over 65 years	=	*4*
Female/aged 16–25 years	=	*5*
Female/aged 26–45 years	=	*6*
Female/aged 46–65 years	=	*7*
Female/aged over 65 years	=	*8*
Information not available	=	*9*

You could then begin to explore whether men and women of different age groups, for example, think they have a healthy diet by creating a simple cross-tabulation of **GENAGE × DIET**.

Age and sex by perceptions of diet (%)	Very healthy	Fairly healthy	Neither healthy nor unhealthy	Fairly unhealthy	Very unhealthy
Male – aged 16–25 yrs					
– aged 26–45 yrs					
– aged 46–65 yrs					
– aged over 65 yrs					
TOTAL MALE					
Fem – aged 16–25 yrs					
– aged 26–45 yrs					
– aged 46–65 yrs					
– aged over 65 yrs					
TOTAL FEMALE					
TOTAL					
Inform. not available					

Coding open questions

Many structured data collection instruments or formats include open questions (**C3**). These are questions that do not have a preset range of answers but allow the participant to give their own answers, often in their own words. In order to be able to work with this data using statistical analysis (which depends on being able to count how many people said or did something), the data from open questions needs to grouped into different types so that a code can be applied. Often an answer will include more than one idea or statement and so have more than one code assigned to it and the question will therefore be multi-coded.

In Example D2.4 below, a set of variables – for example, INFL1 (influence on diet 1), INFL2 (influence on diet 2), INFL3 (influence on diet 3) – would be allocated and those whose answers had only one code assigned (for example, answer G) would only have a code for INFL1 while those with two or more codes (for example, answer A) would also have codes for INFL2, INFL3, etc.

Example D2.4

Coding open questions

Here are some of the answers to the question:

What sorts of things influence what you eat?

A	*I go for the special offers to get the cheapest I can usually but I do check things like the sugar content and we always have lots of fruit. When you have children these things matter.*	2, 1, 6
B	*I don't have much time to think about it really so I just see what's in the fridge or go to the chippy.*	3
C		9
D	*I think it's the way I was brought up really. My mother always cooked a good meal, you know, meat and veg, so I try to do the same thing.*	7
E	*I'm a vegetarian and am very careful about what I eat – it has to be organic if possible and lots of vegetables.*	8,1
F	*Depends how I feel – sometimes I feel like cooking, sometimes I don't so I get a takeaway. Sometimes I just feel too tired to be bothered.*	4
G	*My religion sets out what I can and can't eat so I have to abide by that.*	8
H	*My partner – he cooks for me.*	5
I	*I think it is really important that children have a healthy diet so I make sure that I include lots of fruit and vegetables, watch the fat and sugar content and no fizzy drinks.*	1, 6

After reading through all the answers to the question, a set of codes is drawn up to include most of the answers – it could look like this:

1. Mentions healthy diet including sugar, fat, salt content, fruit and vegetables.
2. Cost of food – cheapest.
3. Time.
4. Feelings about cooking/food.
5. Someone else cooks.
6. Children's health.
7. Family habits.
8. Religious or other beliefs.
9. No answer.

The codes are in the right-hand column – do you agree? Can you suggest other ways of coding this data?

Frequencies

Having checked your data and begun to organise it by allocating variable names and codes, you are now ready to plan your analysis. Whatever statistical analysis (D3) you have in mind, you are likely to begin by producing some frequency tables, so that for each variable you know how many of each answer or code have been given. You can then take a preliminary look at the way in which the answers to your questions are distributed: in the above example, how many in each age group, how many think they are healthy, and so on. At this point you will be able to identify potentially interesting **distributions** of answers which you may wish to explore further.

distribution
An arrangement of the values of a variable showing their observed frequency of occurrence.

Cross-tabulations

As you examine your frequency tables with your research questions in mind, you are likely to begin to look at the relationship between different variables. This is what statistical analysis is all about, and is addressed in much more depth in D3. To get started on your analysis, though, you may want to list any tables or cross-tabulations you will want to do to help you to explore these relationships (see Example D2.3). We usually refer to a table as showing, for example, age (AGE) by gender (GEN), age and gender (GEN AGE) by perception of diet (DIET).

Your research

Relationships and cross-tabulations

Thinking about your own research question, list any relationships between variables you may wish to explore by producing a cross-tabulation.

Variable	By variable	Why might this be interesting?

If you are planning to use a statistical software package (for example, SPSS) or a spreadsheet package like Excel, we suggest that you now also read D9 to help you to prepare your data and plan your analysis to make the most effective use of these packages (then you should come back to this section).

Beginning to organise qualitative data

Qualitative data which is relatively unstructured (or semi-structured) is collected in a variety of ways and typically in its raw state – that is, the way it was spoken, written or observed as it was being collected. Furthermore, most data analysis approaches that are used to work with semi-structured data require the data to be retained in its raw state during at least the initial parts of the analysis process. Any initial organisation of qualitative data, for example, needs to ensure that:

(a) the raw data is always easily accessible to the researcher;

(b) the researcher can find particular data easily.

In this section we suggest a basic initial approach you can take in analysing your qualitative data: labelling your data, creating an index and then beginning to do some initial coding or categorising of your data. We suggest that you then develop a series of charts which will help you to see how different parts of your data relate to each other.

Labelling your data

As we have seen, when you collect qualitative data you can end up with quite a lot of it! In addition to ensuring that each data source has an identifying number, it is useful to also number the pages of each data source and in some cases to number each paragraph, line of text, or audio/video sequence. This will then provide you with a precise reference point for a particular 'chunk' or unit of data. When you are working with qualitative data you often need to refer back to the particular words or phrases used by your data source, be it an interview, a focus group or a document, or indeed a video sequence. An exact reference in the form of a page number and line number or a video counter will help you to do this.

> ### Your research
>
> At this point you should consider whether you will use a software package to assist you in your analysis as each package will have slightly different ways of entering and preparing the data for analysis (D9).

As you become familiar with your data you will begin to assess the size of the data 'chunks' you will be working with and can construct your numbering system accordingly. If you are using computer software to help you work with your data you will find that *most packages provide a variety of ways of labelling your data* (D9). If you are working on paper or with a word-processing package, then you can add reference numbers yourself.

Creating an index

One way to begin to organise data is to create an indexing system which can be applied to the raw data. An index simply lists all the different topics and types of data that may be found in each interview, focus group, document and so on, and assigns a symbol or 'flag' (usually a number or letter combination or colour code) to words, phrases, sentences or sequences in the data where a particular type of data is found.

If you are using a computer software package to help you to analyse your data you will find that most packages include a technique that allows you to do this (D9). If you are using a word processor you can use some of the same search techniques to find data and use your own system of flags or highlighters to mark different types of data. If you are working on paper, then coloured pens, highlighters or symbols can be used. There really isn't a 'right' or 'wrong' way to go about this – you have to choose a system that works for you!

It is important to recognise that *indexing is not the same as coding*. An index simply tells you where the data can be found and should enable you to quickly find the same sort of data in each of your data sources. A basic index can be created by using the headings or questions you have used in your topic guide (**C4** and **C5**). This may then be elaborated as you identify particular aspects of the topic, new ideas or interesting points that you know you will want to come back to and consider further during the analysis process.

Example D2.5 opposite is a short section from an imaginary interview with a young mother as part of research that was studying people's perceptions and understandings of 'healthy eating'.

Example D2.5

A section of a semi-structured interview (indexed)

		Index
I	So, thinking about what you eat during a typical week, what sorts of things influence you in deciding what you eat?	
R	Well, I guess we all get into a bit of a rut with our eating habits – you know, pretty much the same every week, one night it'll be curry, another fish and of course a roast at the weekend – my mother always did a roast on Sundays and she was a really good cook so I try to do the same. Although she never did things like curry or pasta of course because most people just didn't eat that sort of thing then. In fact lots of things we eat now are different from what I ate as a child – things are cooked differently using vegetable oils that are healthier than animal fats, for instance, and we don't have big breakfasts like bacon and eggs except on holidays. But one thing I did learn from my mother was how to cook the basics so I almost always cook from scratch rather than buy ready meals.	4 2 2, 4 4 6 2 4

I	Anything else that influences what you eat?	
R	I suppose time is a big thing. When both partners are out working then there's not much time to do things like roasts except at the weekend. And no time to do pies or cakes – those sorts of thing we don't eat much but if we do we would buy them. I'd love to have more time to really get into cooking – there's so many ideas on TV now – I just wish I had the time and energy to try some new things.	4 1 4

And then the other thing is trying to get the children to eat a balanced diet – or at least to eat less sweets and crisps. I do feel that there should be less advertising of sweets and unhealthy snacks on TV when children are watching – it's hard not to give in to them when they've seen something advertised and there it is on the supermarket shelf. They put on some really good programmes about healthy diets and then the adverts in the break are all about the very things they shouldn't have. Or at least they should be a treat rather than every day. I like a chocolate bar myself occasionally especially if I'm feeling a bit down or stressed but I try not to do that too often.

1
6
3,
6
3,
6

3,
5

I	Does the cost of food influence what you buy?	
R	Oh yes of course – you have to be really well off to buy some cuts of meat or to buy the fancy cakes. But it's not just that – I always look out for the cheap offers – 'buy one get one free' and keep things in the freezer if we don't use then. That does sometimes mean we have something different, you know, if it's cheaper that week. I really ought to go to a greengrocer rather than buy fruit and vegetables at the supermarket – I should think that sort of thing I could get cheaper if I was prepared to shop around. I just don't have the time – it has to be convenient, get everything under one roof!	3 2 2 3

The study could be set in the UK in the early twenty-first century with the current medical and social concerns with regard to the increasing levels of obesity in the population and the consumption of ready-made food. The topic guide could include the following:

- Can you tell me about the food you have eaten in the last 24 hours?
- Can you tell me about your household: who lives with you, who buys food and who prepares food?
- Thinking about a typical week, what sorts of things influence the food you buy and the meals you prepare?
- How important is food to you personally? In what ways is food important to you?
- What do you understand as 'healthy eating'?

An index might include:

1. Household information
2. Examples of food eaten
3. Influences on food bought
4. Influences on food prepared
5. Importance of food
6. Understanding of healthy eating.

An index does not distinguish between different types of information or different ideas or opinions on each topic but simply flags up to you that here is some data you may want to consider when you are looking at a particular issue.

Beginning to code

As you are indexing you will probably become more aware of aspects of your data that you want to explore further and to subject to a more rigorous analysis. As you index, note down the aspects or topics within your data that you want to explore, and observe the different ways in which particular topics are discussed or presented in each data source. You should also have your research questions (A4) in mind and be looking for statements, stories, experiences and opinions in the data that may help you to understand and address your research questions.

The notes or memos to yourself provide the basis for beginning to code or categorise your data. Whatever analytical approach you go on to use, some basic coding – or identifying and gathering together of material on a topic, an opinion or experience – will provide a starting point.

Initially, though, you have to decide what you are looking for – what you are interested in – in the data, and familiarise yourself with the range of data on that topic, before using some exploratory coding to begin to tentatively interpret the data.

In the example above you might begin to take a closer look at the different influences on people when they are deciding what food to buy and prepare. As you read through all your data sources you will probably begin to find some common themes emerging, and you can begin to identify these by developing a basic coding of the data. You should think of this as simply taking your index a stage further and beginning to identify some of the themes in your data that you want to explore further in your analysis.

As with the indexing, it is useful to begin to identify themes by using a coding system and giving each theme a name. In our example we have identified the following initial set of codes with regard to influences on buying and preparing food. Note that each code is clearly defined and the definition attempts to describe all the data that will be included. If you begin to find data that does not match the definition you may want to consider creating a new code to accommodate the data – or possibly to amend your definition so that the data is included. This is where you are beginning to really work with the data and to think about how you are interpreting it.

Example D2.6

Codes

Table D2.3 Examples of codes

Code name	Definition
Childhood family influence (ICF)	Mention of childhood family as influencing positively or negatively the choice of food to buy and/or prepare
Media – negative (IMN)	Mention of media influencing the choice of food that is not regarded as healthy
Media – positive (IMP)	Mention of media influencing the choice of food that is regarded as healthy
Time – buying food (ITB)	Mention of time or lack of time influencing the choice of food to buy
Time – preparing food (ITP)	Mention of time or lack of time influencing the choice of food to prepare

Example D2.7

A section of a semi-structured interview (initial coding)

		Code
I	So, thinking about what you eat during a typical week, what sorts of things influence you in deciding what you eat?	
R	Well, I guess we all get into a bit of a rut with our eating habits – you know, pretty much the same every week, one night it'll be curry, another fish and of course a roast at the weekend – my mother always did a roast on Sundays and she was a really good cook so I try to do the same. Although she never did things like curry or pasta of course because most people just didn't eat that sort of thing then. In fact lots of things we eat now are different from what I ate as a child – things are cooked differently using vegetable oils that are healthier than animal fats, for instance, and we don't have big breakfasts like bacon and eggs except on holidays. But one thing I did learn from my mother was how to cook the basics so I almost always cook from scratch rather than by ready meals.	ICF

ICF |
| I | Anything else that influences what you eat? | |
| R | I suppose time is a big thing. When both partners are out working then there's not much time to do things like roasts except at the weekend. And no time to do pies or cakes – those sorts of thing we don't eat much but if we do we would buy them. I'd love to have more time to really get into cooking – there's so many ideas on TV now – I just wish I had the time and energy to try some new things. | ITP |

> And then the other thing is trying to get the children to eat a balanced diet – or at least to eat less sweets and crisps. I do feel that there should be less advertising of sweets and unhealthy snacks on TV when children are watching – it's hard not to give in to them when they've seen something advertised and there it is on the supermarket shelf. They put on some really good programmes about healthy diets and then the adverts in the break are all about the very things they shouldn't have. Or at least they should be a treat rather than every day. I like a chocolate bar myself occasionally especially if I'm feeling a bit down or stressed it but I try not to do that too often.   IMN   IMP   IMN
>
> I   Does the cost of food influence what you buy?
> R   Oh yes of course – you have to be really well off to buy some cuts of meat or to buy the fancy cakes. But it's not just that – I always look out for the cheap offers – 'buy one get one free' and keep things in the freezer if we don't use then. That does sometimes mean we have something different, you know, if it's cheaper that week. I really ought to go to a greengrocer rather than buy fruit and vegetables at the supermarket – I should think that sort of thing I could get cheaper if I was prepared to shop around. I just don't have the time – it has to be convenient, get everything under one roof!   ITB

Using charts

Having begun to explore your data with some initial coding, you may want to take this a stage further by creating a two-dimensional chart. The type of chart or framework we are introducing here is based on the 'Framework' approach to thematic analysis described in Ritchie and Lewis (2003) (see D4 for more detail). However, we feel that this can be a helpful initial approach to take whatever your analytical approach because through using a chart:

(a) you can see the range of material within any data source on a particular topic

(b) you can compare what one data source (for example, participant) is saying about the topic with what others are saying.

Typically, each chart has a theme or covers an aspect of your research topic and you may want to create a number of charts initially to help you to explore your data. In our example we use the theme of 'What influences people when they are choosing what food to buy and prepare?' We might also have a chart that focuses on 'What people understand as healthy eating'.

You can prepare a chart in many ways, from the simple idea of using a large sheet of paper with a grid drawn onto it to the more sophisticated method of using tables or spreadsheets on your computer to provide the structure. From the example on pp. 338 and 339 you will see that down the side of the chart are listed the numerous data sources (including, in this case, interviews, focus groups and a document) and across the top are the different codes that have been developed.

In the grid you can enter key quotes from your data sources, summaries of points made and factual information about the data source. Note that you may need more than one sheet to each chart if you have more sources than will easily fit. Some boxes in the grid may be empty as there is no relevant material in that data source. You will find it helpful at this stage to add the page number and line or paragraph number to any quotations you include so that you are able to easily find the raw data and look at the quotes in their original context.

> ## Think about it . . .
> ### Charts
>
> Look across Table D2.4 on pp. 338–339 to see what influences were identified by each data source and how the influences were described and discussed. Then look down each column to see how the different data sources described and discussed each of the influences.
>   Write some notes about each of the columns, identifying any similarities and differences in the points made by each of the data sources.

If you are planning to use a qualitative analysis software package (for example, NVivo) we suggest that you now also read D9 to help you to prepare your data and plan your analysis to make the most effective use of these packages.

Your research

Getting started on analysis

Whether you are working with quantitative or qualitative data you are now ready to really get into the analysis process. It is a good idea at this stage to do three things:

1. Revisit your research questions! Think about how your data will enable you to address your research questions or test your hypothesis.

2. Plan your analysis: make a list of the tasks you will do initially. This could include a set of frequency tables and cross-tabulations or it could be to develop a set of charts.

3. Keep a log or list of all the analytical processes you carry out and alongside add your own notes on what you learnt from a particular table, statistical test or chart. Your log should include any new variables you create or codes you identify with their definitions.

CHECKLIST	✓
Is your data *complete*?	
Do you *know your data*?	
Have you decided how to *organise* your data so that you can find what you want?	
Have you *planned* your analysis?	

Table D2.4 Influences on people's choices when buying and preparing food

Data source (identifier)	Household type	Childhood family influences	Positive media influences	Negative media influences	Time	Cost
INT 1	2 parents + 2 children	'my mother always did a roast on Sundays and she was a really good cook so I try to do the same'	'They put on some really good programmes about healthy diets'	'. . . there should be less advertising of sweets and unhealthy snacks on TV when children are watching . . .'	'I suppose time is a big thing. When both partners are out working then there's not much time to do things like roasts except at the weekend. And no time to do pies or cakes – . . . I'd love to have more time to really get into cooking – there's so many ideas on TV now – I just wish I had the time and energy to try some new things.'	'I always look out for the cheap offers . . . That does sometimes mean we have something different, you know, if it's cheaper that week '. . . fruit and vegetables – . . . I could get cheaper if I was prepared to shop around. I just don't have the time – it has to be convenient, get everything under one roof!' **NB Link between time and cost**
INT 2	2 parents + 1 child	'We always go to his mother's for Sunday lunch – it's probably the best meal we have all week'	'There's so much information around now you can't really not know about it.'		'This is the big thing for me, with us both working there really isn't much time. I feel so guilty though I should have time to cook for my child'	'When you don't have much time you really can't afford to be too bothered about cost – you just try to buy the best you can.' **NB Link between time and cost**
INT 3	1 parent + 2 children	'I remember how much I enjoyed my mother's cooking and sitting round the table every evening talking and eating – that's what I want for my children'	'I read all the magazines and watch all the TV programmes – I'm a bit of a healthy foodie!'	'What really gets me down are the adverts for sweets and fizzy drinks during when the children are watching'	'I really enjoy cooking – it's a sort of hobby I suppose.' **NB is this about use of time?**	'I'm a single parent so I don't have a lot of money but I do know how to make a good healthy meal out of cheap ingredients. . . .'

FG 1	All single parent mothers with children under 5	Some have memories of family meals while others recall eating watching TV or each family member getting their own food	Most had seen the Jamie Oliver programmes and thought his meals should be introduced in all schools	'There's always something that's not good for you – you get fed-up of being told you can't have this, that'll make you ill . . . .'	Time was the second most important influence on choice of food	Cost was the most important influence on choice of food
FG 2	All male parents in two-parent families with children under 5	Some felt their partners were not such good cooks as their mothers. Most remembered being told to eat their vegetables and some felt that they didn't want to be so strict with their own children	'What's needed is good straightforward information on what is and isn't good for you – especially for the kids . . .'	'Too many of these cooking programmes, my partner just sits and watches them – she never cooks any of the meals!'	'I really enjoy cooking so we take it in turns and then it's not too much of a burden, it's not everyday . . .' 'Shopping around means spending half the weekend shopping . . .'	Cost was the most important influence on the choice of food. Increase in food prices really begins to put the pressure on other things but food has to be most important
DOC 1	Leaflet issued by Department of Health on children and healthy eating	'Make eating an enjoyable family affair, get together round the table . . .'	'In this leaflet we aim to give you clear information about what is good for your child and you – and it is backed up by medical and scientific evidence'		'Preparing a meal from fresh ingredients doesn't need to take a long time. Try these simple recipes . . .'	'Good food does sometimes cost a little more but it is worth a little extra to know that your child will grow up eating food that is good for him or her . . .'

Your research

Choosing analysis techniques

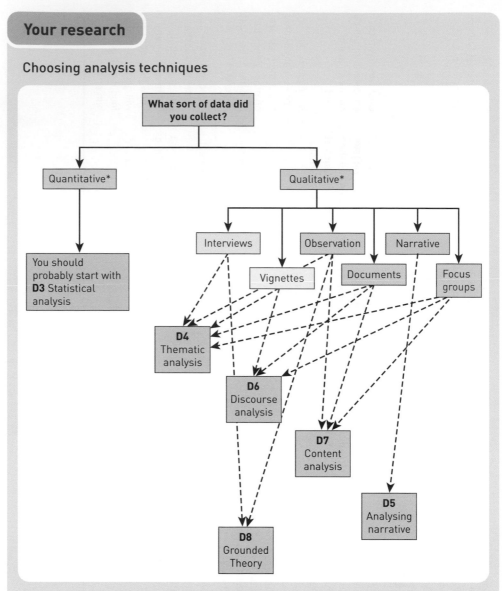

The dashed lines show some of the analysis techniques that *could* be applied to your data. Please remember these are only general guidelines – the data collection techniques you use are specific to your project.

*This chart makes a distinction between quantitative and qualitative data. *This is for clarity only!* (So, for example, observational data might be quantitative as well as qualitative.)

References and further reading

Field, A. (2009) *Discovering Statistics Using SPSS*, 3rd edn, London: Sage.

Grbich, C. (2007) *Qualitative Data Analysis: An Introduction*, London: Sage.

Ritchie, J. and Lewis, J. (2003) *Qualitative Research Practice: A Guide for Social Science Students and Researchers*, London: Sage.

Seale, C., Gobo, G., Gubrium, J. F. and Silverman, D. (2007) *Qualitative Research Practice*, London: Sage.

Wright, D. B. and London, K. (2009) *First (and Second) Steps in Statistics*, 2nd edn, London: Sage.

CHAPTER D3
Statistical analysis

Contents

In context

A statistical analysis of data enables us to:

- summarise the data we have collected and describe the data
- describe the features of the data in ways that help us to identify aspects that are relevant to our research questions
- explore and test relationships between different sets of data.

In this chapter we will look at each of these features of statistical analysis in relation to the process of working with and analysing data to help to answer research questions.

We suggest that you read D2 before reading this chapter.

PART D: Data analysis

	D1:	Beginning to analyse
	D2:	Working with data
▶	**D3:**	**Statistical analysis**
	D4:	Thematic analysis
	D5:	Analysing narrative
	D6:	Discourse analysis
	D7:	Content analysis
	D8:	Grounded Theory
	D9:	Using computers in data analysis
	D10:	So what? Drawing conclusions

In this chapter we introduce statistical analytical techniques which enable you to examine the quantitative data you have gathered. As social research has developed, and, in particular, with the use of both large-scale surveys to find out what people think and do and the government and other organisations collecting and analysing data to inform policy-making and the development and evaluation of services, so statistical techniques have been developed to aid in the understanding of the data collected. This has been facilitated by information technology and the growing use of computers to calculate or compute complex statistics relating to large amounts of data which would be laborious and time-consuming to calculate manually.

Though sometimes complex, statistical techniques are simply tools to help us to work with the data we have gathered in a systematic way. They do not do the analysis for us but rather provide us with some simple, as well as complex, ways of examining and working with our data. Statistical techniques do depend on mathematical statistical theories and formulas and many students of social research do not have the mathematical knowledge and skills to fully understand and use the more complex techniques.

Your research

While computer software packages such as SPSS (D9) do offer students the means of using statistical techniques without fully comprehending the mathematical theory that underpins them, you should recognise that an understanding of the purpose of each statistical technique is required in order to be able to use them effectively and, importantly, to interpret the results.

What we attempt to do here is to introduce you to a range of basic approaches to working statistically with your data which are appropriate for many small-scale pieces of research, and to point you in the direction of more complex approaches should you wish to take your study in this area further. We introduce you to the use of software packages like SPSS in D9 and will make reference to these in this chapter as well.

What is . . .

Statistics

(1) 'quantitative facts or statements' (*OED*)

In social research statistics apply to data that is structured and can be counted or is already expressed in numerical terms. The data is usually collected using a questionnaire or format (**C3**).

(2) 'any of the numerical characteristics of a sample' (*OED*)

Many statistical analytical techniques have been developed and derived from the use of samples from a population (**B5**) as the basis for gathering data in both the physical and social sciences. The statistics are the characteristics of the sample that can be counted, for example, the number of men, the number of people who read the *Daily Mail* newspaper, the number of students with three A levels.

Both definitions are useful as we begin to think about a statistical analysis.

Much of the social research that you will read and make use of in your studies will include some statistical analysis of data. Large-scale surveys and censuses and research using structured questionnaires or formats to gather data lend themselves to being analysed statistically as the data is gathered in a readily structured format. The emphasis is on counting the number of different responses to each question and the findings are usually presented in tables, charts and diagrams. Statistical analysis is most appropriately used for research that gathers data from a probability sample of a known population, as you can apply the statistical analysis techniques to the sample and then extrapolate, or generalise, your findings to apply to the whole population, not just the sample. However, many of the techniques are also appropriate for the sort of small-scale social research projects undertaken by students and others that are not based on a probability sample but have collected structured data from a representative group of cases using an opportunistic sampling approach, for example, a quota sample (**B5**).

❓ What is . . .

Statistical significance

Statistical significance is a statement about the likelihood of the observed result, nothing else. It does not guarantee that something important or even meaningful, has been found.   (Hays, 1993: 68)

1. Tests of statistical significance are designed for use with data gathered from a sample from a population. This sample is usually selected in order to represent statistically a defined population. The main purpose of testing for statistical significance is to provide a measure of the probability that the relationships found in the data from the sample will also be found in the wider population. The test will also show how statistically likely it is that relationships between the data found in the sample would *not* be found in the population.

    The researcher must decide what level of risk he is prepared to take that his sample data is different from that expected to be found in the population. The level of risk most commonly used is p (probability) <0.05, or a 5% chance that the relationships found in the sample data would *not* be found in the population.

    Of course, we cannot be sure that our sample is or is not one of those 5%, but by considering the level of the statistical test we can have some confidence that our findings reflect those that would be found in the population.

2. Statistical significance is also used to describe the likelihood of a particular finding or result, e.g. chi-squared, having occurred by chance. As in the chi-squared example on p. 363, a null hypothesis is set up that there is no relationship between the two variables. If the findings are found to be statistically significant then the null hypothesis can be rejected. The acceptable level of statistical significance used by most social researchers is p (probablility) <0.5, or a 5% chance that there is no relationship between the variables.

Social researchers are also likely to draw on the research of others, so need to be able to read and understand the statistical techniques used by other researchers. This chapter will help you to understand some of the techniques used by other researchers and have a better understanding of their research findings.

Real research

Social Trends

Social Trends is published each year (and currently accessible from www.socialtrends. gov.uk, accessed 2 September 2009). The report presents statistics relating to a range of social themes and the data is taken from a number of government and other sources. The data is presented in a variety of formats – tables, charts and diagrams – and a summary of the main points of interest in the data provides the basis for a discussion. Through reading such reports you can gain an understanding of statistical data and how it can best be presented.

Analysing quantitative data

analysis
A process of working with the data to describe, discuss, interpret, evaluate and explain the data in terms of the research questions or hypothesis of the research project.

process
An on-going, often continuous series of actions intended to achieve a specific result. This often requires the researcher to follow an established set of (usually) routine procedures.

Any analysis of social data is more than simply summarising the data that has been collected. **Analysis** is a process of working with the data to summarise, describe and explain the data in terms of the research questions or hypothesis of the research project. Analysing quantitative data is a **process** in three stages. Each stage is important as we work towards having a set of findings that will help us to answer our research questions or test a hypothesis.

A statistical analysis of data enables us to:

- summarise the data we have collected and describe the data;
- describe the features of the data in ways that help us to identify aspects that are relevant to our research questions;
- explore and test relationships between different sets of data.

In this section we take you through this process as we look at the way an analysis develops. We will use some imagined data from a questionnaire about social networking in parts of this section. The questionnaire could be used to gather data about the way people make social contacts and keep in touch with friends and family, and the researcher is particularly interested in whether men and women differ in the ways they do this and also whether age is linked to the use of different means of communication. An extract of the created questionnaire is presented first, with the variable names attached to each question/variable.

Think about it . . .

A reminder: in D2 we introduced some of the key features of a statistical approach to working with your data:

Structured data

The key characteristics of structured data are:

(a) the questions are the same for each participant or case; and
(b) typically there is a common set of answers for each question.

Variables and creating new variables

- A variable is a *set* of answers to a question.
- New variables can be created from the data by combining the answers given to one or more variables, e.g. age/gender.
- Frequencies for each variable show how often each answer or code is given for each.
- Cross-tabulations show the relationship between two or more variables in a table format.

Codes

Codes are the names or identifiers given to each of the answers in a variable set.

We will be using these in this section and you may wish to refer back to D2.

Example D3.1

Social networking questionnaire

Variable name

1. Are you   male ☐   female ☐   *gen*

2. Which age group are you in?

16–24 years	
25–44 years	
45–64 years	
65 years and over	

agegrp

3. Which of these activities do you take part in during your free time? (please tick all that apply to you)

freetime (multicode)

Watch television	
Listen to music	
Internet (other than computer games)	
Spend time with friends/family	
Go to pubs/bars/clubs	
Sports/exercise activities	
Play computer games	

tv
mus
int
famfri
pub
sport
compgame

4. How frequently do you use the internet in your free time (apart from computer games)?

inttime

Every day	
Three to six days a week	
One or two days a week	
Less than once a week	
Never	

5. About how many hours each week do you spend using the internet?

     hours   *inthours*

6. In what ways do you usually keep in touch with your close friends or family (apart from those who live in the same house as you)? (please tick all that apply to you)

contact (multicode)

Meet in person	
Telephone call	
Text message	
Email	
Letter	
Internet, e.g. chat room; social network site, e.g. Facebook, instant messaging, Twitter	

person
phone
text
email
letter
intcomm

6a)   If you used the internet to use a chat room, social networking site, instant messaging, Twitter and so on yesterday

– how many minutes did you spend on this activity <u>yesterday</u>
Please give your answer to the nearest 15 minutes (quarter of an hour)

hours   minutes

Socnettime

7.   Would you describe yourself as:
     (please circle the number that applies to you)

social

Very sociable	Fairly sociable	Neither sociable or unsociable	Fairly unsociable	Very unsociable
1	2	3	4	5

Different types of quantitative data

In D2 we introduced the idea of a variable as the set of categories or codes of data relating to one question or piece of information: so in the social networking questionnaire, in the first question ('Are you male or female?'), the variable is *gender*. Variables form the basis of a statistical analysis as the data we are working with is the range of answers or codes relating to each variable, and it is to these that we now turn. There are a number of different types of variable, and you can use different techniques in different ways with each type, so we need to distinguish between them. Table D3.1 describes the four main types of variable.

Table D3.1 The four main types of variables

Type of variable	Description
Ratio	A ratio variable is one where the difference between each of the answers or categories is equal and there is an absolute zero on the scale. It is possible to multiply and divide (form ratios) between different variable values. Variable *inttime* in the example asks for a ratio variable because all the answers are in units of one hour, so someone who says he used the internet for ten hours used it for twice as long as someone who used it for five hours and it is possible for someone to not use the internet at all – zero hours.
Interval	An interval variable is similar to a ratio variable in that the difference between each of the answers or categories is equal but there is no absolute zero. For example, the temperature scales of Fahrenheit and Celsius have different temperatures labelled as zero.
Ordinal	An ordinal variable is one where the categories or codes can be ranked in some way – that is, one can be said to be greater or more important than another – but the difference between each pair of categories is not equal. In Q7 *social* is an ordinal variable because there is an order to the answer categories – *very sociable* is more sociable than *fairly sociable* (but not necessarily twice as sociable). Similarly *agegrp* is an ordinal variable as people in category 2 (*25–44 years*) are older than those in category 1 (*16–24 years*), and the categories are not of equal size. The numeric code assigned reflects the order of the categories.

(Continued)

Table D3.1 (*Continued*)

Type of variable	Description
Nominal	A nominal variable is simply a set of names. In other words, the set of categories are not related to each other in terms of quantity. The multicode *freetime* is a nominal variable as each answer is simply the name of an activity and one activity is no more important or larger than another. Quite a lot of variables have just two answers or codes assigned to them – male/female, yes/no. These are known as *dichotomous* variables. In most situations we can regard these as a particular type of nominal variable as the answers are different but not ranked in terms of importance.

Using statistical analysis to summarise and describe your data

As a researcher, you must act as an intermediary between the data you have gathered and the people who will be interested in what you have found out. Your role is to work with the raw data and to provide an account of the data in a form that both summarises it and demonstrates how the data relates to your research questions. The priority for most researchers is to find ways of summarising the data – after all, in most cases your reader will not want to read through all your questionnaires to find out about your respondents.

To help you to do this, we will introduce a number of ways of looking at your data and using what are often called descriptive statistics. These are statistics that summarise the data you have gathered in relation to each variable in terms of

- the frequency of each answer or code;
- how the answers are distributed across the codes;
- summary statistics: for example, means, medians and modes, and percentiles.

In D2 we suggested that you can begin to explore your data by looking at how the answers to your questions or codes are distributed – in other words, how many cases of each code have been recorded. This can be displayed in a frequency table, which is the starting point of your analysis (we include an example of a frequency table in Example D3.2). You can then begin to see the 'shape' of your data, and to describe or summarise the data relating to each variable using simple charts and some descriptive statistics.

Describing the sample

It is useful to start by describing the characteristics of your sample of cases. This may include, for example, a series of charts or frequency tables which set out the age, income levels and gender distributions of the sample. Simple bar charts are often used to show visually the distribution of your sample characteristics – software packages like SPSS and Excel can help you to do this (D9). This will help you to become familiar with your sample so that you can begin to explore the relationships between these characteristics and your other variables.

Example D3.2

Describing the sample

In the social networking example, you may want to first explore differences in social networking between male and female respondents and respondents of different age groups. Start by finding out the distribution of your sample across the age groups by gender, so that you can check whether the distributions of males and females differ in relation to age.

Table D3.2 Social networking respondents by age group and gender (A)

That's interesting!

Age group	No. of males	% males	No. of females	% females	Total	% total
16–24 yrs	14	20%	20	25%	34	22.6%
25–44 yrs	22	31.4%	22	27.5%	44	29.3%
45–64 yrs	18	25.7%	20	25%	38	25.3%
65 yrs and over	16	22.9%	18	22.5%	34	22.6%
Total	70	100%	80	100%	150	99.8%

This can be presented in a bar chart which illustrates the different age distributions of the men and women (and total) in the sample.

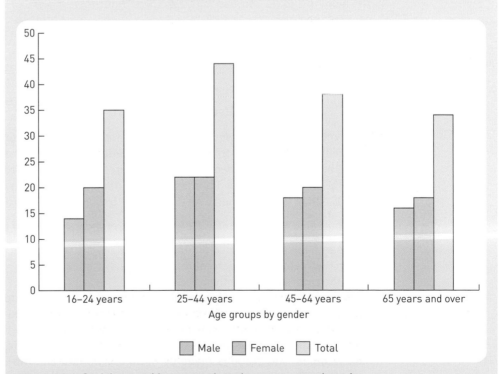

Figure D3.1 Social networking respondents by age group and gender

Example D3.2 describes the distribution of a sample of 150 people. The sample includes slightly more women than men and there are more men *and* women in the middle age groups of 25–44 years and 45–64 years. The age distribution of males and females is slightly different with, for example, only 20% of the males being in the youngest age group compared with 25% of the females. As one of the purposes of our analysis is to look at the differences between men and women and different age groups with respect to their experiences of social networking, we need to stop and think about the possible implications for our analysis of these differences.

We might ask ourselves whether there are sufficient cases (people) in the smallest group for us to be able to say that their answers do represent the group. In this case the smallest group is men aged 16–24 years with 14 cases. The largest groups are men aged 25–44 years and women aged 25–44 years, each with 22 cases. As this is a small-scale piece of research, it is unlikely that we will be able to remedy this by, for example, getting more cases.

At this stage in the analysis we would note the differences and keep them in mind as the analysis progresses. We may later consider combining the age groups into two groups instead of four, so creating groups with larger numbers of people in each.

Example D3.3

Using percentages

A percentage shows each value in your frequency table as a proportion of the whole (with the whole being 100%). Each percentage is worked out by:

$$\frac{\text{Number of cases in category}}{\text{Total number of cases}} \times 100$$

For example, the percentage of men who are in the 16–24 year age group is

$$\frac{14 \text{ (number of men in 16–24 group)}}{70 \text{ (total number of men)}} \times 100 = \mathbf{20\%}$$

Turning your raw data frequencies into percentages can be helpful at this stage as this will enable you to compare groups of different sizes. In the 25–44 age group there are 22 men and 22 women. However, there are 70 men in total and 80 women in total so 22 men makes up a larger percentage or proportion of the total men – 31.4% – than the 22 women who make up 27.5% of the total women.

What if we wanted to know the distribution of men and women in each age group?

The same table can be used but the percentages are worked out on the age groups (each row) rather than each column (gender). Note that the total percentage (100%) is in the right-hand column in this case.

By calculating the percentages in terms of each age group we can see that there is a higher percentage of women in each age group, apart from the 25–44 year age group which is 50% men and 50% women. This is to be expected as there are more women in the sample than men. However, it does also show that the youngest age group is made up of 58.8% women and the smallest group of men (14). This must be noted and borne in mind when looking at the other characteristics of this age group.

Table D3.3 Social networking respondents by age group and gender (B)

Age group	No. of males	% males	No. of females	% females	Total	% total
16–24 yrs	14	41.2%	20	58.8%	34	100%
25–44 yrs	22	50%	22	50%	44	100%
45–64 yrs	18	47.4%	20	52.6%	38	100%
65 yrs and over	16	47%	18	53%	34	100%
Total	70	46.7%	80	53.3%	150	100%

That's interesting!

Your research

Research quality check

- Be cautious about using percentages if the *total* is less than 20 cases as the numbers in each category are likely to be small. Large percentage differences may reflect differences of only one or two cases. Consider combining categories to create larger groups.
- Check that the percentages add up to 100% (or close). When calculating percentages it is common practice to round to one decimal place or to the nearest whole number – when percentages are added they may not be exactly 100, as in the table in Example D3.2.
- Always ensure that you are working on the correct total as 100%, and check the direction of percentages in cross-tabulations – rows or columns?
- When reporting your findings, always say what the percentages relate to – for example, say that *20% of all the men* in the sample were in the 16–24 year age group.

The shape of the distribution

Bar charts and **histograms** can help us to visualise the shape or distribution of the values for each of our variables, and are an effective way of both summarising our data and helping us to identify interesting or anomalous features within the data. In Example D3.4, we will use data from the questionnaire about how frequently the men and women in the sample use the internet to look at the shapes of the distributions of the variable *inttime*.

 What is . . .

Histogram

A histogram is a chart showing the frequency of a ratio or interval variable where the values can be continuous. Each bar in the histogram is centred around the mid point or value of the category it represents. (See Example D3.5 for an example of a histogram.)

Example D3.4

The shape of the distribution

Q4   How frequently do you use the internet in your free time
(apart from computer games)?   *Inttime*

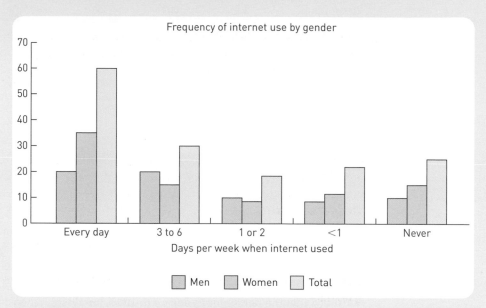

Figure D3.2 Frequency of internet use by gender – bar chart

If we join the mid points of each of the bars of the same colour we can see the shape more clearly. The line representing the total shows that the number of answers is highest at the extremes of *every day* and *never*. However, if we look at the male and female values separately we can see that the shape of the distribution is clearly different for men and women.

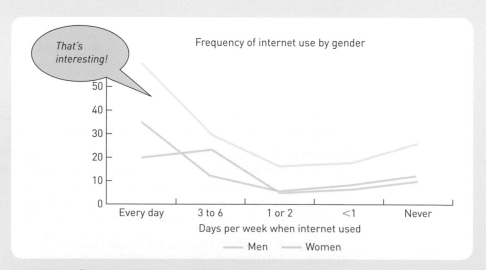

Figure D3.3 Frequency of internet use by gender – line graph

At this stage a finding like this raises further questions:

- *Are there differences between different age groups in terms of frequency of internet use?*
- *Does this finding mean that women spend more time using the internet?*
- *Are there other differences between men and women in terms of the way they use their free time?*

By using charts and graphs as in this example, we can see the way the answers to our questions are distributed across a set of values in terms both of the range – from lowest to highest value – and of where most answers are concentrated. Comparing the shape of the data for different groups, for example, age or gender groups, can be a useful way of beginning to identify interesting differences between them.

Mean, median and mode

central tendency
A statistical measure which summarises the data relating to one variable in one value, such as the mean, median or mode.

There are other ways of summarising the data which may be used to look for differences between different groups or categories. The mean, median and mode are methods of summarising the data relating to one variable in one value. In each case the value relates to a central value of the data, hence they are sometimes called measures of **central tendency.**

mean
A statistical average calculated by totalling all the values and dividing by the number of cases.

- The arithmetic **mean** gives an average of all the values and can be calculated from ratio or interval data.

median
A statistical average calculated by arranging all the values in a sample in numerical order, then noting the middle value of the distribution.

- The **median** is the mid point in a set of data and can be used on ordinal, interval and ratio data.
- The **mode** can be used with any data including nominal data and refers to the most common value.

mode
A statistical average calculated by noting the most common value in the distribution.

While each can be useful in the early stages of analysis, it is important to also look at the way in which the data is dispersed around the mean, median or mode – so ensure that you take account of the shape of the distribution (see Example D3.4) and of the range of values (the gap between the lowest and highest values).

? What is . . .

Normal distribution

In statistical terms a normal distribution is data that is distributed symmetrically around the mean point in a 'bell shape'. (We discussed the normal distribution in B5 in relation to the way characteristics of samples drawn from a population are assumed to be distributed around the real characteristics of the population.)

In real social research, data is rarely distributed exactly in this way although some types of data are likely to closely resemble this shape.

For example:
- If you measured the heights of a representative sample of children of the same age you could expect that most children's heights would cluster around a central point, with few comparatively small and few very tall children.
- Test results or examination marks are often expected to be distributed in this way, with few students getting very high or very low marks.

In a normal distribution the mean, median and mode are all at the central point. Some distributions are *skewed*, that is they have one end or tail of the distribution longer than the other, and the mean, median and mode will be different.

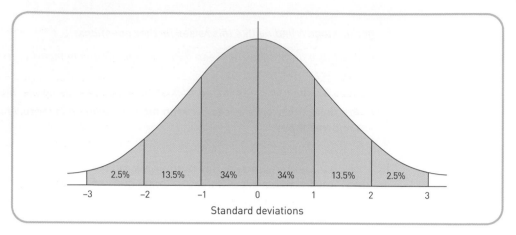

Figure D3.4 Bell-shaped curve showing standard deviations

❓ What is . . .

Standard deviation

The standard deviation is a measure of the dispersion of the cases around the mean. When data is distributed in a normal distribution, about two-thirds of the data values lie within one standard deviation on each side of the mean; 95% of the values lie within two standard deviations of the mean.

The standard deviation is calculated by

standard deviation $=$

$$\sqrt{\text{the sum of } \frac{(\text{deviations of each value of each case from the mean})^2}{\text{number of cases}}}$$

or

$$\sqrt{\frac{\Sigma(X - M)^2}{N}}$$

The mean

A mean is calculated by totalling all the values and dividing by the number of cases. This can be done by using a frequency table, as in Example D3.5. A mean gives an average value for the variable and it can be useful at this stage to compare the means of two groups – for example, men and women – in order to identify differences which may be important. However, the mean does not tell you anything about the range of values or how they are distributed. Very different distributions could have the same mean. For example, if we calculate the mean of two sets of examination marks (say, Sociology and Psychology) for a group of 50 students, both may be 60%. However, the Sociology marks may range from 50% to 70% while the Psychology marks may range from 10% to 90%. In this case we would want to look at the shape of the distribution and calculate the standard deviation to help us understand better the differences between the two sets of marks.

Think about it . . .

Comparing means

In both cases mentioned above, the staff setting the examinations would have some cause for concern about the range of marks. The Sociology staff would consider whether the examination was set at a level to distinguish between 'good' and 'not so good' students as all the students have marks within a 20% range. They may also consider whether the exam markers were making full use of the range of marks and not effectively distinguishing between, for example, the 'good' and the 'very good'.

The Psychology staff would have concerns about the students who have failed when other students have gained very high marks. Perhaps the level and type of teaching did not help the weaker students to learn, while favouring those with particular abilities in the subject or in the type of examination.

To get a better understanding of the marks standard deviations were calculated for each set:

For the Sociology marks, the standard deviation = 5.883217

For the Psychology marks, the standard deviation = 17.54644

Using the standard deviations we can say:

- The Psychology marks were more widely dispersed around the mean of 60% than the Sociology marks which, as we would expect, were clustered around the mean.

- If the Psychology marks were normally distributed, then 68% would lie within 60 ± 17.54644 or marks between 53% and 77%, 95% within 60 ± 35 (approx. $2 \times SD$) or marks between 25% and 95%.

- The Psychology marks were spread across the range and not clustered in a narrow band around the mean with a few extreme values.

Example D3.5

Calculating the mean, median and mode

Q6a) If you used the internet to use a chat room, social networking site, instant messaging, Twitter and so on yesterday
– how many minutes did you spend on this activity yesterday
Please give your answer to the nearest 30 minutes (half an hour)

Fifty people answered this question.

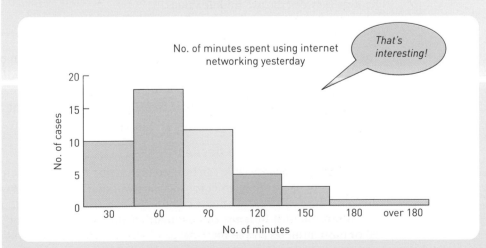

Figure D3.5 Cases of internet networking by number of minutes spent

The histogram shows that the distribution is skewed with a long tail to the right.

Calculating the mean

Table D3.4 Cases of internet networking by number of minutes spent – calculating the mean

No. of minutes X	No. of respondents f	fx (no. of minutes × no. of people)
30	10	300
60	18	1080
90	12	1080
120	5	600
150	3	450
180	1	180
Over 180 (answer given = 300)	1	300
TOTAL	**50**	**3990**

$$\text{MEAN} = \text{fx/Total f} = 3990/50 = 80 \text{ minutes}$$

The *Median* in this case is the two middle values (25th and 26th out of 50) which would both be *60 minutes*. The *Mode* is the most common value which is also *60 minutes*.

In this case the mean is affected by an *outlier* – one extreme value of 300 minutes – which inflates the mean. The median and mode are not affected by this one case.

The median

The median is the middle value of a distribution. In other words, there will be as many cases below as above the median value. If the number of cases is an odd number, the median is the middle value; if there number of cases is even (as in the example), the median value lies halfway between the two middle values.

The mode

The mode is simply the most common value in the distribution. In our example, 60 minutes is the most common time. It is possible to have a distribution with two or more modal points – for instance, in Example D3.4 there could have been as many people who never use the internet as there are who use it every day and the distribution would then have had two modal points.

Quartiles, quintiles and deciles

cumulative frequency
The arrangement of frequency data in categories that add up to 100 per cent.

A **cumulative frequency** table can be used to describe the same data relating to the amount of time spent using the internet for social networking in a different way. You will see from the table that, when calculating a cumulative frequency, we have to rephrase our internet use and think of it in terms of how many people have used it for 30 or more minutes, 60 or more minutes and so on.

Table D3.5 A cumulative frequency table

No. of minutes	No. of people	% of total
30 or more	50	100%
60 or more	40	80%
90 or more	22	44%
120 or more	10	20%
150 or more	5	10%
180 or more	2	4%

That's interesting!

We can use a cumulative frequency table to divide up the cases in a variety of ways. For example, having seen that 44% of our sample used the internet for social networking for 90 minutes or more on the previous day, we could divide our sample into two groups: those who used the internet for social networking for less than 90 minutes (low users) and those who used it for 90 minutes or more (high users). A new variable could be created with these two groups. We could then use this variable to explore whether there are differences between the high and low users.

The example in the 'Real research' box below is based on the household income levels of the respondents and divides the distribution of the respondents into five groups, each representing 20% of the sample. In this case the total sample (100%) is divided into five groups of 20% based on the level of income – each 20% is called a **quintile** (or fifth). Samples can also be divided into four groups (**quartiles**) or ten groups (**deciles**).

Quintiles, quartiles and deciles can also be used as the basis for new variables which can then be used in further analysis as in the 'Real research' example below.

quintile
One-fifth part of a sample or data set.

quartile
One-quarter part of a sample or data set.

decile
One-tenth part of a sample or data set.

Real research

Using quintiles

Government and research reports often divide their samples into four (quartiles) or five (quintiles) groups according to the respondents' household incomes. In this way, a new variable is formed which can then be used to compare the responses of people in each of the income level groups.

The incomes of all respondents are listed in rank order. The 20% of respondents with the lowest incomes are put into a new category – bottom quintile – and the next 20% into the fourth quintile, the next into the third quintile and so on, up to the top quintile comprising the 20% of people with the highest income.

Social Trends 38 (2008) included a chart using the lowest and highest quintiles to compare the two groups in terms of their consumption of different foodstuffs in grams per week. This enables us to see how much of each type of foodstuff is eaten by the highest income households and the lowest income households.

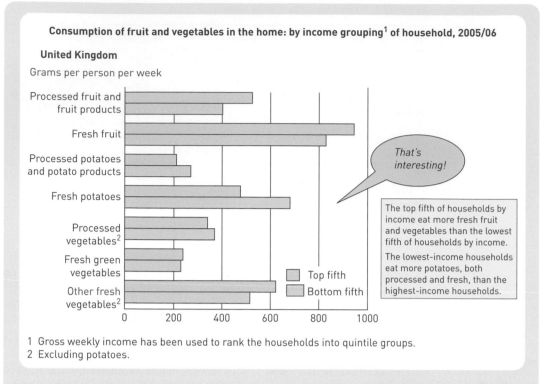

Figure D3.6 Consumption of fruit and vegetables in the home: by income grouping of household, 2005/06

Source: From Office for National Statistics (ONS) (2005) *Social Trends*, 38, Figure 7.9, p. 98. Crown copyright material is reproduced with permission of the controller, Office of Public Sector Information (OPSI) under terms of the Click-Use Licence.

Developing the analysis

The initial stage of analysis has already raised some questions which could be explored further (look at the 'That's interesting!' bubbles as a starting point). Now it is time to do the following:

(a) Consider creating other new variables which combine two variables or combine categories within variables. If, for example, you have categories within one variable with small numbers of cases, you should consider whether for the purposes of the analysis two categories may be combined. You may also consider creating new variables based on the distribution of your sample on one or more variables, for example, using quintiles or quartiles as in the example from *Social Trends 38*.

(b) List the cross-tabulations, scattergrams and bar charts you now want to do to help you to answer the questions that have been raised.

We make some suggestions in Example D3.6.

Example D3.6

Developing the analysis (A)

Questions arising so far from the examples	What to do next
Are there differences between different age groups in terms of frequency of internet use?	Cross-tabulation between (new) variable combining age group and gender and frequency of internet use – *inttime*.

Do women spend more time than men using the internet?	Cross-tabulation between (new) variable combining age group and gender and (new) variable – *inthours* grouped.
Are there other differences between men and women in terms of the way they use their free time?	Cross-tabulation between (new) variable combining age group and gender and the multi-coded variable *freetime* – showing percentages of each gender/age group who take part in each of the activities.
Do people who are high users of the internet for social networking differ in other ways from those who are low users?	Create new variable for those who had used the internet for social networking the day before with two groups – high users (90 minutes or over usage) and low users (less than 90 minutes usage).
Other questions we might have at this stage:	
What means of keeping in touch with friends and family are used by men and women of different age groups?	Cross-tabulation between (new) variable combining age group and gender and the multi-coded variable *contact* – showing percentages of each gender/age group who use each method of communication with their friends and family.
Do women have more 'sociable' free-time activities than men?	Look at the multi-code *freetime* and consider which activities could be considered sociable (those that include some communication between people) and create cross-tabulations of each of these by gender (and age).
Do people who see themselves as fairly or very sociable use particular ways of keeping in touch with their friends and families?	Cross-tabulation between variables *social* and *contact*. This could be followed by doing the cross-tabulation between *social* and *gender*. If there are differences between men and women in terms of their perception of themselves as sociable then the cross-tabulation between *social* and *contact* could be created separately for men and women to look for gender differences.

Your research

Checklist

Have you done frequencies for all your variables?	
Have you looked at the 'shape' of the data for variables that particularly interest you?	
Have you calculated means, medians and modes appropriately?	
Have you considered creating new variables?	
Have you noted down the interesting points from your findings so far?	

At this stage in your analysis it can be helpful for you to write a short account of your findings so far. In it you can summarise your sample and identify any interesting findings that you want to follow up. This account may be used as the first part of your results section in your final report or dissertation.

From your questionnaire or data collection format, list any new variables you now think will be useful in your analysis.

New variable name	Variables used to form new variable	How the new variable is formed	The new variable will help me to . . .

From any questions raised by your analysis so far – and your research questions – make a list of cross-tabulations you could create and what it would help you to explore.

Variable (row)	Variable (column)	This cross-tabulation will help me to . . .

Using statistical analysis to address research questions

Having summarised the data by looking at the frequencies and distribution of values for each variable, you can both return to your research questions to begin to focus your analysis on aspects of the data that are going to help you to address these questions, and look at the questions raised in the first stage. To do this you will probably want to look at two or more variables together. Looking at two variables together is called **bivariate analysis**. Analysing more than two variables together is called **multivariate analysis**.

We have already seen an example of this in D2 where we created a new variable (AGEGEN) combining age groups and gender into one variable. The new variable can then be used in relation to a third variable (in the example, *freetime*) to look at the variation in relation to this variable for both age and gender combined.

bivariate analysis
The analysis of two variables together.

multivariate analysis
The analysis of three or more variables together.

Cross-tabulation

The best way to explore relationships between variables and to begin to identify interesting aspects is to create a series of cross-tabulations. As we stressed earlier (and in D2 and B4), analysis of quantitative data can be planned at an early stage in the research, before the data collection, and a list of potentially interesting cross-tabulations can be prepared using the data collection tool (for example, a questionnaire or other data collection format). Having looked at your frequency tables and newly created variables, you may wish at this point to add to your list other cross-tabulations you now think would be interesting.

A cross-tabulation presents the data from two variables in one table and enables you to identify interesting similarities and differences within the data. As we saw earlier, percentages are often used to facilitate this when we are looking for the similarities and differences between groups of different sizes. In our example using the newly created variable combining age group and gender, we are able to combine three variables – *age*, *gender* and *freetime* (question 3). In fact *freetime* is itself made up of seven variables. *Freetime* is a multi-coded variable in that each person could tick up to seven of the free-time activities. Each of the activities is also a separate variable which can be coded *yes* or *no*.

Think about it . . .

What can you learn from a cross-tabulation?

Table D3.6 shows the numbers, with percentages in brackets, of each age group who take part in each free-time activity.

- Which activity is most common? Which least?
- Which activity shows most difference between men and women? Between different age groups?
- Circle any figures that surprise you or you find particularly interesting.
- Try writing a summary of the table in no more than five sentences.

Table D3.6 Cross-tabulation of age group and sex by type of free-time activity

Age and sex by free-time actvities	Watch TV	Listen to music	Internet (other than computer games)	Friends and family	Pubs/ bars and clubs	Sports/ exercise	Computer games	TOTAL in each group
Male – aged 16–24 yrs	10 (71%)	8 (57%)	12 (86%)	10 (71%)	8 (57%)	8 (57%)	10 (71%)	*14 (100%)*
– aged 25–44 yrs	16 (73%)	16 (73%)	18 (82%)	12 (55%)	12 (55%)	14 (64%)	14 (64%)	*22 (100%)*
– aged 45–64 yrs	16 (88%)	10 (55%)	12 (67%)	12 (67%)	10 (55%)	6 (33%)	6 (33%)	*18 (100%)*
– aged 65 yrs and over	16 (100%)	4 (25%)	6 (38%)	14 (88%)	8 (50%)	4 (25%)	2 (13%)	*16 (100%)*
TOTAL MALE DOING ACTIVITY	58 (83%)	38 (54%)	48 (69%)	48 (69%)	38 (54%)	32 (46%)	32 (46%)	*70 (100%)*

Table D3.6 (Continued)

Age and sex by free-time actvities	Watch TV	Listen to music	Internet (other than computer games)	Friends and family	Pubs/ bars and clubs	Sports/ exercise	Computer games	TOTAL in each group
Female – aged 16–24 yrs	18 (90%)	16 (80%)	18 (90%)	20 (100%)	14 (70%)	10 (50%)	4 (20%)	20 (100%)
– aged 25–44 yrs	16 (73%)	14 (64%)	16 (73%)	14 (64%)	8 (36%)	14 (64%)	4 (18%)	22 (100%)
– aged 45–64 yrs	16 (80%)	10 (50%)	10 (50%)	16 (80%)	10 (50%)	8 (40%)	4 (20%)	20 (100%)
– aged 65 yrs and over	16 (88%)	4 (22%)	8 (44%)	12 (67%)	4 (22%)	8 (44%)	0 (0%)	18 (100%)
TOTAL FEMALE DOING ACTIVITY	66 (83%)	44 (55%)	52 (65%)	62 (78%)	36 (51%)	40 (57%)	12 (15%)	80 (100%)
TOTAL – aged 16–24 yrs	28 (82%)	24 (71%)	30 (88%)	30 (88%)	22 (65%)	18 (53%)	14 (41%)	34 (100%)
– aged 25–44 yrs	32 (72%)	30 (68%)	34 (77%)	26 (59%)	20 (45%)	28 (63%)	18 (41%)	44 (100%)
– aged 45–64 yrs	32 (84%)	20 (53%)	22 (58%)	28 (74%)	20 (53%)	14 (37%)	10 (26%)	38 (100%)
– aged 65 yrs and over	32 (94%)	8 (24%)	14 (41%)	26 (76%)	12 (35%)	12 (35%)	2 (6%)	34 (100%)
TOTAL DOING ACTIVITY	124 (83%)	82 (55%)	100 (67%)	110 (73%)	74 (49%)	72 (48%)	44 (29%)	150 (100%)

NOTE: Percentages are rounded to nearest whole number. Some percentages are based on totals of less than 20 and should be treated with caution. Percentages are of the total in each group, for example, 90% of women aged 16–24 years watch TV in their free time. Percentages do not add up to 100% along the rows because the variable is multi-coded and each person may do more than one activity.

Testing relationships: chi-squared test

Chi-squared is a test that can be used to assess whether the difference between the mean values of two samples is statistically significant (by significant we mean worthy of consideration and note). It can be used to compare variables that are nominal or ordinal, for example, male and female. We will use it to test the statistical significance of the data in the cross-tabulation in Example D3.7. In this example the two samples are the group of men and the group of women.

Example D3.7

How sociable do men and women see themselves to be?

Table D3.7 Perceptions of sociability by gender

Perceptions of sociability by gender	Men	Women	Total
Very sociable	10 (14.3%)	25 (31.3%)	35 (23.3%)
Fairly sociable	20 (28.6%)	30 (37.5%)	50 (33.3%)
Neither sociable nor unsociable	15 (21.4%)	8 (10%)	23 (15.3%)
Fairly unsociable	20 (28.6%)	12 (15%)	32 (21.3%)
Very unsociable	5 (7.1%)	5 (6.3%)	10 (6.7%)
TOTAL	70 (100%)	80 (100%)	150 (100%)

That's interesting!

From this cross-tabulation we can see that almost a third of the women in our sample perceive themselves to be very sociable compared with only 14.3% of the men. Less than half of the men (43%) perceive themselves to be fairly or very sociable.

It seems quite clear from the cross-tabulation that women are more likely to perceive themselves to be sociable than men. But can we say that the relationship between the two variables of *social* and *gender* is significant?

Having looked at the cross-tabulation we could say that we have a research hypothesis that women are more likely to perceive themselves to be sociable than men.

To test for statistical significance we set up a null (or negative) hypothesis that there is no relationship between gender and perceptions of sociability – that the two variables are independent of each other.

The chi-squared test (x^2) is based on measuring how far the observed values (the data collected) differ from those that would be expected if the two groups (in this case men and women) were the same in terms of the variable *social*. The null hypothesis is that there will be no difference. If the null hypothesis is rejected then the differences between men and women are statistically significant.

$$x^2 = \text{sum of (observed − expected)}^2/\text{expected}$$

where observed values are your data.

(It is not advisable to use a x^2 test when either the observed or expected values in the cells of the table are smaller than 5. If there are small numbers it is advisable to group up categories as we will do here. The data will be grouped into three categories: very/fairly sociable; neither sociable nor unsociable; fairly or very unsociable.)

Each expected value is worked out by (row total × column total)/grand total, e.g. row total for *very/fairly sociable* (85) × column total for male (70)/grand total (150) = 39.7.

$$x^2 = 5.59 + 4.88 = 10.47$$

Table D3.8 Testing relationships using chi-squared

	Men		$(O - E)^2/E$	Women		$(O - E)^2/E$	TOTAL
	O	E		O	E		
Very/fairly sociable	30	39.7	*2.37*	55	45.3	*2.08*	85
Neither sociable nor unsociable	15	10.7	*1.73*	8	12.3	*1.50*	23
Very or fairly unsociable	25	19.6	*1.49*	17	22.4	*1.30*	42
TOTAL	70		*5.59*	80		*4.88*	150

degrees of freedom
A statistical measure used with chi-squared tests to calculate statistical significance.

The result of the calculation is then adjusted according to size of the table – the number of categories in each of the variables included (social group has 3 categories and gender has 2). From this, the **degrees of freedom** are worked out. In this case there are $(3 - 1)(2 - 1) = 2$ degrees of freedom.

So is this significant? Chi-squared tables (which can be found in most statistics textbooks) can then be consulted to see whether it is. In this case, chi-squared (two-tailed) tables tell us that with two degrees of freedom a chi-squared value of more than 9.21 is statistically significant at the $p = 0.01$ level. This means that there is a less than a one in a hundred probability that this result occurred by chance, and that in this case the difference between men and women is statistically significant and the null hypothesis is rejected.

Note that all computer software statistical packages, for example, PASW (SPSS) and Microsoft Excel, have functions that enable you to calculate χ^2.

Think about it . . .
Statistical tests – further study

The chi-squared test can be used with two samples that are nominal or ordinal. Other tests that can be used on different types of data include:

Table D3.9 Statistical tests

ANOVA Analysis of variance	Can be used on nominal variables to test for differences between two or more groups
Paired t-test	Can be used to compare differences in ratio or interval variables for two paired groups
Wilcoxon signed-rank test	Can be used to compare ratio or interval data that is not normally distributed

Scattergrams

causal relationship
The assertion that a change in 'A' results in a change in 'B'.

association or associative relationship
The belief that there is a statistical relationship between two concepts, but not necessarily that the relationship is causal.

As part of our analysis we are looking for relationships between variables – in other words, we are interested to find out whether two or more variables may vary or change in relation to each other in a way that can be observed and measured. Relationships between variables may be **causal relationships** if the value of one variable causes a particular value in another variable in many or at least some cases. In social research we can rarely be certain that a causal relationship exists but the evidence of some relationship or **association** between two or more variables can prompt us to explore for possible reasons for the relationship. Note that it is not always clear which variable is dependent on the other.

What is . . .

Independent variable

Independent variables are variables that cannot be changed by other variables, for example, the respondent's age cannot change in relation to how healthy he feels he is.

Dependent variable

Dependent variables can vary in relation to other – independent – variables and there may be a relationship between the variables, for example, the respondent's perception of his own health may be related to his age.

scattergram
A graph that plots two variables to show visually whether and how the variables may be related to each other.

We are repeating here an example box (Relationships) introduced in A4 which looked at the nature of relationships between data in relation to the development of research questions. Research questions often include questions about the possible relationship between two variables and here we look at one way of beginning to identify these possible relationships between two interval or ratio variables by creating a **scattergram**. A scattergram shows us visually whether and how two variables may be related to each other.

Example D3.8

Relationships

Causal relationships

Causal relationship are often shown diagrammatically as:

For example, we could assert that an increase in focused reading results in higher exam marks for university students. We would show this as:

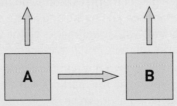

Here an increase in A – focused reading – causes an increase in B – exam marks.

Associative relationships

However, although there may be a statistical relationship between increased focused reading and higher exam marks, we may not be able to prove that A causes B. This could be for a number of reasons:

1. There are many reasons that a student gets high exam marks and it would be difficult to prove that it was focused reading alone that caused the high marks.

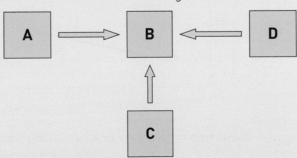

2. It may be the case that students who perform well in examinations are also the students who find focused reading suits their way of learning.

3. A third factor may be at work, influencing both the amount of focused reading and the high exam marks. For example, some of the students may have had a lecturer who has expected her students to undertake regular reading prior to seminars and has set the exam questions. She suggested that they use these readings as revision.

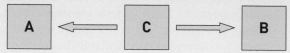

Example D3.9

Scattergrams

A

Students who are training to be professional social workers each have two marks. The first mark is for their Social Work Theory examination and the second is a mark for their performance in their Practice Placement. Looking at each student in the student group, is there a relationship between the two marks? Do students who get high marks in their Social Work Theory examination also have high marks for their Practice Placement performance?

- Each pair of marks is plotted on the scattergram and is represented by a marker. We can see just by looking at the distribution of the markers that, on the whole, students with lower marks on the Social Work Theory examination also get lower marks on their Practice Placement.

- The line drawn through the markers is the line of best fit – the line is as near as possible to all the markers – or the difference between each marker and the line is as small as it can be.

- The slope of the line indicates the direction of the relationship between the two variables – that is, as one variable increases so the other increases.

- We can see that there are some markers that are some distance from the line. These are the outliers or cases that do not fit the general trend so well.

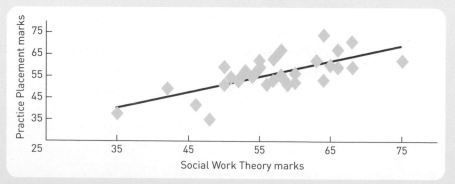

Figure D3.7   Scattergram of Social Work Theory and Practice Placement marks (A)

B

Here is the scattergram of the marks from a different cohort of students. What does this scattergram show?

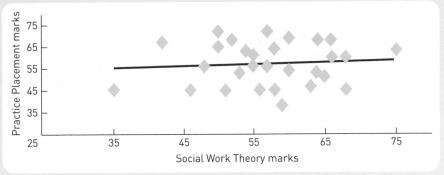

Figure D3.8 Scattergram of Social Work Theory and Practice Placement marks (B)

Testing relationships: correlation coefficient – Pearson's *r*

correlation coefficient
A statistic that provides a measure of the strength and direction of a relationship between two ratio variables.

We have used a scattergram to visually present the possible association between two ratio variables. The **correlation coefficient** is a statistic that provides us with a measure of the strength and direction of the relationship. The correlation is based on the fit of a straight line to the data (see Example D3.9) and the difference of each value from the mean of the set of values. It is calculated using the formula:

$$r = \frac{\Sigma(X_i - \overline{X})(Y_i - \overline{Y})}{\sqrt{\Sigma(X_i - \overline{X})^2 \, \Sigma(Y_i - \overline{Y})^2}}$$

where X_i and Y_i are the values of *x* variable and *y* variable respectively and $\overline{X}$ and $\overline{Y}$ are the means of the *x* variable and *y* variables respectively.

The formula for the calculation of a correlation coefficient is quite complicated and introduces statistical concepts that are beyond the scope of this text. However, the calculation can be described as a way of measuring how each case varies from the mean of all the cases on both the variables and assessing how much of that variance from the mean is shared by both variables – that is, how far it could be considered to be related in some way.

The result of the formula is a value between −1 and +1.

- A result of −1 (minus 1) shows that there is a perfect negative relationship between the two variables – in other words, that as one variable increases, the other decreases.
- A result of +1 shows that there is a perfect positive relationship between the two variables – that as one variable increases, so the other increases.
- A result of zero shows that there is no statistical relationship between the two variables – in other words, there is no discernible pattern to the relation between the two variables.

Of course, the result of the calculation is rarely exactly −1, 0 or +1. The closeness of the result to −1, 0 or +1 shows the strength of the relationship.

In the examples shown as scattergrams in Example D3.9, the correlation coefficients are:

(A) The correlation coefficient (*r*) is +0.701. This shows:

- a positive relationship – as one variable increases so does the other; and that
- there is quite a strong relationship – that many of the cases are close to the line that best fits the distribution.

(B) The correlation coefficient (r) is + 0.074. This shows:

- a very weak positive relationship between the variables – there is no evidence that the two variables are related.

Your research

Remember that a correlation coefficient shows the *statistical* relationship between two sets of data. The researcher can use it to look for possible reasons that the variables may or may not be related but a correlation coefficient does not, by itself, demonstrate that there is an actual relationship.

Note that all computer software statistical packages, for example, SPSS and Microsoft Excel, have functions that enable you to calculate the correlation coefficient Pearson's *r*.

Think about it . . .

Correlation coefficients: further study

The Pearson's *r* correlation coefficient is used on pairs of interval or ratio variables.

There are other coefficients that can be used on different types of data, including those in Table D3.10 below.

Table D3.10 Correlation coefficients

Spearman's *r*	Can be used on pairs of ordinal (ranked) variables or where one variable is ordinal and the other interval or ratio
Phi	Can be used on dichotomous variables
Cramer's *V*	Can be used on nominal variables to indicate strength of association (but not direction)
Gamma	Can be used with ordinal variables

The degree of statistical relationship between groups of variables can be calculated using multivariate analysis techniques, for example, multiple regression and factor analysis.

Statistical analysis as a process

We have introduced statistical analysis as a process rather than as a series of techniques. As with any analytical approach, statistical analysis is a way of working with data to enable the researcher to both explore and address the research questions that have been posed and to present his findings to his audience (E1). The process presented here is suitable for small pieces of research which include quantitative data collected from a sample of cases. Although most statistical analyses will begin with descriptive statistics and progress through to look at relationships between two or more variables, the process is not always so straightforward. As an analysis develops, new ideas about the data can emerge and, although when working with structured, quantitative data it is not possible to add to or reinterpret the data, the researcher can test out possible explanations or ideas by working with the data in different ways. In the example used in this section the finding that women were more likely to describe themselves as sociable than men prompted us to return to the data about free-time activities and consider whether these activities may be associated with our respondents' perceptions of their sociability, as well as to consider whether perception of sociability was also associated with the means of communication used to keep in touch with friends and family.

It is advisable to keep a research journal in which you can note down all the analyses you carry out, new variables created and interesting findings. Add to these your own ideas and 'things to do next'.

Example D3.10

Developing the analysis (B)

In Example D3.7 the cross-tabulation between *social* and *gender* (and the chi-squared test) showed that the women in the sample were more likely to describe themselves as sociable than the men in the sample were. As our research questions concern the use of social networking and communication between friends and family, we might now consider looking more closely at how differently people who describe themselves as sociable communicate compared with those who describe themselves as unsociable. We could do this in a number of stages.

Table D3.11 Developing the research question(s) through cross-tabulations

Questions arising from the analysis so far and the research questions	What to do next
Do they also do more social activities in their free time? *Do they also use particular forms of communication?* *Do they spend more time using the internet for social networking?*	Cross-tabulations of *social* by each of the variables.
Do men who describe themselves as sociable/unsociable behave in similar ways to women who describe themselves as sociable/unsociable?	Create a new variable combining *social* and *gender* and then create cross-tabulations of the new variable by each of the variables as above.
Are there also age differences with regard to sociability? Are women who describe themselves as sociable more likely to come from particular age groups? And men?	Cross-tabulation of combined *age group* and *gender* variable and *social*.

Depending on the findings from the cross-tabulations, we will be able to:

- describe the most common activities and forms of communication of people who describe themselves as sociable/unsociable and identify similarities and differences;

- assess whether there are notable differences between men and women with regard to these similarities and differences;
- assess whether age is a factor that needs to be examined further in relation to social activities and communication.

In a full research project this set of questions would probably relate to a small part of the data collected and other factors would also now need to be considered.

Presenting a statistical analysis

Having developed a statistical analysis you now need to present it to your audience (**Part E**) in a way that will show how you worked with your data, what you found and how the analysis helps you to answer your research questions. As we suggested earlier in this chapter, it is helpful to write an account of your initial analysis as this can provide the first part of your findings. From that you then need to show, by using tables, charts and diagrams from your data, how you developed your analysis. You need to show how you found your results – to tell the story of your analytical process. If there are word restrictions to your report or dissertation which preclude this, you could include this as an appendix. Showing how you worked with and, in particular, interpreted the data is an essential part of your report or dissertation because it provides a check that your analysis and your interpretations are valid. Having presented your findings and your analysis, your discussion is likely to focus on the key findings and how these in some way answer or address your research questions.

Your research

If you are working with quantitative data and doing statistical analysis, try following this process:

1. Organise your data with variable names and codes.
2. Create any new variables you think you will need.
3. Produce frequency tables for each of your variables.
4. Describe the sample in terms of the key characteristics you will use in the analysis, e.g. age and gender.
5. Look at the shape of the data for key variables.

   (HIGHLIGHT INTERESTING FINDINGS)

6. List and create cross-tabulations and scattergrams.

   (HIGHLIGHT INTERESTING FINDINGS)

7. Check for relationships or associations between variables using scattergrams, percentages and appropriate statistical tests.
8. List the questions raised by the analyses so far and how you are going answer them.

9. List and create cross-tabulations and scattergrams.

(HIGHLIGHT INTERESTING FINDINGS)

10. Look for similarities and differences between groups and look for data that will help you to explain the differences and similarities.

(HIGHLIGHT INTERESTING FINDINGS)

11. Check back to your research questions – has the analysis helped you to answer your questions?

Your research

Research quality check

At this stage in the research process you are mainly concerned with the validity of your interpretations and transparency of your analysis.

- Have you checked that your results are accurate throughout the analysis process?
- Have you checked your own understanding of the results with others?
- Can you show others how you conducted the analysis?
- Do your findings make sense in terms of other research and theories in this area?
- Can you justify any claims you make for generalisability of your findings to the population from which your sample was taken?

References and further reading

Bryman, A. and Cramer, D. (2008) *Quantitative Data Analysis with SPSS14, 15, and 16: A Guide for Social Scientists*, London: Routledge.

Field, A. (2009) *Discovering Statistics Using SPSS*, 3rd edn, London: Sage.

Hays, W. (1993) *Statistics*, 4th edn, New York: Holt, Rinehart & Winston.

Hinton, P. R. (2004) *Statistics Explained: A Guide for Social Science Students*, Hove: Routledge.

Social Trends 38 (2008) www.statistics.gov.uk/downloads/theme_social/Social_Trends38/Social_Trends_38.pdf (accessed 21 August 2009).

Wright, D. B. and London, K. (2009) *First (and Second) Steps in Statistics*, 2nd edn, London: Sage.

CHAPTER D4
Thematic analysis

Contents

In context

A variety of approaches can be used to work with qualitative data: the most common (at least as a starting point) is a thematic analysis which will enable you to identify the main themes or issues within the data and to use the data you have collected to refine the themes, look for links within the data, identify typologies and look for similarities and differences within and between cases.

Please read D2 before you read this chapter.

PART D: Data analysis

    D1:   Beginning to analyse

    D2:   Working with data

    D3:   Statistical analysis

 ▶ **D4:   Thematic analysis**

    D5:   Analysing narrative

    D6:   Discourse analysis

    D7:   Content analysis

    D8:   Grounded Theory

    D9:   Using computers in data analysis

    D10: So what? Drawing conclusions

Working with qualitative data

The analysis of qualitative data begins from the time we develop our research question, think about the concepts we are working with and choose our sample of cases. Working with qualitative data is a process that moves between gathering, working with and reflecting upon social data throughout the research. As the primary instrument or data collection tool, the researcher is constantly in touch with and thinking about the data that is being gathered. Because the analysis of qualitative data largely depends on the interpretation of the raw data by the researcher, the process begins as soon as data is being collected. This is why we recommend that you keep a research diary in which you can keep your own record of ideas, notes and reflections during the periods of both data collection and data analysis. In some research projects collection and analysis go on at the same time, with additional cases being introduced to add to the analysis as, for example, themes or theories emerge from the data (see in particular D8). Typically, though, in most small-scale projects there will be distinct periods of data collection and then data analysis.

Qualitative data can take many forms and is relatively unstructured. To ensure that our analysis is credible and transparent to others we need analytical approaches that are:

- *systematic and comprehensive*: the analysis should follow a set of procedures and the same procedures should be applied to all the cases and all the data;
- *grounded*: the data collected is usually in its raw state – that is, as it was said or written and we must be able to return to the data in its raw state throughout the analysis;
- *dynamic*: the full analysis cannot be planned at the beginning of the process as ideas and themes 'emerge' as part of the working process, so the approach itself must be dynamic and flexible and allow for changes;
- *accessible*: the researcher's interpretations and the way these are used to develop the analysis must be open and understandable by others.

In D2 we began to organise and work with the raw data that is usually associated with qualitative approaches to data gathering by creating an index to help us to find pieces (or chunks) of data about particular topics or of particular interest to us. We then began to identify some codes or categories that we could use to help us to look for sections of the data that we wanted to work with and also charted the material around some chosen topics or areas of interest. We now develop the process started there by looking at working with the key ideas or themes that can be identified within the data.

What is a thematic analysis?

thematic analysis
A process of working with raw data to identify and interpret key ideas or themes.

A **thematic analysis** is 'a process of segmentation, categorisation and relinking of aspects of the data prior to final interpretation' (Grbich, 2007: 16).

Working with qualitative data is mainly about interpreting and getting a good understanding of the words, stories, accounts and explanations of our research respondents. We start with each respondent's words and put them alongside the words of other respondents, or the contents of a series of documents are arranged alongside to enable us to

- describe the data;
- get to the meaning of the data for the person who produced it;
- explore the data for meanings;

- look for relationships between different parts of the data;
- explain (tentatively) the similarities and differences and the apparent relationships.

Throughout the analytical process we need to check out our own interpretations and understandings against each successive batch of data.

Thematic analysis is a process, a way of working with data which works from the raw data – the raw verbal or visual data we have gathered – and remains in touch with that raw data throughout. This is an important characteristic of ways of working with qualitative data as, although the data must be interpreted, summarised and categorised, we must remain 'in touch' or 'grounded' in the raw data. So our analytical techniques must enable us to return to the raw data at times throughout the process, to check our interpretations, to look at the data in different ways and to begin to make links between different pieces of data within each case. (In this section we will use the term *case* to apply to each set of data, e.g. each interview, each focus group, each document, each observation event.)

The data is worked with in data (usually text) 'chunks' which may be single words, phrases, sentences or paragraphs. While it is possible to divide your data into chunks prior to working with it, it is more usual and helpful to divide the data as needed and use the index and coding systems to identify meaningful chunks of data.

The process of analysis

In D2 we showed you how to organise the data:

1. By creating an index – a way of finding data when you need to.
2. By creating some initial categories or codes related to some of the themes or issues you had identified in your familiarisation process.
3. By creating summary charts to help you to look at the data in two ways:
   (a) a set of data from within one case;
   (b) a way of looking at each of your initial categories across your cases.

By this time you would be very familiar with the data and probably have ideas about the key themes or issues that are developing.

What are initial themes?

Before you start a thematic analysis you probably have some ideas about the type of data you are going to be interested in. These ideas will have emerged from your research questions, the selection of your sample and the data-gathering process itself. You begin to know the sorts of things people say or write, you have a sense of the issues that are important to at least some of your respondents and you want to explore those further by asking the exploratory questions of your data:

What do they say about . . . ?

Why might they say that . . . ?

What might they mean by . . . ?

You are already moving into the next stage and it is particularly important to record your own thoughts and ideas at this stage because you are beginning to interpret the raw data, beginning to make sense of the data and beginning to ask more questions of it.

The initial indexing, coding and charting will be based on the themes you are beginning to identify and the charts in particular help you to focus on these in more detail because you can bring together the range of data that relates to a particular theme.

Example D4.1

Initial themes

This section will draw on the example used in D2. (If you have not read D2 recently then now would be a good time to return to it before coming back to this section.)

The example used data from imaginary research that was studying people's perceptions and understandings of 'healthy eating' in the UK in the twenty-first century.

Data from interviews, focus groups and documents was included in an initial chart which summarised the different data sources under initial themes of time, cost, influence of childhood/family and media influences. (See pp. 338 and 339)

If you have created a summary chart that includes highlights from each case then you may want to create more detailed charts on some of the themes that are emerging from the initial summary. For example, in the chart we developed in D2, the issue of *time* was raised in most of the cases but it was raised in different ways in relation to people's ideas about healthy food, and at this stage it seems that the theme of *time* will be worth exploring. *Time* can be said to be one of our core initial themes at this point in the analysis. The next thing to do may be to create a more detailed chart focusing on *time* – using some of the ideas that are emerging from reading the data as headings for the chart columns. Example D4.2 shows one way this could be done.

Example D4.2

A chart on the theme of *time*

Table D4.1 A chart on the theme of *time*

	Time priorities reasons for time choices	Healthy food and shopping and cooking time	Feelings about time
INT1	When both partners are out working then there's not much time to . . .	There's not much time to do things like roasts except at the weekend. And no time to do pies or cakes . . .	I suppose time is a big thing. I'd love to have more time.
INT2	This is the big thing for me, with us both working . . .		This is the big thing for me, with us both working, there really isn't much time. I feel so guilty though I should have time to cook for my child.

	Time priorities reasons for time choices	Healthy food and shopping and cooking time	Feelings about time
INT3	I really enjoy cooking – it's a sort of hobby I suppose.		
FG1	Time was the second most important influence on choice of food.		
FG2	I really enjoy cooking so we take it in turns and then . . . it's not too much of a burden, it's not every day	Shopping around means spending half the weekend shopping.	It's not too much of a burden, it's not every day.
DOC1		Preparing a meal from fresh ingredients doesn't need to take a long time.	

This is a suggested chart to help us to explore in more detail some of the comments made. Of course there would probably be more data and at this stage we would be advised to return to our raw data to look for more data that might now fit in the new chart categories. Going back to the data with a focus on the concept of *time,* and the way it is being talked and written about within each case, will help us look at the data in a particular way – as if through a coloured lens – and it is likely that more data will emerge that is related to the *time* theme. We may also find that we want to add columns to our chart – or, on the other hand, we may decide that *time* is not so important as it first appeared and that the chart needs reworking.

There could be other charts to develop: in this example, perhaps, we would look at a chart about each of the other initial themes – influence of media on food choices, childhood and family influences on food and cost of food.

Interpreting the data

Now that you are beginning to interpret the data it is important to record the processes you are going through as you develop categories. Following the example of Ritchie and Lewis (2003), we suggest that you work with this in stages. (Note that in the example below we have added data from two more interviews.)

Stage 1. Read the raw data and then note down your interpretation – what you think is being said here in general terms.

Stage 2. Look at your interpretations across the cases.

Stage 3. Identify categories that are at the next level of conceptualisation and are inclusive of your interpretations.

Interestingly in A4 we looked at operationalising concepts (*time* is a concept) so that we had definitions we could work with and measure or identify when they were present in our data. Now we are working in the opposite direction because we are looking at what the concept of *time* means to our research participants *in terms of the way they talk about or write about healthy eating*. Their words give us a range of examples of the way time and healthy eating interact and, because we are interested in how people understand and make sense of their experience and express it, we want to explore the different ways that *time* is experienced in relation to healthy eating. To help us to do this, a number of categories relating to the way *time* and *healthy eating* interact are identified.

Think about it . . .

In Example D4.3 we have suggested some interpretations of the data and some categories we would want to explore further – what do you think? Would your interpretations be different? Can you identify any other categories that would be interesting to explore?

Example D4.3

Interpreting and identifying theme categories

Table D4.2 Interpreting and identifying theme categories

Initial theme – *TIME*		Initial interpretation	Categories
INT 1	'I suppose time is a big thing. When both partners are out working then there's not much time to do things like roasts except at the weekend. And no time to do pies or cakes ... I'd love to have more time to really get into cooking – there's so many ideas on TV now – I just wish I had the time and energy to try some new things.'	**Cooking is seen as something that takes time.** **Some sorts of cooking take a lot of time.** **Having more time to cook is desirable.** **Cooking could be an enjoyable use of time.**	**Cooking takes time.** **Cooking can be enjoyable.**
INT2	'This is the big thing for me, with us both working, there really isn't much time. I feel so guilty though I should have time to cook for my child.'	**Work roles affect time available.** **Neither with time to taking the cooking role. Guilt relating to child. Cooking for child – being a good parent?**	**Work/household roles.** **Cooking related to 'good' parenting.**

Initial theme – *TIME*		Initial interpretation	Categories
INT3	'I really enjoy cooking – it's a sort of hobby I suppose.' **NB Is this about use of time?**	**Cooking is an enjoyable use of time – can be a leisure activity.**	**Cooking can be enjoyable/leisure activity/prepared to spend time on it.**
INT4	'I think you can do healthy food quickly – it's a matter of being organised and choosing simple dishes, nothing too complicated.'	**Cooking can be quick and simple.** **Healthy food is about organising time.**	**Healthy eating associated with organisation and choice of dishes.** **Time relates to choice of food and dishes.**
INT5	'I'm really not interested in cooking and that sort of thing – it's just not something I want to spend time on. I know I should but it's just not me.'	**Not a time priority.** **Guilt, pressure – from whom?**	**Expectations of cooking – guilt?** **Time priorities.**

Source: Adapted from Ritchie and Lewis (2003: 240). Copyright © 2003 Sage Publications. Reproduced with permission.

Think about it . . .

Working with documents

You are researching the ways people find other people to share a relationship with in the UK in the twenty-first century and one of your data sources is a set of personal ads from a national newspaper. Each of these can be regarded as a mini-document, so first ask yourself:

(a) *Who is the author?*
(b) *What is the author trying to say?*
(c) *To whom is the author speaking?*
(d) *Why has it been written in this way?*
(e) *What does the author want to achieve?*

Then begin to work with the documents by jotting down your interpretations and possible categories.

Table D4.3 Beginning to interpret and categorise (personal ads loosely based on *Guardian* 'SoulMates')

Personal ads	Initial interpretation	Categories
1 Professional, still in possession of own hair and teeth, fit and handsome in a rugged sort of way. Ints include walking, music and cooking.		
2 Pretty teacher seeking handsome hunk to share chocolates.		

3 Don't pass me by – I'm friendly,
   outgoing and practical with a romantic
   streak looking for soulmate between
   35 and 50.

4 Slightly mad and searching for a
   special person to share this crazy life
   with.

5 Caring, sensitive and not boring
   seeking someone to share coffee and
   cakes.

6 Bubbly, blonde, young at heart seeks
   sincere, stylish guy with a GSOH, age
   unimportant.

7 In good condition with a caring heart
   looking for a mature relationship with
   someone 40+ who shares my passion
   for the creative arts.

8 Passionate, blonde 40 seeks sorted
   handsome guy with no strings for
   romance.

9 Easy going, even elegant, would like to
   share time and hopefully more with a
   gorgeous lady under 40.

10 Lawyer 35 seeks irresistible, confident,
    intelligent, adorable woman for LTR.

Looking for relationships in the data

Now that we have explored the concept of *time* in relation to healthy eating we will probably want to look at the other initial themes and how they relate to each other. So similar charts and interpretations and categories relating to, in this example, childhood influences, media and cost could be carried out.

It can be useful to write a descriptive account of your data based on this level of interpretation at this stage as this could provide the basis of your findings. A descriptive account simply sets out what you have found so far:

- that some initial themes have been identified;

and

- from the data it is evident that each theme has a range of ways in which it is related to the central topic (in this example, healthy eating).

You now want to go on to look at the ways the key themes are related and to explore possible similarities and differences between your cases.

It is helpful to many researchers to think of the relationships between the themes and categories in diagrammatic terms and there are various ways of doing this. Most computer software packages for the analysis of qualitative data have some way of exploring the data diagrammatically.

The simplest way to start is by plotting or mapping your themes in relation to each other. This will start in a simple fashion by relating each to the central issue of the research.

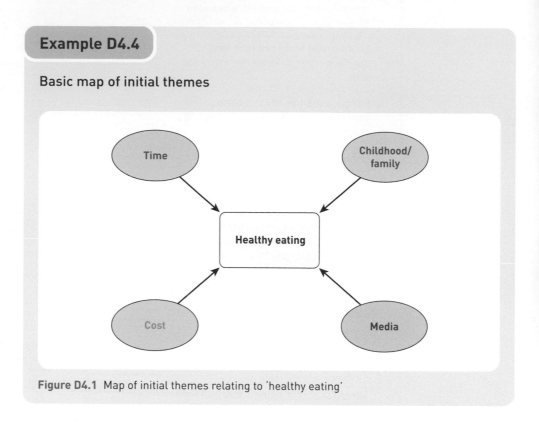

Example D4.4

Basic map of initial themes

Figure D4.1 Map of initial themes relating to 'healthy eating'

Then you could add in the main categories or 'sub-themes' that are emerging in relation to each of the initial themes. In Example D4.5 these are colour coded to the initial themes. These categories or sub-themes are likely to come from your own interpretations and categories. While you are grouping them around each initial theme, think about how they may relate to the other themes. Move them around to help you to explore possibilities. If you look at your charts or a list of all the data you have on each category, you will begin to see possible links – or commonalities.

This is beginning to look quite complicated but the diagram is beginning to reveal some interesting links. For example, if we have a look at the categories surrounding *time* we can see that they have been arranged so that they are in proximity to categories that relate to (a) *childhood and family influences* and (b) *cost*. This suggests that there are two rather different ways in which *time* is being talked about.

- **A** In one way it is about the lack of time as a resource and that healthy food is perceived to be costly in terms of both time and money. The categories are marked A on the diagram.
  - *Time*

    Shopping for healthy food is time consuming.
  - *Cost*

    Shopping for healthy food is costly.

    Memo: Both of these relate to the availability of resources.
- **B** The other way in which time is talked about is in relation to work and household roles and giving time to cook (for others, particularly in some cases for children). This may be

Example D4.5

Mapping the themes and categories

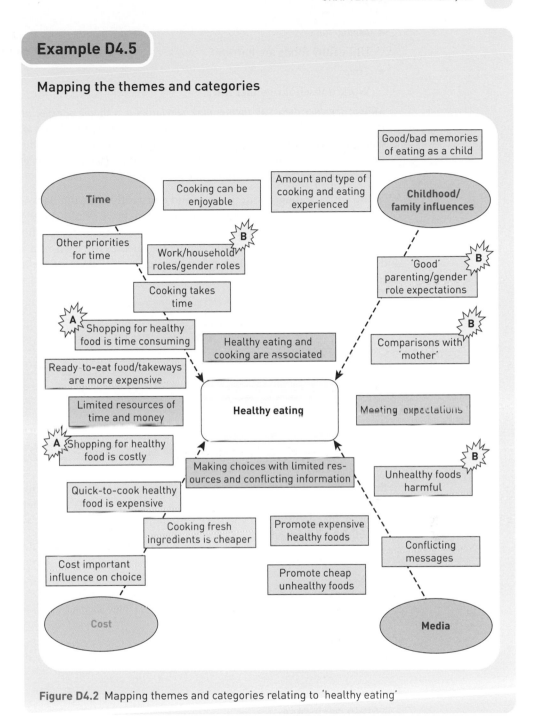

Figure D4.2 Mapping themes and categories relating to 'healthy eating'

linked with experiences from childhood, ideas about parenting and role expectations. There may be gender differences here. In turn, there may be a link between the expectations of being a 'good parent' and the messages from the media about the harmful effects of certain types of food. The categories that may be linked are marked B on the diagram.

- *Influences of childhood and family*

  Good parenting/gender role expectations.

  Comparisons with 'mother'.

- *Media*

  Unhealthy foods are harmful.
- *Time*

  Work/household/gender roles.

Memo: *Together these sub-themes may be relating to a theme of expectations in terms of people (perhaps particularly parents or more specifically mothers?) in relation to providing healthy food and 'guilt' related to not meeting the expectations. This appears to have the following dimensions: gender roles, time priorities, pressure from within (self-perception of childhood influences) and without (media) with regard to the provision of healthy food.*

Working with the diagram in this way and constantly referring back to the raw data to test out the interpretations, we tentatively suggest that we could move from the four initial themes to four (overarching) themes which may help us to explain how people make decisions about eating food. The four overarching themes are each in a sector of the diagram and primarily relate to the relationship between two or three of the initial themes and are shaded in orange on the diagram.

These are:

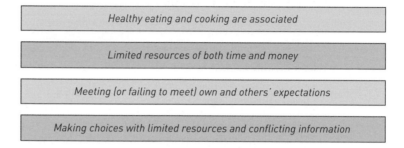

At this point you may feel that we have made some big jumps from the data to a set of statements. This means it is time to check back with the data to see whether these statements adequately include the data you have gathered and to look again at your data through the lenses of these statements.

Example D4.6

Checking back with the raw data

For each overarching theme, list the sub-themes or categories associated with it. Then:

Within each case

Look for instances of the categories across the whole set of data for the case and see whether the overarching theme makes sense in terms of that case.

- For some cases a particular theme may have little relevance or may not have been mentioned. That is OK – each case will be different.
- The theme will work differently for different cases. For example, some people may prioritise cooking healthy food for their children in part because they *did not* have healthy food as children; others may feel guilty that they do not prioritise

> cooking because their mother *did* cook for them and so they have expectations of themselves. These differences are interesting and are key findings for the research.
>
> **Across cases**
>
> Look at the data that relates to each category across all the cases and check whether there are any cases that do not 'fit' with the overarching theme and consider whether the overarching theme needs to be amended.
>
> - This will help you to clarify the range of data that is included within each theme.
> - This may help you to identify similarities and differences between cases.

We now have a framework within which to look for similarities and differences between your cases. You could, for example, look at how men differ from women in terms of the ways they talk about each of these overarching themes. For example:

- Do men tend to emphasise different aspects, or have different understandings of *time?*
- Are women with children more likely to talk in terms of the expectations regarding cooking and healthy food than women without children?

There may be other similarities and differences you have noted or speculated about while working with the data and now is the time to explore these further. This exploration can lead to (tentative) explanations for differences or particular relationships.

You may also consider developing a typology – this is really a way of dividing your cases into linked groupings according to a set of characteristics. In thematic analysis the characteristics refer to where they stand on the themes. One way to explore possible typologies in the example is to plot each of the cases on each of the four overarching themes – see which are similar and then see whether there are other similarities between them. If we found that, on the whole, there were similarities and differences between groupings based on gender and children, we may have a simple typology related to gender and children:

Men with children

Men without children

Women with children

Women without children.

On the other hand, we may find that we can develop a typology drawing on the four overarching themes along the following lines:

1. Food is important regardless of time and cost; enjoys cooking; health is paramount.
2. Food choices have to be made within constraints but will try to do their best to cook healthy meals because of the expectations on self to do so.
3. Feels under pressure and sense of failure or lack of achievement in relation to healthy food.
4. No interest or concern for healthiness of food; time and cost are deciding factors.

Of course you have to test out a typology to see if it (more or less) works for each of your cases but it can provide the basis for discussion in your research report or dissertation.

Think about it . . .

Suppose we were undertaking the research on people's perceptions and under-standings of healthy eating for a government department which wanted to encour-age healthy eating among the UK population. From this example of thematic analysis we have some clues about the reasons that people do or do not eat health-ily and perhaps some ideas about how they could be encouraged: based on the example, what advice would you give a government officer who was thinking about an advertising campaign to encourage healthy eating?

Presenting a thematic analysis

diagram
Presentation of data or findings in a graphical format.

Having developed a thematic analysis, you now need to present it to your audience in a way that will show how you worked with your data, what you found and how the analysis helped you to answer your research questions. As we suggested earlier in this chapter, it is helpful to write an account of your initial thematic analysis as this can provide the first part of your findings. From that you then need to show, perhaps by using **diagrams** and selected verbatim quotations from your data, how your categories were developed, and finally how you worked with these to produce overarching themes and perhaps a typology. Showing how you worked with and, in particular, interpreted the data is an essential part of your re-port or dissertation because it provides a check that your analysis is credible and your in-terpretations are valid. You may want to include some of this in an appendix to your report or dissertation if there are word restrictions. Having presented your findings and your analysis, your discussion is likely to focus on the overarching themes and any typologies and how these answer or address in some way your research questions.

Your research

If you are working with your data using a thematic analysis, try following the same process as we have used in the example:

1. Organise the data.
2. Identify some initial key themes.
3. Explore these using charts.
4. Note down your interpretations.
   (CHECK BACK WITH THE DATA)
5. Compare these across cases.
6. Develop categories into which your data can be put.
   (CHECK BACK WITH THE DATA)
7. Use a diagram to help you think through possible relationships between the categories.
   (CHECK BACK WITH THE DATA)

8. Test out these relationships by returning to the data and looking through different lenses.

9. Look for overarching themes which include within them the relationships you have identified.

(CHECK BACK WITH THE DATA)

10. Check back to your data to see whether the overarching themes are inclusive.

11. Use the overarching themes to explore the data and look for possible explanations of the relationships.

(CHECK BACK WITH THE DATA)

12. Look for similarities and differences between cases and look for data that helps to explain the differences and similarities.

13. Is there a typology emerging?

14. Return to your research questions – has the analysis helped you to answer your questions?

Your research

Research quality check

At this stage in the research process you are mainly concerned with the *validity or credibility* of your interpretations and the transparency of your analysis.

- Have you checked your interpretations with the data throughout the analysis process?
- Can you show others how you decided on and defined your themes?
- Can you show how you decided to categorise 'chunks' of data?
- Do your findings and explanations of the data make sense in terms of other research and theories in this area? Are they credible?

References and further reading

Grbich, C. (2007) *Qualitative Data Analysis: An Introduction*, London: Sage.

Richards, L. (2005) *Handling Qualitative Data: A Practical Guide*, London: Sage.

Ritchie, J. and Lewis, J. (2003) *Qualitative Research Practice: A Guide for Social Science Students and Researchers*, London: Sage.

CHAPTER D5
Analysing narrative

Contents

In context

In **C7** we described narratives as *socially* constructed stories and described how to collect this sort of data. Now we move on to look at how this data can be analysed and used in social research.

PART D: Data analysis

Remember that what we are trying to analyse here is not necessarily the facts of a story, but rather the manner in which the storyteller (narrator) has arranged things.

> *A narrative is the* depiction *of a sequence of past events as they appear in present time to the narrator, after they have been processed, analysed and constructed into stories. This notion of* depiction *is of vital importance; narratives are* not *records of events, they are representations of series of events.* (C7)

Generally, the analysis process for narrative is divided into three sections (see, for example, Riessman, 1993, 2008; or Lieblich *et al.*, 1998). These are:

1. Narration (telling the story) (**C7**).
2. Transcription/organisation – converting the story from audio into the written word (**C2** and **D2**).
3. Analysis (understanding the data and drawing conclusions).

Here we assume that step 1 above is complete and we move on to transcription.

Transcription

After you have collected your narrative data (usually in the form of an audio recording), the first stage of analysis is to transcribe the audio into a word-processor document. This is an essential step in the analysis (though many other qualitative analysis techniques use transcription, it is not always *essential* to do so). Needless to say, this is a very time-consuming process, but it is important for two main reasons (these are discussed in more detail in **D2**):

1. Getting to know your data.
2. Preparing the story for analysis: in particular, it is vital that the story exists as something that can be looked at as a whole.

We would like to emphasise the importance of thinking about these two issues together; knowing your data *and the way that it is organised* is important for the narrative analysis process. Using someone else to transcribe the data is (a) always expensive and (b) potentially risky. Riessman notes:

> *Early in the divorce study when my coinvestigator went back to check the accuracy of the transcriptions, she discovered utterances on the tape that did not appear in the typescript. In response to our query, the transcriber said she left out asides, talk that 'wasn't in answer to the question'. Yet these seeming irrelevancies provided context essential to interpretation and, not infrequently, the asides were narratives, the heart of the matter.*   (Riessman, 1993: 57)

When the narratives have been transcribed, it is possible to move on to the next phase: analysis.

Analysis

Really, analysis started at a much earlier stage of the research and has continued through the transcription phase. Here, however, it becomes a little more organised.

The first stage of narrative analysis is *reading*. This is done in order to fully comprehend the story (you have, of course, read this as you transcribed – however, we believe that a separate reading of the completed transcription is helpful). Of course, you need to read all the stories you have collected – this takes time!

There are a number of techniques that can be used for analysing narratives (see Riessman, 2008, for example), some of which are the same as those for other types of qualitative data (**Part D**). In particular, *thematic analysis* (**D4**) works well.

Real research

A narrative analysis of behaviourally troubled adolescents' life stories

Sanderson and McKeough (2005) undertook a study of 20 young people aged 16 to 21 years who were living on the streets. Their intention was to explore the participants' life histories for evidence that early negative experiences contributed to their present situations.

Narrative data collection sessions were conducted and stories recorded on audio tape in interrupting-style sessions using prompts. The data was analysed using a mixture of thematic (D4) and content analysis (D7) techniques.

The research found that there were strong indications that early negative treatment contributed to the participants' behavioural problems and street-living. The researchers also concluded that narrative research was a particularly effective way to access this population and obtain useful data.

A specific analysis technique that enables you to look at the way the narrative has been constructed is *narrative structural analysis*. This is an examination of the way in which the narrative has been constructed in order to fulfil the narrator's intentions. The most common reasons for telling stories are (**C7**):

- persuading others;
- justifying past behaviour/decisions;
- rationalising;
- explanations/understandings of events;
- 'Set[ting] off on their own paths for their own purposes' (Riessman, 1993);
- raising pity or concern.

In structural narrative analysis, the story will be read while looking for the ways in which the narrator has endeavoured to make her point. This can be done in many ways, but you might look for examples where the narrator uses pathos to gain your pity or a strongly reasoned argument to engage you intellectually. It is worth revisiting the list of 'story styles' (below) and the example that we introduced in **C7**, since they give some indications of the sorts of things to look for when using structural analysis.

Example D5.1

Story styles

History

Overt agenda

Covert agenda

Seeking legitimation

Seeking researcher approval

Seeking information

Imparting information

Criticising

As shown in the 'Real research' examples, a narrative analysis is likely to draw on a range of techniques and approaches to work with the data. Alongside this the researcher is looking at the narrative as it is produced and watching out for indications of the way the narrative was being structured at the time it was produced and why it was structured in that way. In presenting and discussing the findings it is likely that the focus will be on how each narrative came to be structured in this way and how this is demonstrated in the story itself through the way thematic concepts and language are used in descriptions and explanations.

Real research

A narrative analysis of complementary/alternative medicine use by parents for children with Down syndrome

Prussing *et al.*, (2005) conducted narrative data collection sessions with 30 families who had children with Down syndrome, looking at their use of complementary and alternative medicine (CAM).

What the researchers did

The project looked at how parents constructed their identities as 'good' parents through narrative. Narrative data collection sessions ranged in length from 45 minutes to 3 hours (with a mean of 90 minutes) and were conducted using the interrupting method (**C7**) of narrative data collection. The narratives were transcribed and analysed using thematic analysis.

The researchers found that parents were using 'narrative strategies through which they constructed their own definitions of [Down syndrome] and affirmed the essential personhood of their children and themselves' (Prussing *et al.*, 2005: 590).

At the same time, the researchers obtained useful data on the participants' use of CAM, and the ways in which they believed that it had benefited their lives.

Interestingly, they also found that participants told their stories in ways that included most of the 'story styles' (**C7**) common in narratives.

References and further reading

Clandinin, D. J. and Connelly, F. M. (2000) *Narrative Inquiry*, San Francisco: Jossey-Bass.

Czarniawska, B. (2004) *Narratives in Social Science Research*, London: Sage.

Elliot, J. (2005) *Using Narrative in Social Research: Qualitative and Quantitative Approaches*, London: Sage.

Josselson, R. and Lieblich, A. (1999) *Making Meaning of Narratives in the Narrative Study of Lives*, London: Sage.

Lieblich, A., Tuval-Mashiach, R. and Zilber, T. (1998) *Narrative Research: Reading, Analysis and Interpretation*, London: Sage.

Prussing, E., Sobo, E. J., Walker, E., and Kurtin, P. S. (2005) Between 'desperation' and disability rights: a narrative analysis of complementary/alternative medicine use by parents for children with Down syndrome, *Social Science & Medicine*, 60: 587–98.

Riessman, C. K. (1993) *Narrative Analysis*, London: Sage.

Riessman, C. K. (2008) *Narrative Methods for the Human Sciences*, London: Sage.

Sanderson, A. and McKeough, A. (2005) A narrative analysis of behaviourally troubled adolescents' life stories, *Narrative Inquiry*, 15(1): 127–60.

CHAPTER D6
Discourse analysis

Contents

In context

This chapter looks at discourse analysis, a technique that is theoretically based on social constructionism (A2). The chapter discusses the underlying theory and the nature of 'discourse' and describes the techniques that are used to carry out this sort of analysis.

  We suggest that you first read D2.

PART D: Data analysis

  D1:   Beginning to analyse

  D2:   Working with data

  D3:   Statistical analysis

  D4:   Thematic analysis

  D5:   Analysing narrative

▶ **D6:   Discourse analysis**

  D7:   Content analysis

  D8:   Grounded Theory

  D9:   Using computers in data analysis

  D10: So what? Drawing conclusions

What is discourse?

discourse
Text, either spoken or written, in any medium.

Trying to define **discourse** is problematic because it is a controversial and contested term, capable of many different definitions, interpretations and usages. Linguistics uses the term to refer to a speech unit larger than a sentence. However, many commentators see literature as discourse. Similarly, a conversation between two or more people can also be seen as a discourse and the term is used by groups ranging from social scientists to the media and has developed into something both more vague and more wide-ranging. According to Mills, it has

> become common currency in a variety of disciplines: critical theory, sociology, linguistics, philosophy, social psychology and many other fields, so much so that it is frequently left undefined, as if its usage were simply common knowledge.   (Mills, 1997: 1)

Others have used the word differently: some require the discourse to be long; some require it to be two-way (back and forth between at least two individuals) which is remarkably close to the meaning of the Latin root word *discursus*, which can be translated as 'running to and from'; and Foucault uses it as a way of discussing institutionalised boundaries where only limited concepts can be discussed.

We have taken a simpler pathway. For the purposes of this chapter discourse is defined as text, either spoken or written.

Theoretical background

Discourse analysis is used primarily in qualitative research and is theoretically based in social constructionist theory. Social constructivism is complex and, while it is not the purpose of this section to discuss it in detail, we want to set out the basic assumptions:

- *Reality is a social construct.* The scientific approach that the world can be quantified and only the things that can be measured are 'real' is rejected because language and social existence shapes the categories by which such an analysis is accomplished. Therefore our sense of reality is, in turn, constructed by the society in which we live.

- *Individuals can never be truly objective.* However hard we try, we are products of our society and we carry with us 'social baggage' in the forms of norms and assumptions. Inevitably, this means that researchers do not start from a zero position, but have a set of beliefs, values and expectations that impact on any research that is undertaken.

What is discourse analysis?

No single, simple definition of discourse analysis exists. However, all discourse analyses are based on 'texts', although this term may itself be contested. We mean it to be used in terms of spoken or written words, in any medium. This means that we think that discourse analysis can be applied to conversations, letters, emails, television programmes, documents, archives and many other things. We think that it should be used as an inclusive term wherever possible.

Discourse analysis is often used when working with language and with linguistics and is popular in many social sciences, including sociology and political science.

When a discourse or account is analysed, the researcher may be looking at what type of language is being used, what sorts of ideas underlie the text and how those ideas are demonstrated in the language. Some researchers have used discourse analysis to study the way in which ideas develop and change through time or in different cultural settings – in other words, how ideas are socially constructed through the way people think, speak about and experience the social world around them.

> **Think about it . . .**
> 'Green' discourses
>
> If you were to read newspaper accounts of environmental organisations (for exam-
> ple, Friends of the Earth) in the 1970s you are likely to find people supporting them
> being described as rather eccentric, 'tree-hugging' minorities and the ideas about
> global warming or climate change being, in many cases, ridiculed.
>   Is the 'discourse' different now? How did the discourse change?

Gee sums up the nature of discourse analysis when he says:

> *In the end, discourse analysis is one way to engage in a very important human task. The task
> is this: to think more deeply about the meanings we give people's words so as to make our-
> selves better, more humane people and the world a better, more humane place.*   (Gee, 2005)

It is clear then that discourse analysis is a language-based or linguistic method of qualitative analysis.

Using discourse analysis

There are numerous specialist approaches to discourse analysis. We do not discuss them in
detail here, but there are items in the References and further reading section that will inform those who wish to learn about them in more detail. These approaches include:

- critical discourse analysis (CDA);
- socio-cognitive discourse studies;
- political discourse analysis;
- discursive psychology;
- conversational analysis.

Another way to think of this is to consider the types of discourse that could be analysed
with discourse analysis. These include:

- discourses in particular social settings, for example, the discourses used in weather fore-
  casts or school teaching;
- informal conversations between people, either face to face or via some electronic communication system;
- formal conversations/communications, perhaps a doctor–patient discussion;
- permanent and semi-permanent texts, such as letters or newspapers;
- studying the 'shape' of discourse, what Foucault called 'discursive formations' (Hall, 1997).

We think that discourse analysis can be used on two distinct levels for the student researcher. The first of these is for students whose academic discipline routinely uses discourse analysis in specific ways (linguistic analysis, for example) as one of the main ways in
which it collects and processes data. This is quite specialised and is beyond the scope of this
book. However, we list a number of useful texts which can supplement the detailed training that your institution will make available.

The second instance is when students from other disciplines want to use discourse
analysis to help them to answer specific research questions and particularly to work with
documents. If you are considering working with written or spoken discourses, there are
some potential advantages as well as limitations you need to be aware of.

Discourse analysis is applicable to most research topics and situations and can provide
a new perspective to use when analysing data. In particular, 'hidden' meanings in the text
can be revealed by asking different questions of the text. Discourse analysis is reliant on

linguistic and other language-based techniques and this does mean that it tends to be not only language-specific and context-specific, but also culturally specific. For example, there is usually little use in attempting a discourse analysis of a translated text because the changes imposed by the process of translation (and also by the translator himself) cannot be known or understood. In addition, the analysis of a text that is interpreted by a researcher from a different cultural background will be of questionable validity. However, if you are studying a social phenomenon within a particular language and cultural context and are interested in the way ideas about it are socially constructed by those who write and speak about it, then discourse analysis could enable you to use your data to study this.

Think about it . . .

Read the editorial in any newspaper (if you want to be brave and do a comparative analysis, choose two newspapers with opposing political backgrounds – perhaps the *Sun* and the *Guardian*).

Treat the editorial as a text, and try to understand and analyse the use of *language* within it. Ask yourself:

1. What sort of language is used (for example, is it emotional, intellectual, condescending, etc.)? Think about why this sort of language is used.

2. Who are the words aimed at? Think about the delivery of the text.

3. What is the reading age for the newspapers you have chosen? (Use one of the formulae below to calculate this.)

Reading age formulae:

(a) The *forecast* formula:

$$\text{Reading age} = 25 - \frac{N}{10}$$

N is the number of one-syllable words in a passage of 150 words

(b) The *fog* index:

$$\text{Reading age} = \frac{2}{5}\left(\frac{A}{N} + \frac{100L}{A}\right)$$

A – number of words in a passage
N = number of sentences in a passage
L = number of words with three or more syllables (ignore 'ing' and 'ed' endings)

Does the answer to question 3 matter for discourse analysis?

References and further reading

Gee, J. P. (2005) *An Introduction to Discourse Analysis*, London: Routledge.

Hall, S. (1997) The work of representation, in S. Hall (ed.) *Representations: Cultural Representations and Signifying Practices*, London: Sage.

Jorgenses, M. W. (2002) *Discourse Analysis as Theory and Method*, London: Sage.

Macgilchrist, F. (2008) Discourse analysis, available at www.discourse-analysis.de/

Mills, S. (1997) *Discourse*, London: Routledge.

Titscher, S. (2000) *Methods of Text and Discourse Analysis*, London: Sage.

Wetherell, M. (2001) *Discourse as Data: A Guide for Analysts*, London: Sage.

Wetherell, M., Taylor, S. and Yates, S. J. (eds) (2001) *Discourse Theory and Practice: A Reader*, London: Sage.

Woofit, R. (2005) *Conversation Analysis and Discourse Analysis: A Comparative and Critical Introduction*, London: Sage.

CHAPTER D7
Content analysis

Contents

In context

Content analysis is a technique used to analyse texts (though they are usually called 'messages' in this technique). It has some similarities with discourse analysis, but tends to be slightly more rigid in its application. Historically it has been used mostly in literature and media studies, but it is a flexible tool that can be utilised in many social science disciplines.

PART D: Data analysis

D1:   Beginning to analyse
D2:   Working with data
D3:   Statistical analysis
D4:   Thematic analysis
D5:   Analysing narrative
D6:   Discourse analysis
▶ **D7:   Content analysis**
D8:   Grounded Theory
D9:   Using computers in data analysis
D10: So what? Drawing conclusions

What is content analysis?

Content analysis is a technique usually, but not exclusively, applied to 'textual' data (or messages): but it can also be used with other forms of data, for example, the analysis of graphical images (Stemler, 2001). Most analysts agree that it can only be used with data that is enduring, i.e. that is not short-lived. Essentially, it is a technique for examining the categories that the data comprise and condensing them into fewer categories so that they are easier to understand. In other words, content analysis looks for the presence of words (or phrases or concepts) in a text and endeavours to understand their meanings and relationships to each other. You can think of content analysis as a way of discovering patterns in data that aid our understanding of the underlying phenomena. Initially, content analysis was usually thought of as looking for the frequency with which certain words occurred in the text – the words chosen would depend on operational definitions and research questions, of course (A4). This interest in the frequency with which words are used is based on the notion that the words or phrases that are used the most are likely to be the most significant too. Word counting is still important but, as times have changed and the ability to count the occurrences of words in a text by using a computer has become more common, the technique has extended to consider meanings and motives in more detail as well.

? What is . . .

Content analysis

(1) 'Any technique for making inferences by objectively and systematically identifying specified characteristics of messages.' (Holsti, 1969: 14)

(2) 'The systematic, objective, quantitative analysis of message characteristics.' (Neuendorf, 2005: 1)

The word count part of content analysis can be thought of as a quantitative method, but the process can be about much more than word counts, and many argue (see Stemler, 2001, for example) that the strength of this process is in its rigorous categorisation and coding of the data for analysis (D2). Weber (1990: 37) describes categories as 'a group of words with similar meaning or connotations', and notes that they need to be readily identifiable and relate only to one concept. It is important to emphasise that creating robust, accurate codes and categories affects the process of analysis in the same way that operational definitions (A4) affect validity and reliability when collecting data. To be vague is disastrous! (Coding is discussed elsewhere in this book: see D2 and D4, for example.)

Content analysis is particularly useful for determining trends and changes over time, especially in literature (B2), and can also be useful for looking at things such as changes in public opinion (particularly the way in which these are expressed in the media).

How is content analysis used?

Content analysis can be used to analyse any text. Because of this flexibility, it is used in many disciplines within the social sciences. However, historically at least, its home has been in media studies and associated areas.

The detail of content analysis is too complex to enter into here. If you plan to use this technique, we recommend Neuendorf (2005) as being a comprehensive text aimed at the undergraduate student.

Think about it . . .

At party political conferences, journalists will sometimes analyse the party leader's speech in terms of the number of times a particular word or phrase is used – for example, 'new', 'opportunities', 'my responsibility' – and which is used the most times.

What do you think you might learn from an analysis of the ways a particular word or phrase is used in this context?

Real research

Content analysis in leadership research

Insch *et al.* (1997) wrote a paper that discusses the use of content analysis when undertaking research on leadership (the paper includes useful definitions and methodological suggestions, too). Rather interestingly, the project uses content analysis to research content analysis.

They found that there were a number of previous research studies that used content analysis to investigate leadership in research and they undertook a content analysis of these. Although their findings are a little inconclusive, the process they developed to guide themselves – and future researchers – through such an analysis is very useful. In some ways, this reminds us that the outcome of research is *always* useful, even if it does not always find what we expect.

We reproduce their *suggested procedure* (Insch *et al.*, 1997: 8) below:

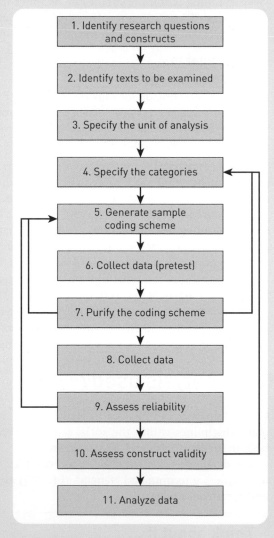

Figure D7.1 Using content analysis

Source: Adapted from Insch, G.S., Moore, J.E. and Murphy L.D. (1997) content analysis in leadership: examples, procedures, and suggestions for future use, *Leadership Quarterly*, 8(1), 1–25. Reproduced with permission of Elsevier Ltd.

Content analysis can be a powerful technique that goes much further than simple word-counting. Properly applied, its formal techniques are rigorous and strong.

Your research

Advantages of content analysis

- It is a reasonably flexible approach which can be applied to most forms of data, particularly unstructured data (A3). It is particularly useful for analysing media data.

- If the project is conducted properly, well coded and with categories designed well, then it should be easily replicable.

- Because it is possible to use content analysis on any data, it can easily be applied to a series of documents (magazines, for example) and therefore can allow some measure of change through time (longitudinal analysis) (Holsti, 1969).

Disadvantages of content analysis

- Content analysis, because of its partial reliance on 'mechanical' techniques such as word-counting, is thought by some to lean towards a positivist paradigm (A2) which is not always considered appropriate in qualitative research.

- The incorrect selection of categories or codes can reduce validity and reliability.

References and further reading

Berelson, B. (1952) *Content Analysis in Communication Research*, Glencoe, II.: Free Press.

Holsti, O. R. (1969) *Content Analysis for the Social Sciences and Humanities*, Harlow: Addison-Wesley.

Insch, G. S., Moore, J. E. and Murphy, L. D. (1997) Content analysis in leadership: examples, procedures, and suggestions for future use, *Leadership Quarterly*, 8(1): 1–25.

Krippendorff, K. (1980) *Content Analysis: An Introduction to its Methodology*, London: Sage.

Neuendorf, K. A. (2005) *The Content Analysis Guidebook*, London: Sage.

Stemler, S. (2001) An overview of content analysis, Practical Research, Assessment & Evaluation, http://PAREonline.net/getvn.asp?v=7&n=17 (accessed August 2009).

Weber, R. P. (1990) *Basic Content Analysis*, 2nd edn, London: Sage.

CHAPTER D8
Grounded Theory

Contents

In context

In many ways, Grounded Theory is 'just' another data collection and analysis method, as we described in B3. However, it is of such unusual popularity – particularly in the USA – that we decided it was worth of a chapter of its own.

We advise you to view this chapter with a certain measure of scepticism since we have some serious concerns about this particular method as a whole. However, we are convinced that the specific processes involved are useful in many forms of research – even if they are not theory-generating.

PART D: Data analysis

We noted in B3 that Grounded Theory's 'big' claim was that social research is atheoretical and that theory emerges (or is 'built') from the data as the process is carried out. We also noted that this claim is not accepted by all researchers. So, although Grounded Theory is an apparently simple process, we want to remind you that it is not as straightforward as it first appears and it is common for the process to be changed so that the 'theory building' element is removed (see B3).

LaRossa (2005: 41) notes that:

> In practice, many researchers have adopted a modified version of grounded analysis drawing upon these approaches but without building a Grounded Theory per se.

This is our experience too. We find the *processes* useful because they are structured, but we have difficulties with much of the underlying theory. Dey (1999: 23) sums up many of these problems when he says:

> There is an irony—perhaps a paradox—here: that a methodology that is based on 'interpretation' should itself prove so hard to interpret.

For us (and for many other researchers), the most important criticism of Grounded Theory is the implication that it is possible to have research *without* a theoretical basis (see A2). We do not think that this is possible in any meaningful way.

Other criticisms of Grounded Theory usually concentrate on its status as 'theory', arguing that what it produces isn't 'theory'. Frankly, we think this is too rarefied an argument for us to pursue here. If you need to see an up-to-date discussion of this and other criticisms, we suggest you see Thomas and James's 2006 article, 'Re-inventing grounded theory: some questions about theory, ground and discovery'.

Critics also question the nature of 'ground' and 'grounded' in research and have reservations about its relevance and importance. Overall, critics suggest that the Grounded Theory process mimics the experimental systems of the natural sciences to too great a degree and therefore is inappropriate for use in social enquiry.

The last item in our explanation of Grounded Theory above was the inference that many researchers use the method without accepting the theory generation aspect. In part, at least, this is because many researchers do not feel that the 'groundedness' (whatever that means) of this method is a significant advantage.

How is Grounded Theory different from other analysis methods?

There is no real agreement about the underlying philosophy of Grounded Theory, some saying that it separates theory and data, others that it combines them. Certainly, in practice, data collection, theory generation and analysis all happen simultaneously. (Of course, most social researchers would argue that data collection and analysis are often concurrent, but they are not always explicitly so.) (See B3, p. 136 for a discussion of the main features of the process.)

Doing Grounded Theory analysis

Data can be collected for Grounded Theory analysis in many different ways. Generally, the technique is used only with qualitative data, although there is no real reason that it should not be utilised for mixed-methods research. As far as we can tell, the method is not used by quantitative researchers.

Grounded Theory research starts when you are in a research setting. As the researcher, your role is to understand the processes that are happening and the ways in which the

constant comparison
Comparing data from different sources and from different places and times to support the analysis, along with the search for negative cases.

coding
The process of 'marking' or identifying data for later analysis.

memo
A way of recording, thinking about and analysing data, or flagging a piece of data for later investigation.

negative cases
Instances that seem to contradict or disprove the emerging theory.

data saturation
The idea that that there are ways in which the researcher can be sure that 'enough' research has been done.

various actors conduct themselves. The most common methods used are such things as interviews and observation, although there is no reason that other qualitative methods should not be utilised. At the end of each data collection session (whatever methods are used), the 'results' are recorded (these could be data, key issues, etc.) and immediately used as part of the **constant comparison** which, along with **coding** and memoing (i.e. using **memos**), is central to the analytical process. Initially, you compare data from different sources (which, of course, may include literature as well as empirical findings). As the process continues it is contended that theory will emerge and that it is then possible to compare data and theory. Whether this can be achieved is contested, but there is no doubt that the processes employed are useful and, for example, constant comparison is often a very good way to identify themes and categories. Some proponents of the process argue that the comparisons made should be recorded with the data and be used as codes (see below). At the same time, the researcher searches for **negative cases** (instances that seem to contradict or disprove the emerging theory). As (and if) these are found, this is seen as an indicator that more research is required (which will, in turn, modify the emerging theory) and that **data saturation** (see below) has not been achieved.

At the heart of Grounded Theory analysis is *coding* and *memoing*. There are many texts that deal with this process in detail and, therefore, we do not intend to do that here. Instead, we will highlight the most significant features so that readers can pursue them in more detail if they need to. In particular, we think that these two processes are very useful for many sorts of qualitative analysis and should not necessarily be thought of as specific to Grounded Theory.

Field notes

In Grounded Theory studies, researchers are encouraged to make notes 'in the field' as the research is conducted. These notes are later used to provide context for the analysis (see the 'Real research' box on p. 401).

Coding

open coding
In Grounded Theory data analysis, this is the first stage of coding data, identifying and describing research phenomena, and assigning them appropriate names.

axial coding
In Grounded Theory data analysis, this is the second stage of coding data, and involves relating codes to each other.

selective coding
In Grounded Theory data analysis, this is the third and final stage of coding data, and is the process of choosing a central or 'core' category and then relating all the other codes, themes and categories to it.

Coding is a process that is used in many different types of analysis, but it is used most commonly in qualitative research. Although coding is very versatile, at its most basic the idea of coding is to mark part of the data that is 'interesting' so that it can be found again for further study – think of using a highlighter to emphasise some text so that you could (a) indicate its importance and (b) find it again when you need to. Coding can be used in a variety of ways; for example, you might wish to note all the occurrences of a particular event or phenomenon or you might want to highlight something for comparison with something else. In Grounded Theory, one of the main purposes of coding is to find the 'core category' (Grounded Theory uses categories and themes interchangeably).

There are three types of coding in Grounded Theory. These are **open coding**, **axial coding** and **selective coding**.

- *Open coding* is the first stage of coding, based, according to Glaser and Strauss (1967), on the principle of *cracking open* the data as a first step in identifying themes and categories. Really, this is about identifying and describing research phenomena, and assigning them appropriate names. If it helps, you can think of the names as labels which are usually nouns (*the things that are being described*) or verbs (*the processes that are being described*). However, it will also be important to identify the properties of these initial codes which will be described by adjectives and adverbs so that we will know the size, shape, duration, frequency, importance, etc., of the things we are discovering. Open codes are usually quite general in nature and, although they are often concrete descriptions of events, it is important (for Grounded Theory at least) to have abstract codes too as it is these that best generate theory.

- *Axial coding* is the second stage of the coding process and is about relating codes to each other. This is something that can only be done by thinking and it will often be best achieved by a combination of deductive and inductive reasoning. Some researchers find that it is easiest to construct a matrix to compare different aspects.
- *Selective coding* is the final part of the coding system and is the process of choosing a central or 'core' category and then relating all the other codes, themes and categories to it. In Grounded Theory there is an assumption that a core category always exists.

As the research continues, the size of the sample is increased by what Glaser and Strauss call **theoretical sampling** (but which is similar to **purposive sampling**). The purpose of this is not only to increase the size of the sample, but also to increase its diversity so that more and different properties will be discovered. When you can no longer find new data for your categories (but especially for your core category), then it is said that data saturation has occurred. At this point you cease adding to the category and move on to sorting. However, before we look at that topic, there is another process that should have been running at the same time as coding and that is memoing.

Memos

The idea of writing research memos is often overlooked, even though it is a wonderful way of recording feelings, ideas, potential links, etc., which we come across when researching. The basic idea is to record your memo (or note or whatever you want to call it) in a way that attaches it to the data. This doesn't have to be a physical attachment (although it might be), but with the widespread use of computers it is quite easy to link different files or to use some sort of indicator to show that a memo is relevant at a particular point. Glaser (1998) says that **theoretical memoing** is the *core stage of grounded theory* (by now you must have noticed that the inventors of this process consider that pretty much every part of it is 'core' in some way), and notes that:

> *Memos are the theorizing write-up of ideas about substantive codes and their theoretically coded relationships as they emerge during coding, collecting and analyzing data, and during memoing.*

Supporters of Grounded Theory say that memoing is especially important in the beginning stages of a project when the researcher is formulating concepts and identifying the incidents and events that will be the basis of the research.

Memos can be in any format, but in Grounded Theory their main functions are to:

- participate in the constant comparison process referred to above;
- let you record the ideas (but particularly the *theoretical* ideas) that occur to you as you participate in the process.

Up to this point, our various processes of data collection, coding and memoing have been running at the same time and have, with theoretical sampling, we hope, resulted in data saturation (see above). Now we can move on to sorting and writing.

theoretical sampling
A sampling technique in which the initial cases are usually selected on a relatively unstructured basis: as 'theory' begins to emerge from the initial data, further cases are selected to explore and test the emerging theory; this continues until there is no new theory emerging and theoretical 'saturation' is reached.

purposive sample
A sample of selected cases that will best enable the researcher to explore the research questions in depth.

theoretical memoing
In Grounded Theory data analysis, 'the theorizing write-up of ideas about substantive codes and their theoretically coded relationships as they emerge during coding, collecting and analyzing data, and during memoing' (Glaser).

Real research

Field notes and memos in Grounded Theory

Montgomery and Bailey (2007) discuss the use of field notes and memos in a Grounded Theory study of mothers with serious mental illness. They conclude that the process is vital to a Grounded Theory approach, and that it also has value in similar studies using other qualitative methods.

They distinguish specifically between the nature and purpose of field notes and memos, noting that the former are records of actual researcher experiences and that the latter are concerned with the development of the Grounded Theory.

They give a number of examples of the differences, and we reproduce two here so that you will be able to appreciate the differences:

Field note

In response to my clarification regarding her efforts to 'protect' her children, Brooke interrupts with an assertive response, 'Definitely.' Then, she becomes tearful and looks away. In a lower tone, she adds that her children are 'normal' with a qualifier 'to the extent that normal can be right now.' Illness 'creates chaos.' There is a pause. I sense discomfort for both of us. Brooke then shifts the flow of the conversation using terms such as 'fun loving,' 'very nurturing,' and 'well-balanced' to describe her children. (68)

Memo

A mother [Brooke] seems to become guarded when she fears that her illness may have inadvertently harmed her children [January field note, Transcript lines (TL): 140–143]. This may demonstrate protection of self-as-mother [TL: 254–258]. A mother's efforts to 'protect' her children unravel in illness [TL: 15-17]. For Brooke and the other initial participants, their illness must not hurt their children. Mothers express emotions of sadness and guilt as they are unable to protect their children from illness. They are searching for guidance re: how to protect their children when their illness is overwhelming. They know of few positive role models in illness. (69)

Sorting and writing

The process of sorting is quite obvious: the things that we have discovered, along with memos and notes, are grouped in logical sequences that make the emerging theory clear. The way in which the components are grouped provides the outline for the final research report.

However, the originators of Grounded Theory argue that there is no single way in which the components of the research must be sequenced for the best results and that it is possible to do this in different ways with the same data. In principle, we think that this is a good idea. However, in practice, there is not usually enough time to use more than one sequence in the analysis.

Real research

Grounded Theory methods and qualitative family research

Ralph LaRossa (2005) looked at the use of Grounded Theory in family research. In the abstract of his paper he says:

Among the different qualitative approaches that may be relied upon in family theorizing, grounded theory methods (GTM), developed by Barney Glaser and Anselm Strauss, are the most popular. . . . My goal is to propose a methodologically condensed but still comprehensive interpretation of GTM, an interpretation that researchers hopefully will find easy to understand and employ.

LaRossa examines the different parts of Grounded Theory procedures and, though he finds them useful, he feels that they are too complex and too difficult to understand to be truly accessible to all researchers. He shares the concern that Grounded Theory methods may not actually produce theory and suggests that the process can be considerably simplified.

In his conclusion, he states: 'GTM are a valuable set of procedures for thinking theoretically about textual materials, but they can be difficult to decipher.' He also notes the importance of Grounded Theory methods because they 'emphasized the centrality of language in social life, the importance of words as indicators, the significance of empirical and conceptual comparisons, the value of thinking about how variables are linked, and the mechanics and aesthetics of crafting a story line.'

Summary

Grounded Theory claims that it is special, but there is some dispute over this because experts do not agree. We take the attitude that some features are useful and others not, as shown below.

✗ The notion that theory emerges from (or is generated by) atheoretical research. Indeed, there is no agreement on what sort of theory this could be.

✗ The nature of the 'groundedness' of Grounded Theory.

✓ The technique can be very useful, particularly because of the processes and concepts of:

Constant comparison

Coding

Memos / field notes

Clear structure.

Your research

How useful is Grounded Theory?

Many of the *processes* used in Grounded Theory are useable, and very useful, in other data and analysis collection systems. In particular, these include:

- *Constant comparison*: the comparing of data from different sources and from different places and times to support the analysis, along with the search for negative cases.

- *Coding*: the (well-known) process of 'marking' or identifying data for later analysis, but split into three useful dimensions (open, axial and selective) in this instance. This could be thought of as a sequential approach to coding.

- *Memos*: ways of recording, thinking about and analysing data (this is like the research journal we discuss elsewhere).

- *Data saturation*: an important concept arguing that there are ways in which the researcher can be sure that 'enough' research has been done. (Really, what this says is that if you keep finding the same data and you're not discovering anything 'new', then you have achieved saturation and your data collection is complete.)

- *Clear structure*: the meticulous way in which the research is structured, undertaken and recorded – an inspiration to us all.

References and further reading

Charmaz, K. (2006) *Constructing Grounded Theory: A Practical Guide Through Qualitative Analysis*, London: Sage.

Dey, I. (1999) *Grounding Grounded Theory: Guidelines for Qualitative Inquiry*, San Diego, CA: Academic Press.

Glaser, B. G. (1994) *More Grounded Theory Methodology*, Mill Valley, CA: Sociology Press.

Glaser, B. G. (1998) *Doing Grounded Theory: Issues and Discussions*, Mill Valley, CA: Sociology Press.

Glaser, B. G., and Strauss, A. (1967) *The Discovery of Grounded Theory: Strategies for Qualitative Research*, Mill Valley, CA: Sociology Press.

LaRossa, R. (2005) Grounded theory methods and qualitative family research, *Journal of Marriage and Family*, 67: 837–57.

Montgomery, P. and Bailey, P. H. (2007) Field notes and theoretical memos in grounded theory, *Western Journal of Nursing Research*, 29: 65–79.

Scott, K. W. (2004) Relating categories in grounded theory analysis: using a conditional relationship guide and reflective coding matrix, *The Qualitative Report*, 9(1) (March): 113–26.

Strauss, A. L. and Corbin, J. M. (1990) *Basics of Qualitative Research: Grounded Theory Procedures and Techniques*, London: Sage.

Strauss, A. L. and Corbin, J. M. (eds) (1997) *Grounded Theory in Practice*, London: Sage.

Strauss, A. L. and Corbin, J. M. (1998) *Basics of Qualitative Research: Techniques and Procedures for Developing Grounded Theory*, London: Sage.

Thomas, G. and James, D. (2006) Re-inventing grounded theory: some questions about theory, ground and discovery, *British Educational Research Journal*, 32(6): 767–95.

CHAPTER D9
Using computers in data analysis

Contents

In context

Whether your data is structured or semi-structured, written, spoken or visual, its analysis is a process of managing and working with the data to produce your findings and address your research questions or test your hypothesis. Even small research projects accumulate quite a lot of material – the data itself, the researcher's notes, notes on literature and other research, and so on. All of this needs to be accessible and drawn upon during the analysis and computers can be helpful in both the management of data and the analysis itself.

In this chapter we look at some of the computer software that has been specially designed to help social researchers analyse their data and also highlight some software you may be using on a day-to-day basis but which has features that could be helpful in your data analysis.

PART D: Data analysis

- **D1:** Beginning to analyse
- **D2:** Working with data
- **D3:** Statistical analysis
- **D4:** Thematic analysis
- **D5:** Analysing narrative
- **D6:** Discourse analysis
- **D7:** Content analysis
- **D8:** Grounded Theory
- ▶ **D9: Using computers in data analysis**
- **D10:** So what? Drawing conclusions

What you can do with computers

Most computer software is designed to enable you to work with particular sorts of material – written text, video, photographs or sound – in a set of defined ways. In other words, the nature of software is that it is designed for use with particular types of material and to enable you to do a standard set of procedures with that material. There is computer software that will help you with each part of the analytical process, some that is designed specifically for the analysis of social research data and some that has wider uses but includes features that are useful to the social researcher.

Basically computer software can help you to:

- organise all your material;
- keep your data and other material in standard labelled formats;
- help you to get the data into a form that is accessible and useable;
- conduct a variety of analytical procedures specific to your type of data;
- enable you to develop your analysis in relevant ways;
- present your findings in formats that are clear and understandable to others.

In addition to these basic features, using computer software can:

- help you to think about and make notes on your analysis;
- keep a log/record of all your analytical activity;
- enable others to see the analytical processes you have been through.

Your research

Note: Computer software cannot do the analysis for you – only *you* can develop the analysis, interpret your findings and present your conclusions.

Statistical analysis

Computer packages for analysing social research data

There are numerous software packages that will help you to organise, analyse and present numerical data. The package most commonly used by social scientists is SPSS, an IBM company.[1] Many university departments use this program and some make it available to their students. Some social research methods modules include tuition in using the package and you may have access to training sessions on the software within your university, college or workplace. In common with most software of this type, it is possible to download trial copies and to use online tutorials at the company website (www.spss.com/uk/statistics/). There are also a number of books on statistical techniques that demonstrate the use of SPSS, some of which are particularly relevant to social scientists and are listed at the end of this chapter.

The package will enable you to:

- create variables (and variable names and descriptions);
- enter your data into a spreadsheet format;
- check your data for, e.g., missing values, inconsistent data;
- create new variables using one, two or more of your original variables;

---

[1] SPSS was acquired by IBM in October 2009.

- create frequency and descriptive statistics (mean, median, mode, standard deviation, percentiles, etc.) for all your variables;
- create cross-tabulations;
- develop complex analyses using a comprehensive range of statistical techniques including chi-squared, correlations, multi-variate analyses and much more;
- present your findings in graphs and charts which can be included in your final document, report or dissertation.

Here we will illustrate some of the key features by showing you some screenshots from the SPSS software to help you to decide whether you should use the package to support the analysis of your data. Note: Screenshots are taken from SPSS 17.0.[2]

Creating variables and entering your data using SPSS

In D2 we showed how each set of answers to a question or activity that has been recorded is called a variable and can be given a variable name. In SPSS a list of all the variables is created in the *Variable View* (Screenshot D9.2). Each variable is listed with information about its type, whether it is nominal, ordinal, ratio and so on, its name (*Label*) and the values (or codes) associated with it. Each value is also given a label or name. Labels can be used in tables or charts produced from the data, making them easier to understand. In the example, code '1' is given the label *yes*.

The data from each of your data cases is then entered in the *Data View* (Screenshot D9.1). Here each line is a different case and each column is a variable headed by its variable name. The codes or values for each variable for each case are entered into the grid.

New variables which combine variables or group values within variables can be created using SPSS. In the example (Screenshot D9.3) the variable *lived*, which can have values of between 1 and 100, is grouped into five-year groupings. The original variable *lived* is selected and a set of new values assigned (1 thru 5 → 1, 6 thru 10 → 2, and so on), creating a new

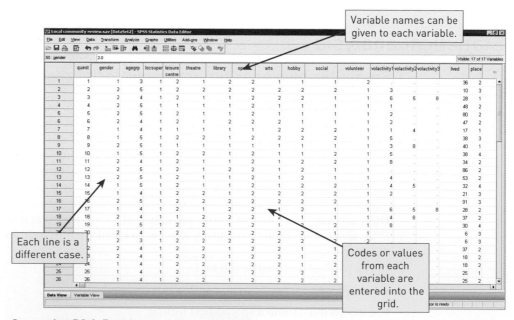

Screenshot D9.1 Entering your data using SPSS

---

[2] SPSS software screenshots are presented with permission of SPSS (UK) Ltd.

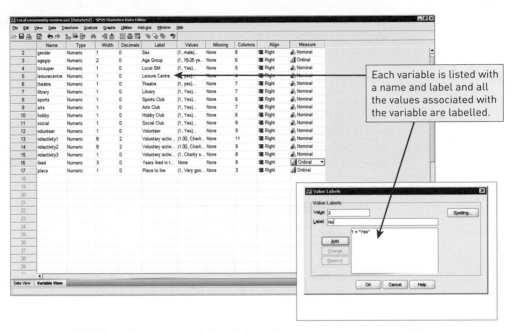

Screenshot D9.2 Creating a list of variables in SPSS

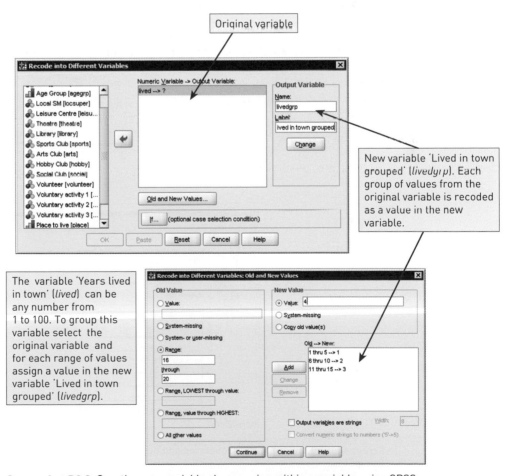

Screenshot D9.3 Creating new variables by grouping within a variable using SPSS

variable *livedgrp*. Using a similar approach, data from two variables can be combined (for example, *age* and *gender*) to create a new variable *genage* (D2).

Producing a range of statistics using SPSS

When the data has been entered in for each case and any new variables have been created, a wide range of calculations can be performed. The first stage of most statistical analyses is to produce frequencies and descriptive statistics, for example, the mean, median, mode and standard deviation (D3) for key variables. In Screenshot D9.4 the researcher has selected a

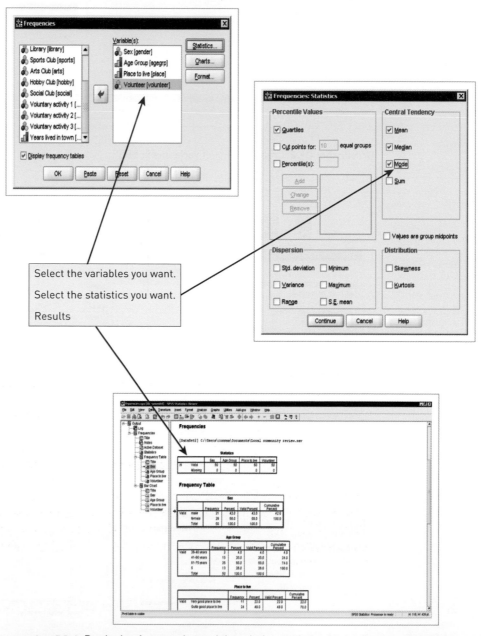

Screenshot D9.4 Producing frequencies and descriptive statistics for a selection of variables using SPSS

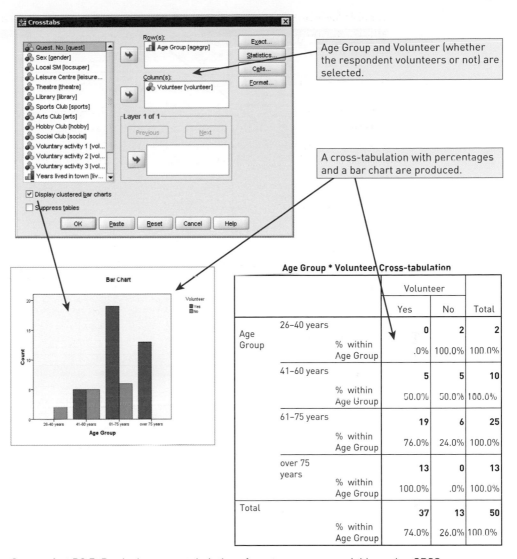

Screenshot D9.5 Producing cross-tabulations from two or more variables using SPSS

list of variables for which certain statistics are required. The output, or result, is in the form of a frequency table for each variable.

Cross-tabulations (D3) are produced by selecting the two variables and specifying which variable is to be in the rows of the table and which in the columns. Additional statistics can be specified using the statistics button and the resulting table can be presented in a number of formats including, as shown in Screenshot D9.5, a bar chart.

As shown in Screenshot D9.6, there are a wide range of statistical analyses that can be performed, starting from a drop-down menu. Having selected a particular statistical technique, a series of boxes enable you to enter the variables and other information required for the analysis to be performed.

Using SPSS to present results in different formats

The results of the statistical analyses can be presented in a range of ways using, for example, the *Chart Builder* as shown in Screenshot D9.7. Having selected the variables for inclusion, the results can be presented in a range of different formats and colours chosen by the

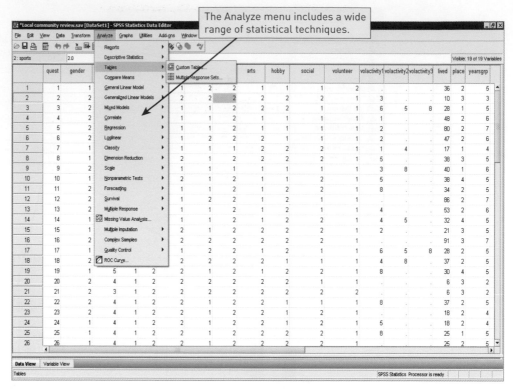

Screenshot D9.6 An extensive range of simple and sophisticated statistical techniques can be used in SPSS

researcher from a *Gallery*. The resulting chart can be labelled and titled so that it is ready for presentation in a document. The final version can be saved for inclusion in a word-processed document or presentation slide.

A package like SPSS can be used at many levels. Some researchers may use it simply to enter and manage their data from, for example, a questionnaire and produce frequencies, descriptive statistics and cross-tabulations to help them to develop their analysis and present their findings. Others will be able to use the complex statistical techniques that these packages offer and which would be lengthy, if impossible, to calculate by hand. As may be seen from the screenshots, SPSS is quite user-friendly and intuitive to use but if you have not used software of this type before you should expect to spend some time becoming familiar with the basic processes before being able to work with your own data effectively.

Alternatives to a statistical software package

If you do not:

- have access to a statistical package . . .
- have time to learn how to use such a package . . .
- have a large number of cases or a large amount of data . . .

you can do some of the same things as you can with a statistical package using a spreadsheet package like Microsoft Excel. As the software is not specifically designed for statistical analysis, it does not have some of the more useful features – for instance, being able to define and label variables – and in particular it is not so easy to find out the frequency of values on a variable

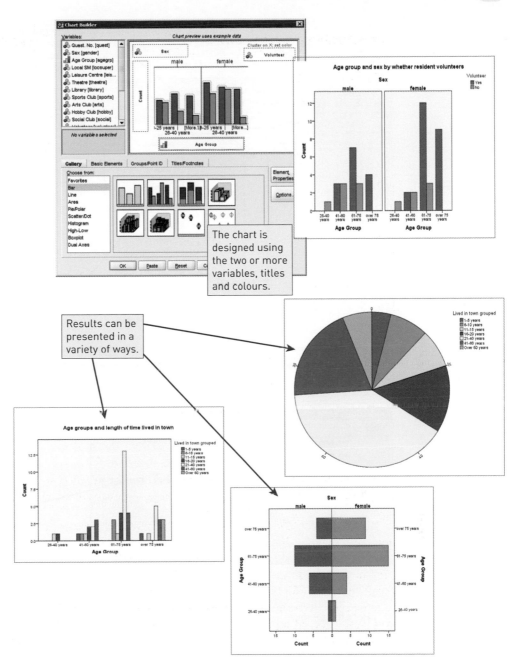

Screenshot D9.7 Using SPSS to present results in different formats

or to produce cross-tabulations. However, spreadsheet software can be useful to:

- enter the data from each case into variable named columns;
- calculate descriptive statistics, such as means, for each variable;
- calculate more complex statistics, chi-squared, correlations and many others from two or more variables;
- present data in charts and graphs within your final document.

You will see from Screenshot D9.8 that a data sheet similar to the *Data View* of SPSS can be produced with a line for each sheet and a column for each variable. However, the variable

Data can be entered into the spreadsheet with a row for each case and a column for each variable.

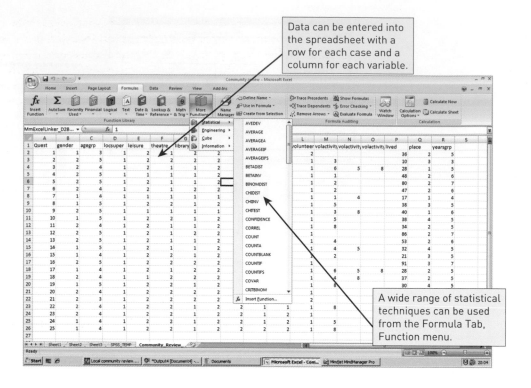

A wide range of statistical techniques can be used from the Formula Tab, Function menu.

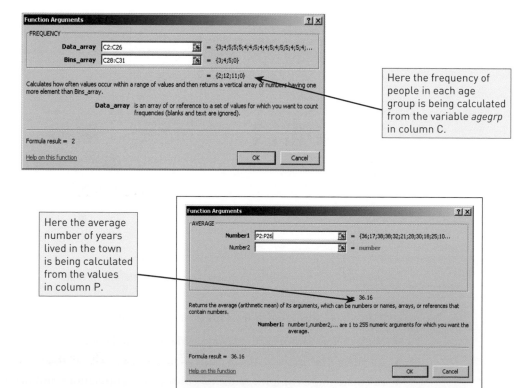

Here the frequency of people in each age group is being calculated from the variable *agegrp* in column C.

Here the average number of years lived in the town is being calculated from the values in column P.

Screenshot D9.8 The data sheet in Excel

names are simply names – they do not have any values attached to them and Excel does not have the facilities to create new variables. The Statistical Function menu includes a range of statistical techniques that can be performed using the data. Note that in Excel each cell in the data screen is defined by its column letter and line number and that each statistical technique is performed on the cells which are included in the Function Arguments box as shown. As shown in the screenshot examples, the average number of years lived in the town is calculated using the values from column P (variable – *lived*) and includes cases from cell P2 through to cell P26 – that is, the values in column P.

Excel can be used to create charts and tables ready to include in your document. However, unlike SPSS, when using Excel you will usually need to prepare the data. In the example in Screenshot D9.9 the data to go into the chart has been prepared, and the frequencies in each cell have been calculated and entered into the table before a chart can be created from the data. A variety of chart styles and colours are available and the chart can easily be labelled, titled and linked to a Microsoft Word document or Microsoft PowerPoint slide.

Although Excel does not have the functions and ease of use of SPSS and other statistical packages, it can help you to manage your data and to create charts and graphs which will help you (and your readers) to understand the data. If you are already familiar with Excel in another setting then you are likely to be able to adapt its features to your requirements as a social researcher. If you are not already familiar then you need to consider whether you are willing to spend some time learning to use the package. As spreadsheets are used in many walks of life, some time spent on developing this transferable skill may well be worthwhile.

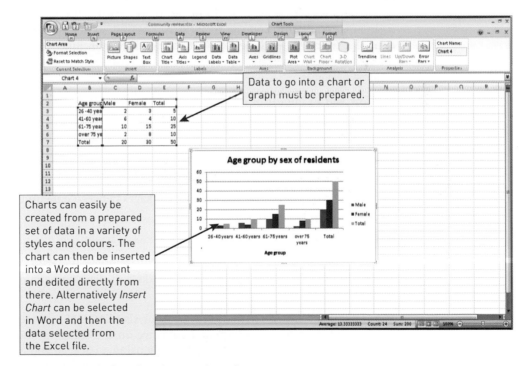

Screenshot D9.9 Creating charts and graphs

Qualitative analysis software

In the early days of social research that gathered and worked with qualitative or raw data, the analysis process was time consuming. Typically transcripts and notes would be typed with a number of carbon copies. The transcripts would be coded, perhaps using different coloured pencils, and then the pages (literally) cut up into 'data chunks'. Data chunks from across the cases which were coded in the same way could then be pasted on a new sheet of paper or chart to enable the researcher to look for similarities, possible relationships and so on. Another approach was to keep a card index system with each code written on a card. References to the points in a particular case or document where the code was used were recorded on the card so that the researcher could easily find the relevant coded data. The card might also include quotations from the data which related to the code. Large sheets of paper would be used to produce charts or diagrams of the relationships between the codes and data.

In many ways the current software available to help with the analysis of raw, semi- or unstructured data does little more than what the researchers then did by hand. However, the use of either generic software like Microsoft Word or a specifically designed package like NVivo can make the process more efficient and enable the researcher to work with the data rigorously and creatively.

Computer packages specifically designed for the analysis of qualitative data

Over the past 20 years a number of software packages have been designed specifically to aid the analysis of qualitative data. To a large extent these have developed alongside the growth of different approaches to analysing qualitative data and the range of data sources now being included in social research. The most commonly used software currently is NVivo (www. qsrinternational.com/products_nvivo.aspx, accessed 30 August 2009) and we look at some examples from this package below. Other examples include: ATLASti www.atlasti.com/, accessed 29 August 2009) and Ethnograph (www.qualisresearch.com/, accessed 29 August 2009).

Most packages:

- allow you to import or create your data sources – these could be transcripts of interviews, documents, audio or video recordings, or notes;
- enable you to segment your data into 'chunks' or units in a variety of ways;
- have coding or indexing systems;
- search and retrieve data units with a particular code;
- facilitate complex searches to establish linkages between data units;
- search for strings, patterns, words and phrases in the text;
- have a facility to attach memos to documents or codes;
- can count number of occurrences of codes, words, etc., in a data source;
- have the facility to produce maps, networks and diagrammatic representations of the links between codes and data.

The Computer Assisted Qualitative Data Analysis (CAQDAS) project at the University of Surrey regularly produces advice and guidance on the selection and use of the range of packages available and if you are considering using a package you are advised to consult their website (http://caqdas.soc.surrey.ac.uk/, accessed 26 August 2009) and the reading suggested at the end of this chapter.

As with the statistical software, trial versions of most packages are downloadable and most have tutorial and sample material to help you to learn how best to use the product (www.qsrinternational.com/products_nvivo.aspx, accessed 30 August 2009). Again, as with

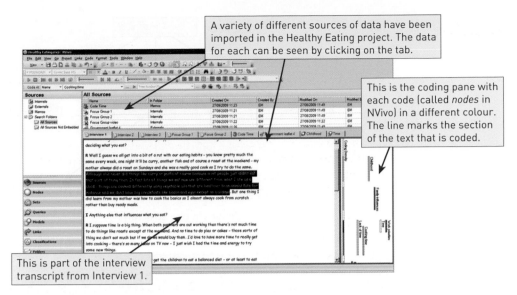

A variety of different sources of data have been imported in the Healthy Eating project. The data for each can be seen by clicking on the tab.

This is the coding pane with each code (called *nodes* in NVivo) in a different colour. The line marks the section of the text that is coded.

This is part of the interview transcript from Interview 1.

Screenshot D9.10 Data sources in the NVivo project

the statistical software, it can be used at different levels: some may use qualitative data software primarily as a way of managing and indexing or coding large quantities of raw data; others will move on to use more of the searching, complex coding and mapping techniques to help them to look for explanations within the data or to develop theory.

The following pages show the early stages of using NVivo to begin an analysis of the healthy food data used in D4. Note: the screenshots are from NVivo 8.[3]

Data sources and NVivo

A range of different types of sources, including interview and focus group transcripts (D2), pictures, video and audio material, can be imported into NVivo and worked with within the software. It is also possible to include offline documents (in the example in Screenshot D9.10 a government leaflet has been included). Here, although the text of the document itself is not imported, the codes and memos applied to the document text can be included and therefore be included within the analysis. Alternatively the document may be scanned and included as a picture. All the data sources connected to the research project are listed and easily accessed by clicking on the labelled tabs. In the central pane of the screen is the transcript of the data source being worked on.

Coding and NVivo

The pane at the right-hand side shows the coding which has already been applied to this data source. Each code (D2, D4) (or *node* as it is called in the NVivo software) is a different colour and the coloured lines in the *coding pane* correspond to the section of text in the data source to which the code has been applied. Each code is listed and has a definition associated with it. The NVivo software enables you to create and work with codes in two different ways. *Free nodes* are often used initially as a way of identifying all the data that may be associated with a particular idea or concept. As the analysis develops and initial codes are divided or combined in different ways, and when relationships between codes begin to emerge, a hierarchical organisation of nodes may be useful. Codes or nodes are

---

[3] NVivo software screenshots are presented with permission of QSR International Pty Ltd. NVivo is a registered trademark of and is designed and developed by QSR International (www.qsrinternational.com).

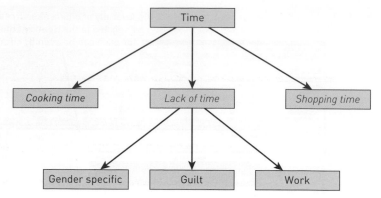

Figure D9.1 Organising codes/nodes in tree structure

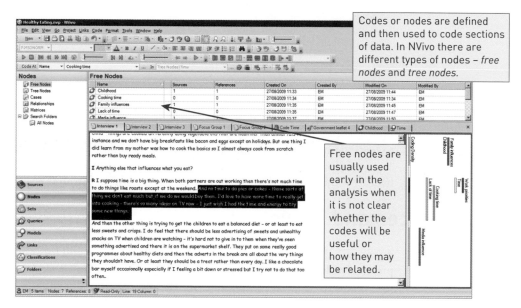

Screenshot D9.11 Using codes (nodes) in NVivo

then organised as a hierarchical *tree* structure (it may be more helpful to think of it as a tree root structure) with a number of hierarchical levels as shown on Figure D9.1.

In the example in Screenshots D9.11 and D9.12 three different aspects or ideas about *Lack of Time* have been identified in the data and are therefore assigned different codes at the next level – in NVivo these are called *child nodes* of the *parent node Lack of Time*.

Using memos in NVivo

Within most qualitative analysis software including NVivo it is possible to attach notes or *memos* (D4) to data being worked with in a number of ways. These memos can include reminders to the researcher, notes on the way a particular code has been defined, interesting ideas that are emerging from the data, and so on. In NVivo each memo is given a label or title and can be attached to a code, a particular section of text in one or more data source or to a specific data source. Each memo can then be edited or added to as the analysis develops and can also be coded using the same codes as the data sources.

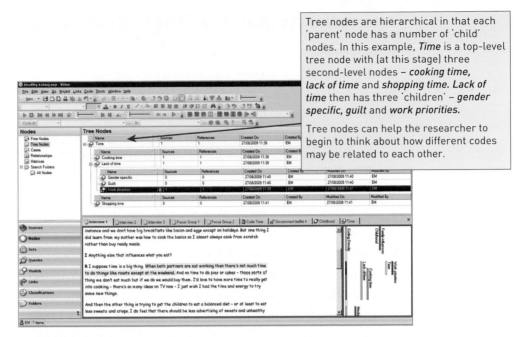

Tree nodes are hierarchical in that each 'parent' node has a number of 'child' nodes. In this example, *Time* is a top-level tree node with (at this stage) three second-level nodes – *cooking time, lack of time* and *shopping time. Lack of time* then has three 'children' – *gender specific, guilt* and *work priorities.*

Tree nodes can help the researcher to begin to think about how different codes may be related to each other.

Screenshot D9.12 Tree nodes in NVivo

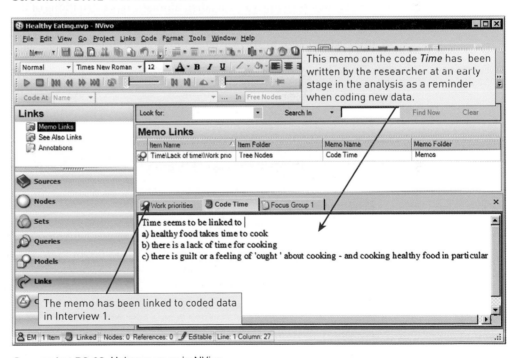

This memo on the code *Time* has been written by the researcher at an early stage in the analysis as a reminder when coding new data.

The memo has been linked to coded data in Interview 1.

Screenshot D9.13 Using memos in NVivo

More recent editions of software like NVivo have focused on making the user interface clear and more user-friendly. Although the screenshots may look complex and some of the terminology is rather strange, the process of importing data sources and developing basic coding is quite straightforward. Using the software at a more complex level depends on the complexity of your analysis and your ability to work with complex ideas and relationships, a process which is as challenging on paper as it is with the help of this type of software. If you have not used software of this type before you should expect to spend some time familiarising yourself with the software and working through some of the examples before working with your own data.

Alternatives to qualitative data analysis software

If you do not:

- have access to a qualitative data analysis package . . .
- have time to learn how to use such a package . . .
- have a large number of cases or a large amount of data . . .

you may want to consider how you can use a package, like Microsoft Word, with which you are familiar to help you to manage the process of working with qualitative data.

Using Word you can:

- transcribe or summarise all of your textual data;
- use the *Line numbers* facility to number all your text;
- organise your data into data chunks by, for example, using a *Table* format;
- highlight coded text using different coloured text, highlighter, symbols or fonts;
- add notes or memos using the *Comment* feature;
- create charts using the *Table* feature;
- cut coded data chunks and paste into a new page or a chart table;
- use the *Find* facility to find words or phrases in your document;
- use the *Shapes* facility to create diagrammatic representations of the links between codes (see D4, for an example);
- use *Book-marking* to mark features in the text and *Cross-reference* facility to link paragraphs in different parts of the document.

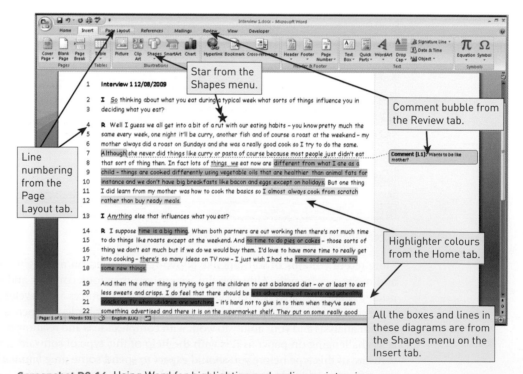

Screenshot D9.14 Using Word for highlighting and coding an interview

Think about it . . .

Visual data

Most software packages that help you to produce photographs or videos have facilities within them that can be useful to a social researcher working with digital visual data, including the facility to:

- arrange or organise photographs;
- change colours or add effects to small sections of a photograph;
- divide video material into small segments, label and reorder them;
- tag or add a memo to a photograph or video still.

And labels can be added to photographs, as we have done with the screenshots in this chapter.

Being able to use the wide range of facilities available on most word-processing software packages will be of value to you, not only in your social research project but in many aspects of your study and everyday life. Not least you will be able to use these facilities in the presentation of your research report or dissertation (**Part E**) and in producing other study assignments.

Your research

Should you use computer software to help you with your analysis?

		✓
Do you use a computer on a daily basis?		
Do you use any of the following types of software regularly?	Word processing, e.g. Word	
	Spreadsheet, e.g. Excel	
	Database, e.g. Access	
Do you have regular access to any of the following types of software?	Statistical analysis software, e.g. PASW (SPSS) Statistics, Minitab	
	Qualitative data analysis software, e.g. NVivo, Ethnograph, ATLASti	
Would you describe yourself as a competent computer user?		
Do you enjoy working on a computer?		
Do you have time to learn how to use new software?		

Think about your data:

- What types of data will you be working with?
- What format is your data in – questionnaires, transcripts, video, notes?

- How many data cases (interviews, questionnaires and so on) do you have?
- What type and level of analysis do you plan to do?

READ about the relevant data analysis techniques (D3 to D8) and this chapter before deciding.

References and further reading

Bazeley, P. (2007) *Qualitative Data Analysis with NVivo*, 2nd edn, London: Sage.

Bryman, A. and Cramer, D. (2008) *Quantitative Data Analysis with SPSS 14,15, and 16: A Guide for Social Scientists*, London: Routledge.

Field, A. (2009) *Discovering Statistics Using SPSS*, 3rd edn, London: Sage.

Lewins, A. and Silver, C. (2007) *Using Software for Qualitative Data Analysis: A Step-by-Step Guide*, London: Sage.

Lewins, A. and Silver, C. (2009) Choosing a CAQDAS package. University of Surrey, CAQDAS, available from http://caqdas.soc.surrey.ac.uk/PDF/2009 (accessed 29 August 2009).

Richards, L. (2005) *Handling Qualitative Data: A Practical Guide*, London: Sage.

CHAPTER D10
So what? Drawing conclusions

Contents

Contents of the conclusion

In context

No matter what social science discipline you work in or what type of project you have undertaken, drawing conclusions from your research is the most important part of the process; in some respects, it is also the most difficult.

Writing a conclusion is much more than simply summarising your work and findings, and is a critical step in ensuring that your work is taken seriously.

In **D1** we noted that analysis was the process by which the data is described, discussed, interpreted, evaluated and explained and a conclusion reached. By now, you will have examined your data in minute detail, discussed and explained what was happening when you collected it and highlighted the things that (a) were interesting and (b) answered your research questions. In this chapter, we come to the final part of analysis: reaching a conclusion.

The overall purpose of a conclusion is to answer your research question(s) and to give a critical reflection on the research project and the contribution that it makes to the issue that has been investigated. It should answer the 'so what?' question that is likely to be applied to evaluate your work and it is likely also to indicate its strengths and shortcomings and, perhaps, to reflect on your role as researcher (see **Part E**, particularly **E4**).

Think about it . . .

The 'so what?' question

Imagine that you are reading your work for the first time and that it is your job to assess it.

When you get to the end and have finished reading the conclusion, you should ask yourself, 'So what?'

- What has this research achieved?
- Has it answered the questions it set out to answer?
- Is it 'good' research?
- Has it left you with unanswered questions?

Simply put, you need to write about what your findings mean and how they apply to the social world. As a student, the conclusion of your research report can also be an opportunity to demonstrate that you have understood the nature of social research and can show how your findings fit into, and impact upon, the wider social world.

Research conclusions often seem difficult to write, perhaps because of the feeling that you've already said everything in your findings and discussion chapters. However, those are not conclusions, but only steps along the way.

Generally, your conclusion should be as concise as possible (but do not abbreviate it to the point that it cannot be clearly understood), while still performing the necessary functions outlined above. Perhaps the most important thing is to remember that you should never introduce new material in your conclusion. As a general rule, everything you discuss should have been mentioned earlier and there should be very few – if any – quotations from others. Some authorities recommend ending your work with an appropriate quote from a leading writer in your area: we strongly advise against it on the basis that the work is *yours* and should not, at this point, need the support of others – after all, wasn't that what the literature review (**B2**) was all about?

We think that there is a major pitfall that catches many unwary students: this is the tendency, in the conclusion, to generalise from results that are not generalisable (see **B5** in particular). This is understandable; you have worked hard and long on your project and you want to maximise its importance to the world (and to the person marking your assignment, perhaps). However, most student projects have small sample sizes (**B5**) so that the sample parameters probably do not truly reflect the population parameters. This is not in itself a problem, of course: difficulties only arise when it is implied that the conclusions reached from (for example) interviewing five schoolteachers in central Birmingham are generalisable to all school teachers in the UK (you will understand by now that suggesting that the experiences of teachers working in a large, diverse city are similar to teachers working, for example, on the island of Mull in the Hebrides is unlikely to be accurate or credible on several levels). However, we do think that it is important to discuss these issues in the conclusion so that future researchers (as well as the person assessing your work) can understand what you have achieved.

Your research

Conclusion

Think about the 'So what?' question and the conclusion of your research project.

- What did you do?
- How well did it work?
- What did you find out that:
  - was important?
  - was new?
  - was the same as other research findings in the area?
  - has added to our understanding of how the social world works?
- How might your work be used or extended by others?

Contents of the conclusion

The contents of *your* conclusion should, of course, reflect *your* research project and every conclusion is unique. However, we suggest below the contents of a typical research report or dissertation conclusion.

1. *Summarise your work.* This part of your conclusion is quite general (item 3 below is more specific) and should be as concise as possible. It is there just to remind the reader of what you have done and how you have done it.

2. *What has been learned? Have you answered your research question(s)?*

3. It is normal for the conclusion to summarise what has been learned from, or discovered in, the research. If you were testing a hypothesis, you will probably attempt to evaluate your success. Remember that even if nothing was discovered in your project, this is still a potentially valuable research finding (the things that are not there may be as important as the things that are!).

4. *What are the strengths and weaknesses of the research? If you were to repeat the project, what changes would you make?* It is always good practice for the researcher to critically evaluate the project as a whole and to discuss particular strengths and weaknesses. This might lead into a discussion of how future researchers might redesign or refine the process.

5. *What are the benefits of the research?* (This links to the next point as well.) This is a useful point to indicate what (and who) will benefit from the research and why.

6. *What suggestions can be made (for example, for changes in policy or practice)?* If the research has a practical application, the researcher may want to make some suggestions for future policy or practice. For example, if this was a research project investigating waiting times at a railway ticket office, suggestions might be made about a revised queuing system.

7. *What needs to be done in the future?* Almost all research projects leave some questions unanswered (or, indeed, ask new questions). Indicating directions for possible future research is useful to other researchers and also indicates that you have been able to think beyond the obvious end-point of a particular project (see E4).

8. *Critical reflection on the research project as a whole.* Although some of this may have been done in item 3 above, it is still useful to evaluate the whole of the project and

to consider the things that went well and those that went less well. This can also be the place where you consider some of the broader questions, for example: Can you generalise from your work? Would you get the same (or similar) results in a different geographical area? Was access difficult or easy?

9. *Personal reflection (this is not always appropriate, but can be useful in some situations, for example, reflecting on the impact you had as a specific individual on the research).* Many social researchers discuss their personal reflections on projects that they undertake. This can take many forms and may not be appropriate for all settings. Common questions that are considered include:

   (a) What impact did I have as an individual person on this research?

   (b) What were my personal experiences as a researcher and what did I learn from them?

   (c) What were my feelings as I went through the project and how might that affect the way I evaluate results?

As we said above, there is no one formula for writing research conclusions; in fact the endpoint of each project is individual and unique. Different aspects will be important in different settings, usually depending on what sort of research issues or questions are being addressed. However, if you bear the points we have made above in mind and use the simple checklist below, you can be confident that your conclusion will contain all the appropriate information (see **Part E**).

Your research

Conclusion checklist

		✓/✗
✓	Have you answered the 'So what?' question?	
✓	Have you answered your research question(s) / demonstrated that you have tested your hypothesis?	
✓	Have you stated what has been learned from your project?	
✓	Have you explained your findings and reasoning?	
✓	Have you explained how your project contributes to knowledge / academic understanding?	
✓	Have you discussed the strengths and weaknesses?	
✓	Have you discussed how your findings impact on the social world?	
✓	Have you stated the benefits of your research (or, for example, the implications for policy or practice)?	
✓	Have you thought about future research (**E4**)?	
✓	Have you critically reflected on the success of your project?	
✓	Have you reflected on your role as researcher?	
✓	Have you explained unexpected findings?	
✓	Have you thought about who will read your conclusion (**Part E**)?	
✗	Have you included new information?	
✗	Have you generalised inappropriately?	

This example checklist cannot take account of all the variables that may be present in your research project. However, if you can tick or cross all the appropriate boxes, then you are probably in a good position to write your conclusion.

PART E
Data presentation and reports

CHAPTER E1
The importance of audience

Contents

In context

Throughout this, the shortest part of the book, we strive to provide you with the tools to complete your research task, because it is not enough to do good research. It is not even enough to discover something completely new or explain something that was not previously understood. The reason for this is simple: you have to tell the world about your research. Throughout **Part E** we will discuss both how to write about your work, why you are writing and – perhaps most importantly – who you are writing to.

Although, obviously, the content of your work is of critical importance, it is also necessary to think about how you will present it to the world. This short part discusses the significance of your 'audience' and gives some simple examples.

We start with the importance of audience and then continue through writing strategies for research, presenting data and, finally, disseminating your research.

PART E: Data presentation and reports

▶ **E1: The importance of audience**

E2: Writing for research: reports and dissertations

E3: Data presentation

E4: Dissemination and further research

Presenting your data, writing your report or preparing your dissertation is the final step in your research project. You have reached the point where all your work is brought to a conclusion and 'published' (this may be for the purposes of your undergraduate dissertation, but the process is the same no matter what level you have been working at). So, it is important to think about why this stage of research is so important.

If you do not tell the world, then (obviously) your work will remain unknown. This almost happened to Charles Darwin and his theory of evolution (see Example E1.1). There have been other, more recent, events too; for example, the publication of the Black Report on Inequalities in Health in 1980 (see the 'Think about it . . .' box on p. 433). Think how different your world might be if this research had not been made public.

It is important, then, to write up and 'publish' your work (as a student it is probably *very* important to your future that you finish and submit your assignments). We talk about the processes of writing in E2, but here we are trying to make a specific point which is that *the audience is important*.

The importance of the audience's perspective cannot be overemphasised. They are the people who will judge the value of your work (and they may be the people who control your future!). Know your audience; try to find out how they think, how they view the topic of your research, what their experience is of the relevant issues and how they are likely to react. If you can then incorporate this in your writing, you will avoid the boring, turgid documents with which some of us will be familiar.

Focusing on the needs and attitudes of the readers will not only help you to get your points across, but will also enable you to have a better understanding of your material; there is no better way to understand your own work than to try to make it understandable to others.

Example E1.1

Charles Darwin and *On the Origin of Species*

Background

Charles Darwin did his fieldwork on evolution between 1831 and 1836 on HMS *Beagle*'s second survey voyage which included much of the South American coastline, the Falkland Islands and the Galapagos Islands. He completed his theoretical work on evolution in about 1845 and wrote a draft of the final book at about the same time. However, he did not publish until 1859.

Why then did Darwin spend 28 years *not* telling the world about his discoveries?

It turns out that the main reason was that, at the time, the Christian Church's influence in Britain was very powerful and there was a risk that a theory such as Darwin's would be seen both as a challenge to the social order and as heresy by denying the role of God as designer and creator.

So why did he publish at all?

Really, it was Darwin's desire to get the recognition for his work. He became aware that other scientists were working with similar ideas (particularly Alfred Wallace who was working in Borneo) and there was a risk that he would not get credit for his original work.

So, he published – what is the point of the story?

The first point is obvious:

- If Darwin had not published, then we would not have known about evolutionary theories unless someone else made the same discovery.

The second point is more difficult:

- Darwin wrote his book to be read by the *scientific establishment* – the famous scientists of the day. It was not welcomed by all (particularly scientists with different opinions and little research experience) and, at its original price of 15 shillings (£0.75), it was beyond the reach of most people. There were reports of working-class people pooling their resources to buy copies. Darwin was angered by this and, eventually, managed to get the price of the much revised sixth edition reduced to 7 shillings and 6 pence (£0.38) which made it affordable to much of the population. As a result, the information was disseminated widely, and ordinary people began to express their opinion and acceptance of the theory.

The emphasis, then, is on the choice of *audience*. Darwin chose to make many alterations to the sixth edition with the result that it was more accessible to people. Coupled with the reduced price, more people could become familiar with the work.

Think about it . . .

The Black Report

The Black Report (Townsend and Davidson, 1982) was commissioned by the Labour Government in 1977 but did not report until April 1980 when a Conservative Government was in power. The findings of the report were not welcomed by the Conservatives. This was a major research project looking at inequalities in health and the publication of such a report would usually be marked by much publicity and the production of impressive documents. In this case only 260 copies of a duplicated typewritten document were released on the eve of the August Bank Holiday, presumably in an attempt to ensure the lowest possible publicity.

Eventually, the authors arranged publication of the report in 1982 by Penguin Books. It continues to sell many copies annually nearly 30 years later, and has been a major influence in the reorganisation of Britain's NHS.

1. Why do you think the government chose such an apparently low-key way to publish this important report?
2. Why do you think the authors chose a publisher that specialises in popular paperback books?
3. How did the idea of 'audience' impact on these decisions?

Audience and clarity

It is, therefore, very important that we produce something that our audience will understand. To some extent (and without being patronising) we make sure that we have written something in a language that they understand, with a clear, obvious structure (which, usually, we will have explained in our introduction and given 'signposts' throughout so that the reader – or listener – knows where he is) and with a clear meaning.

This notion of 'clarity' is important and is a good guide for our style. Our meaning must be clear to our audience and this means that we must have made a good estimate of our audience's

- *Reading level*: so we have 'pitched' our written English where they will understand it – most readers have had the annoying experience of 'clever' writing where one has to have the dictionary to hand while trying to understand confusing or over-complex word use
- *Previous knowledge*: so that we have explained everything we need to, but have assumed a basic level of understanding by the reader; this idea of previous knowledge also embraces whether to include graphs and charts or columns of numerical data (this will depend on the subject area too), and whether pictures enhance our document, for example.

Clarity is important. If our work is not clear, then our reader will quickly get bored. This has a couple of important implications, especially for written work:

1. If our audience is reading for pleasure or to try to get information, then they will stop.
2. If our audience is also assessing our work (as is often the case in education), then unclear work is unlikely to attract high marks.

Of course, this can extend to more than just the written and spoken word (**E3**) and your choice of the methods of presenting other data should also be influenced by your knowledge of the audience.

Your research

Audience

Before you start to write your research report, prepare your poster or write your dissertation, ask yourself a few questions:

- What do I know about my audience?
- What do *they* know about my topic?
- Do they have direct experience of the issues?
- How do I think they may react to my findings/conclusion?
- Do I think that they will understand complicated words/graphs? (Maybe they'd prefer a summary of the data rather than pages of figures?)
- Might they prefer graphics to words?

References and further reading

Crosswaite, C. and Curtice, L. (1994) *Disseminating Research Results: The Challenge of Bridging the Gap between Health Research and Health Action*, Oxford University Press.

Marriott, S. and Palmer, C. (2000) Disseminating healthcare information: getting the message across, *Quality in Health Care*, 9: 58–62.

Townsend, P. and Davidson, N. (1982) *Inequalities in Health: The Black Report*, Harmondsworth: Penguin.

CHAPTER E2
Writing for research
Reports and dissertations

Contents

In context

This chapter is about writing for research. It is aimed at students in further and higher education and its main purpose is to discuss how research writing differs from other student work and how best to go about it. You should read this chapter in conjunction with **E1** and **E3**, since some of the issues are similar.

PART E: Data presentation and reports

E1: The importance of audience

▶ **E2: Writing for research: reports and dissertations**

E3: Data presentation

E4: Dissemination and further research

We do not plan to tell you how to write 'essays' here, although there is some useful information to help you with that, because it would fill a book on its own; this is about writing up your research project as a report, extended essay or dissertation. (There are some useful books on 'general' academic writing listed at the end of the chapter.)

We hope that this chapter will make it clear that there is a difference between a *report* and a *dissertation*. You need to remember that these are not the same, even though they can look similar.

If you try to read this chapter as if it was a chapter in a novel, you'll find it a bit repetitive; we think the best way to approach it is to read the section on the task that you are undertaking and follow the links to anything else that you need.

Why do we write?

We write for a variety of reasons. The basic purpose of writing is communication and, in further and higher education, writing is quite a specialised form of communication that fulfils some specific purposes. These are the most important:

- *Sharing information*: the basic purpose of communication;
- *Measuring progress*: your writing is used by your tutors to establish how much progress you are making in specific areas;
- *Enhancing your understanding and expression*: writing is a learning process that encourages you to express ideas and concepts in your own words;
- *Assessment*: your essays and other written work are assessed by the teaching staff to see whether you have achieved a sufficient mark to pass a course.

What does writing do?

Writing is a specialised form of communication. It is designed to make sure that another person (who understands the basic 'code' that we use – *written language*) can understand what we want to tell them. Writing has some important features:

- It is fixed: that is, once the writing is completed and out of the hands of the author, it cannot be changed.
- It is relatively permanent: this means that the reader can look at the content on more than one occasion.
- However, it is remote from the author: the reader cannot ask questions if something is not clear.
- It enables the writer to include information that cannot always be done with other presentation methods (for example, you can include tables, charts, pictures and references).
- It can be culturally specific: even if someone can read your language it does not mean that they share your view and understanding of how the world works.

The process of writing

Academic writing is, usually, a complex process that includes a number of different dimensions. It is rarely the case that you can sit down at your computer and write your report or other document in one go. There are many reasons for this which will depend on the nature of your project and we have tried to set them out below.

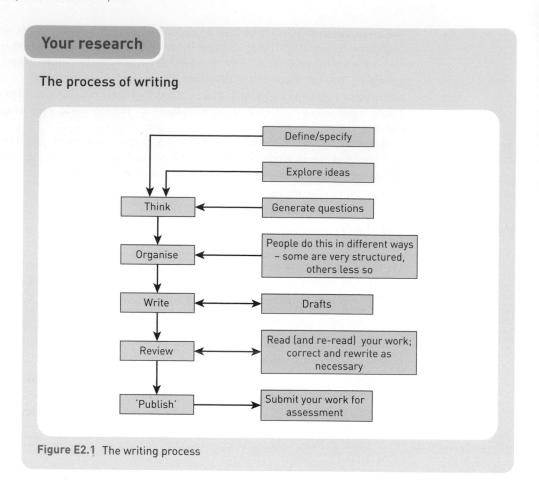

Your research

The process of writing

Figure E2.1 The writing process

Planning and structure

All academic writing starts with the same thing – *planning*. We cannot over emphasise how important this is. Everyone in education who assesses student work will know the joy of reading a document that has been planned and the dejection of reading one that has not.

Planning performs a number of different functions: for example, it tells you what you know about the topic (and, by implication, what you do not). It probably shows you, for example, how complete your literature review is or whether your research has generated the information you need to reach a conclusion.

Everybody plans differently, so we have not tried to tell you how this should be done (you must decide what works best for you), but we have tried to make some suggestions and demonstrate the things that will be a part of most plans.

At its most basic, a plan will set out the purpose of the document and break it down into different areas. You might start out by noting that your work comprises three main sections: an introduction, the main body and a conclusion. In fact this is too simple for almost all research writing, and it is much more likely that your plan will be quite detailed and might include a list of headings such as:

- Introduction
- Literature Review
- Methodology
- Findings
- Discussion
- Conclusion

- Appendices
- References
- Personal Timetable (if you want to, so that you can stay 'on track').

The detail of the planning process for a research paper is very similar to that for any essay so you should make sure that your plan gives you enough detail to write the finished work and that you do not forget the obvious things like the following:

- Have you thought about your audience?
- Has your paper got a proper introduction and conclusion?
- Have you made it clear what you are doing?
- Have you defined key terms?
- Have you included signposts to indicate what takes place in different sections?
- Is your literature review sufficiently comprehensive and critical (see **B2**)?
- Have you established a line of argument? Does your argument follow a logical sequence?
- Have you included enough information?

'Rules' for writing

Although this chapter is not just about writing technique, we think that there are some things that need to be emphasised because they are important in a variety of ways. These are things that, done well, make a report or dissertation a pleasure to read; done badly, they devalue the work and make it difficult to read.

Grammar

Grammar
The 'rules' that control the way that language is structured and, in the case of writing, govern the use of punctuation and syntax so that the writer's meaning will be clear to the reader.

You should aim to write **grammatically** and to use proper punctuation. This section will not give you instruction on the use of punctuation marks or proper sentence construction because these are things that need whole books of their own. There are a number of books listed under References and further reading at the end of the chapter that do an excellent job of this and most are not too stuffy – some are actually fun to read! However, we do want to set out a few things that are important in research writing. We've called them 'rules', but we don't really mean that they are inflexible and must always be applied in a particular way; perhaps calling them 'guidelines' would be better (see below).

The use of language

Choice of words

You need to choose the words you use with care. In particular, don't use long words just for the sake of it – it doesn't make you sound clever and can lead you into difficulties. There's a verbal balancing act here: you need to use the appropriate vocabulary and correct terminology for your subject, but you must strive not to confuse your reader (or yourself) unnecessarily.

In the same way, you should not use *jargon*, which the *Oxford English Dictionary* rather wonderfully defines as:

Applied contemptuously to any mode of speech abounding in unfamiliar terms, or peculiar to a particular set of persons, as the language of scholars or philosophers, the terminology of a science or art, or the cant of a class, sect, trade, or profession. (OED)

or technical terms that will not be understood by your readers.

You should also, to some extent, avoid abbreviations. It is technically correct to define them on their first use in a document and then use the abbreviations, e.g. the National Health Service (NHS), but if you are not careful, the end result can be a page that is so cryptic it defies translation! Likewise, long-windedness and pomposity should be avoided.

The use of symbols (e.g., %, £, €) should not be such a problem – the issue here, as it is so often, is to be *consistent*.

Numbers

The use of numbers in academic writing can be a bit perplexing; some authorities say to use digits (i.e., 1, 2, 3, etc.) for all numbers *unless* it is the first word of a sentence. Others say to use words when the number is less than 10 and after that to use digits; still others to use words (or digits) at all times. Our suggestion is that:

1. You check that there are no special rules for the work you are doing – if there are, obey them.

2. Choose a *consistent* system that *you* like, and stick to it.

Spelling

In these days of computer spell-checkers you might think that spelling mistakes are a thing of the past. Unfortunately, this isn't the case. It does mean, however, that spelling mistakes in word-processed work are completely unacceptable since it indicates (or at least many assessors will assume) that you couldn't be bothered to check your work (see section on drafting below).

One common trap is that (of course) spell-checkers can't tell if you've used the wrong word, provided that the word[1] is spelt correctly. It also leads us into a brief look at words that sound the same, but mean something different (called *homophones*). Take care and look at the 'Think about it . . .' box below.

Think about it . . .

Some words that sound the same (*homophones*) and commonly cause confusion

accept	except	
affect	effect	
cite	sight	site
compère	compare	
draft	draught	
hear	here	
guest	guessed	
knot	not	
passed	past	
principal	principle	
pole	poll	
right	rite	write
their	there	they're
Wales	wails	whales
where	wear	were
whether	weather	
who's	whose	
your	you're	

---

[1] Actually, Microsoft's Word™ 2007 tries to do this. When spelling and grammar are checked it will often indicate when a wrong (but correctly spelled) word has been used.

Legibility and presentation

Again, you might think that problems with legibility went away with pens and ink. Not so: some printers – especially if they're not well maintained – can produce pale print or smeared pages. Equally, some paper is not suitable for inkjet printers.

You should be proud of the way that your work is presented and put some effort into doing it well. This starts with reading the requirements for your submission. (Some universities will require a dissertation, for example, to be hard-bound using a service they provide – and you usually pay for! Others will not specify the way in which work should be presented.) There may be rules about the use of headers and footers too. A bit of thought and effort will often be well repaid. For instance:

- Decide which font is most legible for your work and stick to it (remember that some institutions require the use of specific fonts).

- Look at each page in 'print layout view' on your computer before you print it. Does it look good? Are diagrams the right size? Is there too much or too little white space around the print? Are things where you expect them to be? (Tables are notorious for seeming to move around on their own.) Have titles stayed with the relevant paragraphs?

- If you have a colour printer, have you used it to your advantage? Do pages look dignified and academic (if that's what you are aiming for) or do they remind you of a comic strip?

- Make sure that pages are numbered and that you present your work with the pages in the correct order – you'd be surprised how often this doesn't happen.

- Make sure that you have followed your institution's rules about referencing.

Verb tenses, person and voice

Keep tenses congruent. Don't mix past, present and future in the same sentence or paragraph. This can be quite difficult when writing about research, because the project usually takes place over a significant length of time and the things that we wrote in the *future* tense in the research proposal (B6) that we were planning to do have all been completed and are suddenly *past* tense.

What 'person' should we write in? In academia, we usually avoid writing in the *first person* (I, we) and *second person* (you) and instead use 'one' – technically, this is *third person singular*, but in practice it is used to replace first person.

There are a number of instances where it is useful to write in the first person, for example, when reflecting on your role as the researcher, but they will probably be few and far between in research writing. You should be guided by your supervisor or tutor.

Lastly, we have a choice of whether to write in the 'active' or 'passive' voices. For example:

It was for the benefit of disabled people that the law was enacted. (passive)
Parliament created the law to help disabled people. (active)

Which voice you use will depend on several factors: your discipline might expect you to write in the passive or you might want your work to feel more dynamic and therefore choose the active voice. There is no real rule, but we want you to be aware that there is a choice to be made.

Language that embraces diversity

Your writing should take account of social divisions, so that it is not – for example – sexist or homophobic. There are a number of guides produced by professional associations that can help you: the guide to anti-racist language by the British Sociological Association (1992) is very useful, for example.

The way in which writers in the social sciences have referred to people has changed over time. Cuba and Cocking (1997: 127) note that much of the older work in social science is characterised by the generic use of 'man'. This presents difficulties for contemporary readers. In your own writing, ensure that you do not place a similar burden on your readers. See the 'Think about it . . .' box on p. 440.

> ### Think about it . . .
> #### Embracing diversity in writing
>
> All of the words or phrases below fail to embrace diversity and equality. Try to rewrite them so that they are more accurate (our suggestions are at the end of the chapter).
>
> **1.** The man in the street
> **2.** Masterful
> **3.** Policeman
> **4.** American
> **5.** Forefathers
> **6.** Indian
> **7.** Man-made.

Word limits

Academic writing at all levels is usually constrained by word limits. This is true of writing articles for international journals as well as for the first essays we write at university or college. Failure to observe a word limit will often result in some sanction being applied to your work, usually a reduction in the final mark. In these days of word processors, 'creative' thinking about word limits or the use of the 'approximate' word count is no longer acceptable and honesty is the rule. Usually this means that some things that are relevant in our writing must be omitted and often this means that we cannot tell 'the whole story', but must edit it in some way. This is full of potential problems, but will usually mean that we must assume that the reader has some basic knowledge of our topic. As the author, you must take responsibility for what you include and exclude. It also means that you should be learning to write *concisely*.

Drafting

Drafting is the next stage in writing your dissertation or report. You may go through a series of drafts, but at the least you should aim to produce a *first draft* and a *final draft*. It is important to remember that time spent drafting (rather like time spent planning) is never wasted. It will result in a better document with few 'silly' mistakes.

The first draft

The first draft should be thought of as the detailed outline of the document you need to produce. It should include:

- an *introduction* (though at this stage, this might be very basic, since it is often good practice to write your final introduction when all the other writing is done because you can then be sure that your work delivers what it promises);
- a *conclusion*, though again this might be quite basic;
- your structure (for a report or dissertation, this would be a list of chapter headings);
- all the points you need to make – if possible, in the order you need to make them.

But a first draft is not intended to be the final wording. Your English may be clumsy at the moment, or you may have only written a series of notes that need to be refined into argument, discussion and paragraphs.

> ### Your research
>
> ### 'Rules' for drafting
>
> **DO**
>
> - Begin each section with a sentence that states its purpose.
> - Deal with one key point in each section.
> - Deal with sub-points in individual paragraphs.
> - Illustrate with examples and quotations and reference appropriately.
> - Beware of plagiarism!
> - Be aware of the word limit.
>
> **DON'T**
>
> - Make sections too complex – stick to one issue.
> - Leap from idea to idea: use linking sentences and paragraphs.
> - Make assertions without evidence.
> - Introduce new material in the conclusion.

Revise the draft

As you develop your work, the first draft will become more detailed and the chapters or sections will become complete. Do not hesitate to read your work often (and, if you can, persuade others to do so too) and to rewrite as necessary.

Different people work through this stage in a variety of ways and there can be no fixed rule about the 'best' way to do it: try to develop a process that works for you. However, if you try to bear in mind that you are aiming for a concise (remember the word limit) text that still tells as much of the story as you need, then you will be on the right lines.

Always try to allow yourself plenty of time for this redrafting stage. It isn't so much that the writing itself is time consuming, but rather that you need time away from your text so that it feels 'new' when you look at it again. There is a risk – which seems to have become greater with the use of computers – that we see in front of us what we expect to see rather than what is really there. So, take some time away – you probably have other work to do anyway. Come back refreshed and draft it again!

You should try to think about your style of writing all the time and compare it to other work that you have written and things that you have read. Is it as clear? As academic? Is your layout as good as it can be?

This process of revising your draft leads to the final stage which we call 'publishing' but, for most students, is really the submission of your work for assessment.

When writing is difficult

Sometimes it's really hard to write and getting past this can be difficult. It happens to professional authors who call it *writer's block*, so perhaps it isn't too surprising that it is a widespread

Table E2.1 When writing is difficult – problems and suggested solutions

When writing is difficult

Problem	Possible cause	Solution
Not enough time	Student life is demanding, and there's lots to do; the university/home/leisure balance is difficult	Time management Use some of your leisure time for writing Explain to family and friends that the project is important to you and train them to understand and not to make demands when you are not available
Difficulty with different styles of writing (usually academic)	Familiar only with the sort of writing used in school or work	Read lots of different styles Think about the style when you are reading so that you begin to understand both the style and the conventions associated with it
Not used to writing long pieces of work	More used to one-to-one or face-to-face communication Do not often have to write to argue or justify a position Unfamiliarity with English construction	Read and learn Write short pieces and develop techniques for linking them together to make long pieces Split the work up into sections of a size that you can handle

problem. Everyone has their own way of working, and because of this, different strategies work for different people. Some of the issues that arise can be dealt with fairly easily – others cannot (see Table E2.1).

If you have followed the 'rules' we set out above, then most of your problems will have gone away. You will be well prepared and you will have planned properly. Nevertheless, we think that the most difficult thing about writing is getting started. When you are faced with a blank computer screen (or piece of paper) it can sometimes feel quite daunting.

It isn't important what order you write different parts of your work in (so long as you can link them into a coherent whole at the end), so one strategy is simply to take the 'titles' of different sections from your plan (Introduction, Conclusion, etc.) and write them at the top of a series of blank pages. After this, it is just a question of 'filling in the blanks' which you do from your notes and thoughts. Of course, it still isn't easy, but it works for many people. If this strategy does not work for you, then you need to find something that does! Talk to your tutor and your peers and see what works for them; perhaps you can adapt it for your use.

Whatever you do, try to manage your time. If you don't, then you will always be trying to catch up which isn't usually very productive.

Reports

You're likely to write a lot of reports during your career. In a way, all reports are about research (or, at least, research findings).

Probably the first thing to establish is why to have a report. Reports are a little different from other sorts of writing that you may do at university or college. Although they have a very clear structure that is, superficially at least, very like an essay, their purpose is quite specialised. The most important purpose of a report is that it is supposed to convey information to your reader as quickly as possible and in the most appropriate format.

Why have a report?

Reports may be written for many reasons. They may, for example, be intended to:

- Inform
- Persuade
- Recommend
- Motivate
- Impress
- Prompt debate (or play a part in it)
- Record
- Instruct.

They may also be trying to do more complex things such as change attitudes. (These factors are not mutually exclusive; a report may be multi-functional.)

What's the most important thing about writing a report?

It is always *the audience*! That may sound as though the content of the report does not matter, but of course it does. However, if the reader doesn't understand the report or the message isn't properly targeted, then it's a waste of time!

What makes a good report?

A report should be:

- *Brief.* Something that looks easy to read will be well received. *But* the length must be appropriate for the task. Make it *succinct*.
- *Clear.* The 'audience' must be able to understand it (it must use appropriate language and be clearly structured – a report shouldn't make you feel stupid).
- *Precise.* It should say what it needs to – and no more.
- *Simple.* It should avoid *unnecessary* complexity.
- *Well structured.* So that it proceeds logically through a sequence that is clear and is a sensible way of dealing with the message.
- *Descriptive.* If you need to 'paint a picture' (and many reports do), it must be in a way that gets the 'pictures' over to your audience.
- *Planned.* (and drafted, and redrafted).

All these factors work together to make a report easier to read – if you can also make it clear that you've spent time and effort in making the reader's job easier, so much the better.

Your research

Planning your report

1. List the people who are likely to read your report.
2. List what you think each one expects of the report.
3. Can you accomplish this in one document?

The readers' perspective

The importance of the readers' perspective cannot be overemphasised. They are the people who will judge the value of your report (and they may also be the people who control your funding or your future!). Try to find out how they think, how they view the topic of the report, what their experience is of the relevant issues and how they are likely to react. If you can then incorporate this in your writing, you will avoid the boring, turgid documents with which we are all so familiar.

Focusing on the needs and attitudes of the readers will not only get your points across, but will also enable you to have a better understanding of your material; there is no better way to understand your own work than to try to make it understandable to others.

Your research

Questions about your report

Fill in the blanks in this exercise and use the information to help structure your report.

1. What kind of people are your audience? (e.g. male/female, young/old, managers/ practitioners, etc.)

    _____

2. How well do you know them?

    _____

3. Are they particularly numerate (accountants, for example) or do they prefer words and pictures (maybe teachers)?

    _____

4. What do they know about the issue you are reporting on?

    _____

5. Are they likely to welcome your report?

    _____

6. Do they have personal involvement (and, maybe, axes to grind)?

    _____

7. How important is the report to them?

    _____

8. Is your report likely to cause them to take action or make decisions?

    _____

If you can provide answers to these questions, then you know a lot about the most important part of your report – your audience!

Who is your report audience?

We suggest below a short list of questions for you to consider when compiling your report:

1. *Who is the report for (who is your audience)?* Usually, the answer to this is 'the people who commissioned me (paid!) to create this report' or, at university, 'the person who has set

the assignment and will mark my work'. However, we hope that you will give some detailed consideration to the issues of audience presented here and elsewhere in this book.

2. *Is the audience a homogeneous group or must you meet multiple needs?* Audiences are rarely composed of groups of people who will respond in the same way as each other. Try to take this into consideration with the way that you design your report. For instance, will your audience respond well to charts and graphs or would they rather have tables of figures? Maybe you will need both!

3. *Why does the audience want your report?* If you've been asked to produce a report, then it's very likely that whoever asked wants the information for some specific purpose. Try to make sure that you understand that need and that you completely understand any instructions or briefing.

4. *What sort of things do they want to hear? What will they **not** want to hear?* Nobody likes getting bad news. Unfortunately, that might be what you are presenting. You will need to consider carefully how to 'pitch' your report so that it will be acceptable (suggesting, for example, that the chancellor of your university is to blame for poor results is unlikely to be well received, even if true!).

5. *How much detail is required?* Reports are summaries (though they sometimes contain all the data). You need to decide how much detail will be useful to your audience when they are making their decision on the future or whatever they want to do (see item 3 above).

Report structure

Like many pieces of writing, a report only has three sections:

1. Beginning
2. Middle
3. End.

Of course, this is an oversimplification, but it can be useful to guide the basic structure.

Example E2.1

How to structure a report

Beginning	Where we are now
Middle	1. Literature, methods, findings, etc.
	2. Different possibilities for the future
End	Conclusion/recommendation

Figure E2.2 Report structure

The 'beginning' is simply about an accurate description of the background/context for the report. You may need to explain why the report is being undertaken now or why the issue is important enough to be discussed. You will certainly need to explain who has commissioned the report and for what purpose. Lastly, you will need to describe the current situation that you are reporting on.

The 'middle' is about the *present* and arises from the current situation. For example, your report might say: 'if this situation persists, then the company will be bankrupt by December and we will all be out of a job'. This would, of course, be based on some sort of review of the current situation – probably based on literature or research about the present. It would go on to explain how you planned to gather the information for the rest of the report.

The 'middle' is about the *future*. It will present the results of your research and analysis on the future and will describe/argue possible courses of action (and will list their good and bad features).

The 'end' should set out the 'best' option available and justify its choice. Some reports will need to set out a number of options or a sequence of options. This should also address what is to be done, who needs to do it and what it will require in terms of resources.

As we said above, a report is more or less the same structure as any other piece of formal writing. However, there are a couple of differences which are worth highlighting.

The abstract

Reports (almost) always begin with an abstract which can be thought of as a brief summary of the entire report. Sometimes, especially for government reports, this is known as an 'executive summary'. The abstract condenses the report into about 200 words and should give the reader enough detail to know what the report has done and what it recommends.

The conclusion

Almost always, the conclusion of a report will be more than the summary that we are used to finding at the end of an essay. Most likely, there will be a recommendation (maybe for future action, policy changes, increases in expenditure, etc.) and some justification for the choice of this recommendation. This can be thought of as three separate functions:

1. reaching and presenting the conclusion and/or recommendations;
2. summarising the content (and *not* introducing new material);
3. ending positively (if you can) or, at least, with authority rather than just fading gently away into the distance . . .

When writing your conclusion, there are a couple of traps that you can fall into which are easily avoided:

- *The false ending.* When you say 'finally' or 'in conclusion' – mean it! Few things are more frustrating than reports that are not clear about this.
- *Extending the structure.* Don't go beyond what you said was going to happen in the introduction – this will often be repetition or digression.

The appendices

Most reports will have these. They are repositories for information that is important, but not important enough to be in the main body of the report. For example, if data has been presented graphically, it is likely that the original numeric data will be included as an appendix. Sometimes there will be other things, perhaps questionnaires or explanatory documents. However, the appendices are *not* the receptacle for all the information that you would like to include if there was no word limit. After all, your report should be understandable *without* the appendices.

If you do use appendices, make sure there are appropriate references to them in the text.

Presenting your report

You may have to give a presentation of your report, sometimes at the same time as you deliver it, sometimes later. If your report is to gain acceptance (and this can be thought of as as gaining a good mark for an assessment), then you need to bear a couple of things in mind. When you are reading your report through, but before you send it to whoever will read it, make sure that you:

- *Provide proof.* Explain how you came to your findings and how you are justifying any recommendations or proposals that you are making. It won't be enough to explain that you *believe* something or to imply that your opinion is sufficient. Don't forget that there will often be statistics or findings from other sources that may corroborate your work.

- *Anticipate objections.* Many (maybe most) reports have negative as well as positive findings. Make sure that you have given these proper attention and that you are ready to answer questions on them if the need arises. If you can (and your report format allows it), try to include these answers in the original report.

Your research

How to structure your report

- Try to ensure that your report has a **logical structure**. Try to keep your report as simple as you can (bearing in mind the complexity of the topic and the nature of the audience). Be obvious with the structure. Be chronological if appropriate.
- Use **road mapping**. Make sure you tell your readers where your report is going (and why).
- Use **headings**. The use of headings (and sub-headings) in reports is crucial. They tell the reader where he is and help to break the report into manageable sections that should make it clearer and easier to understand.
- Use **appropriate language** – important at all stages.
- Use **graphics** – using pictures/tables/illustrations/boxes (as well as bold, bigger fonts, etc.) promotes clarity, but also breaks up the text and makes it easier to understand.

Dissertations

What is a dissertation?

When we talk about a dissertation in this book, we specifically mean a dissertation based on research. We have not dealt with the extended essay separately, because they are very similar.

Whatever you do (or are required to do), make sure that you read and understand the rules imposed by your college or university before you start.

It is probably best to think of a dissertation as an in-depth study of any social science (feel free to enter your own discipline here) issue or topic. However, the choice of the issue to study can be a problem for the student. You won't be on your own, though – your college or university will offer you some supervision (we talk about this later). We do recommend that you choose an issue where the study will be manageable and will be likely to keep you interested throughout the year.

How to choose a dissertation topic

It isn't possible for us to list all the potential topics that social science students might choose to study for their dissertations: in any event, it would change from year to year as different issues become topical. What we want to suggest is that dissertations fall into a number of different classifications, no matter what *discipline area* they belong to (Sociology, Political Science, Social Policy, etc.), for example:

- **Historical**
- **Theoretical**
- **Political** (in the sense of national/international politics, rather than of political science which would be the discipline area)
- **National**
- **International/comparative/global**
- **Contemporary debate**
- **Local.**

This classification is really a little too simplistic, because it is possible that a dissertation could belong to more than one category: we think it is helpful, though.

Talking to others can also be helpful at this stage. It can be a useful process to tell people what interests you about your project – if it interests them, then maybe it will be a good choice! In any event, articulating your thought processes in a way that someone else can understand is always useful.

'Doing' your dissertation

It's always difficult to start a project. The first stage is having the idea, but then you must decide how best to proceed.

Most people will start by reading about their subject (**B2**) and that is often useful but, really, you need to have some sense of direction or you may not make the best use of your time.

Another way to begin is to start to formulate your research question. Having a research question is vital for a successful dissertation. Of course, at the beginning the question will probably be a bit general, even vague. Perhaps you want to research about 'working-class women in education'. It's an interesting topic, but you need to be able to ask something more detailed and explicit about it (bearing in mind that an undergraduate dissertation can only have a limited scope and you only have a relatively short time to do it all). So, you will need to develop your research question (**A4**) so that:

1. It is relevant to what you want to find out.
2. It will be manageable: i.e. you can get access to your research population, there is a literature that you can access, there are no insurmountable ethical problems, you know enough about appropriate methodologies, etc. (**Parts A**, **B**, **C** and **D**).
3. It is not too challenging. You are writing a dissertation, not a PhD thesis. No matter how hard you try, you will not be able to tell the full story (see 'word limits' above) of your topic (actually, most PhDs don't manage to either).
4. It can be answered (in the time and with the resources you have available). Be careful not to underestimate the time it will take you to do this work; we suggest that you create a timetable (working back from the submission date) and do your best to stick to it. Don't forget that you'll have other work to do!

Choosing methodology/methods

The choice of methodology and data collection methods will be guided by the nature of your research question (**B4**).

Supervision

Most universities and colleges allocate supervisors for dissertations. This is normally a member of the academic staff who has an interest or expertise in your chosen area. You should make as much use of your supervisor as you are allowed to because they are a useful expert resource.

Their role is to:

- advise you on the feasibility of your project and assist you in choosing an appropriate methodology;
- guide you towards appropriate literature;
- advise you on the design of your data collection and analysis strategies;
- discuss the structure and presentation of the dissertation with you;
- comment on your draft chapters as you write them (the way in which this takes place will depend on your institution: some will only look at a completed draft, others only at selected chapters; check the rules for your institution).

The dissertation structure

- **Preliminaries**
  - **Title page:** which should include:
    - title of the dissertation
    - student identification (might be your student number or name; check the regulations for your dissertation)
    - your degree programme (if appropriate)
    - your department/school/faculty/college
    - the year.
  - **The abstract:** which is usually about 250 words (but check the rules for your dissertation) and should include:
    - information on the topic
    - information on what you have done to research it
    - key findings and conclusions.
  - **Acknowledgements** (usually optional): a chance to write a personal statement, maybe thanking those who have helped and supported you or saying why you decided to undertake this work.
  - **The contents**: this should be a detailed table of contents showing page numbers. It is usual to have separate pages of contents for figures and tables.
- **The main body of the dissertation**: exactly how this is organised will depend on the sort of project that you have done, particularly the sorts of literature you have used and the data that you have collected and analysed. We have set out below a 'typical' list of chapter headings:
  - **Introduction**: This will include details of the nature of your dissertation, the issues that you are addressing and a set of 'signposts' that tell the reader what is in each chapter.
  - **Literature Review**: See B2.

Your research

Don't forget the research question(s)!

At some point, you need to state your research questions clearly. Exactly where you do this is not always obvious and can be different for each dissertation. However, we strongly recommend that it is done before moving beyond this stage.

- **Methodology and methods**: A discussion and description (and justification of the choice) of the methodology and data collection methods; details of your population and sample; a discussion of the analysis strategy you will use for your data; a discussion of ethical issues.
- **Findings**: Basically, what you did in terms of research and what you found out. This can just be a presentation of data but might include some discussion. Can include charts and graphs, maybe pictures or even sound and video files.
- **Discussion**: What your findings mean.
- **Conclusion**: This is a chance for you to give the answer to your research question(s). You might also, for example, be saying how this answer can be used to make proposals for new policy or, perhaps, to instigate changes in practice or inform theory. However, this will depend on the nature of your project.
- **Appendices**: A collection of material that is relevant to your project, but is in a form that would be inappropriate (usually by being too long or too detailed) to include in the main body of the text. It is not a place for putting material that there wasn't room for in the main body! Typically, appendices might be:
  - sample questionnaires
  - sample consent forms
  - detailed tables of data (particularly if you have presented such data graphically elsewhere)
  - excerpts from policy documents
  - an example of collected data (maybe an interview transcript or a completed questionnaire)
  - anything else that *must* be included but was not suitable for the main body.
- **References**: A full list of all the references of the material that you have cited as well as the other material from which you have used ideas, but not quotes. Your institution will have a rule about which of the various referencing systems you must use. Make sure you understand it properly. (Some institutions differentiate between *references* and *bibliography,* some do not. Technically, 'references' are the quotations and other material that you actually cite in your work. The bibliography can be thought of as being all the other works that have informed your thinking, but have not been cited.)

❓ What is . . .

Referencing

Referencing has three main purposes:

1. It shows where you got your ideas and quotes, and thus demonstrates that you have not tried to pass off someone else's work as your own.
2. It allows the reader to follow up your ideas in more depth (if they want to) and to ascertain that you are using appropriate material.
3. It demonstrates that you have learnt how to use other people's work to develop your own ideas and answers.

Example E2.2

Referencing

All references do the same thing: they provide detailed information about where original (or *source*) material comes from. *All* references include the author's name, the date of publication, the title of the work, the place of publication and the publisher (sometimes, for example for journals, the page numbers will be included).

▶

There are a large number of different systems for referencing and you must use the one approved by your institution. However, by way of example, a reference in the Harvard system (our favourite) would look like this:

Deakin, N. Finer-Jones, C. and Matthews, B. (2004) *Welfare and the State: Critical Concepts in Political Science,* **London: Routledge.**

Assessment

Every university and college has a different way of assessing dissertations, but the information should be readily accessible to you. Make sure that you read it *before* you start writing so that you are not caught out by unusual requirements. Reading assessment guidelines is also a good way of seeing what is expected of you.

A final warning: plagiarism

plagiarism
Presenting someone else's work as if it was your own; copying; failing to reference or otherwise attribute the origin.

Plagiarism is, simply, using another person's work and presenting it as if it is your own (that is, without a reference or citation). It is, to say the least, frowned upon by universities and colleges and often carries heavy penalties if you are found out. (The increasing use of sophisticated software to detect plagiarism makes being caught more and more likely.)

However, plagiarism is not just about using someone else's words without acknowledging the source, but also includes (among other things – this is not a complete list):

- using previously published text 'word for word';
- closely paraphrasing the words of a text (usually a book, journal or lecture notes);
- cutting and pasting text from the internet;
- copying another student's work;
- using ideas you have read about, and not quoting their origin;
- using a nice phrase or quote that you have discovered or learnt somewhere, but not saying where;
- using pictures, graphs, diagrams, etc., that you have found (or downloaded) without permission or without acknowledging the source of the material.

Your research

Key points for reports

- Every good report has clear objectives.
- The readers' perspective is more important than the writer's.
- There must be a beginning, a middle and an end.
- There must be a clear, logical structure to the argument/discussion.
- It must be readable!
- Communication is inherently dangerous – think about communicating clearly.
- Your report will only have achieved its end if *you* are clear about its purpose.
- The *audience* is the most important thing!
- Don't write non-reports.

Think about it . . .
Concise language

Write something complex and wordy and then edit it into something simple and short that says the same thing.

Example E2.3

Is complex writing always the best?

(*Translations in brackets*)

1. It is my desire to congratulate you all on a task accomplished with success. (*Well done!*)

2. The operation of this equipment can be instigated by digital pressure on the appropriate push-button. (*Press to start*)

3. Please be aware that it is perilous to approach the periphery of the excavation. (*Danger! Keep back!*)

Think about it . . .
Embracing diversity in writing (suggested answers)

1. People in general

2. Domineering

3. Police officer

4. Remember there is North *and* South America

5. Ancestors

6. OK for people from India: for North America consider Native American (USA), First Peoples (Canada)

7. Manufactured, artificial.

Think about it . . .
Words that sound the same (homophones) exercise

Fill in the blanks by selecting one word from the pairs at the end of the sentence.

1. It was not clear _____ the conclusion was justified. [weather] [whether]

2. Many different activities had been carried out on this _____. [site] [sight] [cite]

3. The participants usually met in ①_____ homes where they discussed the ②_____ of the changes. ①[there] [their], ②[affect] [effect]

4. The college ①_____ told the students that ②_____ behaviour had been exemplary and they would be ③_____ to leave early. ①[Principle] [Principal] ②[their] [there] ③[aloud] [allowed]

5. In a fit of anger the teacher put his ①_____ aside and ②_____ the student outside ③_____ the ④_____ was cold, which had the desired ⑤_____ on him. ①[principles] [principals] ②[threw] [through] ③[where] [wear] ④[weather] [whether] ⑤[affect] [effect]

> ## Your research
>
> ### Research quality check: successful concise writing
>
> - Have you addressed the issues properly (or answered the question)?
> - Is your structure clear and coherent?
> - Have you used signposts?
> - Is your writing clear?
> - Is your grammar and spelling OK?
> - Is your style appropriate?
> - Have you remembered your audience?
> - Have you avoided jargon?
> - Have you been concise?
> - Have you edited and re-drafted?
> - Have you been careful with presentation?

References and further reading

Bell, J. and Opie, C. (2002) *Learning from Research: Getting More from your Data – A Guide for Students*, Buckingham: Open University Press.

Crème, P. and Lea, M.R. (2003) *Writing at University: A Guide for Students*, 2nd edn, Buckingham: Open University Press.

Cuba, L. and Cocking, J. (1997) *How to Write about the Social Sciences*, Harlow: Longman.

Cutts, M. (1995) *The Plain English Guide: How to Write Clearly and Communicate Better*, London: QPD.

Doherty, P. (2006) Problems with apostrophes, available online at www.eng-lang.co.uk/apostrophes.htm (accessed on 21 August 2009)

Fairburn, G.J. and Winch, C. (2000) *Reading, Writing and Reasoning: A Guide for Students*, 2nd edn, Buckingham: Open University Press.

Forsyth, P. (1997) *How to Be Better at Writing Reports and Proposals*, London: The Industrial Society.

Hartley, P. and Bruckman, C. G. (2002) *Business Communication*, London: Routledge.

Joseph, A. (1998) *Put It In Writing: Learn How to Write Clearly, Quickly and Persuasively*, New York: McGraw-Hill.

Lauchman, R. (1998) *Write for Results*, New York: Amacom New Media.

Marsen, S. (2003) *Professional Writing: The Complete Guide for Business, Industry & IT*, Basingstoke: Palgrave.

Murray, R. (2002) *How to Write a Thesis: A Guide for Students*, Buckingham: Open University Press.

Peck, J. and Coyle, M. (2005) *Write It Right: A Handbook for Students*, Basingstoke: Palgrave.

Shelton, J. H. (1994) *Handbook for Technical Writing*, Chicago: NTC Business Books.

Truss, L. (2003) *Eats, Shoots & Leaves: The Zero Tolerance Approach to Punctuation*, London: Profile Books.

Wade, S. (1996) *Studying for a Degree: How to Succeed as a Mature Student in Higher Education*, Plymouth: How To Books.

CHAPTER E3
Data presentation

Contents

In context

Data presentation techniques are important. While it is important to have 'done' your research, you need to think about how to communicate your conclusions to the rest of the world.

The first part of this chapter looks at presenting data graphically, but there are other examples throughout the book (see D3 or D9) and, if you look around, examples are everywhere from advertising to TV documentaries. The second part of this chapter discusses 'other' methods of presenting data and here we have focused on poster presentations and oral presentations, both of which are of increasing popularity both in academia and the outside world.

PART E: Data presentation and reports

    E1: The importance of audience

    E2: Writing for research: reports and dissertations

▶ **E3: Data presentation**

    E4: Dissemination and further research

What is data presentation?

It may seem obvious, but when we have carried out a piece of research, we need to make sure that our findings are available to interested parties. (Who those parties may be is a separate question which depends on a number of issues that we discuss elsewhere – see **E1**.)

Data can be presented in many different ways, a number of which are illustrated in this chapter. However, before going on to the practicalities, there is a question that we need to answer.

Why present data in different ways?

Of course, when we do research we understand our findings. We have been involved in the work since the beginning and what we say in our final document is, to us, blindingly obvious! Unfortunately, this may not be the case for the people that have to read our findings and, maybe, apply them to the real world. We think that the researcher has a duty to make sure that his results are intelligible to the people who need them, and this is the basis for presenting data and choosing the way in which it is presented.

We also think that the most important thing to consider when presenting your data is to take account of your 'audience'. By this, we mean the people who you need to understand your work: maybe because they are assessing and marking, or it maybe because they have employed you to do it. There are many possible reasons. Kumar (1996: 226) says:

> The main purpose in using data display techniques is to make the findings clear and easily understood. There are many ways of presenting the information. The choice of a particular method should be determined primarily by your impressions/knowledge of your likely readership's familiarity with the topic and with research and statistics. If your readers are likely to be familiar with 'reading' data, you can use complicated methods of data display, otherwise it is wise to keep to simple techniques.

So we need to think about how our data will be most easily and clearly understood (see the 'Think about it . . .' box on p. 464). Spreadsheets and tables of figures will probably be more than acceptable to statisticians, economists and accountants – they are their stock in trade, after all. However, it is less likely that they will be easily understood by, for example, social work managers, sociologists and cultural studies experts. Usually, the method we choose to present our data will have a specific purpose: one of the most common is to let us compare populations of different sizes.

There is a warning here as well, though: don't be tempted to swap accuracy for convenience or over-simplification. Usually, what we are doing in presenting data is making sure that our audience understands the findings. Some groups will benefit most from very graphical presentations (see Example E3.4 on p. 461), but others (and of course, they may also be members of the group that like pictures) will want to see the original data from which the image was derived. Often the best way to do this is to include the numerical data as an appendix, but each case must be treated on its own merits.

Processing data for presentation

Usually the 'raw' data that we collect in our research is not suitable for presentation. How data is collected and recorded will have been determined at the research design stage and, while some thought may have been given to the way that it will be presented in the final version, it is likely that no firm decisions will have been taken.

This section shows some basic methods of manipulating numerical data for presentation. The examples used here are very simple, since statistical data analysis is dealt with in D3.

Tables

Using a table (a *matrix*, if you need to sound posh) to present data is often an excellent idea. Carefully created, a table will help your audience to understand your results and (probably) to compare different parts of your findings.

There are some simple rules for tables:

- Tables need an appropriate title.
- Headings should be clear.
- Choose layouts suitable for your project.
- Usually there should be an acknowledgement of the source of the data, especially if you have re-worked someone else's findings.

Example E3.1

A table to compare percentages

Table E3.1 Male and female offenders (%)

Location	Male (%)	Female (%)
Birmingham	73	27
Nottingham	89	11
Total	100	100

Source: Imaginary Tables.

But tables can be used to present non-numerical data too, and can be simple or complex, depending on the job they are trying to do. For example, the table in Example E3.2 shows a way of presenting complex narrative analysis data in a way that allows the audience to compare some of the content of different stories.

Averages

Averages are a useful tool for summarising numeric data simply. There are several different ways of calculating averages, but for simplicity, the one we use here is the arithmetic **mean** – this is what people usually refer to when they say 'average' (see D3 for more detail).

Averages are really useful in presenting data because they allow us to compare groups (or events, or whatever) on the basis of the quantity of a characteristic that they possess, relative to their size.

mean
A statistical average calculated by totalling all the values and dividing by the number of cases.

Example E3.2

Narrative links to manner, tone and structure

Table E3.2 Narrative links to manner, tone and structure

Story	Descriptive	Submissive	Dominant	Resistant	Questioning	Assertive	Informing	Suppressive	Racist	Angry	Confused	Dominant manner, tone and structure
1	■			■								Descriptive/Resistant
2					■	■						Questioning/Assertive
3						■				■		Assertive/Angry
4	■			■								Descriptive/Resistant
5	■	■						■				Descriptive/Submissive/Suppressive
6				■		■				■		Resistant/Assertive/Angry
7		■							■		■	Submissive/Racist/Confused
8	■					■						Descriptive/Assertive
9	■	■										Descriptive/Submissive
10										■	■	Angry/Confused
11	■	■								■		Descriptive/Submissive/Angry
12			■	■		■						Dominant/Resistant/Assertive
13					■			■	■			Questioning/Suppressive/Racist
14	■			■		■						Descriptive/Resistant/Assertive
15					■					■		Questioning/Angry
16						■		■				Assertive/Suppressive
17			■				■	■	■			Dominant/Informing/Suppressive/Racist
18	■		■		■	■	■					Descriptive/Dominant/Questioning/Assertive/Informing
19			■			■	■					Dominant/Assertive/Informing
20	■				■							Descriptive/Questioning
Links	9	4	4	5	3	11	3	4	3	6	2	

Source: Imaginary Tables

We can calculate the mean by adding up all the *values* of the 'observations' (that is, the characteristic we are examining) and then dividing by the *number* of the observations.

Example E3.3

Calculating an average (arithmetic mean)

1. Take a group of five people. Their ages are: 21, 25, 19, 15 and 22 years.

2. Add these ages together (= 102).

3. Divide by the number of people (= 5).

4. Average (mean) = 20.4 years.

Warning!

The arithmetic mean is easily distorted by 'extreme values'. That is, an unusually large or small figure will have a disproportionate effect on the outcome. If we change our example above to 21, 25, 19, 15 and 69 years, then the average rises quite dramatically to 29.8 years. This doesn't have to be a problem, but it does show that there are issues that need consideration when processing even simple data for presentation!

Proportions and percentages

Proportions are the number of cases/observations/instances divided by the total number of instances. For example, if a social worker has a caseload of 70 offenders, 55 of which are male, the proportion of male offenders is:

$$55/70 = 0.785$$

Percentages are proportions multiplied by 100. Using the example above:

$$55/70 = 0.785 \times 100 = 78.5\%$$

Percentages and proportions are particularly useful because they allow the comparison of groups of different sizes.

Graphs and charts

Graphs and charts can be an excellent way of displaying data. Unfortunately, some of the mathematics and statistics that tell us how to produce charts and graphs can be quite complicated (D3).

However, since this is the twenty-first century, most of the graphs and charts you will ever use (and all the ones used in this chapter) can be easily produced using a PC. We discuss the software that can be used for this purpose in D9. However, most students will have access to Microsoft™ Excel which is a very versatile program and can be used for the production of most statistics and charts. Depending on the nature of your studies, you may need to use a dedicated statistical package such as SPSS.

When you use charts, the surface area of the columns or segments (or whatever graphical representation you have decided to use) should be directly *proportional* to the value of the original data. When you create a two-dimensional chart this is fine. However, if you decide to use the three-dimensional graphics facilities that are generously provided with most computer software, then this relationship is destroyed and, technically at least, your chart no longer represents the 'truth'. Sometimes, though, 3-D charts can be stunning so you may decide to use them anyway – just be careful!

Pie charts

Pie charts are a great way of presenting data, especially when comparing different sets of data and particularly to show percentages (think of a sliced cake).

A simple example might be to compare the number of arrests of men and women. Entered into Excel, this might look like:

	Male	Female
No. of arrests	27	14

This is a simple example, so it is quite easy for most people to see that the number of male arrests is far greater than those of females. Still, depending on your audience, it may be better to display the data graphically.

If we then create a **pie chart,** the data looks like this:

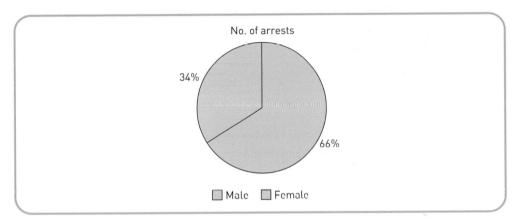

Figure E3.1 Data presented as a pie chart

We can then manipulate the chart in a number of ways, for example, we can change the colour of the 'slices' or their position. The title and legends can be changed too.

One thing that can be very useful is to 'explode' the pie to emphasise a particular point. For example:

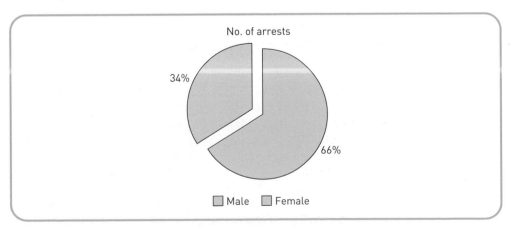

Figure E3.2 Data presented as an exploded pie chart

Column or bar charts

These are really the same type of chart, only their orientation is different. Technically, bar charts consist of horizontal bars and column charts of vertical columns whose surface area represents the original data. This differentiation is unimportant and they will be referred to here as bar charts.

Using the same data from the Excel table above, we can easily produce a simple bar chart which will let us compare the two sets of data and get a clear visual impression of the difference between them:

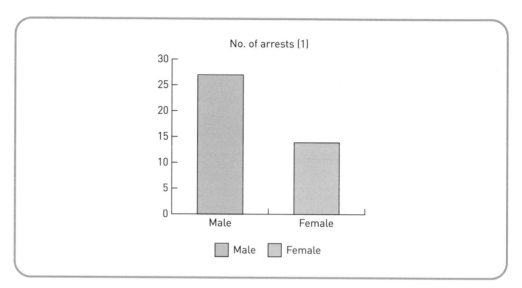

Figure E3.3 Data presented as a bar chart

Interestingly, we could also present this data in a way that makes it look quite different, but is still accurate:

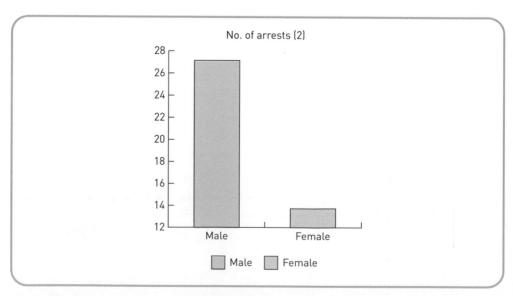

Figure E3.4 Data presented as a bar chart, with a manipulated vertical scale

This format (which is really a deception, much loved by tabloid newspapers) gives the visual impression that the difference between the two sets of data is enormous, yet the original data is the same. We have achieved this very easily; *the vertical scale of the chart has simply been manipulated so that it no longer starts at 0.*

This sort of manipulation is not possible with pie charts which always show the total value of the data.

Of course, bar charts don't have to be as formal as the ones above. Depending on the purpose of your research, you might want to present your data as images – see Example E3.4.

Example E3.4

Elections

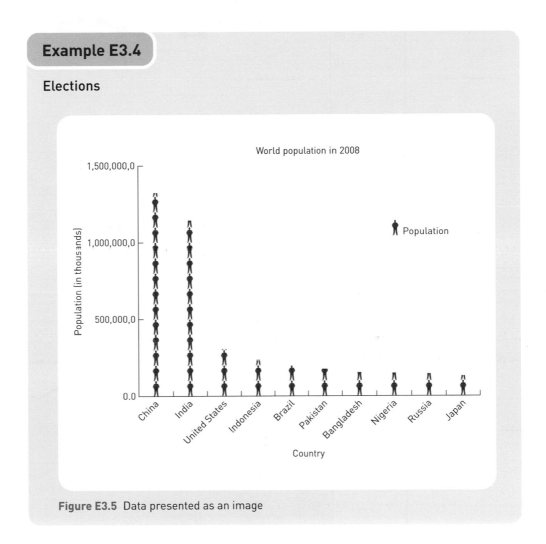

Figure E3.5 Data presented as an image

The opportunities for experimentation are limitless. The important thing, of course, it to remember to use images appropriately.

Other graphs

The two most useful graphs for general use are simple line graphs and area charts – see Figures E3.6 and E3.7.

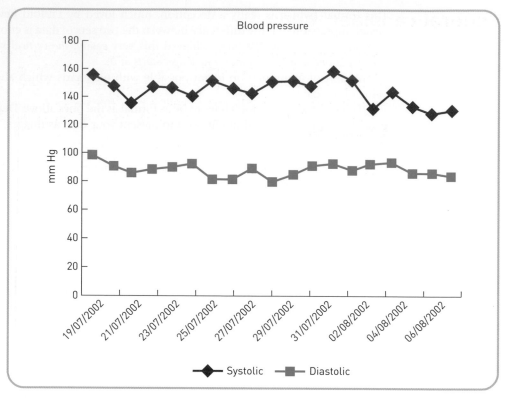

Figure E3.6 Data presented as a line graph

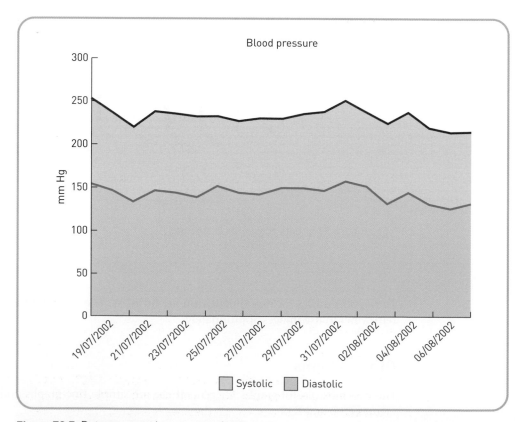

Figure E3.7 Data presented as an area chart

General considerations

There are a number of things that we should consider when we are presenting data which may not be obvious at first thought. As we said earlier, probably the most important thing to think about is the message that you want your audience to take away with them. This means that you must decide what emphasis to give your results.

One way to do this is to use different fonts, colours and backgrounds as we show in the following tables.

No. of Arrests	'White'	'Black'
0	5	8
1	6	1
2	16	4
3	9	1
4	3	4
5	1	9
6	0	1
19	0	1
Total	40	29

No. of Arrests	'White'	'Black'
0	5	8
1	6	1
2	16	4
3	9	1
4	3	4
5	1	9
6	0	1
19	0	1
Total	40	29

No. of Arrests	'White'	'Black'
0	5	8
1	6	1
2	16	4
3	9	1
4	3	4
5	1	9
6	0	1
19	0	1
Total	40	29

No. of Arrests	'White'	*'Black'*
0	5	8
1	6	1
2	16	4
3	9	1
4	3	4
5	1	9
6	0	1
19	0	1
Total	40	29

Your research

Important!

Do *not* use 3-D charts (pie charts, bar charts, etc.) if you need your presentation to be statistically accurate. The 3-D rendering destroys the important relationship between the original data and the area represented on the chart.

> **Think about it . . .**
>
> *There are three kinds of lies: lies, damn lies and statistics.*
>
> (Benjamin Disraeli, but also attributed to Mark Twain)
>
> We are assuming that, as academic researchers, you want your audience to have a full understanding of your results. However, this is not always the case and it is not impossible to present your data 'honestly' while managing to give a false impression about its impact. We illustrate this on p. 460.
>
> We are not advocating this behaviour, which seems to be typical of some tabloid newspapers, but we think that it is important that you understand how accurate results can be presented in a misleading manner!
>
> So, the basic rule is to make sure that graphs and charts start at 0 (unless you are deliberately trying to emphasise or de-emphasise the importance of your results).

Remember that the most important thing that you are doing is making sure that you have presented your data in a way that:

- is appropriate for your audience;
- is accurate;
- is clear.

Other presentation methods

Increasingly, researchers are asked to present their work in innovative ways. In part, this reflects the nature of society in the twenty-first century, where paper has become old-fashioned and electronic media have become of paramount importance. Most conferences encourage delegates to present their results and reports in visual ways and the most common of these is the poster presentation. The spoken word survives, though, perhaps because it is still a familiar and flexible medium and the oral presentation retains its importance. This section provides some straightforward recommendations for these sorts of presentations.

Poster presentations

Posters can be a great way to present your findings, though they are not without their problems; in particular there are three negative issues that should be considered when producing a poster:

1. posters are non-interactive;
2. posters can only represent your work at a single point in time;
3. posters can only carry a limited amount of information.

With this in mind, we set out below some issues to consider when designing and producing posters:

- Posters should grab the attention. You need to think about the composition of your audience (see **E1**) and find some way to make your poster attractive to them.

- Posters can only have a limited amount of information. It is a common mistake to try to cram too much text onto the poster, resulting in print that is too small to read from a distance. Posters full of text rarely appear interesting, so keep the word count as low as you can.

- Make sure that you use fonts that are easy to read (standard non-serif fonts such as Arial or Verdana are good choices). Think about how far away people will stand and make sure that the font size is large enough to read from a distance of at least 1 metre (probably not less than 18 pt).

- Think about colours. Choose the background colour of the board or card that forms your poster with care and use other colours with caution.

- If you are reporting research, it is usually a good idea to use the same sort of structure that you would in a report (i.e. introduction, methods, results/findings, conclusion). If you make sure that your poster tells a story (beginning, middle, end) then you are probably on the right track.

- Think carefully about the images you will use, be particularly careful to ensure that they are relevant to your work.

- Don't forget the obvious things like stating your name(s) and giving contact details.

- Make sure that the title is clear (big and bold!).

We have reproduced some examples of 'real' presentation posters below: ask yourself how well do they do their job.

Example E3.5

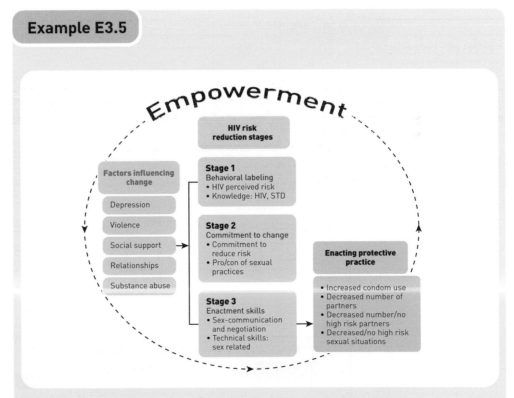

Figure E3.8 Poster (A)

Source: Center for Instructional Technology and Educational Support (CITES) (http://nursing.unc.edu/cites/presentation/example_graphic.jpg) University of North Carolina – Chapel Hill, School of Nursing. Reproduced with permission.

Figure E3.9 Poster (B)

Source: Center for Instructional Technology and Educational Support (CITES) (http://nursing.unc.edu/cites/ presentation/example_ncmap.jpg) University of North Carolina – Chapel Hill, School of Nursing. Reproduced with permission of Dr Jean Goeppinger.

Example E3.7

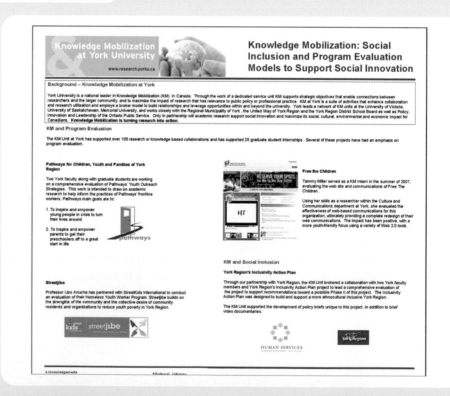

Figure E3.10 Poster (C)

Source: From Research Impact (http://researchimpact.files.wordpress.com/2009/05/april-30-poster-v3mj.jpg). Reproduced with permission.

Example E3.8

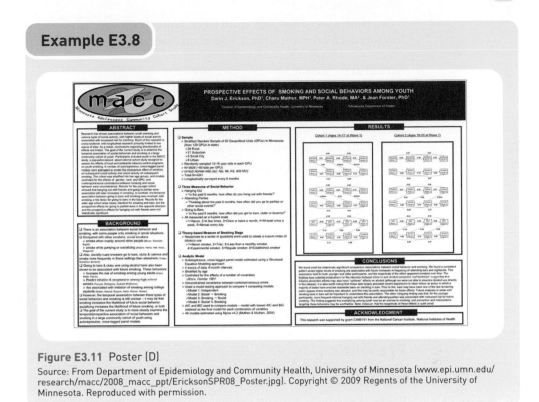

Figure E3.11 Poster (D)

Source: From Department of Epidemiology and Community Health, University of Minnesota (www.epi.umn.edu/research/macc/2008_macc_ppt/EricksonSPR08_Poster.jpg). Copyright © 2009 Regents of the University of Minnesota. Reproduced with permission.

Oral presentations

When students are required to make oral presentations, they are usually apprehensive. Although people vary in their abilities and confidence, hardly anybody likes the idea of being exposed to a potentially critical audience and many are shy. Of course, the first time is the worst and many presenters (and actors) believe that some degree of 'stage fright' is essential to a good performance.

The biggest difference between oral and other sorts of presentations is that it is a dynamic process. There is often a need to interact with the audience – many experienced presenters suggest that this is essential – and there is always the opportunity to change what you say.

Preparing

It is impossible to overemphasise the importance of proper preparation for oral presentations. You need to know your topic well and be clear on the order in which you will deliver your various points. However, you also need to understand the equipment that is available to you and this usually means a trip to the room where you will present, to make sure what facilities are present. We advise you to be careful about relying on technology (especially things like internet connections) as they are not always reliable.

To script or not to script?

Most people, for their first presentation at least, tend to write a script. This is, potentially, a good thing to do when you are starting out, because it offers you a 'safety net' in terms of what you want to say. The main difficulty with scripts is that they tend to restrict the presenter to the words on the paper which means that the presentation is often less dynamic than it could have been. However, it's a great way to prepare.

As your experience and confidence grow, you'll probably move away from a script towards detailed notes. This is a good method too.

Structure

Perhaps the most crucial part of any presentation is its structure. You must make sure that it has a beginning, a middle and an end. Some presenters say that there are three rules for the content of presentations:

1. Tell the audience what you're going to tell them (introduction).
2. Tell them (middle/main body).
3. Tell them what you've told them (conclusion).

If you follow these 'rules' as a guideline, your presentation will, at least, be clearly structured.

Rehearse

You *must* practise your presentation. Not only will this make sure that you are familiar with the content, but it will enable you to keep within your time limit as well as be more confident. There really is no substitute for practice!

Presenting

It's all an act . . .

Public speaking of any sort requires the speaker to present themselves in a particular way that will be attractive to the audience. We think that this is very similar to the craft of acting (as in 'stage fright' above). Speakers choose a persona that will facilitate their role (for example, you could choose to present yourself as an entertainer or an expert). Choose your role carefully, with due consideration for the task that you need to undertake and the setting in which you will present.

Audibility

If your audience can't hear you, then you have failed! If there are aids (radio microphones, for example), make sure beforehand that they work and that you are familiar with their use. At the start of your presentation, check that the people in the back row can hear you.

Clarity

It isn't enough, of course, just to be loud: you need to make sure that your speech is understandable as well. Most of us, when we're anxious, tend to speak too quickly – so try to compensate for this. Again, there is no substitute for rehearsal!

Rapport with your audience

Audiences expect you to be interested in them, and they deserve it – after all, they're listening to you. Individuals in the audience will want to think that you are paying attention to them and they will believe that this is the case if you make eye contact with them.

Eye contact and how to fake it!

Making eye contact with people in the audience can be a problem for the presenter. It is disheartening to see someone texting on their phone or reading a newspaper (though this happens to all presenters at some point). If you are a strong enough personality, by all means make eye contact with individuals (though beware as this can embarrass some people). For the rest of us, we suggest two strategies:

1. *Eyebrows*. Don't look your audience straight in the eye: instead, look at their eyebrows. This really works; they won't know the difference.

2. *Three seconds*. You can maintain 'real' eye contact, but in the three-second method you simply look individuals in the eye for three seconds and then move on to do the same to someone else. If you practise this, it is a reasonably easy technique that is not as distracting as it first sounds.

(Of course, it's a good idea to look at the whole audience from time to time.)

Humour and other tricks

We are not suggesting that you tell jokes for the sake of it (but in an emergency: *How many [insert name of football team] supporters does it take to change a light bulb? Both of them.*). However, people remember things better when they are involved, so making them laugh (or, as an alternative, making them angry) is likely to make your presentation more memorable. We would urge you to make sure that you don't introduce undue levity into serious topics.

Audience involvement

As mentioned above, people who are active are more likely to remember the content of your presentation, so involve them! Get them to participate in a vote or ask questions. Almost any sort of participation will have a positive effect.

Talk – don't read!

Presenters who read from their notes or script tend to be fairly boring, in part because they do not demonstrate that they are aware of their audience. Experienced presenters usually work from a few notes (or without notes at all!) but this takes time and the confidence that comes as experience grows. For the rest of us, there is nothing wrong with using notes, but try not to just read from them.

How to fake it!

There are a couple of strategies that can help (though practice is usually best):

- If you must use detailed notes or a script, then try printing them in a big font and leaving them on the table in front of you so that you can read them without having to hold them in front of your face.
- Put regular reminders in your notes to look at the audience!

Visual aids

Visual aids can be useful. These days, most people are familiar with Microsoft's flexible presentation software PowerPoint and whiteboards and flipcharts. These can be useful, but need to be used with restraint, so that they do not distract from the *oral* part of the presentation.

Appearance

Finally, just a note on 'dress codes'. While it is unlikely to matter how you present yourself for an undergraduate presentation, you should consider the 'messages' that your clothes convey. Some would argue that, for a serious subject, there is some benefit in dressing conservatively. It isn't our task to instruct you in how to dress, but we do think that you should take it into account in your planning stages.

Think about it . . .

Engleberg's '7 Ps' (principles of public presentation)

- **Purpose:** Why are you speaking? What do you want audience members to know, think, believe or do as a result of your presentation?
- **People:** Who is your audience? How do the characteristics, skills, opinions and behaviours of your audience affect your purpose?
- **Place:** Why are you speaking to this group now and in this place? How can you plan and adapt to the logistics of this place? How can you use visual aids to help you achieve your purpose?
- **Preparation:** Where and how can you find good ideas and information for your speech? How much and what kind of supporting materials do you need?
- **Planning:** Is there a natural order to the ideas and information you will use? What are the most effective ways to organise your speech in order to adapt it to the purpose, people, place, etc.?
- **Personality:** How do you become associated with your message in a positive way? What can you do to demonstrate your competence, charisma and character to the audience?
- **Performance:** What form of delivery is best suited to the purpose of your presentation? What delivery techniques will make your presentation more effective? How should you practice?

(Daly and Engleberg, 1994)

References and further reading

Daly, J. and Engleberg, I. (1994) *Presentations in Everyday Life: Strategies for Effective Speaking*, New York: Houghton Mifflin.

Flinn, C. (1999) Developing a poster presentation, George Mason University Writing Center, available at www.gmu.edu/departments/writingcenter/ppt/

Kumar, R. (1996) *Research Methodology*, London: Sage.

Murray, R., Thow, M. and Strachan, R. (1998) Visual literacy: designing and presenting a poster, *Physiotherapy*, 84(7): 319–27.

Tham, M. T. (1997) Poster presentation of research work, University of Newcastle upon Tyne, School of Chemical Engineering and Advanced Materials, available at http://lorien.ncl.ac.uk/ming/Dept/Tips/present/posters.htm

CHAPTER E4
Dissemination and further research

In context

This chapter discusses the ways in which you may choose to tell the world what your research project has achieved. It looks at dissemination as a part of research design (see **B3**) and as an ethical issue (see **A5**). In addition, various aspects of writing which are mentioned here are dealt with in more detail in **E1**, **E2** and **E3**. It looks at different methods of and media for dissemination and discusses the perpetual need for further research. Although this chapter is aimed, predominantly, at researchers who have completed their undergraduate studies, it also provides useful information for everyone.

PART E: Data presentation and reports

    E1: The importance of audience

    E2: Writing for research: reports and dissertations

    E3: Data presentation

▶ **E4: Dissemination and further research**

What is dissemination?

dissemination
The process of spreading the news of research findings so that they become known to a wider audience.

Most research makes a contribution to the body of available knowledge and it is important that findings and conclusions are not lost, but are made available to others. In some cases, researchers will have a duty (often a binding contractual obligation) to report their research to specific people or groups. This is often the case when the research has been funded by an external organisation. In some instances, the researcher will not be allowed to disseminate their work more widely; this is often the case with research undertaken for government departments or for work that is commercially sensitive.

Dissemination spreads the news of your findings to your selected audience (see below) or, perhaps, to the public in general.

Why disseminate?

As we said above, dissemination is an integral part of the research process, not just an after-thought, so it can be seen as the final stage of our project.

The purpose of dissemination is, simply, to make sure that our research results are available to those people who need to know (or who we think should know) about them. There are other purposes for dissemination too; for students, dissemination is usually the process of getting the completed project to the marker so that it can be assessed. For academics, it is usually about putting information into the public sphere so that it can be criticised and assessed by peers and colleagues (often as part of the process of publication).

Thus, dissemination is not without its risks. It could be that:

- your work does not achieve the mark that you hoped for;
- your research is not as original as you hoped;
- your peers do not think that the results are suitable for publication.

Of course, the opposite results are possible too!

Ethical issues

We look at the general relationship between ethics and social research in A5. However, some consideration needs to be given to the notion of dissemination and ethics.

Essentially, there is a potential issue here: should a researcher make a discovery that she believes would have an impact on the general public, what steps should be taken to ensure that the information is successfully shared? Sometimes the answer is simple: if your work is constrained by contractual obligations, then you must abide by them. If not, then the situation is more complex and will require further thought. We do not have the capacity to advise individuals here as each case will be different. However, we urge you to ensure that you consider this (potential) issue at an early stage of your research design (B3) so that it does not come as a surprise.

Deciding on a process

There are, essentially, two main stages in dissemination (so long as you are not forced to use particular processes by the instructions for your assignment or your research contract). These are: deciding on your audience; and deciding how and where to publish.

Deciding on an audience

(We talk about the importance of audience in E1.) The initial decision to make is to answer the questions *Who needs to know?* and *Who are you obliged to tell?* For a student submitting work for assessment, this is easily done as you will have instructions from your university or college telling you how to submit your work.

Table E4.1 Media and methods

Media	Method
Paper	Assignment
	Dissertation
	Report
	Journal article
	Poster
	Book
Electronic	eJournal
	Blog
	Website
	Radio/TV interview
Spoken word	Conference (often linked to paper)
	Seminar

However, if you are planning to let the wider world know about your research, here is a list of those who you might want to (or need to, or be obliged to) tell:

- Research sponsor/funder
- Manager/boss
- Policy-makers
- The public
- Future employer
- Peers/colleagues.

There is a group we have not spoken about before in this section to whom you may have an obligation to report your findings: these are your **research participants**. You may have agreed to share your findings with them in some way or you may just wish to involve them in the outcome. If this is the case, make sure that you have considered the ethical issues outlined in A5, particularly around confidentiality/anonymity and the need to protect your participants from harm.

How and where to 'publish'

If you plan to tell the world about your research, there are some decisions that must be made. The first of these is scale. Will you release your results locally, nationally or internationally (or, of course, some combination of these)?

If you are an undergraduate student, then the likelihood of your research being suitable for international publication is probably low (but you can never be sure: always take the advice of your tutor or supervisor) and it is likely that this issue will be of little concern to you. If you are interested, then we recommend that you consider the methods and media in Table E4.1 above.

Further research

There is *always* a need for more research on a topic. Nothing in the social sciences is ever completely described or explained and every research project will have some limitations or shortcomings.

Therefore your dissemination should indicate that, although you have completed what you set out to do, there is more to be done (by yourself or by others).

References and further reading

Nursing and Health Sciences, 8(1) (March), 2006.
Walker, D. (2001) *Heroes of Dissemination*, Swindon: ESRC.

GLOSSARY

analysis A process of working with the data to describe, discuss, interpret, evaluate and explain the data in terms of the research questions or hypothesis of the research project.

association or **associative relationship** The belief that there is a relationship between two concepts, but not necessarily that the relationship is causal.

asynchronous communication Communication between people where all the communicants are not, necessarily, in contact at the same moment in time.

atheoretical Refers to the absence of an underpinning theory or set of ideas.

axial coding In Grounded Theory data analysis, this is the second stage of coding data, and involves relating codes to each other.

bias Prejudice in favour, or against, a group individual, perspective, etc.

bivariate analysis The analysis of two variables together.

case study The study of a single entity, often a person, an organisation, a situation or a country, wherein the subject is explored in detail and great depth.

causal relationship The assertion that a change in 'A' causes a change in 'B'.

central tendency A statistical measure which summarises the data relating to one variable in one value, such as the mean, median or mode.

chat rooms Online discussion forums allowing synchronous or asynchronous communication.

check boxes On an electronic questionnaire, boxes that can be ticked by respondents in response to a question.

chi-squared A test that can be used to assess whether the difference between the mean values of two samples is statistically significant.

cluster sample A sample consisting of cases selected because of their proximity to one another.

code A way of identifying a specific answer or characteristic. It may be numeric or alphabetic.

coding The process of 'marking' or identifying data for later analysis.

cohort studies A type of longitudinal study which looks at a group of people of the same age and then gathers data about them at set points throughout their lives.

comparative research A research strategy used to study two or more subjects, often countries or cultures.

computer-mediated communication (CMC) The use of computers and the internet for communication between people.

concept An idea, abstraction or construct that encapsulates a way of describing, thinking about or labelling a social phenomenon. Some commonly used concepts in social research are ethnicity, health, family, employment, social class and lifestyle.

constant comparison Comparing data from different sources and from different places and times to support the analysis, along with the search for negative cases.

constructivism An ontological position which asserts that the social phenomena making up our social world are only real in the sense that they are constructed ideas which are continually being reviewed and reworked by those involved in them through social interaction and reflection.

content analysis A technique for examining the categories that the data comprise and condensing them into fewer numbers so that they are easier to understand.

control group In a research design, this is a group of people or materials that are the same as the experimental group in every way *except* the aspect of manipulation or change.

correlation coefficient A statistic that provides a measure of the strength and direction of a relationship between two ratio variables.

covert methods Methods of investigation in which participants are not aware that they are part of a research project, or are perhaps being observed in secret.

credibility The credibility (or believability) of the researcher's interpretations of the data she has gathered is tested by the analysis and interpretation of data being transparent, for example, by testing out the interpretation of the data with the research participants or by setting the interpretations alongside existing theory.

critical approach The way in which we use judgement (and other things such as experience or observation) to evaluate data, information, knowledge, etc. When we say 'critical' we do not mean it in a negative sense, we mean 'evaluate'.

critical realism A position that prioritises identifying structures or mechanisms that result in inequality or injustice and thus offers the opportunity for social change by changing or negating the structural mechanisms that are identified as having these impacts.

critical realist approach This usually means: collecting qualitative and/or quantitative data; revealing hidden structures and mechanisms; uncovering power relations and dominant ideologies; research that leads to action.

cross-sectional research design This research design includes more than one case, collects data at one particular time, and includes within its research participants groups of people or cases that can be compared.

cross-tabulation Presentation of data from two variables in one table, enabling the researcher to identify interesting similarities and differences within the data.

culture Culture is the set of social ideas and behaviours, customs and norms that constitute the way of life of people in a particular society.

cumulative frequency The arrangement of frequency data in categories that add up to 100 per cent.

data A collection of facts (or other information, such as opinions or values) which can be analysed and from which conclusions can be drawn.

data production The way in which social experiences, thoughts, feelings, behaviour and other social phenomena are expressed in words – thus making them available as social data. Individuals and groups can produce data by talking, writing and thinking – using language. This data can then be shared with others using a common language.

data saturation The idea that that there are ways in which the researcher can be sure that 'enough' research has been done.

decile One-tenth part of a sample or data set.

degrees of freedom A statistical measure used with chi-squared tests to calculate statistical significance.

dependability A measure of research quality, meaning, for example, that all data is included, and that no data is lost through unreliable audio recorders or inaccurate transcribers.

diagram Presentation of data or findings in a graphical format.

discourse Text, either spoken or written, in any medium.

discourse analysis A language-based or linguistic method of qualitative analysis.

dissemination The process of spreading the news of research findings so that they become known to a wider audience

distribution An arrangement of the values of a variable showing their observed frequency of occurrence.

documents Written records about people and things that are generated through the process of living. This includes things like film, audio tape or video, but excludes such things as oral histories.

drop-down lists On an electronic questionnaire, a set of possible answers presented as a list from which respondents select one or more applicable responses.

electronic questionnaire A questionnaire that is designed by the researcher, and completed by the participant, via computer-mediated communication (CMC).

epistemology The theory of knowledge and how we know things.

ethics Ethics can be throught of as a set of rules by which individuals and societies maintain moral standards in their lives.

ethnography A research strategy in which the researcher spends time (sometimes a number of years) immersed within the research context, seeing and hearing the data at first hand.

evaluation A research strategy that usually relates to an intervention or change that has been made, and whether the intervention has achieved the change or outcomes that were intended.

experimental group In a research design, the group of people or materials that are manipulated or changed in some way.

experimental research design This type of research assumes that the material or cases that are being studied can be manipulated by the researcher in some way so that some change or difference can be measured.

explanatory research Research that aims to explain why people experience or understand a social phenomenon in a particular way.

exploratory research Research that aims to discover what participants think is important about the research topic.

face to face Research methods which involve researcher and participant meeting in person.

filter questions Questions that are used to help people to find their own way through a questionnaire, and to select respondents according to whether a question is relevant to them.

focus group A data collection method that usually brings together a group of between 5 and 13 people who have something in common, which is connected to the research topic, to take part in a discussion on that topic, which is facilitated by the researcher.

frequency The number of times that each answer has been given, or that a particular outcome occurs.

generalisability A measure of research quality in which the researcher asks 'How far am I able to claim that the results or findings from my research are true for or relevant to the wider population or a different context?' (also known as transferability).

grammar The 'rules' that control the way that language is structured and, in the case of writing, govern the use of punctuation and syntax so that the writer's meaning will be clear to the reader.

grey literature Documents that are produced by (and for) organisations or companies.

Grounded Theory A systematic research approach in which theory is developed – or generated – from data.

harmonised data Data gathered from a range of different sources but which take account of the differences in the way the data has been collected, enabling researchers to access comparative data.

hidden or invisible population Groups who are not easy to identify.

histogram A chart showing the frequency of a ratio or interval variable where the values can be continuous; each bar in the histogram is centred around the mid point or value of the category it represents.

hypothesis A proposal or statement that is intended to explain observations or facts; it can be thought of as an 'informed guess' about the social world that, if true, would explain the phenomenon being researched.

inductive approach A data collection and analysis approach that works with the data in the form it is observed, heard and recorded.

informant interviews A type of interview in which the participant is in control of the interview, and is able to tell their own story, in their own way.

information Knowledge gained through study, experience or instruction: what we are told.

informed consent Making sure that the people who are going to take part in the research understand what they are consenting to participate in.

interpretivism An epistemological position that prioritises people's subjective interpretations and understandings of social phenomena and their own actions.

interpretivist approach This usually means that qualitative data is collected, with a focus on how people interpret the social world and social phenomena and enabling different perspectives to be explored.

interview A data collection method based around a conversation between two or more people. Interviews usually facilitate direct communication between two people, either face to face or at a distance via telephone or the internet and enable the interviewer to elicit information, feelings and opinions from the interviewee using questions and interactive dialogue.

interview guide An agenda for an interview with additional notes and features to aid the researcher.

keywords Terms that tell a database (such as a library catalogue, or a citations search engine) what to look for.

knowledge (1) Information about or awareness of something, an issue, a fact. (2) A understanding of a matter, a fact, an issue.

life history approach A data collection method where participants are asked to tell their life story focusing on common events.

longitudinal study A research design that enables the researcher to look at the same people or situations at key points in time and to consider how the changes over time have affected different groups of people.

macro theories Theories that attempt to cover all aspects of the social world in general terms (also known as grand theories).

mean A statistical average calculated by totalling all the values and dividing by the number of cases.

median A statistical average calculated by arranging all the values in a sample in numerical order, then noting the middle value of the distribution.

memo A way of recording, thinking about and analysing data, or flagging a piece of data for later investigation.

meso theories Middle-level theories relating to social phenomena usually found, such as organisations, institutions, community and family.

micro theories Local theory relating to a specific area, group of people or aspect of the social world.

mixed methods Methods that combine qualitative and quantitative methods in a way that is best for a specific research project.

mode A statistical average calculated by noting the most common value in the distribution.

multi-coded question A question that asks for more than one answer, and to which more than one variable is attached.

multivariate analysis The analysis of three or more variables together.

narrative The depiction of a sequence of past events as they appear in present time to the narrator, after they have been processed, analysed and constructed into stories.

natural sciences The study of the physical world and associated phenomena, including such disciplines as chemistry, physics, etc.

negative cases Instances that seem to contradict or disprove the emerging theory.

node The term used in the NVivo program to refer to codes.

non-response This occurs wherever an invited participant declines to be involved in a research project, perhaps because they refuse, are ill or are inappropriate.

normal distribution Data that is distributed symmetrically around the mean point in a 'bell shape'.

objectivism An ontological position which asserts that the social phenomena that make up our social world have an existence of their own, apart from and independent of the social actors (humans) who are involved.

observation (1) The collection of data through the use of human senses. (2) The act of watching social phenomena in the real world and recording events as they happen. In research, observation is usually divided into *participant observation* and *simple observation*.

online social research The computer-mediated collection of data and typically adapts traditional data collection methods, for example, questionnaires, interviews, focus groups, etc., for use in an online virtual environment.

ontology The 'science or study of being'; in social research, ontology refers to the way the social world is seen to be and what can be assumed about the nature and reality of the social phenomena that make up the social world.

open coding In Grounded Theory data analysis, this is the first stage of coding data, identifying and describing research phenomena, and assigning them appropriate names.

open questions Questions that allow the respondent to answer the question in their own way.

operational definitions Definitions that the researcher can work with and adapt to help to focus the research questions and to decide what data to gather to address those questions.

overt methods Open methods of investigation in which participants are aware that they are part of your research.

paradigm A cluster of beliefs and dictates that for scientists in a particular discipline, influence what should be studied, how research should be done, how results should be interpreted and so on.

participant interviews A type of interview in which the researcher is in control of the interview, asking a set of questions to which the research participant replies.

participant observation A data collection method in which the researcher/observer achieves intimate knowledge of the group of people who are the subjects of the research, in the group's natural setting.

peer review In academic settings, the process by which articles and papers are reviewed and selected for publication.

pilot-test A trial run or an opportunity to try out a data collection method on a small sample of cases before the main research data gathering takes place; question wording, research participant understanding and data collection procedures can all be tried out and amended if necessary before the main research stage.

plagiarism Presenting someone else's work as of it was your own; copying; failing to reference or otherwise attribute the origin.

planning To arrange in advance (an action or proposed proceeding); to devise, contrive, or formulate (a project or manner of proceeding).

population In statistical terms, population refers to the total number of cases that can be included as research subjects.

positivism An epistemological position which asserts that knowledge of a social phenomenon is based on what can be observed and recorded rather than subjective understandings.

positivist approach This usually means that quantitative data is collected; aspects of the social world, social phenomena, are measured; causal relationships between different aspects of the social world are sought; and large data sets and statistical analysis are often used.

primary data The data that a researcher gathers specifically for their own research.

probability sample A sample that can be shown to be highly representative of the whole population – or all the potential cases – in terms of relevant criteria.

process An on-going, often continuous series of actions intended to achieve a specific result. This often requires the researcher to follow an established set of (usually) routine procedures.

prospective longitudinal studies Research studies that are initially designed to be longitudinal.

proxy definition A 'rule of thumb' definition which stands in for a more detailed and sophisticated way of defining something.

purposive sample A sample of selected cases that will best enable the researcher to explore the research questions in depth.

qualitative research methods Methods that are primarily concerned with stories and accounts including subjective understandings, feelings, opinions and beliefs.

quantitative research methods Methods that are primarily concerned with gathering and working with data that is structured and can be represented numerically.

quartile One-quarter part of a sample or data set.

quasi-experiment Literally, 'almost the same as an experiment' but lacking some of the attributes of an experiment.

quasi-experimental research design A research design used in situations where two or more 'naturally' different groups of participants or data can be identified, and one used as the control and the other as the experimental group.

questionnaire (1) A set of questions each with a range of answers; (2) a format which enables standardised, relatively structured, data to be gathered about each of a (usually) large number of cases.

quintile One-fifth part of a sample or data set.

quota sampling A sampling technique that selects a certain number, or quota, of cases, on the basis of their matching a number of criteria.

random controlled study A research design that divides the research participants into broad groups relating to age, gender or ethnicity or other characteristics that are relevant to the research topic, and then randomly allocates people to control and experimental groups.

random sample A sample selected from a population where every case has an equal chance of being included in the sample and the composition of the sample cannot be predicted.

raw data Data that has not been analysed in any way, but is presented in the form it was collected in.

realism (1) An ontological position which asserts that the social world has a reality that is separate from the social actors involved in it, that can be known through the senses as well as the effects of 'hidden' structures and mechanisms. (2) An epistemological approach that asserts that knowledge of a social phenomenon is based on both what can be observed and recorded and 'hidden' structures and mechanisms whose effects can be observed.

reflexive data The data produced by individuals themselves as they think about what they are doing, experiencing and feeling and try to understand their social reality.

reliability A measure of research quality, meaning that another researcher would expect to obtain the same findings if they carried out the research in the same way, or the original researcher would expect to obtain the same findings if they tried again in the same way.

replicability A measure of research quality, meaning that another researcher would expect to obtain the same findings if they carried out the research in the same way.

representative sample A sample that has been selected in order to be representative of a wider population.

research proposal A document that outlines what a research project is about, how it will be undertaken, why it is worthwhile, how long it will take, and why it should be funded.

research quality The reliability, validity, credibility and ethical practice of a piece of research.

research question The initial enquiry from which a research project develops.

research tool Something used to collect data, e.g. a questionnaire, the researcher her/himself or an interview schedule.

retrospective longitudinal study A type of longitudinal study where data is available from the past, for example, where participants can be asked to provide data about their past experiences, or where records may be available.

sampling error The likely variation of the sample mean from the population mean.

sampling frame A list of all the members of a population from which a sample may be drawn.

scattergram A graph that plots two variables to show visually whether and how the variables may be related to each other.

secondary data The data that a researcher uses which has already been produced by others.

selective coding In Grounded Theory data analysis, this is the third and final stage of coding data, and is the process of choosing a central or 'core' category and then relating all the other codes, themes and categories to it.

semi-structured Describes data, or a data collection method (such as an interview or questionnaire), in which questions and answers may vary in wording and length; answers to questions are often in the respondent's own words.

simple observation A data collection method in which the researcher/observer is not part of the process that is being researched, but is an objective outsider.

snowball sampling A sampling technique where members of an initial sample are asked to identify others with the same characteristics as them, who the researcher then contacts.

social phenomenon Anything that influences or is influenced by human beings who interact with and are responsive to each other.

social world The setting or cultural surroundings in which social research takes place.

standard deviation A statistical measure of how values or cases are distributed around the mean value or case.

statistical sampling The process of selecting a probability sample.

statistical significance A measure of the probability that the relationships found in a sample will also be found in the wider population.

statistics Data that is structured and can be counted or is already expressed in numerical terms.

stratification A method of organising a population in order to improve the representativeness of a sample.

stratified sample A sample that is selected to ensure that certain categories and groups of people and cases are included, proportionate to their presence in the population.

structured Describes data, or a data collection method (such as an interview or questionnaire), in which the questions are the same for each participant, and typically there is a common set of answers for each question.

subsidiary research questions These are questions that help you to specify more precisely the areas of the research topic that you will focus on.

synchronous communication Communication between people where all communicants are taking part at the same time and can 'chat'; also known as real-time communication.

thematic analysis A process of working with raw data to identify and interpret key ideas or themes.

theoretical framework The ideas and approaches to viewing and gathering knowledge, and which provide the basic ways of addressing a topic.

theoretical memoing In Grounded Theory data analysis, 'the theorizing write-up of ideas about substantive codes and their theoretically coded relationships as they emerge during coding, collecting and analyzing data, and during memoing' (Glaser).

theoretical sample A sample of selected cases that will best enable the researcher to explore theoretical ideas.

theoretical sampling A sampling technique in which the initial cases are usually selected on a relatively unstructured basis: as 'theory' begins to emerge from the initial data, further cases are selected to explore and test the emerging theory; this continues until there is no new theory emerging and theoretical 'saturation' is reached.

theory A set of ideas or related concepts that can be used to explain and understand an event, situation, social phenomena.

topic guide A set of questions, key points or prompts to be included in a focus group or interview that helps the facilitator to remember the issues/questions to introduce; suggests ways of approaching topics and phrasing questions; reminds the facilitator to probe and follow up comments; includes an introduction and a way of ending; if you are holding more than one focus group or two or more facilitators are involved ensures that the same topics are covered in each group.

transferability A measure of research quality in which the researcher asks 'How far am I able to claim that the results or findings from my research are true for or relevant to the wider population or a different context?' (also known as generalisability).

transparent In a research context, this means that the research process and the decisions made by the researcher are recorded and available to others for scrutiny.

triangulation A measure of research quality, meaning that if different types of data are collected to address the same research question, each set of data can be used to check the findings from the others.

typology A typical model of the way variables tend to be found in relation to each other.

understanding Grasping the meaning of information.

unit The individual respondent or subject about whom a researcher collects data, for example countries, universities, families or individuals.

unstructured Describes data, or a data collection method (such as an interview or questionnaire), in which questions and answers do not follow a guide or template.

validity A measure of research quality, meaning that the data we are planning to gather and work with to address our research questions is a close representation of the aspect of social reality we are studying.

value statements Statements, usually from an individual, that are indications of each person's opinion where they are using their own judgement and criteria.

variable An attribute or characteristic of cases (for example, individuals, organisations, objects or situations) which can vary from case to case.

virtual communities Groupings of people who share some experience but meet virtually online rather than face to face.

INDEX